Dictionary of Antisemitism

From the Earliest Times to the Present

Robert Michael
Philip Rosen

The Scarecrow Press, Inc.
Lanham, Maryland • Toronto • Plymouth, UK
2007

SCARECROW PRESS, INC.

Published in the United States of America
by Scarecrow Press, Inc.
A wholly owned subsidiary of
The Rowman & Littlefield Publishing Group, Inc.
4501 Forbes Boulevard, Suite 200, Lanham, Maryland 20706
www.scarecrowpress.com

Estover Road
Plymouth PL6 7PY
United Kingdom

British Library Cataloguing in Publication Information Available

Library of Congress Cataloging-in-Publication Data

Michael, Robert, 1936–
    Dictionary of antisemitism from the earliest times to the present / Robert Michael,
Philip Rosen.
        p.   cm.
    Includes bibliographical references.
    ISBN-13: 978-0-8108-5862-6 (hardcover : alk. paper)
    ISBN-10: 0-8108-5862-2 (hardcover : alk. paper)
    ISBN-13: 978-0-8108-5868-8 (pbk. : alk. paper)
    ISBN-10: 0-8108-5868-1 (pbk. : alk. paper)
    1. Antisemitism—Dictionaries.   2. Antisemitism—History—Dictionaries.
I. Rosen, Philip.   II. Title.
DS145.M465   2006
305.892′4003—dc22   2006017822

∞ ™ The paper used in this publication meets the minimum requirements of
American National Standard for Information Sciences—Permanence of
Paper for Printed Library Materials, ANSI/NISO Z39.48-1992.
Manufactured in the United States of America.

Contents

Foreword

In the years preceding the establishment of Israel in 1948, Jews opposed to the creation of a Jewish state clashed with Zionists on how best to protect Jewish life in the wake of the Holocaust. Zionists contended that the Nazi extermination of the Jews conclusively proved the failure of assimilation in Europe because, in the opinion of Leon Pinsker, one of the movement's leading theoreticians, and also a physician, antisemitism was a hereditary disease that could never be cured. Antisemitism, he argued, would only disappear when Jews were secure in their own homeland.

Once Israel was in fact established, a coterie of hostile opponents, which included the Arab world, right-wing extremists such as neo-Nazis, Holocaust deniers, as well as traditional antisemites, rejected the very legitimacy of Israel and, as remains the case with Arab extremist groups, such as Hamas and Hezbollah, called for the destruction of the Jewish state. In short, the creation of Israel has not eliminated antisemitism. Quite the contrary, a "new" antisemitism has emerged in the guise of attacks against the state of Israel, holding the Jewish state to a double standard in its efforts to protect itself against those who would destroy it. In France, as is the case in many parts of Europe, increasing incidents against Jews by growing Muslim populations are "justified" on the grounds that all Jews are complicit in the "crimes" of Israel.

Although much of the renewed outbreak of antisemitism is unprecedented in its nature and composition, a great deal of the animus is also old. This is particularly true in regard to the application of conspiratorial design as a means of explaining American policy in the Middle East. That many American neoconservatives, such as Elliott Abrams, Douglas Feith, Richard Perle, and Paul Wolfowitz, are Jewish, only added credence to the belief of political personalities, such as Patrick Buchanan and Congressman Jim Moran of Virginia, that Jewish influence was behind the decision to invade Iraq. Absent from this explanation for the war was the legitimate argument that the overthrow of Saddam would lead not only to the establishment of a democracy, but that the "road-map" to peace in the Middle East ran through Baghdad, and required the removal of Saddam Hussein. Saddam was an obstacle to peace between Israel and the Palestinians, inasmuch as he not only rejected the very existence of Israel, but provided funds for the families of the suicide/ homicide bombers who attacked Israeli civilians.

Antisemitism in its modern form is a case of old wine in new bottles. Although the political conditions that have led to a rebirth of antisemitism are different from the past, nevertheless, much of what is said and believed about Jews is familiar. In the Muslim world, where historically Jews were looked down upon, there was never the intense hatred directed toward them that had existed in Christian Europe. But antisemitism in the Muslim world reveals that many of the contemporary stereotypes of Jews and Israel are imports from the Christian West, ranging from the medieval belief in child ritual murder to, most significantly, the distribution of the forgery known as *The Protocols of the Elders of Zion*.

A staple belief of the conspiracy-minded, the *Protocols* purports to reveal the existence of a Jewish plot to rule the world. This czarist forgery later found its way to the United States, where Henry Ford published it in his *Dearborn Independent*. Hitler believed the *Protocols* to be true, and it became mandatory reading among Nazi officials in the Third Reich. Despite having been proved to be a forgery in a court of law, the *Protocols* continue to be distributed by antisemites who believe that Jewish influence governs American policy. Our own native-born terrorists, such as Timothy McVeigh's Aryan Nations and Matthew Hale's World Church of the Creator, fantasize that Jewish power emanates from their control of the entertainment industry, the news media, and the international banking system, a condition that was predicted in the *Protocols*.

The *Protocols* have also become ubiquitous throughout the Middle East as antisemitism has become a weapon among Arabs in their conflict with Israel. The work is used to encourage Palestinians and other Muslims to engage in murderous attacks against Israelis and Jews. According to the Anti-Defamation League's *Antisemitic Literature in the Islamic World*, some suicide/homicide bombers have been found to have kept copies of the *Protocols*, and "were obviously convinced they were conducting a struggle against a Jewish-world-embracing conspiracy that poses a direct threat to the Muslim nations." Recently, Egyptian television produced a "documentary" on the *Protocols*. The forty-one part series, *Horseman Without a Horse*, fostered the theme that Jews were engaged in secret machinations to take over the world, or that Jews already control the world, a view that is increasingly believed in the Arab world. The program was shown across the Middle East during the Islamic holy month of Ramadan.

The Muslim world is filled with divisions, but regardless of their rivalries (Osama bin-Laden versus the House of Saud, for example), the hatred of Israel and Jews is the single issue on which the most determined Islamic fundamentalist and the most dedicated secularists can find common ground. This explains why governments in the Muslim world continue to use antisemitism as a convenient and useful tool to deflect protests from their populations' profound poverty and economic problems.

By means of modern communication systems such as the Internet, the *Protocols* is widely disseminated throughout the Muslim world and has reached audiences larger than any time in its sordid history. Through the distribution of the *Protocols*, Muslim leaders encourage a delusional conspiratorial view of the world that fosters hatred of Jews and Israel. Accordingly, the modern "Elders of Zion," Elliott Abrams, Douglas Feith, Richard Perle, and Paul Wolfowitz, are alleged to be the actual formulators of Bush's foreign policy, which serves not only Israel's interests but also that of the worldwide Jewish conspiracy. The renewed prominence of the *Protocols* exemplifies the increasing threat of worldwide antisemitism and will continue to remain so in the foreseeable future, regardless of the resolution of the Palestinian-Israeli conflict.

Robert Michael and Philip Rosen have made an important contribution in compiling a dictionary that dramatically demonstrates that antisemitism is not only a thing of the past. Unfortunately, it is alive and well, and this dictionary is a reminder of its origins and the manner in which it is being propagated throughout the contemporary world.

Jack Fischel
Emeritus Professor of History
Millersville University
Millersville, Pennsylvania

Acknowledgments

The authors would like to acknowledge the excellent critical readings of our dictionary by Guillaume de Syon and the exceptional, comprehensive, and detailed historical critique by and editorial contributions of Chana Kotzin.

The following entries were reprinted with permission of the Anti-Defamation League from "Hate on Display: Extremist Symbols, Logos, and Tattoos" (New York: Anti-Defamation League, 2005), available at www.adl.org/learn/default.htm:

- AMERICAN FRONT
- ARYAN BROTHERHOOD
- ARYAN FIST
- BOOTS
- CELTIC CROSS
- CHELSEA
- CONFEDERATE (BATTLE) FLAG
- CROSSED (GERMAN WORLD WAR II) GRENADES
- CRUCIFIED SKINHEAD
- DOC
- EAGLE ATOP SWASTIKA
- ELBOW WEB
- FIVE PERCENTERS
- FOURTH REICH
- GERMAN IMPERIAL FLAG
- KIGY
- LIFE RUNE
- NATIONAL ASSOCIATION FOR THE ADVANCEMENT OF WHITE PEOPLE (NAAWP)
- NATIONALIST MOVEMENT, THE
- ORION
- OTHALA RUNE
- PECKERWOOD
- PHINEAS PRIEST

- ROCK AGAINST COMMUNISM
- SCREWDRIVER
- SKIN
- SKULL AND CROSSBONES
- STORMFRONT
- SWASTIKA
- SWASTIKA WITH IRON CROSS, NAZI
- THUNDERBOLTS/LIGHTNING BOLTS
- TRISKELE, TRISKELION, THREE-BLADED SWASTIKA
- TYR RUNE
- UAO
- "UNSERE EHRE HEISST TREUE"
- VALKNOT
- VOLKSFRONT
- WHITE POWER MUSIC
- WOLFSANGEL

Introduction

WHO IS A JEW?

Who is a Jew?[1] Many Jews have a distinctive consciousness, a sense of sharing a common origin and fate and an awareness of a unique religious, historical, and cultural heritage. The earliest Jewish communal tradition is of a people chosen to keep God's 613 commandments found in their Torah and to bring ethical monotheism to the peoples of the world. Although Jewish identities vary from atheism to ultra-Orthodoxy, many Jews observe rituals, holy days, and social-ethical behavior, including defense of the weak, sympathy for the stranger, aid to the poor, and kindness to humans and animals. Many Jews support education, Jewish charities, Zionist groups, the Anti-Defamation League, and other Jewish organizations, as well as observing traditional ceremonies from birth to death. Many Jews revere the Hebrew language, follow a kosher diet, and eat special foods on Passover and other holy days. Most Jews define a Jew as one born of a Jewish mother. Jews are not members of a biological race, the concept having no anthropological validity. Because of assimilation and intermarriage, Jews tend to resemble the peoples among whom they live.

George Eliot observed:

> On the whole, one of the most remarkable phenomena in the history of this scattered people, made for ages "a scorn and a hissing" is, that . . . they have come out of it . . . rivalling the nations of all European countries in healthiness and beauty of physique, in practical ability, in scientific and artistic aptitude, and in some forms of ethical value. . . . The Jews, whose ways of thinking and whose very verbal forms are on our lips in every prayer which we end with an Amen.[2]

In the same essay, Eliot wrote that "the prejudiced, the puerile, the spiteful, and the abysmally ignorant" admire or abhor "the same motives, the same ideas, the same practices" according to their association with the historical or social accident of whether a human being is regarded as a Jew or not. Harvard psychologist Gordon Allport reported that Abraham Lincoln was admired because people see him as "thrifty, hardworking, eager for knowledge, ambitious, devoted to the rights of the average man, and eminently successful in climbing the ladder of opportunity." He then went on to ask, "Why do so many people dislike the Jews? They may tell you it is because they are thrifty, hardworking, eager for knowledge, ambitious, devoted to the rights of the average man, and eminently successful in climbing the ladder of opportunity."[3]

When all is said and done, it just may be that "the prejudiced, the puerile, the spiteful, and the abysmally ignorant" will be the ones who define who is a Jew—and, therefore, what is antisemitism.

WHAT IS ANTISEMITISM?

In 1879 Wilhelm Marr created the word *Antisemitismus*, and it swiftly found its way into Europe's languages.[4] *Antisemitism* in the broadest sense means hostility toward everything the Jew—not the "Semite"—stands for. There are no Semites; there are only peoples who speak Semitic languages. *Antisemitism* refers to the irrational dislike or hatred of Jews, the attempt to demoralize or satanize them, the rejection of the validity of the Jewish religion, the Jewish way of life, the Jewish spirit, the Jewish character, and, ultimately, the Jewish right to live.[5] As Allport has indicated, antisemitism and anti-Jewishness, like all ethnic prejudices, express themselves as antilocution, avoidance, discrimination, physical attack, and extermination.[6] Assault, expropriation, expulsion, torture, and murder could be added to his list. The German scholar Josef Joffe analyzed these psychosocial aspects of antisemitism: stereotyping, denigration, demonization, obsession, and elimination.[7]

To attempt to define and trace the permutations and combinations of antisemitism, the world's longest and most pervasive hatred, is a daunting task. Three analogies from the chemical, medical, and biological sciences may clarify antisemitism's ideological functions. First, although they exist within different historical contexts, anti-Jewish ideas, emotions, and behaviors are reactive elements easily combining with other ideologies, such as nationalism, racism, social Darwinism, conservatism, fascism, and socialism to form an explosive compound. Second, like a virus, anti-Jewishness rests dormant at different levels of the societal and individual psyche, surfacing especially during the throes of social or personal crisis.[8] Third, although Jews have often been compared to parasites in both medieval and modern antisemitic imagery, antisemitism itself is a parasitic idea, growing more powerful by feeding on the human emotions of fear, anger, anxiety, and guilt. In "Know Thyself," Richard Wagner argued that the Jews represented the multifaceted power of evil, the "plastic demon" responsible for the decadence of all human society.[9] This phrase of Wagner's is better used to describe antisemitism itself, which takes on such variegated forms as to render the concept almost indefinable.

In 2005, the European Union Monitoring Center on Racism and Xenophobia established a "Working Definition of Antisemitism":

> Antisemitism is a certain perception of Jews, which may be expressed as hatred toward Jews. Rhetorical and physical manifestations of antisemitism are directed toward Jewish or non-Jewish individuals and/or their property, toward Jewish community institutions and religious facilities.
>
> In addition, such manifestations could also target the state of Israel, conceived as a Jewish collectivity. Antisemitism frequently charges Jews with conspiring to harm humanity, and it is often used to blame Jews for "why things go wrong." It is expressed in speech, writing, visual forms and action, and employs sinister stereotypes and negative character traits.
>
> Contemporary examples of antisemitism in public life, the media, schools, the workplace, and in the religious sphere could, taking into account the overall context, include, but are not limited to:
>
> - Calling for, aiding, or justifying the killing or harming of Jews in the name of a radical ideology or an extremist view of religion.
> - Making mendacious, dehumanizing, demonizing, or stereotypical allegations about Jews as such or the power of Jews as collective—such as, especially but not exclusively, the myth about a world Jewish conspiracy or of Jews controlling the media, economy, government or other societal institutions.
> - Accusing Jews as a people of being responsible for real or imagined wrongdoing committed by a single Jewish person or group, or even for acts committed by non-Jews.
> - Denying the fact, scope, mechanisms (e.g., gas chambers) or intentionality of the genocide of the Jewish people at the hands of National-Socialist Germany and its supporters and accomplices during World War II (the Holocaust).
> - Accusing the Jews as a people, or Israel as a state, of inventing or exaggerating the Holocaust.
> - Accusing Jewish citizens of being more loyal to Israel, or to the alleged priorities of Jews worldwide, than to the interests of their own nations.

[Although criticism of Israel similar to that leveled against any other country cannot be regarded as antisemitism] examples of the ways in which antisemitism manifests itself with regard to the state of Israel taking into account the overall context could include:

- Denying the Jewish people their right to self-determination, e.g., by claiming that the existence of a State of Israel is a racist endeavor.
- Applying double standards by requiring of it a behavior not expected or demanded of any other democratic nation.
- Using the symbols and images associated with classic antisemitism (e.g., claims of Jews killing Jesus or blood-libel) to characterize Israel or Israelis.

- Drawing comparisons of contemporary Israeli policy to that of the Nazis.
- Holding Jews collectively responsible for actions of the state of Israel.
- Criminal acts are antisemitic when the targets of attacks, whether they are people or property—such as buildings, schools, places of worship and cemeteries—are selected because they are, or are perceived to be, Jewish or linked to Jews.
- Antisemitic discrimination is the denial to Jews of opportunities or services available to others and is illegal in many countries.[10]

Antisemitism is comprised of constituent elements. Although religious, racial, cultural, literary, economic, ethnic, psychosocial, and political antisemitism are usually interwoven, the most basic, vigorous, and longest-lived cause of antisemitism has been religious. Even the aforesaid Wilhelm Marr's secular racism existed alongside his religious antisemitism. On the one hand, Marr despised Jews because of their "disgusting . . . chemical" composition. On the other hand, he associated the "Germanness" he admired with Christianity and contrasted them both to Jewishness. Called "the new Luther" and defending Christian hostility to Jewish domination, Marr believed that Germany was a Christian country, and his goal was to rid Christianity of Judaism's sway. His Antisemites' League used a German oak leaf and a Christian cross as its symbols.[11] In an 1891 article, Marr referred to his movement as composed of "Christians and Aryans."[12]

Christian Antisemitism

Christian scholar Alan Davies has asked whether "centuries of religious anti-Judaism . . . so poisoned the conscience of the ordinary Christian as to blunt his capacity to recognize simple cruelty."[13] John Gager wondered "not simply whether individual Christians had added fuel to modern European antisemitism, but whether Christianity itself was, in its essence and from its beginnings, the primary source of antisemitism in Western culture."[14] Robert Willis concluded that "theological antisemitism [established] a social and moral climate that allowed the 'final solution' to become a reality."[15]

More recent studies have confirmed that anti-Jewish ideology embodied within Christianity provided the fundamental basis for an American antisemitism that on the surface seems so secular.[16] After a careful study of American opinion in the 1960s, Charles Glock and Rodney Stark concluded that "the heart and soul of antisemitism rested on Christianity" and that 95 percent of Americans got their secular stereotypes of Jews from the Christian religion.[17] Gordon Allport concluded that religion stood as the focus of prejudice because "it is the pivot of the cultural tradition of a group."[18] Christianity, unlike any other group in Western history, has dominated the West for the past 1,700 years.

Although bigots have found biblical sanction for their antipathy to women, gays, and blacks, among others, the Church Fathers most effectively used the Christian Scriptures as a warehouse for material against Jews.[19] Jews were no longer merely those annoying people whom a minority of pagans disdained for their "laziness" on the Sabbath or refusal to eat pork.[20] With the establishment of Christianity, Jews became deicides, Christ-killers, God murderers.

Rationally, even Christian antisemites recognize that Jews could not have murdered God. But antisemitism is rarely rational. Besides, Christianity established its own identity in large part by distancing itself from Judaism. St. Jerome called all Jews "Judases"; St. Augustine, "Cains"; St. John Chrysostom, "useless animals who should be slaughtered."[21] By the Middle Ages, Christian Crusaders, townsmen, and authorities defamed, ghettoized, assaulted, expropriated, expelled, physically attacked, tortured, and murdered tens—perhaps hundreds—of thousands of Jews.[22] These *Judenschachter*, Jew-slaughterers, no less than the SS-Totenkopfverbanden or members of the Einsatzgruppen, saw Jews as threats to their very lives, as demons, monsters, plague-rats that had to be killed.[23]

To achieve this separation, Christian writers turned fundamental aspects of Judaism on their heads: Jewish law was obsolete, fulfilled in Jesus; Israel was superseded by Christianity, which now became the new Israel; God's covenant passed from the Jews to the Christian churches.[24] Instead of perceiving Jesus of Nazareth as of the blood and bone and religion of the Jewish people, the Church Fathers accused Jews of rejecting the messiah, of a stiff-necked refusal to see the "truth" of Christianity, of being religious hypocrites, deicides, children of the devil, eternally doomed.[25] The Jews' punishment was meant to be eternal wandering, lives in servitude, and inferiority to the Christians they lived among. Jewish holy books and practices were misread, misinterpreted, and demonized. The Talmud—rabbinic discussions of the meaning of the Jewish Scriptures and Jewish practices—was judged heretical and burned during the Middle Ages and into the 20th century.[26]

It is almost impossible to find examples of antisemitism that are exclusively racial, economic, or political, and free of religious taint. Although Jews are not a "race," antisemites often hate Jews, whom they consider members of a "Jewish race." This kind of antisemitism has existed since the birth of Christianity. Ignoring the salvific power of the sacrament of baptism, several Church Fathers argued that a Jew could no more become a Christian than a leopard change its spots.[27] Spain combined religious and racist antisemitism to establish history's first institutionalized racism from the 15th through the 19th centuries and called the Inquisition.[28] In the latter century, racial antisemitism strengthened all across Europe.[29] Nationalism and racism mixed with religious antisemitism into the potentially explosive brew that would fully erupt during the Holocaust. Many "secular" 19th-century antisemites regarded Jews as a race with inborn evil traits rather than merely a religious community. Neither assimilation nor conversion could save the Jews. Jews did not partake of the national essence—the German Aryan spirit, the Slavic soul, the French esprit.[30] Jews were, are, and would always be dishonest, unscrupulous, clannish, materialistic, unpatriotic, parasitical, domineering, and exploitative. Blood would always tell. Contemporary antisemites often confuse Jews, Israelis, Zionists, and "Semites."[31]

In the fourth century, Church Father St. Jerome identified all Jews as Judas. During the High Middle Ages, because the Church barred Christians from usury, the field was left open to the Jews, who were barred from most other occupations. In the 16th century, Shakespeare's image of Shylock stuck: Jews were stereotyped as ruthless, money-hungry, materialistic, unproductive, exploitive, and cruel. In the 19th century came Dickens's Fagin image: Jews corrupting youth and engaged in criminal activity. Then there was du Maurier's Svengali image: the manipulating Jew, who through occult tricks preyed upon innocent Christian young women, a variation on the ritual-murder myth.

False, contrived, mythical accusations leveled against Jews oftentimes led to mass murder. These defamations included ritual murder (allegedly Jews in every generation killed a Christian child as a repetition of Jesus' crucifixion); blood libel (Jews supposedly used the blood drained from a Christian child to make matzoh for Passover and to drink so that they could rid themselves of their alleged Jew stink); desecration of the Host (Jews allegedly stole and stabbed consecrated wafers in order to maliciously injure Jesus); and poisoning the wells to cause plague as part of the supposed Jewish conspiracy to damage Christians and control the world. Jewish evil was unending. Popes ordered civil authorities to force Jews to wear stigmatic emblems to mark out Jews to prevent Christian fraternization. Jews were confined to ghettos— unhealthy, overcrowded, walled, and guarded—and in Russia to a Pale of Settlement, a circumscribed area where Jews were forced live.

At the mercy of their Christian rulers and townspeople, forbidden to own or train in the use of arms, a tiny and scattered minority, Jews were vulnerable to attack, riots, outright murder, and devastations called *pogroms*. Ghetto residents were subject to proselytizing sermons, forced baptisms, and kidnappings. Social and sexual intercourse with Christians was proscribed. Ghetto dwellers were subject to special restrictions, such as limitations on marriage age and the number of children and synagogues. Jews were subject to genocidal attacks and to mass expulsions from towns, cities, principalities, and whole countries. Crusaders murdered Jews in Europe and the Holy Land. The Inquisition burned thousands of Jews and converted Jews at the stake.

To many modern Christians, no matter how assimilated the Jews became, they were considered the foreigner, the strange one, the alien who does not celebrate Christian rituals or festivals, who may dress differently and speak in a strange language. Mark Twain, whose Austrian critics accused him of being a Jew, wrote that "by his make and ways [the Jew] is substantially a foreigner wherever he may be, and even the angels dislike a foreigner."[32] The young Chaim Weizmann felt that the Jews were like a splinter in the eye: even if it were gold, it was still an incapacitating irritant.[33] The converted Jew Heinrich Heine believed that "Jewishness was an incurable malady."[34]

Jews were caricatured as villainous and dark with exaggerated noses. On the one hand, because the strong sense of social justice among many Jews led them to criticize society in favor of the underdog and minorities, modern antisemites accused Jews of radicalism—in 2006, for many, even liberalism is enough to stir criticism of Jews—trying to upset the traditional order. On the other hand, Jewish success in business and the professions, engendering jealousy, has led to charges that Jews control the economy, especially banking, and are archcapitalists who engage in immoral business practices, war profiteering, and control of the press. Moreover, Jews are charged with engaging in pornography, cheapening culture, and displaying coarse and unrefined nouveau riche habits. Social and economic discrimination, restrictive covenants in housing, and gentlemen's agreements in social clubs, hotels, colleges, corporation boardrooms, and other private organizations excluded Jews.

Among the great literary figures of Europe and the United States, religious antisemitism was widespread. In much of 19th-century literature, Jewish characters are stereotypes, not characters with good and bad traits but universally alien and evil. Authors of this literature, during the century often regarded as the most secular and racist of centuries, reveal their own hostile religious feelings about Jews in their negative Jewish characters—with the authors' antisemitism often confirmed in their letters and essays. The term *Jew* itself became a curse word.

Mark Gelber has observed that "without a truly significant counterbalance to a negative Jewish character or to pejorative references to Jews, such depictions or references must be considered as examples of literary antisemitism."[35] This is the case with Balzac, Trollope, Hawthorne, and hundreds of other important authors who were taught their antisemitism at their mother's knee, their father's table, their teacher's bench, and their priest's or minister's pulpit. Their work is cited in this book and speaks for itself.

What offers hope is the case of the physician, professor, and poet Oliver

Wendell Holmes Sr. An advocate of religious toleration, Holmes observed that it is right that "the stately synagogue should lift its walls by the side of the aspiring cathedral, a perpetual reminder that there are many mansions in the Father's earthly house as well as in the heavenly one."[36] But Holmes confessed that, as a young man, "I shared more or less the prevailing prejudices against the persecuted race," which he traced to Christian teaching and Puritan exclusiveness. In a remarkable poem originally entitled "A Hebrew Tale," Holmes demonstrated how he overcame his early antisemitism. This poem provides us with an important insight into the process of how antisemitism works: how one event can trigger a sequence of hostile thoughts and feelings about Jews. Holmes recounts how he was hemmed in by Jews attending a play. He found their appearance distasteful, reminding him of their deicide, of their perfidy, of their usury, of their murder of Christian children. In this one poem, Holmes captures the two millennia of Jewish history in Christian lands, and the promise of a better future. Holmes mentions the

> hooked-nosed kite of carrion clothes,
> The sneaky usurer, him that crawls
> And cheats . . .
> Spawn of the race that slew its Lord.
> Up came their murderous deeds of old,
> . . . Of children caught and crucified;
> . . . of Judas and his bribe . . .

But when Holmes looked more closely into the faces of the Jews surrounding him, he thought Jesus must have resembled them.

> The shadow floated from my soul,
> And to my lips a whisper stole,—. . .
> From thee the son of Mary came,
> With thee the Father deigned to dwell,—
> Peace be upon thee, Israel.[37]

In the first half of the 20th century, governments sponsored pogroms, passed restrictive immigration laws, ignored talented Jewish candidates for important positions, limited the number of Jews in prestigious schools, and turned a blind eye to persecution and violence against Jews—most notably during the Holocaust. During those terrible days, the U.S. Treasury Department's report entitled "The Acquiescence of This Government in the Murder of the Jews" summarized the relationship between the Western Allies and the Germans and many other Europeans and their governments in discrimination against, and mass murder of, Jews. The "Final Solution of the Jewish Problem" combined religious, nationalist, racist, sociocultural, and economic antisemitism. As Raul Hilberg put it: "The missionaries of Christianity had said in effect: You have no right to live among us as Jews. The secular rulers who followed had proclaimed: You have no right to live among us. The German Nazis at last decreed: You have no right to live."[38]

Islamic Antisemitism

Islam also discriminated against Jews and Christians as *dhimmis*—People of the Book inferior to Muslims—but also afforded them limited protection if they paid special taxes and "behaved." Though Jewish dhimmis were denied full civil and political rights and though pogroms and forced conversions continued in the Muslim world, for centuries during the period of Islamic dominance, Muslims treated Jews better than Christian rulers did. However, as the Islamic world, particularly the Arab nations, approached the 21st century, classic antisemitism invaded its belief system. Many contemporary Muslims fear and hate Jews and believe that Jews are an evil religious community who deserve no homeland and ought to be annihilated.[39] The presence of Israel interrupts the geographic continuity of the Arab world. Many Arabs believe that Israel is a catastrophe imposed imperialistically as an enclave of Western culture—Israeli "depravity" exemplified by liberated Jewish women. Jews are accused of introducing communism into the Middle East since they supported Palestinian, Syrian, Egyptian, and Lebanese communist parties. With no right to exist in a Jewish state, at best Jews should live as they did under caliphs—as dhimmis. At worst, Jews must be destroyed, as some medieval Crusaders proclaimed, down to the last baby at the breast.[40]

Despite the tragic history of antisemitism reflected in the entries of this dictionary, antisemitism is not one unending continuum. There were periods in Jewish history like the Golden Age of Jews in medieval Spain of relative tolerance and peaceful coexistence between Jews and Christians, Jews and Muslims. During the post-Holocaust period, until the last decade, antisemitism has lain dormant. There has been considerable improvement of conditions for Jews since the Holocaust and, since 1965, in the eyes of the Roman Catholic Church. Yet the virus of antisemitism has once again resurrected, and the need to catalogue its manifestations and identify its proponents has never been more necessary.

NOTES

1. Bryan Mark Rigg spends his first two chapters attempting to answer this question in *Hitler's Jewish Soldiers: The Untold Story of Nazi Racial Laws and Men of Jewish Descent in the German Military* (Lawrence: University Press of Kansas, 2002).

2. George Eliot, "The Modern Hep! Hep! Hep!" in *Impressions of Theophrastus Such* (Ames: Iowa University Press, 1994).

3. Gordon Allport, *The Nature of Prejudice* (Reading, MA: Addison-Wesley, 1954), 184.

4. Moshe Zimmermann, *Wilhelm Marr: The Patriarch of Antisemitism* (Oxford: Oxford University Press, 1986).

5. Raul Hilberg, *Destruction of the European Jews*, rev. ed. (New York: Holmes & Meier, 1985).

6. Allport, *Nature of Prejudice*, 48.

7. Josef Joffe, "Nations We Love to Hate: Israel, America and the New Antisemitism," *Posen Papers in Contemporary Antisemitism*, No. 1 (Vidal Sassoon International Center for the Study of Antisemitism, Hebrew University of Jerusalem, 2005), 1–16.

8. What is endemic becomes epidemic. See Imre Hermann, *Psychologie de l'Antisémitisme* (Paris: Eclat, 2006); Danielle Knafo, "Antisemitism in the Clinical Setting: Transference and Countertransference Dimensions," *Journal of the American Psychoanalytic Association* 47, no. 1 (1999), 35–63; Guy Sapriel, "La permanence antisémite: Une étude psychanalytique; La trace mnésique irréductible," *Pardès: Études et culture juive: Psychanalyse de l'antisémitisme contemporain* (2004): 11–20.

9. Richard Wagner, "Know Thyself," in *Richard Wagner's Prose Works*, trans. William Ashton Ellis (London: Routledge & Kegan Paul, 1892–99), 6:264–65, 271.

10. European Union Monitoring Center on Racism and Xenophobia, "Working Definition of Antisemitism," March 16, 2005, http://eumc.europa.eu/eumc/material/pub/AS/AS-WorkingDefinition-draft.pdf.

11. Paul Rose, *Revolutionary Antisemitism in Germany from Kant to Wagner* (Princeton, NJ: Princeton University Press, 1990), 14; Uriel Tal, *Christians and Jews in Germany: Religion, Politics, and Ideology in the Second Reich, 1870–1914* (Ithaca, NY: Cornell University Press, 1975), 264.

12. Moshe Zimmermann, *Wilhelm Marr: The Patriarch of Antisemitism* (Oxford, UK: Oxford University Press, 1986), 83, 88–94, 105, 107, 112.

13. Alan Davies, *Antisemitism and the Christian Mind; The Crisis of Conscience after Auschwitz* (New York: Herder and Herder, 1969), 39.

14. John Gager, *The Origins of Antisemitism: Attitudes toward Judaism in Pagan and Christian Antiquity* (New York: Oxford University Press, 1983), 13.

15. Robert Willis, "Christian Theology after Auschwitz," *Journal of Ecumenical Studies* (Fall 1975): 495.

16. Robert Michael summarizes the argument in his introduction "The United States Is Above All Things a Christian Nation" for his *Concise History of American Antisemitism* (Lanham, MD: Rowman & Littlefield, 2005). See also Egal Feldman, *Dual Destinies: The Jewish Encounter with Protestant America* (Urbana: University of Illinois Press, 1990); and Leonard Dinnerstein, *Antisemitism in America* (New York: Oxford University Press, 1995).

17. Charles Glock and Rodney Stark, *Christian Beliefs and Antisemitism* (New York: Harper & Row, 1966), xvi, 185–87, 50–65, 73–74, 105. See also Rodney Stark et al., *Wayward Shepherds* (New York: Harper & Row, 1971), 5, 9–10, 50; and Alphons Silbermann, *Sind Wir Antisemiten?* (Cologne, Germany: Verlag Wissenschaft und Politik, 1982), 51–52.

18. Allport, *Nature of Prejudice*, 446.

19. Irving Zeitlin, *Jesus and the Judaism of His Time* (Cambridge, UK: Polity Press, 1988), 184–201.

20. Menachem Stern, *Greek and Latin Authors on Jews and Judaism*, 3 vols. (Jerusalem: Israel Academy of Sciences and Humanities,1984).

21. St. Jerome, *De Antichristo in Danielem* 4, 11:21–30, in *Commentarii in Danielem*, ed. Francisci Glorie, Libri 3–4 [*Corpus Christinaorum*, Series Latina] (Turnhout Turnholti: Brepols, 1964), 75A:917–20; St. Augustine, "Reply to Faustus, the Manichaean," in *Disputation and Dialogue*, ed. Frank Talmage (New York: KTAV, 1975), 31; St. John Chrysostom, *Homilies against Judaizing Christians*, 1.2.4–6.

22. Joshua Trachtenberg, *The Devil and the Jews* (Philadelphia: Jewish Publication Society, 1961).

23. Frederick Schweitzer, "The Tap-Root of Antisemitism: The Demonization of the Jews," in *Remembering for the Future: Jews and Christians during and after the Holocaust: Theme One* (Oxford, UK: Pergamon Press, 1988), 879–90.

24. Jacob Neusner, "Christian Missionaries—Jewish Scholars," *Midstream* (October 1991), 31.

25. St. Ambrose, *Epistola* 74:3 (*Patrologiae, Cursus Completus, Series Latina*, ed. J.-P. Migne, 16:1255), cited in Shlomo Simonsohn, *The Apostolic See and the Jews: History* (Toronto: Pontifical Institute of Mediaeval Studies, 1991), 9n29.

26. Robert Chazan, *Medieval Jewry in Northern France* (Baltimore: Johns Hopkins University Press, 1974), 178 and chapters 5 and 6; Solomon Grayzel, ed., *The Church and the Jews in the Thirteenth Century* (New York: Hermon Press, 1966), 32n60, 278n3; Werner Keller, *Diaspora: The Post-Biblical History of the Jews* (New York: Harcourt, Brace & World, 1969), 225; Simonsohn, *Apostolic See and the Jews*, 303–7, 315.

27. St. Isidore of Seville, *Contra Judaeos*, 1, 18, in Rosemary Ruether, *Faith and Fratricide: The Theological Roots of Antisemitism* (New York: Seabury, 1965), 130.

28. Yosef Yerushalmi, *Assimilation and Racial Antisemitism: The Iberian and the German Models* (New York: Leo Baeck Institute, 1982); Léon Poliakov, *The Aryan Myth* (New York: Grosset and Dunlap, 1974); Albert Sicroff, *Les controverses des statuts de "pureté de sang" en Espagne du XVe au XVIIe siècle* (Paris: Didier, 1960); Michael Glatzer, "Pablo de Santa Maria on the Events of 1391," in Shmuel Almog, *Antisemitism through the Ages* (Oxford, UK: Pergamon Press, 1988), 127–37.

29. Johann Gottlieb Fichte, *Reden an die deutsche Nation* (1808), Sixth Address, Point 81; Hans-Joachim Becker, *Fichtes Idee der Nation und das Judentum* (Amsterdam: Rodopi, 2000); Eleonore Sterling, *Judenhass: Die Anfänge des politischen Antisemitismus in Deutschland, 1815–1850* (Frankfurt: Europaische Verlag, 1969), 128–29.

30. Peter Pulzer, *The Rise of Political Antisemitism in Germany and Austria*, rev. ed. (Cambridge, MA: Harvard University Press, 1988), 312.

31. Riccardo Calimani, *Ebrei e pregiudizio: Introduzione alla dinamica dell'odio* (Milan: Oscar Mondadori, 2000).

32. Mark Twain, "Concerning the Jews," *Harper's New Monthly Magazine* (September 1899), reprinted in *The Complete Essays of Mark Twain*, ed. Charles Neider (Garden City, NY: Doubleday, 1963).

33. Fritz Stern, "The Burden of Success: Reflections on German Jewry," in *Dreams and Delusions* (New York: Knopf, 1987), 111n.

34. Heinrich Heine, quoted in Jacob Katz, *Out of the Ghetto* (New York: Schocken, 1973), 210.

35. Mark Gelber, "What Is Literary Antisemitism?" *Jewish Social Studies* 42, no. 1 (Winter 1985); Lionel Trilling, "The Changing Myth of the Jew," *Commentary* 66, no. 2 (August 1978); Alvin Rosenfeld, "What to Do about Literary Antisemitism," *Midstream* 24, no. 10 (1978).

36. Oliver Wendell Holmes, *Over the Teacups* (Boston: Houghton-Mifflin, 1891), 197.

37. Oliver Wendell Holmes, *The Complete Poetical Works of Oliver Wendell Holmes* (Boston: Houghton-Mifflin, 1895), 189.

38. Hilberg, *Destruction of the European Jews*, 1:8–9.

39. Robert S. Wistrich, *Muslim Antisemitism: A Clear and Present Danger* (New York: American Jewish Committee, 2002).

40. An anonymous chronicler of Mainz, quoted in Robert Chazan, "The Hebrew First-Crusade Chronicles," *Revue des Études Juives: Historia Judaica* 33 (January–June 1974): 249–50, 253.

Dictionary

4R. Racist **skinhead** symbol; an abbreviation for "**Fourth Reich**."

4/19. Antigovernment racist date symbol. April 19 is the anniversary of two events: the confrontation between federal agents and the Branch Davidians in Waco, Texas, in 1993, and Timothy McVeigh's 1995 bombing of the Oklahoma City federal building. 4/19 is often used as a tattoo by antigovernment racists.

SUGGESTED READING: Anti-Defamation League, *Hate on Display: Extremist Symbols, Logos, and Tattoos* (New York: Anti-Defamation League, 2006); ADL Law Enforcement Agency Resource Network, *A Visual Database of Extremist Symbols, Logos, and Tattoos*, http://www.adl.org/hate_symbols/default.asp.

4/20. Neo-Nazi date symbol. April 20 is Adolf Hitler's birthday. 4/20 is also used as a tattoo by neo-Nazis to affirm their belief in the ideals of **Nazism**. "4/20" (or 4:20 or 420) is also an unrelated slang term associated with marijuana.

SUGGESTED READING: Anti-Defamation League, *Hate on Display: Extremist Symbols, Logos, and Tattoos* (New York: Anti-Defamation League, 2006); ADL Law Enforcement Agency Resource Network, *A Visual Database of Extremist Symbols, Logos, and Tattoos*, http://www.adl.org/hate_symbols/default.asp.

14/88. White supremacist and **neo-Nazi** symbol. Especially at the close of a letter, it indicates the writer adheres to a belief in white supremacy (**Fourteen Words**) and **Nazism** (**88**).

SUGGESTED READING: Anti-Defamation League, *Hate on Display: Extremist Symbols, Logos, and Tattoos* (New York: Anti-Defamation League, 2006); ADL Law Enforcement Agency Resource Network, *A Visual Database of Extremist Symbols, Logos, and Tattoos*, http://www.adl.org/hate_symbols/default.asp.

18. Neo-Nazi symbol. The first letter of the alphabet is *A*, and the eighth is *H*; "18" thus refers to *AH*, **Adolf Hitler**'s initials. Neo-Nazis use 18 in tattoos. The number is also used by Combat 18, a violent British neo-Nazi group that chose its name in honor of Hitler.

SUGGESTED READING: Anti-Defamation League, *Hate on Display: Extremist Symbols, Logos, and Tattoos* (New York: Anti-Defamation League, 2006); ADL Law Enforcement Agency Resource Network, *A Visual Database of Extremist Symbols, Logos, and Tattoos*, http://www.adl.org/hate_symbols/default.asp.

23. White supremacist symbol. *W* is the 23rd letter of the alphabet. White supremacists and racist **skinheads** use "23" in tattoos to stand for *W*, "white."

SUGGESTED READING: Anti-Defamation League, *Hate on Display: Extremist Symbols, Logos, and Tattoos* (New York: Anti-Defamation League, 2006); ADL Law Enforcement Agency Resource Network, *A Visual Database of Extremist Symbols, Logos, and Tattoos*, http://www.adl.org/hate_symbols/default.asp.

28. The number stands for the name "Blood & Honour" because *B* is the 2nd letter of the alphabet and *H* is the 8th letter. Blood & Honour is an international **neo-Nazi**/racist **skinhead** group started by British white supremacist and singer Ian Stuart. It has chapters around the world, including the United States, but is primarily in Europe. Blood & Honour is associated with the more explicitly violent group Combat 18.

SUGGESTED READING: Anti-Defamation League, *Hate on Display: Extremist Symbols, Logos, and Tattoos* (New York: Anti-Defamation League, 2006); ADL Law Enforcement Agency Resource Network, *A Visual Database of Extremist Symbols, Logos, and Tattoos*, http://www.adl.org/hate_symbols/default.asp.

33/6. Ku Klux Klan symbol. The 11th letter of the alphabet is *K*, and three *K*'s signify "KKK" or Ku Klux Klan. The *6* signifies the sixth or current era of the Klan. "33/6" is also used as a greeting by Klan members. *See also* 311.

SUGGESTED READING: Anti-Defamation League, *Hate on Display: Extremist Symbols, Logos, and Tattoos* (New York: Anti-Defamation League, 2006); ADL Law Enforcement Agency Resource Network, *A Visual Database of Extremist Symbols, Logos, and Tattoos*, http://www.adl.org/hate_symbols/default.asp.

83. Racist "Christian" symbol. The eighth letter of the alphabet is *H* and the third is *C*; "83" stands for "Heil Christ," a greeting used by racists who consider themselves also to be Christian.

SUGGESTED READING: Anti-Defamation League, *Hate on Display: Extremist Symbols, Logos, and Tattoos* (New York: Anti-Defamation League, 2006); ADL Law Enforcement Agency Resource Network, *A Visual Database of Extremist Symbols, Logos, and Tattoos*, http://www.adl.org/hate_symbols/default.asp.

88. Neo-Nazi hate symbol. The eighth letter of the alphabet is *H*, and "88" or *HH* is shorthand for the **Nazi** greeting "Heil Hitler." 88 is often found on hate group flyers, in both the greetings and closing comments of letters written by neo-Nazis, and in e-mail and website addresses.

SUGGESTED READING: Anti-Defamation League, *Hate on Display: Extremist Symbols, Logos, and Tattoos* (New York: Anti-Defamation League, 2006); ADL Law Enforcement Agency Resource Network, *A Visual Database of Extremist Symbols, Logos, and Tattoos*, http://www.adl.org/hate_symbols/default.asp.

100%. White supremacist symbol for an individual's pure **Aryan** or white roots, as well as the "need" for a pure, white race "uncorrupted" by interracial relationships.

SUGGESTED READING: Anti-Defamation League, *Hate on Display: Extremist Symbols, Logos, and Tattoos* (New York: Anti-Defamation League, 2006); ADL Law Enforcement Agency Resource Network, *A Visual Database of Extremist Symbols, Logos, and Tattoos*, http://www.adl.org/hate_symbols/default.asp.

311. Ku Klux Klan symbol. The 11th letter of the alphabet is *K*; thus three times the 11th letter equals "KKK," or Ku Klux Klan. "311" is sometimes used as a greeting to demonstrate membership in the KKK or simply sympathy with the Klan and its ideology. The rock band 311 is not to be confused with this KKK symbol. *See also* 33/6.

SUGGESTED READING: Anti-Defamation League, *Hate on Display: Extremist Symbols, Logos, and Tattoos* (New York: Anti-Defamation League, 2006); ADL Law Enforcement Agency Resource Network, *A Visual Database of Extremist Symbols, Logos, and Tattoos*, http://www.adl.org/hate_symbols/default.asp.

666. (International slur) Symbol of the **Antichrist**, used by Islamic fundamentalists and **neo-Nazis** in reference to Jews.

SUGGESTED READING: "List of Ethnic Slurs," *Wikipedia*, http://en.wiki pedia.org/wiki/List_of_ethnic_slurs.

– A –

AARON OF LINCOLN (1125–1186). English-Jewish financier. During the Middle Ages, Jewish **usury** was indispensable for everyday necessities as well as for cathedrals, pilgrimages, wars, and **crusades**. In 12th-century England, nine Cistercian monasteries, two cathedrals, and the Abbey of St. Albans were built thanks to the moneylending activities of several Jews, particularly Aaron of Lincoln. When Aaron died, his vast fortune was confiscated by King Henry II based on an 1194 cabinet ruling called "The Ordinances of the Jews," which allowed the king to confiscate Jewish wealth at will.

SUGGESTED READING: Cecil Roth, *History of the Jews in England* (London: Oxford University Press, 1941).

ABEGG, WILHELM (1876–1951). In January 1944, an Associated Press interview with a group of anti-**Nazi** German émigrés in Switzerland—later repeated in a 1944 memo entitled "Internal Reorganization of Postwar Germany" from Abegg, a former secretary of state in the Prussian Ministry of the Interior and head of the police and left-wing liberal, given to the U.S. consul in Zurich, and another memo in regard to the solution of the Jewish question in postwar Europe composed in June 1945 by the anti-Nazi **Free Germany Movement**—revealed that Abegg expressed his total opposition to the return of surviving German Jews to Germany. He felt that the German state had to protect itself against *Verjudung*. Abegg argued that Jews had suffered from so much world prejudice that they had developed a unique cunning, especially in money matters; moreover, the Jews were sly and aggressive. **Kurt Eisner**'s Soviet Republic in Bavaria, **Béla Kun** in Hungary, and **Leon Trotsky** in Russia had proved that Jews had "pushed themselves forward and conquered many of the best positions, but they had failed practically everywhere because of their arrogance." Abegg was not a racist in his **antisemitism**, but he ascribed harmful behavior to the Jews as a result of their Jewish traits. Abegg was "blaming" Jews for responsibility for their own persecution. He claimed that the "mass" return of the handful of Jews who survived the Nazi mass murders would destroy the Jews and world peace. He believed that Jews should be settled out of Europe into South America and that the Jewish problem would lessen if most Jews changed their names, assimilated, and became Christians.

SUGGESTED READING: David Bankier, "The Jews in Plans for Postwar Germany," *Jewish Political Studies Review* 14, nos. 3–4 (Fall 2002).

ABELARD, PETER (1079–1142). French theologian and philosopher. Abelard, the author of *The Dialogue of a Philosopher with a Jew and a Christian*, provides a picture of medieval mistreatment of Jews and serves as a plea for tolerance for Jews. In it, he has a Jew complain:

> If we want to travel to the next town, with huge sums of money we have to purchase protection from Christian rulers who really want us dead so that our possessions can be confiscated. The Jews cannot own land or vineyards because they cannot be protected. So all that is left to us as a way to earn a living is moneylending and this in turn brings down on us the hatred of those we lend to.

SUGGESTED READING: Peter Abelard, *Ethical Writings: Ethics and Dialogues between a Philosopher, a Jew and a Christian*, trans. Paul Vincent Spade, with an introduction by Marilyn McCord Adams (Indianapolis, IN: Hackett, 1995).

ABNER OF BURGOS (1270–1348). Also known as Alfonso of Valladolid. Spanish-Jewish physician and apostate. Abner of Burgos was a Jewish convert to Roman Catholicism who, once attacked by his former coreligionists, wrote vituperously against them. He repeated invalid, archaic slanders against Jews, accusing them of blaspheming Christ and cursing Christians. Later apostates used his material.
SUGGESTED READING: Yitzhak Baer, *A History of Jews in Christian Spain*, 2 vols. (Philadelphia: Jewish Publication Society, 1992).

ACTION FRANÇAISE. Antisemitic ultra-rightist, nationalist, royalist movement in France, 1898–1945. Its leader, **Charles Maurras,** founded the movement and newspaper of the same name, which painted Jews as symbols of menacing capitalism and conspirators behind French republicanism. Born during the **Dreyfus** Affair, Action Française supported the **Vichy** regime (1940–44) and collaborated with **Nazi** occupation forces. With the condemnation of Maurras, the movement collapsed in 1945. *See also* BRASILLACH, ROBERT.
SUGGESTED READING: Eugen Joseph Weber, *Action Française, Royalism and Reaction in Twentieth-Century France* (Stanford, CA: Stanford University Press, 1973).

ACTS OF THE APOSTLES. Acts, as it is commonly called, the fifth book of the Christian Scriptures, is an antisemitic morality play written around 80 CE. Portions of it consist of a savage anti-Jewish polemic. Acts described the Jews as being hostile to Roman authority, in league with King Herod and idolaters, and guilty of materialism, refusing to keep the Law, murdering the prophets, and betraying and murdering Jesus. Insisting that Jews who remain Jews are enemies of Christ and unworthy of eternal life, Acts accused all Jews everywhere of crucifying Jesus.

SUGGESTED READING: Joseph A. Fitzmyer, *The Acts of the Apostles* (Woodston, UK: Anchor Books, 1998).

ACTS OF THE MARTYRS. Official court records of the trials of early Christian martyrs from 257–58. The Acts of the Martyrs falsely accused Jews of attacking and persecuting Christians.

SUGGESTED READING: H. Mugurille, *Early Christian Tracts* (New York: Oxford University Press, 1972).

ADAMS, BROOKS (1848–1927). American historian and **social Darwinist**. Brother of **Henry Adams**, Brooks Adams lamented that "England is as much governed by the Jews of Berlin, Paris and New York as the native growth." For him, Jews represented the merchant and banker, that is, pliant, calculating manipulators. He regarded the Jews as conspiring to "control the world."

SUGGESTED READING: David Riesman, "The American Scene in *Commentary*'s Mirror," *Commentary* 15, no. 2 (February 1953); Louis Harap, *The Image of the Jew in American Literature* (Syracuse, NY: Syracuse University Press, 2003); John Higham, "Antisemitism in the Gilded Age: A Reinterpretation," in *American Jewish History: Antisemitism in America*, ed. Jeffrey Gurock (Florence, KY: Rutledge, 1998).

ADAMS, HENRY (1838–1918). American historian and writer. The grandson and great-grandson of presidents **John Adams** and **John Quincy Adams**, respectively, Henry Adams knew very few Jews personally but responded with fear and hatred to the large influx of Orthodox Jewish immigrants into the United States in the last decades of the 19th century. Like his brother, **Brooks Adams**, he felt that Jewish values were distorting modern society and that the Jews conspired to control the world: "I detest them and everything connected with them, and I live only and solely with the hope of seeing their demise, with all their accursed Judaism. I want to *see* all the lenders at interest taken out and executed." From Warsaw he wrote, "[The Jew] makes me creep."

SUGGESTED READING: *The Letters of Henry Adams*, ed. W. C. Ford (New York: Kraus Reprint Co., 1969); Ernest Samuels, *Henry Adams: The Middle Years* (Cambridge, MA: Harvard University Press, 1958).

ADAMS, JOHN (1735–1826). American politician; U.S. president, 1796–1800. Adams sometimes expressed very favorable feelings toward Jews. In a letter to F. A. Van Der Kemp (February 16, 1809), he indicated that "Fate had ordained the Jews to be the most essential instruments for civilizing nations." Despite his admiration for the role of Jewish people throughout the ages and his belief in equal rights, he admitted later in the same letter that "I cannot say that I love the Jews very much." In reply to **Thomas Jefferson**'s negative comments about Judaism, Adams noted that he had no use for the Jews' **Talmud**, "the daemon of hierarchical despotism" (November 15, 1813).

SUGGESTED READING: I. S. Meyer, "John Adams," *American Jewish Historical Society* 37 (1947); N. Taylor Phillips, "Family History of the Reverend David Mendez Macado," *Publications of the American Jewish Historical Society* (1893).

ADAMS, JOHN QUINCY (1767–1848). American politician; U.S. president, 1825–29. Like his father, **John Adams**, John Quincy Adams was ambivalent about Jews. On the one hand, he wrote to Joseph Hume, a British member of Parliament, in 1833 arguing that Jews should be emancipated, for "no set of men can be better subjects." On the other hand, in a diary entry of 1780, he wrote of his visit to an Amsterdam synagogue: "[Jews] are all wretched creatures, for I think I never saw in my life such a set of miserable looking people. And they would steal your eyes out of your head if they could." In his *Letters on Silesia* (London, 1804), Adams described a Silesian town in this manner: "the word filth conveys an idea of spotless purity in comparison with Jewish nastiness." Furthermore, he opposed the plan of Mordecai Noah, the Jewish editor of the *New York Advocate*, to settle Jews in the United States. In a letter, Adams complained to George Joy about "Jew-brokering tricks upon the Royal Exchange."

SUGGESTED READING: *Diary of John Quincy Adams*, ed. David Grayson Allen, 2 vols. (Cambridge, MA: Belknap Press of Harvard University, 1981); John Quincy Adams, *Writings of John Quincy Adams* (New York: Macmillan, 1913).

ADVERSUS HAERESES. See IRENAEUS, ST.

ADVERSUS JUDAEOS. See AUGUSTINE, ST.; CHRYSOSTOM, ST. JOHN; TERTULLIAN.

AFFIRMATIVE ACTION. *See* REVERSE DISCRIMINATION.

AFRICAN-AMERICAN ANTISEMITISM. *See* ANTISEMITISM, BLACK.

AGAINST CELSUS. A tract written in 246–48 by **Origen**, a Christian theologian, attacking **Celsus Philosophus**, a second-century Greek polemicist who criticized Judaism as well as Christianity.

SUGGESTED READING: Hamilton Baird Timothy, *The Early Christian Apologists and Greek Philosophy* (Assen, The Netherlands: Van Gorcum, 1973).

AGOBARD (879–844). Archbishop of Lyons, 814–44. Protested the tolerant treatment of Jews by Emperor **Louis I** in France. Agobard's letter "On the Insolence of the Jews" (826) accused Jews of selling Christians into slavery, cursing Christ and Christians, and forcing Christian servants to adopt Jewish holidays. His solution was strict separation of Jews from Christians in all spheres of life. Agobard feared that if the Court and populace treated Jews with fellowship, the Jews would regard the Church with contempt and the faithful might waver in their loyalty to Christianity. Contrary to church policy of the time, he forced Jewish children to the baptismal font.

SUGGESTED READING: H. H. Ben-Sasson, ed., *A History of the Jewish People* (Cambridge, MA: Harvard University Press, 1976).

AHHH-JEW. (U.S. slur) A false sneeze to indicate a Jew's presence.

SUGGESTED READING: "List of Ethnic Slurs," *Wikipedia*, http://en.wiki pedia.org/wiki/List_of_ethnic_slurs.

AHLWARDT, HERMANN (1845–1914). German politician. Ahlwardt's major work, *The **Aryan** Peoples' Desperate Struggle Against Jewry* (1890), claimed Jews were an octopus strangling Germany. Many of his ideas anticipated **Nazi** ideology. His racist 1895 Reichstag speech proclaimed: "The Jew is no German. Even were he born in Germany, [even] were he to obey German laws and become a dutiful soldier—all this is not decisive for nationality; only race is the determining factor."

SUGGESTED READING: Paul M. Massing, *A Study of Political Antisemitism* (New York: Harper & Row, 1976).

AL-AQSA MARTYRS BRIGADE. Palestinian nationalists who compose the military wing of the secular al-**Fatah** faction of the Palestine Liberation Organization. *Al-Aqsa* literally means "all that is within," and it refers to the Moslem holy site, the Al-Aqsa Mosque, which comprises one-sixth of old Jerusalem, on what Jews call the Temple Mount. The organization grew active after the failure of U.S. president Bill Clinton's initiative to settle the **Intifada** of 2000, the informal Palestinian uprising against Israel in the West Bank. In 2002, the Al-Aqsa Martyrs Brigade began suicide bombings against Israeli civilians. It is listed as a terrorist organization by the U.S. State Department. *See also* ARAFAT, YASSIR.

SUGGESTED READING: Council on Foreign Relations, "Al-Aqsa Martyrs Brigades, Palestinian Nationalists," October 31, 2005, http://www.cfr.org/publication/9127/.

ALBERT THE GREAT. *See* ALBERTUS MAGNUS, ST.

ALBERTUS MAGNUS, ST. (1206–1280). German scientist, philosopher, Dominican, theologian, bishop of Regensburg, papal legate, and mentor of **St. Thomas Aquinas** (1225–1274). Albertus, like Aquinas, became a doctor of the Church (someone whom a pope or an Ecumenical Council has designated as an eminent teacher of the Catholic faith; in two millennia, only 33 Catholics have been so designated). One of the most brilliant minds of his time, Albertus, along with several other Inquisitors, reconfirmed the condemnation of the **Talmud** for blasphemy at Paris. He described the synagogue as having "spilled this same blood [of Christ] and still despises it."

SUGGESTED READING: Isaak Markon, "Albertus Magnus," *Universal Jewish Encyclopedia* (New York: Universal Jewish Encyclopedia, 1939).

ALBIGENSIAN CRUSADE. A crusade called in 1209 by Pope **Innocent III** against the Cathars (also called Albigenses), a **heretical** sect of southern France. It lasted until 1255. Rabbis were falsely accused of influencing the **heresy**. Jews were persecuted, and hundreds were massacred and burned in **autos-da-fé**, forced to wear a yellow circle, or charged by the **Inquisition** with **ritual murder** and **desecration of the Host**.

SUGGESTED READING: Jonathan Sumption, *Albigensian Crusade* (London: Faber & Faber, 2000).

ALBRECHT V (1397–1439). Duke of Austria, 1404–39. Albrecht believed, as did the general populace, that Jews committed every evil, including **desecration of the Host**. In May 1420 Albrecht expelled the poor Jews and imprisoned the wealthy, confiscating their property. Some converted to Christianity, but most he burned at the stake. Others committed suicide. Pope **Martin V**'s only reaction was to decree that Jewish children under the age of 12 should not be forcibly **baptized**. His epitaph boasts that he had ordered the Jews burned ("Jussi Judæos ante cremare meos").

SUGGESTED READING: Gotthard Deutsch, "Austria," *JewishEncyclopedia.com*, http://www.jewishencyclopedia.com/view.jsp?artid=2152& letter=A&search=au stria.

AL-DA'WA (THE CALL). This **Muslim Brotherhood** magazine expresses an extremely intolerant Islamic point of view. It focuses on Jews and "Crusaders" (the Christian West), declares war on them, and provides a rationale for terror. In January 1981, *Al-Da'wa* proclaimed that "democracy contradicts Islam and wages war on it. Those who call for democracy contradict God's plan and attack Islam."

SUGGESTED READING: Bernard Lewis, *Semites and Antisemites* (New York: Norton, 1986).

ALENU PRAYER. Standing Hebrew prayer ("It is our duty"). The last prayer of the daily Jewish liturgy composed in Babylonian exile was denounced by two apostates, Pesach Peter (1399) and Antonius Margarita (1500), as anti-Christian. They referred particularly to the prayer's line that says: "They bow down and pray to vanity and nothingness, and to a god who cannot save." Some Jews spit when they recite this line (the Hebrew word for "emptiness" being the same as for "spit"). From the 14th century to the 18th, Christian authorities banned the line and the spitting. *See also* AMIDAH.

SUGGESTED READING: Ismar Elbogen, *Jewish Liturgy: A Comprehensive History*, trans. Raymond P. Scheindlin (Philadelphia: Jewish Publication Society, 1993); Kaufmann Kohler, "Alenu," *JewishEncyclopedia.com*, http://www.jewishencyclopedia.com/view.jsp?artid=1112&letter=A.

ALEXANDER I (1777–1825). Tsar of Russia, 1801–25. In dealing with Jews, Alexander vacillated between tolerance and persecution. He decreed that government educational institutions were open to Jews and that Jews could have their own schools for secular education. Grateful for Jewish support against **Napoleon** in 1812, he appointed Jewish advisors to his cabinet. In 1816 Alexander denounced **ritual murder** as a false prejudice. However, in 1821 he abolished the *Kahals*, Jewish self-governing bodies, and in 1824–25, believing that Jews corrupted Christian beliefs, he removed Jews from Mogilev and Vitesk, two large provinces.

SUGGESTED READING: Simon Cohen, "Alexander I," *Universal Jewish Encyclopedia* (New York: Universal Jewish Encyclopedia, 1939).

ALEXANDER II (d. 1073). Pope, 1061–73. Although in 1063 Alexander II praised French bishops who had attempted to protect Jews against "holy warriors" en route to attack Muslims in Spain, his same letter noted that the Jews were "by God's grace slaves who, having lost their homeland and their liberty, are living in agony over the whole earth, suffering perpetual punishment, and damned due to their spilling of the Savior's blood."

SUGGESTED READING: Shlomo Simonsohn, *The Apostolic See and the Jews: Documents, 492–1404* (Toronto: Pontifical Institute of Mediaeval Studies, 1988); Gotthard Deutsch and Joseph Jacobs, "The Popes," *Jewish Encyclopedia.com*, http://www.jewishencyclopedia.com/view.jsp?artid = 438&letter = P.

ALEXANDER III (d. 1181). Pope, 1159–81. Alexander III issued a bull of protection during the Third **Crusade** (1187–92) and the years just preceding it (a "bull" is an official papal document, from the Latin *bullum*, "seal"). But Alexander noted the Jews' "stiff-necked obstinacy" and called Judaism a "superstition" and the Jews "enemies of Christ's cross." He also issued a bull that required Jews to keep their doors and windows shut on **Good Friday**, prohibited Jews from employing Christians in their homes, and forced Jews off their lands when they refused to pay traditional tithes to the Church.

SUGGESTED READING: Shlomo Simonsohn, *The Apostolic See and the Jews: Documents, 492–1404* (Toronto: Pontifical Institute of Mediaeval Studies, 1988); Gotthard Deutsch and Joseph Jacobs, "The Popes," *Jewish Encyclopedia.com*, http://www.jewishencyclopedia.com/view.jsp?artid = 438&letter = P.

ALEXANDER III (1845–1894). Tsar of Russia, 1881–94. Convinced that Jewish conspirators had assassinated his father, Tsar Alexander II (1825–1881), he revoked the liberal policies toward Jews he had inherited. Alexander III sponsored **pogroms**, reduction of Jewish residence inside the **Pale**, and denial of Jewish business on Sundays and Christian holidays. A *numerus clausus* was also instituted, dramatically limiting Jewish participation in higher education.

SUGGESTED READING: Salo Baron, *The Russian Jew under Tsars and Soviets*, 2nd rev. ed. (New York: Schocken Books, 1987).

ALEXANDER VI (1431–1503). Pope, 1491–1503. In 1495, Alexander VI approved a statute that excluded New Christians and their descendants down to the fourth generation from membership in the Order of **St. Jerome**. The next year, he conferred the title "Catholic" on the Spanish monarchs Ferdinand and Isabella for their unification of Spain as well as their **expulsion** of the Jews. In 1497, Alexander did not oppose Portuguese

King **Manoel's baptism** of all Jewish children ages 4 to 14 and their removal from their families in an attempt to force their parents to **convert** to Christianity.

SUGGESTED READING: Shlomo Simonsohn, *The Apostolic See and the Jews, Documents: 1465–1521* (Toronto: Pontifical Institute of Mediaeval Studies, 1990); Gotthard Deutsch and Joseph Jacobs, "The Popes," *Jewish Encyclopedia.com*, http://www.jewishencyclopedia.com/view.jsp?artid = 438&letter = P.

ALEXANDRIA RIOTS. Pagans rarely attacked **synagogues**. Only in Alexandria, Egypt, in 38 CE is there sure evidence that Jewish places of worship were destroyed with the acquiescence of the Roman governor. But once Christianity dominated the empire, the number of attacks against synagogues increased dramatically.

SUGGESTED READING: Victor Tcherikover, *Hellenistic Civilization and the Jews* (Philadelphia: Jewish Publication Society, 1959).

ALFONSO X (1221–1284). King of Castile and León, 1252–84. Alfonso allowed Jews in his Court to perform economic, administrative, and intellectual functions that lent them authority over Christians. In 1261, Alfonso supported a seven-part law code, Las **Siete Partidas**. On the one hand, Jews were granted religious freedom, Christians were to respect the **synagogue** "as a house where God's name is praised," Jews were protected from accusations of **ritual murder** and blood libel, Jews could employ Christian laborers, and forced **baptism** was forbidden. On the other hand, Christians who **converted** to Judaism were to be put to death, Jews and Christians could not live together, Jews could not hold positions of authority over Christians, and Jews had to wear **stigmatic emblems**. In 1277, Alfonso ordered all Castilian Jews arrested and fined them 12,000 gold maravedis. In 1279, Pope **Nicholas III** ordered Peter Guerra, bishop of Rieti, to investigate a series of complaints against the king. He was dethroned in 1281 by his son Sancho with the sanction of the Cortes.

SUGGESTED READING: Joseph O' Callaghan, *The Learned King: The Reign of Alfonso X of Castile* (Philadelphia: University of Pennsylvania Press, 1993).

ALHAIZA, ADOLPHE (1839–?). French Utopian Socialist. Alhaiza edited *La Rénovation*, a journal of the **Fourier** movement, whose three dominant themes were nationalism, anti-Marxism, and **antisemitism**. In it, Alhaiza, influenced by **Charles Maurras**, advocated an uprising against the "Jewish race," who were, in his opinion, "eternal destroyers of nations" and "moral corruptors."

SUGGESTED READING: Georgi V. Plekhanov, *Utopian Socialism of the Nineteenth Century* (Berkeley: University of California Press, 2003).

ALIEN RACE. (Nazi German slur) Jews, Africans, Slavs, and other "foreign" or "alien" races residing on German soil; noncitizens.

SUGGESTED READING: "List of Ethnic Slurs," *Wikipedia*, http://en.wiki pedia.org/wiki/List_of_ethnic_slurs.

ALLIANCE ISRAÉLITE UNIVERSELLE. French-based Jewish defense and educational organization. Launched by French Jews and headed by jurist Adolphe Cremieux in 1860, its mission was to defend and aid Jews everywhere. Its establishment was triggered by the **Damascus Affair**. Later, it set up worldwide Jewish educational facilities. Antisemites falsely accused the Alliance of being a front for an international Jewish conspiracy and tool of Jewish subversion.

SUGGESTED READING: Michael Laskier, *The Alliance Israelite and the Jewish Community of Morocco, 1862–1923* (New York: State University of New York Press, 1983).

ALMOHADES (MUWAHADIS). Islamic militant group. A Berber movement of Islamic unitarianism whose military arm conquered and ruled North Africa and Muslim Spain in the 12th and 13th centuries. Fundamentalist and purist, these Moors faced Jews with a choice: convert or die. Traditional Jews such as Maimonides had to flee Cordoba and Fez to find refuge among more tolerant Arabs near Cairo, while other Jews in Spain took refuge in Christian states.

SUGGESTED READING: Mark R. Cohen, *Under Crescent and Cross: The Jews in the Middle Ages* (Princeton, NJ: Princeton University Press, 1994).

AL-QAEDA. Islamic fundamentalist terrorist group formed in opposition to the Soviet invasion of Afghanistan, 1979–1989. Its political goal is pan-Islamic unity with Muslims living under fundamentalist Islamic law. Al-Qaeda leaders, including **Osama bin Laden**, view the world as a struggle between fundamentalist Islam and Western secular ideology. Their spokesmen emphasize the existence of Israel and U.S. support for Israel as major factors justifying their war against the West. Suicide bomber attacks against both Western military and civilian targets, notably the World Trade Center and Pentagon in 2001, are justified as freedom fighting and dying for the holy cause of **jihad**. *See also* MUSLIM BROTHERHOOD; RADICAL ISLAM.

SUGGESTED READING: Samuel P. Huntington, *The Clash of Civilizations and the Remaking of the World Order* (New York: Simon & Schuster, 1998).

ALTER KACKER, ALTER KOCKER. (North American slur) Elderly Jewish people. Although of Yiddish origin (literally meaning "old shit"), the phrase has been adopted by Gentiles as a slur against Jews.

SUGGESTED READING: "List of Ethnic Slurs," *Wikipedia*, http://en.wiki pedia.org/wiki/List_of_ethnic_slurs.

AMBROSE, ST. (340–397). Bishop of Milan. Perhaps the most famous incident of **synagogue** destruction and its political ramifications occurred in 388 when a synagogue in Callinicum was burned by a Christian crowd stimulated by sermons and led by the local bishop; the synagogue was then transformed into a church. The Roman governor punished the arsonists and ordered the bishop to pay to rebuild the synagogue from his own funds. The decision was confirmed by Emperor Theodosius I, who clearly had no legal right to deny the Jews compensation for their loss, as Judaism was still a legally recognized religion in the empire. Ambrose wrote to the emperor that for Christians to destroy a synagogue was a glorious act, so that "there might be no place where Christ is denied." Ambrose despised the Jews, whom he associated with **heresy**, and saw any contact with them as a defilement. He saw the Jews as poisoned serpents and devils.

SUGGESTED READING: Ambrose, "Epistolarum Classis I. XL. 26," in *Patrologiae, Cursus Completus: Series Latina*, ed. Jacques-Paul Migne (Paris: Garnier, 1844–92), 16; Jacob Marcus, *The Jew in the Medieval World: A Source Book, 315–1791* (New York: New York University, 1979).

AMERICA FIRST COMMITTEE (AFC). A conservative isolationist group with ties to Congress, the America First Committee was determined to prevent America's entanglements in Europe's problems during World War II. The AFC did not officially adopt **antisemitism**, although its membership list contained such prominent antisemites as Clara and **Henry Ford**, Fr. **Charles Coughlin**, Rev. **Gerald L. K. Smith**, Rev. **Gerald Winrod**, **William Pelley**, and the leader of the **German-American Bund**, **Fritz Kuhn**. Charles and Anne **Lindbergh** were also notable members. In addition to the Bund, the following pro-**fascist** groups were also aligned with the AFC: American Destiny Party, American Guards, American White Guards, Blackshirts and Italian Fascist Clubs, **Christian Front**,

Christian Mobilizers, Ethiopian-Pacific League, Falangists, Gray Shirts Kyffhaeuser Bund, **Ku Klux Klan**, National Copperheads, National Workers League, Patriots of the Republic, Save America First, Save Our American Clubs, Silver Shirts, Social Justice Clubs, and White Russian Fascists. Gen. Robert Wood, chairman of the AFC prior to Pearl Harbor, opposed all efforts to aid nations threatened by **Nazi** Germany and made no effort to keep out openly pro-Nazi groups. "The Committee has in reality gone underground," FBI Director J. Edgar Hoover reported to the White House. The AFC began planning for the day when they would be the Americans with whom the victorious Nazis would negotiate surrender. However, when the defeat of the Nazis by Allied powers was a foregone conclusion, the committee secretly dissolved itself in 1944.

SUGGESTED READING: Wayne S. Cole, *America First: The Battle against Intervention, 1940–1941* (New York: Octagon Books, 1971).

AMERICAN COALITION OF PATRIOTIC SOCIETIES (ACPS). An organization founded by John Trevor in 1929 to support and maintain tight U.S. immigration restrictions enacted into law in 1924. Trevor was the behind-the-scenes architect of the 1924 **Johnson-Reed Act**, designed to exclude East Europeans, Italians, Jews, and other non-Nordics. The ACPS leadership included those with links to **Nazi** Germany. One associate of Trevor's, zoologist **Madison Grant**, explicitly repudiated "democratic ideals and Christian values in the interest of a Nordic philosophy." Another ACPS director, **Harry Laughlin**, was given an honorary Ph.D. in 1936 by Heidelberg University for his work in the area of racial **eugenics**. In 1942, the ACPS was named by the Justice Department as "a factor" in the sedition charges brought against those thought to be aiding the Axis powers.

SUGGESTED READING: John Higham, *Strangers in the Land: Patterns of American Nativism, 1860–1926* (New Brunswick, NJ: Rutgers University Press, 2002); Marcia Synnott, "Antisemitism and American Universities: Did Quotas Follow the Jews?" in *American Jewish History: Antisemitism in America*, ed. Jeffrey Gurock (Florence, KY: Rutledge, 1998); Arnold Forster and Benjamin R. Epstein, *Danger on the Right* (New York: Random House, 1964).

AMERICAN FASCISTIC ASSOCIATION. *See* SECRET ORGANIZATIONS, 20TH CENTURY.

AMERICAN FRONT. Symbolized by the letters *AF* integrated into a **Celtic Cross**. Led by National Chairman James Porrazzo and based in Harrison,

Arkansas, the American Front believes in **antisemitism** and race separatism. American Front aspires to "secure National Freedom and Social Justice for the White people of North America" and defeat the forces of the "New World Order" and "international capitalists."

SUGGESTED READING: Anti-Defamation League, *Hate on Display: Extremist Symbols, Logos, and Tattoos* (New York: Anti-Defamation League, 2006).

AMERICAN IMMIGRATION CONFERENCE BOARD. A "patriotic" organization that successfully opposed the **Wagner-Rogers Bill**. The bill, sponsored by Sen. Robert Wagner (D-NY) and Rep. Edith Rogers (R-MA), would have permitted 20,000 German **refugee** (Jewish) children under 14 entry into the United States. When President **Franklin Roosevelt** refused to support the bill, it died.

SUGGESTED READING: Arthur Morse, *While Six Million Died* (New York: Overlook Press, 1998); David Wyman, *The Abandonment of the Jews: America and the Holocaust* (New York: New Press, 1998); Rafael Medoff, "Kristallnacht and the World's Response," *Jewish Week*, November 9, 2003, available at http://www.aish.com/holocaust/issues/Kristall nacht_And_The_Worlds_Response.asp.

AMERICAN NAZI PARTY (ANP). George Lincoln Rockwell founded the American **Nazi** Party, originally known as the World Union of Free Enterprise and **National Socialists**, in 1959. He believed all blacks should be deported to Africa and every Jew dispossessed and sterilized. He also believed that "traitors" such as former Presidents **Harry Truman** and Dwight D. Eisenhower should be hanged because they favored civil rights for all, including minorities. In 1967 a disgruntled party member murdered Rockwell. The ANP was renamed the National Socialist White People's Party (NSWPP) just a month or two before Rockwell's assassination. Now led by Rocky Suhayda, the ANP claims to be dedicated to the White Race, an **Aryan** Republic, and Western European cultural heritage. Symbolized by a red flag with a **swastika** in its center and headed by a banner with the words "American Nazi Party."

SUGGESTED READING: David H. Bennett, *The Party of Fear*, 2nd rev. ed. (New York: Vintage, 1995).

AMERICAN PROTECTIVE ASSOCIATION (APA). Nativist organization formed in 1887 with a membership that may have reached 2,250,000. The large influx of Eastern European immigrants prompted the founding of the APA, which came out harshly against Jews and Catholics and promoted restrictive immigration laws. The animosity toward the Jews would become so severe that it "yearned to eliminate Jews from society as a gardener would root out weeds or a surgeon cut out a cancer." They legitimized their racism along the lines of science, "a form of social engineering, which sprang from a conviction that some people could not be improved or controlled. It drew upon centuries of Christian religious prejudice, and gave it a scientific rationale."

SUGGESTED READING: John Higham, *Strangers in the Land: Patterns of American Nativism, 1860–1925* (New Brunswick, NJ: Rutgers University Press, 2002).

AMERICAN VIGILANTE INTELLIGENCE FEDERATION (AVIF). The AVIF was founded in 1927 by Harry Jung, an anti-union spy who believed in a Jewish-Communist conspiracy. With the rise of **antisemitism** in Europe, Jung became the first major distributor in the United States of the antisemitic forgery *The Protocols of the Elders of Zion*.

AMIDAH. Jewish standing prayer. The central portion in the Jewish liturgy, which contains 19 blessings, had a passage condemned by King **John I of Castile** in the 14th century. The part condemning **heretics** he interpreted as anti-Christian. It was expurgated for Spanish Jews. *See also* ALENU PRAYER.

SUGGESTED READING: Mark Cohen, *Under Crescent and Cross: The Jews of the Middle Ages* (Princeton, NJ: Princeton University Press, 1996).

AMIN, IDI (DADA) (1928?–2003). President of Uganda, 1971–79. This military dictator severed relations with Israel in 1972 and established ties with the Palestine Liberation Organization. Amin invited a terrorist-hijacked Air France airliner to stop at Entebbe. He assisted the hijackers, who separated out the many Jews among the passengers. However, before further harm could be done, on July 3, 1976, Israeli paratroopers rescued them.

SUGGESTED READING: Michael Freud, "Remember Entebbe," *Jerusalem Post*, July 9, 2003.

AMULO. Bishop of Lyons about 841. Amulo attempted to influence French king Charles the Bald to discriminate against the Jews. He argued that the Jews must have no authority whatsoever over Christians, slaves or free, that Jews must respect the authority of the Church, and that the faithful should completely shun "these enemies of the cross of Christ." He stated that the

Jews were guilty of "detestable and disgusting unbelief," were "a Godless [and] an unholy people," and were the "worst of all the unbelievers."

SUGGESTED READING: Amulo, "Epistola Seu Liber Contra Judaeos," IIX, in *Patrologiae, Cursus Completus: Series Latina*, ed. Jacques-Paul Migne (Paris: Garnier, 1844–92), 116:141, 170–84; Heinz Schreckenberg, *Die christlichen Adversus-Judaeos-Texte und ihr literarisches und historisches Umfeld, 1.-11 Jh.*, 4th ed. (Frankfurt: Peter Lang, 1999); Bernard Blumenkranz, "The Roman Church and the Jews," in *Essential Papers on Judaism and Christianity in Conflict*, ed. Jeremy Cohen (New York: New York University Press, 1991); Bernard Blumenkranz, *Juifs et Chrétiens dans le Monde Occidental* (Paris: La Haye, Mouton, 1960).

ANCRE, PIERRE DE L' (flourished early 17th cent.). In 1609 Ancre was commissioned as grand inquisitor of witches in France. Denouncing the "superstitious indecency of Judaism," de l'Ancre regarded Jews not only as witches but also as cruel and rapacious murderers of Christians who **poisoned the wells** and who forcibly **circumcized** and ritually murdered Christian children. He wrote that "filth [is] the attribute common to Jews and **pigs**" and that Jews "were more **perfidious** and faithless than demons." He concluded that "the Jews deserve every execration, and as destroyers of all divine and human majesty, they merit the greatest torment."

SUGGESTED READING: H. R. Trevor-Roper, *The Crisis of the Seventeenth Century* (New York: Harper & Row, 1968); H. R. Trevor-Roper, *The European Witch-Craze of the Sixteenth and Seventeenth Centuries* (New York: Penguin, 1969).

ANDERL OF RINN. A 1462 **ritual murder** case in Tyrol, Austria, in which Anderl, a three-year-old boy, was supposedly murdered by Jews. For centuries the church officially sanctioned this invitation to hating Jews. The Church beatified several alleged ritual-murder victims, among them Anderl of Rinn and **Simon of Trent**, thereby implying some truth to the **defamation**.

SUGGESTED READING: Alan Dundes, ed., *The Blood Libel Legend: A Casebook in Anti-Semitic Folklore* (Madison: University of Wisconsin Press, 1991).

ANDREAS OF RINN. *See* ANDERL OF RINN.

ANGLO-CONFORMITY. One of three theories of immigrant assimilation (the other two being melting pot and cultural pluralism), Anglo-conformity is a point of view unsympathetic to immigrants, particularly those from Eastern Europe between 1881 and 1924, that newcomers must shed their native culture—religion, language, dress, and customs—in order to conform to America's white Anglo-Saxon Protestant culture, behavior, and values.

SUGGESTED READING: E. P. Cubberley, *Changing Conceptions of Education* (New York: Riverside Educational Monographs/Houghton-Mifflin, 1909).

ANGRIFF, DER (*THE ATTACK*). Official organ of the **Nazi** Party founded in Berlin in 1927 by **Josef Goebbels**. It served to rally party members and influence the German working class. By 1930 it was a daily and had a circulation of 110,000. Goebbels wrote many antisemitic editorials railing against the "Jewish Press" and "Jewish capitalists," while cartoonist Hans Schweitzer demonized Jews. In 1934 Goebbels bowed out and *Angriff* became an organ of the Reich Labor Front, lasting until the end of the war in 1945.

SUGGESTED READING: George Reuth Rolf, *Goebbels*, trans. Kristin Winston (San Diego: Harcourt, 1994).

ANTICHRIST. "False **messiah**." An antagonist of Christ who simultaneously raised havoc and heralded a "new age" appears in the **Gospels** of Mark and **Matthew** of the Christian New Testament and in the anonymous First Letter to John. Two later professions of faith, written specifically for Jewish **converts** to Christianity, contain a mention of the Antichrist as well: "Above all I renounce Antichrist whom all the Jews await in the figure and form of Christ" and "I invoke every curse and anathema on him whose coming is expected by the Jews as the Christ or Anointed, but is rather Antichrist." An apocalyptic prophecy was that "Satan will be released when a thousand years have passed." This was interpreted to mean that the long-delayed Second Coming and Final Judgment of Christ was about to take place, preceded by a battle between the forces of Christianity and those of the Antichrist. **Church Fathers** believed that the Antichrist would first come to the Jews because they were the ones who had refused to believe in the true messiah, Jesus Christ. According to one prophecy, the Antichrist would be born of a Jewish whore and the Devil.

SUGGESTED READING: James Parkes, *The Conflict of the Church and the Synagogue: A Study in the Origins of Antisemitism* (New York: Atheneum, 1979).

ANTI-DEFAMATION LEAGUE (ADL). Jewish defense organization. The league was founded in 1913 in New York, triggered by the unfair trial of

Leo Frank. The ADL's charge is to combat **antisemitism** in the United States; to expose antisemitic stereotypes in the media, popular culture, and intellectual circles; and to expose **neo-Nazis**. It takes surveys on antisemitic opinions of Americans. The league's website is www.adl.org.

SUGGESTED READING: *Not the Work of a Day: Anti-Defamation League of B'nai B'rith Oral Memoirs* (New York: ADL, 1987); Leonard Dinnerstein, *The Leo Frank Case* (Athens: University of Georgia Press, 1998).

ANTIDREYFUSARDS. French men and women who opposed French captain Alfred Dreyfus during and after his treason trials in 1894–98. Though Dreyfus was wrongfully convicted and later exonerated, the antidreyfusards believed that his being a Jew made him guilty. Also, they persisted in declaring Dreyfus guilty to uphold the honor of the French Army. The culture war pitted devout Catholics, antirepublicans, and antisemites against liberals, republicans, and cosmopolitans. *See also* ACTION FRANÇAISE; BARRÈS, MAURICE; *CROIX, LA*; DREYFUS CASE; DRUMONT, EDOUARD; ESTERHAZY, FERDINAND; HENRY, HUBERT JOSEPH; *LIBRE PAROLE, LA*; MAURRAS, CHARLES; ZOLA, ÉMILE.

SUGGESTED READING: Michael Burns, *France and the Dreyfus Affair: A Documentary History* (Boston: Bedford/St. Martin, 1999).

ANTI-JUDAISM. *See* TRIUMPHALISM.

ANTIOCHUS EPIPHANES (215–164 BCE). Syrian-Greek king of Syria who conquered Jerusalem in 167 BCE and sought to Hellenize Judea. He plundered the Holy Temple, dedicated it to Zeus, and sought to compel Jews to adopt Greek culture. Under the penalty of death, he sought to eliminate Jewish observance of their **Sabbath** and holy days. His Hellenizing led to a revolt by the Maccabees, the Jewish clan who led the revolt in Judea.

SUGGESTED READING: Maccabees 1:21–24; Victor Tcherikover, *Hellenistic Civilization and the Jews* (Philadelphia: Jewish Publication Society, 1959).

ANTISEMITES' LEAGUE. *See* ANTISEMITIC LEAGUE; MARR, WILHELM.

ANTISEMITES' PETITION. Wilhelm Marr's **Antisemitic League**, university students, the Christian Social Party, and most of the **Catholic Center Party** were instrumental in preparing, publishing, and presenting this petition to the German government in 1881–82. Containing nearly a quarter of a million signatures, the document sought to reverse the social and political gains Jews had made in Germany and to free Germany from Jewish "economic servitude" and "alien domination" by limiting or preventing Jewish immigration and by excluding Jews "from all positions of authority."

SUGGESTED READING: George L. Mosse, *The Crisis of German Ideology*. New York: H. Fertig, 1998.

ANTISEMITIC ACCUSATIONS. *See* DEFAMATIONS, ANTI-JEWISH.

ANTISEMITIC CATECHISM. Composed in 1883 by **Theodor Fritsch**, the German publicist who ran the Hammer Publishing House—the first publication of which was the Catechism. Its "Decalogue" included no intermarriage, no social intercourse, no business relations with Jews, and no using of a Jewish teacher, lawyer, or physician. Later, as the "Handbook on the Jewish Question," it served as an inspiration to the **Nazis**.

SUGGESTED READING: William Nicholls, *Christian Antisemitism: A History of Hate* (Northvale, NJ: Jason Aronson, 1995); Paul Massing, *Rehearsal for Destruction: A Study of Political Antisemitism in Imperial Germany* (New York: Fertig, 1967).

ANTISEMITIC CONSPIRACY BELIEFS ABOUT JEWS. Antisemitic beliefs include a Jewish conspiracy to conquer the world, harm Christians, act immorally, control financial institutions and the press, ruin Christians economically, create a godless Communism, murder Christian children and consume their blood, destroy the Christian religion, and betray the nation in which they live. Almost all of these alleged goals stem from the writings of the **Church Fathers** or from the Christian Middle Ages. *See also* DEFAMATIONS, ANTI-JEWISH.

ANTISEMITIC LEAGUE. Organization founded in 1893 by **Wilhelm Marr**; also known as the Social Reich Party. It was a single-issue party, advocating the **expulsion** of Jews from Germany. It failed as an organization. There was also a French antisemitic league founded by **Edouard Drumont** in 1888; it was dissolved by 1890.

SUGGESTED READING: Moshe Zimmerman, *Wilhelm Marr: The Patriarch of Antisemitism* (New York: Oxford University Press, 1985).

ANTISEMITIC LITERATURE. Fiction and nonfiction in which all Jews or the only Jews portrayed are bad, evil, disreputable, or disgusting characters; works in which even minor Jewish characters exhibit negative traditional antisemitic stereotypes; works in which the author's general viewpoint betrays a disdain toward Jews.

ANTISEMITIC POLITICAL PARTIES, GERMAN. *See* ANTISEMITIC LEAGUE; GERMAN NATIONAL PEOPLE'S PARTY; GERMAN WORKERS PARTY; NAZI PARTY; WEIMAR REPUBLIC.

ANTISEMITISM. Irrational dislike, prejudice, hostility, or hatred of Jews. Usually manifested as antilocution, discrimination, expropriation, **expulsion**, violence, murder, and/or genocide of Jews. As part of a history of Jews in Hamburg, Germany, an online glossary of **Nazi** terms at the University of Hamburg's website declares that *antisemitism* is a "misleading" term

> in that hostility was solely directed at Jews and not against all semitic peoples. . . . Enmity towards Jews is not restricted to Christian cultures, however, it is within these cultures that it is most evident. Whereas in the West the spread of antisemitism remained relatively restricted, in Germany and in eastern Europe it was widely disseminated. Following the First World War the Jews were made answerable for all social and political crises. The Nazis consciously built upon this conventional antisemitism and additionally used the modern form of antisemitism.

Many scholars, such as Richard Levy and Michael Marrus, identify antisemitism as occurring only from the 19th century onward, as antisemitism began to involve racist political movements in a society more secularized than before. But research by James Parkes, Rosemary Ruether, Robert Wistrich, Léon Poliakov, and others has shown that anti-Jewish Christian theology, including early forms of racism, influenced Roman Law, persuaded Christian militants (**Crusaders**) to slaughter thousands of Jews, and conditioned a politically powerful Church in general and the papacy in particular during the Middle Ages. By the 15th century, the Spanish government and Roman Church collaborated in a highly politicized **Inquisition** and the enforcement of race laws against Jews. Indeed, every Nazi administrative order had its precedent in Christian societies. *See also* the following entries on various aspects of antisemitism, as well as ANTISEMITIC CONSPIRACY BELIEFS ABOUT JEWS; ANTI-ZIONIST ANTISEMITISM; DEFAMATIONS, ANTI-JEWISH; NEW ANTISEMITISM.

Suggested Reading: William Nicholls, *Christian Antisemitism* (Northvale, NJ: Jason Aronson, 1993); Shmuel Almog, *Antisemitism through the Ages* (Elmsford, NY: Pergamon, 1988); Raul Hilberg, *Destruction of European Jewry* (New York: Holmes & Meier, 1985); Struan

Robertson, "A History of Jews in Hamburg: German and N-S Terminology," *Regionales Rechenzentrum der Universität Hamburg*, http://www1 .uni-hamburg.de/rz3a035/ns_term.html.

ANTISEMITISM, AMERICAN. By the 1880s in the United States, hatred and contempt for the Jew had become a Christian habit of mind, wrought into the very woof of Christianity, intensified by Sunday schools and churches. American **antisemitism**, moderated by traditions of civil liberty and legal equality and by the existence of numerous other scapegoats besides the Jews, was often aggravated by economic, political, and social issues. But it never led to European-style anti-Jewish **pogroms**. During the first half of the 20th century, under the stress of increased Jewish immigration and two world wars separated by an economic depression, U.S. antisemitism grew more radical. Antisemitism would play a crucial role in public attitudes toward European Jews and Jewish **refugees** seeking haven in the United States. *See also CHRISTIAN BELIEFS AND ANTISEMITISM.*

SUGGESTED READING: Seymour Martin Lipset and Earl Raab, *Jews and the New American Scene* (Cambridge, MA: Harvard University Press, 1995).

ANTISEMITISM, ARAB NATIONALIST. Modern secular Arab nationalists envisioning a powerful pan-Arab empire joined with fundamentalist Muslims in regarding Israelis as "aliens and enemies" and melding "international Zionism" with "world Jewry." Incredulous that the *dhimmis* could have established an independent Jewish state and defeated every Arab army sent against them, these nationalists and fundamentalists claim that there exists a metaphysical and ideological battle between the Islamic-Muslim forces of good and the Jewish-Israeli-Western forces of evil embodied in modern libertarianism, music, film, commerce, drugs, and prostitution.

SUGGESTED READING: Israel Gershoni and James Jankowski, eds., *Rethinking Nationalism in the Arab Middle East* (New York: Columbia University Press, 1997); Robert S. Wistrich, *Muslim Antisemitism: A Clear and Present Danger* (New York: American Jewish Committee, 2002).

ANTISEMITISM, BLACK. Despite statements condemning **antisemitism** by the National Association for Advancement of Colored People, the Urban League, Langston Hughes, Booker T. Washington, and W. E. B. Du-Bois (the last two named began their careers exhibiting antisemitism but changed later in life)—and the fact that for decades in the 19th and 20th centuries, Jews and blacks had joined forces to further civil rights for all Americans—there was and is an undercurrent of black antisemitism. Based on their experience with a handful of Jewish landlords, employers, and merchants who exploited the black community, in the mid-20th century blacks in large East Coast and Midwest cities scapegoated Jews. *See also* BLACK CAUCUS; BLACK PANTHER PARTY; BLACK PANTHER PARTY FOR SELF-DEFENSE, THE NEW; CARMICHAEL, STOKELY; FARRAKHAN, LOUIS; MUHAMMAD, KHALID ABDUL; WRIGHT, RICHARD.

SUGGESTED READING: Murray Friedman, *What Went Wrong? The Creation and Collapse of the Black-Jewish Alliance* (New York: Free Press, 1995).

ANTISEMITISM, LEFTIST. Left-wing Jews and non-Jews who view Israel ideologically as a parochial, undemocratic state serving American imperialism. Theirs is a double standard, voicing sympathy to Palestinians but none to Israel, charging Israel as an aggressive, sadistic occupier of Arab land and the cause of terrorism and suicide or homicide bombings.

SUGGESTED READING: George Jochnowitz, "The New Left and Its New Antisemitism," *Midstream* (February 1, 2004); Michael Lerner, *The Socialism of Fools: Anti-Semitism on the Left* (Berkeley, CA: Institute for Labor & Mental Health, 1992); Seth Farber, "The Left-Wing Gatekeepers of the American Anti-Israel Occupation Movement," *Dissident Voice* (October 7, 2005), http://www.dissidentvoice.org/Oct05/Farber1007.htm; Nacha Cattan, "Leftist Jews Gaining Support of the Palestinians," *Forward*, April 12, 2002.

ANTISEMITISM, MUSLIM. Even before the establishment of Israel and modern Muslim **anti-Zionism**, there was a long history of discrimination and violence against Jews in Muslim lands, most of it mirroring Christian **antisemitism**. In 1043 and 1465, Muslim mobs, enraged by alleged Jewish offenses, slaughtered thousands of **ghettoized** Jews. For every Jew who attained a prestige position in Arab lands, a similar number of arbitrary **confiscations of Jewish property**, attempted forced **conversions**, or **pogroms** occurred. Other mass murders of Jews took place in Medina in 627 when Jews refused to convert to Islam; in Morocco in the 8th and 12th centuries, when Jews were either forcibly converted or decimated, and again in 1864 and 1880 as well; in Libya in 1785, when hundreds of Jews were murdered; and in Algiers in 1805, 1815, and 1830. **Synagogues** were destroyed in Egypt and Syria in 1014, 1293–94, and 1301–02; in Iraq in 854–59 and 1344; and in Yemen in 1676. Despite the **Koran**'s prohibitions, forced conversions took place in Yemen in 1165 and 1678; in Morocco in 1275, 1465, and 1790–92; and in Baghdad in 1333 and 1344. *See also* ANTI-ZIONIST ANTISEMITISM.

SUGGESTED READING: Robert S. Wistrich, *Muslim Antisemitism: A Clear and Present Danger* (New York: American Jewish Committee, 2002).

ANTISEMITISM, MYSTICAL. Puzzling, occult, spiritually intuitive **antisemitism**. Unlike other forms of prejudice, antisemitism took on a mystical character with the advent of Christianity. Images of Jews as inhumanly evil and satanically powerful were promulgated by the early **Church Fathers**. The **Crusaders** exploited the ancient theme of Jews as demonic murderers of God, and after **Martin Luther**'s campaign of violent antisemitism in 1543, the stereotype of Jew as primordial sinner became central to the catechism taught to children in Europe.

SUGGESTED READING: Joel Carmichael, *The Satanizing of the Jews* (New York: Fromm International, 1993).

ANTISEMITISM, PAGAN. Widespread pagan **antisemitism** is a myth. Nowhere among the pagans is there an elemental hatred of Jews such as that found among early Christian writers and Christianized Roman officials. Only after Christian influence was felt in the Roman Empire was the "Jew" considered almost universally foul and degrading. Most pagan authors were neutral or friendly toward Jews and accepted Judaism as it was. Pagan Greeks and Romans found many reasons to respect the Jews: their antiquity, their well-documented history, their great sacred literature, the Jews' family and community life, their monotheism, their elevated moral code, and their emphasis on the inherent value of human life. Some pagans identified certain practices as particularly Jewish and ridiculed the **circumcision** procedure, **Sabbath** observance, the eating of kosher foods, the worship of one God, and Jewish separatism. Of the 179 pagan authors (writing 576 fragments) who mention Jews or Judaism or Judaea/Galilee, only 28 include negative statements in their work.

SUGGESTED READING: Menahem Stern, ed., *Greek and Latin Authors on Jews and Judaism* (Jerusalem: Israel Academy of Sciences and Humanities, 1984).

ANTISEMITISM, POSTWAR GERMAN. Surveys taken by the Allied military authorities shortly after the war revealed a "massive persistence of **antisemitism**" similar to the situation with American antisemitism. Surveys that followed showed again, as in other nations such as Romania and

Hungary, that about one-third of the West German population was openly antisemitic, one-third was "somewhat," and one-third was not antisemitic. From the 1950s to the 1990s, West German tolerance of public antisemitism declined along with the public expression of antisemitism, although there was a corresponding increase of private antisemitism. Whereas age, education, and political orientation were the major factors influencing antisemitism in both parts of Germany, anti-Jewish attitudes declined more sharply in the former Democratic Republic (East Germany) than in the Federal Republic (West Germany), and there were fewer feelings of guilt for the **Holocaust** in East Germany. There are three possible reasons for this: First, dictatorial Communist anti-**fascism** in the East may have been able to diminish prejudice more effectively than the free exchange of ideas in democratic West Germany. Second, East Germany declared fascism to be a result of capitalism, thereby exonerating its population from any historical responsibility for **Nazism**. Third, East Germany's condemnation of fascism precluded discussion of Jews or antisemitism in any regard, whereas West Germany permitted intensive debates in education and in public life on the nature and history of the **Third Reich**. This kept anti-Jewish stereotypes and antisemitic ideas in the forefront. In 1998, when Jews in Germany numbered in the tens of thousands, a study sponsored by the newspaper *Die Woche* indicated about a third of Germans surveyed imagined the Jews to number in the millions.

SUGGESTED READING: Werner Bergmann and Rainer Erb, *Antisemitism in Germany: The Post-Nazi Epoch since 1945* (New Brunswick, NJ: Transaction, 1997); Sidney Bolkosky, review of Bergmann and Erb, *Antisemitism in Germany*, H-Net Reviews, July 1997, http://www.ess.uwe.ac.uk/genocide/reviewas5.htm; John Rosenthal, "Anti-Semitism and Ethnicity in Europe," *Policy Review*, no. 121 (October–November 2003), http://www.policyreview.org/oct03/rosenthal.html.

ANTISEMITISM, RACIAL. Writers have often used the word *race* as a synonym for *people* or *nation*. Racism holds that

1. different groups of human beings (races) are permanently, genetically different
2. each individual within a group always manifests the same traits as all other members of their group
3. inevitable consequences (intellectual, moral, social, and physical) follow from the differences between groups

From the first centuries of the Christian era onward, many Christian writers found an inherent theological repulsiveness as well as a horrible physical

Otherness in Jews. The **Church Fathers** claimed that each and every single Jew was fundamentally and repugnantly un-Christian and that Jews transmitted indelibly and permanently evil characteristics to their offspring. Such beliefs were later adopted by **Wilhelm Marr**, the German writer who coined the term *antisemitism* in 1873 to provide a more polite word to express hatred of Jews. *See also* ANTISEMITISM, AMERICAN; ANTISEMITISM, PAGAN; CHAMBERLAIN, HOUSTON STEWART; CHRISTIAN RACISM; EUGENICS; GOBINEAU, ARTHUR DE; HAECKEL, ERNST; HITLER, ADOLF; LAGARDE, PAUL ANTON DE; LIEBENFELS, LANZ VON; PAN-SLAVISM; SOCIAL DARWINISM; VÖLKISCH NATIONALISM; WAGNER, RICHARD.

SUGGESTED READING: Gavin Langmuir, *Toward a Definition of Antisemitism* (Berkeley: University of California Press, 1990).

ANTISEMITISM, WORKING DEFINITION OF. The Organization for Security and Cooperation in Europe's definition of *antisemitism* was intended as "a template for police forces and antiracist campaigners, for use on the streets." It reads:

Antisemitism is a certain perception of Jews, which may be expressed as hatred toward Jews. Rhetorical and physical manifestations of antisemitism are directed toward Jewish or non-Jewish individuals and/or their property, toward Jewish community institutions and religious facilities.

In addition, such manifestations could also target the state of Israel, conceived as a Jewish collectivity. Antisemitism frequently charges Jews with conspiring to harm humanity, and it is often used to blame Jews for "why things go wrong." It is expressed in speech, writing, visual forms and action, and employs sinister stereotypes and negative character traits.

Contemporary examples of antisemitism in public life, the media, schools, the workplace, and in the religious sphere could, taking into account the overall context, include, but are not limited to:

- Calling for, aiding, or justifying the killing or harming of Jews in the name of a radical ideology or an extremist view of religion.
- Making mendacious, dehumanizing, demonizing, or stereotypical allegations about Jews as such or the power of Jews as collective—such as, especially but not exclusively, the myth about a world Jewish conspiracy or of Jews controlling the media, economy, government or other societal institutions.
- Accusing Jews as a people of being responsible for real or imagined wrongdoing committed by a single Jewish person or group, or even for acts committed by non-Jews.
- Denying the fact, scope, mechanisms (e.g. gas chambers) or intentionality of the genocide of the Jewish people at the hands of National-Socialist Germany and its supporters and accomplices during World War II (the **Holocaust**).

- Accusing the Jews as a people, or Israel as a state, of inventing or exaggerating the Holocaust.
- Accusing Jewish citizens of being more loyal to Israel, or to the alleged priorities of Jews worldwide, than to the interests of their own nations.

Although criticism of Israel similar to that leveled against any other country cannot be regarded as antisemitism, examples of the ways in which antisemitism manifests itself with regard to the state of Israel taking into account the overall context could include:

- Denying the Jewish people their right to self-determination, e.g., by claiming that the existence of a State of Israel is a racist endeavor.
- Applying double standards by requiring of it a behavior not expected or demanded of any other democratic nation.
- Using the symbols and images associated with classic antisemitism (e.g., claims of Jews killing Jesus or blood-libel) to characterize Israel or Israelis.
- Drawing comparisons of contemporary Israeli policy to that of the Nazis.
- Holding Jews collectively responsible for actions of the state of Israel. However, criticism of Israel similar to that leveled against any other country cannot be regarded as antisemitic.
- Anti-Semitic acts are criminal when they are so defined by law (for example, denial of the Holocaust or distribution of antisemitic materials in some countries).
- Criminal acts are antisemitic when the targets of attacks, whether they are people or property—such as buildings, schools, places of worship and cemeteries—are selected because they are, or are perceived to be, Jewish or linked to Jews.
- Antisemitic discrimination is the denial to Jews of opportunities or services available to others and is illegal in many countries.

(European Union Monitoring Center on Racism and Xenophobia, "Working Definition of Antisemitism," March 16, 2005, http://eumc.europa.eu/eumc/material/pub/AS/AS-WorkingDefinition-draft.pdf)

See also BERLIN DECLARATION.

ANTISEMITISM IN THE CHRISTIAN SCRIPTURES. Pagan **antisemitism** was founded on secular Jewish nonconformity, but Christian antisemitism was defined first in the Christian Scriptures, the foundation of the Christian faith. Crucial passages in the four **Gospels**, in **Acts of the Apostles**, and in some Pauline letters deemed the Jews alien to the Christian cause and looked on Judaism as Christianity's enemy. These passages damned the Jews as rapacious hypocrites, children of hell and the Devil, God-haters in turn rejected by God, and murderers of Jesus the Christ, God incarnate. Nearly all Christian writers of the apostolic and patristic periods—the first seven or eight centuries of the Common Era—employed the

Christian Scriptures as a warehouse of anti-Jewish material. Accordingly, Christians designated themselves as God's new chosen people through their faith in Jesus; they displaced the Jews, now cut asunder from God's grace and abandoned to play out their devilish role in history. These perceptions, known as **triumphalism** or theologia gloriae, have dominated Christian attitudes toward the Jews for nearly two thousand years. A sea change occurred among many Protestants after the **Holocaust** and among Roman Catholics in 1965 with **Vatican Council II** and *Nostra Aetate. See also* JOHN, ST.; MATTHEW, ST.; PAUL, ST.

SUGGESTED READING: James Parkes, *The Conflict of the Church and the Synagogue: A Study in the Origins of Antisemitism* (New York: Atheneum, 1979).

ANTISEMITISMUS. *See* ANTISEMITISM.

ANTISEMITISM VERSUS ANTI-SEMITISM. Jewish historian Shmuel Almog pointed out:

> If you use the hyphenated form, you consider the words "Semitism", "Semite", "Semitic" as meaningful. They supposedly convey an image of a real substance, of a real group of people—the Semites, who are said to be a race. This is a misnomer: firstly, because "semitic" or **"aryan"** were originally language groups, not people; but mainly because in antisemitic parlance, "Semites" really stands for Jews, just that. And "Jews are not a race at all."

SUGGESTED READING: Shmuel Almog, *Antisemitism through the Ages* (Elmsford, NY: Pergamon, 1988).

ANTI-ZIONISM IN THE USSR. *See* ANTI-ZIONIST ANTISEMITISM.

ANTI-ZIONIST ANTISEMITISM. Those who oppose the creation and existence of the State of Israel are not necessarily antisemites. Many anti-Zionists attack the Jewish people through Israel; they scapegoat and condemn Israel for the world's problems. The key to this form of **antisemitism** is the double standard held for Israel apart from the other nations of the international community. As Martin Luther King Jr. proclaimed in 1968: "When people criticize Zionism, they mean Jews. . . . What is anti-Zionism? It is the denial of the Jewish people of a fundamental right that we justly claim for the people of Africa and freely accord all other nations of the globe." Anti-Zionist antisemites hold these views in common:

1. They complain that Arabs living in Israel do not have full rights while at the same time they demand that Jews be expelled from areas where Arabs dominate.

2. They use deceptions, disinformation, exaggerations, and selective omissions to attack Israel, and to identify its self-defense to **Nazi** practices.
3. They have a double standard for suffering—greater concern for Arabs, while virtually ignoring Jewish suffering.
4. They minimize or excuse the preaching and teaching of murderous hate toward Israel or Zionism.
5. They argue that Jews plot to influence public opinion in the West to support Israel and that such support opposes the national interest.
6. Arab clerics have negated the distinction between antisemitism and anti-Zionism. They claim that there is no essential difference between Israelis and Nazis.

Anti-Zionist Arab cartoonists learned from classic Christian anti-Jewish stereotypes, portraying Jews as demons and murderers, the fount of all evil and corruption, eternally conspiring to penetrate and destroy Muslim society and control the world. Jews are drawn as stooped, black-bearded, crooked nosed, loathsome men—straight out of the pages of **Julius Streicher**'s *Der Stürmer*, the Nazi journal that was not only **Adolf Hitler**'s favorite reading but also the most oriented toward attacking Jews in traditional Christian antisemitic terms. Judaism is shown as an evil, bloodthirsty, cabalistic religion. Zionists are labeled criminals, racists, or Nazis.

The goals of these anti-Zionist antisemites are to delegitimize Israel, to dehumanize Judaism, and to diabolize the Jewish people. Anti-Zionist antisemitism's goals are shared by many, if not most, Arab Muslim politicians, intellectuals, and religious leaders and the Arab in the streets. As Fiamma Nirenstein has written:

> The effect of this relentless vilification [is that] Israel has been transformed into little more than a diabolical abstraction, . . . a malignant force embodying every possible negative attribute—aggressor, usurper, sinner, occupier, corrupter, infidel, murderer, barbarian. As for Israelis themselves, they are seen not as citizens, workers, students, or parents but as the uniformed foot soldiers of that same dark force.

See also ANTISEMITISM, WORKING DEFINITION OF.

Suggested Reading: Bernard Lewis, *Semites and Anti-Semites* (New York: W. W. Norton, 1999); Robert S. Wistrich, *Muslim Antisemitism: A Clear and Present Danger* (New York: American Jewish Committee, 2002); Fiamma Nirenstein, "How Suicide Bombers Are Made," *Commentary*, September 2001.

ANUSIM. Hebrew for "forced ones." These were Spanish Jews, most of whom were forced to become Christians. Other names given were New

Christians, *conversos*, **Judaizers**, and **Marranos** (**"pigs"**). They were subject to the Spanish **Inquisition**. *See also* AUTO-DA-FÉ; TORQUE-MADA, TOMÁS DE.

SUGGESTED READING: Cecil Roth, *History of the Marranos* (New York: Sepher Herman, 1992).

APHRAATES (fl. 4th cent.). Christian Armenian writer. Aphraates misquoted the **Gospel** of **John**, claiming that Jesus said to the Jews, "You are the children of Cain, and not the children of Abraham." He called Christians the authentic "descendants of Abraham" and derided Jewish "sensuality, carnal desires and cupidity."

SUGGESTED READING: James Parkes, *The Conflict of the Church and the Synagogue: A Study in the Origins of Antisemitism* (New York: Atheneum, 1979); Frank Talmage, ed., *Disputation and Dialogue* (New York: Ktav, 1975); Louis Ginsberg, "Aphraates: The Persian Sage," *JewishEncyclopedia.com*, http://www.jewishencyclopedia.com/view.jsp?=p637&letter =A-31k.

APION (20 BCE–45 CE). Egyptian-Greek grammarian and historian. Apion appeared before the Roman emperor Caligula to attack the Jews of Alexandria. His five-volume *History of Egypt* has a long section against the Jews. It repeated slurs by earlier writers, including that Moses was a sun worshipper, a seducer, and wizard; that the Jews' **expulsion** from Egypt was because they were lepers; that the Holy of Holies (room of the Jewish high priest) in the Jerusalem Temple housed a golden ass that Jews worshipped; that Jews practiced **ritual murder** in the Holy Temple and drank Gentile blood; and that the observance of the **Sabbath** grew out of a Jewish groin disease. Apion also claimed that tenets of Judaism encouraged Jews to hate the rest of humankind. Much of what is known about Apion comes from the work of the Jewish historian Josephus, *Against Apion*. *See also* MA-NETHO.

SUGGESTED READING: Josephus, *Against Apion* (Cambridge, MA: Harvard University Press, 1926).

APP, J. AUSTIN (1902–1984). Former professor of English literature; a theoretician of **Holocaust denial**. App claimed that the Allied publicity about the **Holocaust** was a hoax, an attempt to hide Allied "outrages" against the German people during World War II. Alluding to *The Protocols of the Elders of Zion*, App accused Jewish leaders of controlling the Allies, provoking war, encouraging massive bombings, and even raping German women. His *The Six Million Swindle* (1973) denied the Holocaust and exonerated the **Nazi** regime of **genocide**.

SUGGESTED READING: Deborah Lipstadt, *Denying the Holocaust* (New York: Free Press, 1993).

AQUARIUS, AGE OF. *See* BAILEY, ALICE A.

AQUINAS, ST. THOMAS (1226–1274). Catholic theologian. The Italian **Dominican** cleric Thomas Aquinas stated in his "On the Governance of the Jews" that Jews should not be treated as regular neighbors but should live in perpetual servitude. Sovereigns could treat Jews as property. He considered Jewish rejection of Jesus as the **messiah** (he claimed Jews knew of his divinity) as the basis of Jewish woes. He also argued that the Jews were inherently cruel.

SUGGESTED READING: Henk Schoot and Pim Valkenberg, "Thomas Aquinas and Judaism," *Modern Theology* 20, no. 1 (January 2004).

ARAB LEAGUE. Loose organization of independent Arab states. The Arab League is an association of 22 Arab countries whose territories encompass a land area 675 times the size of Israel. Formed in 1945 with the encouragement and support of Great Britain to win Arabs over to their side, its purpose is to coordinate the political interests of Arabs, among them the rejection of the existence of a Jewish state as an affront to the collective Arab nation. The league portrays Israel as expansionist and imperialistic. In 1948, it launched an unsuccessful military attack on Israel and promoted boycotts and isolation of that state. Currently, the league supports the Palestine Liberation Organization, which it formed in 1964, and has moderated its eliminationist stand on the Jewish state. *See also* ARAFAT, YASSIR; SIX DAY WAR; TORQUEMADA, TOMÁS DE.

SUGGESTED READING: Dan Cohn-Sherbok and Dawoud el Alami, *The Palestinian–Israeli Conflict* (New York: One World Press, 2002); Robert W. Macdonald. *The League of Arab States* (Princeton, NJ: Princeton University Press, 1965).

ARAFAT, YASSIR (1929–2004). Head of the Palestine Liberation Organization (PLO) and Palestinian Authority until his death in 2004. Born in Cairo, Arafat began his anti-Israel activity in 1946, smuggling arms to insurgents against the Jews and British. He fought as an officer in the Egyptian Army at Suez in 1956. In 1958 Arafat founded **Fatah**, a guerrilla organization harassing the state of Israel (*fatah* means "conquest"; *hataf* means "death" and is also an acronym for Harakat al-Tahrir al-Falistiniya, or Palestine Liberation Organization). In 1964, the **Arab League** formed the PLO. Fatah took over control of the PLO in 1969. Its goal was the expulsion of Israel from Palestine and Arab sovereignty. Expelled from Jordan, Arafat and the PLO settled in Lebanon. Guerrilla incursions led Israel to invade Lebanon in 1982, and Arafat fled to Tunis. In 1988 a popular uprising in the Palestinian territories called the **Intifada** brought Arafat back to Palestine. In that year, Arafat renounced violence and moderated his demands, accepting a two-state solution with Arab self-rule in Gaza and the West Bank. In 1993 progress was made toward a peace settlement. However, the assassination of Israeli prime minister Yitzhak Rabin (1922–1995) and extreme elements on both sides slowed progress toward a settlement. In 2000 U.S. president Bill Clinton tried to broker a peace settlement, but Arafat found it unacceptable. Soon afterward, the **Al-Aqsa** Intifada broke out, with suicide or homicide bombers employed against Israel. U.S. President George W. Bush and Israeli Prime Minister Ariel Sharon declared Arafat irrelevant. With Arafat's death, new initiatives toward peace have been made, with a resulting reduction of violence. Those who favor Arafat termed him a freedom fighter; his detractors viewed him as a terrorist.

SUGGESTED READING: Barry M. Rubin and Judith Colp Rubin, *Yassir Arafat: A Political Biography* (New York: Oxford University Press, 2003); "A Life in Retrospect: Yassir Arafat," *Time*, November 12, 2004.

ARAGÓN. Kingdom within medieval Spain. A 12th-century town charter in Aragón confirmed that "the Jews are the slaves of the crown and belong exclusively to the royal treasury." *See also* FERDINAND V.

SUGGESTED READING: Yitzhak Baer, *A History of Jews in Christian Spain*, 2 vols. (Philadelphia: Jewish Publication Society, 1992).

ARENDT, HANNAH (1906–1975). Secular German-Jewish political theorist. In her reporting of the 1961 **Adolf Eichmann** trial for the *New Yorker*, she used the phrase "banality of evil" to describe the involvement of Eichmann in the Nazi **Final Solution**. Eichmann, like other **Nazis** and their collaborators, was not a malevolent Jew-hater, she believed; rather, he failed in critical judgment—he followed orders. Detached, he ignored the moral ramifications of his actions on his human victims.

SUGGESTED READING: Hannah Arendt, *Eichmann in Jerusalem: A Report on the Banality of Evil* (London: Faber & Faber, 1963).

ARGENTINA. After 1930 with the advent of a military coup, this South American country fell into the pro-Axis camp. It refused entry to Jewish

refugees. Yet, under President Juan Perón, dozens of **Nazi war criminals** found refuge there in the years following World War II, including **Adolf Eichmann**. Bombings have taken place at the Israeli Embassy (1992) and Jewish Cultural Center (1994). *See also* BUENOS AIRES PROGROMS; RATLINE.

SUGGESTED READING: Daniel Feierstein and Miguel Galante, "Argentina and the Holocaust: The Conceptions and Policies of Argentine Diplomacy, 1933–1945," *Yad Vashem Studies* 27 (2000).

ARMED FORCES OF THE UNITED STATES. Jews have served in the U.S. armed forces in all of its wars, and they were subject to **antisemitism**. Uriah Levy's and **Hyman Rickover**'s promotions were held back by the Navy until Congress intervened. Gen. **Ulysses S. Grant** during his **Civil War** campaign in Kentucky and Tennessee barred Jews from those areas with his Order Number 11, which was reversed by President Abraham Lincoln. Senior officers of the U.S. Army in World Wars I and II were for the most part small-town Protestants. They considered Jews, particularly those of Eastern European background, inferior and probable **Bolsheviks**. They were annoyed at Jewish soldiers' concerns about the Nazi **genocide**, considering any attempt to help the civilian victims detrimental to the war effort, and obstructed rescue efforts. Jewish **displaced persons** after the war were held in contempt. *See also* BROWN, GEORGE S.; EUGENICS; MORGENTHAU, HENRY; PATTON, GEORGE S.

SUGGESTED READING: Joseph W. Mendersky, *The Jewish Threat: Anti-Semitic Policies of the United States Army* (New York: Basic Books, 2000); Leonard Dinnerstein, *Antisemitism in America* (New York: Oxford University Press, 1995).

ARMLEDER MASSACRE. In 1336–37, German bands of "Jew killers" (*Judenschlächter*) in Swabia, Alsace, and Franconia were stirred to bloody action by alleged Jewish **desecration of the Host** and other anti-Jewish propaganda. A noble called King Armleather (Armleder) exhorted the people to avenge the death of Christ by wounding Jews as they had wounded Christ and by spilling Jewish blood as Christ's blood had been shed. The slaughter spread throughout southern Germany and Austria, where more than a hundred Jewish communities were destroyed.

SUGGESTED READING: Edward Flannery, *The Anguish of the Jews* (New York: Paulist Press, 1985); Richard Gottheil and Gotthard Deutsch, "Armleder Persecutions," *JewishEncyclopedia.com*, http://www.jewishencyclopedia.com/view.jsp?artid = 1790&letter = A&search = armleder; Paul E.

Grosser and Edwin G. Halperin, *Anti-Semitism: The Causes and Effects of a Prejudice* (Secaucus, NJ: Citadel Press, 1979).

ARNDT, ERNST MORITZ (1769–1860). German patriot and author. Arndt saw the Jews as being behind the disturbing social changes occurring in 19th-century Germany: the Jews hated "folkdom and Christianity," he said, and "labor[ed] untiringly to destroy and dissolve [sacred German] patriotism and fear of God."

SUGGESTED READING: Alfred D. Low, *Jews in the Eyes of Germans: From the Enlightenment to Imperial Germany* (Philadelphia: Institute for the Study of Human Issues, 1979).

ARNIM, ACHIM VON. Arnim's 1812 story "Isabella von Ägypten" was the first German literary text to feature a Golem. By activating anti-Jewish stereotypes, Arnim makes the Jewish creation a deficient being. The animated Golem-woman and sex-slave Bella is unspiritual and instinctual, the "crude embodiment" of "pride, lust and avarice." Golem Bella thus reveals the destructive potential of carnal beings by fully displacing Isabella, who embodies the values of Romantic love. Arnim chose as his protagonist the German Holy Roman Emperor Charles V (1500–1558). When Charles prefers the Golem to the gypsy queen Isabella, he symbolically gambles away Arnim's Romantic dream of a unified European empire.

SUGGESTED READING: Cathy Gelbin, "Horror Narratives of Transgression, from Jewish Folktales to German Cinema," *Kinoeye: New Perspectives on European Film* 3, no. 11 (October 13, 2003); Gerald Gillespie, Manfred Engel, and Bernard Dieterle, "Artificial Life and Romantic Brides," paper presented at the International Comparative Literature Association 16th Congress, Pretoria, South Africa, August 13–19, 2000.

ARNOLD, MATTHEW (1822–1888). English poet and social and literary critic. In *Culture and Anarchy* (1882), he wrote that Christians are better than Jews because spiritual growth results from contact with "the main stream of human life." In *Democratic Education* (1860), Arnold proclaimed that thousands of years of Jewish history were nothing more than "speculative opinion." Arnold adhered to **St. Augustine**'s dictum of the Witness People: that because the Jews had rejected and killed Christ, they were no longer God's chosen people. The Jews had to exist in misery. Jews are irrelevant, and Judaism is blind to the future course of civilization.

SUGGESTED READING: Edward Alexander, "Dr. Arnold, Matthew Arnold, and the Jews," *Judaism* (Spring 2002).

ARNOLD, THOMAS (1795–1842). English educator, headmaster of Rugby, and intellectual leader of the liberal branch of the Church of England. Arnold was convinced that Christianity should be the law of England. In 1834, Arnold insisted that he "must petition against" Jewish emancipation because **citizenship** is not a right acquired "by the accident" of a man living in England or paying taxes. "I would pray that distinctions be kept up between Christian and non-Christian," he wrote. Jews had no political rights because

> the Jews are strangers in England, and have no more claim to legislate for it, than a lodger has to share with the landlord in the management of his house. . . . England is the land of Englishmen, not of Jews . . . [and] my German friends agree with me.

Only if Jews converted to Christianity could they become English citizens. Jews should leave England, he believed, and he would contribute to the cost of their deportation. In "The Oxford Malignants and Dr. Hampden," Arnold condemned

> formalist, **Judaizing** fanatics, . . . the zealots of **circumcision** and the ceremonies of the law. . . . The poisonous plant of Judaism was cut down or withered away; but the root was left in the ground; and thus, when its season returned, it sprung up again, and is now growing rankly.

Finding himself the sole member of the London University senate opposed to giving Jews degrees, Arnold resigned his position.

SUGGESTED READING: Arthur Penrhyn Stanley, *Life and Correspondence of Thomas Arnold, D.D.* (London: John Murray, 1887).

ARNULF. Bishop of Lisieux. When Cardinal Pietro Pierleoni was elected Pope Anacletus II (antipope, *R.*1130–38), Arnulf argued that his Jewishness could be seen in his face and that his family "had still not been purified from the yeast of Jewish corruption."

SUGGESTED READING: Mary Stroll, *The Jewish Pope: Ideology and Politics in the Papal Schism of 1130* (Leiden: Brill, 1987).

AROUET, FRANÇOIS MARIE. *See* VOLTAIRE.

ARROW CROSS. Hungarian **antisemitic** party, formed in 1937, that assumed power in October 1944 with the aid of the German occupation of Hungary. Pro-**Nazi** and **fascistic**, it persecuted Jews and aided in **deportations** to death camps. The Arrow Cross was responsible for a **death march** of 80,000 Jews to the Austrian border beginning November 1944. It was disbanded with the end of the war.

SUGGESTED READING: Randolph L. Braham, *The Destruction of Hungarian Jewry: A Documentary Account* (New York: Columbia University Press, 1963).

ARYAN BROTHERHOOD (AB). A white supremacist prison gang. Its symbol is a three-leaf clover or a shamrock with an "AB" or "**666**" inscribed on the leaves. The **Aryan** Brotherhood originated in 1967 at San Quentin in California. Many members profess white supremacist ideology, but they are first and foremost a criminal gang involved in the methamphetamine trade. The AB has also spawned other white gangs in the prison system. Sometimes, AB tattoos will identify a member's state of origin. Several common nicknames for AB members are Alice, Alice Baker, Tip & Brand, and the Brand.

SUGGESTED READING: David Grann, "The Brand," *New Yorker*, February 16 and 23, 2004; Anti-Defamation League, *Hate on Display: Extremist Symbols, Logos, and Tattoos* (New York: Anti-Defamation League, 2006).

ARYAN FIST. Also known as the white power fist, a twist on the fist representing the Black Power movement and the battle against racial oppression. The **Aryan** fist is a symbol of white power used by hate groups who promote their racist agenda as white pride activism.

SUGGESTED READING: Anti-Defamation League, *Hate on Display: Extremist Symbols, Logos, and Tattoos* (New York: Anti-Defamation League, 2006).

ARYAN IDENTITY RELIGION. Antisemitic U.S. hate group formed in 1946. The members claim that **Aryans** were the true people of the Bible and that Jews are children of Satan. Their ideology has been adopted by the **Ku Klux Klan** under the leadership of Pastor Robert Sawyer and by the **neo-Nazi** group **Posse Comitatus**.

SUGGESTED READING: Southern Poverty Law Center, *Klanwatch Intelligence Report* no. 77, March 1995.

ARYANIZATION. The **Nazi** concept of removal of Jews from the German economy as well as the economies of occupied Europe and nations allied with the **Third Reich**, including the **confiscation of Jewish property** during the **Holocaust**. Because Jews were not compensated, the net effect of Aryanization was theft on a grand scale.

SUGGESTED READING: Lynn H. Nicholas, *The Rape of Europa* (New York: Knopf, 1994).

ARYAN NATIONS. The contemporary incarnation of the Church of Jesus Christ–Christian, an Idaho-based racist, **antisemitic** group founded by Dr. **Wesley Swift** after World War II and since 1970 led by the "Rev." **Richard G. Butler** (a mail-order minister). Butler preached that white people are the true descendents of the Lost Tribes of Israel and that the Jews were sons of Satan and Cain, "hooked-nosed **Antichrists**" who control the press and judiciary and must be eliminated from the United States. Symbolized by a crown topping a two-edged sword piercing a revolving resurrection cross on the face of a shield.

SUGGESTED READING: David Bennett, *Party of Fear*, 2nd rev. ed. (New York: Vintage, 1995); Anti-Defamation League, "Aryan Nations/Church of Jesus Christ Christian," http://www.adl.org/learn/ext_us/Aryan_Nations .asp?xpicked = 3&item = 11.

ARYANS. The first thinkers to develop ideas about an Aryan myth were German nationalists. They wrote that their language and history derived from an archaic Aryan people. In his *Essay on the Language and Wisdom of the Indians* (1808), the German **Karl Wilhelm Friedrich von Schlegel** argued that Aryans, led by Sanskrit warrior-priests, had civilized Europe and colonized early German peoples. Schlegel elucidated the concept that language, race, and culture combined to create human identity. He used the word *Aryan* because he identified it with the German *Ehre* (honor). Other scholars such as **Georg Wilhelm Friedrich Hegel** and **Christian Lassen** developed this theme. Frenchman Adolphe Pictet in 1859 asserted that a common root meant a common race: the White Indo-European language group. During his years in Vienna, **Adolf Hitler** was a regular reader of **Lanz von Liebenfels**'s journal *Istara*, which wrote of blond Aryans as against dark *Tschandalas*. White supremacists, **Nazis**, and racists misuse the term to mean the Nordic type, a superior person, or a non-Jewish person. Note that Aryans are unrelated to Arians, the followers of Arius and Arianism, a **heretical** offshoot of Christianity that held that Jesus Christ was divine but theologically inferior to God the Father. *See also* ARYANIZATION; CHAMBERLAIN, HOUSTON STEWART; GOBINEAU, ARTHUR DE; WAGNER, RICHARD; VOLK.

SUGGESTED READING: Léon Poliakov, *The Aryan Myth* (New York: Barnes & Noble, 1996).

ARYAN THEATER. Adam Müller-Guttenbrunn, author of the **antisemitic** pamphlet *Wien war eine Theaterstadt* (*Vienna Was a City of Theater*), blamed the corruption of the Viennese theater on the Jews. Between 1898 and 1903, Müller-Guttenbrunn directed the so-called Aryan Theater of Vienna (officially, the Kaiserjubiläums-Stadttheater; now the Vienna Volksoper). This was the first and, so far as we know, the only antisemitic theater ever. Müller-Guttenbrunn's antisemitism was reflected in the theater repertoire, where all plays authored by Jews were excluded. In 1938, one of Müller-Guttenbrunn's sons wrote in the chief **Nazi** newspaper that his father would have been pleased that the theater, then under Nazi leadership, was accomplishing what his father would have wanted it to do.

SUGGESTED READING: Richard S. Geehr, *Adam Müller-Guttenbrunn and the Aryan Theater of Vienna, 1893–1903: The Approach of Cultural Fascism* (Göppingen, Germany: Verlag Alfred Kümmerle, 1973).

ASHKENAZIM. Predominantly Eastern European Jews; a Hebrew-Yiddish term for German Jews, later applied to Polish and Eastern European Jews, as opposed to descendants of Sephardim, or Spanish, Jews. Some **antisemites** claim that the Ashkenzim descend from Khazars, a Turkic-Mongolian tribe from the Russian Caucasus who converted to Judaism.

SUGGESTED READING: David Biale, *Cultures of the Jews: A New History* (New York: Schocken, 2003).

ASSEMBLY OF NOTABLES. A conclave called by French emperor **Napoleon** in 1806 in Paris. Prominent Jews were asked 12 questions in order to determine whether the religion of the French Jews undermined their responsibility as French citizens. The carefully worded replies indicated that Judaism in no way interfered with French citizenship. Napoleon then revived a **Sanhedrin** (Jewish religious court) that endorsed the answers of the Notables.

SUGGESTED READING: Paul R. Mendes Flohr and Jehuda Reinharz, eds., *The Jew in the Modern World: A Documentary History* (New York: Oxford University Press, 1995).

ATHANASIUS, ST. (296–373). Bishop of Alexandria. In an instance of Christian **triumphalism**, Athansius wrote:

> The Jews are afflicted like some demented person. . . . What more is there for their Expected One [**messiah**] to do when he comes? What has not come to pass that the Christ must do? What is there left out or unfulfilled that the Jews should disbelieve so light-heartedly? The plain fact is, as I say, that there is no longer any king or prophet nor Jerusalem nor sacrifice nor vision among them.

SUGGESTED READING: Steven Bowman, *The Jews of Byzantium* (Tuscaloosa: University of Alabama Press, 1985); St. Athanasius Study Archive, http://www.preteristarchive.com/StudyArchive/a/athanasius_alone.html.

AUF GUT DEUTSCH (*IN PLAIN GERMAN*). A weekly news sheet edited and published by **Dietrich Eckart**. It blamed Jews for the recent defeat in World War I, the **Versailles** Treaty, and war profiteering. These ideas greatly influenced **Adolf Hitler**.

SUGGESTED READING: George Mosse, *Toward the Final Solution: A History of European Racism* (New York: Fertig, 1997).

AUGUSTINE, ST. (354–430). Bishop of Hippo, North Africa. Augustine, the author of the 22-volume *City of God* vindicating the Catholic Church, believed that the dispersion of Jews from Judea was a punishment for Jewish complicity in the murder of Jesus. Augustine's *Adversus Judaeos* stated that Jews were Cains, cast off by God. However, Jews should survive—but suffer as a witness people to the truth of Christianity.

SUGGESTED READING: Augustine, *City of God*, trans. Henry Bettenson (San Francisco: Image, 1958).

AUSCHWITZ-BIRKENAU. Nazi death camp (1940–45) near Oswiecim in southern Poland. The last stop for many Jews in the **Final Solution** was Auschwitz. It was a complex of three major camps and 36 subcamps. One major adjunct camp, Birkenau, housed four **gas chambers**, where 1.3 million Jews were murdered. *See also* HIMMLER, HEINRICH; HÖß, RUDOLF; ZYKLON.

SUGGESTED READING: Yisrael Gutman and Michael Birenbaum, *Anatomy of the Auschwitz Death Camp* (Bloomington: Indiana University Press, 1994).

"AUSCHWITZ LIE, THE" (**DIE AUSCHWITZ-LÜGE**). A 1973 essay written by Thies Christophersen, a pioneer **Holocaust denier**. Christophersen was sent to **Auschwitz**, not as a prisoner but as a Sonderführer **SS**. He wrote: "I never in the least observed anything that even indicated mass killings in **gas chambers**." In the 1980s Christophersen was imprisoned for "insulting the state" and "insulting the memory of the dead." **Holocaust** denial is known in Germany as the Auschwitz lie.

SUGGESTED READING: Deborah Lipstadt, *Denying the Holocaust: The Growing Assault on Truth and Memory* (East Rutherford, NJ: Plume, 1994); "Shofar FTP Archive File: people/c/christophersen.thies/heil-hitler-thies," *The Nizkor Project*, http://www.nizkor.org/ftp.cgi/people/c/ftp.py?people/c/christophersen.thies/heil-hitler-thies.

AUSTRALIA. Australian Jews have experienced little institutional or organized **antisemitism**. Jewish civil liberties have not been restricted. Jews play a prominent role in Australian public life. During the **Holocaust** and the decade following, 40,000 Jewish **refugees** were allowed to enter Australia despite informal restrictions based on a conscious desire to minimize the number of Jews entering the country. As in many other nations, when opposition to other minorities increases, so does antisemitism. The antisemitism that exists in Australia today is minimal, consisting of scattered attacks on **synagogues**, Jewish cemeteries, and homes, along with increased Internet harassment.

SUGGESTED READING: Paul R. Bartrop, *Australia and the Holocaust, 1933–1945* (Melbourne: Australian Scholarly Pub., 1994).

AUSTRIA. German-speaking central European country; once part of the Austro-Hungarian Empire. At the time of the *Anschluss* (annexation by **Nazi** Germany) in March 1938, more than 185,000 Jews lived in the republic. Immediately, wholesale arrests took place and many Jews were sent to **Dachau,** a concentration camp near Munich. The anti-Jewish decrees visited upon Germany's Jews over many years fell upon Austrian Jews immediately. Jews were forced to move into Vienna, and a Jewish Council was set up to administer Nazi laws. Lt. Col. **Adolf Eichmann** set up an emigration bureau, but few countries would accept Jewish **refugees**. After the **confiscation of Jewish property** by **Aryanization**, Jews were sent east— deported to **ghettos** or concentration camps. Whereas Austrians constituted only 8 percent of the Greater German Reich, 40 percent of Austrians were involved in the **Final Solution**. *See also* SEYSS-INQUART, ARTUR.

SUGGESTED READING: Eugene Davidson, *The Trial of the Germans* (New York: Macmillan, 1966).

AUTO-DA-FÉ. Spanish for "act of the faith." Auto-da-fé was the ritual public pronouncement of sentences imposed by the **Inquisition** on **heretics** and apostates, along with the execution of those sentences. Punishments ranged from wearing a **stigmatic emblem**, through imprisonment, to public burning by the secular authority. Those prisoners who refused to "confess their sins" were burned, but those who reconciled to the Roman Catholic Church were privileged to be strangled at the stake before their bodies were burned. The first burnings occurred in 1451 when six **Marranos** were executed near Seville, Spain, for the "**heresy**" of returning to their Judaism. The last horror of the Spanish Inquisition took place in 1826. More than 2,000 autos-da-fé claimed up to 50,000 lives. *See also* ANUSIM; CONVERSOS.

SUGGESTED READING: Yitzhak Baer, *A History of Jews in Christian Spain*, 2 vols. (Philadelphia: Jewish Publication Society, 1992).

– B –

BABI YAR. Ravine located outside the city of Kiev, Ukraine, the scene of mass murder on September 29–30, 1941. Nearly 40,000 Jews were machine-gunned by the mobile killing units of the **SS Einsatzgruppe** C. Other mass killings of non-Jews brought the total number of dead to 100,000.

SUGGESTED READING: Othniel Seiden, *The Survivor of Babi Yar* (Denver: Stonehenge Books, 1980).

BACH-ZELEWSKI, ERIC VON DEM (1899–1972). **SS** general. As head of **Einsatzgruppe** B and the Order Police, Bach-Zelewski was instrumental in the mass murder of Belorussian Jews in 1941–42. In October 1942 he headed the Bandenkampf ("war against bandits"), an anti-partisan effort that also murdered many Jews who were considered potential partisans. After the war, he served merely 10 years in prison.

SUGGESTED READING: Harris R. Whitney, *Tyranny on Trial* (New York: Barnes & Noble, 1995).

BACON, FRANCIS (1561–1626). English philosopher, essayist, and statesman. In *The New Atlantis*, Bacon's conception of a utopian state, he wrote:

> I was fallen into straight acquaintance with a merchant of that city, whose name was Joabin. He was a Jew and **circumcised**. . . . They hate the name of Christ, and have a secret inbred rancor against the people among whom they live.

SUGGESTED READING: Myriam Yardeni, *Anti-Jewish Mentalities in Early Modern Europe* (Lanham, MD: University Press of America, 1990).

BADGE OF SHAME. *See* JEW BADGE.

BAGEL; BAGEL DOG. (North American slur) A Jew; a reference to a traditional Jewish food, bagels.

SUGGESTED READING: "List of Ethnic Slurs," *Wikipedia*, http://en.wiki pedia.org/wiki/List_of_ethnic_slurs.

BAILEY, ALICE A. (1880–1949). Bailey wrote more than 20 books that established the foundation of World Goodwill, the major international **New Age** organization. In books filled with anti-Jewish stereotypes, including *Esoteric Psychology*, *The Unfinished Autobiography*, *Problems of Humanity*, *Esoteric Healing*, and *The Rays and the Initiations*, Bailey directly and indirectly attacked Jews, Jewishness, and Judaism, accusing the Jews of being grasping racists, selfish, manipulative, materialistic, and cruel; their Judaism was described as loveless, obsolete, useless, and undesirable. From all of these characteristics, she wrote:

> The Jews, by their illegal and terroristic activities, have laid a foundation of great difficulty for those who are seeking to promote world peace. . . . The Jews have partially again opened the door to the Forces of Evil, which worked originally through **Hitler** and his evil gang. . . . These Forces of Evil work through a triangle of evil, one point of which is to be found in the Zionist Movement in the United States, another in central Europe, and a third in Palestine.

SUGGESTED READING: Clifford Denton, "The Subtle Antisemitism of the New Age Movement," *Tishrei* (July 2003) and *Community* 2, no. 4 (Summer 1994).

BAKER, RAY STANNARD (1870–1945). U.S. journalist. Baker's book *The Disintegration of the Jews* (1909) is highly critical of Orthodox Jews in New York City. He criticizes them as "still living in the Middle Ages" and bringing "tribal instincts and tribal conceptions of God and setting up tribal institutions."

SUGGESTED READING: Judah Gribetz, Edward L. Greenstein, and Regina S. Stein, *The Timetables of Jewish History* (New York: Simon & Schuster, 1993).

BAKUNIN, MIKHAIL (1814–1876). Russian anarchist and former aristocrat, landlord, and officer in the tsarist army. Bakunin attacked Jews not merely as bourgeois but in general as bloodsucking parasites and an exploiting sect that controlled all the newspapers and produced nauseating literature. His followers justified **pogroms** as popular protest against exploiters. *See also* YOUNG HEGELIANS.

SUGGESTED READING: Peter Avrich, *Anarchist Portraits* (Princeton, NJ: Princeton University Press, 1988).

BALDWIN, JAMES (1924–1987). African-American author. In a 1967 essay, "Negros Are Antisemitic," Baldwin wrote that the Christian faith "shaped and molded the black experience in America. [Among blacks], the traditional accusation that the Jews killed Christ is neither questioned nor doubted." He also noted, "The root of **antisemitism** among Negroes is . . . the relationship of colored people . . . to the Christian world."

SUGGESTED READING: James Baldwin, "Negroes Are Antisemitic Because They Are Anti-White," *New York Times*, April 9, 1967.

BALDWIN OF EXETER. *See* BENEDICT OF YORK.

BANKING. Only during the Middle Ages were Jews dominant in money-lending, the reason being that the Church prohibited Christians from the field at that time. Even after Jews no longer dominated the industry, anti-semites accused them of doing so, pointing to the **Rothschilds**, Warburgs, Schiffs, and a few other Jewish families still prominent in the banking field. Antisemites accused Jewish bankers falsely of starting wars and revolutions and singled them out as conspiring against the Gentile world. The fact was that, at least before 1945, Jews were discriminated against in banking. *See also* POPULISTS, U.S.; *PROTOCOLS OF THE ELDERS OF ZION, THE*; SOMBART, WERNER.

SUGGESTED READING: Norman Cohn, *Warrant for Genocide: The Jewish World Conspiracy and the "Protocols of the Elders of Zion"* (Hudson, NH: Serif, 1996); Gordon Allport, *The Nature of Prejudice* (Reading, MA: Addison-Wesley, 1954).

BANNA, HASSAN AL- (1906–1949). Islamic scholar. Banna was a teacher of Islam in Cairo, Egypt, until he founded the **Muslim Brotherhood** in 1929. Disturbed by what he saw as immorality in modernizing Egypt, his goal was to re-Islamicize society by teaching fundamentalist Islam to the average Muslim. He was a frequent writer for the Cairo magazine *Al Manar*. Banna's major theme was to impose Muslim religious law on all Arab states, including their Jewish residents. He was assassinated in 1949. *See also* RADICAL ISLAM.

SUGGESTED READING: Jason Burke, *Al-Qaeda: The True Story of Radical Islam* (London: Penguin, 2004).

BAPTISM, FORCED. Conversion by coercion. Frustrated by Jews not flocking to Christianity despite their "persuasions," various Christian monarchs deemed that as a precondition for Jews to remain in their realms, or perhaps to keep their lives, Jews had to undergo baptism. In 613, King Sisebut of Spain decreed that all Jews who did not accept the ritual would be whipped and their property seized, as did King **Erwig** in 694. At Clifford's Tower in York, England, in 1190, 150 Jews took their own lives rather than face baptism. During the **Crusades** Jews were often faced with death if they did not convert. In 1348, in Basel, Switzerland, 140 Jews were forcibly converted. In 1497 King **Manoel** of Portugal, his country inundated by fleeing Spanish Jews, instituted baptism for all children up to age four. In Toledo, Spain, in 1449, following a **pogrom**, the Jews succumbed to accepting the cross. In tsarist Russia, **Nicholas I** decreed in

1825 that a quota of Jews from all cities, towns, and villages must serve in the army for 25 years, where the recruits were pressured to convert. *See also* MARRANOS; MORTARA ABDUCTION CASE.

SUGGESTED READING: Jane S. Gerber, *The Jews of Spain: A History of the Sephardic Experience* (New York: Free Press, 1992); Larry Domnitch, *The Cantonists: The Jewish Children's Army of the Czar* (New York: Devora, 2004); James Parkes, *The Conflict between the Church and the Synagogue* (New York: Atheneum, 1979).

BARABBAS. Gospel references to Barabbas, most likely a member of the Jewish Zealot party whose traditional first name was Jeshua, may have indicated that the Jews wanted to reprieve Jesus of Nazareth from the Roman sentence of crucifixion, but all four Gospels transformed this desire into its opposite. Barabbas's name is properly bar Abbas, or "son of the father," a phrase by which the Gospel of **John** identifies Jesus himself. When the Gospels portray the Jews as selecting Barabbas for pardon rather than Jesus, they are made to appear to choose Judaism over Christianity, that is, eternal damnation over redemption. But, historically more likely, when the Jewish crowd before Roman governer Pontius Pilate chose to free Barabbas, they were simply choosing a more violent approach to ridding Judea of the Romans than Jesus offered.

SUGGESTED READING: Haym Maccoby, "Jesus and Barabbas," *New Testament Studies* (October 1969).

BARBIE, KLAUS (1913–1991). **Gestapo** officer. The "Butcher of Lyons," Barbie was noted for his tortures and executions. He deported thousands of Jews from France. In 1943 he was notorious for his cruel **deportation** of the Jewish children of Izieu. Convicted of **crimes against humanity** after his extradition from Bolivia, Barbie died in a French prison in 1991. *See also* KLARSFELD, SERGE AND BEATE; RATLINE.

SUGGESTED READING: Tom Bower, *Klaus Barbie, Butcher of Lyon* (New York: Pantheon, 1984); Marcel Ophuls, *Hotel Terminus: The Life and Times of Klaus Barbie* (New York: Holiday House, 2004).

BAR CODE. (U.S. slur) A reference to the tattoos of **Nazi** concentration camp victims.

SUGGESTED READING: "List of Ethnic Slurs," *Wikipedia*, http://en.wikipedia.org/wiki/List_of_ethnic_slurs.

BARDÈCHE, MAURICE (1909–1998). **Robert Brasillach**'s friend, coauthor, and brother-in-law; **fascist** and neo-fascist author and literary critic and **Holocaust denier**. After 1945, Bardèche regarded right-wing thought as threatened by liberal European governments. In his journal *Défense de l'Occident*, he advocated non-**Nazi** organic, idealistic fascist states to defend Europe against Communism and U.S.-sponsored liberalism. He attributed Europe's and the world's problems to a Jewish conspiracy that controlled U.S. financial power *and* **Bolshevism**.

SUGGESTED READING: Ian Barnes, "Antisemitic Europe and the 'Third Way': The Ideas of Maurice Bardèche," *Patterns of Prejudice* 34, no. 2 (April 1, 2000).

BAR KOCHBA REVOLT. The destruction of the Second Temple dealt a nearly fatal blow to Jewish national and religious life, and Jews prayed for the arrival of a **messiah** to save them from Roman oppression. In 132 CE, the leading rabbi of the time, Rabbi Akiba, endorsed Simon Bar Kochba ("Simon, Son of the Star") as the promised messiah. Many people were skeptical, but other rabbis also acclaimed Simon as Messiah. Bar Kochba led a revolt against Rome in 135 CE. Those who believed that Jesus was the promised messiah—that is, Christians—naturally opposed the revolt. Bar Kochba regarded them as enemies to his cause, further alienating Christians from Jews.

SUGGESTED READING: John Haralson Hayes and Sara Mandell, *The Jewish People in Classical Antiquity: From Alexander to Bar Kochba* (Westminster, England: John Knox Press, 1998); J. Alberto Soggin, *A History of Israel: From the Beginnings to the Bar Kochba Revolt, AD 135* (London: SCM Press, 1984); Gary M. Grobman, "Classical and Christian Anti-Semitism," 1990, http://www.remember.org/history.root.classical.html.

BARON, SALO. *See* LACHRYMOSE THEORY OF JEWISH HISTORY.

BARRÈS, MAURICE (1862–1923). Writer and French nationalist politician. In 1889, Barrès ran for office in Nancy, France, on an **antisemitic** and xenophobic platform. He believed Jews had too much power, were monopolists, and controlled public offices. Earlier, he was an **antidreyfusard**. Barrès opposed Jewish citizenship. He wrote: "Deep down in our hearts, Jewish is only an adjective we use to designate **usurers**, hoarders, speculators on the stock market—all those who abuse the omnipotence of money."

SUGGESTED READING: William I. Brustein, *Roots of Hate: Antisemitism in Europe before the Holocaust* (Cambridge: Cambridge University Press, 2003).

BARRUEL, AUGUSTIN (1741–1820). French Jesuit. In 1803, Barruel advised the French government and Pope **Pius VI** against offering any rights to Jews. He saw a Jewish–**Freemason–Illluminati** conspiracy behind the **French Revolution** and the Revolution's attacks on Christianity, and he forged letters to this end. Barruel urged **Napoleon** to dissolve the newly created Jewish **Sanhedrin**. *See also PROTOCOLS OF THE ELDERS OF ZION, THE.*

SUGGESTED READING: Barry Coward and Julian Swann, *Conspiracies and Conspiracy Theory in Early Modern Europe: From the Waldensians to French Revolution* (Aldershot, England: Ashgate, 2004).

BARTELS, ADOLF (1862–1945). German writer, philologist, and racist. Bartels bemoaned the alleged dominance of Jews in professions such as **banking**. He compiled a list of 800 Jewish writers who were supposedly displacing German writers from their *völkisch* Christian culture. In 1913, Bartels coined the term *Deutschchristentum* (German Christianity) when he issued the slogan: "More German Christianity [Deutschchristentum]; less Jewish Christianity." In other words, Christianity needed to become **Aryan** and Germanic. Bartels influenced the aristocratic **Nazi** Baldur von Schirach.

SUGGESTED READING: Wolfgang Hardtwig, "Political Religion in Modern Germany: Reflections on Nationalism, Socialism, and National Socialism," *Bulletin of the German Historical Institute*, no. 28 (Washington, DC, 2001); Uwe Puschner, "One People, One Reich, One God: The *Völkische Weltanschauung* and Movement," *German Historical Institute London Bulletin* 24, no. 1 (May 2002).

BARTH, KARL (1886–1968). Swiss theologian. Barth was perhaps the most influential Protestant theologian of the 20th century. Although he later became active in relief agencies to rescue Jews and wrote a prologue to the Auschwitz Protocols (the 1944 Vrba-Wetzler Report) exposing Nazi atrocities, his theological **antisemitism** was so strong that in 1942 he wrote that Jews deserved their fate. Judaism was "outmoded and superseded." Jews had revolted against God and therefore experienced "the sheer, stark judgment of God. . . . The Jews of the **ghetto** . . . have nothing to attest to the world but the shadow of the cross of Christ that falls upon them."

SUGGESTED READING: Richard Gutteridge, *Open Thy Mouth for the Dumb!* (Oxford, England: Blackwell, 1976).

BARUCH, BERNARD MANNES (1870–1965). Financial advisor to six U.S. presidents, from **Woodrow Wilson** to John F. Kennedy, and in his later years highly regarded as an elder statesman. Baruch's father was a German immigrant who came to the United States in 1855. During World

War I, Bernard advised President Wilson on national defense, and in 1918 he became the chairman of the War Industries Board. After the war he accompanied Wilson to the **Versailles Peace Conference**. Baruch was a member of the "Brain Trust" in President **Franklin D. Roosevelt**'s "New Deal." As World War II approached, he proposed a number of brilliant economic measures, including a pay-as-you-go tax plan, rent ceilings, stockpiling of rubber and tin, and a synthetic rubber program, all of which helped the United States win the war. In 1946 President **Harry S. Truman** appointed him representative to the United Nations Energy Commission, where he proposed international control of atomic energy. Antisemites often accused him of having too much influence on the U.S. government and using his position for evil purposes.

SUGGESTED READING: James Grant, *Bernard Baruch: The Adventures of a Wall Street Legend* (Indianapolis, IN: Wiley, 1997).

BASEL, COUNCIL OF. At the Ecumenical Council at Basel, Switzerland, in 1431–43, the Roman Catholic Church affirmed that there could be no fellowship between Christians and Jews, that Christians could not serve Jews nor hire them as physicians, and that Jews were to be excluded from holding offices, were confined to **ghettos**, and had to wear **stigmatic emblems**. The Council added new canons preventing Jews from obtaining university degrees and forcing them to attend mandatory **sermons**.

SUGGESTED READING: Paul E. Grosser and Edwin G. Halperin, *Anti-Semitism: The Causes and Effects of a Prejudice* (Secaucus, NJ: Citadel Press, 1979).

BASIL (THE GREAT), ST. (329–379). Bishop of Caesarea. He wrote:

> When Jews stretch forth their hands in prayer, they only remind God-the-Father of their sin against His Son. And at every stretching-forth of their hands, they only make it obvious that they are stained with the blood of Christ. For they who persevere in their blindness inherit the blood-guilt of their fathers; for they cried out: "His blood be on us and on our children."

SUGGESTED READING: Basil the Great, "On Prayer," Sermon IX, in *Patrologiae, Cursus Completus: Series Graeca*, ed. Jacques-Paul Migne (Paris: Garnier, 1857–66), 32, Sermon 9; E. A. Livingstone, *The Concise Oxford Dictionary of the Christian Church* (New York: Oxford University Press, 2000).

BASILISK. A most fearsome animal of medieval legend. It was believed that the look or odor of a basilisk could kill. Benadictine abbot **Peter the Venerable** called Jews basilisks, likening them to "a monstrous animal" and "brute beast." "You [Jews] hatch basilisks' eggs, which infect you with the mortal poison of ungodliness. . . . They will be so evilly hatched by you as at last to produce **Antichrist**, the king of all the ungodly."

SUGGESTED READING: Peter the Venerable, "Tractatus Adversus Judeorum Inveteratam Duritiem," in *Patrologiae, Cursus Completus: Series Latina*, ed. Jacques-Paul Migne (Paris: Garnier, 1844–92), 189; Robert T. Mason, "The Divine Serpent in Myth and Legend," 1999, http://www.geocities.com/Athens/Delphi/5789/serpent.htm.

BASNAGE DE BEAUVA, JACQUES (1653–1723). French Protestant historian who condemned the Jews and Judaism as hag-ridden (tormented by fear) with belief in demons, spirits, and the most extreme fanaticism and **xenophobia**.

SUGGESTED READING: Myriam Yardeni, *Anti-Jewish Mentalities in Early Modern Europe* (Lanham, MD: University Press of America, 1990).

BAUER, BRUNO (1809–1882). German Protestant theologian. Bauer's book *On the Jewish Question* (1843) argued that Jews must give up Judaism and their religious identity, for only then could they receive emancipation. For him, there was an impossible divide between Christians and Jews. Bauer denied that Christianity emerged from Judaism and argued that Jews contributed nothing to civilization.

SUGGESTED READING: Leopold Davis, "The Hegelian Antisemitism of Bruno Bauer," *History of European Ideas* 25 (1999): 179–206.

BAYLE, PIERRE (1647–1706). French philosopher. Bayle advocated tolerance for Jews, although he regarded them not only as stupid but also as materialistic and cruel. He believed that whereas the Christian Scripture advocated peace and charity, the Jewish Scripture was essentially vengeful, insidious, cruel, and treacherous.

SUGGESTED READING: Adam Sutcliffe, *Judaism and Enlightenment* (New York: Cambridge University Press, 2003).

BAYREUTH FESTIVAL. German annual operatic event, consisting of performances of **Richard Wagner**'s works. The opera house is located in Bavaria, Germany, where the stage is specially constructed for Wagner's pageant. During the **Nazi** period, Nazi-tainted conductors led the productions, and the site was a source of **Aryan** exaltation and devotion to **Adolf Hitler**. At the conclusion of World War II, the festival was closed, but it reopened in 1951, without the **antisemitism** and Nazism.

SUGGESTED READING: Frederic Spotts, *Bayreuth: A History of the Wagner Festival* (New Haven, CT: Yale University Press, 1994).

BEAMISH, HENRY HAMILTON. Son of an admiral, brother of a Conservative member of Parliament, and a soldier in the Boer War who was influenced by the extreme **antisemitism** of the Boers. In 1918 Beamish founded the Britons Society, an English organization dedicated to "exposing Jewish conspiracies" and eradicting "alien" influences from British life. Beamish also published his antisemitic views in a periodical sometimes titled *Jewry Uber Alles*, other times *The Hidden Hand* and the *British Guardian*. His publishing company printed 85 editions of *The Protocols of the Elders of Zion*. Beamish was described as a "traveling salesman of international antisemitism." The Britons Society was part of the self-styled "Jew Wise" group that included the Imperial Fascist League and the Nordic League, aided by the Duke of Northumberland who published their antisemitic outpourings and fantasies in his *Morning Post* and weekly *The Patriot. See also* MARSDEN, VICTOR.

SUGGESTED READING: Richard Thurlow, *Fascism in Britain: A History, 1918–1985* (Oxford: Blackwell, 1987).

BEASTIE BOY. (U.S. slur) Jews who "act black"; from the music group Beastie Boys, whose members were Jews.

SUGGESTED READING: "List of Ethnic Slurs," *Wikipedia*, http://en.wiki pedia.org/wiki/List_of_ethnic_slurs.

BEILIS CASE. Russian **ritual murder** and blood libel case of 1911–13. Mendel Beilis (1874–1934) supervised a brick-making kiln outside of Kiev, then part of tsarist Russia. A boy was found stabbed to death, murdered in a cave. Arrested on the basis of the testimony of two habitual drunkards, Beilis, a Jew, was incarcerated for two years while police officials withheld evidence of the true murderer. After a trial of 34 days in 1913, a jury of simple folk acquitted Beilis, though they believed a ritual murder did take place. Faced with threats from the ultranationalist organization the **Black Hundreds**, Beilis made his way to the United States. *See also* DREYFUS CASE.

SUGGESTED READING: Maurice Samuel, *Blood Accusation: The Strange History of the Beilis Case* (London: Weidenfeld & Nicholson, 1967).

BEKENNENDE KIRCHE. *See* CONFESSING CHURCH.

BELLOC, HILAIRE (1870–1953). Member of Parliament from 1906 to 1910, British novelist, historian, poet, Roman Catholic polemicist, and antisemite. Belloc saw Jews in everything and everywhere, and he predicted an uprising in New York against them. In 1922, in his book *The Jews*, he wrote these lines:

> Here Rothschild lives, chief of the tribe abhorred
> Who tried to put to death Our Blessed Lord
> But on the third day, as the Gospel shows
> Cheating their machinations, He arose
> In Whose commemoration now and then,
> We persecute these curly-headed men.

He added, "If or when the New Yorkites rise against the Jews there will be a **pogrom**."

Sailing to New York he wrote: "Talking of Yids the swarm of Yids on board this sparsely populated craft is extraordinary: there are hardly 100 people on board and at least 81 are incredible: monsters of the deep." He regarded capitalism as the result of two evils, Judaism and Protestantism.

SUGGESTED READING: Jay P. Corin, *G. K. Chesterton and Hilaire Belloc: The Battle against Modernity* (Athens: Ohio University Press, 1981).

BELZEC. Death camp where deportees were quickly gassed. Located in eastern Poland near Lublin, it operated from March 17 to December 1942. Jews from Lublin, Krakow, and other Galician areas were the main victims and totaled 680,000, leaving only two survivors. In 1943, fearful of exposure, the Nazis ordered the mass graves opened and the corpses burned.

SUGGESTED READING: Konnilyn G. Feig, *Hitler's Death Camps: The Sanity of Madness* (New York: Holmes & Meier, 1981).

BENEDICT XIII (1348–1422). Antipope, 1394–1417. The former Spanish cardinal Pedro de Luna, Benedict XIII's goal was to make the Spanish Jews disappear through **conversion**. He abused the Jews as "blind" and Judaism as "an execrable rite" and "damnable." In this spirit, Benedict presided over the **Tortosa Disputation** between churchmen and Jews in 1413–14, where the **Talmud** was condemned and the social contact between Christians and Jews was reduced. Jews were increasingly **ghettoized** and pressured to convert.

SUGGESTED READING: Shlomo Simonsohn, *The Apostolic See and the Jews: Documents, 1394–1464* (Toronto: Pontifical Institute of Mediaeval Studies, 1989); Hyam Maccoby, *Judaism on Trial: Jewish Christian Disputation in the Middle Ages* (Oxford, England: Littman Library of Jewish Civilization, 1993).

BENEDICT XIV (1675–1758). Pope, 1740–58. In 1747 Benedict wrote that Jewish children over seven could be **baptized** against the will of their parents and contrary to the procedures of **canon law**. In 1751 he punished Jews who changed their minds about becoming Christians. This stimulated Christian kidnapping of Jewish children and their forced baptism.

SUGGESTED READING: Dagobert Runes, *The War against the Jews* (New York: Philosophical Library, 1968); Paul E. Grosser and Edwin G. Halperin, *Anti-Semitism: The Causes and Effects of a Prejudice* (Secaucus, NJ: Citadel Press, 1979); Owen Chadwick, *The Popes and European Revolution* (New York: Oxford University Press, 1981).

BENEDICT OF YORK. In the 12th century, Benedict of York, an English Jew, had been baptized under the threat of death but recanted before King **Richard I**. At that point, Baldwin of Exeter, the archbishop of Canterbury, burst out, "Since he does not wish to be a Christian, let him be the Devil's man." The chronicler wrote that Benedict "returned to the Jewish depravity . . . like a dog to his vomit."

SUGGESTED READING: Joseph Jacobs, *The Jews of Angevin England: Documents and Records* (London: David Nutt, 1893).

BEN-HUR. *See* WALLACE, LEW.

BENIGNI, UMBERTO (d. 1918). Antimodernist Roman Catholic priest who founded the Sodality of St. **Pius V**, which functioned as an international secret service for Pope **Pius X**. Benigni wrote in *Piccolo Monitore* that Jews were "a rabbinical race that still today in 1891 slits the throats of little Christians for the **Synagogue**'s Passover." Later, Benigni was honored with a powerful position in the **Vatican**'s Secretariat of State.

SUGGESTED READING: David I. Kertzer, *The Popes against the Jews* (New York: Knopf, 2001).

BEN JUJU. Antisemitic reference to British prime minister **Benjamin Disraeli** (1804–1881). *See also PUNCH.*

BENN, GOTTFRIED (1886–1956). Racist German writer and physician. Concerned with the "vitality" of the German "race," Benn welcomed the **Nazi** creed of "the emergence of a new biological type, a mutation of history and a people's wish to breed itself."

SUGGESTED READING: Robert Jay Lifton, *The Nazi Doctors: Medical Killing and the Psychology of Genocide* (New York: Basic Books, 2000).

BENNY. (North American slur) A male Jew, deriving from the number of Jewish men named Benjamin, Benny, or Ben and/or a reference to Jewish comedian Jack Benny, noted for his tight-fisted nature.

SUGGESTED READING: "List of Ethnic Slurs," *Wikipedia*, http://en.wiki pedia.org/wiki/List_of_ethnic_slurs.

BÉRARD, LÉON. Vichy ambassador to the **Vatican** during World War II. Justifying French antisemitic laws during the Vichy regime, Bérard noted to Marshal Pétain, understating the intensity of **St. Thomas Aquinas**'s antagonism to Jews, that St. Thomas had believed "it would be unreasonable in a Christian state to allow [Jews] to have any political power, especially over Catholics. It is legitimate to discriminate against them in terms of public office, admission to university, and in the liberal professions." Bérard added, "In fact, this practice was strictly adhered to in the Middle Ages." *See also* STATUT DES JUIFS.

SUGGESTED READING: Léon Poliakov, *Harvest of Hate* (London: Elek Books, 1956).

BERGEN-BELSEN. Nazi concentration camp located outside Hanover, Germany, that opened August 2, 1943. Bergen-Belsen was transit camp for sick deportees. Camp II, a camp for Jews, had the worst physical conditions of the entire complex of concentration camps. Fifty thousand inmates were liberated by British forces on April 15, 1945—too late for diarist Anne Frank, who died there a few weeks earlier. *See also* GRESE, IRMA; KRAMER, JOSEF.

SUGGESTED READING: Jo Reilly, David Cesarani, Tony Kushner, and Colin Richmond, *Belsen in History and Memory* (Essex, England: Frank Cass, 1997).

BERGSON BOYS. Members of a breakaway Jewish Palestinian military organization. A group of Irgun (a pre-Israel dissident group) representatives came to the United States in 1940 to help create a Jewish army to fight against the **Nazis**. Peter Bergson (Hillel Kook, 1915–2001) recognized that nothing was being done to rescue the Jews of Europe. His group formed the Emergency Committee to Rescue the Jews of Europe, and their political action led to the U.S. **War Refugee Board** in January 1944. Although funded almost exclusively from Jewish sources, the board circumvented the antisemitic U.S. **State Department** and rescued an estimated 200,000 Jews. *See also* LONG, BRECKINRIDGE.

SUGGESTED READING: David Wyman and Rafael Medoff, *The Race against Death: Peter Bergson, America and the Holocaust* (New York: New Press, 2002).

BERLIN, TREATY OF. The 1878 treaty that marked the disintegration of the newly formed Three Emperors' League of Germany, Austria, and Russia and the renewal and intensification of the Austro-Russian rivalry in the Balkans. Bulgaria became autonomous, and Serbia, Montenegro, and Romania gained complete independence and additional territory. The treaty stipulated that the sovereignty of the new state, Romania, was to be contingent upon the admission of the Jews to full civil and political rights. Romania, however, circumvented this obligation; the Romanian constitution of 1879, though it apparently repudiated the 1866 provision limiting naturalization to "foreigners of the Christian rite," stipulated that "noncitizens might be naturalized only by vote of both houses of the legislature," except in the case of veterans. Of course, only a handful of Jews were naturalized under these provisions.

SUGGESTED READING: Paul E. Grosser and Edwin G. Halperin, *Anti-Semitism: The Causes and Effects of a Prejudice.* (Secaucus, NJ: Citadel Press, 1979).

BERLIN DECLARATION. An April 29, 2004, statement by the Organization for Security and Cooperation in Europe (OSCE), representing 55 nations: Albania, Andorra, Armenia, **Austria**, Azerbaijan, Belarus, Belgium, Bosnia-Herzegovina, **Bulgaria**, **Canada**, **Croatia**, Cyprus, the Czech Republic, Denmark, Estonia, Finland, France, Georgia, Germany, Greece, the Holy See, Hungary, Iceland, Ireland, Italy, Kazakhstan, Kyrgyzstan, Latvia, Liechtenstein, Lithuania, Luxembourg, Macedonia, Malta, Moldova, Monaco, the Netherlands, Norway, Poland, Portugal, Romania, Russia, San Marino, Serbia-Montenegro, the Slovak Republic, Slovenia, Spain, Sweden, Switzerland, Tajikistan, Turkey, Turkmenistan, Ukraine, the United Kingdom, the United States, and Uzbekistan. In this declaration, these nations:

- opposed discrimination of any kind, based on race, religion, or other status
- reaffirmed the right to freedom of thought, conscience, and religion
- dedicated themselves to combating **antisemitism** "in all its manifestations and to promote and strengthen tolerance and non-discrimination"
- recognized that antisemitism, "following its most devastating manifestation during the **Holocaust**, has assumed new forms and expressions, which, along with other forms of intolerance, pose a threat to democracy, the values of civilization and, therefore, to overall security"
- expressed concern that "this hostility toward Jews—as individuals or collectively—on racial, social, and/or religious grounds, has manifested itself in verbal and physical attacks and in the desecration of **synagogues** and cemeteries"

- condemned without reserve "all manifestations of antisemitism, and all other acts of intolerance, incitement, harassment or violence against persons or communities based on ethnic origin or religious belief, wherever they occur"
- condemned "all attacks motivated by antisemitism or by any other forms of religious or racial hatred or intolerance, including attacks against synagogues and other religious places, sites and shrines"
- declared "unambiguously that international developments or political issues, including those in Israel or elsewhere in the Middle East, never justify antisemitism"

The OSCE states further committed themselves to

> strive to ensure that their legal systems foster a safe environment free from anti-semitic harassment, violence or discrimination in all fields of life; promote, as appropriate, educational programs for combating antisemitism; promote remembrance of and, as appropriate, education about the tragedy of the Holocaust, and the importance of respect for all ethnic and religious groups; [and] combat hate crimes, which can be fuelled by racist, xenophobic and antisemitic propaganda in the media and on the Internet.

See also ANTISEMITISM, WORKING DEFINITION OF.

SUGGESTED READING: Jonathan Weizman, "European Institutions Support Open Access with the 'Berlin Declaration,'" *Scientist* (November 2003).

BERLIN MOVEMENT. By the end of the 1880s, many of the Berlin Movement's radical leaders were best-selling authors—including **Wilhelm Marr** (*Der Sieg des Judentums über das Germanentum*, 1873) and **Otto von Glagau** (*Der Börsen- und Gründungsschwindel in Berlin*, 1876–77). The movement published several articles in the reactionary journal *Kreuzzeitung*, the Catholic *Germania*, and the *Gartenlaube* supposedly demonstrating the subversive power of Germany's Jews to Germany's Christian life. These writers and publicists—some of whom were influential members of the Prussian establishment such as **Heinrich von Treitschke** (*Ein Wort über das Judentum*, 1880) and the Court preacher **Adolf Stöcker**—interwove traditional Christian stereotypes of Jews with contemporary hatreds. In 1880 Max Liebermann von Sonneberg, Bernhard Förster, and **Ernst Henrici** began a campaign to collect a quarter-million signatures for the **Antisemites' Petition**, which they presented to German Chancellor **Otto von Bismarck**.

SUGGESTED READING: George Mosse, *The Culture of Western Europe: The Nineteenth and Twentieth Centuries* (Boulder, CO: Westview Press,

1988); Stephen C. J. Nicholls, "The Burning of the Synagogue in Neustettin: Ideological Arson in the 1880s," 1999, http://www.sussex.ac.uk/units/cgjs/publications/nic.html.

BERMUDA CONFERENCE. A meeting held on the Atlantic island of Bermuda April 19–28, 1943, to discuss action regarding news of Jewish **genocide**. Only British and U.S. representatives were present. Their purpose was to find solutions to the "**refugee problem**" (Jews in Europe). The American government made no changes in its restrictive immigration policy while the British kept Palestine closed to Jewish refugees. The policy of no diversion from the war effort to aid persecuted Jews was to continue. Mainstream Jewish organizations were convinced now that rescue efforts were futile.

Suggested Reading: David Wyman, *The Abandonment of the Jews: America and the Holocaust* (New York: New Press, 1998).

BERNARDINO DA SIENA (1380–1444). One of the Church's great preachers, Bernardino was violently opposed to the Jews. He felt that Jewish moneylenders deprived Christians of their wealth and Jewish physicians deprived Christians of their "health and life." "There can be no concrete love towards Jews," he said.

Suggested Reading: H. H. Ben-Sasson, ed., *A History of the Jewish People* (Cambridge, MA: Harvard University Press, 1976).

BERNARDINUS OF FELTRE (BERNARDINO DA FELTRE) (1439–1494). Franciscan monk; self-proclaimed "scourge of the Jews." Bernardinus wanted the Jews expelled from Christian society. In the mid-1470s in Italy, he predicted that Easter would not pass without Christians fully understanding Jewish evildoing. Predictably, a two-year-old boy named Simonino (later called **Simon of Trent**) disappeared on Holy Thursday in 1475. The boy's death led to a **ritual-murder** accusation against the local Jews and some visiting German Jews. This **defamation** led to the torture and death of some Jews and **expulsion** of others. Simon's murder was assumed to be a reenactment of the crucifixion of Christ. A little over a hundred years later, Simon was beatified as the Blessed Simon of Trent. Bernardinus's agitation seemed to spread beyond Italy's borders, and ritual-murder trials took place within a few years at Regensburg, Ratisbon, Endingen, and Ravensburg and in Spain.

Suggested Reading: Po-Chia Hsia, *Trent, 1475: Stories of a Ritual Murder Trial* (New Haven, CT: Yale University Press, 1992).

BERNARD OF CLAIRVAUX (1090–1153). Cistercian monk and French theologian. Bernard led the Second **Crusade** and approved a policy that Crusaders should have their debts to Jews wiped out. He agreed that Jews were punished (for their supposed **deicide**) by their dispersion, but would serve as witnesses to Jesus. Bernard clearly rejected anti-Jewish violence, although he did not attempt to save Jewish lives because of mercy, charity, or human decency but because their suffering serves Christians as constant reminders of Jewish sin and of Christian redemption. *See also* AUGUSTINE, ST.; CONRAD III.

SUGGESTED READING: G. R. Evans, *Bernard of Clairvaux* (New York: Oxford University Press, 2000).

BERTHOLD OF REGENSBURG (c. 1210–1272). Attracting huge audiences for more than 30 years in Central and Western Europe, the Franciscan Berthold sermonized against the Jews. Berthold associated Jews with those whom Christendom directly sought to exterminate—**heretics** and pagans—and his virulent rhetoric had a great impact. He associated the **Talmud** with **heresy**, and the Jews with the **Antichrist** and the Devil as the public enemies of Christendom. Berthold argued, "Talmud is completely heretical, and it contains such damned heresy that it is bad that [the Jews] live."

SUGGESTED READING: Joshua Trachtenberg, *The Devil and the Jews* (Philadelphia: Jewish Publication Society, 1961); Jeremy Cohen, *The Friars and the Jews* (Ithaca, NY: Cornell University Press, 1982); Berthold von Regensburg, *Berthold von Regensburgs Deutsche Predigten* (Jena, 1924), Sermon 42.

BEST, WERNER (1903–1989). **Reinhard Heydrich**'s deputy, who helped **deport** French Jews to concentration camps. In 1943 Best of the **SS** became **Adolf Hitler**'s representative to Denmark. That September, he received the final order to proceed with deportation of the 7,500 Danish Jews to **Terezín** (Theresienstadt) concentration camp. The operation was to commence at 10 p.m. on October 1, 1943, on Rosh Hashanah, the Jewish New Year. Before the operation was begun, Georg F. Duckwitz, the German naval attaché, leaked the order to Hans Hedtoft, a Danish Social Democrat, who in turn warned C. B. Henriques, the head the Jewish Community. On September 29, Dr. Marcus Melchior, the acting chief rabbi of the Krystalgaade **Synagogue**, implored the whole Danish-Jewish community to go into hiding immediately. Thousands of individual Danes representing all aspects of Danish society, from churchmen to firemen, from the government to the police, from teachers to fishermen, helped hide and then ship the Jews out of the country to Sweden. Many Wehrmacht soldiers and Kriegsmarine sailors looked the other way. After the war, Best was sentenced to death, but he was released in 1951.

SUGGESTED READING: Leo Goldberger, *The Rescue of Danish Jews: Moral Courage under Stress* (New York: New York University Press, 1987).

BETTAUER, HUGO (1872–1925). Bettauer's 1922 *Die Stadt ohne Juden: Ein Roman von Ubermorgen* (*The City without Jews*) is a novel that postulates a time when Vienna passes a law making it illegal for any Jew to exist in the city. Foreshadowing the **Holocaust**, but with much humor, Bettauer imagined a Jew-free Vienna, satirizing **antisemitism** as ridiculous. Jews in Vienna were crucial elements in the city's creative, business, and professional community. In Bettauer's "alternate history," Vienna is transformed from a world center of the arts to a wasteland. Bettauer envisioned a Vienna that had murdered its own soul. However, he also imagined that Vienna quickly realized its mistake in deporting all its Jews. A reviewer commented:

> He naively imagined that once Vienna realized how essential Jews were to the city's continued cosmopolitan well-being, there would be a city-wide outcry for the return of the Jews, a sentimental nostalgia for the Good Old Days causing Jewish physicians, teachers, artists, and journalists to return with honors— resulting in a happy-ever-after ending.

In 1925, a self-proclaimed "Nordic," believing Bettauer to be a menace to German *Kultur*, shot and killed Bettauer. At the murderer's trial, he was unrepentant, as unrepentant as most Viennese.

SUGGESTED READING: Hugo Bettauer, *The City without Jews: A Novel of Our Time* (New York: Bloch, 1997); Jessica Amanda Salmonson, "Hugo Bettauer's 1922 Dystopian Satire *The City without Jews* and Austrian Anti-semitism," 2000, http://www.violetbooks.com/REVIEWS/jas-bettauer .html.

BÉZIERS, COUNCIL OF. In 1246 the Catholic Church council of the province of Béziers, France, claimed that Jews practiced black magic and that Jewish physicians and Jews in general were always out to murder Christians.

SUGGESTED READING: Solomon Grayzel, *The Church and the Jews in the XIII Century*, ed. Kenneth R. Stow, vol. 2, *1254–1314* (Detroit: Wayne State University Press, 1989).

BIARRITZ 1868. **Hermann Goedsche,** a postal clerk and Prussian spy, wrote this fantasy novel under the pen name of Sir John Retcliff. Its most important chapter, "In a Jewish Cemetery in Prague," contains speeches of rabbis telling the assembled Jews how to control and exploit Gentiles. This section became one of the bases for *The Protocols of the Elders of Zion*. Antisemites considered the event in Prague as literally true.

SUGGESTED READING: Norman Cohn, *Warrant for Genocide* (London: Serif, 1996).

BIG NOSE. (U.S. slur) Jews are stereotyped as having big noses.

SUGGESTED READING: "List of Ethnic Slurs," *Wikipedia*, http://en.wiki pedia.org/wiki/List_of_ethnic_slurs.

BILBO, THEODORE (1877–1947). Racist senator from Mississippi (1935–47) connected with the **America First Committee**. Bilbo claimed to like the Jews of his state but railed against the "**kike** Jews" of New York.

SUGGESTED READING: Chester M. Morgan, *Redneck Liberal: Theodore Bilbo and the New Deal* (Baton Rouge: Louisiana State University Press, 1985).

BILLROTH, THEODOR (1829–1894). In 1876, Billroth, the chief surgeon at the University of Vienna, published a well-received book on medical education containing long passages of **antisemitic** diatribe that triggered widespread anti-Jewish discrimination in Austrian universities. He attacked Jewish medical students from Hungary and Galicia, arguing "that the Jews are a sharply defined nation, and that no Jew . . . can ever become a German." Jewish-Germans are only Jews who happen to speak German and happened to be educated in Germany, Billroth said, no matter how well they write German literature or think in the German language. We should not expect nor even desire Jews to become "true Germans in the sense that during national battles they feel the way we Germans do." Jews lack authentic "German sentiments." Billroth admitted that even though he liked some Jews as individuals, "the gap between purely German and purely Jewish blood is just as wide as the gap a Teuton may have felt between himself and a Phoenician."

SUGGESTED READING: Karel Absolon, *Theodor Billroth, 1829–1894* (Rockville, MD: Kabel Publishers, 1999); Brigitte Hamann, *Hitler's Vienna: A Dictator's Apprenticeship*, n.d., http://www.porges.net/jewsin vienna/1historicalbackground.html.

BINGEN, HILDEGARD VON (1098–1179). Benedictine German nun and mystic, religious order founder, abbess, poet, musician, and scientist. One of the most remarkable women of any time or religion, Hildegard in her book *Scivias* (1151) adopted a **triumphalistic** stance when she commented that **circumcision** was replaced by grace, and "the yoke of the Law" with mercy. The Law was "shadow," but the **Gospel** was "truth." Judaism was of "fleshly things," whereas the Church was of "spiritual things." Judaism was "the servant," the Church the "master." "The **Synagogue** went before as a foreshadowing sign, and the Church came after in the light of truth."

SUGGESTED READING: Hildegard of Bingen, *Scivias*, trans. Columba Hart and Jane Bishop (New York: Mahwah, 1990).

BINGHAM, THEODORE. New York police commissioner, 1906–09. In 1908, in the *North American Review,* Bingham claimed that 50 percent of the criminals in New York City were Russian Jews, who numbered 25 percent of the population. "Jews are fire bugs, burglars, pick pockets and robbers when they have the courage," he wrote. A storm of Jewish protest followed, and Bingham hastily discovered that his figures were in error. He was, nevertheless, removed from office.

SUGGESTED READING: Judah Gribetz, Edward L. Greenstein, and Regina S. Stein, *The Timetables of Jewish History* (New York: Simon & Schuster, 1993).

BIN LADEN, OSAMA. Leader of **Al-Qaeda**. A native of Saudi Arabia, bin Laden achieved notoriety fighting against the Soviets in Afganistan. In 1998, he declared "**Jihad** [Holy War] against Jews and Crusaders" (the West). Bin Laden has no qualms against attacking civilian as well as military targets, citing the existence of Israel and the Palestinian cause among his motives. He organized the most notorious attack on the United States (New York's World Trade Center and the Pentagon) since Pearl Harbor on September 11, 2001. *See also* ISLAMIC JIHAD; MUSLIM BROTHERHOOD; RADICAL ISLAM.

SUGGESTED READING: Bernard Lewis, *The Crisis of Islam: Holy War and Unholy Terror.* New York: Random House, 2004.

BIROBIDZHAN. This was a city set up in 1928 for Soviet Jews as a Jewish Autonomous Region of the USSR consisting of 36,000 sq. km. (14,000 sq. mi.). At most, this eastern Siberian experiment near the Chinese border housed only 30,000 Jews (20 percent of the total population). **Joseph Stalin** and the Kremlin advertised it as an alternative to a Jewish homeland in Palestine; actually, they intended to stamp out the Jewish religion and assimilate Jews into Soviet Communism.

SUGGESTED READING: Robert Weinberg and Bradley Berman, *Stalin's Forgotten Zion: Birobidzhan and the Making of a Jewish Homeland* (Berkeley: University of California Press, 1984).

BISMARCK, OTTO VON (1815–1898). German statesman. The first chancellor of a united Germany in 1871, Bismarck favored a complete emancipation of Jews and was friendly to some Jews, but singled out Jewish **bankers** as being engaged in a world conspiracy. He believed the U.S. **Civil War** was engineered by the **Rothschild family** and the **Illuminati**. While Bismarck was chancellor, the Court chaplain was the antisemite **Adolf Stöcker**.

SUGGESTED READING: Peter Pulzer, *Jews and the German State: The Political History of a Minority, 1848–1933* (Detroit: Wayne State University Press, 2002).

BLACK CAUCUS. The Congressional Black Caucus represents African-American members of the U.S. Congress. The organization was founded in January 1969 by black members of the House of Representatives. The caucus is officially nonpartisan, but in practice it has been almost exclusively composed of Democrats who lobby the Democratic Party for legislation on behalf of African Americans. In 2003 the caucus contained 38 members. Although most members support Israel, some of the members have been accused of **antisemitism** because of their public and private stands against Israel and for the Palestinians.

SUGGESTED READING: Robert Singh, *The Congressional Black Caucus: Racial Politics in the U.S. Congress* (Thousand Oaks, CA: Sage, 1997).

BLACK DEATH. Bubonic plague, which spread across Europe in 1347–50. Seeking a scapegoat for the disease that eventually claimed up to half of Europe's population, Christians accused Jews of **poisoning the wells**. This false accusation seemed credible because Jews had a lower mortality rate (because of ritual sanitation rules). Jews were subject to torture, and large numbers were put to death. Whole communities were annihilated. Many Jews, particularly in Germanic states, fearing extreme persecution, committed suicide.

SUGGESTED READING: Barabara Tuchman, *Distant Mirror: The Calamitous Fourteenth Century* (New York: Ballantine Books, 1987).

BLACK HUNDREDS. Xenophobic, antidemocratic, racist, antirevolutionary, **antisemitic**, and government-controlled gangs active in tsarist Russia in 1903–17. The Black Hundreds' goals were to support the tsarist government, the Orthodox Church, and the empire and to suppress reform and revolution in Russia—in part by murdering all Jews. Supported by the agencies of the government, including the tsar (**Nicholas II** himself wore a badge), its strong antisemitic propaganda led its gangs to institute **pogroms** against Jews. Members murdered Jewish industrialists and two Jewish representatives in the Duma (Russian Parliament). The group's antisemitic policies included exclusion of Jews from the military, a special Jewish **tax**, denial of Jews' right to vote, a ban on printing presses, and restrictions on Jewish trading and commerce. They chanted "Kill the **Zhids**." In 1905 alone, the Black Hundreds committed 50 pogroms, blaming that year's defeat of the Russian army and navy by the Japanese on the Jews. They publicized the forgery ***Protocols of the Elders of Zion***, as well the antisemitic **defamations** of **ritual murder** and blood libel. The Kiev cell organized mass demonstrations against the innocent Mendel **Beilis** in 1911. The pogroms encouraged Jews toward Zionism and mass migration to the United States.

SUGGESTED READING: Walter Laqueur, *Black Hundreds: The Rise of the Extreme Right in Russia* (New York: HarperCollins, 1993).

BLACK LEGION. *See* SECRET ORGANIZATIONS, 20TH CENTURY.

BLACK PANTHER PARTY. Formed by Huey Newton and Bobby Seale in Oakland, California, in 1966, the Black Panther Party combined militant black nationalism with Marxism and advocated black empowerment and self-defense, often through confrontation. By 1969, the group had an estimated 5,000 members in 20 chapters around the country. At this time, in a story on Al **Fatah**, the party's magazine, *The Black Panther*, claimed that the Palestinians "pioneered . . . the road of armed struggle which brooks no false solutions, does not recognize the so-called peaceful solution, and knows only the gun as the sole means to achieve victory." The story was headlined "Palestine Guerrillas versus Israeli Pigs." *The Black Panther* also printed antisemitic poems and articles whose major impact on the black community was to discourage moderates and encourage violence. In the early 1970s, however, the group lost momentum and most of its support because of internal disputes, violent clashes with police, and infiltration by law enforcement agencies. Despite the collapse, the group's mystique continued to influence radicals, and by the early 1990s a new generation of militant activists calling themselves the New **Black Panther Party for Self-Defense** began to model themselves after the original Black Panthers.

SUGGESTED READING: Nathan Glazer, "Blacks, Jews, and the Intellectuals," *Commentary* 47, no. 4 (April 1969); Charles E. Jones, ed., *The Black Panther Party: Reconsidered* (Baltimore: Black Classic Press, 1998); Southern Poverty Law Center, "Snarling at the White Man," 2005, http://www.splcenter.org/intel/intelreport/article.jsp?aid=214.

BLACK PANTHER PARTY FOR SELF-DEFENSE, THE NEW. Party founded in 1990 by Aaron Michaels. It espouses a mix of black nationalism, Pan-Africanism, and racist **antisemitic** bigotry, following in the footsteps of the **Black Panther Party** of the 1960s. Since the late 1990s, it has become the largest organized antisemitic black militant group in the United States. After the death of its former leader **Khalid Muhammad** in February 2001, Malik Zulu Shabazz, a Washington, DC–based attorney, took over leadership of the group. Under Shabazz, the group continues to organize demonstrations across the country that blend inflammatory bigotry with calls for black empowerment and civil rights. Its symbol is a leaping black panther superimposed over a green Africa on a red circle.

SUGGESTED READING: Jeffrey Ogbar, *Black Power, Radical Politics and African American Identity* (Baltimore: Johns Hopkins University Press, 2004).

BLACK SEPTEMBER. Palestine terrorist group. This organization, made up of various Palestinian resistance groups loosely attached to the Palestine Liberation Organization, was responsible for the murder of Israeli athletes at the 1972 Munich **Olympic Games**. The group also assassinated the Jordanian prime minister and in Khartoum, Sudan, murdered two U.S. diplomats. The Israeli secret service tracked down the assassins and killed them.

SUGGESTED READING: Aaron Klein, *Striking Back: The 1972 Munich Olympics Massacre and Israel's Deadly Response* (New York: Random House, 2005).

BLACK SHIRTS. *See* SECRET ORGANIZATIONS, 20TH CENTURY.

BLAINE, JAMES. *See* HARRISON, BENJAMIN.

BLAKE, WILLIAM (1757–1827). English poet, engraver, and painter. Blake contrasted Jesus's forgiving nature to the hardness of Jews in general and the **Pharisees** in particular. In his works *Milton* and *Jerusalem*, Blake called Jesus "the Lamb of God . . . forgiving trespasses and sins" lest Jews "With Moral & Self-righteous Law / Should Crucify in Satan's Synagogue!" Blake suggested that Jesus died because he contested the evils of Judaism. He also called the Jewish Torah a "bloody shrine" and Judaism an invalid religion. Blake wrote that "a **Pig** has got a look / That for a Jew may be mistook." He compared the Jews' ancestors to creatures of Satan who "Rioted in human gore, / In offerings of Human life." He implored Jews to "Take up the Cross . . . & follow Jesus."

SUGGESTED READING: Frank Felsenstein, *Antisemitic Stereotypes: A Paradigm of Otherness in English Popular Culture, 1660–1830* (Baltimore: Johns Hopkins University Press, 1995).

BLASTARES, MATTHEW. A 14th-century Greek monk who tried to reduce **canon law** to a handy and accessible form. In 1335 Blastares called Jews "stiff-necked" and "uncircumcised in the heart." He said that Christians who participated in Jewish rites, used Jewish doctors, bathed with Jews, or associated with Jews in any friendly way should be excommunicated.

SUGGESTED READING: Steven Bowman, *The Jews of Byzantium* (Tuscaloosa: University of Alabama Press, 1985); Matthew Blastares, "Against the Jews," in *Byzantine Monastic Foundation Documents*, ed. John Thomas and Angela Constantinides Hero (Washington, DC: Dumbarton Oaks Research Library, 2000).

BLAVATSKY, HELENE (1836–1891). Spiritualist and occultist. Blavatsky, cofounder of the Theosophical Society, wrote many books on her occult experiences. Her writings about an ancient race of **Aryans** (supermen) and their symbol, the **swastika**, were adopted by **Guido von List** and **Lanz von Liebenfels,** both authors who greatly influenced the young **Adolf Hitler**. In her *Secret Doctrine* (1888), Blavatsky viewed the Jewish religion as "one of hatred and malice of everyone except itself."

SUGGESTED READING: Dara Ekland, ed., *H. P. Blavatsky: Collected Writings* (Wheaton, IL: Quest Books, 2002).

BLOIS. City in west-central France where, after a **ritual murder** accusation in 1177, 51 Jews were burned, 17 women among them. They died chanting the **Alenu prayer**. This was the first city in continental Europe to experience the blood libel defamation. Dirges written to commemorate the tragedy were incorporated into Jewish prayers.

SUGGESTED READING: Abraham I. Shinedling, "Blois," *Universal Jewish Encyclopedia* (New York: Universal Jewish Encyclopedia, 1940).

BLOOD ACCUSATION. *See* DEFAMATIONS, ANTI-JEWISH; RITUAL MURDER.

BLOOD & HONOUR. *See* 28; TRISKELE; TRISKELION; THREE-BLADED SWASTIKA; WHITE POWER MUSIC.

BLOOD AND SOIL (*BLUT UND BODEN*, BLUBO). The **Third Reich** considered German peasants the backbone of a pure **Aryan**/Nordic race. Only they had the right and duty to grow food on German soil to nourish healthy and strong Germans. In 1930, **Richard Walther Darré** proclaimed that "the unity of blood and soil must be restored." Blood and soil referred to a mystical connection between the blood of the German race or *Volk* on the one hand, and the land and the natural environment unique to Germanic peoples on the other. The advocates of *Blut und Boden* regarded the Jews as rootless wanderers capable of having neither German blood nor of any true relationship with the sacred German land.

SUGGESTED READING: Gustavo Corni, *Blut und Boden: Rassenideologie und Agrarpolitik im Staat Hitlers* (Idstein, Germany: Schulz-Kirchner, 1994).

BLOOD FOR TRUCKS. This was a plan negotiated between Joel Brand of the Budapest Jewish Rescue Committee and **Adolf Eichmann** in the spring of 1944. Eichmann, sent by **Heinrich Himmler** to bring the **Final Solution** to Hungarian Jews, also had another agenda—to negotiate a separate peace with the British and the Americans. The plan called for the end of **deportation** and release of up to one million Jews in exchange for 10,000 trucks (to be used against the Russians only). Nothing came of the affair. Brand was arrested by the British, who, along with the Americans saw the Nazi offer as a ruse to break up the Allies. Brand believed the rescue plan was an opportunity the Allies deliberately avoided.

SUGGESTED READING: Yehuda Bauer, *Jews for Sale: Nazi-Jewish Negotiations, 1939–1945* (New Haven, CT: Yale University Press, 1981); Alexander Weissberg, *Desperate Mission: Joel Brand's Story* (New York: Criterion, 1958).

BLOOD LIBEL. *See* DEFAMATIONS, ANTI-JEWISH; LA GUARDIA BLOOD LIBEL; NORWICH BLOOD LIBEL; RITUAL MURDER.

BLOODSUCKERS. (International slur, esp. among Muslim extremists) A reference to the medieval Christian **defamation** that Jews drank the blood of Christian children. The modern myth holds that Israelis murder Palestinian children and drink their blood. *See also* DRACULA; RITUAL MURDER; WANDERING JEW.

SUGGESTED READING: "List of Ethnic Slurs," *Wikipedia*, http://en.wiki pedia.org/wiki/List_of_ethnic_slurs.

BLUT UND EHRE. *See* 28.

B'NAI BRITH. Jewish organization founded in 1843 in New York by American Jews dedicated to combating **antisemitism**, racism, and bigotry, protecting human rights, developing positive intercommunity relations, and eliminating discrimination. Working in association with the **Anti-Defamation League**, the **B'nai Brith** accomplishes its goals through legal legislative initiatives, intercultural dialogues, community coalitions, and educational programming. Right-wing extremists and **neo-Nazis** attack it, claiming it violates the law by spying and taking part in Jewish conspiracies. Its website is http://bnaibrith.org.

BÖCKEL, OTTO (1815–1894). German political agitator and scholar. In 1889 Böckel attended an **antisemitic** conference at Bochum, Germany, and soon thereafter founded a radical political party, Antisemitischer Volkspartei. (The conference led to the founding of a second antisemitic party as well, the Deutsch-Soziale Partei led by **Max Liebermann von Sonnenberg**.) Called "the Hessian Peasant King," Böckel saw the Jews as causes of Germany's economic problems, whose solution consisted of a "Jew-Free" Germany; this appealed as well to the German lower middle classes. The first radical antisemite in the Reichstag (1887–1903), Böckel's slogan was "Peasants, free yourself from Jewish middlemen."
SUGGESTED READING: Philip Rees, *Biographical Dictionary of the Extreme Right since 1890* (New York: Simon & Schuster, 1990).

BODO. Bishop and chaplain of Emperor **Louis I**. Bodo converted to Judaism in 839. One chronicler dismissed Bodo's treachery as "succumb[ing] to the Jewish perfidy, . . . the Jewish madness." Another chronicle described Bodo's actions: "Allured by the enemy of mankind, he now abandoned Christianity and declared himself a Jew. . . . [A] plan of treachery and depravity with the Jews." Because of Bodo's apostasy, **Agobard**, the archbishop of Lyons, declared that the Jews posed a threat to the Church as dangerous as that of the **Antichrist** himself.
SUGGESTED READING: Jacob Marcus, *The Jew in the Medieval World: A Source Book, 315–1791* (New York: New York University Press, 1979).

BOER WAR. *See* BEAMISH, HENRY HAMILTON.

BOLSHEVIKS. The Communist Party of Russia at the turn of the 20th century. For the short term, Bolshevism was beneficial to Jews. The party's policy for a while was anti-**antisemitism**. In power after their revolution of 1917, the Bolsheviks eliminated antisemitic laws and restrictions going back to the tsars. During the Russian **Civil War**, with the Whites (pro-tsarist forces), they protected Jews. However, in the long run, the Bolsheviks and Communist Party set about to destroy Jewish autonomy, culture, and religion and the Zionist movement. *See also* BELLOC, HILAIRE; BIROBIDZHAN; BUND; CHURCHILL, WINSTON; COSMOPOLI-TANISM; KUN, BÉLA; STALIN, JOSEPH; TROTSKY, LEON; YEV-SEKTSIA; ZINOVIEV, GREGORY.

SUGGESTED READING: Robert Wistrich, *Antisemitism in the Soviet Union: Its Roots and Consequences* (Jerusalem: Hebrew University Press, 1972).

BONALD, LOUIS DE (1754–1840). French reactionary, counterrevolutionary, and theocratic apologist. In 1806, attempting to undo the aim of the **French Revolution** in freeing Jews, Bonald wrote: "Jews sought to reduce all Christians until they are nothing more than their slaves." This prompted **Napoleon** to reexamine the Revolution's legislation in regard to the Jews and ultimately to call the **Assembly of Notables**. Later, during the Restoration, Bonald held that "Jews could not become French citizens without consequences," and, one historian noted, "he was probably right in the eyes of Catholic believers."

SUGGESTED READING: David Klinck, *The French Counterrevolutionary Theorist, Louis De Bonald (1754–1840)*, Studies in Modern European History, vol. 18 (New York: P. Lang, 1996); Gotthard Deutsch, "Bonald, Louis," *JewishEncyclopedia.com*, http://www.jewishencyclopedia.com/view.jsp?artid=1263&letter=B.

BONHOEFFER, DIETRICH (1906–1945). Eminent German Lutheran minister and theologian. While Bonhoeffer was sympathetic to and later helped German Jews and was himself executed by the **Nazis**, he defended the **Third Reich**'s early anti-Jewish actions:

> The state's measures against the Jewish people are connected . . . in a very special way with the Church. In the Church of Christ, we have never lost sight of the idea that the "Chosen People," that nailed the Savior of the world to the cross, must bear the curse of its action through a long history of suffering.

SUGGESTED READING: Kenneth Barnes, "Dietrich Bonhoeffer and Hitler's Persecution of the Jews," in Robert Eriksen and Susannah Heschel, *Betrayal: German Churches and the Holocaust* (Minneapolis, MN: Augsburg-Fortress, 1999); Edwin Hanton Robertson, *The Shame and the*

Sacrifice: The Life and Martyrdom of Dietrich Bonhoeffer (New York: Macmillan, 1987).

BONIFACE VIII (1235–1303). Pope, 1295–1303. In 1298 Boniface ordered the **Inquisition** to persecute as relapsed **heretics** those Jews who had been **baptized** as children or as a result of coercion. This principle soon found its way into **canon law**. His bull *Unam sanctam* of 1302 reiterated that "there is one holy, Catholic and apostolic Church . . . and that outside this Church there is no salvation or remission of sins."

SUGGESTED READING: Judah Gribetz, Edward L. Greenstein, and Regina S. Stein, *The Timetables of Jewish History* (New York: Simon & Schuster, 1993).

BONIFACE SOCIETY (BONIFATIUS-VEREIN). A German, Roman Catholic society founded in 1901 whose object was "to promote the spiritual interests of Catholics living in Protestant parts of Germany, and the maintenance of schools." The society often went beyond these goals to express **antisemitic** ideas, however. Despite the critiques of contemporary theologians such as Franz Delitzsch, the Boniface Society widely published the defamatory *The Talmud Jew* of the antisemitic priest **August Rohling**, which has resulted in a negative effect on Catholic minds even until today.

BOOK BURNING. Throughout time in the Christian world, the **Talmud** has been burned. The rationale was that the work debased Christianity and mocked Jesus. Popes and other Christian prelates wanted the Jews to be living witnesses to Jesus and to restrict themselves to the Jewish Scriptures admired by both religions. The prelates believed the Talmud superceded the Hebrew Scriptures in Jewish life and hence discouraged its study. Often an apostate would make accusations and debate with rabbis in a forced **disputation**. This was followed by the burning of the Talmud. There is evidence that those who burned Jewish books thereafter burned Jews. On May 10, 1933, the **Nazis** burned many books, particularly those on Jewish themes and written by Jewish authors. *See also* DONIN, NICHOLAS; FRANKISTS; GREGORY IX; JUSTINIAN I; LOUIS IX; PAUL IV; PFEFFERKORN, JOHANNES.

SUGGESTED READING: Stephen J. Whitfield, "Where They Burn Books . . . ," *Modern Judaism* 22 (2002).

BOOTS. Racist and nonracist **skinhead** symbol. Until recently, skinheads could be identified by their colored shoelaces and Doc Martens boots, often made with steel tips and used as "weapons." A "boot party" is a gathering where skinheads commit acts of violence.

SUGGESTED READING: Anti-Defamation League, *Hate on Display: Extremist Symbols, Logos, and Tattoos* (New York: Anti-Defamation League, 2006).

BORMANN, MARTIN (1900–1945?). Head of the **Nazi Party** Chancellery and private secretary of **Adolf Hitler**. By the end of World War II, Bormann had become second only to Hitler himself in terms of real political power. He was involved in **Aryanization** and **deportations**. Bormann was invariably the advocate of radical measures when it came to the treatment of Jews, the conquered Eastern peoples, and prisoners of war. He signed the decree of 1942 prescribing that "the permanent elimination of the Jews from the territories of Greater Germany can no longer be carried out by emigration but by the use of ruthless force in the special camps of the East."

SUGGESTED READING: Jochen Von Lang, *The Secretary—Martin Bormann: The Man Who Manipulated Hitler* (Athens: Ohio University Press, 1981).

BÖRNE, LUDWIG (JUDAH BARUCH) (1786–1837). German political essayist. A convert to Lutheranism, Börne bitterly summed up the predicament of Jews who were making their way into German Christian society: "Some reproach me with being a Jew, some praise me because of it, some pardon me for it, but all think of it."

SUGGESTED READING: Ludwig Börne, *Briefe aus Paris*, Letter 74; Hannah Arendt, *The Origins of Totalitarianism* (Cleveland: Meridian, 1958).

BOSCH, HIERONYMUS (1450?–1516). Dutch painter. Bosch's Prado Epiphany portrayed the **Antichrist** as the Jewish **messiah** and as the epitome of evil. Bosch also painted "The Crucifixion," which shows Jesus en route to Golgotha; his face at peace, he is spiritually transported beyond the frenzied Jewish mob that surrounds him. In sharp contrast to the sublime Jesus, the Jewish crowd is portrayed as a collection of dehumanized monstrosities.

SUGGESTED READING: Lotte Brank Philip, "The Prado Epiphany by Jerome Bosch," in *Bosch in Perspective*, ed. James Snyder (Englewood Cliffs, NJ: Prentice-Hall, 1973).

BÖTTICHER, PAUL. *See* LAGARDE, PAUL ANTON DE.

BOUSQUET, RENÉ (1910–1993). Secretary-general of the French National Police. Appointed by Pierre Laval, prime minister during the **Vichy** regime

(1940–44), to head the National Police, Bousquet was responsible for the **deportation** and deaths of 60,000 Jews. After the war, unpunished, he directed the Bank of Indochina. *See also* KLARSFELD, SERGE AND BEATE.

SUGGESTED READING: Susan Zucotti, *The Holocaust, the French and the Jews* (New York: Basic Books, 1993).

BOYCOTT OF 1912. In 1912, the founder of Endejca (a Polish right-wing nationalistic movement), **Roman Dmowski**, organized a boycott of Jewish businesses in Poland. Confined mainly to Warsaw, the boycott continued until 1914. This economic boycott was later incorporated as a plank in the Endejca's party platform in interwar Poland. Dmowski also advocated an ethnically homogeneous and intensely Catholic Poland, excluding Jews. He sought to make Poland so inhospitable for Jews that they would "voluntarily" emigrate from Poland. In 1916, Dmowski publicly spoke against the Jews: "Why is there such dislike for the Jews in Poland? The Jews are [supposedly] the salt of the earth. [But as everyone knows,] if there is too much salt in the soup, nobody can eat it." Intellectual and popular publications carried Dmowski's anti-Jewish message across Poland, accusing Jews of lacking patriotism and seeking to dominate Poland at the expense of the Polish people and Polishness. Newsletters encouraged Catholic Poles to patronize only "their own." The boycott and the continuing campaign against the Jews helped to impoverish the most vulnerable members of the Jewish community. But most Jews refused to allow this verbal **pogrom** to force them into leaving Poland, since their ancestors had fought for Poland during the nation's wars of liberation and they considered Poland their nation and themselves citizens.

SUGGESTED READING: Robert Blobaum, "The Politics of Antisemitism in Fin-de-Siècle Warsaw," *Journal of Modern History* 73, no. 2 (June 2001).

BOYCOTT OF JEWISH SHOPS, GERMAN. In 1933, **Adolf Hitler** ordered a boycott of Jewish shops to begin on April 1. Hitler's pretext was that the boycott was in response to "atrocity propaganda" disseminated by "international Jewry." Most active in the plan's coordinating committee were **Josef Goebbels** and **Julius Streicher**. The **Nazis** placed stormtroopers or other thugs in front of each Jewish store to dissuade shoppers, although many shoppers refused to honor the boycott. This was the first major action against Germany's Jews. Negative publicity, hard economic times, and poor response led to the termination of the boycott.

SUGGESTED READING: Marion Kaplan, *Between Dignity and Despair: Jewish Life in Germany* (New York: Oxford University Press, 2000); David Bankier, ed., *Probing the Depths of German Antisemitism: German Society and the Persecution of Jews* (Jerusalem: Yad Vashem and Leo Baeck Institute, 2000).

BRACTON, HENRY DE (1210–1268). Also known as Henry of Bratton, Henricus de Brattona, and Henricus de Bractona. The greatest of Catholic jurisprudents. In *On the Laws and Customs of England*, Bracton wrote that Jews were wards of the king and "the Jew can have nothing of his own, for whatever he acquires, he acquires not for himself, but for the king." *See also* EDWARD I; RITUAL MURDER; *SERFS.*

SUGGESTED READING: Henry de Bracton, *On the Laws and Customs of England*, ed. Samuel Thorne (Cambridge, MA: Belknap Press, 1968).

BRANDT, RUDOLPH (1909–1947). **Nazi** physician. Brandt was the prime **war criminal** at the **Nuremberg War Crimes Trial** of doctors charged with **crimes against humanity** in 1946. He was convicted and hanged for his role in performing inhumane experiments resulting in the death of deportees at **Dachau** and **Mauthausen**.

SUGGESTED READING: Robert Lifton, *The Nazi Doctors* (New York: Basic Books, 2000).

BRASILLACH, ROBERT (1909–1945). French author and journalist. In 1931, when he was just 21, the precocious Brasillach was named literary editor at the openly antisemitic *Action Française.* As editor-in-chief of François Coty's antisemitic tabloid *Je Suis Partout,* Brasillach wrote in favor of collaboration with the **Nazis** and establishment of a new European order governed by Nazi ideology. In 1941, the German embassy in Paris, recognizing Brasillach's sympathies, ordered his release from a prisoner-of-war camp. While still a prisoner-of-war, he had written an article identifying certain fellow officers as Jewish. Once released from camp, he maintained his attack against the "Judeo-Gaullist" forces threatening France. In the context of the roundup of more than 8,000 Jewish children kept at the Velodrome d'Hiver bicycle stadium that was transformed into a transit camp in July 1942, Brasillach demanded that France separate itself from "the Jews en bloc and not keep any little ones." Brasillach collaborated fully and willingly with the genocidal **Third Reich**. He was tried by the High Court, sentenced to death for collaboration, and executed in 1945.

SUGGESTED READING: Alice Kaplan, *The Collaborator: The Trial and Execution of Robert Brasillach* (Chicago: University of Chicago Press, 2000).

BRAUCHITSCH, WALTHER VON (1881–1948). German Army field marshal. Brauchitsch was charged at the **Nuremberg War Crimes Trials** with complicity in **Adolf Hitler**'s aggression. Acting as commander-in-chief (1938–41), he signed the **Commissar Order** that called for summary murder of Communists and Jews.

SUGGESTED READING: Joachim Fest, *Plotting Hitler's Death: The Story of German Resistance*, trans. Bruce Little (New York: Metropolitan Books, 1996).

BRENTANO, CLEMENS (1778–1842). German poet and author. Although he admired ancient Judaism, Brentano hated contemporary Jews, calling them ugly, traitorous, and nasty. He cofounded the Christian-German Dining Club, which barred "Jews, converted Jews, and the descendents of converted Jews" from membership. There is evidence that, like **Johann von Goethe**, he softened toward Jews in his old age.

SUGGESTED READING: Alfred Low, *Jews in the Eyes of the Germans* (Philadelphia: Institute for Study of Human Issues, 1979).

BRESLAU, COUNCIL OF. Roman Catholic Church council in 1266. The council found that "since Poland is a new plantation on the soil of Christianity there is reason to fear that her Christians will fall prey to the superstitions and evils of the Jews living among them." It ordered that Jews residing in Poland must not live side by side with Christians and that the Jewish section must be separated from the Christian section by a hedge, wall, or ditch. The Jews owning houses in the Christian quarter had to sell them within the shortest time possible. Jews were required to lock themselves up in their houses while church processions were marching through the streets. In each Polish city, Jews could have only one **synagogue**. They were required to wear a distinctive hat (*cornutum pileum*, or *Judenhut*) with a hornlike shield; any Jew showing himself on the street without this would be penalized. Christians were forbidden to invite Jews to eat or drink, or to dance or make merry with them at weddings or other celebrations. Christians were also forbidden to buy meat and other food from Jews, since the latter might poison them.

BREVIARY OF ALARIC II. Set of laws proclaimed in 506 by Alaric II, Arian king of Spain, 484–507. The Breviary ordered that Jews were not to **circumcize** Christian slaves (the penalty was the freeing of the slave) nor could the Jews harass Jewish apostates to Christianity (in this case, the punishment was "according to the nature of the crime committed"). Christians were not permitted to participate in Jewish rituals. Intermarriage among Christians and Jews was forbidden. Secular issues under litigation were required to be brought before Roman law courts. **Synagogues** were to be protected and Jewish holidays respected. The harshest of these laws forbade Jews from holding imperial office, from constructing new synagogues, and from converting Christians to Judaism on pain of death. This last law may have been inspired by the Christian piety aroused when **Church Father St. John Chrysostom**'s bones were returned to Constantinople. The code remained in force until 654.

SUGGESTED READING: Clyde Pharr, *The Theodosian Code and Novels* (Greenwich, CT: Greenwood Press, 1952).

BREW. (U.S. slur) A Jew. Shortened form of the word *Hebrew*.

SUGGESTED READING: "List of Ethnic Slurs," *Wikipedia*, http://en.wiki pedia.org/wiki/List_of_ethnic_slurs.

BREWER, DAVID (1837–1910). U.S. Supreme Court justice, 1899–1910. Like fellow Supreme Court justices Joseph Story and William Strong, Brewer was a dedicated Calvinist. The son of a minister, he lived his early life in Connecticut and attended the then passionately Protestant Yale University. His **Holy Trinity Church** opinion, for a unanimous Supreme Court, was that in "American life as expressed by its laws, its business, its customs, and its society, we find everywhere a clear recognition of the same truth. . . . This is a Christian nation." In *The United States: A Christian Nation* (1905), Justice Brewer made the same points by detailing the state constitutional provisions, statutes, and legal decisions that proved Americans lived in a Christian state: "We constantly speak of this republic as a Christian nation—in fact, as the leading Christian nation of the world."

SUGGESTED READING: David J. Brewer, *The United States: A Christian Nation* (Philadelphia: John C. Winston, 1905).

BRIGHAM, CARL (1890–1943). American raceologist. A Princeton University psychologist, Brigham's major work was *A Study of American Intelligence* (1922). He based a great deal of it on **Madison Grant**'s *Passing of the Great Race* (1916), which purported that the most desirable immigrants were Nordics. Soon after, Brigham adapted the heavily cultural-biased Army Alpha tests for a college entrance exam. This became the Scholastic Aptitude Test (SAT). Jews scored on the moron level in the Alpha test even if they were literate in Yiddish. He later recanted his racist views, but too late to undo the damage done regarding Jewish immigration and students.

SUGGESTED READING: Edwin Black, *The War against the Weak* (New York: Four Walls, Eight Windows, 2003).

BRITISH BROTHERS LEAGUE. The British Brothers League, formed in 1902, was one of several British antisemitic, nativist, **fascist** organizations established at the turn of the 20th century seeking to curtail Jewish immigration. In 1932, it became part of the **British Union of Fascists**.

SUGGESTED READING: William J. Fishman, *East End Jewish Radicals, 1875–1914* (Nottingham, England: Five Leaves Publishers, 2005).

BRITISH UNION OF FASCISTS (BUF) (1918–1940). **Xenophobic**, racist, and pro-**Nazi**, the British Union of Fascists became a political party under the leadership of Sir Oswald Mosley (1896–1980), a British member of Parliament and **fascist**. After the Russian Revolution, several conservative British politicians associated Jews and **Bolshevism** in an attempt to discredit both. In 1932, the British Union of Fascists combined the **British Brothers League**, the Britons Society, the Imperial Fascist League, and the British Empire Union with Sir Oswald Mosley's New Party. The BUF took its cues from **Benito Mussolini**'s Italian Fascists. At its height, it boasted 40,000 members, particularly in London's poor East End. In 1934–35, **antisemitism** became its dominant theme. It held marches in Jewish sections, stirring violence against Jews. Parroting **Adolf Hitler**, it claimed that Jewish financiers were behind threats of war. Thuggish actions led to a dramatic loss of its support and membership. In 1940, the BUF was banned. *See also* JOYCE, WILLIAM.

SUGGESTED READING: Thomas Lineham, *Fascism in Britain, 1918–1939: Parties, Ideology, and Culture* (Manchester, England: Manchester University Press, 2000).

BROWN, GEORGE S. (1918–1979). U.S. Army general and chairman of the Joint Chiefs of Staff. Brown spoke to Duke University on October 10, 1975, and was asked a question by a student: "How can we stop Israel from obtaining from the Congress more foreign aid than any other nation in the world?" General Brown responded: "When they get tough-minded enough to set down the Jewish influence in this country and break that lobby. It is so strong, you wouldn't believe it. . . . They own—you know—the banks in this country, the newspapers. Just look at where the Jewish money is."

SUGGESTED READING: Edgar Puryear, *George S. Brown, General, U.S. Air Force: Destined for Stars* (New York: Random House/Presidio Press,

1983); Mark Franklin, "Gentile Leaders Have Not Liked Jews," *History News Network*, 2005, http://www.hnn.us/comments/15664.html.

BRUDER SCHWEIGEN. *See* SILENT BROTHERHOOD.

BRUNNER, ALOIS (1912–?). **SS** officer. *Hauptsturmführer* (captain) Brunner was second in command to **Adolf Eichmann** and aided him in implementing the **Final Solution**. He bore direct responsibility for the **deportation** to death camps of 128,000 Jews from Austria, Greece, France, and Slovakia. After hiding out on his own, in 1954 the U.S. Central Intelligence Agency helped Brunner reach Syria safely to evade capture.

SUGGESTED READING: Richard Rhoads, *Masters of Death: The SS Einsatzgruppen and the Invention of the Holocaust* (New York: Vintage, 2003).

BRUNO, FILIPPO GIORDANO (1548–1600). Italian philosopher and priest. Claiming to advocate a new faith, Philosophy, with more love of humanity and wisdom than Catholicism or Lutheranism, Bruno left the **Dominican** order in 1576. In 1584–85, he wrote *Lo Spaccio della Bestia Trionfante* (The Expulsion of the Triumphant Beast) in which his character Wisdom states: "The Jews are so pestilent, leprous, and generally so pernicious as to merit being aborted rather than born." The book passed almost without notice. However, another of his books supporting Copernicus and challenging the Catholic Church's geocentric conception of the universe led to his being burned at the stake in Rome in 1600.

BRYAN, WILLIAM JENNINGS. *See* POPULISTS, U.S.

BRYANT, WILLIAM CULLEN (1794–1878). American poet. Bryant held ambivalent views on Jews. On the one hand, he asserted that Jews had "an unquenchable lust for lucre" and a "lust for money"; they were like snakes "in search of prey." Yet he also stereotyped Jews as "noble" and "spiritual," with affectionate family relations and great contributions to the world in religion, law, poetry, and music. "Their disposition is to triumph by intellect rather than violence."

SUGGESTED READING: Allan Gould, *What Did They Think of the Jews?* (Northvale, NJ: Jason Aronson, 1991).

BUBIS, IGNATZ (1927–1999). The late head of the German Jewish community. In an interview with the Austrian weekly *Profil* (August 3, 1997) the revisionist **Jörg Haider**—using information that *after the war* Bubis smuggled gold into Germany—claimed that "various circles [*verschidene Kreisen*, rightist code phrase for Jews] do not want to have the Swiss gold issue fully discussed because . . . Bubis may have smuggled gold from Switzerland to Germany, [gold] taken from his former friends [*seine fruehere Freunden*, rightist code phrase for murdered Jews], to start his fortune." Haider was suggesting that Bubis smuggled **Nazi** gold *during* the war and attempting to draw an analogy between a Jewish survivor and Swiss collaborators with the Nazis—that is, that both the Swiss and Jews like Bubis made their fortunes from the assets of murdered Jews. According to historian Anat Peri, "Haider is clearly drawing on the classic Christian image of **Judas [Iscariot]** who betrayed Christ and sold his life for thirty pieces of silver."

SUGGESTED READING: Anat Peri, "Jörg Haider's Antisemitism," Vidal Sassoon International Center for the Study of Antisemitism, 2001, http://sicsa.huji.ac.il/acta18.htm.

BUCER, MARTIN (1491–1551). Strasbourg religious reformer. Bucer believed that Jews threatened Christian society, and he convinced Landgrave Philipp of Hesse to institute discriminatory regulations against the Jews.

SUGGESTED READING: John Kleiner, "The Attitudes of Martin Bucer and Landgrave Philipp toward the Jews of Hesse," in *Faith and Freedom*, ed. Richard Libowitz (Oxford: Oxford University Press, 1987); Hastings Eells, "Bucer's Plan for the Jews," *Church History* 6 (1937).

BUCHANAN, PATRICK (1935–). U.S. journalist and former presidential candidate. The **Anti-Defamation League** and William Buckley have charged him with **antisemitism**. Buchanan has claimed that the Israel lobby, dominated by American Jews, promotes a pro-Israel U.S. foreign policy at the expense of American interests. He has called Capitol Hill "Israel's Occupied Country" and has defended Nazi **war criminals**, seeing them as innocent victims of Jewish conspiracies. According to Buchanan, **Adolf Hitler** was "an individual of great courage, a soldier's soldier" (*The Guardian*, January 14, 1992). He set himself in agreement with **Holocaust deniers** when he wrote that thousands of Jews were not killed at Treblinka because "Diesel engines do not emit enough carbon monoxide to kill anybody" (*New York Post*, March 17, 1990). He called for closing the U.S. Justice Department's Office of Special Investigations, whose role was to prosecute **Nazi** war criminals, because it was "running down 70-year-old camp guards" (*New York Times*, April 21, 1987). After Cardinal O'Connor of New York criticized antisemitism, Buchanan wrote:

If U.S. Jewry takes the clucking appeasement of the Catholic cardinalate as indicative of our submission, it is mistaken. When Cardinal O'Connor seeks to soothe the always irate Elie Wiesel by reassuring him "there are many Catholics who are anti-Semitic" . . . he speaks for himself. Be not afraid, Your Eminence; just step aside, there are bishops and priests ready to assume the role of defender of the faith. (*New Republic*, October 22, 1990)

In a September 1993 speech to the Christian Coalition, Buchanan declared: "Our culture is superior. Our culture is superior because our religion is Christianity" (*ADL Report*, 1994). *See also* DONAHUE, WILLIAM.

SUGGESTED READING: Jacob Weisberg, "The Heresies of Pat Buchanan," *New Republic*, October 22, 1990.

BUENOS AIRES PROGROMS. In reaction to the police killing several demonstrators during a march by FORA (the Federación Obrera Regional **Argentina**, an anarchist-socialist federation) in 1909, Simón Radowitzki, a young anarchist Jew, killed both the chief of police Col. Ramón Falcón and his secretary. As a result, in 1910 the government arrested thousands, deported foreigners, many of them Jews, and declared martial law. Police mentioned the confiscation of leaflets printed in Hebrew (more likely in Yiddish) calling for violence and rioting. In January 1919, "La Semana Trágica" (Tragic Week), police attacked striking workers, and in retaliation a general strike was called. Reacting to the scattered labor unrest, police, army, and right-wing civilians attacked the Russian-Jewish community of Buenos Aires, resulting in 700 deaths and a further 4,000 casualties.

SUGGESTED READING: David Rock, *Politics in Argentina, 1890–1930: The Rise and Fall of Radicalism* (Cambridge: Cambridge University Press, 1975).

BULGARIA. Bulgaria, home to 50,000 Sephardic Jews at the onset of World War II, was an ally of the **Third Reich**. But all elements of Bulgaria's population of five million resisted the **Final Solution**—parliament, clergy, workingmen, and the monarchy, particularly King Boris III, who was possibly assassinated by the Nazis. Nevertheless, many Jews were rounded up and taken to labor camps. Angelo Roncalli, the **Vatican** representative in Turkey, pleaded with King Boris against the **deportations**. Only 11,384 Jews from Thrace and Macedonia were ultimately deported. By the time the Russian army entered Bulgaria in September 1944, only 14 percent of Bulgaria's Jews had perished.

SUGGESTED READING: Frederick B. Chary, *The Bulgarian Jews and the Final Solution* (Pittsburgh, PA: University of Pittsburgh Press, 1984).

BUND. The Jewish Workers Union, formed in Vilnius, Lithuania, in 1897. The Bund sought full Jewish economic, civil, and cultural rights in the **Pale of Settlement**. This socialist movement favored national rights for Jews, communal autonomy, a language of their own (Yiddish), and their own union, schools, press, and self-defense units. It was the first Jewish political party. Zionists opposed it, favoring Jewish autonomy in Palestine, not in the **Diaspora**. Mainline **Bolsheviks**, such as **Joseph Stalin**, disliked it because he believed Jews were not a nation; communists believed workingmen had no ethnicity or nation. In 1922 the Bund was suppressed by Vladimir Lenin. However, in Poland, the Bund remained vital until the **Nazi**-Soviet invasions in September 1939.

SUGGESTED READING: Jack Jacobs, ed., *Jewish Politics in Eastern Europe: The Bund at 100* (New York: New York University Press, 2001).

BURCKHARDT, JACOB (d. 1897). Like many German conservatives, Burckhardt associated the Jews with the potentially destructive changes in modern industrialized society. Progress, materialism, and urbanization were threats that he perceived as stemming from Judaism. His revulsion at what he stereotyped as a typically ugly Jewish face symbolized his antagonism to the Jews as the antitype of "the spiritual essence of the age."

SUGGESTED READING: George Mosse, *Germans and Jews* (Detroit: Wayne State University Press, 1987).

BURKE, EDMUND (1729–1797). Anglo-Irish politician, essayist, and philosopher. In *A Letter from Mr. Burke to a Member of the National Assembly* (1791), Burke wrote of "the whole gang of **usurers**, pedlars, and itinerant Jew-discounters at the corners of streets."

SUGGESTED READING: Frank Felsenstein, *Antisemitic Stereotypes: A Paradigm of Otherness in English Popular Culture, 1660–1830* (Baltimore: Johns Hopkins University Press, 1995).

BURSCHENSCHAFTEN. The Allgemeine Deutsche Burschenschaft (Young Germany Movement) was a group of ultranationalistic German student fraternities that organized the Wartburg Festival of 1817, where 500 students from 12 universities met to burn symbols of tyranny, for example, copies of the Code **Napoleon** and a corporal's cane, as well as hundreds of books written by reactionary authors. They excluded foreigners from their ranks, refused to accept Jewish students as members, and participated in antisemitic outbursts in Frankfurt in 1819. Their antirationalism, **antisemitism**, intolerance, terrorism, and **xenophobia** were precursors, *mutatis mutandis*, of the **Nazis**.

BUTLER, RICHARD G. (1918–2004). Butler led the **Aryan Nations** and the Church of Jesus Christ–Christian—the nation's most well-known bastion of **neo-Nazism** and **Christian Identity**—which accused Jews of being Satan's children. The Southern Poverty Law Center, an American human rights organization, won a $6.3 million lawsuit against Butler's organization in September 2000 that bankrupted the group, leading to its downfall.

SUGGESTED READING: James Ridgeway, *Blood in the Face: The Ku Klux Klan, Aryan Nations, Nazi Skinheads, and the Rise of a New White Culture* (New York: Thunder's Mouth Press, 1995); Anti-Defamation League, "Richard Butler," n.d., www.adl.org/learn/ext_US/Butler.asp?xpicked = 2&idem = 2.

BUTZ, ARTHUR (1889–1968). American **Holocaust denier** and associate professor of electrical engineering and computer science at Northwestern University. Although Butz lacks a background in history, his 1976 book *The Hoax of the Twentieth Century: The Case against the Presumed Extermination of European Jewry* is a mainstay of the Holocaust Denial Movement in the United States. *See also* NOONTIDE PRESS.

SUGGESTED READING: Deborah Lipstadt, *Denying the Holocaust: The Growing Assault on Truth and Memory* (East Rutherford, NJ: Plume Books, 1994).

BUXTORF, JOHANNES, THE ELDER (1564–1629). German Protestant scholar at the University of Basel who contrasted the carnal reign of the Jewish **messiah** with the spirituality of the Christian messiah, Jesus Christ. Buxtorf alleged that Jews cursed and urinated on the meat they sold Christians.

SUGGESTED READING: Frank Manuel, *The Broken Staff: Judaism through Christian Eyes* (Cambridge, MA: Harvard University Press, 1992); Solomon Grayzel, *The Church and the Jews in the XIII Century*, ed. Kenneth R. Stow, vol. 2, *1254–1314* (Detroit: Wayne State University Press, 1989).

– C –

CAESAREA. City in ancient Judea. The spark that triggered the Jewish revolt against pagan Rome and Hellenism was ignited in Caesarea, where there was considerable tension between the large Roman-Greek community and the smaller community of Jewish residents. When non-Jewish Caesareans sacrificed a bird outside the door of a **synagogue** in 66 CE, this led to a fight and then an anti-Jewish riot. News of the event spread and sparked a revolt against Rome throughout Judea.

SUGGESTED READING: Paul Johnson, *A History of the Jews* (New York: HarperPerennial, 1987).

CAESAR'S COLUMN. *See* DONNELLY, IGNATIUS.

CALLINICUM. *See* AMBROSE, ST.

CALVIN, JOHN (1509–1564). Also known as Jean Cauvin. French Protestant reformer. Calvin's hostility toward Jews was mild compared to **Martin Luther**'s. Calvin claimed Jews were liars, braggarts, and falsifiers of Scriptures. Judaism was a faith of the past and had been superceded by the Christian church. Jews were punished because of their rejection of Jesus. Historically, however, Calvinists have been less hostile to Jews than many other Protestant denominations. *See also* TRIUMPHALISM.

SUGGESTED READING: Jack Hughes Robinson, *John Calvin and the Jews* (New York: Peter Lang, 1992).

CAMELOTS DU ROI (THE KING'S NEWSBOYS). A paramilitary youth organization and violent monarchist street gang recruited in 1908 to sell the newspaper *Action Française*. In 1908–09, these French royalists destroyed the monuments of Ludovic Trarieux, **Émile Zola**, Charles Auguste Scheurer-Kestner, and Bernard Lazare, all important figures in the attempt to attain justice for Alfred Dreyfus. The Camelots attempted to revise the legacy of the **Dreyfus Case** by working to carry out the reactionary goals of Action Française, the first French **fascist** movement, comprising conservatives, monarchists, and other antirepublicans dedicated to overthrowing the values of liberty, equality, and fraternity. In 1934, 15 Camelots were killed by the Paris police during a demonstration. *See also* BARRÈS, MAURICE; BRASILLACH, ROBERT; MAURRAS, CHARLES; STAVISKY AFFAIR.

SUGGESTED READING: Brooke Stacey Rosenblatt, "Manipulating History: The Camelots du Roi's Campaign to Quash Dreyfusard Monuments," thesis, University of Maryland, 2005.

CAMPERS. (U.S. slur) Reference to Jews as inmates of concentration camps; also, a reference to the alleged inclination of Jews to send their children to summer camp.

SUGGESTED READING: "List of Ethnic Slurs," *Wikipedia*, http://en.wiki pedia.org/wiki/List_of_ethnic_slurs.

CANADA. Between 1880 and 1930, Canada's Jewish population grew from minuscule to 155,000, with Jewish immigrants seeking asylum from Eastern European **pogroms**. In the 1920s and 1930s, organized **antisemitism** grew among liberals and rightists in both the English-speaking and French-speaking populations. The Canadian **Ku Klux Klan** and **Aryan Nations** developed in the same period. In 1935 the anti-Jewish restrictionist Canadian government appointed Frederick Charles Blair—like **Breckinridge Long** in the U.S. **State Department**—director of immigration to ensure restrictions on immigration. As in the United States, when "safe havens" were most needed for the Jews of Europe, Canadian authorities shut the door to Jewish immigration, following a "none is too many" policy. In 1938, Prime Minister Mackenzie King noted in his diary that any significant immigration of Jews would "undermine the unity of the nation. . . . This is no time for Canada to act on humanitarian grounds." After the war, the government passed antidiscrimination laws, and today's Jewish population of 371,000 participates fully in Canadian life. Nevertheless, antisemitic incidents have increased 200 percent since 1988. A 2004 audit recorded 857 anti-Jewish incidents, the highest number in 22 years. A Jewish elementary school in Montreal was firebombed, and relations between Jewish and Muslim students at Concordia and McGill universities deteriorated. *See also* HAMMERSKIN NATION; REFUGEE PROBLEM; ZUNDEL, ERNST.

SUGGESTED READING: Irving Abells, *A Coat of Many Colors* (Toronto: Key Porter Books, 1990); Gerald Dirks, *Canada's Refugee Policy: Indifference or Opportunism?* (Montreal: McGill Queen's University Press, 1977); Joanna Sloame, "The Virtual Jewish History Tour: Canada," 2006, http://www.jewishvirtuallibrary.org/jsource/vjw/canada.html.

CANON LAW. Beginning in the 11th century, the medieval Church began to exploit both canon law and secular law to destroy whatever legal and social privileges the Jews still possessed. By the 12th century, the status of the Jews in Christian Europe dropped below that of all Christians. According to canon 24 of the Third Lateran Council of 1179, for example, "Jews should be slaves to Christians and at the same time treated kindly due to humanitarian considerations." Canon 26 held that "the testimony of Christians against Jews is to be preferred in all causes where they use their own witnesses against Christians. And we decree that those are to be anathematized whosoever prefer Jews to Christians in this regard, for they ought to be under Christians."

SUGGESTED READING: Edward Peters, *Inquisition* (Berkeley: University of California Press, 1989); H. H. Ben-Sasson, "Effects of Religious

Animosity on the Jews," in *A History of the Jewish People*, ed. H. H. Ben-Sasson (Cambridge, MA: Harvard University Press, 1976); Gavin Langmuir, "Anti-Judaism as the Necessary Preparation for Antisemitism," *Viator: Medieval and Renaissance Studies* 2 (1971); Bernhard Blumenkranz, "The Roman Church and the Jews," in Jeremy Cohen, ed., *Essential Papers on Judaism and Christianity in Conflict* (New York: New York University Press, 1991).

CAPHEAD. (Australian slur) A reference to Jewish men wearing yarmulkas.
SUGGESTED READING: "List of Ethnic Slurs," *Wikipedia*, http://en.wikipedia.org/wiki/List_of_ethnic_slurs.

CAPISTRANO, ST. GIOVANNI DI (1386–1456). Also known as John of Capistrano and Juan Capistrano. A Franciscan who believed that Jews were not really needed in Christendom. Known as "the scourge of the Jews," Capistrano carried on an anti-Jewish propaganda campaign in royal and papal courts. Instrumental in coercing the Jews to wear the **Jew badge**, he also managed to obtain the cancellation of pro-Jewish protective charters. He attacked the Jewish means of living by forbidding Jewish moneylending in Spain and Italy and further alienated Jews from their neighbors by reinforcing the social separation between Christian and Jew. He spread rumors of **ritual murder** and **desecration of the Host** that led to the destruction of the Jews of Breslau and **Passau** in 1453. He argued that without baptism the conflict between Christians and Jews could only be solved by sending the Jews to their death on the high seas. *See also PRIVILEGIA.*
SUGGESTED READING: Shlomo Simonsohn, *The Apostolic See and the Jews: History* (Toronto: Pontifical Institute of Mediaeval Studies, 1991).

CAPOTE, TRUMAN (1924–1984). American writer. In a *Playboy* interview of March 1968, Capote assailed "the Zionist mafia" that allegedly monopolized publishing and suppressed writing that did not meet with Jewish approval.
SUGGESTED READING: Norman Podhoretz, "Is It Good for the Jews?" *Commentary* 52, no. 2 (February 1972).

CAPPO; CAPO. (North American slur) Jews who turn against or exploit their own people. From the **Nazi**-German word for a concentration camp inmate overseer.

SUGGESTED READING: "List of Ethnic Slurs," *Wikipedia*, http://en.wiki
pedia.org/wiki/List_of_ethnic_slurs.

CARAFFA, GIOVANNI PIETRO. *See* PAUL IV.

CARAN D'ACHE. *See* POIRÉ, EMMANUEL.

CARLYLE, THOMAS (1795–1881). British historian and essayist. In *On Heroes* (1840), Carlyle wrote:

> The wild Bedouin welcomes the stranger to his tent . . . and then, by another law
> as sacred, kill him if he can. . . . They are, as we know, of Jewish kindred: but
> with that deadly terrible earnestness of the Jews they seem to combine something
> graceful and brilliant, which is not Jewish.

Standing in front of Baron **Rothschild**'s London house in 1861, Carlyle
told Charles Dickens, "If you ask me which mode of treating these people
[Jews] to have been nearest to the will of the Almighty about them—to
build them palaces like that, or to take pincers for them, I declare for the
pincers." (In the Middle Ages, heretics were clawed with red hot pincers.)
Carlyle imagined Rothschild at his mercy: "Now Sir, the State requires
some of these millions you have heaped together with your financing work.
'You won't? Very well'—and Carlyle gave a twist with his wrist—'Now
will you?' and then another twist till the millions were yielded."

SUGGESTED READING: Edward Alexander, "Dr. Arnold, Matthew Arnold, and the Jews," *Judaism*, Spring 2002; Frank Modder Montagu, *The
Jew in the Literature of England* (Philadelphia: Jewish Publication Society,
1960).

CARMICHAEL, STOKELY (1941–1998). Also known as Kwame Ture.
Black activist West Indian immigrant. Carmichael led young Turks in the
civil rights movement in pushing Martin Luther King Jr. aside, denouncing
him as an Uncle Tom. In 1966, Carmichael emerged as the chief spokesman for the Black Power movement, which replaced King's goals of integration and a colorblind society with images of political violence and race
hatred. In 1967, when Israel was attacked by six Arab nations, Carmichael
announced that "the only good Zionist is a dead Zionist." Carmichael promoted armed warfare in American cities and was briefly made prime minister of the **Black Panther Party**. In the late 1980s, he attacked Jews,
whites, and the United States. He became a protégé of Nation of Islam
head **Louis Farrakhan**.

SUGGESTED READING: Jonathan Tobin, "Good News and Bad News: Antisemitism's Only Stronghold in America," *Jewish World Review*, November 30, 1998.

CARTO, WILLIS (1926–). Influential antisemite and **Holocaust denier** involved with dozens of far-right organizations, front groups, and publications, such as the Congress of Freedom, Liberty and Property, **Liberty Lobby**, John Birch Society, National Youth Alliance, **Institute for Historical Review, Populist** Party, *Right*, *Western Destiny*, *Liberty Letter*, *Washington Observer*, *American Mercury*, *The Spotlight*, *IHR Newsletter*, and *Journal for Historical Review*; he is currently associated with the American Free Press, *The Barnes Review*, **Noontide Press**, "Radio Free America," and "Editor's Roundtable." In a letter revealed in 1966, Carto wrote:

> Hitler's defeat was the defeat of Europe. And of America. How could we have been so blind? The blame, it seems, must be laid at the door of the international Jews. It was their propaganda, lies and demands which blinded the West to what Germany was doing. . . . If Satan himself, with all of his super-human genius and diabolical ingenuity at his command, had tried to create a permanent disintegration and force for the destruction of the nations, he could have done no better than to invent the Jews.

SUGGESTED READING: Michael Shermer and Alex Grobman, *Denying History* (Berkeley: University of California Press, 2000).

CASABLANCA CONFERENCE. *See* ROOSEVELT, FRANKLIN D.

CASHEWS. (U.S. Catholic slur) Offspring of a Jew and a Catholic. First used by Jewish comedian Jack Carter in the 1960s.
SUGGESTED READING: "List of Ethnic Slurs," *Wikipedia*, http://en.wiki pedia.org/wiki/List_of_ethnic_slurs.

CASIMIR III THE GREAT. *See* JEWISH CONDITION IN POLAND.

CASSIUS DIO. *See* DIO CASSIUS.

CASTILE. *See* ARAGÓN.

CATHER, WILLA (1873–1947). American novelist. Cather's biographer, Phyllis Robinson, pointed out that Cather had a "deep-seated" prejudice against Jews that was not uncommon for her time. "She romanticized other nationalities and cultures, . . . but where Jews were concerned, she seemed to have a blind spot." In her 1920 story "Scandal," Cather's description of the Jewish millionaire Sigmund Stein was that "he was a vulture of the vulture race, and he had the beak of one."

SUGGESTED READING: Phyllis Robinson, *Willa: The Life of Willa Cather* (Garden City, NY: Doubleday, 1983); James Woodress, *Willa Cather: A Literary Life* (Lincoln: University of Nebraska Press, 1987); Loretta Wasserman, "Cather's Semitism," in *Cather Studies*, vol. 2, ed. Susan J. Rosowski (Lincoln: University of Nebraska Press, 1993).

CATHERINE I (1689–1727). Russian tsarina, 1725–27. The widow of **Peter the Great** (who forbade immigration of Jews into Russia but tolerated those living in his Baltic and Ukrainian territories), Catherine was impelled by popular pressure to expel "those Jews of masculine and feminine sex who are found in the Ukraine and in Russian cities. . . . Henceforth they will not be admitted into Russia upon any pretext, and the closest watch will be kept upon them in all places."

SUGGESTED READING: Salo Baron, *The Russian Jews under Tsars and Soviets*, 2nd rev. ed. (New York: Schocken Books, 1987).

CATHOLIC CENTER PARTY (DEUTSCHE ZENTRUMSPARTEI). Today, the "oldest political party of Germany." A Roman Catholic political party founded in Germany in 1870–71 whose goals were to preserve the Church's autonomy and rights. The party, itself divided into left (sometimes calling for anti-Jewish measures) and right wings, collaborated with a variety of other political parties so long as its goals were advanced. In the **Weimar Republic**, the party helped draw up the Weimar Constitution. The party accepted **Adolf Hitler** as chancellor based on his promises to protect Catholic rights and supported the Enabling Act in the Reichstag. Many party members defected to the National Socialists, and the German bishops lifted their ban on cooperation with the **Nazis**. Cardinal Pacelli, **Vatican** secretary of state for Pope **Pius XI**, acquiesced in the party's dissolution as the Concordat negotiations were concluding. The dissolution of the party freed many German Catholics to express their **antisemitism** by joining the Nazi Party. After the war, the Center Party was refounded but remains marginal. Many Catholic Center politicians, such as Konrad Adenauer, joined other parties.

SUGGESTED READING: Ellen Lovell Evans, *The German Center Party, 1870–1933* (Carbondale: Southern Illinois University Press, 1996).

CÉLINE, LOUIS-FERDINAND (LOUIS-FERDINAND DESTOUCHES) (1894–1961). Pessimistic French writer and doctor. His novels are filled with scenes of dismemberment and murder. Though personally compassionate, Céline was a vicious racist and antisemite, during the German occupation calling for the extermination of the Jews and ranting about miscegenation and the possible extinction of the white race. In 1944, accused of collaboration, Céline fled France to live in Germany. In 1950 the French government condemned him to one year in prison and declared him a national disgrace.

SUGGESTED READING: Bettina Knapp, *Céline: Man of Hate* (Tuscaloosa: University of Alabama Press, 1974).

CELSUS PHILOSOPHUS (fl. 2nd cent.). Greek philosopher. Celsus wrote that Jews "worship angels and are addicted to sorcery taught to them by Moses." He regarded the Jews as rebels against the established Egyptian religion because of their seditious and revolutionary temperament. He ridiculed the founding myths of Jewish religious history and noted that there are no external signs that God had chosen the Jews as his people. "Ignorant of the truth," Celsus wrote, "enchanted by illusion, and condemned for their arrogance, Jews have been driven from their own nation."

SUGGESTED READING: *Greek and Latin Authors on Jews and Judaism*, ed. Menahem Stern (Jerusalem: Israel Academy of Sciences and Humanities, 1984).

CELTIC CROSS. The Odin's Cross of **neo-Nazi** and white supremicist groups. First used as a hate symbol by the **Ku Klux Klan**, the symbol was later adopted by the National Front in England, Stormfront, and Skrewdriver to represent "white pride." The Celtic Cross is also used widely in a nonracist manner as a symbol of the Celts of ancient Ireland and Scotland and as a Christian symbol.

SUGGESTED READING: Anti-Defamation League, *Hate on Display: Extremist Symbols, Logos, and Tattoos* (New York: Anti-Defamation League, 2006).

CENTRAL ASSOCIATION OF GERMAN CITIZENS OF JEWISH FAITH (ZENTRALVEREIN DEUTSCHER STAATSBÜRGER JÜDISCHEN GLAUBENS). Once the modern organized antisemitic movement formed in Germany in the later 19th century, Jews employed a spectrum of means to combat **antisemitism**. One, the nationalist and assimilationist Central Association of German Citizens of Jewish Faith, formed in 1893, lobbied the national government; brought libel and slander suits against every major anti-Jewish leader in an attempt to force them and their organizations into bankruptcy; sued publishers of anti-Jewish works; wrote and distributed to Christians pamphlets defending Jews, Jewishness, and Judaism; and funded academic articles and secular organizations opposed to antisemitism. The **Third Reich** forcibly converted the Central Association into the government-controlled Reich Representation of German Jews, which recommended emigration. In November 1938, its doors closed.

SUGGESTED READING: Karl A. Schleunes, *The Twisted Road to Auschwitz: Nazi Policy toward German Jews, 1933–1939* (Champaign: University of Illinois Press, 1990); S. Ragins, *Jewish Responses to Anti-Semitism in Germany, 1870–1914* (Cincinnati: Hebrew Union College Press, 1980).

CHALALA. (French slur) A young, fashionable Jew.

SUGGESTED READING: "List of Ethnic Slurs," *Wikipedia,* http://en.wiki pedia.org/wiki/List_of_ethnic_slurs.

CHALCEDON, COUNCIL OF. Ecumenical council in Russia in 451. The Roman Catholic assemblage issued Canon XIV, a decree that stated:

> Since in certain provinces it is permitted to the readers and singers to marry, the holy Synod has decreed that it shall not be lawful for any of them to take a wife that is heterodox. But those who have already begotten children of such a marriage, if they have already had their children baptized among the **heretics**, must bring them into the communion of the Catholic Church; but if they have not had them baptized, they may not hereafter baptize them among heretics, nor give them in marriage to a heretic, or a Jew, or a heathen, unless the person marrying the orthodox child shall promise to come over to the orthodox faith.

SUGGESTED READING: V. C. Samuel and Peter Farrington, *The Council of Chalcedon Re-Examined* (Philadelphia: Exlibris Corp., 2001).

CHAMBERLAIN, HOUSTON STEWART (1855–1927). British-German political writer. The son-in-law of composer **Richard Wagner**, Chamberlain's magnum opus was the *Foundations of the Nineteenth Century*. An advocate of **Aryan** supremacy and **antisemitism**, Chamberlain believed Jews were culture destroyers, the enemy of the German Aryan who would make Gentiles slaves. *See also* SOCIAL DARWINISM.

SUGGESTED READING: Geoffrey G. Field, *Evangelist of Race: The Germanic Vision of Houston Stewart Chamberlain* (New York: Columbia University Press, 1981).

CHANNING, WILLIAM (1810–1884). Progressive U.S. minister and early Unitarian leader. Despite his liberal credentials, Channing saw Jews as a stumbling block to Christian progress. He stated, "The dispensation of

Moses, compared with that of Jesus, we consider as adopted to the child-hood of the human race, a preparation for a nobler system."

SUGGESTED READING: Egal Feldman, *Dual Destinies: The Jewish Encounter with Protestant America* (Chicago: University of Illinois Press, 1990).

CHARLEMAGNE (742–814). King of the Franks, 800–814. In Carolingian France, because of their prior Roman citizenship, Jews were considered freemen, the king's subjects, and were granted some of the privileges of free Christians. Although Jews could not hold power over Christians, Jews served the monarch, including Charlemagne, in political, financial, and scholarly ways. Once Charlemagne became Holy Roman emperor, however, the Jews lost much of their status. The Jews could not take the new loyalty oath of 802 because it mentioned "God" and "the Lord," referring to Jesus Christ.

SUGGESTED READING: Simon Dubnov, *History of the Jews*, vol. 2, *From the Roman Empire to the Early Medieval Period*, trans. Moshe Spiegel (South Brunswick, NJ: Thomas Yoseloff, 1968).

CHARLES III (THE SIMPLE) (848–929). King of France, 879–929. Charles confiscated Jewish-owned vineyards, salt mines, and houses in Narbonne and donated them to the Catholic Church. This signaled the end of the period when the Carolingian kings dealt favorably with the Jews.

SUGGESTED READING: Simon Dubnov, *History of the Jews*, vol. 2, *From the Roman Empire to the Early Medieval Period*, trans. Moshe Spiegel (South Brunswick, NJ: Thomas Yoseloff, 1968).

CHATEAUBRIAND, FRANÇOIS-RENÉ (1768–1848). French writer and diplomat. Meditating on Venice's Jewish cemetery in 1833, Chateaubriand thought about "everyone's contempt and hate for those who sacrificed Christ. A quarantine of the Jewish race has been proclaimed from the height of Calvary and will remain until the end of time."

SUGGESTED READING: Béatrice Philippe, *Être Juif dans la société française* (Paris: Montalba, 1979).

CHAUCER, GEOFFREY (1343–1400). English author, philosopher, diplomat, and poet. Chaucer was familiar with the traditional religious sources of theological **antisemitism** on which **ritual murder** defamations were based. He read the **Church Fathers** and often quoted from the Christian Scriptures, the Apocrypha, and the lives of the saints. "The Prioress's Tale" from *The Canterbury Tales* (1390) was based on the anti-Jewish allegations surrounding the affair of Hugh of Lincoln. Chaucer gave the accusation renewed respectability when he included it in his famous book, roughly a century after the Jews had been brutally forced out of England.

SUGGESTED READING: Sheila Delany, *Chaucer and the Jews* (New York: Routledge, 2000).

CHELSEA. Female **skinhead**. Chelsea is the image of the typical female skinhead or skinhead associate with her hair shaved on top and the hair that frames her face grown long, this style referred to as Chelsea, Renee, and Fringe.

SUGGESTED READING: Anti-Defamation League, *Hate on Display: Extremist Symbols, Logos, and Tattoos* (New York: Anti-Defamation League, 2006).

CHINTILA. King of **Visigothic** Spain, 636–40. In 638, at the sixth Toledo Council, rules were enacted to stop Christians from using Jewish doctors, eating the unleavened bread of Jews, or bathing with Jews. Converts promised the king to be more vigilant against relapses.

SUGGESTED READING: Karl Joseph von Hefels, *A History of the Councils of the Church from Original Documents* (New York: Ams Pres, 1975).

CHMIELNICKI MASSACRES. Pogroms in Poland and Ukraine in 1648–49. The Cossack Ukrainian leader Bodan Chmielnicki (1595–1657) launched a series of vicious, murderous attacks on Jews in the Ukraine and Poland that destroyed 300 Jewish communities and left 100,000 to 300,000 dead. The Cossack chieftain claimed Jews were Polish agents exploiting the common Ukrainian people, whereas he was their liberator. He charged the Jews with **ritual murder** and **desecration of the Host**.

SUGGESTED READING: Nathan Hanover and Abraham Mesch, *Abyss of Despair/Yeven Metzulah: The Famous 17th-Century Chronicle Depicting Jewish Life in Russia and Poland during the Chmielnicki Massacres of the 16th Century* (New Brunswick, NJ: Transaction Publishers, 1983).

CHRISTIAN BELIEFS AND ANTISEMITISM. Groundbreaking work published in 1966. Using modern public-opinion polling, Charles Glock and Rodney Stark found that roughly half of the American people manifested religious **antisemitism** and most of these people got even their secular stereotypes of Jews—whether positive or negative—from religion. In 1920, for example, a Jewish student in Illinois was refused permission to use the university's athletic field on Sundays on the grounds that "this is a Christian country established upon *Christian* traditions and this is an institution backed largely by Christian communities." Further research by scholars in Catholic, Protestant, and secular universities in the United States and Europe in the past 30 years has verified these conclusions.

SUGGESTED READING: Charles Glock and Rodney Stark, *Christian Beliefs and Antisemitism* (1966; reprint, Westport, CT: Greenwood Press, 1979).

CHRISTIAN CENTURY. This prominent American Protestant weekly has been compared in the 1930s and 1940s to **Henry Ford**'s antisemitic *Dearborn Independent*. In the mid-1930s, the writers of the *Christian Century* explicitly opposed the religious pluralism that many liberal Protestants had supported and that American Jews depended on to maintain their freedom and equality. Although Protestants traditionally opposed Roman Catholics on the grounds of "popery," the Jews were considered the more obvious alien body in Protestant America. In 1936 the journal threatened to put aside tolerance unless Jews Christianized themselves. It called Judaism a racial, religious, and nationalist prototype of **Nazism**. In a February 1944 article entitled "A Reply to Screamers," the magazine objected to emotional public protests against the **Holocaust**. In 1945, the *Christian Century* implied that Nazis should beware lest they develop a self-image as a martyred chosen people like the Jews.

SUGGESTED READING: E. Ross, *So It Was True! The Protestant Press and the Nazi Persecution of the Jews* (Minneapolis: University of Minnesota Press, 1980).

CHRISTIAN DEFENSE LEAGUE. In 1977, **Gerald L. K. Smith**—an assistant in the 1930s to the antisemitic "radio priest" Fr. **Charles Coughlin**, a member of the **American Nazi** group the Silver Shirts, and an ordained Disciples of Christ minister—founded the Christian Defense League, a survivalist group that accused Jews of undermining civilization and U.S. sovereignty. Smith spread **Christian Identity** theology in his periodical, *The Cross and the Flag*.

SUGGESTED READING: Michael Barken, *Religion and the Racist Right* (Chapel Hill: University of North Carolina Press, 1994); Glen Jeansonne, *Gerald L. K. Smith, Minister of Hate* (Baton Rouge: Louisiana State University, 1997).

CHRISTIAN FRONT. Formed from the followers of the antisemitic radio priest **Charles Coughlin**. Under the banner of anticommunism, this **antisemitic** and pro-**Nazi** organization encouraged boycotts of Jewish merchants, used the slogan "Buy Christian," and published the Christian

Index, a directory of non-Jewish merchants in part of New York City. As late as 1943, it sponsored attacks on Jews in Boston and New York.

SUGGESTED READING: Ronald Carpenter, *Father Charles E. Coughlin: Spokesman for the Disaffected* (Westport, CT: Greenwood Press, 1998).

CHRISTIANI, PABLO (d. 1274). French **Dominican** and Jewish apostate. Christiani was sent by **Raymond of Peñaforte** to convert Jews of **Aragón**, Spain. Nachmanides, the famous rabbi, was forced into a **disputation** at Barcelona in 1263. Then Christiani traveled about, forcing Jews to hear his **sermons**. The apostate denounced the **Talmud** to Pope **Clement VI**, resulting in the confiscation of the Holy Book. In 1269 the friar persuaded King **Louis IX** of France to enforce the wearing of the **Jew badge**.

SUGGESTED READING: Hyam Maccoby, *The Disputation* (London: Caldor, 2001).

CHRISTIAN IDENTITY MOVEMENT (CI). 20th-century American **antisemitic** and racist movement. Its basic tenets are that the Jews are descendants of Satan and that the real Israelites are the English-speaking and Germanic tribes. This idea is derived from the teaching that after the Assyrian captivity, 10 Hebrew tribes scattered in the Caucasus Mountains later settled Europe and were the true Israelites. Blacks, Asians, and other minorities are considered pre-Adam, that is, inferior creations. Some CI groups have decided that minorities are on the same level as animals, and therefore have no soul. Some CI churches advocate separation of the races, while others call for the extermination of all nonwhites. The movement teaches that Jesus, when talking about the Jews, was literally talking about the descendants of the Devil. Since the Devil is a liar and a murderer, Jews are liars and murderers like their father. According to this belief, Jews became descendants of Satan when Satan seduced Eve and Eve gave birth to Cain. Satan's plan is to destroy the pure white race by causing other races (called "mud people") to sexually mix with the white race. **Ku Klux Klan** members and **neo-Nazis** appear to be strongly attracted to this "religion." **Gerald L. K. Smith** spread CI theology in his periodical, *The Cross and the Flag*. Groups associated with the CI movement have perpetrated numerous violent and deadly hate crimes with the avowed purpose of stopping an alleged Zionist-Communist conspiracy from subverting the United States.

SUGGESTED READING: Michael Barkun, *Religion and the Radical Right: The Origin of the Identity Movement* (Chapel Hill: University of North Carolina Press, 1996); Glen Jeansonne, *Gerald L. K. Smith, Minister of Hate* (Baton Rouge: Louisiana State University, 1997).

CHRISTIAN MOBILIZERS. A 20th-century pro-**fascist** and **antisemitic** group aligned with the **America First Committee**.

SUGGESTED READING: Stephen Norwood, "Marauding Youth and the Christian Front: Antisemitic Violence in Boston and New York during World War II," *American Jewish History* 91, no. 2 (June 2003); "Christian Affronters," *Time*, November 27, 1939.

CHRISTIAN NATIONALIST CRUSADE. *See CROSS AND THE FLAG, THE.*

CHRISTIAN PATRIOTS DEFENSE LEAGUE (CPDL). 20th-century antisemitic survivalist group involved in paramilitary activity and martial-arts training, founded by John Harrell and based in Illinois. Gordon "Jack" Mohr, a retired U.S. Army colonel who exploits Christian terminology for his own extremist purposes, has described the CPDL as "made up primarily of Christians and/or Patriots, who *see* what is happening in our government and are preparing for difficult times we believe are ahead." For many years, he has stridently promoted **antisemitism**, **anti-Zionism**, and white supremacy as a leader of the Christian Identity Movement. *See also* CITIZENS EMERGENCY DEFENSE SYSTEM.

SUGGESTED READING: "Christian Patriots," *The Nizkor Project*, http://www.nizkor.org/hweb/orgs/american/adl/paranoia-as-patriotism/mohr-cpdl.html.

CHRISTIAN RACISM. From the first centuries of the Christian Era onward, many Christian writers found an inherent theological repulsiveness as well as "a horrible and fascinating physical otherness" in Jews. The **Church Fathers** claimed that each Jew was fundamentally and repugnantly un-Christian and that Jews transmitted indelibly and permanently evil characteristics to their offspring. Because Jews were permanently evil, many Christians believed the sacrament of Christian baptism would not wash away the "stink" of Jewish unbelief. Associating the Jews with **heresy**, the second-century Christian apologist **Justin Martyr**, for instance, argued that God had given Moses' Law to the Jews because God wanted to keep the inherently sinful Jews' evil in check. **St. Augustine** observed that no Jew could ever lose the stigma of his forebears' denial and murder of Christ. He wrote that the evil of the Jews, "in their parents, led to death." His contemporary **St. Jerome** claimed that all Jews were **Judas** and were innately evil creatures who betrayed the Lord for money. **St. John Chrysostom** also approached racist thinking in regard to the Jews when he called them **deicides** with no chance for "atonement, excuse, or defense"; citing Jeremiah 13:23, he asked, "Can the Ethiopian change his skin or the leopard his spots?" **St. Isidore of Seville** declared that the Jews' evil character never changes. A seventh-century Byzantine proverb stated that "when a Jew is baptized, it is as if one had baptized an ass." St. John of Damascus (d. 754) wrote that God gave the Jews the **Sabbath** because of their "absolute propensity for material things." *See also* ANTI-SEMITISM, RACIAL; INQUISITION, SPANISH; LUTHER, MARTIN.

SUGGESTED READING: Jacques-Paul Migne, ed., *Patrologiae, Cursus Completus: Series Graeca* (Paris: Garnier, 1857–66); Jacques-Paul Migne, ed., *Patrologiae, Cursus Completus: Series Latina* (Paris: Garnier, 1844–92).

CHRISTIAN SCIENCE MONITOR. A leading newspaper published by Christian Scientists. Grounded in theological anti-Judaism, the *Christian Science Monitor* became a leading skeptic in regard to the **Holocaust**. In April 1933 the *Monitor* launched a vituperative attack on U.S. Jews who protested the **Nazi**-instigated **German boycott of Jewish shops**. It accused American Jews of rejecting Jesus's commandment to "love one another." On June 2, 1939, the *Monitor* attacked Jewish refugees as being the cause of their own troubles and blamed **antisemitism** on Jewish business practices.

SUGGESTED READING: Robert Ross, *So It Was True! The Protestant Press and the Nazi Persecution of the Jews* (Minneapolis: University of Minnesota Press, 1980).

CHRISTIAN SOCIAL PARTY (Austria). *See* LUEGER, KARL.

CHRISTIAN SOCIAL PARTY (Germany). *See* ANTISEMITES' PETITION.

CHRISTIE, AGATHA (1890–1976). English mystery writer. The ultraconservative Christie associated Jews with liberal politics. In *The Mystery of the Blue Train* (1928), Christie wrote about a Polish Jewish anarchist: "A little man with a face like a rat. . . . This man, negligible and inconspicuous as he seemed, played a prominent part in the destiny of the world. In an Empire where rats ruled, he was the king of the rats." In the *Mysterious Mr. Quinn* (1930), she described "men of Hebraic extraction, sallow men with hooked noses, wearing flamboyant jewellery." In *Peril at End House* (1932), a character is referred to as "the long-nosed Mr Lazarus," and, again, "he's a Jew, of course, but a frightfully decent one." In *And Then There Were None* (1940), originally titled *Ten Little Niggers*, her character

Philip Lombard had this to say: "The little Jew had not been deceived—that was the damnable part about Jews, you couldn't deceive them about money—they knew!" However, in her novel *Giant's Bread* (1930), written under the pseudonym of Mary Westmacott, Christie sympathetically portrayed the Levinnes as a Jewish family suffering from English **antisemitism**.

SUGGESTED READING: Charles Osborne, *The Life and Crimes of Agatha Christie* (New York: HarperCollins, 2000); Johann Hari, "Agatha Christie—Radical Conservative Thinker," *Independent on Sunday*, October 4, 2003.

CHRIST-KILLER. (Christian slur) Reference to the **Church Fathers'** interpretation of the Christian Scriptures as holding all Jews collectively guilty for murdering Jesus of Nazareth. *See also* CHRIST-KILLERS.

SUGGESTED READING: "List of Ethnic Slurs," *Wikipedia*, http://en.wiki pedia.org/wiki/List_of_ethnic_slurs.

CHRIST-KILLERS. The main religious charge against the Jews over the past two millennia. The **Gospels** assaulted the Jewish people, their leaders, and their institutions and indicted them for rejecting and crucifying Jesus. By neglecting the historical facts of Jesus' Jewishness and the involvement of the Romans in his crucifixion, Mark and other writers of the New Testament transformed the crucifixion into an exclusively Jewish event, describing Pontius Pilate as an innocent pawn completely controlled by the malicious Jews. When Pilate wanted to release Jesus, asking "Why, what evil has he done?" the priests "stirred up the crowd," which called repeatedly, "Crucify him!" Anti-Jewish Christians most frequently cite the passage in which the Jewish people cry, "Let him be crucified! . . . His blood be on us and on our children" (Mark 15:11–15, Matthew 27:22–25, John 18–19). This passage, according to one Jewish scholar quoted by Samuel Sandmel in *A Jewish Understanding of the New Testament* (Cincinnati: Hebrew Union College Press, 1956), has "been responsible for oceans of human blood and a ceaseless stream of misery and desolation." **Matthew** refers to the **triumphal** Christian belief that because of the Jews' rejection and murder of the Christ, they will lose not only their spiritual election as the chosen people but also all their worldly valuables, nationhood, government, capital city, house of worship, priesthood, and system of worship: Israel, king, Jerusalem, Temple, and Judaism. Calling the Jews "the **Synagogue** of Christ-killers," **St. John Chrysostom** upbraided those Christians who had anything to do with "those who [nearly 400 years before] shouted, 'Crucify him. Crucify him.'" The charge is still current in the 21st century among many antisemites.

SUGGESTED READING: Gerhart Ladner, "Aspects of Patristic Anti-Judaism," *Viator: Medieval and Renaissance Studies* 2 (1971).

CHRYSOSTOM, ST. JOHN (347–407). Founding patriarch of the Greek Orthodox Church and the **Church Father** most bitterly hostile to the Jews. Chrysostom's sermons addressed Christian **Judaizers**. Choosing to discourage judaizing by damning Jews and Judaism, Chrysostom labeled Christian judaizers diseased enough or mad enough "to enter into fellowship with those who have committed outrages against God himself." He sought to alienate any Christian feelings of affinity with, or common humanity toward, the Jews. In his sermons, he considered the Jews not ordinary members of the human race but congenitally evil people who "danced with the Devil." He believed that the Jews were **deicides** who had no chance for "atonement, excuse, or defense." Chrysostom denied any good use for Jews. Because "Jews rejected the rule of Christ," he wanted these useless Jews killed. Chrysostom justified such an atrocity by arguing that "what is done in accordance with God's will is the best of all things even if it seems bad. . . . Suppose someone slays another in accordance with God's will. This slaying is better than any loving-kindness." His major contribution to Jewish–Christian relations was an encouragement of violence against the Jewish people and their **synagogues**.

SUGGESTED READING: John Chrysostom, *Discourses against Judaizing Christians*, trans. Paul W. Harkins, in *The Fathers of the Church*, vol. 8 (Washington, DC: Catholic University Press, 1979).

CHURCH FATHERS. Christian theologians between the second and ninth centuries from Rome, North Africa, and the Middle East who borrowed from Judaism to supply Christianity with an unimpeachable history and a prestige the new Church would not have otherwise possessed. When these Christian authors wrote about Jews, Judaism, and Jewishness for a Christian audience and not in argument against pagans, nearly all of them demonstrated an almost compulsive hostility to the Jewish spirit. These writers quashed whatever neighborly relations had existed between Christians and Jews, clearly crossing the boundary from reasoned debate to emotional polemic. Christian writings were part of a theological war to the death and beyond. Although several Church Fathers knew individual Jews, they portrayed Jews as satanic adversaries. They imagined that Jews insulted Christ and the Blessed Virgin each day in their **synagogue** prayers. For these crimes, Christian theologians argued, Jews must suffer continual punishment on Earth and eternal damnation in the afterlife, unless they sought salvation through the one true faith, Christianity. They proclaimed that the Jews are, have always been, and will always be, paragons of evil. *See also* CHRYSOSTOM, ST. JOHN; CYPRIAN; CYRIL OF ALEXANDRIA; IRENAEUS, ST.; ISIDORE OF SEVILLE, ST.; JEROME, ST.; JUSTIN MARTYR; ORIGEN; TERTULLIAN.

SUGGESTED READING: William Nicholls, *Christian Antisemitism: A History of Hate* (Northvale, NJ: Jason Aronson, 1995); Jacques-Paul Migne, ed., *Patrologiae, Cursus Completus: Series Latina* (Paris: Garnier, 1844–92).

CHURCHILL, WINSTON (1874–1965). British statesman and prime minister. Although Churchill was friendly to Jews and called himself a Zionist, he held some negative stereotypes about Jewish power. He wrote that Jews are "the most formidable and the most remarkable race which has ever appeared in the world," but in the same article in the *Illustrated Sunday Herald* (London) of February 8, 1920, he stated:

> The [**Bolshevik**] movement among the Jews is not new. . . . [This] world-wide conspiracy for the overthrow of civilisation and for the reconstitution of society on the basis of arrested development, of envious malevolence, and impossible equality, has been steadily growing. It played, as a modern writer, Mrs. [Nesta] Webster [an English antisemite], has so ably shown, a definitely recognisable part in the tragedy of the **French Revolution**. It has been the mainspring of every subversive movement during the Nineteenth Century; and now at last this band of extraordinary personalities from the underworld of the great cities of Europe and America have gripped the Russian people by the hair of their heads and have become practically the undisputed masters of that enormous empire. Terrorist Jews. There is no need to exaggerate the part played in the creation of Bolshevism and . . . the actual bringing about of the Russian Revolution: by these international and for the most part atheistical Jews. It is certainly a very great one; it probably outweighs all others.

In 1922, Churchill awarded 80 percent of a potential home for Jews in Palestine as Transjordan to Emir Abdullah. During the **Holocaust**, he upheld the **White Paper of 1939** and his attempts to help the Jews during this period were foiled by his foreign secretary Anthony Eden and other British bureaucrats in the Foreign Office. *See also PROTOCOLS OF THE ELDERS OF ZION, THE.*

SUGGESTED READING: Michael J. Cohen, *Churchill and the Jews* (London: Frank Cass, 1985).

CHURCH OF JESUS CHRIST–CHRISTIAN. *See* ARYAN NATIONS.

CICERO, MARCUS TULLIUS (106–43 BCE). Roman orator, writer, and politician. Cicero wrote of the "odium attached to Jewish gold" and of Judaism as a "barbaric superstition." "The practice of their sacred rites was at variance with the glory of our empire, the dignity of our name, the customs of our ancestors," he wrote. Jews and Syrians were "peoples born to be slaves."

SUGGESTED READING: Hans Conzelmann, *Gentiles, Jews, Christians: Polemics and Apologetics in the Greco-Roman World*, trans. Eugene Boring (Minneapolis, MN: Fortress Press, 1992).

CIRCUMCISION. Jewish ritual cutting of a male infant's foreskin. Christian writers claimed that circumcision no longer symbolized the Jews' Covenant with God; instead, it marked the Jews as devils or Cains. **Justin Martyr** wrote in his *Dialogue with Trypho*: "Circumcision was given to you as a sign that you may be separated . . . from us, and that you alone may suffer that which you now justly suffer, and that your land may be desolate, and your cities burnt with fire. These things have happened to you in fairness and justice." The fourth-century theologian Ephraem of Syria called the Jews "circumcised dogs"; **St. John Chrysostom** called them "circumcized beasts." **Aphraates** held that circumcision was not necessary to mark out the authentic Israel, since Abraham had not been circumcised. **Tertullian** suggested that God intended that the circumcision would identify the Jews so that they could never reenter Jerusalem.

SUGGESTED READING: Robert S. Wistrich, *Anti-Semitism: The Longest Hatred* (New York: Schocken, 1994); Jacques-Paul Migne, ed., *Patrologiae, Cursus Completus: Series Graeca* (Paris: Garnier, 1857–66); Jacques-Paul Migne, ed., *Patrologiae, Cursus Completus: Series Latina* (Paris: Garnier, 1844–92).

CITIZENS EMERGENCY DEFENSE SYSTEM (CEDS). 20th-century militant civilian "defense" group restricted to white Christians. Associated with Gordon "Jack" Mohr, a retired U.S. Army colonel. *See also* CHRISTIAN PATRIOTS DEFENSE LEAGUE.

CITIZENSHIP, JEWISH. In Carolingian France, because of their prior Roman citizenship, Jews were considered freemen, the king's subjects, and were granted some of the privileges of free Christians. Although Jews could not hold power over Christians, Jews served the monarch, including **Charlemagne**, in political, financial, and scholarly service. In the High Middle Ages, Jews had few if any citizenship rights and were allowed to live in Christendom based primarily on their usefulness to secular rulers and on the **Augustinian** principle of the Witness People. The Church had made the Jews stateless beings long before the **Nazis** did so with their **Nuremberg Laws**; just as in Germany there had been no legitimate place for the Jews, so too in the medieval *societas Christiana*, Jews were excluded from the mystical **Corpus Christi** of the Church. The Church therefore established administrative and legal precedents for handling Jews that later served as a model for the Nazis.

During the early years of the **French Revolution**, the most ardent advocate of Jewish emancipation was Stanislas, Duke of Clermont-Tonnerre. A few months after France's Declaration of the Rights of Man and the Citizen, he argued before the National Assembly on December 23, 1789, that only the prejudiced opposed freedom for all citizens, including Jews. "You have, by the Declaration of Rights, secured the rights of men and of citizens." He demanded that individual Jews become citizens of France and adhere to a moral religion. In January 1790, the Assembly granted citizenship to the 3,000 or so Sephardic Jews living in southwest France and in September 1791 to 30,000 **Ashkenazic** Jews of Alsace and Lorraine. But the French goverment's generosity was limited. Freedom was awarded only to those Jews who explicitly renounced their membership in Jewish communities.

In England, the High Court of Chancery ruled that Judaism was a religion contrary to the established Christian Church. Indeed, full citizenship was withheld until the mid-19th century. In the 1800s, most liberal European thinkers thought that Jews deserved the rights of citizenship but had to convert to Christianity to receive them. German Jewish poet Heinrich Heine called **conversion** "an admission ticket to western culture." On the one hand, a lingering fear haunted German liberals that Jews would persist in their "alien" ways. Liberals, however, were not contemplating individual rights that would guarantee Jews the freedom to express and enjoy their Jewishness openly. The more Jews assimilated—as the **conversos** in 15th-century Spain had—the more they resembled "regular" Germans and the more of a threat they were to German Christian society once anti-Jewish restrictions were removed. The governments of Germany, France, Italy, Poland, Hungary, and Romania issued religiously based anti-Jewish legislation during the **Holocaust**.

SUGGESTED READING: Pierre Birnbaum and Ira Katzenelson, eds., *Paths of Emancipation* (Princeton, NJ: Princeton University Press, 1998).

CITY WITHOUT JEWS, THE. See BETTAUER, HUGO.

CIVILTÀ CATTOLICA (1849–). Catholic journal. The **Jesuit** journal was the semiofficial voice of the **Vatican**. From 1880 on, it published attacks on Jews, including the old canard, **ritual murder**. It was strongly **anti-dreyfusard**.

SUGGESTED READING: David I. Kertzer, *The Popes against the Jews* (New York: Knopf, 2001).

CIVIL WAR, RUSSIAN. After the **Bolsheviks** took power in 1917, the anti-Bolshevik forces sought to bring back the tsarist regime. During the 1918–20 civil war, these forces, called Whites, identified the Bolsheviks with the Jews and instituted **pogroms**, massacring 30,000 Jews and destroying 28 percent of Jewish homes. *See also* WHITE TERROR (RUSSIA).

SUGGESTED READING: Salo Baron, *The Russian Jew under Tsars and Soviets*, 2nd rev. ed. (New York: Schocken Books, 1987).

CIVIL WAR, U.S. Thousands of Jews served in both the Union and Confederate armies, fighting in a Civil War that was considered from the start a Christian battle for the sake of Christian principles. The speeches, songs, prayers, and proclamations for fast-days, the laws, and the military decrees, all recognized the supremacy of Christianity. Southern and Northern government officials and armies referred to their own Jewish civilians, enlisted men, officers, and politicians in **antisemitic** phrases. The war unleashed a previously latent anti-Jewishness on both sides that had existed from the founding of America. Fear of foreigners, antagonism to change, and the need to find scapegoats for inflation and shortages led to an increased articulation of widely held anti-Jewish sentiments. *See also* GRANT, ULYSSES S.

SUGGESTED READING: Bertram Korn, *American Jewry and the Civil War* (New York: Atheneum, 1970).

CLARK, CHAMP. *See* NYE, GERALD.

CLASS, HEINRICH. *See* PAN-GERMAN LEAGUE.

CLAUDIUS (10 BCE–54 CE). Fourth Roman emperor, 41–54. Though in general Claudius treated the Jews with great indulgence, in the middle of his reign (49) he banished them from Rome. In trying to deal with political turbulence and anti-Roman subversion at **Alexandria**, Claudius urged Roman officials in Alexandria

> that, on the one hand, the Alexandrians show themselves forebearing and kindly towards the Jews who for many years have dwelt in the same city, and dishonor none of the rites observed by them in the worship of their god, but allow them to

observe their customs as in the time of the Deified Augustus, which customs I also, after hearing both sides, have sanctioned; and on the other hand, I explicitly order the Jews not to agitate for more privileges than they formerly possessed, and not in the future to send out a separate embassy as though they lived in a separate city (a thing unprecedented), and not to force their way into gymnasiarchic or cosmetic games, while enjoying their own privileges and sharing a great abundance of advantages in a city not their own, and not to bring in or admit Jews who come . . . from Egypt or from Syria, a proceeding which will compel me to conceive serious suspicions. [If this happens,] I will by all means take vengeance on them as fomenters of . . . a general plague infecting the whole world.

SUGGESTED READING: *Epistolae*, in *Select Papyri II*, ed. A. S. Hunt and G. C. Edgar (Cambridge, MA: Loeb Classical Library, 1934).

CLAUSEWITZ, CARL PHILLIP GOTTLIEB VON (1780–1831). German military theorist. Clausewitz observed that the "filthy German Jews, who swarm in dirt and misery like vermin, are the patricians of this country."

SUGGESTED READING: Victor Farías, *Heidegger and the Nazis* (Philadelphia: Temple University Press, 1989); Alfred Low, *Jews in the Eyes of the Germans* (Philadelphia: Institute for Study of Human Issues, 1979).

CLEMENT IV (d. 1268). Pope, 1265–68. Clement IV's bull of July 27, 1267, *Turbato corde*, renewed several times by later popes, gave the **Inquisition** full authority to examine the Jews and their books for **heresy**. Another letter, which Clement sent to **James I**, King of **Aragón**, just 12 days before, *Damnabili* **perfidia** Judaeorum, condemned the Jews' ingratitude and their "damned and treacherous faithlessness." He called the Jews

a repudiated, a blind, and a terribly sinful people who had rejected and murdered their true **Messiah** . . . and who have been forced to wander the earth like the fratricide Cain, guilty of a crime too great even for the Lord to forgive. . . . They had brought him down, they had whipped him, they had sacrilegiously killed him by crucifixion, calling down His blood upon themselves and their children.

Clement ordered the ecclesiastical and civil authorities of Aragón to force the Jews to surrender their copies of the **Talmud** to the **Dominicans** and the Franciscans, who were to examine it for heresies and errors.

SUGGESTED READING: Shlomo Simonsohn, *The Apostolic See and the Jews: Documents, 492–1404* (Toronto: Pontifical Institute of Mediaeval Studies, 1988).

CLEMENT VI (1291–1352). Pope, 1342–52. Clement VI threatened to excommunicate any Christian who killed Jews without trial, who forced **bap-**

tisms, or who robbed Jews. But he also addressed Jews as a **"perfidious,"** "stubbornly hard-hearted" people, who, "unwilling to understand the words of their prophets and their own arcane Scriptures and to come over to Christianity, deserve to be despised." Clement suppressed the **flagellants,** not to protect Jews but to protect the Church from them.

SUGGESTED READING: Shlomo Simonsohn, *The Apostolic See and the Jews: Documents, 492–1404* (Toronto: Pontifical Institute of Mediaeval Studies, 1988).

CLEMENT VIII (1536–1605). Pope, 1592–1605. Clement VII's bull of February 1593 emphasized **Augustine**'s doctrine of Jewish degradation: "Christians had tolerated Jews despite their wickedness . . . in witness to the true faith and in memory of the passion of the Lord."

SUGGESTED READING: Marianne Calmann, *The Carrière of Carpentras* (Oxford: Oxford University Press, 1984); SIDIC, "Most Significant Papal Bulls about the Jews," n.d., http://www.sidic.org/en/dossierview.asp?id = 74.

CLERMONT-TONNERRE, STANISLAS, DUKE OF. *See* FRENCH REVOLUTION.

CLIP-TIP. (U.S. slur) Reference to the Jewish religious ritual of **circumcision.**

SUGGESTED READING: "List of Ethnic Slurs," *Wikipedia,* http://en.wiki pedia.org/wiki/List_of_ethnic_slurs.

CODREANU, CORNELIU (1899–1938). Romanian political leader. Codreanu was a proto-**Nazi** who founded the antisemitic **Legion of Archangel Michael** in 1927, dedicated to the elimination of Jews. The Legion engaged in **pogroms,** and out of it evolved the National Christian Party, which assumed power in 1937 for 44 days. In that short time, the country's 750,000 Jews were denaturalized and eliminated from many areas of Romanian life. The party evolved into the **Iron Guard,** which engaged in numerous murderous anti-Jewish activities.

SUGGESTED READING: Alex Bennent, *Romanian Nationalism: The Legionnaire Movement* (Baton Rouge: Louisiana University Press, 1998).

COKE, EDWARD (1552–1634). Eminent English solicitor-general. When Lord Coke commented that "Christianity is part and parcel of the common law of England," he set a precedent for American jurisprudence. Lord Coke's reference to the Jews reflected a widely held belief: that Jews were "*perpetui inimici*, perpetual enemies, for between them, as with the devils, whose subjects they be, and the Christian, there is a perpetual hostility, and can be no peace." This lasted as a legal principle in English courts until 1818. In prosecuting Roderigo Lopez for attempting to murder Queen Elizabeth I, Coke argued, "[This] murderous Jewish doctor is worse than **Judas** himself . . . of a religious profession fit for any execrable undertaking."

SUGGESTED READING: David Katz, *The Jews in the History of England* (New York: Oxford University Press, 1997).

COLERIDGE, SAMUEL TAYLOR (1772–1834). English poet. In 1833 Coleridge remarked in his *Table Talk*:

> The two images farthest removed from each other which can be comprehended under one term, are, I think, Isaiah "Hear, O heavens, and give ear, O earth!" and Levi of Holywell Street "Old clothes!" Both of them Jews, you'll observe. *Immane quantum discrepant* [how immensely they differ].

At other times he seemed to explain the Jews' concern with money by their treatment in Christian society.

SUGGESTED READING: Frank Felsenstein, *Antisemitic Stereotypes: A Paradigm of Otherness in English Popular Culture, 1660–1830* (Baltimore: Johns Hopkins University Press, 1995).

COLONIAL NORTH AMERICA. There can be no doubt that the European powers responsible for settling North America—the Spanish, French, Dutch, and English—intended Christianity to be the colonies' religion. As in Europe, Protestant may have hated Catholic and Catholic may have detested Protestant—but both regarded the Jews as corrosive to their society and to their churches. Throughout the colonial period and after, despite many instances of good Jewish–Christian relations, most Americans seemed to hold the belief that Jews were cast out of the economy of salvation because Jews rejected and crucified Christ and continued to do so in every generation. This anti-Jewish ideology was carried by European immigrants to the New World from the Old. During the colonial period, anti-Jewish prejudice spread to black slaves and Native Americans indoctrinated into the Christian religion. Although the American brand of anti-Jewish bigotry was milder than its European progenitor, nevertheless Jews were commonly denigrated in the press, "Jew" being considered a dirty word. Although no **pogroms** against Jews occurred in the American colonies, Jewish cemeteries were desecrated and Jews were insulted because of their Jewishness. Many of the teachings of the Sunday schools and other religious institutions were anti-Jewish. After the American Revolution, many Jews and Christians felt that the Jews deserved a share in the prosperity and pride of the new nation, but the vast majority of states continued to discriminate against Jews in allowing them fewer rights than Christian citizens, following the old Christian tradition that Jewish authority over Christians was sinful. By the end of the 19th century, all legal disabilities had been removed from the American Jews. All that remained was for Jews to find full social equality in America.

SUGGESTED READING: Jacob Marcus, ed., *United States Jewry* (Detroit: Wayne State University Press, 1989); Jacob Rader Marcus, *The Colonial American Jew, 1492–1776*, 3 vols. (Detroit: Wayne State University Press, 1970); Henry Feingold, ed., *The Jewish People in America*, 5 vols. (Baltimore: Johns Hopkins University Press for the American Jewish Historical Society, 1992).

COLUMBIA JEWNIVERSITY. (U.S. slur) Columbia University.

SUGGESTED READING: "List of Ethnic Slurs," *Wikipedia*, http://en.wiki pedia.org/wiki/List_of_ethnic_slurs.

COMBAT 18. *See* 28.

COMMISSAR ORDER. Prior to Operation Barbarossa, the invasion of the Soviet Union, **Adolf Hitler** issued a decree to his armed forces on June 6, 1941. All Soviet commissars—Communist Party members whose role was to ensure proper loyalty to the **Joseph Stalin** regime—were to be summarily executed. This order was also interpreted to include all Jews, for in **Nazi** eyes "Jews were the carriers of **Bolshevism**." It acted as a charter for the **Einsatzgruppen**. These murderous actions stood in direct violation of the Hague and Geneva Conventions and made the Wehrmacht (the German Army) complicit in Nazi **war crimes**.

SUGGESTED READING: Omer Bartov, *Hitler's Army: Soldiers, Nazis and the War in the Third Reich* (New York: Oxford University Press, 1991); Robert Conot, *Justice at Nuremberg* (New York: Carroll & Graf, 1983).

COMMITTEE FOR OPEN DEBATE ON THE HOLOCAUST, THE (CODOH). *See* SMITH, BRADLEY.

CONCENTRATION CAMPS. *See* EXTERMINATION CAMPS; FORCED LABOR CAMPS.

CONCERNING THE CIVIC AMELIORATION OF THE JEWS. *See* DOHM, CHRISTIAN WILHELM VON.

CONFEDERATE (BATTLE) FLAG. Some U.S. Southerners regard this flag as a symbol of Southern pride, but it is often used by racists to represent white supremacy. Some Southern states still fly the flag from public buildings or incorporate it into their state flag's design. Georgia's and Mississippi's flags incorporate the Confederate flag, and Florida's state flag contains the St. Andrew's cross. The flag is also used by racists as an alternative to the U.S. flag, which they consider an emblem of the allegedly Jewish-controlled government.

SUGGESTED READING: Anti-Defamation League, *Hate on Display: Extremist Symbols, Logos, and Tattoos* (New York: Anti-Defamation League, 2006).

CONFESSING CHURCH (BEKENNENDE KIRCHE). The most significant dissenting institution in Germany during the **Nazi** regime. Led by pastors **Dietrich Bonhoeffer** and **Martin Niemöller**, it opposed **Adolf Hitler**, although early on it sympathized with the **Third Reich**'s Jewish policy. Some members of the Confessing Church joined the Nazi **SA** (Sturmabteilung).

SUGGESTED READING: Richard Gutteridge, *Open Thy Mouth for the Dumb: The German Evangelical Church and the Jews, 1879–1950* (Southhampton, England: Camelot, 1976).

CONFISCATION OF JEWISH PROPERTY. In addition to confiscatory **taxes** on Jews during the Middle Ages by kings and princes, there were attacks on, and confiscations of, **synagogues**. These were often instigated by the local bishop, through anti-Jewish sermons or the Jewish reaction to them, and resulted in forced **conversion**, exile, or death of the Jewish congregants. Such attacks occurred especially in the early Middle Ages in France, Italy, and the Christian Near East. During the **Holocaust**, *Aryanization* was the euphemism for confiscation of Jewish property.

SUGGESTED READING: Shlomo Simonsohn, *The Apostolic See and the Jews: Documents, 492–1404* (Toronto: Pontifical Institute of Mediaeval Studies, 1988); Ethel Mary Tinnemann, "German Catholic Bishops' Knowledge of Nazi Extermination of Jews," in Sanford Pinsker and Jack Fischel, *Holocaust Studies Annual, 1990* (New York: New York University Press, 1990).

CONINGSBY. See DISRAELI, BENJAMIN.

CONRAD III (c. 1093–1152). German Holy Roman emperor, 1138–52; founder of the Hohenstauffen dynasty. In 1144 Conrad III was a leader of the disastrous Second **Crusade**. This crusade, like most, began with massacres of Jewish civilians in Europe. *See also* BERNARD OF CLAIRVAUX; RODOLPHE.

SUGGESTED READING: Shlomo Eidelberg, *The Jews and the Crusades: The Hebrew Chronicles of the First and Second Crusades* (New York: Ktav, 1993).

CONSTANTINE I (312–337). Roman emperor, 312–337. Constantine I made Christianity the official creed of the Roman Empire. Toleration ended, and Jews could not intermarry or proselytize. **Conversion** became rampant. Constantine summoned the Council of **Nicaea** in 325, which contained a number of anti-Jewish provisions. *See also* EDICT OF MILAN.

SUGGESTED READING: Charles Freeman, *The Closing of the Western Mind: The Rise of Faith and the Fall of Reason* (New York: A. A. Knopf, 2003); W. H. C. Frend, *The Early Church* (Philadelphia: Fortress Press, 1982).

CONSTANTINE POGROM. When the French colonized Algeria in 1830, the Jewish community, which had resided there since biblical times, was liberated from Islamic persecution. For a millennium, Muslims had been the political masters over the Jewish *dhimmis*, who were subjected to legal and popular discrimination. The Cremieux Decree of 1870 granted Algerians citizenship rights, but whereas the Muslims disdained to take advantage of these civil liberties, the Jews did. In Constantine, Algeria, in August 1934, in the context of Muslim envy, anti-Jewish broadcasts from Radio Berlin and Radio Stuttgart, and the laizzez-faire attitude of local Muslim authorities, three days of Muslim looting of Jewish property took place, with the murder of 23 Jews and wounding of 35. Further riots took place in 1965 under the direction of Muslim authorities.

SUGGESTED READING: Michel Abitbol, *The Jews of North Africa during the Second World War* (Detroit: Wayne State University Press, 1989).

CONSTANTIUS (317–361). Roman emperor, 337–61. Constantius, the son of **Constantine I**, issued a number of anti-Jewish decrees. They included no Jewish visitation to Jerusalem, no **circumcision** of non-Jewish slaves, no recovery of Jews who **converted**, and no marriage between a Jew and Christian woman.

SUGGESTED READING: P. Schafer, *The History of the Jews in Antiquity* (Luxembourg: Harwood Academic Publishers, 1995).

CONTRA HAERSES. See IRENAEUS, ST.

CONVERSIONS. Writing in the fourth century, **St. Augustine** hoped that the principle of Christian love would attract Jewish converts. This was generally unsuccessful, however, and Augustine saw three areas as sticking points:

1. the Jews' resistance to conversion
2. the fact that they were the first keepers of Scriptures sacred to Christians
3. the attraction they held for the Christian faithful

In response, Augustine developed these doctrines:

1. "there is no salvation outside the Church"—implying that Jews who refused to convert were damned to hell
2. proof of the Jews' inherent evil existed in their own sacred writings, and the Jews who rejected Jesus as the Christ were not true Jews
3. Christians who observed even minor Jewish rituals (**judaized**) were **heretics**

Two Christianized Roman laws of 383–84 punished Christian conversion to Judaism by exile, expropriation, or death. "Those Christians who have insulted the dignity of their own religion and name and have contaminated themselves with the Jewish disease will be punished for these shameful acts," the first declared. The second law noted that "to convert a Christian to Judaism meant contaminating him with Jewish sacraments."

In the fourth and fifth centuries, the Latin Church changed its baptismal rites to reflect the belief that the Jews were more satanic and less receptive to Christian truth than any other converts. Not only was the conversion process more protracted for Jews, but the Church also required only the Jewish converts to curse themselves, the Jewish people, and its history. Several Byzantine emperors unsuccessfully attempted to convert Jews forcibly, including emperors Maurice (d. 602), Phocas (d. 610), Heraklios (d. 641), Leo III (d. 741), Basil I (d. 886), Romanos I Lekapenos (*R.* 920–44), and later John Vatatzes (d. 1254). In the High Middle Ages and thereafter, the conversion of a Jew to Christianity was usually the cause of great celebration since it confirmed to the faithful the "truth of Christianity." *See also* OATHS, JEWISH.

SUGGESTED READING: James Parkes, *The Conflict of the Church and the Synagogue: A Study in the Origins of Antisemitism* (New York: Atheneum, 1979).

CONVERSOS. Term given by Christians in Iberian Peninsula to Jews who **converted** to Catholicism, particularly in the 9th to 15th centuries. It had no negative connotation. Another term used was *New Christians*. *See also* ANUSIM; FERDINAND V; INQUISITION, SPANISH; MARRANO.
    SUGGESTED READING: Yitzhak Baer, *A History of Jews in Christian Spain*, 2 vols. (Philadelphia: Jewish Publication Society, 1992).

COOPER, JAMES FENIMORE (1789–1851). American novelist. Although most famous for his novel *Last of the Mohicans*, Cooper's novel *The Bravo* (1831) contained traditional anti-Jewish stereotypes: "bearded old rogue," "knave of a Jew," "a grasping Hebrew," "greedy," "habitual cupidity and subdued policy completely mastered every other feeling."
    SUGGESTED READING: Louis Harap, *The Image of the Jew in American Literature* (Syracuse, NY: Syracuse University Press, 2003).

CORPUS CHRISTI. Latin for "body of Christ." The Feast of Corpus Christi commemorates the institution of the Holy **Eucharist**. This stimulated many Christians to fantasize that the Jews, who obviously denied transubstantiation, were guilty of **desecration of the Host**. *See also* CORPUS CHRISTI PLAYS; *CORPUS MYSTICUM CHRISTI*.
    SUGGESTED READING: Miri Rubin, *Gentile Tales: The Narrative Assault on Late Medieval Jews* (Philadelphia: University of Pennsylvania Press, 2004).

CORPUS CHRISTI PLAYS. Medieval **Corpus Christi** plays celebrated the power of the consecrated Host by dramatizing miracles involving the **eucharist**. These dramas portrayed the Jews in distinctive Jewish costume as protagonists who viciously attacked the host, driving nails through it and making it bleed.
    SUGGESTED READING: Miri Rubin, *Gentile Tales: The Narrative Assault on Late Medieval Jews* (Philadelphia: University of Pennsylvania Press, 2004).

CORPUS MYSTICUM CHRISTI. Christian belief that all of Christendom was a holy mystical body of Christ (**Corpus Christi**) without a legitimate place for the Jews. This conception led to attempts to **convert** Jews, expel them, or exterminate them.
    SUGGESTED READING: Miri Rubin, *Gentile Tales: The Narrative Assault on Late Medieval Jews* (Philadelphia: University of Pennsylvania Press, 2004).

COSMOPOLITANISM (1949–1953). A 19th-century slur against the Jews, cosmopolitanism was employed by Stalinists as a charge against Jews, particularly after World War II. Drummed up by state-controlled newspapers, cosmopolitanism was the first attack on Jews as Jews. It meant Jews were not loyal to the Soviet Union, were unpatriotic, and were tied to other Jews in other countries, particularly Israel. The cosmopolitanism campaign threatened Jewish existence, but ended with the death of **Joseph Stalin** in 1953. *See also* JEWISH ANTI-FASCIST COMMITTEE.

SUGGESTED READING: Harrison E. Salisbury, *Moscow Journal: The End of Stalin* (Chicago: University of Chicago Press, 1961).

COSMOPOLITE. (Former Soviet Union slur) Reference to the alleged rootless nature of Jews.

SUGGESTED READING: "List of Ethnic Slurs," *Wikipedia*, http://en.wiki pedia.org/wiki/List_of_ethnic_slurs.

COUGHLIN, CHARLES (1891–1979). Priest and demagogue. A **Canadian** priest who worked out of the Detroit diocese, Coughlin traveled the United States spreading his message of hatred toward Jews in person and on the radio. His popularity was so great among the American public that he received even more letters of support (tens of thousands a week) from Protestants than he did from Catholics. Coughlin claimed to be fighting for the Christian nature of public life against a Jewish assault. He, along with his Protestant colleagues **Gerald Winrod** and **William Pelley**, believed that the Jews were out to destroy Christian society and deserved their divinely ordained punishment. **Adolf Hitler**, his friend **Julius Streicher**, and German foreign minister Joachim von Ribbentrop admired Coughlin, who praised Hitler's ruthless prescriptions for "social justice." Although several leading Catholic hierarchs opposed Coughlin's ideas, the Church allowed him great latitude in expressing his anti-Jewish beliefs. Coughlin's monthly, *Social Justice*, had a circulation of 750,000. Arguing that the Jews stood behind the Communist takeover in Russia, Coughlin published a **Josef Goebbels** speech in 1935. In 1938, *Social Justice* claimed that Hitler and **fascists** were "the champions of Christian social order." Blaming the Jewish victims instead of Hitler for persecutions in the mid-1930s, Coughlin spoke before meetings of the **Nazi**-front organization the **German-American Bund**. At first friendly with President **Franklin D. Roosevelt**, when Coughlin opposed the war, the U.S. government clamped down and convinced the bishop of Detroit to shut Coughlin's activities down.

SUGGESTED READING: Leo Ribuffo, *Protestants on the Right: William Dudley Pelley, Gerald B. Winrod and Gerald L. K. Smith* (New Haven, CT: Yale University Press, 1976).

COURT JEWS. Between the Middle Ages and the 17th century, Christian nobles frequently recognized the economic advantages of having Jewish financial advisors. This advantage always had to be weighed against the political upheavals created by the Church and the Christian faithful against the Jews. In the early 17th century, Court Jews became institutionalized in several courts in Europe. Their chief privileges were direct access to the prince, freedom to travel, and exemption from any rabbinic jurisdiction—they were the first autonomous Jews in Europe. They were primarily responsible for providing the prince and his court with goods and money, supplying metal for the mint, provisioning the army, undertaking commercial and diplomatic missions, and investigating proposals for the promotion of trade and industry. Creative and ambitious, these hardworking Jews assimilated into the secular Gentile world. They preferred marriages with the families of other Court Jews and attempted to secure their positions for their descendants. The Court Jew often acted as an intercessor with authorities on behalf of the Jewish community.

SUGGESTED READING: Jacob Marcus, *The Jew in the Medieval World: A Source Book, 315–1791* (New York: New York University, 1979).

COX, WILLIAM HAROLD. Judge who presided over the "Mississippi Burning" case of the murder of three young civil rights workers—James Chaney, Andrew Goodman, and Michael Schwerner—on June 21, 1964. After the jury returned its guilty verdict in 1967, Judge Cox declared, "I very heartily endorse the verdict of the jury." Nevertheless, when he sentenced the defendants to extremely light terms ranging from three to ten years, Cox said, "They killed one nigger, one Jew, and a white man. I gave them all what I thought they deserved."

SUGGESTED READING: Joel Norst, *Mississippi Burning* (New York: New American Library, 1989); "U.S. vs Cecil Price et al. ('Mississippi Burning' Trial)," http://www.law.umkc.edu/faculty/projects/ftrials/price&bowers/price&bowers.htm .

CRANE, CHARLES. Commissioner sent by President **Woodrow Wilson** after World War I to the Middle East. Crane was an arch-antisemite whose views reflected many of the anti-Jewish views dominating important political circles in the United States early in the 20th century: the association of the Jews with the Russian-**Bolshevik** political threat to the West and their religious threat to Christianity. Crane sought to organize a coalition of Arabs, Muslims, the **Vatican**, and **Adolf Hitler** against the Jews.

SUGGESTED READING: F. W. Brecher, "Charles R. Crane's Crusade for the Arabs, 1919–1939," *Middle East Studies* (January 1988).

CRANE, STEPHEN (1871–1900). American writer. Crane did not deal often with Jews, but in his 1893 novel, *Maggie, a Girl of the Streets*, he described the following scene: "She swelled with virtuous indignation as she carried the lighter articles of household use, one by one under the shadows of the three gilt balls, where Hebrews chained them with chains of interest."

SUGGESTED READING: Stephen Crane, *Maggie, a Girl of the Streets* (New York: D. Appleton, 1896).

CREATIVITY MOVEMENT. *See* WORLD CHURCH OF THE CREATOR.

CREMATORIA. Furnaces at **Nazi** concentration camps where dead bodies were taken to be cremated. Inmates called *Sonderkommandos* manned them.

SUGGESTED READING: Robert Jay Lifton, *The Nazi Doctors: Medical Killing and the Psychology of Genocide* (New York: Basic Books, 2000).

CRIMES AGAINST HUMANITY. The major criminal charge against defendants at **Nuremberg War Crimes Trials**. It involved enslavement, extermination, **deportation**, and maltreatment not directly connected to warfare. The **genocide** of the Jews hence was included, though not the **Nazi** persecution before September 1939, when the war began. International law at the time (to 1948) allowed for nations to practice what they pleased upon their own citizens. *See also* FINAL SOLUTION OF THE JEWISH PROBLEM; GAS CHAMBERS; HOLOCAUST; WAR CRIMINAL; ZYKLON.

SUGGESTED READING: Robert Falk, Gabriel Kolko, and Robert Jay Lifton, *Crimes of War* (New York: Vintage, 1971).

CRIMES AGAINST HUMANITY, FRENCH. The trials of former **SS** officer **Klaus Barbie** in 1987; of former head of the **Vichy** *milice* (Vichy's paramilitary police) Paul Touvier in 1994; and of Maurice Papon, responsible for Jewish affairs in Bordeaux, in 1997–98 have raised questions about the collaboration of the Vichy regime, as well as ordinary French people, in the murder of more than 73,000 Jews rounded up in France and **deported**, via French transit camps, to be murdered in **Nazi** death camps such as **Auschwitz**. Barbie, a German SS officer stationed in Lyons during the Occupation, was accused of the persecution, torture, and murder of French Jews. But the trial of the Frenchman Touvier was for rounding up Jews and other "undesirables." Barbie and Touvier both received life sentences and died in prison. Another Frenchman, Papon, a bureaucrat, was tried for **crimes against humanity**, specifically, the ordering of 1,560 French Jews, including 223 children, to deportation and ultimately to their deaths at the hands of the Nazis. The trial served as an opportunity to investigate the degree of complicity of the Vichy regime with the rounding up, deportation, and murder of Jews resident on French soil. Papon was found guilty of complicity in crimes against humanity and received a 10-year prison sentence. This established precedents so that in the future no perpetrator could claim that he was only obeying orders, no statute of limitation contained in the laws of any state would apply, and no one would be immune from prosecution for such crimes, even a head of state.

SUGGESTED READING: Henry Rousso, *The Haunting Past: History, Memory, and Justice in Contemporary France* (Philadelphia: University of Pennsylvania Press, 2002); A. Kaspi, *Les Juifs pendant l'occupation*, 2nd ed. (Paris: Seuil, 1997).

CRISTEA, MIRON. Patriarch of the Romanian Orthodox Church. In January 1938, at the time the Romanian government was revoking Jewish citizenship, Cristea declared, "The Jews are sucking the marrow from the bones of the nation."

SUGGESTED READING: Radu Ioanid, *The Holocaust in Romania: The Destruction of Jews and Gypsies under the Antonescu Regime, 1940–1944* (Chicago: Ivan Dee, 2000).

CROATIA. With the occupation of Yugoslavia by the German Army in April 1941, Croatia became an independent state. It remained so until May 1945, when liberation came by Tito's Partisans joined by the Soviet Red Army. Almost immediately upon German occupation, the **fascist**, pro-**Nazi Ustasha** regime headed by **Ante Pavelic** instituted discriminatory **Nuremberg Law**–style restrictions on the country's 38,000 Jews, impoverishing and harassing them. Concentration camps were established, the most notorious being Jasenovac. More than 30,000 Croatian Jews perished, with about 5,000 saved because the Italian Army occupying the Dalmatian Coast saved them.

SUGGESTED READING: Anthony Rhodes, *The Vatican in the Age of the Dictators, 1922–1945* (New York: Holt, Rinehart and Winston, 1973); Leon Poliakov and Jacque Sabille, *Jews under Italian Occupation* (New York: H. Fertiq, 1983).

CROIX, LA. The Catholic newspaper *La Croix* had many provincial editions, hundreds of thousands of readers, and was extremely influential in France at the end of the 19th century. Its editorial policy was ferociously **antisemitic** before, during, and after the **Dreyfus Case** in the late 1890s.

SUGGESTED READING: David I. Kertzer, *The Popes against the Jews* (New York: Knopf, 2001); Stephen Wilson, *Ideology and Experience: Antisemitism in France at the Time of the Dreyfus Affair* (Rutherford, NJ: Fairleigh Dickinson University Press, 1982); Pierre Sorlin, *"La Croix" et les Juifs* (Paris: Grasset, 1967).

CROSS AND THE FLAG, THE. **Antisemitic** monthly periodical published by the Christian Nationalist Crusade and edited initially by **Gerald L. K. Smith** and later by his disciple **Wesley Swift**.

CROSSED (GERMAN WORLD WAR II) GRENADES. **Neo-Nazi**, racist **skinhead** symbol; the emblem of the World War II anti-partisan "Dirlewanger Brigade" (also the 36th **SS** Division) known for cruelty and atrocities and the racist band Dirlewanger.

SUGGESTED READING: Anti-Defamation League, *Hate on Display: Extremist Symbols, Logos, and Tattoos* (New York: Anti-Defamation League, 2006).

CROSSES, DESECRATION OF. *See* DEFAMATIONS, ANTI-JEWISH.

CROWLEY, LEO (1889–1972). Catholic economist, head of the Federal Deposit Insurance Corporation, and wartime alien property custodian. One day in January 1942, President **Franklin D. Roosevelt** proclaimed to a shocked Crowley, who later recorded the president's statement in his diary: "Leo, you know this is a Protestant country, and the Catholics and the Jews are here on sufferance. It is up to both of you [Crowley and Henry Morgenthau, a Jew and secretary of the treasury] to go along with anything that I want at this time."

SUGGESTED READING: Michael Beschloss, *The Conquerers* (New York: Simon & Schuster, 2002).

CRUCIFIED SKINHEAD. Skinhead crucified on the **tyr rune**, the "Warrior Rune"; **neo-Nazi**, racist, and non-racist skinhead metaphor symbolizing the plight of the working class. SHARPs (SkinHeads Against Racial Prejudice) use the symbol to express their pain at being confused with neo-Nazi skinheads. As a prison tattoo, it may signify that its bearer has served prison time or committed a murder.

SUGGESTED READING: Anti-Defamation League, *Hate on Display: Extremist Symbols, Logos, and Tattoos* (New York: Anti-Defamation League, 2006).

CRUCIFIXION. *See* DEICIDE ACCUSATION.

CRUSADERS FOR ECONOMIC LIBERTY. *See* SECRET ORGANIZA-TIONS, 20TH CENTURY.

CRUSADES. In the Middle Ages, armed Christian pilgrimages, later called Crusades, went to war against Muslims to make the Holy Land safe for pilgrims and to restore the Christian holy places to Christian control. In 1096, the First Crusade and the People's Crusade made their way through Germany toward the Holy Land but decided en route to kill Jews, "Christ's worst enemies." They murdered, forcibly **converted**, and coerced into suicide thousands of Jews, destroying the German Jewish communities in **Worms**, Mainz, Speyer, and Cologne. Famines, epidemics, and civil wars were factors in the anti-Jewish **pogroms** that broke out with the onslaught of the Second Crusade in 1146–48. Crusaders "fought" an "infidel" without having to face the expense and danger of a long journey to the Holy Land, or an armed enemy who could fight back. An additional factor was the existence of a new group of Christian merchants eager to rid themselves of Jewish competition. There were a dozen crusades through 1291, all of them beginning with the murder of Jews across Europe. The popes' letters of protection were too little and too late. *See also* BERNARD OF CLAIRVAUX; EMICHO; GODFREY OF BOUILLON; *KIDDUSH HA SHEM*.

Suggested Reading: August Krey, ed., *The First Crusade: The Accounts of Eye-Witnesses and Participants* (Princeton, NJ: Princeton University Press, 1921); Hans Mayer, *The Crusades* (New York: Oxford University Press, 1988).

CULTURE DESTROYER. (Nazi German slur) Reference to the alleged destructive nature of Jews, especially their supposed corruption of German **Aryan** culture.

Suggested Reading: "List of Ethnic Slurs," *Wikipedia*, http://en.wiki pedia.org/wiki/List_of_ethnic_slurs.

CUMMINGS, E. E. (1894–1962). American poet. His **antisemitic** poetry began in the 1920s and lasted 30 years. "There are some specimens of humanity," he wrote of a Jew he called the Fighting Sheeny, "in whose presence one instantly and instinctively feels a profound revulsion." Cummings played with Jewish names and associated Jews with money in his 1926 poem, "Ikey." In "No Thanks" (1935), he called a Jew a "kike." In

Xaipe (1950), Cummings associated Jews with money, manipulation, and corruption.

SUGGESTED READING: Marc Miller, "Jews and Antisemitism in the Poetry of E. E. Cummings," *Spring*, no. 7 (1998).

CUM NIMIS ABSURDUM. Pope **Paul IV**'s 1555 anti-Jewish bull reinstituted the Jewish **ghetto** and severely limited Jewish economic activity in the **Papal States**. It stated that it was

> utterly absurd and impermissible that the Jews, whom God has condemned to eternal slavery for their guilt [in the crucifixion], should enjoy our Christian love and toleration . . . [that Jews] strive for power . . . that Jews venture to show themselves in the midst of Christians and even in the immediate vicinity of churches without displaying any [**Jew**] **badge**.

SUGGESTED READING: Sam Waagenaar, *The Pope's Jews* (LaSalle, IL: Open Court Publishers, 1974); Judah Gribetz, Edward L. Greenstein, and Regina S. Stein, *The Timetables of Jewish History* (New York: Simon & Schuster, 1993).

CURLEYS; CURLIES. (U.S. slur) Hassidic/Orthodox Jewish men; a reference to their characteristic curls, or to Moe "Curly" Howard (Moses Horwitz) of the Three Stooges.

SUGGESTED READING: "List of Ethnic Slurs," *Wikipedia*, http://en.wiki pedia.org/wiki/List_of_ethnic_slurs.

CURL MERCHANT. (U.S. slur) Hassidic/Orthodox Jewish men; rhymes with "pearl merchant." *See* CURLEYS.

SUGGESTED READING: "List of Ethnic Slurs," *Wikipedia*, http://en.wiki pedia.org/wiki/List_of_ethnic_slurs.

CUZA, ALEXANDRU (1859–1946). Romanian political organizer and economist. Cuza was a racist and extreme nationalist who started **antisemitic** organizations at the turn of the 20th century. He formed the first openly antisemitic party in Romania. When briefly in power in 1938, Cuza initiated anti-Jewish laws that paralleled the **Nuremberg Laws** in Nazi Germany, including denaturalization and **Aryanization** (Romanianization). *See also* CODREANU, CORNELIU.

SUGGESTED READING: I. C. Butnaru, *The Silent Holocaust; Romania and Its Jews* (Westport, CT: Greenwood Press, 1992).

CYPRIAN, ST. (d. 549). Bishop of Toulon, France. Cyprian, a **Church Father**, asserted that "the Bible itself says that the Jews are an accursed people . . . the devil is the father of the Jews." In 1936 his assertion became the masthead of **Julius Streicher**'s *Der Stürmer*—**Adolf Hitler**'s favorite reading. *See also* PSEUDO-CYPRIAN.

SUGGESTED READING: James Parkes, *The Conflict of the Church and the Synagogue* (New York: Atheneum, 1979).

CYRIL OF ALEXANDRIA (d. 414). Roman Catholic **Church Father**. A "fanatically strict patriarch," Cyril himself led riots against the Jews and expelled them from his city, stated that the Jewish "**Sabbath** was rejected by God." He also wrote, "Note that the shadow of the law [Jewish Torah] is reversed and the ancient things of the law are made ineffective."

SUGGESTED READING: Heinrich Graetz, *History of the Jews*, vol. 5 (Philadelphia: Jewish Publication Society, 1942).

CYRIL OF JERUSALEM (315–386). Bishop of Jerusalem; doctor of the Roman Catholic Church. The early Apostles' Creed emphasized that the true **Messiah** was Jesus Christ, whom the Jews had rejected and murdered. As Cyril of Jerusalem explained, the Apostles' Creed was directed not at pagans, who did not believe in the coming of any Messiah, but at the Jews.

SUGGESTED READING: Jean Juster, *Les Juifs dans l'empire romain* (Paris: P. Geuthner, 1914); Dom Touttée, "Saint Cyril, Confessor, Archbishop of Jerusalem" (Paris, 1720).

– D –

DACHAU. Concentration camp near Munich, Germany, opened on March 20, 1933, for **Adolf Hitler**'s political opponents. It trained future camp administrators and guards in inhumane behavior toward inmates. Ten thousand Jews were detained there after **Kristallnacht**, and thousands more before liberation in April 1945. Dachau also served as a medical facility for sadistic "medical experiments" on its inmates.

SUGGESTED READING: Konnilyn G. Feig, *Hitler's Death Camps: The Sanity of Madness* (New York: Holmes & Meier, 1981).

DAHN, FELIX (1834–1912). German novelist. Dahn, along with Gustav Freytag, wrote historical novels whose negative images of Jews contributed to the growth of German nationalism and **antisemitism**.

SUGGESTED READING: George Mosse, *Germans and Jews: The Right, the Left, and the Search for a "Third Force" in Pre-Nazi Germany* (New York: Grosset & Dunlap, 1971).

DAMASCUS AFFAIR. False murder charge against Jews in 1840. When an Italian monk, Father Thomas, disappeared in Damascus, Syria, a number of Jews were charged by the French consul and other monks with **ritual murder** and blood libel. The manufactured charge led to the imprisonment and torture of Jews, including children, by Egyptian authorities. The affair became a cause célèbre and led to diplomatic intervention. The efforts of Adolphe Cremieneux and Moses Montefiore with the Egyptian Pasha Ali led to the resolution and freeing of Jews.

SUGGESTED READING: Ronald Florence, *Blood Libel: The Damascus Affair of 1840* (Madison: University of Wisconsin Press, 2004).

DAMASUS I, ST. (304–383). Pope, 366–83. After the Synod of Rome in 382, Pope Damasus decreed the 73 books of the Jewish and Christian Scriptures as holy. He also stated, "What is found in the Father and Son is good, but what is not resident in the Holy Spirit is **heretical**, because all heretics from the Son of God and evil opinions from the Holy Spirit may be found in the **perfidious** disbelief of the Jews and Gentiles."

SUGGESTED READING: Shlomo Simonsohn, *The Apostolic See and the Jews: History* (Toronto: Pontifical Institute of Mediaeval Studies, 1991).

DAMOCRITUS (1st cent. CE). Greek historian and tactician. Damocritus stated that the Jews "worship an ass's golden head and every seventh year they catch a foreigner and sacrifice him. They kill him by cutting his flesh into small pieces."

SUGGESTED READING: Kaufmann Kohler, "Ass-Worship," *JewishEncyclopedia.com*, http://www.jewishencyclopedia.com/view.jsp?artid = 2027&letter = A.

DANIEL DERONDA. *See* ELIOT, GEORGE.

DANTE ALIGHIERI (1265–1321). Florentine poet, author of *La divina commedia* (*The Divine Comedy*). In Canto 23 of *The Inferno*, Dante described the hypocrites, preeminent among them the chief Jewish priest, Caiaphas. In Dante's final circle, the Heart of Hell—named Giudecca after **Judas**—the centerpiece is Judas himself, being tortured in the mouth of the Devil. Here, in contrast to most medieval writers, who associated Judas with all Jews, Dante indicates that Judas represents all traitors to lords and benefactors, not the Jews.

SUGGESTED READING: Cecil Roth, *Jews in the Renaissance* (Philadelphia: Jewish Publication Society, 1978).

DARNAND, JOSEPH (1897–1945). A member of the royalist **Action Française**. At the beginning of World War II, Darnand served in the French Army. He became a leading figure in the **Vichy** French organization Légion Française des Combattants (Legion of French Fighters) and recruited fighters against "**Bolshevism**" into a right-wing group, Service d'Ordre Légionnaire, which supported the Vichy regime. In 1943 his organization, the *milice*, became the secret police for Vichy, enforcing German and French anti-Jewish race laws and carrying out roundups of Jews. Although Pierre Laval was its official president, Darnand was its actual leader. Darnand took an oath of loyalty to **Adolf Hitler** in October 1943 and received a rank of *Sturmbannführer* (major) in the Waffen **SS**. In December 1944 he became head of police and later minister of the interior. He was captured after the war and returned to France, where he was executed. *See also* DEPORTATION; STATUT DES JUIFS.

SUGGESTED READING: Ed Morgan, *An Uncertain Hour: The French, The Germans, the Jews and the Klaus Barbie Trial* (New York: William Morrow, 1990).

DARRÉ, RICHARD WALTHER (1895–1953). One of the **Nazi** Party's chief "race theorists." Advocating a ruralization of Germany and Europe to ensure the health of the **Aryan** race, Darré popularized the *völkisch* slogan "**Blood and Soil**" as a crucial principle of Nazi thought. He advocated a gardener whose function was "ruthlessly eliminating the [human] weeds that would deprive the better [human] plants of nutrition, the air, light, sun." From 1933 to 1942 Darré led the Reich Peasants and the Ministry of Agriculture—the fourth largest of the Nazi ministries. Darré synthesized the Nazi opposition to Western civilization, liberalism, modernism, and **cosmopolitanism** into an "agrarian mystique." He argued, "The concept of Blood and Soil gives us the moral right to take back as much land in the East as is necessary to establish a harmony between the body of our **Volk** and the geopolitical space [Lebenstraum]." Ironically, Darré's influence led to the **Third Reich**'s support of ecologically safe farming and land use.

SUGGESTED READING: Zygmunt Bauman, *Modernity and the Holocaust* (New York: New York University Press, 1992); Anna Branwell, *Blood and Soil* (London: Kensal Press, 1985).

DAS IST DER JUDE! Anti-Jewish pamphlet written by **Dietrich Eckart** and published by *Auf Gut Deutsch*. **Martin Luther**'s name and **antisemitic** ideas were invoked in several passages of this book and on nearly every page of Eckart's *Bolshevism from Moses to Lenin: A Dialogue between Adolf Hitler and Me*. Both books quote Luther's *Von die Juden und*

Ihren Lügen word for word. Just about every anti-Jewish book printed during the **Third Reich**, such as **Theodor Fritsch**'s 1933 *Handbuch der **Judenfrage***, contained citations to and quotations from Luther.

DAUDET, LÉON (1867–1942). French author and monarchist. Daudet was an **antisemitic** conservative, a leading polemicist for the antisemitic **Action Française** who gleefully described Alfred **Dreyfus**' degradation. He regarded the captain as a **ghetto** creature, not authentically French.

SUGGESTED READING: Eugen Weber, *Action Francaise: Royalty and Reaction in Twentieth-Century France* (Palo Alto, CA: Stanford University Press, 1962).

DAVENPORT, CHARLES BENEDICT (1866–1944). American psychologist. In 1917 Davenport was a cofounder of the **eugenics** movement in the United States. Hostile to the recent wave of immigrants from Southern and Eastern Europe, which included many Jews, Davenport wrote in his 1911 book *Heredity in Relation to Eugenics* that children of Jewish-Christian marriages were "half-breeds . . . dissatisfied, restless, and ineffective." He contrasted the individualism and ruthlessness of Russian and Balkan Jews with English and Scandinavian "fear of God and love of country." He lobbied for a very restrictive immigration policy against non-Nordics. *See also* GRANT, MADISON; LAUGHLIN, HARRY; STODDARD, LOTHROP.

SUGGESTED READING: Edwin Black, *War against the Weak* (New York: Four Walls, Eight Windows, 2003).

DAVID IRVING CASE. *See* IRVING, DAVID.

DEARBORN INDEPENDENT. *See* FORD, HENRY.

DEATH CAMPS. *See* EXTERMINATION CAMPS.

DEATH MARCHES. Evacuations of **Nazi** concentration camp inmates. As World War II was drawing to a close in late 1944, the German forces were squeezed between the Red Army in the east and Allied troops in the west. Wishing to avoid liberation of camp inmates—living evidence of their **crimes against humanity**—the Nazis marched surviving inmates from the east into central Germany under deplorable conditions, employing extreme brutality and privation, thus leading to the deaths of thousands more victims.

SUGGESTED READING: Daniel Jonah Goldhagen, *Hitler's Willing Executioners* (New York: Knopf, 1996).

"DECENT JEW." Nazi **antisemitism** both domestic and overseas dedicated itself to destroying the concept of "a good Jew," "a loyal Jew," or "a decent Jew." In a 1937 "Letter to an Englishman," Hanns Oberlindober summarized the **Nazi** campaign against the Jews:

> Jews are a foreign body in every people. . . . There were times when Jews . . . could buy titles, **citizenship**, religion and stature, just as . . . plastic surgery for . . . nose or devices for flat feet. The National Socialist people's and state leadership has only done its simple duty to the German people, . . . to ensure that there will never again be a time of unlimited or concealed Jewish domination. . . . We German National-Socialists *see* the public controversy with Jewry not only as the answer to a question that is the result of a new social order and the solution of the racial struggle between host peoples and parasitic manifestations, but also as a major contribution to the moral, physical, and economic health of the world. . . . Never was the level of public morality lower than during the time in which your [Jewish] racial comrades had nearly complete control over film, the stage and the arts. . . . The damage done to our youth by **Magnus Hirschfeld** . . . one of a legion of Jewish corrupters of the youth, sexual criminals, pseudo-scientists, playwrights and novelists, painters and sculptors, theater and cabaret directors, publishers and distributors of pornographic literature. . . . There is no crime, from pickpocketing to bank robbery, from train robbery to brutal murder, from drugs to the defilement of corpses, from document forgery to perjury, from embezzlement to counterfeiting, in which the names of [the Jews] are not written large as perpetrators or accomplices in the history of criminality. . . . Bearing the mark of Cain, [Jews] must wander until [their] fate is fulfilled. Only then will the age of true peace between the peoples of this earth begin!

See also AUGUSTINE, ST.

SUGGESTED READING: Hanns Oberlindober, *Ein Vaterland, das allen gehört! Briefe an Zeitgenossen aus zwölf Kampfjahren* (Munich: Zentralverlag der NSDAP, 1940), from the German Propaganda Archive at Calvin College, collected by Randall Bytwerk, 2003.

DECLARATION ON THE RELATIONSHIP OF THE CHURCH TO NON-CHRISTIAN RELIGIONS. This declaration, entitled *Nostra Aetate* (*In Our Time*), was released by the **Vatican Council II** in 1965. The council asserted that the Jews have a spiritual heritage in common with Christians, that Jews had no collective guilt in the death of Christ, that Israel was not cursed nor rejected by God, and that Catholic teachings should be free of prejudice and should note the special loving relationship between Christians and Jews. The results since 1965 have been mixed because nearly 2,000 years of religious **antisemitism** cannot be expunged in a generation or two. Although Vatican II refused to ask forgiveness from the Jews for past Catholic behavior—as it had from Protestants, Orthodox

Christians, and Muslims—and although the council neglected to assert the contemporary value of Judaism, it still attempted to improve Catholic attitudes toward the Jews. *See also* JOHN XXIII.

SUGGESTED READING: David I. Kertzer, *The Popes against the Jews* (New York: Knopf, 2001).

DEFAMATIONS, ANTI-JEWISH. False charges defaming the Jews have existed at least from the early Middle Ages. The main charges are **ritual murder**, blood libel, **desecration of the Host**, **poisoning the wells**, and the **Judensau**. Papal letters denying the validity of these anti-Jewish defamations were often ambivalent or ambiguous. Christians have murdered hundreds of thousands, perhaps millions, of Jews over two millennia as a result of these defamations. Religious hatred of Jews was not the only motivation for defamations. Christian fear, mistrust, anger, envy, and self-doubt may also have led to such charges.

SUGGESTED READING: Edward Flannery, *The Anguish of the Jews* (New York: Paulist Press, 1985).

DEFOE, DANIEL (1660–1731). English essayist, political propagandist, journalist, poet, and novelist. In *Roxana: The Fortunate Mistress* (1724), a Jewish jewel dealer recognizes Roxana's jewels as stolen and seeks to have Roxana arrested. Defoe continued:

> As soon as the Jew saw the jewels he falls a-jabbering in Dutch or Portuguese to the merchant. . . . The Jew . . . put himself into a thousand shapes, twisting his body and wringing up his face this way and that way in his discourse, stamping with his feet and throwing abroad his hands . . . ; then he would turn and give a look at me like the devil; I thought I never saw anything so frightful in my life.

This character has no name, being called only "the Jew," "devil of a Jew," "cursed," "dog of a Jew," "traitor," "villain," and the like; "after that rogue of a Jew, whose very name I hated, and of whose face I had such a frightful idea, that Satan himself could not counterfeit a worse."

SUGGESTED READING: Frank Felsenstein, *Antisemitic Stereotypes: A Paradigm of Otherness in English Popular Culture, 1660–1830* (Baltimore: Johns Hopkins University Press, 1995); Daniel Defoe, *Roxana: The Fortunate Mistress*, http://www.blackmask.com/books12c/roxana.htm.

DEGAS, EDGAR (1834–1917). French painter and sculptor. According to one researcher, Degas was a regular reader of **Edouard Drumont**'s antisemitic *Libre Parole* newspaper and an active opponent of **Alfred Dreyfus**.

SUGGESTED READING: Linda Nochlin, *The Politics of Vision* (New York: Harper & Row, 1989).

DE GAULLE, CHARLES (1881–1970). French general and statesman. As president of France, seeking to befriend the Arabs, de Gaulle insulted Jews by calling them "people responsible for ill will and domineering." He refused to deliver Israel's 76 prepaid Mirage planes and four missile boats in 1967. This was a major break in the friendly relations between Israel and France.

SUGGESTED READING: Raymond Aron, *De Gaulle, Israel and the Jews* (New York: Praeger, 1968).

DEGENERATE ART (*ENTARTETE KUNST*). In National Socialist theory, propaganda, and policy, art that was alien, racially corrupted, un-German, un-*völkisch*, Jewish; art that was not coherent with the Nordic ideal of culture and morals; modern, avant-garde art; or art that **Adolf Hitler** determined was decadent and subversive or simply did not like. In the broadest sense, this forbidden category included works of art in literature, theater, film, architecture, and music (the latter category comprising "non-German" music, jazz, modern music, and music composed by Jews). During the Entartete Kunst campaign, more than 20,000 works by more than 200 artists were confiscated. In 1927, the National Socialist Society for German Culture was founded to halt the "corruption of art" and to inform the German people about race and art.

In 1937, German officials purged Germany's museums of thousands of works the Nazis considered degenerate. They chose 650 for a special exhibit of Entartete Kunst that opened in Munich and then traveled to 11 other cities in Germany and Austria. In each installation, the "degenerate" art was surrounded by graffiti and mocking labels. More than three million visitors attended the exhibition. Many of the artists included in the Entartete Kunst exhibition are now considered masters of the 20th century, including Marc Chagall, Max Ernst, Vassily Kandinsky, Paul Klee, Franz Marc, Edvard Munch, George Grosz, Oskar Kokoschka, and Piet Mondrian. *See also DEGENERATION.*

SUGGESTED READING: Stephanie Barron, ed., *Degenerate Art: The Fate of the Avant Garde in Nazi Germany* (New York: Harry Abrams, 1991).

DEGENERATION. Book written in 1892 by Max Nordau (1849–1923), born Simon Maximilian Sudfeld, a Jewish physician, journalist, and Zionist. Nordau based his book on research into the hereditary criminal by Cesare Lombroso (1836–1909), a Jewish professor of psychology at the University of Turin. Nordau attacked dissident poets and artists as depraved and classified them by pathologies such as egomania, sadism, exhibitionism, and mysticism. He claimed they had the same mental characteristics as insane criminals. Nordau later wrote, "Whoever looks upon civilization as a good, having value and deserving to be defended, must mercilessly crush under his thumb the anti-social vermin." Ironically, the **Nazis** adopted many of Nordau's ideas and applied them against Jews and modern artists, prohibiting what they called "**degenerate art**" and calling Jews a criminal race.

SUGGESTED READINGS: Frederic Spotts, *Hitler and the Power of Aesthetics* (Woodstock, NY: Overlook, 2003); David Horn, *The Criminal Body: Lombroso and the Anatomy of Deviance* (New York: Routledge, 2003); John S. Moore, "*Degeneration*, Nordau, and Nietzsche," paper presented to the fourth annual conference of the Friedrich Nietzsche Society, April 1994.

DEGESCH. An abbreviated form of Deutsche Gesellschaft für Schädlingsbekämpfung (German Society for Combatting Vermin). Degesch was a pesticide manufacturer controlled by **I. G. Farben**. This subsidiary produced **Zyklon** for use in Nazi **gas chambers**.

SUGGESTED READING: Josiah DuBois, *The Devil's Chemists* (Boston: Beacon, 1952).

DEGRELLE, LÉON (1906–1994). Belgian politician. Degrelle founded and headed the **fascist**, pro-**Nazi** Rexist Party, which actively collaborated with the German occupiers and formed a Waffen **SS** unit. After the war, Degrelle found sanctuary in Franco's Spain.

SUGGESTED READING: Stanley G. Payne, *A History of Fascism, 1914–1945* (Madison: University of Wisconsin Press, 1995).

DEGUSSA (DEUTSCHE GOLD- UND SILBER-SCHEIDEANSTALT). The German Gold and Silver Separation Institute. Degussa was among the most prominent of the German industrial and insurance companies, banks, and other institutions contributing to the rise of the **Nazi Party**, the German war effort, and the **Holocaust**. During the Holocaust, connections existed between Degussa and its subsidiaries, the **SS**, and Jews' gold (including from teeth) and silver. After the war, Degussa collaborated in supplying Egypt, Iraq, Pakistan, and other Muslim countries with materials for use in their atomic bomb projects—bombs that Egypt and Iraq most likely intended to use against Israel.

SUGGESTED READING: Peter Hayes, *From Cooperation to Complicity: Degussa in the Third Reich* (Cambridge: Cambridge University Press, 2004); Susanne Urban, "How German Banks and Industry Profited from 'Aryanization' and Slave Labor," *Jewish Political Studies Review* 17, nos.

3–4 (Fall 2005); Ralf Banken, "National Socialist Plundering of Precious Metals, 1933–1945: The Role of Degussa," University of California (Berkeley) Institute of European Studies, 2006, Paper 060402 posted at the University of California eScholarship Repository, http://repositories.cdlib.org/ies/060402.

DEICIDE ACCUSATION. Matthew's Gospel implicates the whole Jewish people in crimes against God and humanity both before and during the present generation. The most significant single crime—deicide, the murder of God—was but one manifestation of the inherent and preexisting Jewish evil, from Cain's crime onward. **St. John Chrysostom** believed that the Jews were deicides who had no chance for "atonement, excuse, or defense" because they had "crucified the Christ whom you [Christians] adore as God." He thought that Jewish God-murder was "the crime of crimes" or "sin of sins," and called the Jews "the Synagogue of Christ-killers."

SUGGESTED READING: Frederick B. Davis, *The Jew and Deicide: Origin of an Archetype* (Lanham, MD: University Press of America, 2003); Marvin Perry and Frederick M. Schweitzer, *Antisemitism: Myth and Hate from Antiquity to the Present* (New York: Palgrave Macmillan, 2002).

DE LAPOUGE, GEORGES VACHER. *See* LAPOUGE, GEORGES VACHER DE.

DELASSUS, HENRI. *See* PAPAL JEWISH POLICY.

DELAY, JEAN. Bishop of Marseille and **Vichy** supporter. Delay's view was typical of the French Church's attitudes toward Jews during the **Holocaust**. In September 1942 he wrote that he recognized the difficult problems that the Jewish question posed for the Vichy government, and he justified the government's right "to take all measures needed to defend itself against those who, especially in the last few years, have done so much evil and whom [the government] has the duty to punish severely. . . . But the rights of the state are limited."

SUGGESTED READING: Béatrice Philippe, *Être Juif dans la société française* (Paris: Montalba, 1979).

DELBRÜCK, HANS (1848–1929). Conservative German historian and politician. Delbrück reflected common anti-Jewish attitudes when he opposed Jews gaining positions of power in Christian society "because they are Jews, and education, teaching, or the judiciary are regarded in our culture as the product of the Christian spirit."

SUGGESTED READING: George Mosse, *Germans and Jews* (Detroit: Wayne State University Press, 1989).

DE LYRA, NICHOLAS (1270–1340). Familiar with the commentaries of Rashi and other rabbis, the eminent Franciscan biblical scholar Nicholas of Lyra argued that traditional rabbinic Judaism as well as contemporary Jews had maliciously deviated from Jewish Scripture and were essentially **heretics**.

SUGGESTED READING: Jeremy Cohen, *The Friars and the Jews* (Ithaca, NY: Cornell University Press, 1982).

DEMOCRATIC PARTY PLATFORM OF 1896. In 1896 the Democratic and **Populist** Party platforms declared: "The influence of European moneychangers has been more potent in shaping legislation than the voice of the American people," and they attacked a conspiracy of "the money-lending [code for Jewish **bankers**] class at home and abroad."

SUGGESTED READING: Donald Bruce Johnson, *National Party Platforms, 1898–1976* (Urbana: University of Illinois Press, 1973).

DEMONSTRATIO ADVERSUS JUDAEOS. See CHRYSOSTOM, ST. JOHN.

DENIKIN, ANTON (1872–1947). White Russian general. During the last half of 1919, Denikin's armies occupied the Ukraine. He and his tsarist forces (Whites) identified Jews with the **Bolsheviks**, and his troops engaged in 213 **pogroms**, which murdered 50,000 Jews.

SUGGESTED READING: Dimitry V. Lehovitch, *White against Red; The Life of General Anton Denikin* (New York: Norton, 1974).

DEPORTATION. Euphemism for a stage in the Nazi **Final Solution**. Jews were taken from their homes or **ghettos** and sent "to the East" by the **Nazis**—meaning to concentration camps, where most of them died. **Joseph Stalin**'s regime also deported Jews to the Gulag, his version of concentration camps. *See also* ARROW CROSS.

SUGGESTED READING: Martin Gilbert, *Final Journey: The Fate of the Jews in Nazi Europe* (New York: Mayflower Books, 1979).

DERZHAVIN, GAVRIL ROMANOVITCH (1743–1816). Russian poet and senator commissioned by Tsar Paul to investigate the Jews' role in a famine in White Russia. Derzhavin's prejudice against the Jews, that "stubborn race," was carried to extremes. From the custom of the Orthodox Jews of keeping their heads covered, he concluded that they considered themselves "of all peoples the most excellent." He associated the frequent occurrence of certain names, such as Moses and Abraham, with the Jews' intent to conceal their individual identities, and he concluded that the Jews hoard money to rebuild the Temple in Palestine. His report, *An Opinion on How to Avert the Scarcity of Food through the Curbing of Jewish Usury*, considered the Jews "as fanatic and stiff-necked enemies of the Christians [and] destined by fate to remain eternally scattered." He recommended their **expulsion**.

SUGGESTED READING: Simon Dubnow, *History of the Jews in Russia and Poland* (Philadelphia: Jewish Publication Society, 1920).

DESECRATION OF THE HOST. The Host is the wafer used in Christian communion. It is consecrated by the priest during the **Eucharist** ceremony of the mass. Catholics believe that, through transubstantiation, it becomes the actual body of Jesus Christ. From the 15th century on, Jews were falsely accused of stabbing it, reenacting the passion of Jesus. **Pogroms**, torture, and burnings of Jews resulted from these accusations. *See also* LATERAN COUNCIL, FOURTH; RINDFLEISCH.

SUGGESTED READING: Robert Stacey, "From Ritual Crucifixion to Host Desecration: Jews and the Body of Christ," *Jewish History* 12 (1998).

DESTROYER, THE. *See* CULTURE DESTROYER.

DEUTSCHE CHRISTEN. *See* GERMAN-CHRISTIANS.

DEUTSCHES WÖRTERBUCH. *See* GRIMM, JACOB AND WILHELM.

DHIMMI. "Protected people" in Arabic. Jews and Christians were second-class citizens in Muslim lands, though they were considered better than other non-Muslims since they were People of the Book (Bible) or *dhimmi*. **Muhammad**, when in 628 CE he conquered the Jewish oasis of Khaybar, decreed that such protected people could live among Muslims but were subject to discrimination. This included a poll **tax**, restrictions on religious institutions, and legal disabilities—for example, murder of a Jew is merely manslaughter, and Jews could not testify against a Muslim. Jews also could not build new **synagogues**. The **yellow** stigmatic **Jew badge** was first instituted in Muslim lands. Although in Umayyad Spain, Fatimid Egypt, and the Ottoman Empire they at times experienced better protection than under Catholic kings, in the outskirts of the Arab world, especially in Morocco, Iran, and Yemen, dhimmis experienced degradation, contempt, restrictions, violence, and murder even into the early 20th century. Islamic rule allowed periods of relative tolerance of Jewish intellectual advances, economic prosperity, and minimal political influence, but this kind of Jewish success alternated with the same sort of misery and violence Jews experienced in Christian lands.

SUGGESTED READING: Norman Stillman, *The Jews in Arab Lands: A History and Sourcebook* (Philadelphia: Jewish Publication Society, 1979); Robert S. Wistrich, *Muslim Antisemitism: A Clear and Present Danger* (New York: American Jewish Committee, 2002); Bernard Lewis, *Semites and Antisemites* (New York: Norton, 1986).

D'HOLBACH, PAUL HENRI (1723–1789). **Enlightenment** figure Baron D'Holbach believed that the Jews were a greedy, "ignorant, savage people . . . cowardly and degraded Asiatics." The Jewish Bible was unsociable, senseless, and superstitious. The Jews deserved the contemporary horrors perpetrated by the Spanish and Portuguese **Inquisitions** on the **conversos** because "all the ferocity of the Judaic priesthood seems to have passed into the heart of the Christian priesthood."

SUGGESTED READING: Frank Manuel, *The Broken Staff: Judaism through Christian Eyes* (Cambridge, MA: Harvard University Press, 1992); Léon Poliakov, *The History of Antisemitism*, 4 vols. (New York: Vanguard, 1965–86).

DIASPORA. Greek for "dispersion." *Diaspora* refers to the scattering of a culture, especially the scattering of the Jews to countries outside of Palestine beginning with the sixth-century BCE Babylonian Captivity. **Church Fathers**, Christian theologians, and popes saw in this Diaspora God's punishment upon the Jews for their rejection of the Christ. **St. Augustine**, for example, wrote that, as Cains, the Jews should wander endlessly while suffering punishment for their murder of Jesus. "The Jews have been scattered throughout all nations as witnesses to their own sin and to our truth. . . . 'Scatter them abroad, take away their strength. And bring them down O Lord.'" In his *Dialogue between a Philosopher, a Jew, and a Christian*, **Peter Abelard**—along with Giovanni Boccaccio and **Dante Alighieri** one of the few medieval writers *not* **antisemitic**—put these words into the mouth of a Jew: "We are in *Diaspora* among all nations without our own king or ruler, and we are burdened down with **taxes** so heavy that it seems we must buy our own lives every day." *See also* WANDERING JEW.

SUGGESTED READING: Frederic Brenner, *Diaspora: Homelands in Exile* (New York: HarperCollins, 2003); Amotz Asa-El, *The Diaspora and the Ten Lost Tribes of Israel* (Westport, CT: Hugh Lauter Levin, 2004).

DIASPORA REVOLT. Unsuccessful Jewish revolt against Rome, 114–17 CE. Between 38 CE and 135 CE, the Jews came into serious conflict with Rome in four major crises: in 38, the riot in **Alexandria** in the time of emperor Caligula; in 67, the victory of **Vespasian** and **Titus** over the Jews in the Jewish war under Nero; the Diaspora Revolt under Trajan; and in 131–35, the **Bar Kochba Revolt** under **Hadrian**. In 114, in the context of the Roman destruction of Jerusalem and **messianic** expectations, the Jews of Alexandria, Cyprus, and North Africa rebelled against Trajan's Rome. The revolt was aggravated by religious and cultural conflict between Diaspora Jews and their Hellenistic neighbors.

SUGGESTED READING: Victor Tcherikover, *Hellenistic Civilization and the Jews* (Philadelphia: Jewish Publication Society, 1959); Ernst Baltrusch, *Die Juden und das Römische Reich: Geschichte einer konfliktreichen Beziehung* (Darmstadt, Germany: Wissenschaftliche Buchgesellschaft, 2002).

DICKENS, CHARLES (1812–1870). British novelist. Dickens, the author of *Oliver Twist*, placed a Jew, **Fagin,** as a main character in the novel. Fagin is a despicable person who corrupts youths by leading them to steal and fence goods. Fagin is no ordinary villain: he mirrors the medieval Christian view of Jew as devil. He became a stereotype for Jews as criminal characters and moral seducers. Although Dickens denied it, his comments and other work indicate that early on, he was an **antisemite**.

SUGGESTED READING: Milton Kerker, "Charles Dickens, Fagin and Riah," *Midstream* (December 1999), http://learn.jtsa.edu/topics/luminaries/monograph/wr_dickens.shtml.

DICKSTEIN, SAMUEL (1885–1954). Jewish immigrant from Russia elected to the U.S. House of Representatives from New York, 1923–45; chaired the House Committee on Immigration and Naturalization, 1931–45. Exasperated by congressional, governmental, and popular **antisemitism** during the **Holocaust**, Dickstein lamented:

> The silence shown by the American people at large. . . . Heavenly Father! Where is the Christian world? Where are all the fine Christian people? Where is America, which is supposed to be the champion of liberty? Why has not our voice been raised in protest against the inhuman treatment of millions of innocent victims of Nazism? . . . The Jews were the first target of Nazi propaganda, but you Catholics, you Protestants are next.

His bills favoring a more generous refugee immigration policy were never passed.

SUGGESTED READING: Herbert Druks, "Congressional Responses to the Holocaust in 1943," *Martyrdom and Resistance* (March–April 1981).

DIDASCALIA APOSTOLORUM. A treatise not written by the Apostles at the time of the Council of Jerusalem, as originally believed, but actually a composition of the third century. The patristic *Didascalia* indicated that Christians should continually recall the crimes of the Jews: Jesus's trial on "Wednesday, when [the Jews] began to lose their souls," the crucifixion on "Friday, . . . when they crucified [Jesus Christ] as part of their Passover festival," and Saturday, the **Sabbath** day that God imposed on the Jews not as a day of joy and rest but as "mourning for their damnation."

Suggested Reading: Jean Juster, *Les Juifs dans l'empire romain* (Paris: P. Geuthner, 1914).

DIDEROT, DENIS (1718–1784). French philosopher. His article, "Juifs," was one of the longest in his *Encyclopédie* and provided literate men with knowledge about the development of Judaism. Diderot blamed the Jews for Jesus' crucifixion. He admired traditional Jewish moral principles but claimed that contemporary Judaism was devoid of "any rightness of thought, exactness of reasoning, or precision of style." The Jews' "unhealthy philosophy" consisted of "a confused mixture of reason and revelation, an intentional obscurantism, and often unfathomable principles that led to fanaticism, a blind respect for the authority of their rabbis and for tradition; in a word, of all the faults that proclaim an ignorant and superstitious people."

Suggested Reading: Arthur Hertzberg, *The French Enlightenment and the Jews* (New York: Columbia University Press, 1990).

DIES, MARTIN (1900–1972). U.S. congressman (D-TX), 1931–45, 1953–59. Dies was chairman of the House Committee on Un-American Activities (HUAC) from its inception in the late 1930s. The HUAC investigated **fascist**, Communist, and other so-called extremist or subversive political organizations. The Dies Committee, as it was first called, investigated the **German-American Bund** and the Silver Shirt Legion, both pro-**Nazi** organizations, and the U.S. Communist Party's infiltration of the Federal Theatre Project and the Federal Writers Project. Its original intent was to halt Axis propaganda in the United States, but much of its attention was eventually centered on New Deal liberals, artists and intellectuals, and labor leaders, many of whom were Jews. In October 1947 it presented evidence that 10 Hollywood writers and directors had Communist affiliations. The Hollywood Ten, of whom nine were Jews, refused to affirm or deny the charges made against them and were jailed for contempt. In 1975 the HUAC was abolished.

Suggested Reading: August Raymond Ogden, *The Dies Committee: A Study of the Special House Committee for the Investigation of Un-American Activities, 1938–1941* (Westport, CT: Greenwood Press, 1984).

DIETARY LAWS, JEWISH. Kosher foods, ritually accepted. **Antisemites** claimed Jews were **misanthropic**, elitist, and unwilling to break bread with their Gentile neighbors. The Roman emperor **Claudius** criticized Jews as having superstitions, the dietary laws being one of them. Five European countries today prohibit processing of kosher meat. Antisemites charge that kosher foods place a Jewish "food tax" on Gentiles.

Suggested Reading: Samuel Dresner and Seymour Siegel, *Jewish Dietary Laws* (New York: United Synagogue Book Service, 1980); Veronika Grimm, "On The Dietary Habits of the Roman Empire as Seen by Outsiders, Jews and Christians," *Classics Ireland*, http://www.ucd.ie/classics/classicsinfo/99/grimm.html.

DILLINGHAM COMMISSION (1907–1911). U.S. congressional committee, headed by Sen. William Paul Dillingham (R-VT) and established by Congress for the examination of the "new immigration" (from Eastern and Southern Europe), it was guided by racist and **eugenic** assumptions in claiming the inferiority of these newcomers. Their recommendations eventually led to immigration restrictions from areas populated largely by Jews. *See also* BERMUDA CONFERENCE; BRIGHAM, CARL; DAVENPORT, CHARLES BENEDICT; EVIAN CONFERENCE; IMMIGRATION RESTRICTION LEAGUE; JOHNSON-REED ACT; LAUGHLIN, HARRY; REFUGEE PROBLEM; ROOSEVELT, FRANKLIN D.

Suggested Reading: Roy Lawrence Garis, *Immigration Restriction: A Study of the Opposition to and Regulation into the United States* (Englewood, NJ: J. S. Ozer, 1971).

DINING SOCIETY. *See* BRENTANO, CLEMENS; PRINCETON UNIVERSITY EATING CLUBS.

DINTER, ARTUR (1876–1948). Extreme **antisemitic** racist German novelist and **Nazi** *Gauleiter* (governor) of Thüringen. Dinter's racial novel, the best-selling *Die Sünde wider das Blut* (*Sin against the Blood*, 1934), deals with Jewish-**Aryan** intermarriage. The novel indicated how Nazis regarded intermarriage as

> passing its curse not only to the mixed race offspring, rather to the defiled mother, never leaving her for the rest of her life. Racial defilement is racial death. Racial

defilement is bloodless murder. A woman defiled by the Jew can never rid her body of the foreign poison she has absorbed. She is lost to her people.

The mother, who has had relations with a Jew, commits suicide on seeing her baby, which looks "typically Jewish, even in the cradle." The Nazi concept of **Rassenschande**, race defilement, followed this line of thought. *See also* CHAMBERLAIN, HOUSTON STEWART; LAGARDE, PAUL ANTON DE; LIEBENFELS, LANZ VON; THULE SOCIETY.

SUGGESTED READING: John Weiss, *Ideology of Death* (Chicago: Ivan Dee, 1996); George L. Mosse, "The Mystical Origins of National Socialism," *Journal of the History of Ideas* 22, no. 1 (January–March 1961): 81–96; Richard Sleigman-Gall, *The Holy Reich: Nazi Conceptions of Christianity, 1919–1945* (New York: Cambridge University Press, 2003).

DIO CASSIUS (160–230 CE). Greco-Roman historian. Dio Cassius claimed that Jews "would eat the flesh of their victims, make belts for themselves of their entrails, anoint themselves with their blood and wear their skins for clothing."

SUGGESTED READING: Fergus Miller, *A Study in Cassius Dio* (New York: Oxford University Press, 1964).

DIODORUS SICULUS (THE SICILIAN) (d. 21 BCE?). Greek historian. Diodorus produced a 40-volume history of the world. He repeated numerous **defamations**:

> The race of Jews . . . alone of all nations avoided dealings with any other people and looked upon all men as their enemies. [Their ancestors] had been driven out of all Egypt as men who were impious and detested by the gods. [Those who had] leprous marks on their bodies [were] considered cursed and driven across the border. [They] made their hatred of mankind into a tradition. [Their laws were] not to break bread with any other race, nor to show them any good will at all. [Found in] the innermost sanctuary of the[ir] god's temple . . . a marble statue of a heavily bearded man seated on an ass, with a book in his hands . . . Moses . . . who had ordained for the Jews their **misanthropic** and lawless customs.

SUGGESTED READING: Paul Johnson, *A History of the Jews* (New York: Harper, 1988).

DIRLEWANGER EMBLEM. *See* CROSSED (GERMAN WORLD WAR II) GRENADES.

DISPLACED PERSONS ACT. A 1948 Act of Congress authorizing 200,000 displaced Europeans (those unwilling to repatriate) to enter the United States, essentially opening U.S. borders to refugees from nations occupied after World War II by the Soviet Union. The Act had three morally questionable results: First, it made it easier for Nazi **war criminals** to immigrate to the United States. Second, it specifically benefited Baltics, Ukrainians, and ethnic Germans—all of whom had a high level of collaboration with the **Nazis**. Third, it allowed into the United States only displaced persons who had been registered in displaced-person camps after December 22, 1945. Because almost all of the Jewish survivors had been in camps before this date, Jews were basically excluded. When the bill was debated in the 80th Congress, many representatives, as well as officials of the departments of **State**, Justice, and the Interior, indirectly expressed their anti-Jewish discrimination publicly and, more clearly, in private.

SUGGESTED READING: Raul Hilberg, *Destruction of European Jewry* (New York: Holmes & Meier, 1985).

DISPUTATIONS. Public debates between Jews and Christians on theological subjects during the Middle Ages, Renaissance, and Reformation. These debates were dangerous for the Jews, because the intent was **conversion**. Often the Christian debater was a former Jew, an apostate, misquoting or misinterpreting Jewish holy books. This lose-lose situation often resulted in a threat to the lives and well-being of the Jewish debaters (rabbis) and the censorship or destruction of the **Talmud**. *See also* APION; CHRISTIANI, PABLO; DONIN, NICHOLAS; FRANKISTS.

SUGGESTED READING: Jane S. Gerber, *Jews of Spain: A History of the Sephardic Experience* (New York: Free Press, 1994).

DISRAELI, BENJAMIN (1804–1881). British prime minister and novelist. Like **Karl Marx**'s father, Disraeli's father converted him and his siblings as a child to Christianity so that he would gain more opportunities for success in a Christian society. Later, Disraeli completely identified himself with the Church of England. In speeches, letters, and his novels, he refers to Christianity as the completion of Judaism. His oddly formulated defense of Jewish emancipation was due to his gratitude for Jews and Judaism being the foundations of Christianity. He shared the 19th-century doctrines of race and wrote of the Jews as a superior race, a great creative force collectively and individually in history, and he writes dismissively of other "races," making all the great figures in history Jews or their descendants (and therefore still "Jewish"), even Mozart and **Napoleon**. When these racial notions are joined to Disraeli's belief that the world was governed by conspiracies, his writing has been employed by **antisemites** to "prove" that the Jews were a conspiratorial race and dangerous—**Richard Wagner**, **Houston Stewart Chamberlain**, **Adolf Hitler**, **Julius Streicher**, and many others do just that. The Jews used to be victims of persecution but, Disraeli warns, will not tolerate that any longer.

Disraeli's novel *Coningsby* (1844) described Jews as industrious citizens, temperant, energetic, and vivacious of mind, supporters of the English king, "deeply religious," yet believers in human equality even at the risk of their own life and property. They threatened only antisemites who threatened them: "Do you think that the quiet humdrum persecution of a decorous representative of an English university can crush those who have successively baffled the Pharaohs, Nebuchadnezzar, Rome, and the Feudal ages . . . and Christian Inquisitors[?]" Jews were influential in terms of their laws, their intellect, their literature: "You never observe a great intellectual movement in Europe in which the Jews do not greatly participate." And they often worked behind the scenes politically. This book is often cited by antisemites as proof of Jewish conspiracy to control the world.

SUGGESTED READING: Todd M. Endelman and Tony Kushner, *Disraeli's Jewishness* (London: Vallentine Mitchell, 2002).

DMOWSKI, ROMAN (1864–1939). Polish political leader, founder of the **National Democratic Party** in Poland in 1891 and publisher of the periodical *Gazeta Polska*. Dmowski advocated a social and economic boycott of Jews. He saw them as treasonous, secret plotters against Polish interests. Dmowski also helped to organize and support the Blue Army (American and European Poles comprising an army of 100,000 men, led by Gen. Jozef Haller), which in 1919 attacked Jewish towns in eastern Galicia.

SUGGESTED READING: Ezra Mendelsohn, *The Jews of East-Central Europe between the World War*s (Bloomington: Indiana University Press, 1983).

DOC. Racist **skinhead** symbol for "Disciples of Christ," after a fictional **neo-Nazi** skinhead gang appearing in the movie *American History X*. Some racist skinheads tattoo themselves with the acronym DOC. The term "Disciples of Christ" also has nonextremist meanings, referring also to the Disciples of Christ (D.O.C.) Christian Church, a nonracist mainstream Protestant religious sect founded in the early 19th century in the United States. The Disciples of Christ is also the name of a nonracist Christian-oriented hip-hop R&B band.

SUGGESTED READING: Anti-Defamation League, *Hate on Display: Extremist Symbols, Logos, and Tattoos* (New York: Anti-Defamation League, 2006).

DOCTORS' PLOT. Joseph Stalin's 1953 anti-Jewish campaign. In an attempt by Stalin to destroy the Soviet Jewish community, doctors were arrested on the phony charge that they killed the military leaders whom they treated while they worked for an international Jewish-American-Israeli bourgeois espionage organization. Nine doctors were accused of killing Andre Zhandov (d. 1953), a prominent Soviet Communist leader, At first, only 37 doctors, most of them Jews, were arrested, but the numbers quickly increased into the hundreds. Hundreds of Soviet Jews were fired from their jobs, arrested, sent to gulags, or executed. With Stalin's death in 1953, the new government admitted that the charges were completely an invention of Stalin's.

SUGGESTED READING: Arkady Vaksberg, *Stalin against the Jews* (New York: Knopf, 1994).

DODD, WILLIAM (1869–1940). U.S. ambassador to Germany, 1933–37. Dodd wrote to the antisemitic **Charles Crane** that he, Dodd, had told the Germans "unofficially" that "they had a serious [Jewish] problem but that they did not know how to solve it. The Jews had held a great many more of the key positions in Germany than their numbers or their talents entitled them to."

SUGGESTED READING: F. W. Brecher, "Charles R. Crane's Crusade for the Arabs, 1919–1939," *Middle Eastern Studies* 24 (January 1988).

DOHM, CHRISTIAN WILHELM VON (1751–1820). Prussian constitutional law scholar. The author of "On the Civic Improvement of the Jews" (1781), Dohm postulated that for political equality and emancipation, Jews must change their ways. For Dohm, that meant dramatically changing their moral outlook and economic practices. He believed maltreatment made Jews unfit for **citizenship**. He cited Jewish disobedience of the laws of trade, forgery, and love of **usury**. Therefore, he urged the end of persecution of Jews, an education program, and full civil rights.

SUGGESTED READING: Paul Mendes Flohr and Jehuda Reinharz, eds., *The Jew in the Modern World: A Documentary History* (New York: Oxford University Press, 1995).

DOMINICANS. Roman Catholic order of friars, one of whose roles was the suppression of **heresy**. Dominicans became prominent in the **Inquisition** and particularly against the **Marranos** (**conversos** who were secret Jews). They studied the Hebrew language and **Talmud** to enable them better to **convert** Jews.

SUGGESTED READING: Jeremy Cohen, *The Friars and the Jews* (Ithaca, NY: Cornell University Press, 1982).

DONAHUE, WILLIAM. President of the Catholic League for Civil Rights. Referring to the Mel Gibson movie *The Passion of the Christ*, Donahue commented:

> It's not a secret, OK? And I'm not afraid to say it. That's why they [Jews in Hollywood] hate this movie. It's about Jesus Christ, and it's about truth. . . . Hollywood is controlled by secular Jews who hate Christianity in general and Catholicism in particular. It's not a secret, OK? . . . Hollywood likes anal sex. They like to see the public square without Nativity scenes.

SUGGESTED READING: Transcript, *Scarborough Country*, MSNBC-TV, December 8, 2004, http://msnbc.msn.com/id/6685898.

DONIN, NICHOLAS. 13th-century French Franciscan. Donin was a Jewish convert who denounced the **Talmud** to Pope **Gregory IX** as blasphemous, claiming the book advocated cheating and deceiving Christians, even murder. The pope ordered an examination of the religious text; only **Louis IX** complied. A **disputation** was ordered between Donin and well-known rabbis. The outcome was the burning in France of 24 carloads of the Talmud in 1240.

SUGGESTED READING: Solomon Grayzel, *The Church and the Jews in the XIII Century*, ed. Kenneth R. Stow, vol. 2, *1254–1314* (Detroit: Wayne State University Press, 1989).

DONNELLY, IGNATIUS (1831–1901). **Populist** leader and author. Running for governor of Minnesota in 1894, Donnelly insisted, "We are fighting Plutocracy, not because it is Jewish or Christian, but because it is Plutocracy." But the underlying and supportive basis of **antisemitism** was recognized at the time. Donnelly wrote the best-selling *Caesar's Column*, a utopian novel showing how "the nomadic children of Abraham . . . fought and schemed their way, through infinite pains of persecution . . . to a power higher than the thrones of Europe." The Jews were the international **bankers** and rulers of Europe in "a vast conspiracy against mankind" and "rapidly taking possession of the world" in revenge for Christian antisemitism. "They were as merciless to the Christian as the Christian had been to them."

SUGGESTED READING: John Higham, "Antisemitism in the Gilded Age: A Reinterpretation," *Mississippi Valley Historical Review* 43, no. 4 (1957): 559–78.

DORÉ, GUSTAVE (1832–1883). Doré illustrated **Eugène Sue**'s 19th-century novel *Le Juif Errant* (*The Wandering Jew*). This most striking and haunting of Doré's imaginative works has propagated the **Wandering Jew** legend.

SUGGESTED READING: David Biale, *Cultures of the Jews: A New History* (New York: Schocken, 2002); Joseph Gaer and Gustave Doré, *The Legend of the Wandering Jew* (New York: New American Library, 1961).

DOSTOYEVSKY, FYODOR (1821–1881). Russian novelist. This ideological **antisemite** claimed that Jews were dedicated to the destruction of Christian civilization. Dostoyevsky condemned them for nihilism, being the driving force behind revolutionary movements, and as agents of socialist subversion. He also accused Jews of disrespecting all non-Jews and humiliating Russian peasants. Dostoyevsky felt that the Jews were the people chosen to bring the **Messiah** to the world, but having done this, they were no longer needed. The Jew who dared outlive his usefulness and stubbornly maintained his Jewish identity instead of disappearing into Christianity was, Dostoyevsky imagined, a bundle of negative stereotypes. This **Yid**, or *zhid*, was a **usurer** and **ritual murderer**, a betrayer of nations, and a force that stood fundamentally opposed to Christian values. In 1877, Dostoyevsky wrote:

> there is certainly no other people in the whole world who complains so much about their own lot . . . their humiliation, their sufferings, their martyrdom. [Yet is it not they who] are reigning in Europe, is it not they who control the stock exchanges . . . and, hence, the policy, the domestic affairs, the moral conduct of the states?

In 1880 Dostoyevsky's *Notebooks* proclaimed that the Yid is

> the master of all, the master of Europe. . . . The Yid and his bank are now reigning over everything: over Europe, education, civilization, socialism—especially socialism, for he will use it to uproot Christianity and destroy its civilization. And when nothing but anarchy remains, the Yid will be in command of everything. . . . The **Antichrist** will come and stand above the anarchy.

Dostoyevsky developed these ideas in his fiction and in his journalism. Through his friend **Konstantin Petrovich Pobedonostsev**, Dostoyevsky achieved an influence in the royal household and on several other Russian government officials.

SUGGESTED READING: David I. Goldstein, *Dostoyevsky and the Jews* (Austin: University of Texas Press, 1981).

DRACONET DE MONTAUBAN, JEAN. Mid-13th-century French aristocrat. In order to extract money from the Jews, Draconet had without evidence "cut some of them [Jews] in two, others he burned at the stake, [as to] others he castrated the men and tore out the breasts of the women." *See also* INNOCENT IV.

.SUGGESTED READING: Solomon Grayzel, *The Church and the Jews in the XIII Century*, ed. Kenneth R. Stow (Detroit: Wayne State University Press, 1989).

DRACULA. The figure of the vampire stems from the medieval blood libel **defamation** of Jews. In the late-19th-century Gothic novel, especially in *Dracula*, a "Vampire Empire" exists in which ambivalent attitudes about the modern world are projected upon powerfully mysterious and threatening characters—such as Augustus Melmotte, Count Dracula, and **Fagin**. Wherever vampires appear in fiction or film, they are often unconsciously associated with Jews. Although probably not antisemitic himself (in 1905, he protested against **antisemitism**), author Bram Stoker associates Count Dracula with the "alien" Jew, the racial Other, residing in ghettos such as Whitechapel, where Jack the Ripper, Stoker's vampiric model, did his dirty work. *See also* WANDERING JEW.

SUGGESTED READING: Joseph Valente, *Dracula's Crypt* (Urbana: University of Illinois Press, 2002); Carol Davison, *Anti-Semitism and British Gothic Literature* (New York: Palgrave Macmillan, 2004); Patrick Bratlinger, "Anti-Semitism and British Gothic Literature," *Shofar* 23, no. 1 (Fall 2004).

DREISER, THEODORE (1871–1945). American novelist and playwright. Dreiser's Jewish characters were "wrecks and cripples," or a molester and murderer of little girls, or a **Shylock**. In 1922, Dreiser wrote his friend and kindred spirit, journalist **H. L. Mencken**, that New York was "a Kyke's dream of a **Ghetto**." In letters, he described the Jews as **wanderers**, stubbornly holding onto their religion and "race," and sharply "money-minded." He opposed tolerance for Jews in the United States because it would allow Jews to "possess America by sheer numbers, their cohesion, their race tastes and, as in the case of the Negro in South Africa, really [to] overrun the land." Dreiser argued further that the Jew should leave America, since when he "invades" a country, he never assimilates.

SUGGESTED READING: Richard Tuerk, "The American Spectator Symposium Controversy: Was Dreiser Anti-Semitic?" *Prospects* 16 (1991): 367–89.

DREXLER, ANTON (1884–1943). German political activist and one of the founders of the **German Workers Party** in 1919. A toolmaker, and a non-veteran, he saw himself as a champion of workingmen. A non-Marxist, he believed Jews were the enemy of the common man, and Germany was in the middle of a Jewish capitalist-Masonic conspiracy. **Adolf Hitler**, working for the German Army, was hired to spy on the Party, was attracted to its ideas, and soon became its president. *See also* FREEMASONS; NAZI PARTY; THULE SOCIETY.

SUGGESTED READING: Charles B. Flood, *Hitler: The Path to Power* (Boston: Houghton Mifflin, 1990).

DREYFUS CASE (1894–1906). French treason trial. Capt. Alfred Dreyfus (1859–1935), a Jew on the French General Staff, was falsely accused of passing military secrets to the Germans. A court-martial convicted him on trumped-up evidence and sentenced him to military degradation and solitary confinement on Devil's Island. The case divided France into dreyfusards, who supported Dreyfus, and **antidreyfusards**, who believed in Dreyfus's guilt and included many antisemites. In 1906 a civilian appeals court overturned his conviction and restored Dreyfus to full honors. He volunteered and fought in World War I at Verdun. Theodore Herzl, a Hungarian-Jewish journalist, was so traumatized by the case and despairing of an end to **antisemitism** in Europe that he founded the modern Zionist movement. It took the French Army a hundred years to admit it had erred in this case and had falsely accused Dreyfus of treason. *See also* DAUDET, LÉON; DEGAS, EDGAR; DRUMONT, EDOUARD; ESTERHAZY, FERDINAND; HENRY, HUBERT JOSEPH; PICQUART, GEORGES; ZOLA, ÉMILE.

SUGGESTED READING: Guy Chapman, *The Dreyfus Case: A Reassessment* (Westport, CT: Greenwood Press, 1979).

DROSTE-HÜLSHOFF, ANNETTE VON (1797–1848). German poet from an aristocratic Catholic Westphalian family. When she was 21 in 1818, Droste-Hülshoff traveled with her father to Kassel to meet **Jacob and Wilhelm Grimm**. In 1842 she wrote *The Jews' Beech-Tree*, a story that reveals the anti-Jewish attitudes of late 18th-century Germans and of Droste-Hülshoff herself. Her letters also reveal her German aristocratic **antisemitism**. "Every **banker** must be a Jew," she writes, and she describes a bride in terms of her physical Jewishness.

SUGGESTED READING: Karin Doerr, "The Specter of Antisemitism in and around Annette von Droste-Hülshoff's *Judenbuche*," *German Studies Review* 17, no. 3 (October 1994).

DRUMONT, EDOUARD (1844–1917). French journalist and politician. Drumont authored the best-selling French book *La France Juive* (*Jewish*

France, 1886) and ran the daily *Libre Parole* in 1892. Both were filled with racist and religious **antisemitism** that asserted that Jews controlled French political and economic life. He called for a social revolution that would confiscate and expropriate Jewish property. His works were a major source for the **antidreyfusards**.

SUGGESTED READING: Malcolm Hay, *Europe and the Jews* (Boston: Beacon Press, 1960); Guy Chapman, *The Dreyfus Case: A Reassessment* (Westport, CT: Greenwood Press, 1979).

DÜHRING, EUGEN KARL (1833–1921). German economist and social theorist. Dühring connected **antisemitism** with the natural sciences in his book *The Jewish Question as a Racial, Moral, Cultural Problem* (1881). Hence, undesirable traits attributed to Jews, such as unethical behavior and parasitism, made Jews a biological and cultural danger to the German people. These alleged traits were inborn and ineradicable. Dühring had a profound influence on racial antisemitism. He wrote:

> The contempt felt for the Jewish race lies in its absolute inferiority in all intellectual fields—even music. Loyalty and respect to anything great and noble are alien to [Jews]. As a race [Jews are] inferior and depraved. [It is] the duty of the Nordic peoples to exterminate such parasitic races just as we exterminate snakes and beasts of prey.

SUGGESTED READING: Paul Mendes Flohr and Jehuda Reinharz, *The Jew in the Modern World* (New York: Oxford University Press, 1995).

DUKE, DAVID (1950–). U.S. politician and founder of the White Youth Alliance, a group affiliated with the neo-Nazi National Socialist White People's Party; founder and self-appointed Imperial Wizard of the Louisiana-based Knights of the **Ku Klux Klan**. In early 1980s Duke established the **National Association for the Advancement of White People** and the European-American Unity and Rights Organization (originally named the National Organization for European American Rights) in January 2000. In 1989 Duke won a seat representing Metairie in the Louisiana state legislature. Five unsuccessful political campaigns followed: a 1990 bid for the U.S. Senate, a 1991 campaign for the governorship of Louisiana, a bid for the U.S. presidency in 1992, another senatorial race in 1996, and a 1998 attempt to win a congressional seat in Louisiana. In both the 1990 and 1991 races, he attracted a majority of Louisiana's white voters. America's best-known racist, he was instrumental in the Klan resurgence of the 1970s. Duke has since continued to propagandize white supremacist views as a frequent political candidate, with a variety of fringe organizations, and, in recent years, in Russia, Europe, and the Middle East. He was one of the first **neo-Nazi** and Klan leaders to discontinue the use of **Nazi** and Klan regalia and ritual, as well as other traditional displays of race hatred, and to cultivate media attention. Since 2001 he has been based in Russia and Ukraine, where he has participated in **Holocaust denial** conferences and argued, in writings and lectures, that Israel perpetrated the September 11, 2001, attacks on the World Trade Center and the Pentagon.

SUGGESTED READING: John Kuzenski et al., *David Duke and the Politics of Race in the South* (Nashville, TN: Vanderbilt University Press, 1995).

DU MAURIER, GEORGE (1834–1896). French-British novelist. Du Maurier, the author of the 1894 novel *Trilby*, introduced the sinister character **Svengali**, who hypnotizes the young innocent Trilby. Du Maurier, also an illustrator, drew the Svengali character with exaggerated stereotypical Jewish features. This novel illustrated the negative view of the Jew whose occult power corrupts virtuous white women.

SUGGESTED READING: Richard Kelly, *George Du Maurier* (Boston: Twayne, 1983).

DUNS SCOTUS, JOHN (1266–1308). A Franciscan theologian and philosopher. Duns Scotus advocated forced **baptism** and Jewish **expulsion** on the grounds that Jews were not needed in Christian society; their presence only contaminated the Christian soul.

SUGGESTED READING: Malcolm Hay, *Europe and the Jews* (Chicago: Chicago Academy Publications, 1952).

DURBAN CONFERENCE AGAINST RACISM. September 2001 conference held in South Africa allegedly opposed to racism but exhibiting, as a result of Muslim **antisemitism**, the highest level of antisemitism since the end of the **Holocaust**. At the conference, Arab, Palestinian, and Muslim organizations falsely accused Israel of **genocide** against the Palestinians, ethnic cleansing, and "racism." Arab organizations distributed propaganda pamphlets depicting Jews with bloody fangs and wearing Nazi **swastikas**.

SUGGESTED READING: Robert S. Wistrich, *Muslim Antisemitism: A Clear and Present Danger* (New York: American Jewish Committee, 2002).

DUTCH WEST INDIA COMPANY. In March 1656, this trading corporation centered in Amsterdam explicitly instructed **Peter Stuyvesant** to limit the Jews in New Amsterdam (later New York) to the freedom they had in old Amsterdam. That is, although the Jews would be allowed to trade on an equal footing with all the other inhabitants and to "exercise in all quietness their religion within their houses," they were not permitted "free and public exercise of their abominable religion," for "the wolves [must] be warded off from the tender lamb of Christ." Largely because there were so many Jewish investors in the company, Stuyvesant, under orders from the home office, had to accept Jews.

SUGGESTED READING: Marc Angel, *Remnant of Israel: A Portrait of the First Jewish Congregation, Shearth Israel* (New York: Riverside Book Co., 2004).

– E –

EAGLE ATOP SWASTIKA. National Socialist symbol representing the power and strength of the **Third Reich**. Generic **neo-Nazi** symbol.

SUGGESTED READING: Anti-Defamation League, *Hate on Display: Extremist Symbols, Logos, and Tattoos* (New York: Anti-Defamation League, 2006).

EASY-BAKE. (U.S. slur) Reference to Jewish **Holocaust** victims' bodies being burned.

SUGGESTED READING: "List of Ethnic Slurs," *Wikipedia*, http://en.wikipedia.org/wiki/List_of_ethnic_slurs.

ECCLESIA. *See* SYNAGOGA.

ECCLESIASTICAL JOURNAL. *See* LEO XII.

ECK, JOHANN VON (1486–1543). German Roman Catholic theologian; **Martin Luther**'s Catholic opponent. Eck regarded Jews as murderous by nature: bloodthirsty magicians who reveled in the demonic. In his eyes, Jews were the very image of the Devil. He believed that Jews seek Christian blood to wash away their stigma for having murdered Christ. He concluded that Christian persecutions of Jews were justified as self-defense. His "Refutation of a Jewish Book" (1541) recycled old canards about **ritual murder** and Jewish **desecration of the Host**.

SUGGESTED READING: Fritz Voll, "A Short Review of a Troubled History," *JCRelations.net*, http://www.jcrelations.net/en/?id = 836.

ECKART, DIETRICH (1868–1928). German playwright and **Adolf Hitler**'s mentor. Eckart was the leader of the **German Workers Party** before Hitler. He was the author of the **Nazi** battle-cry poem "Germany Awake" and editor of the Nazi newspaper, *Auf gut Deutsch*. Hitler borrowed a number of ideas from Eckart, such as notions that the Jews were responsible for Germany's defeat in World War I and that Jews should be totally excluded from German life. Eckart also introduced Hitler to party contributors and to other **antisemitic** personalities. *See DAS IST DER JUDE!*

SUGGESTED READING: Nicholas Goodrick-Clarke, *The Occult Roots of Nazism* (New York: New York University Press, 1992); Peter Viereck, *Metapolitics: From Wagner to German Romantics to Hitler* (Piscataway, NJ: Transaction Press, 2003).

ECONOMIC CRIMES. Soviet anti-Jewish accusations. Under Nikita Khrushchev and the Soviet 21st Congress, laws were enacted in 1961 that delineated economic crimes (e.g., financial manipulation, parasitism), making them subject to the death penalty. Jews were prominent among those arrested and executed. Novelist Boris Pasternak's woman friend was one indicted on such trumped-up charges.

SUGGESTED READING: Nathan Sharansky, "On Hating the Jews," *Commentary* 116, November 2003.

EDICT OF MILAN. The proclamation of Christianity as the religion of the Roman Empire. In 312, under a Christian symbol for Christ, **Constantine** defeated his rival for the imperial throne. In 313, he and Eastern emperor Licinius agreed to recognize Christianity as a lawful religion. Judaism's position in the Roman Empire declined greatly after this edict.

SUGGESTED READING: Fordham University, *Medieval Sourcebook*: Galerius and Constantine: Edicts of Toleration, 311/313, http://www.fordham.edu/halsall/source/edict-milan.html.

EDWARD I (1239–1307). King of England, 1272–1307. In 1275 Edward I decreed the *Statutum Judaismo*, which banned Jews from money-lending at interest and forced them to wear a **yellow** star patch and to pay an Easter poll **tax** (that is, a head tax for the privilege of living there). In 1278, on a false charge of coin clipping, 680 Jews were imprisoned in the Tower of London. In 1290 Edward expelled all 3,000 Jews from England.

SUGGESTED READING: Robin R. Mundill, "Edward I and the Final Phase of Anglo-Jewry," in *The Jews in Medieval Britain: Historical, Literary and Archeological Perspectives*, ed. Patricia Skinner (Suffolk, England: Boydell Press, 2003).

EDWARDS, JONATHAN (1703–1758). Congregational minister and theologian; the leading light of the Great Awakening, the revolutionary period in early American religious thought. Edwards argued that the Jews "had crucified the Lord of Glory, with the utmost malice and cruelty, and persecuted his followers." For this, the Jews must continually be punished.

SUGGESTED READING: Morton Borden, *Jews, Turks, and Infidels* (Chapel Hill: University of North Carolina Press, 1984).

EGICA (c. 610–701). Also spelled Ergica. Spanish king, 687–701. In 694 Egica accused Jews of aiding Muslims; he then confiscated all Jewish property and declared all Jews, baptized or not, to be slaves and distributed them as gifts among Christians. Jewish children over seven years of age were taken from their parents and given as gifts.

EICHE, THEODORE (1893–1943). **Nazi** concentration camp inspector. Eiche founded and trained the Nazi Totenkopfverbände, the **SS** Deaths Head Brigade, which administered the concentration camps. Eiche originated the slogan "Arbeit Macht Frei" (Work brings freedom), a motto intended to deceive the prisoners. He ran **Dachau** as a model camp, ruling with maximum impersonal severity, including corporal punishment, solitary confinement, and shootings. His other motto was "Tolerance is a sign of weakness."

SUGGESTED READING: Tom Segev, *Soldiers of Evil: The Commandants of the Nazi Concentration Camps* (New York: McGraw-Hill, 1987).

EICHMANN, ADOLF (1906–1962). SS Colonel. As head of the Jewish section of the RSHA (the Reichssicherheitshauptamt, the **Third Reich**'s Main Security Administration in charge of all security, **SS**, and police operations, which included the Intelligence Division, the **Gestapo**, Kriminalpolizei, and the **SD**), Eichmann was in charge of **deporting** and transporting Jews to **ghettos** and concentration camps. He was a major implementer of the **Final Solution**. Using a **Vatican** passport after the war, he escaped to **Argentina**. The Israeli secret service successfully kidnapped him to bring him to trial in Israel for **war crimes** and **crimes against humanity**. Eichmann was the first **Nazi** mass murderer to be tried in Israel, and he was hanged on June 1, 1962. *See also* ARENDT, HANNAH; HEYDRICH, REINHARD; RATLINE; WANNSEE CONFERENCE.

SUGGESTED READING: Jochen Lang, ed., *Eichmann Interrogated: Transcripts from the Archives of the Israeli Police* (New York: Vintage, 1984); Hannah Arendt, *Eichmann in Jerusalem: A Report on the Banality of Evil* (New York: Viking Press, 1963); Haim Goui, Michael Swirsky, and Alan Mintz, *Facing the Glass Booth: The Jerusalem Trial of Adolf Eichmann* (Detroit: Wayne State University Press, 2004).

EINSATZGRUPPEN. Special **SS** mobile killing groups. These specially trained assassins followed the German Army and murdered Jews, Communists, and Nazi political opponents in the Balkans and Eastern Europe. The Einsatzgruppen murdered 1.5 million to 2 million Jews between 1941 and early 1943 until **extermination camps** replaced them. *See also* BABI YAR; BACH-ZELEWSKI, ERIC VON DEM; OHLENDORFF, OTTO; REICHENAU, WALTER VON; SONDERKOMMANDO.

SUGGESTED READING: Yitzhak Arad, Shmuel Krakowski, and Shmuel Spector, eds., *The Einsatzgruppen Reports: Selections from the Dispatches of the Nazi Death Squads in Occupied Territories of the Soviet Union, July 1941–January 1943* (New York: Holocaust Library, 1989).

EISENMENGER, JOHANN ANDREAS (1654–1704). German professor of Oriental languages. Eisenmenger charged Jews as **poisoners** and **ritual murderers** and stated that the Jewish religion was far inferior to Christianity. Using excerpts from the **Talmud**, he sought to prove that Jews were immoral. Eisenmenger's most **antisemitic** and damaging work was *Entdecktes Judentum* (*Judaism Unmasked*), which has been quoted widely by antisemites. *See also* ROHLING, AUGUST; *TALMUD JEW, THE.*

SUGGESTED READING: Simon Dubnov, *History of the Jews*, vol. 4, *From Cromwell's Commonwealth to the Napoleonic Era*, trans. Moshe Spiegel (South Brunswick, NJ: Thomas Yoseloff, 1971).

EISNER, KURT (1867–1919). German statesman and socialist who opposed German involvement in World War I. Having engineered a bloodless coup, Eisner became prime minister of the new republic of Bavaria. A member of the **Thule Society** and Bavarian army officer murdered him in January 1919. **Adolf Hitler** pointed to Eisner's Jewish identity, claiming Jews fomented disorder and were Marxists.

SUGGESTED READING: Richard Grunberger, *Red Rising in Bavaria* (London: Alan Barker, 1973).

ELBOW WEB. Spider web prison tattoo. Racist convicts may "earn" this tattoo by killing a minority person. Nonracists may wear this tattoo unaware of its racist symbolism.

SUGGESTED READING: Anti-Defamation League, *Hate on Display: Extremist Symbols, Logos, and Tattoos* (New York: Anti-Defamation League, 2006).

ELIOT, GEORGE (1819–1880). English novelist. On the basis of her novel *Daniel Deronda* (1876), Eliot is usually identified as a great champion of

Jewry. But in reaction to Prime Minister **Benjamin Disraeli**'s pronouncements of Jewish superiority in his novels, she wrote in 1847 to her friend
John Sibree:

> My Gentile nature kicks most resolutely against any assumption of superiority in
> the Jews and is almost ready to echo **Voltaire**'s vituperation. I bow to the suprem-
> acy of Hebrew poetry, but much of their early mythology and almost all of their
> history is utterly revolting. . . . Everything specifically Jewish is of a low grade.

SUGGESTED READING: Saleel Nubhal, Kim Newton, and George Eliot,
Judaism and the Novels: Jewish Myth and Mysticism (Basingstoke, England: Palgrave Macmillan, 2003).

ELIOT, T[HOMAS] S[TEARNS] (1888–1965). Anglo-American poet and
Christian conservative who longed for a "Christian world-order." Christian **triumphalism** permeated Eliot's work. He believed that Christ was
the **Messiah** who fulfilled the old Law, consummates Israel's history, and
caused the destruction of Jerusalem. Eliot condemned Jews as corrupters
of Christian civilization, without roots in, or loyalty to, the nation in which
they live. They were animalistic and ruthless in their quest for power over
Gentiles. Some of Eliot's poetry described the Jews as worse than prehis-
toric monsters and rats and contended that their compulsive greed undermined Christian society. Eliot saw the Jews as the fundamental "Forces of
Evil," the "diabolic," "the Evil Spirit today," who should not be allowed
to corrupt Christian culture. In *After Strange Gods* (1934), he wrote:
"What is still more important is unity of religious background; and reasons
of race and religion combine to make any large number of free-thinking
Jews undesirable. . . . A spirit of excessive tolerance is to be deprecated."
Despite his denials, Eliot used the metaphor of "Jew" to represent the most
despicable and corruptive principles.

SUGGESTED READING: Anthony Julius, *T. S. Eliot, Antisemitism and Literary Form* (Cambridge: Cambridge University Press, 1996).

ELIZABETH II (1709–1762). Tsarina, 1741–62. Under pressure from Mus-
covites who wanted no competition from Jews, in addition to Elizabeth's
feeling that Jews "were an evil influence on Russian peasants," the tsarina
confined Jews to a **Pale of Settlement**, arguing, "I seek no gain at the
hands of the enemies of Christ."

SUGGESTED READING: Simon Dubnov, *History of the Jews*, vol. 4, *From
Cromwell's Commonwealth to the Napoleonic Era*, trans. Moshe Spiegel
(South Brunswick, NJ: Thomas Yoseloff, 1971).

ELLENIKE. (Greek slur) A Jew.
SUGGESTED READING: "List of Ethnic Slurs," *Wikipedia*, http://en
.wikipedia.org/wiki/List_of_ethnic_slurs.

EMANCIPATION, JEWISH. *See* REVOLUTIONS OF 1848.

EMERSON, RALPH WALDO (1803–1882). American essayist. Despite
rejecting many aspects of Christianity, this transcendental Unitarian nevertheless adopted traditional anti-Jewish attitudes. His early sermons reflected his belief that the Jews were responsible for murdering Jesus, who
was the founder of a set of religious beliefs far superior to those of Judaism. For him, the Jewish God was cruel; the Jewish Law was stifling. What
was bad about Christianity was its Jewish substance. In his journal entry
for July 3, 1839, he wrote: "In the Allston [Massachusetts, art] gallery the
Polish Jews are an offense to me; they degrade & animalize."
SUGGESTED READING: Ralph Waldo Emerson, *The Journals and Miscel-
laneous Notebooks*, 16 vols. (Cambridge, MA: Harvard University Press,
1960–82).

EMICHO (1076–1123). Also known as Emmerich von Leiningen. Count of
Leiningen, Germany. The Christian chronicler Ekkehard of Aura described
Emicho as a brute who, once "called to religion," took up the cross and
slaughtered Jews. His 12,000 Crusaders campaigned throughout the cities
on the Rhine, Main, and Danube rivers, "either utterly destroy[ing] the execrable race of the Jews wherever they found them (being even in this matter zealously devoted to the Christian religion) or forc[ing] them into the
bosom of the Church." In May 1096, Emicho's Crusader army massacred
the Jewish community of **Worms**. Many Jews killed themselves. A small
remnant was "**converted** forcibly and **baptized** against their will." A few
days later, the Crusaders slaughtered hundreds of Mainz's Jews, stripping
them naked and throwing them, "still writhing and convulsing in their
blood," from windows until the dying Jews were piled in heaps on the
ground. *See also* RUTHARD.
SUGGESTED READING: Robert Chazan, *In the Year 1090: The First Crusade and the Jews* (Philadelphia: Jewish Publication Society, 1997).

ENDECJA. *See* NATIONAL DEMOCRATIC PARTY (POLAND).

ENGELS, FRIEDRICH (1822–1895). English mill owner and Marxist
thinker. **Karl Marx**'s friend and collaborator, Engels followed the Marxist
ideology that the Jews were not a nation but a caste, and Jewish national-

ism was a diversion from the class struggle. Engels commented that the "Jewish so-called Holy Writ was an expression of Arab tribal traditions." Referring to French Jewish **bankers**, he said, "I begin to understand French **antisemitism**." Engels believed "Jews from Poland were the dirtiest of all races." *See also* YOUNG HEGELIANS.

SUGGESTED READING: Albert S. Lindermann, *Esau's Tears: Modern Antisemitism and the Rise of the Jews* (Cambridge: Cambridge University Press, 2000).

ENLIGHTENMENT. 17th- and 18th-century European intellectual movement when the European world moved away from religion toward secularism, rationalism, humanism, and empirical science. Enlightenment had mixed blessings for Jews. Though it preached toleration, the movement was generally intolerant of Jews. It was not until the 19th century that Jews were released from the **ghetto**, were granted civil rights, and became more accepted in the working world—and even then, they were still not fully accepted socially. Several Enlightenment philosophers, among them **Denis Diderot** and **Voltaire**, attacked Jews and Jewish customs and holy books. *See also* MISANTHROPY.

SUGGESTED READING: Arthur Hertzberg, *The French Enlightenment and the Jew* (New York: Columbia University Press, 1990).

ENTDECKTES JUDENTUM (*JUDAISM UNMASKED*). Book by German writer **Johann Eisenmenger**. Using quotations out of context, misquotations, misinterpretations, and references to pagans, the author presented an anti-Christian interpretation of the **Talmud**. His work was adopted by German theologian **August Rohling** in his *Talmud Jew* and is widely quoted by **antisemites** to this day.

SUGGESTED READING: Uriel Tal, *Christians and Jews in Germany* (Ithaca, NY: Cornell University Press, 1975).

ERASMUS, DESIDERIUS (1466–1536). Dutch religious humanist. The writer of the book *In Praise of Folly* and a noted figure in the history of toleration, Erasmus was unsympathetic to the Jewish religion. A translator of the Bible into Latin, he considered Judaism too ceremonial, full of "egregious formalism." Erasmus attacked Jewish **usurers** for excessive interest. He claimed that no place existed in Christian society for "the most pernicious plague and bitterest foe of the teachings of Jesus Christ." He believed that the Jews' stubborn refusal to **convert** jeopardized the most fundamental values of Christian society.

SUGGESTED READING: Simon Markish, *Erasmus and the Jews* (Chicago: University of Chicago Press, 1986).

ERWIG (d. 687). **Visigothic king** of Spain, 680–87. Erwig removed Jews from public offices as well as the stewardship of large estates.

SUGGESTED READING: Simon Dubnov, *History of the Jews*, vol. 2, *From the Roman Empire to the Early Medieval Period*, trans. Moshe Spiegel (South Brunswick, NJ: Thomas Yoseloff, 1968).

ESPINA, ALFONSO DE. Spanish Franciscan monk. In 1460 Espina wrote a work titled *Fortalitium Fidei* (*Fortress of the Faith*), in which he called for the establishment of an **Inquisition** to root out **converso heresy** (newly converted Jews who kept elements of Judaism) and Jewish blasphemy. Following his advice, Isabella and **Ferdinand**, the Catholic rulers who were to unite Spain, reinforced the Spanish Inquisition already established with papal approval. The Inquisition attacked Jews, **heretics**, Muslims, free thinkers, and Protestants as un-Christian elements.

SUGGESTED READING: Susan Myers and Steve McMichael, *Friars and Jews in the Middle Ages and Renaissance* (Leyden, The Netherlands: Brill, 2004).

ESSAY ON THE INEQUALITY OF THE HUMAN RACES. Major work of French diplomat **Arthur de Gobineau**, 1853–55. The essay justified racist notions of Nordic-**Aryan** superiority. It postulated that decisive events of history were determined by the iron law of race. Human destiny was decreed by nature expressed in race. All civilization came from the white race, the best part of which was the Aryan. To remain superior and in control, race mixing had to be avoided. *See also* SKINHEADS; SOCIAL DARWINISM; VÖLKISCH NATIONALISM.

SUGGESTED READING: George Mosse, *Toward the Final Solution* (Madison: University of Wisconsin Press, 1988); Léon Poliakov, *The Aryan Myth* (New York: Barnes & Noble, 1996).

ESTERHAZY, FERDINAND (1847–1923). As a major on the French General Staff, Esterhazy offered the Germans French military secrets in the 1890s. The memorandum in his handwriting was misread as that of Alfred **Dreyfus**, the only Jew on the General Staff. Alhough Esterhazy's espionage was discovered by Intelligence chief Col. **Georges Picquart**, the General Staff ignored it. Esterhazy escaped justice by fleeing to England, where he confessed his guilt. The collusion of the military high command to keep Dreyfus on Devil's Island indicated the depth of **antisemitism** in France. *See also* MONUMENT HENRY.

SUGGESTED READING: Louis Snyder, *The Dreyfus Case: A Documentary History* (New Brunswick, NJ: Rutgers University Press, 1973).

ETERNAL JEW, THE. *See EWIGE JUDE, DER.*

EUCHARIST. The sacrament of the Lord's Supper; the solemn act of ceremony of commemorating the death of Christ by using bread and wine as the appointed emblems; the communion. Catholics and others who take this sacrament literally believe the bread and wine become the actual body and blood of Christ through transubstantiation. This ritual lent credence to the blood libel hoax and the false charge of **desecration of the Host** during the Middle Ages. *See also* ANTISEMITISM, MYSTICAL.

SUGGESTED READING: Shlomo Simonsohn, *The Apostolic See and the Jews: Documents, 492–1404* (Toronto: Pontifical Institute of Mediaeval Studies, 1988).

EUGENICS. Scientific human breeding. This term was first used in 1883 by Englishman Francis Galton. It referred to the attempts to improve the genetic structure of the human race. American eugenicists argued that Jews and others immigrating into the United States at the turn of the 20th century were inferior and should be restricted. Asserting that Nordics were superior, the **Nazis** sought the destruction of the "anti-race" Jews as imperative to **Aryan** survival and domination. *See also* DAVENPORT, CHARLES BENEDICT; DILLINGHAM COMMISSION; EUTHANASIA; FINAL SOLUTION OF THE JEWISH PROBLEM; IMMIGRATION RESTRICTION LEAGUE; JOHNSON-REED ACT; LAUGHLIN, HARRY.

SUGGESTED READING: Stefan Kuehl, *The Nazi Connection: Eugenics, American Racism and German National Socialism* (New York: Oxford University Press, 1994).

EUGENIUS III (d. 1153). Pope, 1145–53. Though he issued a papal letter of protection, Eugenius's decree did not prevent anti-Jewish attacks during the Second **Crusade**. Furthermore, as Eugenius also decreed that Crusaders did not need to repay interest on any debts to Jews, it is likely that **Louis VII** of France felt justified in forgiving Crusaders their obligations to pay back their loans from Jews.

SUGGESTED READING: Max L. Margolis and Alexander Marx, *A History of the Jewish People* (Philadelphia: Jewish Publication Society, 1927).

EUGENIUS IV (1388–1447). Pope, 1431–47. In 1442 Eugenius IV attacked the Jewish means of living by forbidding Jewish money-lending in Spain and Italy. He further alienated Jews from their neighbors by reinforcing the social separation between Christian and Jew and diminished their safety by abolishing earlier charters. The next year, he issued a bull prohibiting Jews from studying the **Talmud**.

SUGGESTED READING: Max L. Margolis and Alexander Marx, *A History of the Jewish People* (Philadelphia: Jewish Publication Society, 1927).

EUSEBIUS OF ALEXANDRIA (d. 444). Fifth-century ecclesiastical writer. Eusebius indicated that Sundays should remind Christians of "the resurrection of the Lord, the victory over the Jews." He began every paragraph in the first half of his sermon on the Resurrection in this way:

> Woe to you wretches, . . . you were called sons and became dogs. Woe to you, stiff-necked and [spiritually] uncircumcised, from being the Elect of God you became wolves, and sharpened your teeth upon the Lamb of God. You are estranged from His Glory; woe to you, ungrateful wretches, who have loved Hell and its eternal fires. . . . Hell . . . shall imprison you with your father the devil.

SUGGESTED READING: Simon Dubnov, *History of the Jews*, vol. 2, *From the Roman Empire to the Early Medieval Period*, trans. Moshe Spiegel (South Brunswick, NJ: Thomas Yoseloff, 1968).

EUTHANASIA. Mercy killing. Although the term comes from the Greek for "good death," the **Nazi** T-4 euthanasia program was far from it. The first killing centers were established in 1939 where those whom the Nazi doctors deemed mentally and physically "unfit," or life unworthy of life, were gassed. At first, it involved predominantly German Gentiles, not Jews. This program paved the way for the **Holocaust** by rationalizing government-sponsored killing of those who could spread "defective" genetic materials, thereby endangering "**Aryan**" stock. It also corrupted the German medical profession until some German doctors became part and parcel of the mass murder of Jews and others in the Nazi camps. The T-4 program led to the development of **gas chambers** (using carbon monoxide to kill) and crematoriums. *See also* PIUS XII; ZYKLON.

SUGGESTED READING: Saul Friedlander, *The Origins of Nazi Genocide from Euthanasia to Final Solution* (Chapel Hill: University of North Carolina Press, 1995).

EVANS, HIRAM (1881–1966). Colorado **Ku Klux Klan** leader. In 1922, Hiram Evans, a dentist from Dallas, became imperial wizard of the Ku Klux Klan. In 1925 Evans sponsored a Klan day in Noblesville, Indiana, with Hoosier Klansmen joined by delegations from Illinois, Kentucky, Michigan, and Ohio. Evans had just returned from the Washington, DC, Klan parade, in which 40,000 robed men and women marched down Pennsylvania Avenue. He praised the recently passed **Johnson-Reed Act**, which sharply restricted the immigration of certain national and ethnic groups, for building "a stone wall around the nation so tall, so deep and so strong that the scum and riff-raff of the old world cannot get into our gates." "If the Klan is dead," he said, "then America is dead."

SUGGESTED READING: Wyn Craig Wade, *The Fiery Cross: The Ku Klux Klan in America* (New York: Oxford University Press, 1998).

EVIAN CONFERENCE. At President **Franklin Roosevelt**'s suggestion, 32 nations met at the French resort town of Evian on Lake Geneva July 6–15, 1938, to find a solution to the "**refugee problem**," meaning a safe harbor for persecuted Jews. The U.S. delegation was headed not by a government official but by a businessman, Myron Taylor, making it clear the United States would not change its immigration laws. Britain stated it would not accept refugees to Palestine nor its colonies. The other participating nations took the hint—nothing substantial was expected—and closed their doors. The Nazis were then emboldened to pursue their anti-Jewish policies. *See also* BERMUDA CONFERENCE.

SUGGESTED READING: Henry Feingold, *The Politics of Rescue* (New York: Holocaust Library, 1980).

EVIDENCE OF THE HOLOCAUST, SUPPRESSION OF. The U.S. **State Department** made every effort to prevent evidence of the **Holocaust** from being sent to the United States. In January 1943, it relayed to Rabbi Stephen Wise a copy of a telegram detailing the increasing mass murder of Jews in Europe. But on February 10, 1943, a State Department cable was sent to the U.S. legation in Bern attempting to shut down further information about the Holocaust, even though throughout the war, State transmitted without compunction hundreds of private messages from Switzerland to the United States when the subject matter was not atrocity against the Jews. Secretary of the Treasury Henry Morgenthau's staff described the cable as "the most vicious document we have ever read," designed "by diabolical men" to suppress information on the **Final Solution**. Secretary Morgenthau observed, in exasperation, "When you get through with it, the attitude [of members of the State Department] to date is no different from **Hitler**'s attitude." Assistant Secretary of State **Breckinridge Long** initialed the cable, along with four other State Department officials: Ray Atherton, acting chief of State's European Affairs Division;

James Dunn, State's advisor on political relations; and Elbridge Durbrow and John Hickerson, also in the European Affairs Division. Randolph Paul, general counsel of the Treasury Department, described State Department officials involved in America's refugee policy as an "underground movement . . . to let the Jews be killed." Paul was referring to George Brandt, Long's executive assistant; Wallace Murray, another State Department advisor on political affairs; Howard Travers, chief of the Visa Division; and a lesser officer, R. Borden Reams.

Moreover, the U.S. **Office of War Information** (OWI) refused to release information on "barbarous actions and cruelties not serving to directly illuminate the nature of the enemy, but merely to excite horror and hatred of all members of the races guilty of such actions." At the same time, OWI approved American films that attacked the Germans and the Japanese—that is, that accomplished precisely this allegedly proscribed behavior of exciting horror and hatred.

SUGGESTED READING: David Wyman, *The Abandonment of the Jews* (New York: New Press, 1998); Henry Feingold, *The Politics of Rescue: The Roosevelt Administration and the Holocaust* (New York: Holocaust Library, 1980).

EVOLUTIONARY PSYCHOLOGY. Kevin B. MacDonald (1944–), a professor of psychology at California State University–Long Beach, claims that Jews use a "group evolutionary strategy." In his study of "evolutionary psychology," MacDonald asserts that Jewish conscious or unconscious ethnic selfishness and ruthlessness enables Jews to outcompete Gentiles. In *The Culture of Critique*, he argues that such Jewish genetic traits as "high IQ, their ambitiousness, their persistence, their work ethic, and their ability to organize and participate in cohesive, highly commited groups" has enabled Jews to outcompete Gentiles for resources while undermining Gentile power and self-confidence. Although unscientific and flawed, MacDonald's work has found an audience among white supremacists.

SUGGESTED READING: David Lieberman, "Scholarship as an Exercise in Rhetorical Strategy: A Case Study of Kevin MacDonald's Research Techniques," *H-Antisemitism: Occasional Papers* (January 2001).

EWIGE JUDE, DER (*THE ETERNAL JEW*). Nazi propaganda film from 1940. It was one of three films (*Ewige Jude*, *Jud Süss*, and *Die Rothschilds*) commissioned by **Josef Goebbels**'s Propaganda Ministry to mobilize **antisemites** across Europe, the German people, and the Wehrmacht to support the **Third Reich**'s views of the "Jewish Problem" and the necessity to solve it. In *The Eternal Jew*, the filmmaker focused on Jews in the Polish **ghettos** soon after the **Nazis** conquered Poland and created the ghettos in 1939–40. The production was advertised as "the authentic Jew in his native habitat." Under the guise of a documentary, the camera focused on the filth and ugliness of conditions of the Nazi-imposed ghetto. Jews were compared to rats coming out of a sewer. *See also* SUBHUMAN.

SUGGESTED READING: Rolf Giesen, *Nazi Propaganda Films: A History and Filmography* (Jefferson, NC: McFarland, 2003); "*The Eternal Jew*: A Blueprint for Genocide in Nazi Film Archive," Mellon Sawyer Lecture at Yale Genocide Studies Program, October 15, 1998.

EXCOMMUNICATION OF JEWS. Cutting of fellowship between Jews and Christians. During the Middle Ages, the papacy had religious authority all across Europe. It also ruled areas where no effective secular authority existed, both within the **Papal States** and elsewhere. This put many Jews under the papacy's direct jurisdiction. The Church could fine, mutilate, beat, or hang Jews "by order of a bishop or prince." Also, the Church managed to excommunicate Jews by forbidding Christians from sharing "fellowship and drinking, standing together and speaking, coming or going, buying or selling, eating in any location, affection or intercourse" with Jews. In other words, Jews were to be totally separated from "the communion of the faithful in Christ." This boycott was called a "judgment of the Jews," *judicium Judaeorum*, and every pope of the 13th century issued such decrees.

SUGGESTED READING: William Chester Jordan, "Excommunication of the Jews in the Middle Ages," *Jewish History* (Spring 1986): 31–38.

EXETER, COUNCIL OF. The 1287 Church Council of Exeter decreed that Christian women were not to serve in Jewish homes, because "consorting with evil corrupts the good."

SUGGESTED READING: Solomon Grayzel, "Legislation from Provincial and Local Councils Concerning the Jews," in *The Church and the Jews in the XIIIth Century* (Detroit: Wayne State University Press, 1989).

EXODUS 1947. Blockade running displaced persons ship. The *President Warfield*, a converted ferryboat bought by the Palestinian Jewish defense organization Haganah, was renamed *Yetziat Eiropah Tasha—Exodus 1947*. Holding 4,500 survivors of the **Holocaust** and manned by green American Jewish sailors, the crew sought to discharge its refugee passengers in Palestine in July 1947, but was intercepted by British destroyers and boarded by Royal Marines. After a four-hour battle, with several deaths among the passengers and injuries to the crew, the passengers were brought back to internment camps in Germany. The episode drew international attention to the plight of the displaced persons, prompting Great Britain to turn the Palestinian problem over to the United Nations. *See also* WHITE PAPER OF 1939.

SUGGESTED READING: Yoram Kaniuk and Seymore Simeka, *Commander of the* Exodus (New York: Grove Press, 2000).

EXPULSIONS AND BARRING OF ENTRY AND DEPARTURE OF JEWS. Jews were forced to leave and/or refused entry from many polities over the millennia, including Africa (in 1147 and 1790), Arabia (624), Austria (1298), Babylon (586 BCE), Bavaria (1551), Belgium (1370), Czechoslovokia (1745), Denmark (not allowed in until the 17th century), Egypt (1571 BCE, 38 BCE, 3 BCE, 66), England (not allowed in until the 12th century, expelled in 1290), France (561, 1182, 1242, 1306, 1394, 1540, 1682), Germany (1012, 1096, 1146, 1298, 1510, 1614; citizenship revoked in the 1930s; deportations to concentration and death camps in the 1940s), Hungary (1360, 1582, 1717), Iraq (not allowed to emigrate until 2003), Italy (1492, 1540, 1550, 1846), Lebanon (Jews not allowed entrance), Lithuania (1495), the Netherlands (1444), Norway (1814), Palestine (70, 324), Poland (1453, 1772), Portugal (1498), Prussia (1510), Rome (315, 379), Russia (1772, 1881), Saxony (1349), Slovakia (1380, 1744), Spain (612, 694, 1391, 1492–1968), Sweden (until 1782), Switzerland (1939), Syria (Jews not allowed entrance), and the United States (in 1940, Assistant Secretary of State **Breckinridge Long** ordered U.S. consuls to "postpone and postpone and postpone" Jewish visas). *See also* PALE OF SETTLEMENT.

SUGGESTED READING: Paul E. Grosser and Edwin G. Halperin, *Anti-Semitism: The Causes and Effects of a Prejudice* (Secaucus, NJ: Citadel Press, 1979).

EXTERMINATION CAMPS. Nazi death camps. These were concentration camps whose main purpose was to murder Jews and others. The most efficient way to kill, the Nazis discovered, was to subject inmates or newly arrived to poison **gas chambers**. These killing centers consisted of **Auschwitz-Birkenau**, **Belzec**, Chelmno, **Majdanek**, **Sobibor**, and Treblinka. *See also* EICHE, THEODOR; EICHMANN, ADOLF; FINAL SOLUTION OF THE JEWISH PROBLEM; GENOCIDE; GERSTEIN, KURT; GRESE, IRMA; HÖß, RUDOLF; LEUCHTER, FRED; MANDEL, MARIA; MENGELE, JOSEF; NUREMBERG WAR CRIMES TRIALS.

SUGGESTED READING: Yitzhak Arad, *Belzec, Sobibor, Treblinka: The Operation Reinhard Death Camps*, Bloomington: Indiana University Press, 1987.

– F –

FABRICIUS, LAURENTIUS. 16th-century professor of Hebrew at the University of Wittenberg, Germany. Fabricius took up **Martin Luther**'s **antisemitic** ideas, arguing that "the Lord came specially for them, . . . but they made themselves unworthy of eternal life. . . . They . . . opened their mouths and all their senses to the Devil who filled them with all the lies, impiety, and blasphemy." He wrote that Judaism "is . . . 'dung,' stinking animal excrement, which Satan has set before the blind Jews to drink and eat, so as to make those who were nauseated by the dishes of divine mysteries sated with the most stinking excrements."

SUGGESTED READING: Isaiah Shachar, *The Judensau: A Medieval Anti-Jewish Motif and Its History* (London: Warburg Institute, 1974).

FADLALLAH, HUSAYN. *See* HEZBOLLAH.

FAGIN. Fictional character in *Oliver Twist* (1836). Throughout this novel by **Charles Dickens**, the character of Fagin is repeatedly identified as Jewish through the use of negative Jewish stereotypes. Fagin is portrayed as villainous, repulsive, greedy, unkempt, and exploitive of boys, contributing to their moral downfall. Illustrations show a hook-nosed shabby dark figure. The Fagin image became a fixture in stereotyping Jews.

FALANGA. Polish irredentist right-wing organization formed in 1935, part of Obóz Narodowo-Radykalny [National Radical Camp] Falanga. Falanga sought to reestablish a greater Poland. Banned, it went underground. It influenced students to attack Jews in the streets and in universities, with the goal of re-**ghettoizing** the Jews. Falanga was anticommunist as well as anticapitalist. Its gang attacks on Jews persisted until after World War II.

SUGGESTED READING: Yisrael Gutman and Shmuel Krakowski, *Unequal Victims: Poles and Jews during World War II* (New York: Holocaust Library, 1986).

FALWELL, JERRY (1933–). American evangelical Protestant leader. Although Falwell defends Israel and is friendly to Jews, in January 1999, he addressed a pastor's conference in Kingsport, Tennessee, in which he asserted that "the **Antichrist** may possibly be alive on the earth today. . . . When he appears during the Tribulation period he will be a full-grown counterfeit of Christ. Of course, he'll be Jewish."

SUGGESTED READING: Merrill Simon, *Jerry Falwell and the Jews* (Middle Village, NY: Jonathan David, 1999).

FARE, HENRY DE LA. Bishop of Nancy, France. Fare opposed Jewish emancipation during the early **French Revolution**. He wrote that "the people detest [Jews]. . . . They claim that the Jews speculate in grain, they take up too much room, they buy the most beautiful houses, and soon they will own the whole city."

SUGGESTED READING: Jay R. Berkovitz, "The French Revolution and the Jews: Assessing the Cultural Impact," *Association for Jewish Studies Review* 20, no. 1 (1995).

FARHUD. Arabic for "**pogrom**" or "violent dispossession." A pogrom against the 2,600-year-old Jewish presence in Iraq in June 1941. A group of pro-**Nazi** Iraqi officers led by Gen. Rashid Ali staged a coup, forcing the regent, Abdul Illah, to flee. When he returned, a mob attacked a delegation of Iraqi Jews sent to meet the regent at Baghdad airport. Violence quickly spread, and the next day Iraqi policemen joined the attacks on the Jewish community. Shops belonging to Jews were burned, a synagogue was destroyed, and rape, torture, and mutilations were reported. British forces finally quelled the violence by imposing a curfew and shooting violators on sight. As a result of Farhud, hundred of Jews were killed and thousands wounded. The Iraqi government condemned to death eight rioters, including army officers and police. In the decade following this event, Jews were targeted for violence, persecution, boycotts, confiscations, and **expulsion**. The population of Jewish communities in the Muslim Middle East and North Africa has been reduced from almost a million in 1948 to less than 8,000 today.

SUGGESTED READING: Edwin Black, *Banking on Bagdhad* (New York: Wiley, 2004).

FARRAKHAN, LOUIS (1933–). Black Muslim leader. In the African-American community, **antisemitism** seems to be centered in Farrakhan's **Nation of Islam**. Although Farrakhan denies being antisemitic, his divisive approach of focusing on a small proportion of Jews who owned slaves or belonged to organized crime and expanding on them as representatives of all Jews certainly speaks to an antisemitic base. In a 1994 speech, he stated that "The Jews don't like Farrakhan, so they call me **Hitler**. Well, that's a good name. Hitler was a very great man."

SUGGESTED READING: Arthur J. Magida, *Prophet of Rage: The Life of Louis Farrakhan and His Nation* (New York: HarperCollins, 1997).

FASCISM. Rule by dictatorship characterized by hypermilitarism, ultranationalism, state terrorism, and contempt for civil liberties, as seen in **Adolf**

Hitler's Germany and **Benito Mussolini**'s Italy. All aspects of a country's political, social, and cultural life are subordinate to the policies of the dictatorship. During the **Holocaust** years, fascist states such as Italy, Slovakia, Croatia, Hungary, **Vichy** France, and Romania collaborated with the Nazis in persecuting and murdering Jews. *See also* BRITISH UNION OF FASCISTS; FASCIST INTELLECTUALS, FRENCH; ISLAMIC FASCISM.

SUGGESTED READING: Stanley G. Payne, *A History of Fascism, 1914–1945* (Madison: University of Wisconsin Press, 1995).

FASCIST INTELLECTUALS, FRENCH. French **fascism** may be traced from its possible roots in **Maurice Barrès** and **Georges Sorel**, through French fascist **Mussolini**-admirers in the 1920s, to unique French political forms in the 1930s and the **Vichy** regime. Native French fascism is not only a racist, mystical, organic, **blood-and-soil** nationalism but also a transcendence of class. Fascism in France attracted more intellectuals, writers, and theorists than in any other country. **Louis-Ferdinand Céline**, Pierre Drieu la Rochelle, and **Robert Brasillach** conceived of politics as a means to unify the French people, reifying the disparate elements of society into an organic "work of art."

SUGGESTED READING: Zeev Sternhell, *The Birth of Fascist Ideology: From Cultural Rebellion to Political Revolution* (Princeton, NJ: Princeton University Press, 1994); Robert Soucy, "French Fascist Intellectuals in the 1930s: An Old New Left?" *French Historical Studies* 8 (1974); David Carroll, *Nationalism, Antisemitism, and the Ideology of Culture* (Princeton, NJ: Princeton University Press, 1998).

FASSBINDER, RAINER WERNER. *See GARBAGE, THE CITY, AND DEATH, THE.*

FATAH. Arabic for "conquest," specifically by means of *jihad* (Islamic holy war); also a reverse acronym for Harakat al-Tahrir al-Falistiniya, or Palestine Liberation Organization). The Palestine Liberation Organization's military arm. Founded in 1958 in Algeria and headed until his death by **Yassir Arafat**, it was a terrorist organization supported for a time by Syria. Fatah joined the PLO in 1968 and dominated it a year later. Extremely **anti-Zionist** and anti-Israel, it was as the PLO's armed faction that Fatah sought the destroy of the Jewish state. During the 1990s, Fatah renounced terrorism, but it has reverted to violence.

SUGGESTED READING: Walter Laqueur and Barry Rubin, *Israel-Arab Reader* (New York: Penguin, 2001).

FAULHABER, MICHAEL VON (1869–1952). Cardinal and leading Roman Catholic prelate in Germany during the **Third Reich**. During the anti-Jewish activities of the German government in April 1933, Faulhaber opined that there were more important issues for the Church than protecting Jews. He even declined to defend Jews converted to Catholicism because he thought that baptism gave no one leave to expect earthly advantage from it. In his Advent sermons for 1933, he pointed out that

> Israel had repudiated and rejected the Lord's annointed, [and] had . . . nailed Him to the Cross. Then the veil of the Temple was rent, and with it the covenant between the Lord and His people. The daughters of Sion received the bill of divorce, and from that time forth Assuerus [the **Wandering Jew**] wanders, forever.

Faulhaber also proclaimed that "blood and race supplement one another."

SUGGESTED READING: Guenter Lewy, *The Catholic Church and Nazi Germany* (Cambridge, MA: Da Capo Press, 1964); Saul Friedlander, *Nazi Germany and the Jews* (New York: HarperCollins, 1997).

FAULKNER, WILLIAM (1897–1962). American novelist and short-story writer. Over time, Faulkner's portraits of Jewish characters changed to a more tolerant view. Contrasting his early novel *The Sound and the Fury* (1929) with *The Mansion*, written 30 years later, there is a change from the stereotypical association of Jews with the corruptions of capitalism to a picture of courageous Jewish soldiers fighting **fascism** in Spain.

FAURISSON, ROBERT (1929–). Former professor of literature at the University of Lyons, a major **Holocaust denier**. Convinced by **Fred Leuchter**'s false and misleading studies on **gas chambers**, Faurisson concluded that the chambers were not used to murder Jews. He also considered the *Diary of Anne Frank* a work of fiction. Faurisson is a frequent contributor to the *Journal for Historical Review* and testified as a friendly witness for **Ernst Zundel** at his Canadian trial.

SUGGESTED READING: Deborah Lipstadt, *Denying the Holocaust* (New York: Free Press, 1993).

FEDER, GOTTFRIED (1883–1941). German political activist. Feder was one of the founders of the **German Workers Party** in 1919, which **Adolf Hitler** joined and subsequently dominated. Feder helped draft the Twenty-Five Points, a platform in 1920 that would deny Jews civil and political rights. A crusader against interest capitalism and an **antisemite**, Feder advised Hitler on economics. By 1934 he had fallen out of favor as Hitler began to cultivate big business.

SUGGESTED READING: John Dornberg, *Munich 1923* (New York: Harper Books, 1982).

FERDINAND V (1452–1516). King of Castile, 1474–1504; as Ferdinand II, he was also king of Sicily (1468–1516) and of **Aragón** (1479–1516), and as Ferdinand III, king of Naples (1504–16). The union of the Spanish kingdoms of Aragón and Castile was effected in 1469 by Ferdinand's marriage to his cousin Isabella I, queen of Castile. In 1492 the Spanish monarchs expelled the Spanish Jews, though not the **conversos**. *See also* EXPULSIONS AND BARRING OF ENTRY AND DEPARTURE OF JEWS.

SUGGESTED READING: J. H. Elliott, *Imperial Spain, 1469–1716* (New York: Penguin Books, 2002).

FERRER, VINCENT (1350–1419). Spanish **Dominican** friar and preacher. Evangelist Ferrer aggressively sought to **convert** Jews. He converted **synagogues** into churches, fomented riots against Jews, and encouraged princes to establish **ghettos**, particularly in Spain. A mob of **flagellants** usually followed him. Two notable Ferrer converts were **Paul de Burgos** and Geronimo de Santa Fé.

SUGGESTED READING: Yitzhak Baer, *A History of Jews in Christian Spain*, 2 vols. (Philadelphia: Jewish Publication Society, 1992).

FETTMILCH, VINCENT (d. 1616). Fettmilch was a butcher who in 1614 led a mob that attacked the **Frankfurt Ghetto**—where Jewish residences were already marked by insulting signs of **pigs** and scorpions—for two days and nights, leading to the massacre of nearly 3,000 of Frankfurt's Jews; the rest had their property expropriated and were expelled. The German emperor Mathius stepped in and restored order, hanged Fettmilch, and then welcomed back the Jews.

SUGGESTED READING: Christopher Friedrichs, "Politics or Pogrom? The Fettmilch Uprising in German Jewish History," *Central European History* 19, no. 2 (June 1986): 180–225.

FEUJ. (French slur) A Verlan (a form of French slang, with words comprised of adjusted reversed syllables) inverting the two syllables of the French word for Jew, *Juif.*

SUGGESTED READING: "List of Ethnic Slurs," *Wikipedia*, http://en .wikipedia.org/wiki/List_of_ethnic_slurs.

FEURBACH, LUDWIG (1804–1872). German philosopher. Although Feurbach critiqued Christianity, he regarded it as superior to Judaism, which he saw as egotistical, materialistic, self-centered, and unfriendly to any outsiders. He wrote in *The Essence of Christianity*: "Judaism is worldly Christianity; Christianity, spiritual Judaism. The Christian religion is the Jewish religion purified from national egoism." **Karl Marx** and **Frederick Engels** were heavily influenced by his writings. *See also* MISANTHROPY.

SUGGESTED READING: Uriel Tal, *Christians and Jews in Germany: Politic and Ideology in the Second Reich, 1870–1914* (Ithaca, NY: Cornell University Press, 1975).

FEYDEAU, ERNEST (1821–1873). French writer. In "Les mémoires d'un coulissier," Feydeau described Bordeaux as "always the great nursery that fed the Stock Exchange of the sons of Israel." Starting with nothing, suddenly the Jews became "masters of the marketplace. Soon they ruled it like tyrants. . . . Christian beasts, who have good backs, . . . do not know how to defend themselves."

SUGGESTED READING: Béatrice Philippe, *Etre Juif dans la société française* (Paris: Montalba, 1979).

FICHTE, JOHANN GOTTLIEB (1762–1814). German philosopher, writer, and student of **Immanuel Kant**. In 1793 Fichte argued that Judaism comprised a "state within the state" hostile to, and at war with, all other states of Europe. Later, he maintained that only Germans could be genuine Christians. He advocated **expulsion** of Jews from Germany or one night Christians could "chop off all their heads and replace them with new ones, in which there would not be one single Jewish idea." His explosive combination of Christian **antisemitism** and German nationalism would become the fundamental ideological stimulus of the **Holocaust**. *See also* YOUNG HEGELIANS.

SUGGESTED READING: Uriel Tal, *Christians and Jews in Germany* (Ithaca, NY: Cornell University Press, 1975).

FIELDING, HENRY (1707–1754). English novelist, playwright, essayist, journalist, lawyer, jurist, and magistrate. In several places in his work, Fielding makes **antisemitic** remarks reflecting English popular culture. In *Tom Jones* (1748)—a novel without a Jewish character—when a £100 note falls from a pocketbook offered to Tom Jones, Fielding quips that "a *Jew* would have jumped to purchase it at five shillings less than £100." In *Enquiries into the Causes of the Late Increase of Robbers* (1751), Fielding refers to Jews as fences for stolen goods, which may have influenced **Charles Dickens**'s *Oliver Twist* and its **Fagin** character.

SUGGESTED READING: Frank Felsenstein, *Antisemitic Stereotypes: A Paradigm of Otherness in English Popular Culture, 1660–1830* (Baltimore: Johns Hopkins University Press, 1995).

FIELDS, EDWARD. *See* NATIONAL STATES RIGHTS PARTY.

FIERY CROSS. *See* KU KLUX KLAN.

FILM INDUSTRY, NAZI PURGE OF. Universum Film Aktiengesellschaft (UFA) was the home of the German film industry from 1917 to 1945 during the **Weimar Republic** and the **Third Reich**. Under the Third Reich, UFA, controlled by **Josef Goebbels**'s Propaganda Ministry, produced musicals as well as vicious **antisemitic** propaganda. In March 1933, as part of the **Nazi** assault on Jews in German culture, UFA purged its Jewish employees, which aggravated the flight of Jewish, part-Jewish, and other artists and intellectuals from Nazi Germany. Director Fritz Lang joined Peter Lorre and others in Hollywood. *See also* DEGENERATE ART; THEATER, NAZI PURGE OF.

SUGGESTED READING: Rolf Giesen, *Nazi Propaganda Films: A History and Filmography* (Jefferson, NC: McFarland, 2003); Linda Sculte-Sasse, *Entertaining the Third Reich* (Durham, NC: Duke University Press, 1996).

FINAL SOLUTION OF THE JEWISH PROBLEM (*ENDLÖSUNG DER JUDENFRAGE*). A euphemism for the mass murder of Jews after World War II began. The very presence of Jews was a problem for Germany, a "harmful nation within a nation" that demanded resolution. **Hermann Goering** used the term *Endlösung* in a letter to **Reinhard Heydrich** charging him at the **Wannsee Conference** (January 20, 1942) with making arrangements for the already-decided "complete solution" of the Jewish problem. *See also* FICHTE, JOHANN GOTTLIEB.

SUGGESTED READING: Christopher R. Browning and Jurgen Matthaus, *The Origins of the Final Solution: The Evolution of Nazi Jewish Policy, September 1939–March 1942* (Lincoln: University of Nebraska Press, 2004).

FISCUS JUDAICUS. *See* TAXATION OF JEWS.

FITZGERALD, F. SCOTT (1896–1940). American short-story writer and novelist. In Fitzgerald's 1937 essay "Echoes of the Jazz Age," Fitzgerald wrote:

By 1928, Paris had grown suffocating. With each new shipment of Americans spewed up by the boom, the quality fell off, until toward the end there was something sinister about the crazy boatloads. . . . I remember a fat Jewess inlaid with diamonds, who sat behind us at the Russian ballet and said as the curtain rose, "That's luffly, they ought to baint a picture of it." This was low comedy. . . . There were citizens traveling in luxury in 1928 and 1929 who, in the distortion of their new condition, had the human value of Pekinese, bivalves, cretins, goats.

Fitzgerald's finest novel, *The Great Gatsby* (1925), has been denounced by Milton Hindus as reading "virtually like an **antisemitic** tract." Later in life, Fitzgerald's antisemitism relented when he visited **Nazi** Germany and then spent years writing in Hollywood, where he met a variety of Jews.

SUGGESTED READING: Alan Margolies, "The Maturing of F. Scott Fitzgerald," *Twentieth-Century Literature* (Spring 1997); Milton Hindus, "F. Scott Fitzgerald and Literary Antisemitism: A Footnote on the Mind of the Twenties," *Commentary* 3 (1947).

FIVE PERCENTERS. Universal Flag of Islam, Five Percent Nation, the Nation of Gods and Earths. The number 7 superimposed over a five-pointed Islamic star and Islamic crescent image, itself superimposed on a sun image. Clarence Smith (also known as Father Allah), a former Nation of Islam (NOI) member, founded the Five Percenters in New York City in 1964. The Five Percenters derives its name from the belief that only 5 percent of the population is righteous. Five Percenters are racists who believe that blacks are the original people of Earth, that they founded all civilization, and that the "blackman" is god. They also believe that whites have deceived the whole world, causing it to honor and worship false gods and idols.

SUGGESTED READING: Anti-Defamation League, *Hate on Display: Extremist Symbols, Logos, and Tattoos* (New York: Anti-Defamation League, 2006).

FIVE WORDS. "I have nothing to say." Alex Curtis, a San Diego–based white supremacist, coined the phrase, indicating that white racists in the United States should use the five words to demonstrate a "code of silence" to help avoid prosecution by law enforcement agencies.

SUGGESTED READING: Anti-Defamation League, *Hate on Display: Extremist Symbols, Logos, and Tattoos* (New York: Anti-Defamation League, 2006); ADL Law Enforcement Agency Resource Network, *A Visual Database of Extremist Symbols, Logos, and Tattoos*, http://www.adl.org/hate_symbols/default.asp.

FLAGELLANTS. European penitents inflicting pain on themselves and each other—and on other, less cooperative victims. Sometimes 10,000 strong, they traveled from town to town doing public penance. They believed the Black Plague was a manifestation of God's anger and sought to appease Him. Starting in the Italian States in 1260, the Flagellants spread into Europe and continued until Pope **Clement VI** banned them in 1360. When they arrived in a town, they often attacked the Jewish **ghetto** and murdered Jews, accusing them of **poisoning the wells**. *See also* FERRER, VINCENT.

SUGGESTED READING: Norman Cantor, *In the Wake of the Plague* (New York: Perennial, 2002).

FLIEGENDE BLÄTTER. German humor magazine. Between the world wars, favorite topics for German cartoons were the economy, the bourgeoisie, the power of money, bribery, corruption, and the aristocracy. European and German cartoonists found a wealth of subject matter to ridicule in the Jews. Cartoonists caricatured European Jews as inconsistent symbols of cheapness, black marketeering, **usury**, and Marxism, portraying them with satanic red hair, huge hooked noses, thick eyebrows, fat lips and bellies, and dirty clothes. Jews were stereotyped as having no loyalty to their nations, only money serving as their native land. Judaism was portrayed as hollow and hypocritical. This "Jewish monster" of caricature and cartoon may have worsened the indifference Europeans felt to the mass murder of Jews during the **Holocaust**.

SUGGESTED READING: Zel Rozental, "Cartoon's Role in the 20th Century," http://www.nd-karikaturvakfi.org.tr/yiryuzkar.htm.

FLORENCE, COUNCIL OF. In 1442, the Council of Florence held that "no one remaining outside the Catholic Church, not only pagans, but Jews, **heretics**, or schismatics, can become partakers of eternal life; but they will go to the 'eternal fire prepared for the devil and his angels' [Matthew 25:41]."

SUGGESTED READING: Richard McBrien, *Catholicism* (Minneapolis, MN: Winston Press, 1981).

FOETOR JUDAICUS. Latin for "Jew stink." People in the Middle Ages claimed Jews had a distinct body odor—a stink associated with Judaism. It was further believed that the Jews needed to drink Christian blood to rid themselves of the Jew smell, thus the **ritual murder** defamation.

SUGGESTED READING: Robert Chazan, *Medieval Stereotypes, Modern Antisemitism* (Berkeley: University of California Press, 1997).

FONTANE, THEODOR (1819–1898). German writer. Fontane was the first master of the realistic novel in Germany. He revealed the situation of contemporary Berlin society. Although his writing contains elements of **philosemitism**, he inconsistently wished for a *"schwere Heimsuchung"* (serious misfortune) to befall the Jews.

SUGGESTED READING: Irving Massey, "Philo-Semitism in Nineteenth-Century German Literature," in *Condicio Judaica*, vol. 29 (Tübingen, Germany: Max Niemeyer, 2000).

FORAIN, JEAN-LOUIS (1852–1931). French artist. One of the world's great etchers, Forain's cartoons and caricatures appeared frequently in the anti-Jewish publications of **Edouard Drumont**. The three greatest cartoonists of the 19th century—**Adolphe Willette**, **Emmanuel Poiré** (Caran d'Ache), and Forain—drew anti-Jewish material that elicited in many **antisemitic** emotions.

SUGGESTED READING: Robert Byrnes, *Antisemitism in Modern France* (New Brunswick, NJ: Rutgers University Press, 1950); Norman Kleeblatt, "The Dreyfus Affair: A Visual Record," in *The Dreyfus Affair: Art, Truth, and Justice* (Berkeley: University of California Press, 1987).

FORBY (Australian slur) Rhyming slang for Jew. "Forby" is short for four-by-two (a piece of wood four inches by two), which rhymes with Jew.

SUGGESTED READING: "List of Ethnic Slurs," *Wikipedia*, http://en .wikipedia.org/wiki/List_of_ethnic_slurs.

FORCED LABOR CAMPS. More than seven million foreign workers were conscripted for labor under **Nazi** occupation policies. Some were paid; many were not. Often, they were impressed, along with prisoners of war. Those Jews who were allowed temporarily to survive were forced into slave labor. Frequently, sites of slave labor, industries, mines, and so forth were near Jewish **ghettos** and concentration camps. The most notorious was Monowitz, near **Auschwitz-Birkenau**. The practice of forced labor was generally inhumane, with the aim of working prisoners to the maximum—often to death—with the absolute minimum of food or care. One example of an exception to this rule was the experience of those workers under Oskar Schindler of the famous *Schindler's List*. *See also* LEY, ROBERT; SAUCKEL, FRITZ.

SUGGESTED READING: Joseph Borkin, *The Crime and Punishment of I. G. Farben* (New York: Free Press, 1978).

FORD, HENRY (1863–1947). American industrialist, inventor, and financier. In his autobiography, Ford wrote that Jews were "a sinister element" in this country. "We must not suffer [this] stranger, the destroyer, the hater of happy humanity, to divide our people." Ford claimed that the Jews had corrupted American "literature, amusements, and social conduct" and that Jews possess

> a nasty Orientalism which has insidiously affected every channel of expression— and to such an extent that it was time to challenge it. The fact that these influences are all traceable to one racial source is a fact to be reckoned with. [The Jews have persisted in an] economic or intellectually subversive warfare upon Christian society. . . . If they are as wise as they claim to be, they will labor to make Jews American, instead of laboring to make America Jewish. The genius of the United States of America is Christian in the broadest sense, and its destiny is to remain Christian.

Ford anticipated **Adolf Hitler**'s ideas that the Jews had conspired to start World War I. On May 22, 1920, Ford's *Dearborn Independent* began a series of more than 90 **antisemitic** articles based on *The Protocols of the Elders of Zion*. The series helped turn the newspaper into America's leading anti-Jewish journal, with a nationwide circulation of a half-million readers. **Ku Klux Klan** editors later collected several of the *Independent*'s articles into a four-volume book, *The International Jew*, which sold 10 million copies in the United States and millions more in South America, the Near East, and Europe. The **Nazi** World Service distributed *The International Jew* widely in Germany as *The Eternal Jew*. Hitler was reported in the American press to have said, "We look to Heinrich Ford as the leader of the growing **Fascist** movement in America," and "I regard Henry Ford as my inspiration." Despite his later claims to be rid of antisemitism, by 1939 signs like these appeared on the parking-lot gates of Ford's Rouge River plants: "Jews are traitors to America and should not be trusted—Buy Gentile."

SUGGESTED READING: Neil Baldwin, *Henry Ford and the Jews* (Cambridge, MA: Perseus/Public Affairs Press, 2002).

FÖRSTER-NIETZSCHE, ELISABETH. In the 1880s, Förster-Nietzsche left Germany for Paraguay with her husband, the notorious **antisemite** Bernhard Förster, to found a German-**Aryan** colony free of Jews and based on antisemitic principles. She would later become a **Nazi Party** member and an admirer of **Adolf Hitler**.

SUGGESTED READING: H. F. Peters, *Zarathustra's Sister* (New York: Crown, 1977).

FORTALITIUM FIDEI. See ESPINA, ALFONSO DE.

FOUNDATIONS OF THE NINETEENTH CENTURY. A two-volume work published in 1899 by **Houston Stewart Chamberlain**, accusing

Jews of corrupting and degenerating German society, whereas all great accomplishments of civilization were achieved by **Aryans**. In Chamberlain's view Jesus was an Aryan. The Germans, purest of Aryans, were the master race. **Adolf Hitler** and Nazi ideologists borrowed heavily from *Foundations*. *See also ESSAY ON THE INEQUALITY OF THE HUMAN RACES*; GOBINEAU, ARTHUR DE.

FOUNDING MYTHS OF THE STATE OF ISRAEL, THE (*LES MYTHES FONDATEURS DE LA POLITIQUE ISRAÉLIENNE*). *See* GARAUDY, ROGER.

FOURIER, CHARLES (1772–1837). French utopian socialist. Fourier wrote: "Ah! Has there ever been a nation more despicable than the Hebrews, who have achieved nothing in art and science, and who are distinguished only by a record of crime and brutality which at every page of their loathsome annals makes you sick!" They are "parasites, merchants, usurers." He called the Jews "the enemies of God." The Jewish religion, he wrote, "furthers vices [and] gives its adherents a dangerously immoral character." *See also* ALHAIZA, ADOLPHE.

SUGGESTED READING: Edmund Silberner, "Charles Fourier on the Jewish Question," *Jewish Social Studies* 8, no. 4 (1946).

FOURTEEN WORDS. "We must secure the existence of our people and a future for white children." A white supremicist slogan coined by the now imprisoned racist David Lane, a member of the **Silent Brotherhood**. It has become the battle cry and rallying slogan for the white supremacist movement.

SUGGESTED READING: Anti-Defamation League, *Hate on Display: Extremist Symbols, Logos, and Tattoos* (New York: Anti-Defamation League, 2006); ADL Law Enforcement Agency Resource Network, *A Visual Database of Extremist Symbols, Logos, and Tattoos*, http://www.adl.org/hate_symbols/default.asp.

FOURTH REICH. "Fourth Reich" alludes to **Hitler's Third Reich** and to the goal of establishing another society ruled by **Nazi** ideology. A California-based **neo-Nazi** skinhead gang active in the early 1990s adopted the name "Fourth Reich Skins," but appears to have largely disbanded after leaders in the gang were arrested and convicted in 1993 for conspiring to commit bombings and murders. In more recent years, Fourth Reich Skins have been active in Arizona. Gang members or affiliates may sport tattoos with the words "Fourth Reich" or the Fourth Reich symbol **4R**. In addition, nonassociated white supremacists may sometimes use "Fourth Reich" symbolism as well.

SUGGESTED READING: Anti-Defamation League, *Hate on Display: Extremist Symbols, Logos, and Tattoos* (New York: Anti-Defamation League, 2006).

FRANCE JUIVE, LA (*JEWISH FRANCE*). Two-volume diatribe (1886) by the French journalist **Edouard Drumont** that catalyzed the preexisting **antisemitic** movement in France and set the stage for the **antidreyfusards**. Drumont blamed Jews for the **French Revolution**, for the collapse of the leading Catholic bank, and for planning to destroy Christianity. This polemicist believed Jews were obscenely wealthy and exploited Christians. The "alien body" of Jews should be driven out of France in a savage way, he said, and then France's social problems would end. The book is replete with racist stereotypes. Drumont presented his parish priest with the manuscipt before it was published to ensure that it conformed to traditional Catholic antisemitism. *See also* DREYFUS CASE.

SUGGESTED READING: Malcolm Hay, *Europe and the Jews* (Boston: Beacon Press, 1968).

FRANCO, G. G. In 1896, Franco, a French Catholic priest, wrote that in the Jewish-controlled lodges of the **Freemasons**, "the obscene worship of objects . . . is always a part of the cult of Satan . . . and of hatred of the Christ of God." Franco accused Jewish organizations in Germany, France, and the United States (the **B'nai B'rith**), along with the Masons, of being dedicated to the worship of the Devil. He suggested that "the race of [**Judas**] **Iscariot**" be awarded the status of strangers, with legal protection but without full rights of **citizenship**. He saw the solution to the Jewish problem in "the abolition of their civic equality," their re-**ghettoization**, **confiscation of Jewish property**, and "the return of temporal rule to the Holy Throne of the Papacy." *See also CIVILTÀ CATTOLICA.*

SUGGESTED READING: "Le logge israelitiche secrete pienamente illustrate," *Civiltà Cattolica* 16a, ser. 6 (1896).

FRANK, HANS (1900–1946). **Nazi** legal and administrative official who wrote anti-Jewish legislation in the 1930s. As governor of Occupied Poland during World War II, Frank participated in the **ghettoization** and internment of Jews in concentration camps, and hence in the **Final Solution**. He was one of the very few defendants at the **Nuremberg War Crimes Trials** who admitted his guilt for involvement in the mass murders of Jews. *See also* SEYSS-INQUART, ARTHUR.

SUGGESTED READING: Eugene Davidson, *The Trial of the Germans* (New York: Macmillan, 1966).

FRANK, LEO (1884–1915). American victim of anti-Jewish violence. Although anti-Yankee feelings, economic jealousies, and political opportunism were factors in the arrest, wrongful conviction, and murder of Leo Frank in Atlanta in 1913–15, religious **antisemitism** was the crucial cause. An educated Brooklyn Jew and president of the Atlanta **B'nai B'rith**, Frank was arrested and convicted of murdering a Christian girl, Mary Phagan, his employee and the daughter of a poor tenant farmer. Although the Georgia governor commuted Frank's death sentence, he was lynched by a crowd of "respectable" Southern gentlemen.

SUGGESTED READING: Leonard Dinnerstein, *The Leo Frank Case* (Athens: University of Georgia Press, 1998).

FRANKFURT GHETTO. On January 14, 1711, a huge fire destroyed the entire Jewish **ghetto** of Frankfurt am Main, Germany. Thirty-six Torah scrolls went up in flames. The German magistrate put all sorts of obstacles in the way of rebuilding the ghetto. After temporary shelter in nearby homes, all Jews had to return to the ghetto (Judengasse). *See also* FETTMILCH, VINCENT.

SUGGESTED READING: Simon Dubnov, *History of the Jews*, vol. 4, *From Cromwell's Commonwealth to the Napoleonic Era*, trans. Moshe Spiegel (South Brunswick, NJ: Thomas Yoseloff, 1971).

FRANKISTS. Heretical Jewish cult. The Frankists were a mystical faction, a Sabbatarian and Kabalistic movement in mid-18th century Europe that downplayed Torah and **Talmud** in favor of a Judaism based on the Zohar, a book of mysticism. Their "services" included unrestrained sexual behavior. They believed salvation came through promiscuous behavior. Frankists discarded Jewish laws and customs. They were excommunicated for **heresy** by a congress of rabbis in Brody, Russia. The movement's founder, Jacob Frank (1726–1791), led a debate with rabbis in Poland in 1757 with Catholic clerics as judges. When, after the debate the cult converted to Christianity, the Polish Catholic bishop who sponsored the debate burned more than 1,000 copies of the Talmud.

SUGGESTED READING: "The Visions of the Lord, Jacob Frank," *Proceedings of the Tenth World Congress of Jewish Studies*, 1990.

FRANTZ, CONSTANTINE. 19th-century German writer. Frantz argued that "Jews have excluded themselves from the community founded by

Christianity, and no one can ever free them from that punishment. . . . The Jews by rejecting Christian authority cannot have any right of **citizenship**."

SUGGESTED READING: John Weiss, *Ideology of Death* (Chicago: Ivan Dee, 1995); Paul Rose, *Revolutionary Antisemitism in Germany from Kant to Wagner* (Princeton: Princeton University Press, 1990).

FREE GERMANY MOVEMENT IN SWITZERLAND (BEWEGUNG "FREIES DEUTSCHLAND" IN DER SCHWEIZ). A movement in Switzerland during World War II that consisted of almost every stripe of anti-Nazi, including Catholic exiles, followers of **Karl Barth**, former members of the German State Party, Social Democrats, Communists, and apoliticals. *See also* JEWISH QUESTION IN POSTWAR GERMANY.

SUGGESTED READING: David Bankier, "The Jews in Plans for Postwar Germany," *Jewish Political Studies Review* 14, nos. 3–4 (Fall 2002).

FREEMASONS. Secret fraternal order founded in England in 1717. It had international links and held liberal beliefs such as racial equality, universalism, and humanitarianism. Anti-Freemasonry rhetoric became common for right-wing organizations beginning in 1840. The Masonic lodges were falsely accused of being a cover for the mythical Jewish conspiracy to destroy Christianity as well as traditional conservative society. This bizarre charge was asserted in the notorious forgery known as ***The Protocols of the Elders of Zion***.

SUGGESTED READING: Jacob Katz, *Jews and Freemasons in Europe, 1723–1939* (Cambridge, MA: Harvard University Press, 1970).

FREIKORPS. Unofficial paramilitary groups of German army veterans (1918–1923). The Freikorps blamed Germany's defeat in World War I and the **Versailles** Treaty on Social Democrats and Jews. Extremely right-wing and supranationalist, Freikorpsmen, after their discharge from service in World War I, aided in defeating the Spartacus rebellion. They murdered Spartacus Party (communist) leader **Rosa Luxemburg** in 1919. Many Freikorps members joined the **Nazi** Sturmabteilung (**SA**) in the 1920s.

SUGGESTED READING: Nigel H. Jones, *Hitler's Heralds: The Story of the Freikorps* (New York: Dorset Press, 1992).

FRENCH REVOLUTION. Overthrow of the old monarchy and aristocratic order in France, 1789–1804. The most ardent advocate of Jewish emancipation was Stanislas, Duke of Clermont-Tonnerre, a French parliamentary member. A few months after France's Declaration of the Rights of Man and the Citizen, he argued before the National Assembly on December 23, 1789, that only the prejudiced opposed freedom for all citizens, including Jews. Maximilien Robespierre, then a representative to the Assembly, also favored providing the Jews with "the self-respect of men and of citizens." But a combination of anti-ecclesiastical radicals such as the Alsacian deputy **Jean-François Rewbell** and traditional Catholics like Abbé **Jean Maury** and Bishop **Henry de la Fare** of Nancy persuaded the deputies to defeat the extension of full civil liberties to Jews. On December 24, the day after the debate on Jewish emancipation, the Assembly awarded civil rights to Protestants, but not to Jews. In January 1790, the Assembly granted **citizenship** to 3,000 Sephardic Jews living in southwest France and in September 1791 to 30,000 **Ashkenazic** Jews of Alsace and Lorraine. Freedom was awarded only to those French Jews who explicitly renounced their membership in Jewish communities, and although the French government assumed the debts of the Christian Churches, they refused to do so for the Jewish communities. The Revolution also established civil rights temporarily for Jews in the nations that **Napoleon** conquered all across Europe.

SUGGESTED READING: Michael Graetz, *The Jews in Nineteeth-Century France from the French Revolution to the Alliance Israelite Universelle*, trans. Jane Marie Todd (Stanford, CA: Stanford University Press, 1996).

FREUD, SIGMUND (1856–1938). Viennese founder of psychoanalysis. Freud entered psychiatry in part because there was discrimination against Jewish physicians in the Austro-Hungarian Empire in the more prestigious medical fields. His colleagues in the movement were mostly Jewish, as were his audiences and patients. Freud appointed **Carl Jung**, a Swiss Protestant, as president of the Psychoanalytical Association to make the movement seem less Jewish and more universal. However, Jung left to flirt with **Aryan** collective unconsciousness.

SUGGESTED READING: Peter Gay, *Freud, Jews, and Other Germans* (New York: Oxford University Press, 1978).

FREYTAG, GUSTAV. German novelist. His 1855 realistic and humorous novel *Soll und Haben* (*Debit and Credit*), translated into almost all the languages of Europe, was hailed as the best German novel of its day. It contrasts middle-class Germanic virtues with the shiftless Pole and the rapacious Jew.

SUGGESTED READING: Klaus L. Berghahn, "Literarischer Antisemitismus: Untersuchungen zu Gustav Freytag und anderen burgerlichen

Schriftstellern des 19. Jahrhunderts," *Shofar: An Interdisciplinary Journal of Jewish Studies* 19, no. 4 (Summer 2001).

FRIENDS OF THE NEW GERMANY. Pro–Nazi Germany group organized in the United States in 1936 that evolved from a series of nationwide German-American groups formed after World War I. The Free Society of Teutonia was organized in 1924, followed by the Friends of the **Hitler** Movement and the Friends of the New Germany. Carrying flags emblazoned with **swastikas**, the emblem of the Nazi movement, older bundists and young campers paraded in uniform—displaying stiff-armed salutes and singing the Nazi marching song, "Horst Wessel." Later, it was discovered that plans to commit espionage and sabotage in the future were also discussed. *See also* GERMAN-AMERICAN BUND.

SUGGESTED READING: Robert E. Herzstein, *Roosevelt and Hitler: Prelude to War* (New York: Paragon Books, 1989).

FRIES, JACOB (1773–1843). Fries published a pamphlet, *On the Danger Posed to the Welfare and Character of the German People by the Jews*, portraying the Jews as bloodsuckers of the people and contaminants of the purity of German life. He advocated the suppression of Jewish educational institutions; prohibition of Jewish immigration into Germany as well as encouragement of Jewish emigration from Germany; prevention of Jews from marrying Gentiles; prohibition of Christian servants, especially maids, to work for Jews; and **stigmatic emblems** for Jews.

SUGGESTED READING: Paul Johnson, *A History of the Jews* (New York: HarperPerennial, 1987).

FRITSCH, THEODOR (1852–1933). German historian. Fritsch founded an **antisemitic** publishing house, Hammer, whose major publication was the **Antisemitic Catechism**, and was leader of the Reichshammerbundes. Fritsch's major ideas were adopted by the **Nazis**, including a dejudaized Christianity; no physical or social intercourse with Jews; no business relations with them; no use of Jewish doctors, lawyers, or teachers; and a **boycott of Jewish shops**. Fritsch became a member of the Nazi Reichstag (German parliament) and was honored by Nazis as the "Old Master." *See also DAS IST DER JUDE!*

SUGGESTED READING: Paul Massing, *Rehearsal for Destruction: A Study of Political Antisemitism in Imperial Germany* (New York: Fertig, 1967).

FRUMMER. (British slur) A Hasidic Jew, from the Yiddish word *frum*, meaning "devout."

SUGGESTED READING: "List of Ethnic Slurs," *Wikipedia*, http://en
.wikipedia.org/wiki/List_of_ethnic_slurs.

FUGU PLAN. Having received *The Protocols of the Elders of Zion* from
White Russian émigrés who had fought with the Japanese against the Soviets after World War I, five of the most powerful men in Japan—Prime Minister Prince Konoye, Foreign Minister Arita Hachiro, Army Minister
Itagaki Seishiro, Naval Minister Yonai Mitsumasa, and Ikeda Shigeaki,
minister of finance, commerce, and industry—in 1938, believing the *Protocols* to be a valid description of Jewish power and wealth, theorized that
world Jewry would be grateful for a haven from the **Nazis** and would persuade U.S. president **Franklin Roosevelt** to adopt a hands-off policy
toward Japan's imperialist expansion in Asia and that the Jews would help
them build a Greater East Asia Co-Prosperity Sphere. *Fugu* is a deadly
poisonous blowfish which, after it is carefully detoxified, the Japanese eat
as a delicacy. The Japanese considered that the Jews, once their "poison"
was removed, would be a highly valuable "nation." The goal was to settle
Jews in Manchuria. The plan was never put into effect, but Shanghai, a
Chinese port captured by Japanese forces in 1937, already contained an
international section and proved more convenient. The Japanese government allowed 20,000 refugee Jews to settle there without visas or other
documents. Chiune Sugihara, using his position as Japan's consul in
Kovno, Lithuania, gave thousands of exit and transit visas to fleeing Jews
in 1939–40.

SUGGESTED READING: James Ross, *Escape to Shanghai: A Jewish Community in China* (New York: Free Press, 1994); Marvin Tokayer and Mary
Swartz, *The Fugu Plan: The Untold Story of the Japanese and the Jews
during World War II* (London: Paddington Press, 1979); Hillel Levine, *In
Search of Sugihara: The Banality of Good* (New York: Free Press, 1996).

FÜHRER. *See* HITLER, ADOLF.

FULDA. Town in the Prussian province of Hesse-Cassel; the site of massacres of Jews. In 1238 **Crusaders** murdered Jews in Fulda after charging
them with blood libel. In 1309 more than 600 Jews were killed because
they supposedly brought on the plague. In 1671 Jews were expelled, but
later reinstated. The Nazis deported the Fulda Jewish community during
the **Holocaust**. Since 1829, Fulda has been the site of the annual German
Catholic bishops conference.

SUGGESTED READING: Gavin Langmuir, *Toward a Definition of Antisemitism* (Berkeley: University of California Press, 1990).

– G –

GABARDINE-STROKING MONKEY. (U.S. slur) Reference to Jews in the clothing business.

SUGGESTED READING: "List of Ethnic Slurs," *Wikipedia*, http://en .wikipedia.org/wiki/List_of_ethnic_slurs.

GALLICO, PAUL (1897–1976). U.S. novelist and sportswriter; sports editor for the *New York Daily News*. In 1938, in his book *Farewell to Sport,* Gallico wrote, "The reason, I suspect, that basketball appeals to the Hebrew with his Oriental background is that the game places a premium on an alert scheming mind, flashy trickiness, artful dodging and general smart aleckness."

SUGGESTED READING: Paul Gallico, *Farewell to Sport* (London: International Polygonics, 1990); Jon Entine, *Taboo: Why Black Athletes Dominate Sports and Why We're Afraid to Talk about It* (New York: Public Affairs, 2001); *Journal of Sport History* 26, no. 1 (Spring 1999).

GARAUDY, ROGER (1913–). French **Holocaust denier**. In 1998, a French court found Garaudy, a convert to Islam, guilty of Holocaust denial and racial **defamation**, fining him $40,000 for his 1995 book, *The Founding Myths of the State of Israel* (*Les mythes fondateurs de la politique israélienne*). Endorsing the views of **Robert Faurisson**, Garaudy's book declared that during the **Holocaust**, Jews were not killed in **extermination camps**. The book was quickly translated into Arabic and Persian, and a Muslim legal team represented Garaudy at his trial. He became a hero in much of the Muslim world, with the **Iranian** government and United Arab Emirates paying his fine.

SUGGESTED READING: Robert S. Wistrich, *Muslim Antisemitism: A Clear and Present Danger* (New York: American Jewish Committee, 2002).

GARBAGE, THE CITY, AND DEATH, THE. Rainer Werner Fassbinder's play *The Garbage, the City, and Death* concerns a poor prostitute, Roma, who begins to prosper when she finds a wealthy client referred to as "The Rich Jew." The Rich Jew is a real estate speculator and works for the city government. Roma's husband and pimp, Franz, becomes discouraged by Roma's success and leaves her, and Roma convinces the Rich Jew to kill her rival. The Rich Jew avoids being charged with the crime through his connections with the city government. Fassbinder's play was blocked from performance in Germany four times, in 1975, 1984, 1985, and 1998, on the grounds that the play would antagonize the relationship between the German Christian and German Jewish communities. German critics accused the play of **antisemitism** when it was printed in the *Frankfurter Allgemeine Zeitung*. The publisher withdrew all copies of the play and announced that it would not be reprinted until Fassbinder changed the name of the Rich Jew character.

SUGGESTED READING: "Censorship," in *A World Encyclopedia* (London: Fitzroy Dearborn, 1999).

GARRISON, WILLIAM LLOYD (1805–1879). Noted American abolitionist minister. Garrison called the ancient Jews an exclusivist people "whose feet ran to evil," and he thought that Jews deserved their "miserable dispersion in various parts of the earth, which continues to this day."

SUGGESTED READING: William Lloyd Garrison, *The Letters of William Lloyd Garrison*, 6 vols. (Cambridge, MA: Belknap Press of Harvard University Press, 1971–81).

GARTENLAUBE, DIE. A right-wing, **antisemitic**, anti-French German newspaper. The first German newspaper with mass circulation, in 1876 it had five million readers. In a letter of April 1890, **Friedrich Engels** wrote: "I myself was dubbed a Jew by the *Gartenlaube* and, indeed, if given the choice, I'd as soon be a Jew as a 'Herr von.'" *See also* BERLIN MOVEMENT.

SUGGESTED READING: Hazel E. Rosenstrauch, "Zum Beispiel Die Gartenlaube," in *Trivialliteratur,* ed. Annamaria Rucktäschel and Hans Dieter Zimmermann (Munich: Fink, 1976).

GAS CHAMBERS. Murder facilities in Nazi **extermination camps**. Gassing took place in a sealed chamber, often labeled as showers, where **Zyklon** or diesel fumes were used to murder Jews. In **Auschwitz-Birkenau**, one and one-half million Jews were murdered this way. Those who could not perform slave labor, the injured, the disabled, children, or the sick were "**selected**" for the chambers. If no labor was needed at the time of the arrival of the Jews, then even the able-bodied were killed. The Nazis built six large gassing facilities at Auschwitz, **Belzec**, Chelmno, **Majdanek, Sobibor**, and Treblinka. The reaction of officials and the public in the so-called free world, even when informed, varied from indifference and collaboration with the murderers, to opposition. Despite convincing information that reached the British and U.S. Allies, no effort was made to bomb either the facilities or the tracks leading to them. *See also* CREMATORIA; EUTHANASIA; EVIDENCE OF THE HOLO-

CAUST, SUPPRESSION OF; GENOCIDE; HOLOCAUST; SOCIAL DARWINISM; SONDERKOMMANDO; SONDERWAGON.

SUGGESTED READING: Jean Claude Pressac, *Auschwitz: Technique and Operation of the Gas Chambers* (New York: Beate Klarsfeld Foundation, 1989); Walter Laqueur, *The Terrible Secret* (New York: Penguin, 1981).

GAXOTTE, PIERRE (1895–1982). Royalist French Catholic historian. Gaxotte called the Jewish French premier Léon Blum "a man accursed" who "incarnates all that revolts our blood and makes our flesh creep. He is evil. He is death."

SUGGESTED READING: Stephen Schuker, "Origins of the 'Jewish Problem,'" in *The Jews in Modern France*, ed. Frances Malino and Bernard Wasserstein (Hanover, NH: Brandeis University Press, University Press of New England, 1985).

GEMLICH LETTER. Adolf Hitler's first **antisemitic** writing consists of a letter of September 16, 1919, to a certain Herr Adolf Gemlich. After the **Freikorps** repression of the 1918–19 Marxist Munich revolt, Gemlich sent an inquiry about the "Jewish question" to Capt. Karl Mayr, the officer in charge of the Reichswehr News and Enlightenment Department in Munich. Mayr referred the letter to Hitler, who had distinguished himself in a Reichswehr-sponsored course for demobilized soldiers focusing on nationalism, antisemitism, and antisocialism. A few days before responding to Gemlich, Hitler, as a secret Reichswehr agent, had paid his first visit to the **German Workers Party**—which would become the National Socialist German Workers (**Nazi**) Party. As a result of this letter, Hitler's political career was launched as a radical rightist and nationalist conservative whose antisemitism could help discredit the democratic **Weimar Republic**.

In sum, Hitler wrote that the Jews are an unscrupulous, pitiless, alien, un-German race competing by means of money and material possessions in a merciless struggle for all that authentic Germans prize most highly: individual worth determined by character, achievement, morality, and spirituality. Antisemitism must be based on a systematic legal discrimination against Jews, who must be removed (*Entfernung*) from German society. To achieve this goal, Germany needs a moral and spiritual rebirth led by personalities with an inner sense of responsibility.

SUGGESTED READING: Eberhard Jäckel, ed., *Hitler: Sämtliche Aufzeichnungen 1905–1924* (Stuttgart, 1980); J. P. Stern, *Hitler: The Führer and the People* (Berkeley: University of California Press, 1975).

GENERAL CHARTER OF JEWISH LIBERTIES. *See* JEWISH CONDITION IN POLAND.

GENERAL COMMISSARIAT FOR JEWISH AFFAIRS. An office of the **Vichy** regime in France. With the encouragement of **Nazi** Germany, this department was established by the collaborationist Vichy French government in March 1941. It oversaw the **Aryanization** of Jewish businesses and played a major role in the **deportation** of 75,000 foreign Jews residing in France to their doom in concentration camps. *See also* PELLEPOIX, LOUIS DARQUIER; STATUT DES JUIFS; VALLAT, XAVIER DE.

SUGGESTED READING: Michael Marrus and Robert Paxton, *Vichy France and the Jews* (New York: Schocken Books, 1983).

GENOCIDE. Ethnic killing. The term *genocide* was coined by Raphael Lemkin, a Jew who escaped the **Holocaust** in Poland and used the word in his 1943 book, *Axis Rule in Occupied Europe*. Whereas the word *Holocaust* is used specifically to refer to the **Nazi** mass murder of Jews, genocide is a broader term, referring to the attempt to eliminate any racial, religious, or ethnic group. A United Nations Genocide Convention in 1948 made the planned killing of a whole people an international crime, but nations have generally ignored it. Genocide remains an ever-present threat for all peoples. *See also* CRIMES AGAINST HUMANITY; FINAL SOLUTION OF THE JEWISH PROBLEM; WANNSEE CONFERENCE.

SUGGESTED READING: Samantha Power, *A Problem from Hell: America and the Age of Genocide* (New York: Basic Books, 2002).

GENUFLECTION. Amalarius of Metz (d. 850), archbishop of Trier, was the first expositor of the details of the Christian liturgy. He explained why Christians do not genuflect after the prayer for the Jews during the **Good Friday** Mass:

> When we pray for the **perfidious** Jews, we do not genuflect. For they had genuflected in mockery [of Christ in His Passion]. Let us demonstrate our revulsion at this act by not genuflecting when we pray for the Jews. In like manner, let us abstain from the kiss of peace . . . so as not to duplicate the evil **Judas** kiss, which led to Christ's suffering. . . . We should abstain from doing things that associate us with the Jews. As **St. Augustine** has said, Easter should be commemorated on a Sunday so that it will be distinguished from the Jewish holiday.

See also OREMUS.

SUGGESTED READING: John Osterreicher, "Pro Perfidis Judaeis," *Theological Studies* (1947); Erik Peterson, "Perfidia Judaica," in *Ephemerides Liturgicae* 50 (1936); Bernhard Blumenkranz, *Archivium Latinitatis medii Aevi*, vol. 22 (1952).

GEORGE, STEFAN (1868–1933). German poet. Although George had many Jews in his circle, some of his comments on Jews are quite antisemitic: "One Jew is very useful, but as soon as there are more than two of them, the tone becomes different and they tend to their own business." "Jews are the best conductors. They are good at spreading and implementing values. To be sure, they do not experience life as deeply as we do. They are in general different people."

SUGGESTED READING: Justin Cartwright, "Stefan George, Prophet of Doom," *The Guardian*, January 14, 2006.

GERLIER, PIERRE-MARIE (1880–1965). Cardinal and archbishop of Lyons. Gerlier ordered Catholic institutions to hide Jewish children during World War II and earned the title "Righteous Gentile." Nevertheless, he held some negative views on Jews. In October 1941 he told the commissioner-general for Jewish affairs, **Xavier de Vallat**, that the anti-Jewish law was "not unjust, [merely lacking in] justice and charity in its enforcement" and that "no one recognizes more than I the evil the Jews have done to France."

SUGGESTED READING: Michael Marrus and Robert Paxton, *Vichy France and the Jews* (Stanford, CA: Stanford University Press, 1995).

GERMAN-AMERICAN BUND (*DEUTSCH-AMERIKANISCHER VOLKSBUND*). An openly pro-**Nazi** organization of ethnic Germans living in the United States, founded in 1936. Aside from its veneration of **Adolf Hitler**, its program included **antisemitism** and anticommunism. The Bund invited the antisemitic Catholic priest **Charles Coughlin** to speak at a meeting. Instead of Hitler, he blamed the Jews for their own persecution. A February 1939 rally in New York's Madison Square Garden attracted 20,000, many of whom chanted "Heil Hitler." *See also* FRIENDS OF THE NEW GERMANY.

SUGGESTED READING: Robert E. Herzstein, *Roosevelt and Hitler: Prelude to War* (New York: Paragon House, 1989).

GERMAN BIG BUSINESS. *See* FEDER, GOTTFRIED; HUGENBERG, ALFRED; I. G. FARBEN.

GERMAN CANDLE; GERMAN OVEN MITT. (U.S. slur) Jews. Reference to **Holocaust crematoriums**.

SUGGESTED READING: "List of Ethnic Slurs," *Wikipedia*, http://en.wikipedia.org/wiki/List_of_ethnic_slurs.

GERMAN-CHRISTIANS. Officially the Faith Movement of German-Christians (*Glaubensbensbewegung Deutschen Christen*). Most German

Protestants belonged to this organization during the **Third Reich**, 1933–45. Their Christian beliefs were seen as consistent with **Nazi** ideology and state **antisemitism**. Two thirds of German Protestants joined the German-Christian movement or voted for it. Hans Schemm—a Protestant schoolteacher, Nazi Party member of the Reichstag, and founder of the movement—proclaimed, "Our politics are Germany and our religion Christ." *See also* BONNHOEFFER, DIETRICH; CONFESSING CHURCH; REICHSTHEOLOGIE.

SUGGESTED READING: Doris Bergen, *The Twisted Cross: The German Christian Movement in the Third Reich* (Chapel Hill: University of North Carolina Press, 1996).

GERMANENORDEN (GERMANIC ORDER). The ultraright-wing, *völkisch*, occultist, and elitist German Aryan Masonic Lodge. The National Socialist Party from the very beginning was a mixture of politics and occultism. Some of the party's ideology derived from the German **Freemason** lodge Germanenorden, which was founded in 1912 in Leipzig by **Theodor Fritsch** with 1,000 members and by 1916 had 100 lodges. The master for this order was Herman Paul. By 1918 the order was reorganized by **Philip Stauff**, a cultural nationalist who believed Jews were alien. Germanenorden allied with other anti-Jewish organizations such as the **Thule Society**. Its **swastika** symbol and occult antisemitic ideology were adopted by **Adolf Hitler** and the National Socialists. It faded away with the growth of the **Nazi Party**.

SUGGESTED READINGS: Richard Cavendish, ed., *Man, Myth and Magic: An Encyclopedia of the Supernatural* (New York: Cavendish Corp., 1970); Nicholas Goodrick-Clarke, *The Occult Roots of Nazism* (New York: New York University Press, 1992).

GERMAN FAR-RIGHT ROCK MUSIC. Far-right German **neo-Nazi** bands see themselves as *Neue deutsche Härte* (new German hardness), possibly a reference to **Heinrich Himmler**'s assertion that his **SS** troops were to be *"hart wie Krupp stehl"* (hard as Krupp steel). Some bands adopt only a **Nazi** aesthetic and symbolism, while others glorify violence and war and fill their lyrics with Nordic mythologies and racist slogans. All result in stimulating **antisemitic** radicalization in their audiences. Stirred by "hardcore/hatecore" music of American neo-Nazi bands like the Blue Eyed Devils, German far-right music has become more racist and antisemitic. The song "We Believe," recorded by Strength thru Blood, states: "We believe in National Socialism. We believe in white supremacy. We believe we'll smash Zion's occupation." National Socialist black metal bands are more brutal, glorifying violence and war, **Social Darwinist** advocacy of the supposed laws of nature and the principle of "might makes right," and hostile to the Judeo-Christian tradition. The black metal band Magog sings, "We are marching into a new age that will free us from Jews and Christians"—a new age that can only be achieved by the "total annihilation of the existing Jewish-Christian system." In March 2005, Germany's highest court, the Federal Court of Justice in Berlin, ruled that the neo-Nazi rock group Landser (Soldier) is a criminal organization, and it upheld a three-year prison sentence for the leader of the band, Michael Regener. The court ruled that Landser incited racial hatred and spread Nazi propaganda. *See also* WHITE POWER MUSIC.

SUGGESTED READING: Christian Dornbusch and Jan Raabe, eds., *Rechts-Rock: Bestandsaufnahme und Gegenstrategien* (Far-Right Rock: Stocktaking and Countermeasures) (Hamburg: Rat/Unrast Verlag, 2002).

GERMANIC ORDER. *See* GERMANENORDEN.

GERMAN IMPERIAL FLAG. Imperial War Ensign, Reichskriegsflagge. One of the flags (portraying an iron cross, an eagle, and black, white, and red stripes) used by the German Empire (1871–1918), now a **neo-Nazi** symbol. After postwar Germany and other European nations banned the **swastika**, some neo-Nazis in Germany and some white supremacists use the Imperial flag as a substitute for the **Nazi** flag and swastika.

SUGGESTED READING: Anti-Defamation League, *Hate on Display: Extremist Symbols, Logos, and Tattoos* (New York: Anti-Defamation League, 2006).

GERMAN NATIONAL PEOPLE'S PARTY (DNVP). The German National People's Party was established in 1918 from supporters of the Prussian monarchy, with much of its membership coming from Protestant rural areas. The 1920 platform pledged the party to fight the "hegemony of Jews in government and public life." The party was a member of **Adolf Hitler**'s coalition when he came to power in 1933. *See also* WEIMAR REPUBLIC.

SUGGESTED READING: Michael Burleigh, *The Third Reich: A New History* (London: Pan, 2001).

GERMAN PEOPLE'S PROTECTION AND DEFENSE LEAGUE (DEUTSCHVÖLKISCHE SCHUTZ- UND TRUTZBUND). Also called the German National Protective and Defensive League. In 1920 the league published millions of racist and **antisemitic** leaflets. It was a nationwide political party whose goal was the repression of Jewish influence. *See also* WEIMAR REPUBLIC.

SUGGESTED READING: William Brustein, *The Logic of Evil: The Social Origins of the Nazi Party, 1925–1933* (New Haven, CT: Yale University Press, 1996); Proceedings of the Nuremberg War Crimes Trials, Avalon Project at Yale Law School, http://www.yale.edu/lawweb/avalon/imt/proc/07-12-46.htm.

GERMAN RESISTERS TO HITLER. Most conservative German resisters were **antisemitic**: early on **Dietrich Bonhoeffer** and **Martin Niemöller**, then Claus von Stauffenberg, Carl Goerdeler, Adam von Trott, and the Kreisau Circle, believed that Germany was and should be based on Christian values. Like the **Nazis** and their German collaborators, these German resisters regarded the Jews as unwanted aliens, never to be permitted German **citizenship**.

SUGGESTED READING: John Weiss, *Ideology of Death* (Chicago: Ivan Dee, 1995).

GERMAN REVISIONISM, POST-HOLOCAUST. German revisionist historians claim that histories of World War II and, in particular, of the **Holocaust** are written from the winners' point of view and should be revised within their historical, that is, relativistic, context. Revisionists equate the Holocaust with **Joseph Stalin**'s crimes. Ernst Nolte, for example, claimed that the Holocaust only emulated Stalin's mass murder of the Russian bourgeoisie. Revisionists also regard Allied "crimes" during World War II as identical to the crimes of the Nazis. They draw analogies, for example, between Dresden's bombing and **Auschwitz**, and between the postwar expulsions of Germans from Eastern Europe with the extermination of the Jews. A third revisionist strategy compares Jewish and Israeli "crimes" to those of the Nazis. *See also* HAIDER, JÖRG; HISTORIANS' CONTROVERSY.

SUGGESTED READING: Eberhard Jäckel, ed., *Historikerstreit* (Munich: Piper, 1987).

GERMAN STUDENT ORGANIZATIONS (*BURSCHENSCHAFT*). Although German Jews had been welcome to fight against **Napoleon**, nationalistic German student organizations later expressed a high degree of **antisemitism**. Their leaders—**Ernst Moritz Arndt, Friedrich Ludwig Jahn, Jacob Fries**, and Lorenz Oken (1779–1851)—coupled traditional anti-Jewishness with a reborn nationalism fostered by both Lutheran and Catholic theology. At the Wartburg Festival of 1817, the German students conducted a **book burning** associated with Napoleon and freedom for Jews.

SUGGESTED READING: Stephen J. Whitfeld, "Where They Burn Books," *Modern Judaism* 22, no. 4 (October 2003).

GERMAN WORKERS PARTY (DEUTSCHE ARBEITERPARTEI). Obscure German political group founded in 1919 by **Anton Drexler** and **Dietrich Eckart** at the end of World War I. **Adolf Hitler** joined the party after he spied on it for the German Army. Several of the party's Twenty-Five Points (1920) referred to Jews, advocating that they be deprived of all citizenship rights and driven out of the economy. Point 24 read:

> We demand freedom of religion for all religious denominations within the state so long as they do not endanger its existence or oppose the moral senses of the Germanic race. The Party as such advocates the standpoint of a positive Christianity without binding itself confessionally to any one denomination. It combats the Jewish-materialistic spirit within and around us.

Soon after he became Führer—head of the party—Hitler changed its name to National Socialist German Workers Party—abbreviated in German as "**Nazi**." *See also* THULE SOCIETY.

SUGGESTED READING: Dick Geary, "Nazis and Workers before 1933," *Australian Journal of Politics and History* 48 (2002).

GERSTEIN, KURT (1905–1945). German Waffen **SS** officer. Although Gerstein joined the **Nazi Party** and the SS, as a former member of Lutheran Church groups he found that Nazism did not fit well with his Christian beliefs. Gerstein headed the SS Institute of Hygiene. He worked with **Zyklon** and viewed firsthand the murders in the **gas chambers** at the **Belzec**, **Sobibor**, and Treblinka **extermination camps**. He tried to alert the Berlin papal nuncio and other church leaders and diplomats, but to no avail. After the war, he died under mysterious circumstances as an Allied prisoner-of-war.

SUGGESTED READING: Saul Friedlander and Kurt Gerstein, *The Ambiguity of Good* (New York: Knopf, 1969).

GESTAPO (GEHEIME STAATSPOLIZEI). Secret State Police. The Gestapo was the most feared agency in **Adolf Hitler**'s Germany and **Nazi**-controlled areas. It was a police force directed not against common criminals but against real or perceived enemies of Nazism. A subsection of Reichssicherheitshauptamt (the office in charge of Reich security under **Reinhard Heydrich**), IVB4 under **Adolf Eichmann**, dealt with Jews and the **Final Solution**. It had enormous powers of investigation, arrest, interrogation, incarceration, and operation without judicial review or without any due process of law. *See also* GOERING, HERMANN; HIMMLER, HEINRICH; MÜLLER, HEINRICH; SS.

SUGGESTED READING: Edward Crankshaw, *Gestapo: Instrument of Tyranny* (New York: Viking Press, 1956).

GHETTO BENCHES. Separate sections of seats for Jewish students in all lecture halls and laboratories set up by the university and technical college authorities of Warsaw in 1937 and 1938. Polish Jewish and some Catholic students, as well as overseas academics, protested this violation of the Polish Constitution that guaranteed equal rights to all citizens. In 1938, **antisemites** boycotted and picketed Jewish stores, terrorizing Poles who patronized the Jewish shops. Street assaults on Jews became an everyday occurrence despite the Polish president Ignaz Moscicki stating that neither antisemitic terrorism nor the **confiscation of Jewish property** would be tolerated by the Polish government. Newspapers printed articles advocating large-scale emigration of Poland's Jews because Poland had the largest percentage of Jews in the world (3.5 million out of a total population of 35 million).

SUGGESTED READING: William Zukerman, "Jews and the Fate of Poland," *Nation* 146, no. 10 (April 2, 1938).

GHETTOS. Compulsory Jewish quarter. Ghettos were set up at various times and places in Europe and Islamic North Africa. In 1090, the streets in Venice assigned to Jews were known as "Judaca" or "Giudaca." Some scholars claim the word comes from the Italian term *gietto*, the cannon foundry where the Jewish quarter was located in Venice in 1516. Ghettos were an expression of **antisemitism**, intolerance, and distrust by Christians. Their locations were usually near rivers, which flooded the streets. The ghettos were overcrowded, dirty, narrow, and unhealthy, sealed off by walls and gates. The Prague Ghetto was famous for its self-sufficiency, with its own town hall, police force, **Talmudic** courts, schools, scholars, and **guilds**. Many ghettos were torn down during the **Napoleonic** era, but rebuilt after Napoleon's fall in 1815. The **revolutions of 1848** in Europe eliminated most ghettos. The **Nazis** reinstituted them with the purpose of housing Jews for slave labor, to slowly starve them to death, and to collect them before shipping them to concentration and death camps. *See also* DREISER, THEODORE; FRANKFURT GHETTO; NAPOLEON; PAPAL STATES; SONDERKOMMANDO; WARSAW GHETTO UPRISING, THE *NEW YORK TIMES* TREATMENT OF.

SUGGESTED READING: Cecil Roth, "The Ghetto," in *Antisemitism* (Jerusalem: Keter Publishing, 1974).

GIBSON, MEL (1956–). Actor, filmmaker. Son of Hutton Gibson, a noted **Holocaust** denier, Gibson in 2004 produced *The Passion of the Christ*, a film that many feel distorted the **Gospels** and the Jewish role in the crucifixion. In July 2006 in Malibu, California, Gibson was arrested for drunk driving. The arresting Los Angeles Sheriff's Department deputy stated that Gibson "blurted out a barrage of antisemitic remarks," such as "fucking Jews" and "the Jews are responsible for all the wars in the world." Even though Gibson claimed that his conservative Catholic religion helped him "beat his demons" of alcoholism, Abraham Foxman, head of the Anti-Defamation League, noted that "liquor loosens the tongue of what's in the mind and in the heart, and in his mind and in his heart is his conspiracy theory about Jews and hatred of Jews."

SUGGESTED READING: Allison Hope Weiner, "Mel Gibson Apologizes for Tirade After Arrest," *New York Times* (July 30, 2006).

GIUDEO. (Italian slur) A Jew.

SUGGESTED READING: "List of Ethnic Slurs," *Wikipedia*, http://en.wikipedia.org/wiki/List_of_ethnic_slurs.

GLAGAU, OTTO VON (1834–1892). German journalist and one of the central figures in the birth of modern German **antisemitism**. Glagau worked at the antisemitic magazine *Der Kulturkämpfer* (*Culture Warrior*). He claims to have uncovered the "swindlers" and "hyenas" of the Jewish stock exchange and recognized the monstrous crime of **ritual murder**. "Today the social question is essentially the Jewish question. All other explanations of our economic troubles are fraudulent cover-ups." His work led to the first Antisemitic Congress held in Dresden in 1882.

SUGGESTED READING: John Weiss, *Ideology of Death* (Chicago: Ivan Dee, 1995).

GLOBKE, HANS (1898–1973). **Nazi** jurist. Globke coauthored anti-Jewish laws in Germany during the 1930s—laws to exclude, denaturalize, and segregate Jews from society. He wrote the requirement that forced all Jews to use the middle names "Sarah" and "Israel" on all official documents. He crafted "legal" ways for **confiscation of Jewish property**, while Jews were sent to concentration camps. *See also* NUREMBERG LAWS OF 1935.

SUGGESTED READING: Ingo Mueller, *Hitler's Justice: The Courts of the Third Reich*, trans. Deborah Schneider (Cambridge, MA: Harvard University Press, 1991).

GLOCK, CHARLES. *See CHRISTIAN BELIEFS AND ANTISEMITISM.*

GOBINEAU, ARTHUR DE (1806–1882). French philosopher and minor diplomat. Gobineau's magnus opus was his *Essay on the Inequality of the Human Races* (1853–55). He was not an **antisemite**, but modern racist thought is greatly indebted to him. He believed the **Aryans** were superior to all other peoples, having greater intelligence, energy, instinct for order and honor, and better work habits. He lamented racial mixing. Gobineau's political and racist views were adapted and adopted by the **Nazis**. *See also* CHAMBERLAIN, HOUSTON STEWART; *FOUNDATIONS OF THE NINETEENTH CENTURY*; *MEIN KAMPF*; SOCIAL DARWINISM.

SUGGESTED READING: Arthur de Gobineau, *The Inequality of Human Races* (New York: Howard Fertig, 1999); Léon Poliakov, *The Aryan Myth*, trans. Edmund Howard (New York: Barnes & Noble, 1974).

GODFREY OF BOUILLON (1060–1100). French **Crusader**. Before departing on the First Crusade, Godfrey "swore wickedly that he would not depart on his journey without avenging the blood of the Crucified with the blood of Israel and that he would not leave 'a remnant or residue.'" While in Europe, he extorted funds from the Jews of Cologne and Mainz. He then took his revenge on the Jews of Jerusalem by permitting his troops to murder them along with the Muslim residents of the city. These Crusaders, after receiving communion, spent the day murdering Jews. Burning some of the Jews alive in the great **synagogue**, the Crusaders marched around it singing "Christ, We Adore Thee."

SUGGESTED READING: Meron Benveniste, *Crusaders in the Holy Land* (Jerusalem: Israel Universities Press, 1970).

GOEBBELS, JOSEF PAUL (1897–1945). **Nazi** minister of propaganda. Goebbels, **Adolf Hitler**'s friend, was a key figure in the dictator's rise to power. Once in charge of all cultural activities and media, he produced **antisemitic** propaganda urging the elimination of Jews from German society. **Kristallnacht** in 1938 was his brainchild. His diaries provide much inside information on the **Holocaust**.

SUGGESTED READING: Roger Mandell and Heinrich Frankel, *Doctor Goebbels: His Life and Death* (New York: Simon & Schuster, 1960).

GOEDSCHE, HERMANN (1816–1878). Prussian novelist. Goedsche published a novel entitled *Biarritz* in 1808 under the pseudonym Sir John Retcliff. A highly antisemitic chapter was entitled "In the Jewish Cemetery in Prague." The fictional "Rabbi's Speech" describes a cabal representing the 12 tribes of Israel plotting to destroy Gentile society and preparing for Jewish domination in the 20th century. The novel was treated as an authentic record, adapted, and published in Russia as *The Protocols of the Elders of Zion* (1899) by the tsarist secret police. *See also* FORD, HENRY; FREEMASONS.

SUGGESTED READING: Herman Bernstein, *The Truth about "The Protocols of the Elders of Zion"* (New York: Ktav, 1971); Norman Cohen, *Warrant for Genocide* (New York: Harper & Row, 1967).

GOERING, HERMANN (1893–1946). **Nazi** deputy Führer and head of the Luftwaffe. Goering, an early Nazi and part of **Adolf Hitler**'s inner circle, had a major role in the **Holocaust**. He established the **Gestapo**, created the first concentration camps, convened the **Wannsee Conference**, and charged it with the **Final Solution**. Goering was unrepentant at the **Nuremberg War Crimes Trials**, escaping the hangman by taking poison.

SUGGESTED READING: Leonard Mosely, *The Reich Marshal* (New York: Dell, 1975).

GOETHE, JOHANN VON (1749–1832). German Romantic poet, novelist, and playwright; perhaps Germany's foremost literary figure. Léon Poliakov suggests that Goethe's rage at Jewish emancipation summarized the Western Christian tradition: "The most serious and most disastrous consequences are to be expected . . . all ethical feelings within families, feelings which rest entirely on religious principles, will be endangered." Goethe respected some Jewish intellectuals, who were perhaps his greatest readers, but he expressed contempt for the mass of Jews. He called Judaism "ancient nonsense" and the modern Jewish language, Yiddish, the vehicle of a rabbinic, anti-Christian fanaticism. "We tolerate no Jew among us, because how could we grant him participation at the highest level of [Christian] culture, whose very origin and tradition he denies." As an old man, he reminisced that he had been especially fearful of the Jews in his youth because of the **ritual murder** charges. At other times he called the Jews "the chosen people of God" and noted that Jews "also were men, active and obliging; and, even to the tenacity with which they clung to their peculiar customs one could not refuse one's respect." He admitted:

> My contempt [for the Jews] was more the reflection of the Christian men and women surrounding me. Only later, when I made the acquaintance of many intel-

lectually gifted, sensitive men of this race, did respect come to join the admiration I cherish for the people who created the Bible and for the poet who sang the Song of Songs.

See also YELLOW.

Suggested Reading: Alfred Low, *Jews in the Eyes of the Germans* (Philadelphia: Jewish Publication Society, 1979).

GOGA, OCTAVIAN (1881–1938). Former head of the **Iron Guard**, short-lived premier of Romania, and leading Romanian **antisemite** in 1930s. In 1937, Goga, along with **Alexandru Cuza** and **Corneliu Zelea Codreanu** (head of the **fascist** Iron Guard), led 300,000 antisemites in a mass demonstration blessed by the head of the Romanian Orthodox Church, **Miron Cristea**.

Suggested Reading: I. C. Butnaru, *The Silent Holocaust* (Westport, CT: Greenwood Press, 1992); Radu Ioanid, *The Sword of the Archangel: Fascist Ideology in Romania*, trans. Peter Heinez (New York: Columbia University Press, 1990).

GOGOL, NIKOLAI (1809–1852). Ukrainian-Russian writer. In Gogol's novel *Taras Bulba* (1835), the title character was a Cossack warrior chief. Gogol describes a Jew whom Taras convinced to lead him to Warsaw in search of Taras's son:

> This Jew was the well-known Yankel. . . . He had gradually got nearly all the neighbouring noblemen and gentlemen into his hands, had slowly sucked away most of their money, and had strongly impressed his presence on that locality. . . . as if after a fire or an epidemic. . . . He was ashamed of his avarice, and tried to stifle within him the eternal thought of gold, which twines, like a snake, about the soul of a Jew. . . . "You Jews . . . would deceive the very devil."

GOLDBERG. (U.S. slur) Goldberg is an **Ashkenazic** (Eastern or Central European) Jewish name used to stereotype Jews as money-hungry.

Suggested Reading: "List of Ethnic Slurs," *Wikipedia*, http://en.wikipedia.org/wiki/List_of_ethnic_slurs.

GOLDIE. (U.S. slur) Reference to the emblems—**yellow** stars of David— with which the **Nazis** stigmatized Jews.

Suggested Reading: "List of Ethnic Slurs," *Wikipedia*, http://en.wikipedia.org/wiki/List_of_ethnic_slurs.

GONDEBAUD, LAW OF (*LOI GOMBETTE*). Roman Law of the Burgundians that, among other things, forbade all marriage between Jews and

Christians in 502. Such unions, in accordance with the law of Roman emperor Theodosius IX, were declared adulterous. The law also prescribed that any Jew who struck or kicked a Christian should be punished by having his hand cut off, though he might compromise by paying a compensation of 75 sous and a fine of 12 sous. For striking a priest, the penalty was death and **confiscation of property**.

SUGGESTED READING: Joseph Jacobs and Israel Levi, "France," *JewishEncyclopedia.com*.

GOOD FRIDAY. In Christianity, the day during Holy Week when Jesus' crucifixion is commemorated. Repeated reports of violence Christians had perpetrated against Jews over the course of history from the Middle Ages into the modern period on, or just after, Good Friday provide ample evidence of the anti-Jewish feelings the Good Friday service provoked. Even when violence was not the result of the service, the negative impact on Catholics has been noted: the congregation was ordered to **genuflect** and say "Amen" after prayers for pagans, infidels, and atheists, but was commanded to omit these respectful rituals when it came to the Jews. *See also* OREMUS.

SUGGESTED READING: Jacob Rader Marcus and Marc Saperstein, *The Jew in the Medieval World: A Source Book* (Cincinnati, OH: Hebrew Union College Press, 2000).

GOSPEL OF PETER. Early noncanonical Christian writing. The Gospel of Peter, though fragmentary, reveals an apparent split in the Jewish leadership over the wisdom of having Jesus crucified. This Gospel absolves Pilate of guilt for the crucifixion, placing the blame squarely upon the Jews.

SUGGESTED READING: John Dominic Crossan, *The Cross That Spoke: The Origins of the Passion Narrative* (San Francisco: Harper & Row, 1998).

GOSPELS. First four books of the Christian Scriptures: **Matthew**, Mark, Luke, and **John**. Many anti-Jewish passages occur in the Gospels. Although these books are essentially expressions of Christian faith, they leave the dangerous impression that they are objective history. Some passages refer only to a few Jews as evil, or make positive statements about Jews. More often, however, Jews are dramatically portrayed as antagonists or disloyal followers of Jesus, or as persons or a people who misunderstood him. Jesus is reported to have repudiated them, calling them "hypocrites" and "evil-speakers" who deserved to die. Written generations after the actual events they purport to document, these books appear to offer eyewitness accounts of the events they detail, which helps account for their subsequent power.

SUGGESTED READING: Peter Richardson and David Granshaw, *Anti-Judaism in Early Christianity* (Waterloo, OH: Wilfred Laurier University Press, 1986).

GOUGENOT DE MOUSSEAUX, HENRI ROGER (1805–1876). French aristocrat and writer. Gougenot thought Jews to be "the representatives on earth of the spirit of darkness," who conspired along with the **Freemasons** to destroy Christian values and control the world. In 1869, in *Le juif, la judaisme et la judaisation des peuples chrétiens* (*The Jew, Judaism, and the Judaization of the Christian People*), he wrote that the world was being taken over by a group of Satan-worshipping Jews, out of which a man would emerge whom the Jews would worship as their **messiah.**

> Masonry, that immense association, the rare initiates of which, that is to say, the real chiefs of which, whom we must be careful not to confound with the nominal chiefs, live in a strict and intimate alliance with the militant members of Judaism, princes and imitators of the high cabal. . . . The majority [are] Jewish members which the mysterious constitution of Masonry seats in its sovereign counsel.

He continued: "Judaism (more properly called **Phariseeism**) has two esoteric movements within the movement. One is **Talmudism**; the other is Cabalism; the former is anti-Christ while the other is pro-Lucifer."

SUGGESTED READING: Léon Poliakov, *The History of Antisemitism*, 4 vols. (New York: Vanguard, 1965–86).

GRAHAM, BILLY. *See* NIXON, RICHARD M.

GRAND MUFTI OF JERUSALEM. *See* HUSSEINI, HAJJ AMIN EL.

GRANT, MADISON (1865–1937). Zoolgist and premier American racist writer. In his 1916 magnum opus, *Passing of the Great Race*, Grant wrote, "Asia, in the guise of **Bolshevism** with Semitic leadership and Chinese executioners, is organizing an assault upon western Europe." The mixing of European races disgusted him; he believed the foundation of American national and cultural life lay in racial purity. Grant warned that the ruling white race was beginning to fail because different races do not blend; miscegenation "gives us a race reverting to the more ancient and lower type." A "cross between any of the three European races and a Jew is a Jew . . . whose dwarf stature, peculiar mentality, and ruthless concentration of self-interest are being engrafted upon the stock of the nation."

SUGGESTED READING: Madison Grant, *Passing of the Great Race; or, The Racial Basis of European History* (1916; reprint, Manchester, NH: Ayer, 1970).

GRANT, ULYSSES S. Civil War general and president of the United States, 1869–77. Grant believed that Jews were engaged in smuggling, theft, speculation, vagrancy, and possibly treason. On December 17, 1862, he wrote to C. P. Wolcott, assistant secretary of war:

> Regulations of the Treasury Department have been violated . . . mostly by the Jews and other unprincipled traders. So [I have refused] all permits to Jews to come South, and I have frequently had them expelled from the department. . . . The Jews seem to be a privileged class that can travel anywhere.

On the same day, Grant issued General Order No. 11, which expelled all Jews from Tennessee's Western Military District within 24 hours.

SUGGESTED READING: Leonard Dinnerstein, *Antisemitism in America* (New York: Oxford University Press, 1994).

GRATIAN (d. 1159). Italian monk and famous canonist (religious lawmaker). Gratian is credited with shaping **canon law**. He wrote *Decretum* (1140), a collection of 4,000 patristic texts. Rediscovering **St. Isidore of Seville**'s anti-Jewish ideas, he transmitted these ideas to the whole Middle Ages through his prodigious output.

SUGGESTED READING: Lou Kessler and Neal Weinbaum, *Dictionary of Jewish-Christian Relations* (Cambridge: Cambridge University Press, 2005); James Parkes, *The Conflict of the Church and the Synagogue: A Study in the Origins of Antisemitism* (New York: Atheneum, 1979).

GREAT SATAN. (Islamic slur) Reference to the Islamic identification of Jews with the Devil.

SUGGESTED READING: "List of Ethnic Slurs," *Wikipedia*, http://en .wikipedia.org/wiki/List_of_ethnic_slurs.

GREENE, GRAHAM (1904–1991). English novelist. Greene, along with **Agatha Christie**, **T. S. Eliot**, **Rudyard Kipling**, **Wyndham Lewis**, and **H. G. Wells**, created offensive Jewish characters in their work. Although he later condemned **Nazi** persecutions, Greene's novels in the 1930s ridiculed "Jewesses" as "little bitches." He wrote in *Brighton Rock* (1938): "He had been a Jew once, but a hairdresser and a surgeon had altered that." And in *The Confidential Agent* (1939), Greene opined that a female character "deserved something better than a man named Furtstein. . . . The domed Semitic forehead, the dark eyes over the rather gaudy tie." In the *Spectator*

(April 7, 1939), he condemned "large fat foreign" Jewish refugees and noted that "the financial crisis has improved English films! They have lost their tasteless Semitic opulence and are becoming—English." Greene was personally aware of the Nazi assault on the Jews—his brother was Berlin correspondent of the *Daily Telegraph*—yet his **antisemitism** continued even after **Kristallnacht**.

SUGGESTED READING: Michael Shelden, "Greene and Antisemitism," *New York Review of Books* 42, no. 14 (September 21, 1995).

GRÉGOIRE, HENRI-BAPTISTE (1750–1831). French clergyman and politician. Although a proponent of Jewish emancipation and **citizenship**, the **Jesuit** Abbé Gregoire wanted the Jews to **convert** to Catholicism so that they would lose their degenerative physical, moral, and political traits. Even so, he found much to admire in the Jews "wherever they begin to be treated as men." Yet he believed the **deicide accusation** to be true, and he wrote in *Essai sur la régéneration physique, morale, et politique des Juifs* (1789) of the Jews' "wretched corruption." He wanted to force Jews out of urban areas and into the professions in order to break the hold of the tyrannical rabbis, to mollify Jewish animosity against Christians, and to make Jews more honest in their business practices. He called Yiddish a "Teutonic-Hebraic rabbinic jargon German Jews use, which only serves to deepen ignorance or to mask trickery." He condemned the **Talmud** as a "vast reservoir, I almost said a cesspool," that prevented Jews from converting to Christianity.

SUGGESTED READING: Ruth Necheles, "The Abbé Grégoire and the Jews," *Jewish Social Studies* 33 (1971).

GREGORY I (THE GREAT) (540–604). Pope, 590–604. Gregory's Jewish policy, later incorporated into **canon law**, was laid out in his letter "Sicut Iudaeis" of June 598. Gregory argued that Jews should not be killed, and although they did not have license to do everything they wanted, they were nevertheless permitted what the Church had already conceded to them. Jews could follow their religious practices but must never be allowed to tempt Christians away from the true faith toward **perfidious** Judaism; they must never have authority over Christians, never in any way try to demonstrate the superiority of Judaism over Christianity, and never blaspheme Christianity. His writings described Judaism as "superstition," "vomit," "perdition," and "treachery" and the Jews as "enemies of Christ," as "criminal," "cursed," and "satanically perverse," "dragons of poisonous ideas," "wicked," "people of Satan," "of the **Antichrist**," and "of the Devil." *See also* RECCARED.

SUGGESTED READING: Shlomo Simonsohn, *The Apostolic See and the Jews: Documents, 492–1404* (Toronto: Pontifical Institute of Mediaeval Studies, 1988).

GREGORY VII, ST. (1025–1085). Pope, 1073–85. Gregory VII's first letter on the subject of Jews condemned King Alfonso VI of Castile and Léon, who allowed Jews in his court: "You must not permit Jews in your land to dominate Christians. . . . For what is it to set Christians beneath Jews . . . except to oppress the Church of God and to exalt the Synagogue of Satan; you must realize that your desire to please the enemies of Christ is to condemn Christ himself?"

SUGGESTED READING: Bernhard Blumenkranz, ed., *Les auteurs chrétiens latins du moyen age sur les Juifs et le Judaisme* (Paris: Mouton, 1963).

GREGORY IX (1227–1241). Pope, 1227–41. Obsessed with **heresy**, Gregory IX established an **Inquisition** in 1231 and in 1232 turned over its administration to the **Dominicans** and Franciscans. He issued an edict commanding there be no friendly relations between Christians and Jews. In 1233 and 1236, Gregory complained to the French bishops about the torture and murder of Jews, but he put no sanctions in his letter of protection and refused to suggest excommunication. He also severely reprimanded minor Jewish offenses against Christians and threatened to use secular military forces against the Jews. In March 1233, Gregory commanded the bishops of Germany "completely to suppress" Jewish attempts to **convert** Christians, hold public office, and avoid their stigmatizing **Jew badges**. He added: "[So that the Jews] should not again dare to straighten their neck bent under the yoke of slavery and dispute with Christians about their faith, [the bishops] may call in for this purpose the secular arm." In 1233, when Christians tortured Jews by tearing out their fingernails and teeth as part of the Inquisition process, the pope beseeched the French bishops to "warn all the faithful Christians . . . and induce them not to harm the Jews . . . so long as they do not presume to insult the Christian faith." Alas, the very fact of persistence in one's Judaism and regard for the **Talmud** (commentary on Old Testament) was presumptive insult to the Christian faith. In 1240, informed by **Nicholas Donin** about the "blasphemies" in the Talmud, Gregory ordered monarchs to confiscate the Jews' holy book. *See also* BOOK BURNING.

SUGGESTED READING: Bernhard Blumenkranz, ed., *Les auteurs chrétiens latins du moyen age sur les Juifs et le Judaisme* (Paris: Mouton, 1963).

GREGORY XVI (1765–1846). Pope, 1831–46. In 1832, Gregory XVI condemned the liberal principle of "freedom of conscience [and] emancipation" of Jews and others as an "absurdity."

SUGGESTED READING: David I. Kertzer, *The Popes against the Jews* (New York: Knopf, 2001).

GREGORY NAZIANZUS, ST. (325–389). A Doctor of the Church who saw **heresy** as essentially Jewish.

SUGGESTED READING: Edward Kessler and Neil Wenborn, *A Dictionary of Jewish–Christian Relations* (Cambridge: Cambridge University Press, 2005); Carol Krinsky, *Synagogues of Europe: Architecture, History, Meaning* (New York: Dover, 1996).

GREGORY OF NYSSA, ST. (d. 385). Bishop of Nyssa in Asia Minor. Gregory implicated all Jews, past and present and future, in mythological crimes against Christianity. Gregory described the Jews as

> murderers of the Lord, killers of the prophets, enemies and slanderers of God; violators of the law, adversaries of grace, aliens to the faith of their fathers, advocates of the devil, progeny of poison snakes, . . . whose minds are held in darkness, filled with the anger of the **Pharisees**, a **Sanhedrin** of satans. Criminals, degenerates, . . . enemies of all that is decent and beautiful. They are guilty of shouting: Away with him, away with him. Crucify him. He who was God in the flesh!

SUGGESTED READING: Gregory of Nyssa, "In Christi Resurrectionem, Oratio V," in *Patrologiae Cursus Completus: Series Graeca*, ed. Jacques-Paul Migne (Paris: Garnier, 1857–66).

GREGORY OF TOURS, ST. (538–594). French bishop. Gregory spread tales into Western Europe from the Byzantine Empire that the Jews had maliciously assaulted the sanctums of Christianity by stealing and then defiling a Christian image or relic.

SUGGESTED READING: Lou Kessler and Neal Weinbaum, *Dictionary of Jewish–Christian Relations* (Cambridge: Cambridge University Press, 2005).

GREISER, ARTHUR (1897–1946). **Nazi** executive. As president of the Danzig Senate in 1938–39, Greiser initiated anti-Jewish laws. After the German conquest of Poland, as *Gauleiter* (party regional governor), he played a major role in establishing the **extermination camp** Chelmno and deporting Jews there.

SUGGESTED READING: Lucjan Dobroszycki, *The Chronicle of the Lodz Ghetto, 1941–1944* (New Haven, CT: Yale University Press, 1984).

GRESE, IRMA (1921–1945). SS matron. Grese was known as the "Blond Angel of Hell" and "the Beautiful Beast." She assisted doctors in their inhumane deadly experiments at Ravensbrück concentration camp. Placed in charge of female prisoners at **Auschwitz-Birkenau** and **Bergen-Belsen**, she treated them with great brutality, devising sadistic exercises for them and often beating them to death. At Birkenau, the **extermination camp** of Auschwitz, she assisted camp commandant **Josef Kramer** with **selections** for the **gas chambers**.

SUGGESTED READING: Daniel P. Brown, *The Beautiful Beast: The Life and Times of SS-Aufseherin Irma Grese* (Ventura, CA: Golden West Historical Publications, 1996).

GRIMM, JACOB AND WILHELM (1785–1876, 1786–1859). Philologists and story writers. The Brothers Grimm collaborated in compiling and editing *Kinder- und Hausmärchen* (*Children's and Household Tales*, 1812–14). The fairytales exhibited a cultural nationalism that portrayed the outsider in Germany as repulsive. Jews were characterized as malevolent and scheming. The tales affirmed the preexisting negative Jewish stereotype. In their dictionary *Deutsches Wörterbuch*, begun in the 19th century and not finished until after World War II, the long entry under *Jude* (Jew) states in part: Jews

> are especially unclean as well as greedy and extortionate [as used] in a whole variety of idioms—dressed dirty or messy like an old jew; he stinks like a jew; . . . to taste like a jew; . . . to taste like a dead Jew; . . . to practise **usury**, to cheat, to profiteer, to borrow like a Jew.

Reflecting German 19th-century usage, almost obsession with things Jewish, the dictionary contains nearly a hundred words prefixed by "Jew." *See also* MOTHER GOOSE.

SUGGESTED READING: Louis L. Snyder, "Cultural Nationalism: The Grimm Brothers Fairy Tales," in *Roots of German Nationalism* (Bloomington: Indiana University Press, 1978).

GROSS, WALTHER (1904–1945). Head of the **Nazi** Racial Policy Office, 1935–45. In 1932, directing the Nazi Doctors Alliance, Gross sought to remove all Jewish doctors. As a member of the Reichstag (parliament), he encouraged anti-Jewish laws enacted during the 1930s. While in the Racial Policy Office in 1943, Gross wrote the prophetic **"Final Solution,"** a work advocating **euthanasia** for Jews.

SUGGESTED READING: Robert S. Wistrich, *Who's Who in Nazi Germany* (Independence, KY: Routledge, 1995).

GROTIUS, HUGO (1583–1645). Dutch jurist and humanist. In good mercantilist fashion, Grotius defended Jewish settlement in Holland as economically useful, and he suggested that the Catholic **ritual murder** defamation was false, caused by Jew-hatred. However, he opposed the establishment of public **synagogues**, sexual contact between Christians and Jews, Jews in public office, and the conversion of Christians to Judaism.

SUGGESTED READING: Jonathan Israel, *European Jewry in the Age of Mercantilism* (Oxford: Oxford University Press, 1989).

GUENTHER, HANS F. K. (1891–1968). German racist historian. Guenther's *Racial Elements in European History* (1927) is a work like **Arthur de Gobineau**'s, extolling the Nordic race as superior. Guenther decried the presence of other peoples in Germany, fearing amalgamation with them. He favored all the Jews going to Palestine, believing they "presented a grave danger to the life of European people." His pictures and descriptions of races were used by **Nazi** racial "scientists." *See also* CHAMBERLAIN, HOUSTON STEWART; DAVENPORT, CHARLES BENEDICT; EUGENICS.

SUGGESTED READING: Hans F. K. Guenther, *Racial Elements of European History* (1927; reprint, Port Washington, NY: Kennikut Press, 1970).

GUI, BERNARDO (1261–1331). Notorious Italian **Francisan** inquisitor. After the **Shepherds' Crusade** was suppressed, Pope **John XXII** authorized Gui to place the **Talmud** on trial, since, as the pope insisted, Christians must be kept away from the Jewish "pestilence." The Talmud had to be examined, and if blasphemies were found therein, it had to be burned, and both **judaized** Christians and Jews were to be punished according to **canon law**. Found guilty of blasphemy, the books of the Talmud were burned on Gui's orders in Toulouse and Perpignan, France, in the early 14th century. *See also* BOOK BURNING.

SUGGESTED READING: Shlomo Simonsohn, *The Apostolic See and the Jews: History* (Toronto: Pontifical Institute of Mediaeval Studies, 1991).

GUIBERT OF NOGENT (1064–1124). French abbot. Guibert wrote about a monk who fell sick and had to call upon a Jewish doctor, who "promised to be his mediator with the devil."

SUGGESTED READING: Joshua Trachtenberg, *The Devil and the Jews* (Philadelphia: Jewish Publication Society, 1961).

GUICCIARDINI, FRANCESCO (1483–1540). Spanish historian, states-man, and humanist. Guicciardini applauded the **expulsion** of the Jews from Spain in 1492 and judged the forced exile as one of the Spanish monarchy's major accomplishments. He was profoundly disturbed that Jews were occasionally chosen to administer Castile's finances and felt that the Jewish presence would soon lead to the destruction of Spanish Catholicism. As a result, Guicciardini praised the **Inquisition**, even when it burned 120 Jews in Cordova in one day.

SUGGESTED READING: Shlomo Simonsohn, *The Apostolic See and the Jews: History* (Toronto: Pontifical Institute of Mediaeval Studies, 1991).

GUILDS. Associations of skilled European craftsmen. Jews were excluded from membership in guilds everywhere in Europe throughout medieval times. This Judeophobia grew out of an economic root. Such exclusion encouraged Jews to enter one of the few fields open to them, money-lending. In 16th- and 17th-century Poland, Jews had a great deal of self-government, including guild membership. In Muslim lands, Jewish artisans played an important economic role. *See also* USURY.

SUGGESTED READING: H. H. Ben-Sasson, ed., *A History of the Jewish People* (Cambridge, MA: Harvard University Press, 1976).

GWYNNE, H. A. Editor of the openly **antisemitic** British periodical *The Morning Post* and author of *The Cause of World Unrest* (1920). In this book, Gwynne reported the myth that "the **Bolsheviks** were not sincere Socialists or Communists, but Jews, working for the ulterior motives of Judaism." Although he knew *The Protocols of the Elders of Zion* was a forgery, he accepted the antisemitic fantasy offered by the head of Special Branch at Scotland Yard, Sir Basil Thomson, that the *Protocols* was a "series of political formulae concocted by Lenin, **Trotsky**, Leibnecht, **Rosa Luxemburg** . . . and other prominent Anarchist Jews [Bolsheviks]." Gwynne intended to portray Russian Bolshevism as further proof of a Jewish conspiracy against the world's social order. With support from other British antisemites such as **Nesta Webster**, Gwynne published *The Protocols* in the *Morning Post* in July 1920. Later that year, **Victor Marsden**, the *Morning Post*'s Russian correspondent, published the most popular English translation of *The Protocols*, which by 1930 sold more than a half-million copies in Britain and the United States. Gwynne's publications stirred British fears of a Jewish conspiracy to destroy the British Empire.

SUGGESTED READING: Keith Wilson, "*The Protocols* and the *Morning Post*, 1919–1920," *Patterns of Prejudice* 19, no. 3 (1985); Colin Holmes, "The *Protocols* of 'The Britons,'" *Patterns of Prejudice* 12, no. 6 (1978).

GYP (1850–1932). Pseudonym for Sibylle Aimée Marie Antoinette Gabrielle de Riqueti de Mirabeau, Comtesse de Martel de Janville, an extremely popular French novelist, cartoonist, and playwright. Gyp lampooned crooks, bankers, and Marxists, both Jewish and Gentile. Her later plays were devoted to nationalism and **antisemitism**.

SUGGESTED READING: "Gyp," *LoveToKnow 1911 Online Encyclopedia*, 2003, http://83.1911encyclopedia.org/g/gy/gyp.htm.

– H –

HADITH. Muslim oral tradition. The Hadith contain passages accusing the **perfidious** Jews of murdering the prophet **Muhammad** and claiming that these malicious Jews were the cause of the Islamic **heresies** that threatened the integrity of all Islam. These accusations paralleled the Christian charges that the Jews killed Christ and were responsible for Christian heresies. Such principles form the basis of modern Islamic **antisemitism**. *See* KORAN.

SUGGESTED READING: Robert S. Wistrich, *Muslim Antisemitism: A Clear and Present Danger* (New York: American Jewish Committee, 2002).

HADRIAN (76–138). Roman emperor, 119–38. Hadrian hoped to destroy the Jews once and for all. He ordered the destruction of the Second Temple in Jerusalem and that a pagan temple be constructed in its place. He also forbade the Jews entry into Jerusalem, the practice of **circumcision**, the observance of Jewish holidays, public performance of Jewish ritual, and Jewish education. His campaign resulted in the deaths of perhaps a half-million Jews and the destruction of hundreds of Jewish communities in Judaea. He renamed the city of Jerusalem Aelia Capitolina.

SUGGESTED READING: Moshe Aberback, *The Roman Wars and Jewish Cultural Nationalism* (New York: Palgrave, 2000).

HAECKEL, ERNST (1834–1919). German zoologist, philosopher, **Social Darwinist**, racist, and nationalist. Haeckel's slogan, "Politics is applied biology," became a favorite with the **Nazis**. He believed in Nordic race superiority, opposed any racial mixing, and advocated racial **eugenics**. A **völkisch nationalist**, Haeckel held that Jesus could not be fully Jewish because he exhibited superior **Aryan** traits. He argued that Jews were too separatist and alienated from German life, and he viewed the Russian Jewish immigrant as the worst example of Jewishness. To him, they were "filthy people with outlandish appearance." Haeckel's view was that the Jews must either stop being Jewish and conform completely or leave Germany. **Antisemitism**, he concluded, was a good thing, for it encouraged Jews to assimilate. His ideas on eugenics, evolution, Social Darwinism, Aryan purity, infanticide, and immigration were an inspiration to the Nazis. *See also* BRIGHAM, CARL; DAVENPORT, CHARLES BENEDICT; GRANT, MADISON; GOBINEAU, ARTHUR DE; GUENTHER, HANS F. K.; *MEIN KAMPF.*

SUGGESTED READING: Daniel Gasman, *Haeckel: Monism and the Birth of Fascist Ideology* (New York: Peter Lang, 1998).

HAGGARD, H. RIDER (1856–1925). British writer most noted for his *King Solomon's Mines* (1885). The novel *Benita: An African Romance* (1906) paints an unsympathetic picture of a Jewish character, Jacob Meyer:

> There was something in the man's personality which repelled and alarmed Benita, something wild and cruel. When asked, "What do you mean by a better life, Mr. Meyer?" Meyer responded, "I mean . . . great wealth, and the power that wealth brings. Ah! I see you think me very sordid and materialistic, but money is God in this world, Miss Clifford—money is God."

HAHN, DIEDERICH (1859–1918). Noted German agrarian politician and bureaucrat. Hahn was first elected to the Reichstag in 1893. An innovative and boisterous politician, he was also the director of the Agrarian League, Germany's largest and best-funded interest group. As the director of the league and the most well-known political figure of the time, Hahn participated in all the major political controversies of the period. A typical political cartoon portrays Hahn as a Don Quixote leading his followers against the forces of modernity. Although Hahn was a virulent antisemite from his student days, **antisemitism** was neither widespread nor popular in the region when his political career began.

SUGGESTED READING: Hans-Jürgen Puhle, *Von der Agrarkrise zum Präfaschismus* (Wiesbaden: Steiner, 1972); George S. Vascik, "Diedrich Hahn and German Agrarians: Computer-Assisted Plotting and Analysis of Village Returns in German National Elections, 1893–1912," *Journal of the Association for History and Computing* 4, no. 1 (April 2001), http://mcel.pacificu.edu/jahc/jahciv1/articles/vascik%20/vascikindex.html#anchor-44591.

HAIDAMACKS. 18th-century Russian brigade bands composed of Cossacks and runaway serfs and those who opposed Polish nobles and Jews. Haidamacks massacred many Jews in Kiev, Volhynin, and Podolia. In

1734, 1735, and 1768, horrendous scenes of mass slaughter took place. At Uman, 20,000 Jews met horrible deaths.

SUGGESTED READING: S. M. Dubnow and Saul Friedlander, *History of the Jews of Russia and Poland from Earliest Times until the Present (1915)* (Bergenfield, NJ: Avotaynu, 2000).

HAIDER, JÖRG (1950–). Leading postwar Austrian revisionist, governor of the Austrian province of Carinthia, and former leader of the rightist Austrian Freedom Party (FPÖ). In 2005 he founded a new party, the Alliance for the Future of Austria (BZÖ). Haider was born after the **Holocaust**, both his parents unrepentant Austrian **Nazis**. Haider regarded his parents and their generation as victims. He claims that the wartime bombing of German and Austrian cities and the postwar expulsions of Germans from Eastern Europe were morally worse than the crimes against the Jews during the Holocaust itself. Furthermore, he believes that the Germans and Austrians should be compensated for their wartime suffering. Haider has also alleged that many Holocaust survivors had collaborated with the Nazis, and therefore these Jews have no moral grounds to blame the Nazis. Haider is significant not only in Austrian and European politics but also in German cultural **antisemitism**. See also BUBIS, IGNATZ.

SUGGESTED READING: Anat Peri, "Jörg Haider's Antisemitism," Vidal Sassoon International Center for the Study of Antisemitism, 2001, http://sicsa.huji.ac.il/acta18.htm.

HAKIM BI-AMR ALLAH, AL- (985–1021). Caliph (996–1021) and founder of the Druze faith and ruler of most of North Africa and Middle East in early 11th century. Hakim was at first a protector of Jews. In 1008, Hakim, the third Fatima ruler (of the dynasty descended from Fatima, **Muhammad**'s daughter), enforced the **Pact of Omar** (638), which protected but discriminated against **dhimmis**. Jews and Christians had to wear **stigmatic emblems** around their necks. After 1012, Hakim persecuted the Jews by burning **synagogues** and forcing **conversions** to his sect.

SUGGESTED READING: A. J. Arberry, ed., *Religion in the Middle East* (Cambridge: Cambridge University Press, 1969); Norman A. Stillman, *The Jews of Arab Lands: A History and Source Book* (Philadelphia: Jewish Publication Society, 1979).

HALDEMAN, H. R. See NIXON, RICHARD M.

HALSUADA, AL. (Palestinian slur) Arabic dialect for "evil dogs."

SUGGESTED READING: "List of Ethnic Slurs," *Wikipedia*, http://en.wikipedia.org/wiki/List_of_ethnic_slurs.

HAMAN. Biblical character; Persian noble. In the Book of Esther, Haman, the chief minister to the Persian king Ahasuerus, accuses the Jews of being disloyal, unpatriotic, unlawful, and unreliable. Haman's attempt to exterminate the Jews of Persia is foiled by Queen Esther. The Jewish holiday of **Purim** celebrates Jewish survival and Haman's death.

HAMAS. Arabic for "devotion" or "zeal" in the path of Allah; acronym for Harakat al-Muqawama al-Islamiyya (Islamic Resistance Movement). The Hamas movement, a Palestinian offshoot of the Egyptian **Muslim Brotherhood**, is now a Palestinian terrorist organization. The Hamas Covenant of 1988 states:

> The Islamic Resistance Movement calls on Arab and Islamic nations to . . . warn the people of the danger eminating from leaving the circle of struggle against Zionism. Today it is Palestine, tomorrow it will be one country or another. The Zionist plan is limitless. . . . When [the Zionists] have digested the region . . . , they will aspire to further expansion. . . . Their plan is embodied in the *Protocols of the Elders of Zion*. . . . Leaving the circle of struggle with Zionism is high treason, and cursed be he who does that. . . . There is no way out except by concentrating all powers and energies to face this Nazi, vicious Tatar invasion.

Hamas alleges that the Jews control the world's wealth and mass media; caused the **French Revolution** and Russian Revolution as well as the two world wars; and established cabalistic organizations such as the **Freemasons**, the Lions' Clubs, and the League of Nations to destroy Islam and achieve the Zionist goal of world domination. Hamas draws an analogy between **Muhammad**'s 628 conquest of "treacherous" Jews and its own war to destroy Israel. Hamas fought against Israel in its 1948 War of Independence. Believing in violence as a method to achieve its aims, Hamas seeks to "liberate" all of Palestine, eliminate the sovereign state of Israel, and replace it with a fundamentalist Islamic Arab state. Hamas has used suicide bombers against Israel and murdered collaborating Arabs. In 2006 Hamas won the majority of seats in the Palestinian Parliament and became the ruling party in both the West Bank and Gaza. *See also* RADICAL ISLAM; YASSIN, AHMED.

SUGGESTED READING: Simon Robinson, "How Will Hamas Rule?" *Time*, February 27, 2006; Dan Cohn-Sherbok and Dawoud el-Alami, *The Palestine-Israeli Conflict* (New York: One World [Oxford], 2002); "Hamas Covenant, 1988," Avalon Project at Yale Law School, http://www.yale.edu/lawweb/avalon/mideast/hamas.htm.

HAMMERSKIN NATION. The most violent and best-organized **neo-Nazi skinhead** group in the United States. A number of its members have been convicted of harassing, beating, or murdering minorities. Many popular racist **white power music** bands are affiliated with the Hammerskin Nation, and the group regularly sponsors concerts. The name and symbol of the Hammerskin Nation came from *The Wall*, a 1979 album by the rock group Pink Floyd that was made into a film in 1982. In it, a rock singer turns to **fascism** and performs a song in which he expresses a desire to line all of the "queers," "Jews," and "coons" in his audience "up against the wall" and shoot them. In obvious references to the **Holocaust**, he sings of the "**final solution**" and "waiting to turn on the showers and fire the ovens." The **swastika** is replaced by his symbol: two crossed hammers, which he boasts will "batter down" the doors behind which frightened minorities hide from his fascist supporters. Chapters exist in several countries, including **Canada**, England, France, Germany, and The Netherlands. *See also* FRITSCH, THEODOR.

SUGGESTED READING: Michael Reynolds, "Hammerskin Nation," *Intelligence Report* (Southern Poverty Law Center), 2005, http://www .splcenter.org/intelreport/article.jsp?aid = 310.

HAMMOND, JAMES (1807–1864). The Thanksgiving proclamation of Governor James H. Hammond of South Carolina in 1844 stated, "I invite and exhort our Citizens of all [Christian] denominations to Assemble at their respective places of worship to offer up their devotions to God the Creator, and his Son Jesus Christ, the redeemer of the world." Local Jews wrote to him "sternly and solemnly to protest against the language and spirit of the Proclamation," calling it "as unusual as it was offensive." The governor replied:

> I have always thought it a settled matter that I lived in a Christian land! And that I was the temporary chief magistrate of a Christian people. That in such a country and among such a people I should be, publicly, called to an account, reprimanded and required to make amends for acknowledging Jesus Christ as the Redeemer of the world, I would not have believed possible, if it had not come to pass. . . . I know that the civilization of the age is derived from Christianity, that the institutions of this country are instinct with the same spirit, and that it pervades the laws of the State as it does the manners and I trust the hearts of our people.

American Jews, who had inherited "the same scorn for Jesus Christ which instigated their ancestors to crucify him," Hammond said, had no grounds for objecting to the Christian holiday of Thanksgiving.

SUGGESTED READING: Jacob Marcus, *United States Jewry, 1776–1985* (Detroit: Wayne State University Press, 1989); "The Israelite of South Carolina," *Occident and American Jewish Advocate* 11, no. 10 (January 1945).

HARNACK, ADOLF VON (1851–1930). German humanist and church scholar; specialist in patristic history. Denying the Jewish roots of Christianity, Harnack argued that because the connection between Jesus Christ's teaching and Judaism was "only a loose one, . . . the Old Testament should be deposed from canonical rank."

SUGGESTED READING: Andrew Irving, "Adolf von Harnack," in *Dictionary of Modern Western Theology* (Boston: Boston University Press, 1996).

HARRINGTON, JOHN (1561–1612). British statesman. As a member of the House of Lords, Harrington opposed admission of Jewish immigrants in 1858. He accused British Jews of promoting the national debt and thought that their money-lending made them enemies of freedom.

SUGGESTED READING: Myriam Yardeni, *Anti-Jewish Mentalities in Early Modern Europe* (Lanham, MD: University Press of America, 1990).

HARRISON, BENJAMIN (1833–1901). U.S. president, 1889–93. Harrison's message to the Congress on December 9, 1891, expressed concern that multitudes of Jews were about to invade the United States from Russia. He reported that his government had informed St. Petersburg that "the harsh measures now being enforced against the Hebrews in Russia" would force a million Jews to seek haven in the United States. The attitude of Harrison and his secretary of state, James Blaine, was that the Russian Jews were contaminated beings. The government of the United States made it clear it considered it an unfriendly act for Russia to force on the United States "large numbers of degraded and undesirable persons."

SUGGESTED READING: Louise Mayo, *The Ambivalent Image* (London: Associated University Press, 1988).

HASKALAH. Hebrew for "enlightenment." An 18th-century European Jewish movement toward abandoning Jewish exclusiveness and seeking instead assimilation through secular public education and adopting the manners and aspirations of the nations in which they lived. It included the study of Biblical Hebrew and Hebrew literature but substituted modern subjects for intensive, all-encompassing **Talmud** study. It opposed the ultra-Orthodox Jewish Hasidim. Exponents of the movement were called *Maskilim*, enlighteners. They advocated Jewish involvement in agriculture and crafts and an awareness of current events. They also urged Jews to follow the path of **Moses Mendelssohn**, the brilliant German philosopher and most prominent German Jew, in abandoning the **ghetto** for more secular involvements. Maskilim met with more success in Western Europe.

Such integration brought many Jews together with Christians, but also stimulated new waves of **antisemitism** because many Christians were fearful the assimilated Jews would serve as rivals.

SUGGESTED READING: Paul Mendes and Jehuda Reinharz, *The Jew in the Modern World* (New York: Oxford University Press, 1995).

HAUPTMANN, HANS. 20th-century German writer. Hauptmann wrote that the Jews did the Devil's work on Earth and that Jews had the Germans hypnotized. He believed that an "**Aryan** Christ" had been crucified by "Semitic Jews." His book *Bolshevism in the Bible* was adopted as a **Nazi** text.

SUGGESTED READING: Carl Lamson Carmer, *The War against God* (New York: Holt and Co., 1943).

HAWTHORNE, JULIAN (1846–1934). Popular **antisemitic** American novelist, son of novelist **Nathaniel Hawthorne**. Julian Hawthorne depicted Jews as extremely base characters whose financial speculation was the key to their power and was thinly disguised theft.

SUGGESTED READING: Alan G. James, "The Master and the Laureate of the Jews: The Brief Friendship of Henry James and Emma Lazarus," *Henry James Review* 21, no. 1 (Winter 2000).

HAWTHORNE, NATHANIEL (1804–1864). American novelist. Perhaps the most egregious examples of **antisemitism** in 19th-century literature occur in Hawthorne's work. Although he had almost never directly experienced Jews, he discussed them more extensively than his colleagues. In the novel *The Marble Faun*, Hawthorne refers to the Jews as "the ugliest, most evil-minded" people, "resembling . . . maggots when they over-populate a decaying cheese." In an essay in *English Notebooks* (1853–56), he described the Jewish lord mayor of London's elder brother in this way:

> There sat the very Jew of Jews; the distilled essence of all the Jews that have been born since Jacob's time; he was **Judas Iscariot**; he was the **Wandering Jew**; he was the worst, and at the same time, the truest type of his race, and contained within himself, I have no doubt, every old prophet and every old clothesman, that ever the tribes produced; and he must have been **circumcised** as much as ten times over. I never beheld anything so ugly and disagreeable, and preposterous, and laughable, as the outline of his profile; it was so hideously Jewish, and so cruel, and so keen. . . . I rejoiced exceedingly in this **Shylock**, this Iscariot; for the sight of him justified me in the repugnance I have always felt towards his race.

Two of Hawthorne's images—the Jew as maggot and as devil—are echoed in the work of **Adolf Hitler**. *See also* HAWTHORNE, JULIAN.

SUGGESTED READING: Augustus M. Kolich, "Miriam and the Conversion of the Jews in Nathaniel Hawthorne's *The Marble Faun*," *Studies in the Novel* 33 (December 2001).

HAY, JOHN (1838–1905). American writer and diplomat. An intimate of Abraham Lincoln's, ambassador to Great Britain, and later secretary of state, Hay in 1868 described the Jews in the Vienna **Ghetto**: "This coquetry of hideousness is most nauseous. . . . These slouching rascals are as idle as they are ugly. . . . I suppose the curse of the nation has lit on these fellows especially."

SUGGESTED READING: Louis Harap, *The Image of the Jew in American Literature* (Syracuse, NY: Syracuse University Press, 2003).

HAY SEED. (U.S. slur) Intentional mispronounciation of *Hasid*(ic Jew).

SUGGESTED READING: "List of Ethnic Slurs," *Wikipedia*, http://en.wikipedia.org/wiki/List_of_ethnic_slurs.

HEBE; HEEB; HEEBIE; HEEBO. (North American slur) Short for Hebrew.

SUGGESTED READING: "List of Ethnic Slurs," *Wikipedia*, http://en.wikipedia.org/wiki/List_of_ethnic_slurs.

HEEBSPANIC. (U.S. slur) Mixed Jewish and Hispanic parentage, or a person of Hispanic ethnicity/national origin who practices Judaism.

SUGGESTED READING: "List of Ethnic Slurs," *Wikipedia*, http://en.wikipedia.org/wiki/List_of_ethnic_slurs.

HEGEL, GEORG WILHELM FRIEDRICH (1776–1831). German philosopher. In Hegel's *Philosophy of History*, he ranks the Jews low on the scale of civilization. He saw the Jewish soul as a withering leaf in his dialectic of the evolving world soul. As Judaism holds no further historical role, he believed it must be replaced by Christianity. *See also* YOUNG HEGELIANS.

SUGGESTED READING: Yovel Yirmiyahu, *Dark Riddle: Hegel, Nietzsche and the Jews* (University Park: Pennsylvania State University Press, 1998).

HEIDEGGER, MARTIN (1889–1976). German philosopher. Heidegger joined the National Socialist Party shortly after **Adolf Hitler**'s accession to power in 1933, and after he himself had become chancellor of Freiburg University. During his administration, Jewish teachers were excluded from the university, and public **book burnings** were held by the students. Heidegger rejected in 1929—that is, before the **Nazis** came to power—the "'Jewification' of the German spirit." He removed the dedication of *Being and Time* (an existentialist critique of rationalism) to the "inconveniently Jewish" Edmund Husserl (a convert to Christianity). There are various stories of Heidegger not signing the dissertations of his Jewish graduate students, although he was very enthusiastic about some Jewish students, such as **Hannah Arendt**, with whom he had an affair, and he did decline to take some Nazi anti-Jewish measures. Heidegger applied the logic of his own glorification of the German *Volk* and often conformed to the political direction of the Führer.

SUGGESTED READING: Jean Francois Lyotard, *Heidegger and the Jews* (Minneapolis: University of Minnesota Press, 1990); Victor Farías, *Heidegger and the Nazis* (Philadelphia: Temple University Press, 1987).

HEINE, HEINRICH (1797–1856). One of Germany's greatest poets. A converted German Jew, Heine observed that "Jewishness was an incurable malady." For many Germans, despite his apostasy, he remained a Jew. *See also* HEINE MONUMENT CONTROVERSY

SUGGESTED READING: Michael Meyer, "The German Jews: Some Perspectives on Their History," in *Judaism within Modernity: Essays on Jewish History and Religion*, ed. Michael Meyer (Detroit: Wayne State University Press, 2001).

HEINE MONUMENT CONTROVERSY. After World War I, **antisemites** severely defaced a marble statue to **Heinrich Heine** located in a private park. Once it was removed, in 1926 the city had a bronze monument to Heine created by Hugo Lederer (1871–1940), and it was set up in the city park (Stadtpark). In August 1933, some months after the **Nazis** came to power, Hamburg authorities ordered its removal, and it was melted down as scrap metal in 1943.

SUGGESTED READING: Ritchie Robertson, *Heinrich Heine* (London: Halban, 1988); Robert Herzenberg, "An meinen Sohn Leonhard Herzenberg," trans. Leonardo Herzenberg, 1998, http://www.herzenberg.net/leo/htmlrh/postwar.html.

HEMINGWAY, ERNEST (1899–1961). American novelist. Writer Hemingway was fashionably **antisemitic**, which occasioned his hostility toward Robert Cohen in *The Sun Also Rises* (1926). Hemingway may have grown away from this easy antisemitism if his changed attitude toward art critic Bernard Berenson is any measure. Whereas in 1928 Hemingway had called

Berenson "an empty asshole and **kike** patron of the arts," by 1949 he regarded Berenson as "one of the living people that I respect the most."

SUGGESTED READING: Ron Berman, "Protestant, Catholic, Jew: *The Sun Also Rises*," *Hemingway Review* 18 (1998).

HENDRICK, BURTON (1875–1949). American Pulitzer Prize–winning author. Reacting to the large-scale immigration of Jews in previous decades, Hendrick called for the barring of further Jewish immigration into the United States in his 1923 *The Jews in America*.

HENRICI, ERNST (1854–1915). German *völkisch* demagogue, schoolteacher, racist, and founder of the Social Imperial Party (Soziale Reichspartei). In February 1881, Dr. Henrici visited Neustettin, Germany, and made an inflammatory **antisemitic** speech, campaigning against what he called *Judenherrschaft* (Jewish supremacy):

> If we can protect against livestock disease, why can't we take similar measures against the uncontrolled spread of Jewry? . . . Our private property will soon be in Jewish hands, and [real] Germans will be reduced to **pig** farmers for the Jews. [You must] boycott Jewish businesses and newspapers, sign the **Antisemites' Petition**, and prepare for unconditional war against the Jews so as to make their lives as difficult as possible and force them to leave the country. . . . Fear not, for we 42 million Germans will get the better of the 700,000 Jews.

His speech was quoted in full in the *Norddeutsche Presse*, and five days later the local **synagogue** was burned, a unique event during the German Second Reich. Henrici's visits to Eastern Pomerania spread the rabble-rousing slogans of Berlin's antisemitism to Neustettin, which proved to be fertile ground for such propaganda. In Henrici's address to Berlin antisemites in the Reichshall Meeting of 1880, Henrici had called for physical attacks on Jews attending the meeting. Henrici's title was "Lecture on the Means for Maintaining Christian-German Interests," and his talk stands as a summary of centuries of antisemitic defamations. Running for office in 1881, Henrici's extreme form of antisemitism gained him fewer than 900 votes. In 1883, after his failure to make a political career in Berlin, he turned his back on public life and emigrated to the United States. Germany was not yet ready for the volatile mixture of economic, völkisch, political, and racist antisemitism that became so effective after World War I.

SUGGESTED READING: Paul W. Massing, *Rehearsal for Destruction: A Study of Political Antisemitism in Imperial Germany* (New York: Harper, 1949); *Die Tribüne*, December 19, 1880, reprinted in *Der 'Berliner Antisemitismusstreit', 1879–1881*, ed. Karsten Krieger, trans. Erwin Fink (Munich: Saur, 2003).

HENRY II (1333–1379). King of Castile, 1369–79. Also known as Henry of Trastámara. Henry was the first nobleman to use **antisemitism** as a political tool in Spain. This led to an end to the *convivencia*—the period of great peaceful coexistence from 786 into the 1300s—and a period of riots and **pogroms**, which can be seen as sowing the seeds of the Spanish **Inquisition**'s persecution of the Jews, beginning a century later. Henry ordered Jews not to take Christian names, not to hold public office, and to wear a distinctive **Jew badge**.

SUGGESTED READING: Vivian B. Mann et al., *Covivencia: Jews, Muslims, and Christians in Medieval Spain* (New York: George Braziller, 1992).

HENRY III (1207–1272). King of England, 1216–72. Henry ruled that all the Jews of England were guilty of the **ritual murder** of Hugh of Lincoln in 1255 and seized this opportunity to extort money from them.

SUGGESTED READING: Robert C. Stacey, "The English Jews under Henry III," in *The Jews in Medieval Britain: Historical, Literary and Archeological Perspectives*, ed. Patricia Skinner (Suffolk: Boydell Press, 2003).

HENRY, HUBERT JOSEPH (d. 1898). Chief of French General Staff Intelligence. During the **Dreyfus Case** (1894–99), Henry falsely accused Capt. Alfred Dreyfus of giving secrets to the German ambassador, a fabrication leading to Dreyfus's arrest. Later, he forged documents claiming Dreyfus's complicity in espionage. Eventually, the truth came to light, largely through the efforts of Intelligence Chief **Georges Picquart** (Henry's successor); when the forgeries were detected, Henry committed suicide in 1898. *See also* ESTERHAZY, FERDINAND; ZOLA, ÉMILE.

SUGGESTED READING: Guy Chapman, *The Dreyfus Case* (Westport, CT: Greenwood Press, 1978).

HENTSCHEL, WILLIBALD (1858–1947). Radical racial propagandist; a student of **Ernst Haeckel**. "That which preserves health is moral," Hentschel said. "Everything that makes one sick or ugly is sin." He advocated a racially pure utopia free of Jews. *See also* BLOOD AND SOIL.

SUGGESTED READING: Richard Weikart, *From Darwin to Hitler* (New York: Palgrave Macmillan, 2004).

HEP HEP RIOTS. Anti-Jewish riots in Germany and Denmark in 1819, led by university students. The words "Hep Hep" may be an acronym from the Latin *"Hierosolyma est perdita"* (Jerusalem is destroyed). The students were joined by peasants and unemployed factory workers. Jews were blamed for famine, unemployment, and hard times. The House of **Rothschild** was also attacked. *See also* POGROM.

SUGGESTED READING: Peter Vierck, *Metapolitics: The Roots of the Nazi Mind* (New York: Capricorn, 1961).

HERDER, JOHANN GOTTFRIED VON (1744–1808). German romanticist and clergyman. A pacifist, internationalist, and admirer of the Hebrew Bible and **Moses Mendelssohn,** Herder was the coiner and founder of the *Volk* cult. His term *Volkgeist*—the spirit of an ethnic people, a Volk soul— was adapted to mean intolerant aggressive nationalism by the **Nazis**.

SUGGESTED READING: Peter Vierck, *Metapolitics: The Roots of the Nazi Mind* (New York: Capricorn, 1961).

HERESY. Opinion at variance with accepted doctrine. According the Christian definition, a heretic was a person whose intelligence and will had been perverted by the Devil or his Jewish agents. A long Christian tradition existed associating the Jews with the **Antichrist**. In an attempt to establish the orthodoxy of Christian doctrine, early Christian writers associated Jews with condemned sectarians and **heretics**. **St. Paul** wrote that factious people are "perverted and sinful." **Acts of the Apostles** accuses the **Pharisees**, the most popular and scrupulous Jews, and the Sadducees, the priestly aristocracy of the Temple, as heretics or "parties." **Origen, Eusebius of Alexandria, St. Irenaeus, Gregory of Nyssa, St. Basil, Gregory Nazianzus, Justin Martyr**, and other **Church Fathers** saw heresy as essentially Jewish. **Tertullian** explained that "from the Jew the heretic has accepted guidance in this discussion [that Jesus was not the Christ]. Let the heretic now give up borrowing poison from the Jew . . . the asp, as they say, from the adder." **St. Ambrose** argued that all Jews were heretics because Jews should have recognized in Jesus their **messiah**. **Pseudo-Ambrose** saw all Jews as "apostates, for denial of Christ is essentially a violation of the Law." Anastasius (d. 700) called Christian heretics "Jews," and they in turn insulted other heretics as "Jews." The Christian emperor **Justinian** also classified Judaism as a kind of heresy. In response to Christian depredations, the Jews may have supported some Christian heretics, for example, the Arian Christians.

SUGGESTED READING: William Nicholls, *Christian Antisemitism: A History of Hate* (Northvale, NJ: Jason Aronson, 1995); Alan Davies, ed., *Antisemitism and the Foundations of Christianity* (New York: Paulist Press, 1979).

HERETIC. Professed believer who rejects church doctrine. The **Inquisition** defined a heretic also as a backsliding Jew—one who converted to Christianity but reverted to some Jewish rituals and practices, thus secretly practicing Judaism. In Roman Catholic Canon XLV (Church law), any bishop, presbyter, or deacon who prays with a heretic (defined as a Jew) was to be excommunicated.

HEYDRICH, REINHARD (1904–1942). **SS** lieutenant general. Heydrich became the head of the RSHA (Reichssicherheitshauptamt), the **Third Reich**'s Main Security Administration; the **SS**; and police operations, including the Intelligence Division, the **Gestapo**, Kriminalpolizei, and the **SD**. He was also the *Reichsmarschall* (military governor) of Bohemia-Moravia. Heydrich initiated the murderous **Einsatzgruppen** and chaired the **Wannsee Conference**. He developed the plan for **ghettoization** and extermination of the Jews of Europe. Heydrich was assassinated by Czech commandos in May 1942.

SUGGESTED READING: Günter Deschner, *Heydrich: The Pursuit of Total Power* (London: Orbis, 1988).

HEZBOLLAH. Arabic for "Party of God." Lebanese Shiite movement. Hezbollah, like **Hamas**, views Judaism as Islam's most dangerous enemy. It opposes "Western arrogance" and advocates the destruction of Israel so that Islamic unity can be reestablished. Hezbollah spokesman Sheikh Husayn Fadlallah argues that Israel is, as Robert Wistrich puts it, "the ultimate expression of the corrupt, treacherous, and aggressive 'Jewish' personality." Jews are "the enemy of the entire human race" and congenitally "racist." Fadlallah alleges that "diabolical" Israel stands as the military arm for the worldwide Jewish conspiracy to achieve economic and cultural domination. Hezbollah believes that the "**final solution** to the Jewish problem" is a successful Islamic war, including suicide bombings against Israel, Zionism, and the Jews. Hezbollah draws much of its ideology from contemporary **Iranian** attitudes toward Jews as demonic infidels. Its military leader was Shiite cleric Sayyed Hassan, who also held the office of secretary general. The nonpartisan Council on Foreign Relations considers Hezbollah "a terrorist group believed responsible for nearly 200 attacks since 1982 that have killed more than 800 people." *See also* ISLAMIC JIHAD.

SUGGESTED READING: Robert S. Wistrich, *Muslim Antisemitism: A Clear and Present Danger* (New York: American Jewish Committee, 2002); Cyril Glasse, *The New Encyclopedia of Islam* (Walnut Creek, CA: Rowman & Littlefield, 2002).

HFFH. Abbreviation for "Hammerskins Forever, Forever Hammerskins." *See* HAMMERSKIN NATION.

HILARY (315–398). Bishop of Poitiers, France; Doctor of the Catholic Church. Hilary would neither acknowledge the greeting of a Jew in the street nor accept food from one because he believed that "the Jews were possessed of an unclean devil." For him, Judaism was "ever . . . mighty in wickedness; . . . when it cursed Moses; when it hated God; when it vowed its sons to demons; when it killed the prophets, and finally when it betrayed to the Praetor and crucified our God Himself and Lord. . . . And so glorying through all its existence in iniquity."

SUGGESTED READING: James Everett Searer, *The Persecution of the Jews in the Roman Empire, 300–428* (Lawrence: University Press of Kansas, 1952).

HIMMLER, HEINRICH (1900–1945). *Reichsführer-SS* (leader of the **Third Reich**'s **SS**) and chief of the Reich's police. Himmler was second only to **Adolf Hitler** and was the major architect of the **Holocaust** of European Jews. As chief of antipartisan warfare, he ordered the summary execution of Jews. All Jewish inmates of concentration and death camps came under the jurisdiction of Himmler's SS. In October 1943, Himmler defined Germany's goal of murdering all Jews. He distinguished between **genocide** and Holocaust (without using those terms). First, he defined genocide:

> Whether the other nations live in prosperity or croak from hunger interests me only insofar as we need them as slaves for our culture. . . . We shall never be brutal or heartless where it is not necessary—obviously not. We Germans, the only people in the world who have a decent attitude toward animals, will also take a decent attitude toward these human animals.

Himmler then defined Holocaust:

> A really grave matter. Among ourselves, this once, it shall be uttered quite frankly; but in public we will never speak of it. . . . I am referring to the evacuation of the Jews, the annihilation of the Jewish people. . . . In our history, this in an unwritten and never-to-be-written page of glory. . . . The wealth they had we have taken from them. . . . We had the moral right, we had the duty toward our people, to kill this people which wanted to kill us.

See also GAS CHAMBERS; ZYKLON.

SUGGESTED READING: *Trial of the Major War Criminals before the International Military Tribunal, Nuremberg, 14 November 1945–1 October 1946* (Buffalo, NY: William S. Hein, 1995), 29:110–73; Richard Breitman, *The Architect of Genocide: Himmler and the Final Solution* (New York: Knopf, 1991).

HIRSCHFELD, MAGNUS (1868–1935). Director of the Berlin Institute of Sexual Science. In 1933, the **Nazis** destroyed Hirschfeld's Sexualwissenschaft (scientific project to study sexual interactions founded and developed mainly by Jews or by Christians of Jewish descent). In 1939, Hanns Oberlindober, head of the Nazi organization for wounded veterans, wrote about Hirschfeld: "The damage done to our youth by Magnus Hirschfeld alone, and the fact that the rest of Jewry tolerated him, is by itself sufficient to justify the harshest measures against the Jews."

SUGGESTED READING: J. Edgar Bauer, "Hirschfeld, Magnus," in *An Encyclopedia of Gay, Lesbian, Bisexual, Transgender, and Queer Culture*, http://www.glbtq.com/social-sciences/hirschfeld_m.html; from the *German Propaganda Archive at Calvin College*, collected by Randall Bytwerk, 2003.

HISTORIANS' CONTROVERSY (HISTORIKERSTREIT). German historians Ernst Nolte and Andreas Hillgruber, respectively in Nolte's *Deutschland und der kalte Krieg* (*Germany and the Cold War*, 1974) and Hillgruber's *Zweierlei Untergang* (*Two Kinds of Defeats*, 1986), historicized the **Holocaust** by dispassionately asserting that **Nazi** atrocities were no worse than other atrocities—the Turkish war on Armenians in 1918, the Stalinist attack on Ukrainians in the 1930s, the U.S. war in Vietnam in the 1960s and 1970s, and the Khmer Rouge genocide of the 1970s. They wrote with empathy about the German disasters on the Eastern Front, attempting to integrate Nazism into the rest of German history and denying the uniqueness of Nazism and the Holocaust. In 1986, German leftist social philosopher Jürgen Habermas began the Historians' Controversy by critiquing Nolte on the grounds that his writing of German history was revisionist. Debate divided historians along political and historiographical lines; the Liberal-left, Socialists, and Social Democrat Party accused conservatives like Nolte, Hillgruber, Michael Stürmer, Joachim Fest, Klaus Hildebrand, and Hagen Schulze of trying to "normalize," "relativize," even gloss over the Nazi past; of attempting to create a new national identity and reestablish the continuity of German history according to a conservative political agenda; conservatives and the Christian Democratic Union accused Habermas, Hans-Ulrich Wehler, Jürgen Kocka, Eberhard Jackel, Hans Mommsen, and Wolfgang Mommsen of dwelling on guilt, weakening Germany, distorting German identity, and not recognizing the achievements of the Second Reich and **Weimar** Germany. *See also* GERMAN REVISIONISM, POST-HOLOCAUST.

SUGGESTED READING: Peter Baldwin, ed., *Reworking the Past: Hitler, the Holocaust and the Historians' Controversy* (Boston: Beacon Press, 1990).

HISTORY OF EGYPT. *See* APION.

HITLER, ADOLF (1884–1945). Dictator of **Nazi** Germany. Hitler conceived, initiated, and implemented the most destructive **antisemitic** policies history has ever known. From 1920 on, he was the leader of the National-Socialist German Workers (Nazi) Party. From 1933 to 1945, he was the chancellor, then dictator (Führer) of Germany. Central to his policies was a race struggle against the Jews. The destruction of the European Jews came in stages, from exclusion, expropriation, and isolation to **ghettoization**, slave labor, and murder in concentration camps. As Germany engaged in a war of conquest, Nazi-controlled areas implemented extermination. *See also* ARYANIZATION; BAYREUTH FESTIVAL; BLAVATSKY, HELENE; BORMANN, MARTIN; BRAUCHITSCH, WALTHER VON; BRITISH UNION OF FASCISTS; DREXLER, ANTON; ECKART, DIETRICH; EISNER, KURT; FEDER, GOTTFRIED; *FOUNDATIONS OF THE NINETEENTH CENTURY*; GOEBBELS, JOSEF PAUL; GOERING, HERMANN; HITLER'S PROPHECY; HITLER'S SPEECHES, CHRISTIAN CONTENT OF; HITLER'S *TABLE TALK*; HOLOCAUST; HORTHY, MIKLÓS; HUSSEINI, HAJJ AMIN EL; LIEBENFELS, LANZ VON; LIST, GUIDO VON; *MEIN KAMPF*; NAZI PARTY PLATFORM; NUREMBERG LAWS OF 1935; WAGNER, RICHARD.
 SUGGESTED READING: Raul Hilberg, *The Destruction of European Jews*, rev. ed. (New York: Holmes & Meier, 1985).

HITLER'S PROPHECY. Addressing the Reichstag on January 30, 1939, the sixth anniversary of his assuming power as German chancellor, **Adolf Hitler** predicted:

> Once again I will be a prophet: should international Jewry of finance succeed both within and beyond Europe in plunging mankind into yet another world war, the result will not be the **Bolshevization** of the earth and the victory of Jewry, but the annihilation [*Vernichtung*] of the Jews of Europe.

In his bunker in 1945, with the end in sight, Hitler stated: "I told them that, if they precipitated another war, they would not be spared and that I would exterminate the vermin throughout Europe, once and for all."
 SUGGESTED READING: Alan Bullock, *Hitler and Stalin: Parallel Lives* (New York: Knopf, 1991).

HITLER'S SPEECHES, CHRISTIAN CONTENT OF. Adolf Hitler's public speeches and private conversations indicate that Christian **antisemitism** inspired many of his anti-Jewish ideas, which paralleled those of his listeners. He sometimes expressed himself in the words of the **Gospels** themselves, as in this speech on April 12, 1922:

> I would be no Christian . . . if I did not, as did our Lord two thousand years ago, turn against those by whom today this poor people [Christian Germany] is plundered and exploited. . . . My feeling as a Christian points me to my Lord and Savior as a fighter. It points me to the man who . . . recognized these Jews for what they were and summoned men to fight against them. . . . In boundless love, as a Christian and a human being, I read through the passage which tells us how the Lord rose at last in His might and seized the scourge to drive out of the Temple the brood of vipers and adders. How terrific was His fight against the Jewish poison. Today, after two thousand years, with deepest emotion I realize more profoundly than ever before the fact that it was for this that He had to shed His blood upon the Cross.

Through at least 1938, Hitler's public statements continued to contain biblical allusions. *See also* GEMLICH LETTER.

SUGGESTED READING: Adolf Hitler, *My New Order*, ed. Raoul de Roussy de Sales (New York: Octagon Books, 1973).

HITLER'S *TABLE TALK.* Hitler's informal remarks and private conversations were recorded by his secretary, **Martin Bormann**, and others. The notes encompass a period from July 5, 1941, to November 1944. Hitler talked about destroying **Bolshevism**, establishing a huge German empire covering the Eurasian heartland, breeding an **Aryan** elite of *Ubermenschen*, enslaving whole nations to serve his empire, invading Russia, *Einsatzgruppen*, the genocide of the Slavic *Untermenschen*, and the destruction of the "Jewish spirit" (Jews, Jewishness, Judaism). Hitler's worldview as expressed in his *Table Talk* was consistent with his beliefs in *Mein Kampf*.

SUGGESTED READING: Hugh Trevor-Roper, *Hitler's Table Talk, 1941–1944: His Private Conversations* (New York: Enigma Books, 2002).

HIZBALLAH. *See* HEZBOLLAH.

HLINKA, ANDREJ (1864–1938). Catholic priest and Slovakian nationalist. Hlinka reestablished the Slovak Peoples' Party, an **antisemitic** Slovakian nationalist organization whose purpose was autonomy for Slovakia, part of Czechoslovakia, just before World War II. After Hlinka's death and with **Adolf Hitler**'s conquest of Czechoslovakia in 1939 and creation of the satellite state of Slovakia, the party was renamed the **Hlinka Peoples' Party**. *See also* HLINKA GUARD; TISO, JOSEF; TUKA, VOJTECH.

SUGGESTED READING: Emanuel Frieder, *To Deliver Their Souls* (New York: Holocaust Library, 1987).

HLINKA GUARD. Hlinka Peoples' Party militia in Slovakia in 1939–44, operated against Jews, Czechs, and leftists. From 1942 on, the Hlinka Guard aided local police and German authorities in **deporting** Jews to Poland. After the Slovakian National Revolt in August 1944, the **SS** took control. Nearly 85,000 Slovakian Jews (80 percent) perished.

SUGGESTED READING: David Hogan, *Holocaust Chronicle* (Chicago: Publications International, 2000).

HLINKA PEOPLES' PARTY. Collaborationist Slovakian political party, 1939–44. **Josef Tiso**, a Catholic priest, led this party, which established a pro-**Nazi** government in March 1939. Hlinka People's Party policy was to persecute Jews and eventually **deport** them to Poland.

SUGGESTED READING: David Hogan, *Holocaust Chronicle* (Chicago: Publications International, 2000).

HLOND, AUGUST (1888–1948). Polish prelate. In 1935 Cardinal Hlond called for a Christian boycott of Jewish businesses. In 1936 in a letter entitled "Principles of Catholic Morality," Hlond claimed that Polish Jews battle against the Church and are the "vanguard of atheism and communism." He condemned Jews for "corrupting morals and disseminating pornography." After the terrible Kielce **pogrom** in 1946, the cardinal blamed Jews for the event, asserting that they occupied important positions and sought to impose communism.

SUGGESTED READING: Carol Ritter and Stephen Smith, eds., *The Holocaust and the Christian World* (New York: Continuum, 2000).

HOBSON, JOHN A. (1858–1940). Hobson's original vision of imperialism insisted that a cabal of Jewish financiers drove expansionist policy. He argued that imperialists are dupes of these Jewish financiers. In *Imperialism* (1902), Hobson also wrote of "countries occupied by 'lower' or unprogressive peoples," that "interference on the part of civilised white nations with 'lower races' is not prima facie illegitimate," and that "civilized Governments may undertake the political and economic control of lower races."

HÖβ, RUDOLF (1900–1947). **SS** commandant at **Auschwitz** death camp. Höβ was responsible for the introduction of **Zyklon** gas and enlarging the camp's capacity for mass gassing. A major prosecution witness at the **Nuremberg War Crimes Trials**, Höβ provided details on the camps and their murder process.

SUGGESTED READING: Steven Paskuly, ed., *Rudolph Hoess, Death Dealer: The Memoirs of SS Kommandant at Auschwitz*, trans. Andrew Pollinger (Buffalo, NY: Prometheus Books, 1992).

HOFFMANN, E. T. A. (1776–1822). German writer, composer, caricaturist, painter, and jurist, best known for his stories that inspired Jacques Offenbach to compose his opera *The Tales of Hoffmann*. Hoffman's story "The Golden Pot," based on the Jewish folk tale of the Golem, reveals the common perception of Jews as uncanny and corrupt. This story and two others reveal that Hoffman could not free himself from the **antisemitism** prevalent in his culture.

SUGGESTED READING: Karin Doerr, "The Specter of Antisemitism in and around Annette von Droste-Hülshoff's *Judenbuche*," *German Studies Review* 17, no. 3 (October 1994); Eveline Goodman-Thau, "Golem, Adam oder Antichrist—Kabbalistische Hintergründe der Golemlegende in der jüdischen und deutschen Literatur des 19 Jahrhunderts," in *Kabbala und die Literatur der Romantik*, ed. Eveline Goodman-Thau, Gert Mattenklott, and Christoph Schulte (Tübingen, Germany: Max Niemeyer, 1999).

HOGARTH, WILLIAM (1697–1764). English caricaturist. In Hogarth's 1732 "A Harlot's Progress," plate 2, Moll appears as the mistress of a wealthy Jewish merchant. Hogarth's distaste for the "corrupt" merchant class and their lifestyle is symbolized by his Jewish merchant, whose mahogany table, monkey, and black houseboy were all derived from colonial trade. The portraits on the Jew's wall of the deist Thomas Woolston and philosopher Samuel Clarke, who were considered enemies of Christianity, confirms the Jew's antagonism to the Christian religion. In plate 5, a Passover matzoh is affixed as a flytrap to a wall. In 18th-century England, Jews were experiencing emancipation, assimilation, and economic progress—all of which disturbed English Christians, especially those who regarded Britain as a "second and better Israel." Hogarth used unflattering depictions of Jews while attacking English politics and immorality.

SUGGESTED READING: Jenny Uglow, *Hogarth* (London: Faber & Faber, 1997); Stuart Bingham, "William Hogarth: Art and Documentary in the 18th Century," http://www.stuartbingham.info/pages/research/hogarth .html; Sheldon Rothblatt, "Jewish Life in the Eighteenth Century," *Eighteenth-Century Life* 21, no. 1 (February 1997); Isaac Land, "Jewishness and Britishness in the Eighteenth Century," *History Compass* 3 (January 2005).

HOLLYWOOD HITLERS. *See* WHEELER, BURTON.

HOLMES, OLIVER WENDELL (1809–1894). Essayist, humorist, novelist, poet, and physician. In his poem "At the Pantomime" (1891), Holmes recounted the story of his attending a play and being hemmed in by Jews whose very appearance he found distasteful. He thought of their **deicide**, of their **perfidy**, of their **usury**, of their murder of Christian children. "Ah, cursed unbelieving Jew!" Then he had an epiphany. When he looked closely into the faces of the Jews who surrounded him, he thought Jesus must have looked like them. He turned from curses to blessings, stating, "From the son of Mary came, / with thee the Father deigned to dwell— / Peace upon thee, Israel." Such later-in-life conversions from **antisemitism** have occurred in several writers, from **Johann von Goethe** to **F. Scott Fitzgerald** to **William Faulkner**.

SUGGESTED READING: Eleanor Tilton, *Amiable Autocrat: The Biography of Dr. Oliver Wendell Holmes* (New York: Henry Schuman, 1947).

HOLOCAUST. Term that refers to the planned systematic discrimination, expropriation, forced **deportation**, and mass murder of six million Jews by the **Nazis** and their collaborators across Europe between 1933 and 1945. While persecution began in 1933 with the coming to power of **Adolf Hitler**, the mass murder phase began with the invasion of the Soviet Union in June 1941. Gypsies were also marked for death, as were the handicapped and male homosexuals. Until the end of the war, most Germans, and thousands, perhaps millions, of non-German nationals willingly collaborated in the Nazi Reich's discrimination against Jews, the **confiscation of Jewish property**, and mass murder, serving as political allies, guards in camps, members of **Einsatzgruppen**, engineers, doctors, scientists, railroad workers, and bureaucrats. Although the Holocaust occurred during, and under the cover of, World War II, it was a separate mobilization of resources that sometimes aided but oftentimes impeded the German war effort. The Red Cross and neutral nations, as well as the Allied nations fighting Nazi Germany, often turned a blind eye to the horrors of the Holocaust and sometimes indirectly aided the German efforts to destroy the Jews. Even though each historical event is unique in its own way, the scope and organization of the Holocaust, and the determination of the murderers suggest that this historical event was unprecedented. *See also* EVIDENCE OF THE HOLOCAUST, SUPPRESSION OF; FINAL SOLUTION OF THE JEWISH PROBLEM; GENOCIDE; HOLOCAUST DENIAL; LONG, BRECKINRIDGE; MASSACRES DISBELIEVED, HOLOCAUST; ROOSEVELT, FRANKLIN D.

SUGGESTED READING: Yehuda Bauer, *Rethinking the Holocaust* (New Haven, CT: Yale University Press, 2001); Raul Hilberg, *The Destruction of the European Jews* (New York: Holmes and Meier, 1985); Michael Berenbaum, *A Mosaic of Victims* (New York: New York University Press 1990).

HOLOCAUST DENIAL. Those who claim, despite the mass of authentic evidence to the contrary, that the Jewish **genocide** did not happen at all and that there were no **gas chambers**. Some play down and dramatically reduce the numbers murdered. Others deny **Adolf Hitler**'s personal responsibility and consider the survivor testimonies lies. Deniers accuse Jews of a hoax and Israelis of using the Holocaust to steal Arab land and milk reparations.

Holocaust denial has become central to **anti-Zionist antisemitism**. Hoping to undermine the moral basis of the founding of Israel, the Arab world has come to believe that a "Holocaust myth" is part and parcel of a diabolical Jewish plan to achieve world domination. In 1983, Mahmoud Abbas wrote *The Other Side: The Secret Relationship between Nazism and the Zionist Movement.* In 1987, the Swedish-based Moroccan exile Ahmed Rami, creator of the Radio Islam website, used a Swedish radio station to broadcast anti-Zionist antisemitism. Rami has joined with **David Irving**, **Robert Faurisson**, **Bradley Smith**, **Louis Farrahkan**, Saddam Hussein, and the **Institute for Historical Review** in claiming that the "so-called 'holocaust'" was a tool of "Zionists . . . to oppress and vilify" Palestinians. These Zionists, according to Radio Islam's propaganda, have a monopoly over "information services in the West" and bribe Western politicians to support them in their "Anti-Arab and anti-Moslem racism" and "hatred against everything German." Rami claims that the world Jewish conspiracy is proved by *The Protocols of the Elders of Zion*, and he has called for "a new Hitler" to lead the world against the Jews.

Beginning in the early 1980s, denying the Holocaust, **Iranian** radicals led a campaign against the "**Talmudic** Jew," featuring the *Protocols*, and called for the destruction of Israel and Zionism. Iranian leader Ayatollah Ali Khameini claimed that "Zionists had close relations with German Nazis and exaggerated statistics on Jewish killings" and that the Israelis are not Jews but Eastern European "hooligans and thugs" exported to Palestine to establish "in the heart of the Islamic world an anti-Islamic state under the guise of supporting the victims of racism."

See also BUCHANAN, PATRICK; BUTZ, ARTHUR.

SUGGESTED READING: Michael Shermer and Alex Grobman, *Denying History* (Berkeley: University of California Press, 2000); Deborah Lipstadt, *Denying the Holocaust: The Growing Assault on Truth and Memory* (New York: Penguin Books, 1994); Robert S. Wistrich, *Muslim Antisemitism: A Clear and Present Danger* (New York: American Jewish Committee, 2002); Marvin Perry and Frederick M. Schweitzer, *Antisemitism: Myth and Hate from Antiquity to the Present* (New York: Palgrave Macmillan, 2002); ADL Law Enforcement Agency Resource Network, "Poisoning the Web: Hatred Online: Internet Bigotry, Extremism and Violence— Holocaust Denial: Ahmed Rami," http://www.adl.org/poisoning_web/rami.asp.

HOLY TRINITY CHURCH CASE. The same year in which Congress passed the **Immigration Act of 1891** excluding Jewish refugees, the U.S. Supreme Court in October reaffirmed in the Holy Trinity Church case that the United States was a Christian nation and that Americans were a Christian people. Henry Carroll, a director of the U.S. census for 1890, estimated that more than 90 percent of Americans were religious (that is, observing Christians) to one degree or another. Jewish leaders such as Louis Marshall insisted that despite the religious preferences of most Americans, the Founding Fathers intended church and state to be separate. In 1942, the Supreme Court finally held that state and city governments were subject to the First Amendment freedom of religion. In the 1960s, the Court held that religious activities in public schools, such as reading the Bible and praying, were unconstitutional.

SUGGESTED READING: Anson Phelps Stokes, *Church and State in the United States* (Westport, CT: Greenwood Press, 1964).

HONORIUS III (d. 1227). Pope, 1216–27. In 1220 Honorius III remarked on

> the **perfidia** of the Jews, [who are] condemned to perpetual slavery because they damned themselves and their children when they cried out for the blood of Christ. They are hardly worthy of papal nurturance . . . nevertheless . . . we forbid anyone from molesting [them] in person or goods so long as you [they] refrain from blaspheming Christ and his faith.

Of course, since Jews were frequently accused of blaspheming Jesus in their daily prayer, the conclusion a Christian could draw from Honorius's remarks was that Jews could, and perhaps should, be molested.

SUGGESTED READING: Shlomo Simonsohn, *The Apostolic See and the Jews: Documents, 492–1404* (Toronto: Pontifical Institute of Mediaeval Studies, 1988).

HONORIUS IV (1210–1287). Pope, 1285–87. In 1286 Honorius IV wrote to Archbishop of Canterbury John Peckham that the "damned Jewish **perfidia**" was being treated too leniently in England. Learning all sorts of vices from the **Talmud** and associating with converts, the Jews "curse Christians and commit other evils. [Judaism] is a dangerous plague." Four years later, the Jews were expelled from England. As a result of the papal initiative, the Talmud was also attacked by Churchmen and princes in France—where it was tried, convicted, and burned at the stake for containing **heresy**—and later in Spain, Germany, and Italy.

SUGGESTED READING: Shlomo Simonsohn, *The Apostolic See and the Jews: History* (Toronto: Pontifical Institute of Mediaeval Studies, 1991).

HOOK NOSE. (U.S. slur) Stereotype of Jewish facial features.

SUGGESTED READING: "List of Ethnic Slurs," *Wikipedia*, http://en.wikipedia.org/wiki/List_of_ethnic_slurs.

HORTHY, MIKLÓS (1868–1957). Regent of Hungary, 1920–44. Horthy became ruler after defeating **Béla Kun**'s Hungarian Communist dictatorship in 1920. He passed anti-Jewish legislation in 1938–41, following the Nazi **Nuremberg Laws of 1935**. However, he rejected taking **Adolf Hitler**'s advice on a Hungarian Jewish **genocide**. Jews were forced into the Hungarian Army's labor battalions and then mistreated by Hungarian and German officers, with thousands losing their lives on the Russian Front. After the German invasion in March 1944, Horthy lost power and a half-million Hungarian Jews were **deported** to death camps in Poland.

SUGGESTED READING: Thomas L. Sakmyste, *Hungary's Admiral on Horseback, Miklós Horthy, 1918–1944* (New York: Columbia University Press, 1994).

HORTUS DELICARIUM. A 12th-century Latin book takings its name from the Garden of Delights, a common medieval gathering place. An illustration in this book showed Jews roasting in the first cauldron of Hell.

SUGGESTED READING: Paul E. Grosser and Edwin G. Halperin, *Anti-Semitism: The Causes and Effects of a Prejudice* (Secaucus, NJ: Citadel Press, 1979).

HOUGHTELING, MRS. JAMES. *See* WAGNER-ROGERS BILL.

HOWELLS, WILLIAM DEAN (1837–1920). American novelist and critic. Howells repeatedly associated Jews with money. Although he claimed to be ridiculing this belief, in *The Rise of Silas Lapham*, the title character said that the Jews

> have got in. . . . And when they get in, they send down the price of property. Of course, there ain't any sense in it. . . . You tell folks that the Saviour himself was one, and the twelve apostles, and all the prophets . . . and it don't make a bit of

difference. They send down the price of real estate. Prices begin to shade when the first one gets in. . . . Oh, yes, they've all got the money.

Howells argued that he was simply reflecting what most Americans believed, although he did cut the offending passages from later editions of his work.

SUGGESTED READING: William Dean Howells, "The Rise of Silas Lapham," *Century Magazine*, November 1884.

HUDAL, ALOIS (1885–1963). Pro-**Nazi** German Catholic bishop. After World War II and the defeat of the Nazis, Hudal ran an underground organization, **Ratline**, to aid Nazi **war criminals** to escape from Europe. Working out of the **Vatican**, Hudal supplied false papers and safe hiding places for the fleeing Nazis.

SUGGESTED READING: Christopher Simpson, *Blowback: America's Recruitment of Nazis and Its Effects on the Cold War* (London: Weidenfeld & Nicolson, 1988).

HUGENBERG, ALFRED (1865–1951). Cofounder of the **Pan-German League**, financier, and politician. He was president of the directorate of the Krupp firm from 1909 to 1918, during World War I endorsed Germany's most aggressive war plans, entered the Reichstag in 1919, and was chairman of the conservative German Nationalist Party 1928–33. Control of the Hugenberg Combine, a media and financial conglomerate—including 1,600 newspapers with millions of readers, and Germany's largest and most influential film corporation, UFA, which controlled distribution of films to scores of theaters—enabled him to mount a powerful propaganda campaign against communists, socialists, and the **Versailles** Treaty. Hoping to control **Adolf Hitler**, Hugenberg was a major financial backer of the **Nazis**, especially when the party was failing in 1928. His support opened the door for Hitler to gain subsidies from other industrialists. Hugenberg's promise to serve in a Hitler cabinet helped convince German president Paul von Hindenburg that Hitler could be used to unify German conservatives. His party was dissolved and his combine gradually absorbed by the Nazi state. *See also* FILM INDUSTRY, NAZI PURGE OF.

SUGGESTED READING: John Leopold, *Alfred Hugenberg: The Radical Nationalist Campaign against the Weimar Republic* (New Haven, CT: Yale University Press, 1977).

HUGO, VICTOR (1802–1885). French dramatist, poet, and novelist. In the play *Cromwell* (1827), Rabbi Manassé ben Israël (who actually petitioned Oliver Cromwell to allow Jews to reenter England) is portrayed as Cromwell's agent and evil genius, astrologer, "spy from heaven," and all-around master of evil. But this does not prevent the rabbi from indulging in counterespionage for the benefit of Cromwell's enemies when it is profitable: "Of the two rival parties, does it matter which succumbs? Either way, Christian blood will flow in torrents! At least, I hope so! That's the advantage of conspiracies. . . . To steal from Christians is a meritorious thing."

HUMANITARIANISM IN REGARD TO JEWS. In December 1940 T. E. Latham of the British Foreign Office's Refugee Section opined that Jewish refugees cannot be "let into the U.K. on merely humanitarian grounds." **Nazi** Minister of Propaganda **Josef Goebbels** wrote: "You just cannot talk humanitarianism when dealing with Jews." In 1941, Sir John Shuckburgh, undersecretary in the British Colonial Office, wrote, "We cannot be deterred by the kind of prewar humanitarianism that prevailed in 1939." Britain had closed the gates of Palestine to Jewish refugees.

SUGGESTED READING: Bernard Wasserstein, *Britain and the Jews of Europe, 1939–1945* (London: Institute of Jewish Affairs; Oxford, England: Clarendon Press, 1979).

HUMBOLDT, CAROLINE. Wife of German humanist **Karl Wilhelm von Humboldt**. In a letter, she wrote, "The Jews in their depravity, their usury, their inherited lack of courage, which springs from **usury**, are a stain upon humanity." She felt the Jews controlled "all the money of the country" and called them the "stigmata of the human race."

SUGGESTED READING: Alfred Low, *Jews in the Eyes of the Germans* (Philadelphia: Institute for Study of Human Issues, 1979); Léon Poliakov, *The History of Antisemitism*, 4 vols. (New York: Vanguard, 1965–86).

HUMBOLDT, KARL WILHELM VON (1767–1835). German humanist, politician, and spokesman for Jewish rights in Prussia and at the Congress of Vienna. Humboldt revealed in his letters to his wife, **Caroline Humboldt:**

> I love even the Jews—in general—but I go out of my way to avoid them as individuals. . . . I work with all my strength to give the Jews full **citizenship** rights, so that I no longer need to go into Jews' houses out of kindness. Besides, they don't love me at all.

He felt that only when the Jews abandoned Judaism and became Christians could they fully assimilate into German culture and become true German citizens. Humboldt, like **Immanuel Kant**, looked at Judaism as an inferior, legalistic religion that would soon be abandoned by the assimilated Jews in favor of "a loftier faith," as he put it.

SUGGESTED READING: Jacob Katz, *Out of the Ghetto: The Social Background of Jewish Emancipation, 1770–1870* (New York: Schocken Books, 1978).

HUME, DAVID (1711–1766). Scots economist, philosopher, and historian. In his *Essays, Moral, Political, and Literary* (1742), Hume allowed that the dispersal of the Jewish people may have had a singular influence on their bad character that would have nothing in common with the people among whom they lived: "Thus the Jews in Europe, and the Armenians in the East, have a peculiar character; and the former are as much noted for fraud as the latter for probity."

SUGGESTED READING: Eric Morton, "Race and Racism in the Works of David Hume," *Journal on African Philosophy* (2002); John Immerwahr, "Hume's Revised Racism," *Journal of the History of Ideas* 53 (July–September 1992).

HUNGARY. *See* ARROW CROSS; HORTHY, MIKLÓS; KUN, BÉLA.

HUSSEINI, HAJJ AMIN EL (1895–1974). Grand Mufti of Jerusalem, a religious-political leader. Appointed mufti by the British Mandate commissioner Sir Herbert Samuel in 1920, the British official falsely believed this would make Husseini moderate and feel part of the establishment. However, Husseini continued to attack both the Jewish pioneers and British in 1929 and 1936–39. After fleeing to Iraq, Husseini engineered a **pogrom** there. When the British entered Iraq, Husseini fled to Berlin in 1940 where he was welcomed by **Adolf Hitler**. He broadcast from Berlin urging Muslims to support Nazi forces and raised an **SS** division (Handsar) that saw service in the Balkans and Russia. Husseini advised **Heinrich Himmler** to vigorously pursue the mass murder of Jews. In November 1943, Husseini proclaimed:

> The Germans know how to get rid of the Jews. . . . The Germans have never harmed any Muslim, and they are again fighting our common enemy. . . . But most of all they have definitely solved the Jewish problem. [This **Final Solution**] has made our friendship with Germany . . . a permanent and lasting friendship based on mutual interest.

SUGGESTED READING: Joseph Boris Schectman, *The Mufti and the Fuehrer: The Rise and Fall of Hajj Amin el Husseini* (New York: Thomas Yoseloff, 1965); Robert S. Wistrich, *Muslim Antisemitism: A Clear and Present Danger* (New York: American Jewish Committee, 2002).

HYMIE; HEIMY. (U.S. slur) A Jew from New York City, from Jewish first names "Hyman" or "Chaim" (Hebrew for "life").
SUGGESTED READING: "List of Ethnic Slurs," *Wikipedia*, http://en .wikipedia.org/wiki/List_of_ethnic_slurs.

HYMIETOWN. (U.S. slur) New York City.
SUGGESTED READING: "List of Ethnic Slurs," *Wikipedia*, http://en .wikipedia.org/wiki/List_of_ethnic_slurs.

– I –

ICONOGRAPHY, CHRISTIAN. Iconography is a symbolic code that unites past, present, and future. Beginning with catacomb frescoes in the early centuries of the Christian era, Christian iconongraphy deals with episodes from the life and passion of Jesus (the Nativity, the Descent from the Cross, the Pietà), the Virgin Mary (the Sacred Conversation, the Visitation), the saints (St. Francis Receiving the Stigmata, **St. Jerome** in the Wilderness, the Martyrdom of St. Agatha), and symbolic scenes of ultimate beatitude (the Majesty, the Savior of the World, the Coronation of the Virgin). This iconography is intended to inculcate in every Christian mind the goals and fundamental principles of Christianity. For two millennia, Christian iconography has also served as anti-Jewish propaganda, affecting Christian minds and behaviors and emphasizing the image of Jesus Christ's crucifixion as "proof" of the Jews' collective guilt.
SUGGESTED READING: Norman Manea, "Some Reflections on Antisemitism in the Second Half of the Twentieth Century," Vidal Sassoon International Center for the Study of Antisemitism, http://sicsa.huji.ac.il/ 99an1.html; A. N. Didron, *Christian Iconography*, trans. E. J. Millington, 2 vols. (1851–86; reprint, New York: F. Ungar, 1965).

IDENTITY CHURCHES. *See* CHRISTIAN IDENTITY MOVEMENT.

IF I WERE KAISER. Written by Heinrich Class, this 1912 book was the manifesto of the **Pan-German League**. Regarding Jews, it advocated measures taken by the **Nazi** regime: make Jewish citizens aliens, stop all Jewish immigration into Germany, eliminate Jews in government, expel foreign Jews, bar Jews from the professions, and restrict Jews from German cultural life. *See* NAZI LEGAL MEASURES AGAINST JEWS.
SUGGESTED READING: Geoffrey Eleg, *Reshaping the German Right: Radical Nationalism and Political Change after Bismarck* (Ann Arbor: University of Michigan Press, 1991).

I. G. FARBEN (INTERESSEN-GEMEINSCHAFT FARBENINDUS-TRIE AG).

German chemical conglomerate. I. G. Farben was composed of Agfa, Casella, BASF (Badische Anilin und Soda Fabrik), Bayer, Hoechst, Huels, Kalle, and several smaller companies. I. G. Farben built a factory for producing synthetic oil and rubber (from coal) in **Auschwitz**. At its peak in 1944, this factory made use of 83,000 slave laborers. The pesticide **Zyklon**, for which I. G. Farben held the patent and which was used in the **gas chambers** for mass murder, was manufactured by **Degesch** (Deutsche Gesellschaft für Schädlingsbekämpfung), a company owned by I. G. Farben. Of the 24 directors of the company indicted in the so-called I. G. Farben Trial before a U.S. military tribunal at the subsequent **Nuremberg War Crimes Trials**, 13 were sentenced to prison terms of between 18 months and eight years. At Monowitz, an Auschwitz subcamp built on the Farben campus, the chemical giant exploited its laborers, mainly Jewish, under horrendous conditions.

SUGGESTED READING: Joseph Borkin, *The Crime and Punishment of I. G. Farben* (New York: Free Press, 1978); Peter Hayes, *Industry and Ideology: IG Farben and the Nazis*, 2nd ed. (Cambridge: Cambridge University Press, 2001).

IGNATIEV, NIKOLAI PAVLOVITCH (1832–1908). Russian count and statesman; one of the prime movers in the reactionary anti-Jewish Russian legislation of the last quarter of the 19th century, the alleged instigator of anti-Jewish riots, and the author of the notorious **May Laws**. As minister of the interior, Ignatiev extorted money from wealthy Jews. He sought to create the impression that Jews were a danger to the rest of the population. Ignatiev stated:

> While protecting the Jews against violence, the government recognizes the need of equally vigorous measures for changing the existing abnormal relations between the Jews and the native population, and for protecting the people from that injurious activity of the Jews which has been the real cause of the agitation.

Ignatiev told Tsar **Alexander III** that the government had "recognized how harmful to the Christian population of the country is the economic activity of the Jews, their tribal seclusion and religious fanaticism."

SUGGESTED READING: Simon Dubnow, *History of the Jews in Russia and Poland from the Earliest Times to the Present Day* (New York: Ktav, 1975).

IGNATIUS OF ANTIOCH, ST. (d. 115). Pious letter writer. Ignatius was very concerned with **Judaizing**. In chapter 6 of his *Epistle to the Philadel-*

phians, he wrote,"If any one preaches the one God of the law and the prophets [that is, Judaism], but denies Christ to be the Son of God, he is a liar, even as also is his father the devil."

IKEY-MO (British, U.S. slur) A Jew; from two common Jewish names, Isaac and Moses.

SUGGESTED READING: "List of Ethnic Slurs," *Wikipedia*, http://en .wikipedia.org/wiki/List_of_ethnic_slurs.

ILLUMINATI. Secret conspiratorial society that is accused of seeking to rule the world. Supposedly formed in 1776 by Adam Weiskauf, a former Bavarian Jesuit, it is allegedly a power behind the governments of the world and is hostile to Christianity. Conspiracy believers insist that **Freemasons** and **Ashkenazi** Jews aid the Society through **banking**, intellectual pursuits, and their occult knowledge.

SUGGESTED READING: Jim Marrs, *Rule by Secrecy* (London: Perennial, 2001).

IMMIGRATION ACT OF 1891. U.S. law aimed at Russian Jewish immigrants. Under the Act, immigrants had to prove that they were not destitute, had a useful skill, and would not be a burden to the state. It restricted the financing of Jewish emigration from Europe by preventing the entry of immigrants whose passage had been paid by overseas organizations.

SUGGESTED READING: Roger Daniels, *Guarding the Golden Door* (New York: Hill & Wang, 2004).

IMMIGRATION LAW OF 1924. *See* JOHNSON-REED ACT.

IMMIGRATION RESTRICTION LEAGUE. New England nativist group, 1894–1920. Frightened by the huge numbers of immigrants from Eastern and Southern Europe, upper-class American nativists sought to cut it down. Advised by **eugenicists**, they sought legislation to eliminate "defectives" and illiterates. They agitated for restrictions for those likely to be a public charge and a literacy test that they hoped would eliminate undesirables from immigration.

SUGGESTED READING: Edwin Black, *The War against the Weak* (New York: Four Walls, Eight Windows, 2003).

IMPROPERIA. Also known as the Reproaches. A portion of the **Good Friday** liturgy. The Improperia, or Reproaches, were first mentioned in the sixth century by Bishop Gregory of Tours; introduced into Western liturgy from the East, perhaps Jerusalem, in the eighth century; and fully developed by the 11th century. They consist of a series of contrasting parallels between the good deeds God had done for the Jews and the Jews' supposed malicious behavior in return. Purportedly spoken from the cross, this portion of the Easter Week liturgy was delivered in emotional and devastatingly anti-Jewish language.

SUGGESTED READING: F. L. Cross, ed., *The Oxford Dictionary of the Christian Church* (New York: Oxford University Press, 1997).

INFAMOUS DECREE. Issued by Napoleon in 1808, this decree canceled all debts to Jews owed by those in military service. Jews who wished to trade needed permits from local prefects, a requirement that made trade difficult.

SUGGESTED READING: Paul Mendes-Flohr and Jehuda Reinhartz, *The Jew in the Modern World* (New York: Oxford University Press, 1995).

INHUMAN. *See* SUBHUMAN.

INNOCENT III (1160–1216). Pope, 1198–1216. Innocent III stated in his protective bull *Constitutio pro Judeis* of 1199 that "the Jews shall not be destroyed completely, [but] only those who have not presumed to plot against the Christian Faith [will be protected]." In a letter of 1205, Innocent proclaimed that Jews should not be killed, even though they were dangerous and evil beings who should barely be tolerated in Christian society. He also enumerated other Jewish blasphemies and insults to Christianity that he assumed all Jews were guilty of: money-lending, having Christian servants, building a new **synagogue** higher than a nearby church, engaging in overly loud religious rites, insulting Christians by saying that they "believe in a peasant who had been hanged by the Jewish people," appearing in public on **Good Friday** and laughing at the Christian adoration of the cross, opening their doors to thieves in order to fence stolen goods, and murdering Christians at every opportunity. He also claimed that "when [Jews] remain living among the Christians, they take advantage of every wicked opportunity to kill in secret their Christian hosts." Innocent insisted that the French king **Philip Augustus** stop these Jewish blasphemies or remove the Jews from his kingdom. This letter supplied the king with the additional pretext he needed almost to destroy the Jewish community in France by expropriations, **expulsions**, and mass murder. He instituted a **genocide** against the **Albigensians** in southern France and Jews living among them. Innocent also insisted on Jews wearing a **Jew badge**. *See also* LATERAN COUNCIL, FOURTH.

SUGGESTED READING: Leonard B. Glick, *Abraham's Heirs: Jews and Christians in the Middle Ages* (Syracuse, NY: Syracuse University Press, 1999).

INNOCENT IV (d. 1254). Pope, 1243–54. Innocent IV rejected the blood libel and appealed for piety and kindness toward the Jews. Yet he specified no punishment for **Jean Draconet de Montauban**, who had tortured and murdered Jews. Innocent also ordered the bishop of Constance to force the Jews to wear the **Jew badge**.

SUGGESTED READING: Lynn Thorndike, ed., *University Records and Life in the Middle Ages* (New York: Columbia University Press, 1944).

INQUISITION, PAPAL. "Courts" to root out and punish **heresy**. Inquisition courts were established by Pope **Innocent III** when he recruited St. Dominic, after whom the **Dominican** order was named, to investigate, or inquire into, the authentic Catholic beliefs of the **Albigensians**. Inquisitors were recruited from the Dominican and Franciscan orders. Those charged with heresy would be arrested and tortured, then imprisoned or executed. The arrestation, torture, and penalties were performed by the secular authority in collaboration with the Church. The **Talmud** was subject to the Inquisition and burning. Most papal courts operated in Central and Western Europe; the Spanish Inquisition fell under the broad umbrella of the papal Inquisition but was a separate undertaking backed by the Spanish Crown. Started in 1215, the Inquisition ended in 1858. *See also* AUTO-DA-FÉ; DONIN, NICHOLAS; FRANKISTS; GUI, BERNARDO; INQUISITION, SPANISH; MARRANOS.

SUGGESTED READING: Stephen O'Shea, *The Perfect Heresy: The Revolutionary Life and Spectacular Death of the Medieval Cathars* (New York: Walker & Co., 2005).

INQUISITION, SPANISH. Nationwide investigation instituted by Spanish monarchs **Ferdinand** and **Isabella** in collaboration with the Roman Catholic Church. Its mission was to discover and to stamp out **heresy**, and it was specifically aimed at the **conversos**—many of whom may have been crypto-Jews who secretly practiced Judaism—and to a lesser extent at Moriscos, crypto-Muslim converts to Christianity. The Spanish version of the **Inquisition** was far more severe than the papal one. Started in 1481, thousands of conversos were caught in the inquisitorial net. **Tomás de Torquemada** was appointed inquisitor-general. More than 90 percent of the Spanish Inquisition's victims were of Jewish origin. Rather than accept the new Christians into Spanish life and culture, the Inquisition set out to destroy the Jewish presence in Spain. In 1492, Isabella and Ferdinand signed the Edict of **Expulsion** of the Jews on the grounds that their very presence encouraged the conversos in their reversion to Judaism. In a dozen years, 13,000 conversos, some of them crypto-Jews, were burned. The last **auto-da-fé** in Spain occurred in 1826; in its long history, the flames took 30,000 lives. *See also* ADAMS, HENRY; ANUSIM; HERETIC; MARRANOS; SIXTUS IV.

SUGGESTED READING: Cecil Roth, *Spanish Inquisition* (New York: W. W. Norton, 1996).

INSTITUTE FOR HISTORICAL REVIEW (IHR). Pseudo-academic enterprise known for its **Holocaust denial**, or **Holocaust** revisionism. It was founded by **Willis Carto** in 1979, but has been independent of him since a bitter 1993 dispute with staffers. When the IHR called for an "open debate on the Holocaust" in the United States in 1979, there were already other groups or individuals claiming that the Holocaust was simply a hoax. Some revisionists claimed that **Adolf Hitler** had no knowledge of mass extermination taking place and that there was never any master plan for Jewish extermination. Others argued that facilities at the various **extermination camps**, notably the **gas chambers**, really were showers. Still other revisionists doubted whether the Germans had murdered as many as six million Jews. *See also* BUTZ, ARTHUR; IRVING, DAVID; SMITH, BRADLEY.

SUGGESTED READING: Frank Mintz, *The Liberty Lobby and the American Right, Race, Conspiracy and Culture* (Westport, CT: Greenwood Press, 1985).

INSTITUTE FOR THE STUDY AND ERADICATION OF JEWISH INFLUENCE ON GERMAN RELIGIOUS LIFE. In 1939, Walter Grundmann, professor of New Testament at the University of Jena, established—along with ministers, bishops, religion teachers, and professors of theology from all over the German Reich—this institute with funds from the Lutheran Church. Its goal was finally to destroy every bit of Judaism involved in Christianity. The institute's publications were sold to hundreds of thousands of German Christians. It was a marriage of **swastika** and cross. John 4:22, "Salvation comes from the Jews," became "The Jews are our misfortune." "Amen" disappeared, and Jesus became an **Aryan**.

SUGGESTED READING: Susannah Heschel, "Nazifying Christian Theology: Walter Grundmann and the Institute for the Study and Eradication of Jewish Influence on German Church Life," *Church History* 63 (1994).

THE INTERNATIONAL JEW. See FORD, HENRY.

INTERNATIONAL SOCIALIST CONGRESS OF 1891. See MARX, KARL.

INTERNET, ANTISEMITISM ON THE. The Stephen Roth Institute reports that in 2006, the Internet remained a major vehicle for **antisemitic** ideas. Through thousands of blogs, websites, chat rooms, bulletin boards, and e-mails, hundreds, perhaps thousands, of individuals and groups antagonistic to Jews communicated hate literature and antisemitic conspiracy theories (from September 11 through the war in Iraq). *See also* HAMMERSKIN NATION.

SUGGESTED READING: Jordan Kessler, *Poisoning the Web: Hatred online; An ADL Report on Internet Bigotry, Extremism and Violence* (New York: Anti-Defamation League, 1999); Stephen Roth Institute for the Study of Antisemitism and Racism, "United States of America," http://www.tau.ac.il/Anti-Semitism/asw2003-4/usa.htm.

INTIFADA. Loosely, "uprising" or "sweeping out" in Arabic. The first Palestinian Intifada began spontaneously in December 1987. It was fed by rumors and incidents on both the Israeli and Arab Palestinian sides. It lasted until 1992 and the coming of the Oslo Accords. Violence by the Palestinians included not only rock throwing but weapons use as well, and attacks against military in addition to civilian targets. **Yassir Arafat**, the Palestinian Liberation Organization leader, entered soon after its beginning and encouraged it. The second Intifada began soon after Israeli Prime Minister Ariel Sharon visited the Temple Mount (the al-Aqsa Mosque) in Jerusalem. A May 2001 report by former U.S. senator George Mitchell exonerated Sharon as the cause of the Intifada.

SUGGESTED READING: Cyril Glasse, *The New Encyclopedia of Islam* (Walnut Creek, CA: Rowman & Littlefield, 2002).

INVOCATION, THE GREAT. Alice Bailey was the author of a "prayer" known as the Great Invocation, still widely used in **New Age Movement** circles:

> Let the Lords of Liberation issue forth
> Let the Rider from the secret place come forth
> And coming, save.
> Come forth, O Mighty One
> Let Light and Love and Power and Death
> Fulfill the purpose of the Coming One.

From the center where the Will of God is known
Let purpose guide the little wills of men
The purpose which the Masters know and serve.
Let the Plan of Love and Light work out
And may it seal the door where evil dwells.
Let Light and Love and Power restore the Plan on Earth.

In her book *Esoteric Healing* (1953), Bailey explains about "the Plan" that "the Jewish race, who loved the possessions of the world more than they loved the service of Light, joined ranks with the rebels against God. Thus the history of the **Wandering Jew** began and the Jew since has known no lasting peace."

SUGGESTED READING: Yonassan Gershom, "Antisemitic Stereotypes in Alice Bailey's Writings," 2005, http://www.pinenet.com/rooster/bailey.html.

IRAN. Iranian president Mahmoud Ahmadinejad is following a public campaign against Israel and Jews. He is planning a conference on the "scientific evidence" for the **Holocaust** and has called the **Nazis'** World War II slaughter of six million European Jews a "myth," saying that Israel should be "wiped off the map." In the Iranian Foreign Ministry–affiliated *Tehran Times*, columnist Hossein Amiri wrote "Lies of the Holocaust Industry," timed to coincide with the international commemoration of the liberation of **Auschwitz**, in which he accused Israel and Europe of exploiting the Holocaust to justify the Palestinian suffering. In December 2004, the official Iranian news agency published articles describing Jews as a "subversive element in human history" and as "satanic," "anti-human," "dangerous to both Christians and Muslims," and the source of "all corrupt traits in humanity." In "Zahra's Blue Eyes," aired on Iranian television, the "Zionists" are shown kidnapping Palestinian children and harvesting their organs. In "The People of the Cave," the Jews are portrayed maliciously abusing Christ on the cross. In "Al-Shatat," the Jews are responsible for all the ills of the world, through political, economic, and sexual conspiracies, warmongering, and political assassinations.

SUGGESTED READING: Middle East Media Research Institute, "Antisemitism and Holocaust Denial in the Iranian Media," January 28, 2005, http://memri.org/bin/articles.cgi?Page = archives&Area = sd&ID = SP85505.

IRENAEUS, ST. (c. 120–200). Bishop of Lyons. Many Latin and Greek **Church Fathers**—among them Irenaeus—saw **heresy** as essentially Jewish. Based on passages in the **Gospels** of **Matthew** and Mark in which Jesus warned his followers about the arrival of false **messiahs** and a time of chaos, Irenaeus believed that the **Antichrist** would first come to the Jews because they were the ones who had refused to believe in the true messiah, Jesus Christ.

SUGGESTED READING: Edward Kessler and Neil Wenborn, *A Dictionary of Jewish–Christian Relations* (Cambridge: Cambridge University Press, 2005).

IRON CROSS. *See* SWASTIKA WITH IRON CROSS, NAZI.

IRON GUARD. Romanian **fascist** party, 1927–44. This political organization grew out of the **Legion of Archangel Michael** founded by **Corneliu Codreanu**. In 1940 it formed the **antisemitic** National Legionary Government. In 1941 the Iron Guard instituted murderous riots in Bucharest, then fled to Germany because of a failed coup.

SUGGESTED READING: I. C. Butnaru, *The Silent Holocaust* (Westport, CT: Greenwood Press, 1992).

IRVING, DAVID (1938–). Controversial British historian and **Holocaust-denial** activist. Irving is unique among modern Holocaust deniers for having first established a reputation as a popular, if controversial, chronicler of World War II. The governments of **Canada**, Austria, Germany, and Australia have barred him from entering their countries, and he has been convicted of defaming the memory of the dead in Germany. In April 2000 Irving sued American historian Deborah Lipstadt and her publisher, Penguin Books, for defamation because Lipstadt attacked Irving's credibility on several historical points. The court found against Irving and for the defendants on all counts. The reasons the finding went against Irving, according to the presiding judge, were that

> Irving has for his own ideological reasons persistently and deliberately misrepresented and manipulated historical evidence; that for the same reasons he has portrayed **Adolf Hitler** in an unwarrantedly favorable light, principally in relation to his attitude towards and responsibility for the treatment of the Jews; that he is an activist; that he is antisemitic and racist and that he associates with right wing extremists who promote **neo-Nazism**.

Irving has founded his own publishing house, Focal Point Publications. He also lectures internationally and has appeared at conferences held by the **Institute for Historical Review** and the **neo-Nazi** National Alliance. In February 2006, after a jury trial for violating an Austrian law against Holocaust denial, an Austrian judge sentenced Irving to three years' in Vienna's Josefstadt prison.

SUGGESTED READING: D. D. Guttenplan, *The Holocaust on Trial: History, Justice and the David Irving Libel Case* (London: Granta, 2004); "Austria Imposes 3-Year Sentence on Notorious Holocaust Denier," *New York Times*, February 26, 2006; Deborah E. Lipstadt, *History on Trial: My Day in Court with David Irving* (New York: HarperCollins, 2005).

ISIDORE OF SEVILLE, ST. (560–636). The last of the major **Church Fathers**. Isadore declared that the Jews' evil character never changes. He regarded Jews as **Christ-killers** condemned to slavery and eventual extermination. Isadore presided over the Fourth Council of **Toledo** in 633, and his thought dominated its deliberations and its canonical legislation. Like **St. Augustine**, Isadore identified the Jews with Cain and called Judaism the "pernicious **perfidy** of the Jews"; like **St. John Chrysostom**, he centered his attack on the **deicide** charge against the Jews; and like **Cyril of Alexandria**, he associated the Jews with the Devil and the **Antichrist**. He believed that Jews—all of whom were inherently evil—who remained Jews were to be enslaved and ultimately destroyed. *See also* GRATIAN.

SUGGESTED READING: B.-S. Albert, "Isidore of Seville: His Attitude towards Judaism and His Impact on Early Medieval Canon Law," *Jewish Quarterly Review* (January–April 1990).

ISLAM AND THE JEWS. *See* BANNA, HASSAN AL-; DHIMMI; IRAN; ISLAMIC DIASPORA, JEWS IN; ISLAMIC FASCISM; KORAN; MUHAMMAD; MUSLIM BROTHERHOOD; RADICAL ISLAM.

ISLAMIC DIASPORA, JEWS IN. Although Jewish communities in Islamic countries were less oppressed than Jews in Christian lands, Jews certainly experienced persecution and humiliation among the Muslims. According to Princeton University historian Bernard Lewis, Jewish rights in Muslim countries are a "myth." Because Jews refused to **convert** to Islam, the **Koran** demeans them as "consigned to humiliation and wretchedness" (Sura 2:61), corrupt (5:64), disobedient (5:68), and enemies of Allah, the Prophet, and the angels (2:97–98). Jews as **dhimmis**, "People of the Book," are allegedly protected under traditional Islamic law, although one would not know this, because for more than a thousand years, whenever Jews were perceived as experiencing "too much" cultural and economic harmony, **antisemitic** discrimination and violence would result—from the 1066 crucifixion of Joseph HaNagid, the Jewish vizier of Granada, Spain, the destruction of the Jewish quarter of the city, and the slaughter of its 5,000 inhabitants, through the 19th-century **ghettoization** of Jews in North Africa, to the thousands of Jews killed in 1940s Iraq,

Libya, Egypt, Syria, and Yemen and hundreds of thousands of Jews exiled from their homes in Islamic lands, up to the anti-Jewish homicide bombings of the 20th and 21st centuries. *See also* BANNA, HASSAN AL-; IRAN; MUHAMMAD; MUSLIM BROTHERHOOD; RADICAL ISLAM.

SUGGESTED READING: Mitchell Bard, "The Treatment of Jews in Arab/ Islamic Countries," *Jewish Virtual Library*, http://www.jewishvirtual library.org/jsource/anti-semitism/Jews_in_Arab_lands_(gen).html.

ISLAMIC FASCISM. Marking the parallels between Nazi **fascism** and Muslim fascism, Robert Wistrich notes, "These [fascist] Muslim radicals have consciously chosen a cult of death, turning the motif of sacrifice and martyrdom into something urgent, elemental, pseudoreligious, and even mystical." Muslim fascists allegedly represent the Muslim masses. For these fascists, American and Israeli Jews—the devil incarnate—conspire with capitalistic finance, **Freemasonry**, secularism, Zionism, communism, Christianity, heretics, dissenters, America, Europe, modernism, and women to destroy Islam and Muslims. Just as **Nazis** quoted from *Mein Kampf*, so Islamic fascists quote from the **Koran** to justify their homicides. Both the Nazis and these Muslim fascists are totalitarians, seeking to conquer the world and commit genocide against Jews. For Islamic groups such as **Al-Qaeda**, **Hamas**, and **Hezbollah**, **antisemitism** and **anti-Zionism** are an essential aspect of their totalitarianism. *See also* IS-LAMIC FUNDAMENTALISM; RADICAL ISLAM.

SUGGESTED READING: Robert S. Wistrich, *Muslim Antisemitism: A Clear and Present Danger* (New York: American Jewish Committee, 2002).

ISLAMIC FUNDAMENTALISM. Religious and political thought that espouses extreme anti-Western, anti-Israel, and anti-Jewish views. The primary radical Islamists are the **Muslim Brotherhood**, **Al-Qaeda**, **Hamas**, **Hezbollah**, and **Islamic Jihad**. Their goal is to establish governments and culture based on their interpretation of the **Koran** and Islamic law. They oppose secularism, democracy, and the Western way of life. For them Western nations are imperialist, colonialist, morally degenerate **crusaders**. *The Protocols of the Elders of Zion* for them are genuine, and they fear that Jews wish to dominate the world and prevent Islamic hegemony. They favor *jihad*, holy war resulting in complete annihilation of all "Zionists" and Jews. *See also* ISLAMIC FASCISM; RADICAL ISLAM.

SUGGESTED READING: Fatima Merrissi, *Islam and Democracy, Fear of the Modern World*, trans. Mary Jo Lakeland (New York: Perseus Books,

2002); Tibi Bassum, *The Challenge of Fundamentalism, Political Islam and the New World Disorder* (Berkeley: University of California Press, 2002).

ISLAMIC JIHAD. Arab organization listed as a terrorist organization by the U.S. government. Islamic Jihad is guilty of committing bloody acts, including bombing the U.S. embassy in Beirut in 1980. It has been particularly active militarily against Israeli Army posts in Lebanon and against Israeli citizens and soldiers.

The Palestinian Islamic Jihad (PIJ) is another Islamic terrorist group, formed in 1979 by Fathi Shaqaqi and Palestinian students living in Egypt. Egypt expelled the PIJ to the Gaza Strip as a result of their involvement in the assassination of Egyptian president **Anwar al-Sadat** in 1981. The PIJ is dedicated to replacing Israel with an Islamic Palestinian state. The group has carried out many attacks against Israel, including suicide-terrorist bombings. In 1995, Israeli agents assassinated Shaqaqi. Despite its ideological affinity to **Hamas**, PIJ is a separate organization headquartered in Syria and funded mostly by **Iran**. *See also* ISLAMIC FUNDAMENTALISM; JIHAD; RADICAL ISLAM.

Suggested Reading: Andrew Bostom, *The Legacy of Jihad: Islamic Holy War and the Fate of Non-Muslims* (New York: Prometheus Books, 2005); Tamra Orr, *Egyptian Islamic Jihad: Inside the World's Most Infamous Terrorist Organizations* (New York: Rosen, 2002); "Palestinian Islamic Jihad (PIJ)," *ynetnews.com*, January 2005, http://www.ynetnews.com/articles/0,7340,L-3020637,00.html.

ISTOUCSZY, GYOZO (1882–1915). Hungarian **antisemitic** politician. In 1872 as a member of the Diet (parliament), Istoucszy opposed Jewish emancipation, accusing Jews of seeking world domination. Six years later he urged transporting all Hungarian Jews to Palestine. Istoucszy urged college students to demonstrate against Jewish students. In 1880, he founded a highly antisemitic paper called *Twelve Pamphlets* as well as an antisemitic party whose members gained seats in the Diet.

Suggested Reading: Andrew Handler, *An Early Blueprint for Zionism* (Cooperstown, NY: Willis Monie Books, 1989).

IVAN III (THE GREAT) (1440–1505). Grand duke of Moscow, 1462–1505. Ivan initiated a policy of "quarantining" Jews.

Suggested Reading: Simon Dubnov, *History of the Jews*, vol. 3, *From the Later Middle Ages to the Renaissance*, trans. Moshe Spiegel (South Brunswick, NJ: Thomas Yoseloff, 1969).

IVAN IV (THE TERRIBLE) (1530–1584). Grand duke of Moscow, 1533–84, and first tsar of Russia, 1547–84. Ivan the Terrible had Muscovite Jews who refused to **convert** to Christianity drowned in the Moscow River. In 1550 he rejected Jewish entry into Moscow, even when requested by his ally, Polish king Sigismund Augustus. Ivan wrote "of the vile actions of the Jews, who have turned our people away from Christ, introduced poisonous drugs into our state, and caused much harm to our people. You should be ashamed, our brother, to write us about them."

SUGGESTED READING: Léon Poliakov, *The History of Antisemitism*, 4 vols. (New York: Vanguard, 1965–86).

– J –

JACKSON-VANIK AMENDMENT. Congressional human rights legislation of 1974. In an American attempt to reduce Russian **antisemitism**, the Jackson-Vanik Amendment to the 1974 Trade Act denies normal trade relations to certain countries, including Russia, that restrict emigration rights. As a result of this amendment, 573,000 refugees—many of them Jews, evangelical Christians, and Catholics—from areas of the former Soviet Union have resettled in the United States.

SUGGESTED READING: Judah Gribetz, Edward L. Greenstein, and Regina S. Stein, *The Timetables of Jewish History* (New York: Simon & Schuster, 1993).

JAHN, FRIEDRICH LUDWIG (1778–1852). German educator and gymnast. Jahn was a fanatic nationalist, exponent of an organic *völkisch* society, coiner of term *folkdom*, and believer in a Führer. He was a founder of gymnastic societies and a National Student League, all **antisemitic**. He stated, "A state without a *Volk* is nothing, a lifeless, frivolous phantom like the vagabond Gypsies and Jews."

SUGGESTED READING: Peter Viereck, *Metapolitics: The Roots of the Nazi Mind* (New York: Capricorn Books, 1961).

JAMES I (1208–1276). King of **Aragón** and Catalonia, 1214–76. James I used Jews in various functions at court and in his government, but in 1228 he forbade them from holding public office and decreed that Jews must not employ Christian women as servants. In 1241, James issued a law code that vilified Jews. The next year, he ordered Jews to endure conversionary **sermons**, and in 1254 he confiscated all debts owed to Jews as an act of piety "for the salvation of our soul and the souls of our forebears."

SUGGESTED READING: Yitzhak Baer, *A History of Jews in Christian Spain*, 2 vols. (Philadelphia: Jewish Publication Society, 1992).

JAMES, HENRY (1843–1916). American novelist. Reacting to the introduction of Yiddish words such as *chutzpah, kibitzer,* and *meshuga* into everyday vocabulary, James believed that Yiddish-speaking Jews were ruining the English language. In 1905 he told the Bryn Mawr College graduating class that Jews "dump[ed] their mountain of promiscuous material into the foundation of the American." To him, the Jewish "denizens of the New York Ghetto" seemed like "small, strange animals . . . snakes or worms . . . who, when cut into pieces, wriggle away and live in the snippet as completely as in the whole."

SUGGESTED READING: Everett Carter, "Realists and Jews," *Studies in American Fiction* 22 (1994).

JAP. (U.S. slur) Acronym for **Jewish-American princess** or Jewish-American prince.

SUGGESTED READING: "List of Ethnic Slurs," *Wikipedia,* http://en .wikipedia.org/wiki/List_of_ethnic_slurs.

JAPAN. *See* FUGU PLAN.

JAZEERA, AL-. Popular Arab TV station. On a daily basis, Al-Jazeera provides millions of Arab homes with malicious, fantastic images, as Robert Wistrich indicates, of "a demonic Israel that deliberately spreads drugs, vice, and prostitution into the Arab world and gasses the Palestinians or deliberately poisons their food and water."

SUGGESTED READING: Robert S. Wistrich, *Muslim Antisemitism: A Clear and Present Danger* (New York: American Jewish Committee, 2002).

JEFFERSON, THOMAS (1743–1826). President of the United States, 1801–09. Jefferson spoke and wrote eloquently on behalf of equal rights and religious freedom. However, his personal views on Judaism were hostile. Writing to the eminent revolutionary leader and physician Benjamin Rush (d. 1813), Jefferson called Jewish ethics "repulsive and anti-social, as respecting other nations." To **John Adams** on October 13, 1813, Jefferson wrote that Judaism was "a wretched depravity of sentiment and manners." Although he criticized the Christian sects for persecuting Jews—at least when he wrote to Jews—Jefferson regarded Judaism as barbarous and futile and Jews as murderous; he believed that Mosaic Judaism related to the worst of human qualities, whereas Jesus' religion, Christianity, took "the best qualities of the human head and heart, wisdom, justice, goodness." In a letter to William Short (lawyer, diplomat, financier, and Jefferson's friend, protégé, and private secretary) on August 4, 1820, Jefferson wrote:

> Jewish ceremonies were idle . . . mummeries . . . of no effect towards producing the social utilities which constitute the essence of virtue. . . . The fumes of the most disordered imaginations were recorded in their religious code, as special communications of the Deity, . . . vague rhapsodies . . . tricks upon words. . . . Jesus had to walk on the perilous confines of reason and religion; and a step to right or left might place Him within the grasp of the priests of the [Jewish] superstition, a bloodthirsty race, as cruel and remorseless as the Being whom they represented as the family God of Abraham, of Isaac and of Jacob, and the local God of Israel. They were constantly laying snares, too, to entangle Him [Jesus] in the web of the law.

This background of antipathy toward biblical Jews and Judaism led Jefferson to stereotype contemporary Jews. His distaste for what he imagined of Judaism moved him to observe to the Marquis de Lafayette in 1817 that the Jews continued to be dispersed and still form "one nation, foreign to the land they live in." He assumed that Judaism had not changed in any significant way since Moses' time and that Jews were forever aliens.

SUGGESTED READING: Michael Feldberg, *Jefferson and the Jews* (Cleveland, OH: Jewish Federation of Cleveland, 2004).

JEFFRIES, LEONARD (1937–). Professor and political scientist. In 1991 Jeffries, chair of the City University of New York's Black Studies Department, recited to a Black Arts and Cultural Festival that whites are "ice people" inclined to violence and cruelty, while blacks are "sun people" prone to peace and compassion. He also stated that Jews controlled the slave trade and that there is a Hollywood conspiracy of Russian Jews and the Mafia to destroy black people. In 1992 Jeffries was removed as chair of his department, a move upheld in 1995 after his appeals. In 1955, he had spoken at the **antisemitic**, anti-white Black Holocaust Nationhood Conference.

SUGGESTED READING: Robert George, "Academic Freedom: The Grounds for Tolerating Abuses," *Mind and Heart of the Church* 4 (1991); Anti-Defamation League, "Schooled in Hate: Antisemitism on Campus," 1997, http://www.jewishvirtuallibrary.org/jsource/anti-semitism/Black _student_groups.html.

JEHOVAH'S WITNESSES. On June 25, 1933, the leadership of the German Jehovah's Witnesses, under pressure from the **Nazi** government to renounce their religious beliefs, wrote this letter to **Adolf Hitler**:

The circles which led horror propaganda in the United States (commercialistic Jews and Catholics) are also the most eager persecutors of our Society's work and its administration. These and other statements in our Declaration are meant to serve as a rejection of the slanderous claim that the Bible Students are supported by Jews. [We request] that a commission of men be appointed by you, Mr. Chancellor . . . who would alone truly examine our concerns without prejudice and according to the just principles enunciated by the Chancellor of the Reich himself. By these principles we mean the statements in Section 24 of Platform of the National Socialist German Workers Party: ". . . The Party, as such, represents the viewpoint of positive Christianity without associating itself with a specific confession. It opposes the Jewish-materialist spirit domestically and abroad. . . ." With anticipation of an early, positive assent [to our requests] and with the assurance of our highest esteem, most honored Mr. Chancellor, we remain, Most respectfully, Watch Tower Bible and Tract Society.

Nevertheless, an international convention of Witnesses in Lucerne, Switzerland, in September 1936 condemned the Nazi regime. Other Jehovah's Witnesses material denounced the persecution of German Jews and Communists, as well as the Nazification of schools, universities, and churches.

SUGGESTED READING: Christine King, "Jehovah's Witnesses under Nazism," in *A Mosaic of Victims: Non-Jews Persecuted and Murdered by the Nazis*, ed. Michael Berenbaum (New York: New York University Press, 1990.

JEROME, ST. (340–420). Born Sophronius Eusebius Hieronymus. **Church Father**, writer, and translator. Jerome's most important contribution to **antisemitism** was his identification of the Jews with **Judas Iscariot** and with the immoral use of money, two themes that would bedevil Christian–Jewish relations for a millennium. Jerome associated materialism with Judas's sin, which, with his punishment, symbolized Jewish behavior and fate: "Christ is saying: 'Judas betrayed Me, the Jews persecuted and crucified Me.' . . . In particular, this is the story of Judas; in general it is that of the Jews. . . . Judas, in particular, was torn asunder by demons—and the [Jewish] people as well. . . . Judas is cursed, that in Judas the Jews may be accursed." Jerome wrote:

[Even] the repentance of Judas became worse than his sins. [Just as] you see the Jew praying; . . . nevertheless, their prayer turns into sin. . . . Whom do you suppose are the sons of Judas? The Jews. The Jews take their name, not from Juda who was a holy man, but from the betrayer. . . . From this Iscariot, they are called Judaeans. . . . Iscariot means money and price. . . . Synagogue was divorced by the Savior and became the wife of Judas, the betrayer.

SUGGESTED READING: James Everett Seaver, *Persecution of the Jews in the Roman Empire, 300–428* (Lawrence: University of Kansas Press, 1952).

JESUITS. The Society of Jesus, a Roman Catholic order founded in 1534 by Ignatius Loyola (1491–1556). Initially, it stood as a standard anti-Jewish organization, arguing that Jews were evil **Christ-killers** but would be redeemed if they **converted** authentically to Roman Catholicism. But by the early 17th century, the order had ruled that Jews were racially evil. The Jesuits' major mission was to propagate the faith and counter Protestantism. However, it was also hostile to Jews and Judaism. It accused Jewish people of **ritual murder** and **desecration of the Host**. Jesuits fomented hatred, accusing Jews and **Freemasons** of engineering the **French Revolution**. They were strong **antidreyfusards**; they burned Hebrew books and railed against the **Talmud**. During the **Holocaust**, the Jesuits kept up their anti-Jewish crusade. *See also CIVILTÀ CATTOLICA.*

SUGGESTED READING: James Reites, "St. Ignatius of Loyola and the Jews," *Studies in the Spirituality of Jesuits* (September 1981).

JEW, TO; TO JEW DOWN. (British, U.S. slur) To bargain aggressively or deceptively.

SUGGESTED READING: "List of Ethnic Slurs," *Wikipedia*, http://en.wikipedia.org/wiki/List_of_ethnic_slurs.

JEWBACCA. (U.S. slur) A hairy Jew; a reference to Chewbacca from *Star Wars*.

SUGGESTED READING: "List of Ethnic Slurs," *Wikipedia*, http://en.wikipedia.org/wiki/List_of_ethnic_slurs.

JEW BADGE. An identification badge that the Jews have been forced to wear in order to distinguish them from non-Jews at various times in history. Singling out Jews by degrading symbols is centuries old. In 807 CE, Arbassid caliph Haroun al-Raschid ordered Jews to wear a **yellow** belt and cone-like hat in Muslim areas. At the Fourth **Lateran Council** of 1215, the Church required secular princes to brand Jews with a **stigmatic emblem**, and the kings of Europe followed the papal will. In 1257 Jews wore the badge in the **Papal States**. King **Louis IX** of France demanded a circular yellow badge in 1269. English king **Edward I** in 1275 commanded that Jews wear a piece of yellow taffeta depicting the Tablets of the Law over their hearts. By the time of the Spanish **expulsion** in 1492, all Jews were marked out. All Jews in Germany wore it in 1520 and in Austria in 1551. Pope **Paul IV** reinstituted the badge in the Papal States in 1555; not until 1798, when the French invaded, was the rouelle abolished there.

The medieval badge took various shapes and colors—often red (for hell) or yellow (for gold)—sewn on the coat. The badge was usually round (called, in French, the *rouelle*), probably signaling the association of Jews with money, with **Judas Iscariot**'s alleged betrayal of Jesus for 30 silver coins, with **usury**, and with the **desecration of the Host**. It was sometimes tablet-shaped, evocative of the Tablets of the Law. Other times, as in Portugal in the early 14th century, the six-pointed Star of David was introduced. Such signs marked out perjurers, witches, whores, and **heretics** as well.

The *Judenstern* (Jewish star) of the Middle Ages was replicated by the **Nazis** in areas under their control, both inside and outside of concentration camps; Jews were required to wear badges of various sorts in Poland in 1939, in Czechoslovakia and Germany in 1941, in France in 1942, and in Hungary in 1944. The Nazis used various signs, including a blue armband stamped with the six-pointed Star of David in Eastern European **ghettos** and a yellow six-pointed star with the letter *J* in Western Europe. In many concentration camps, Jews were marked with a red triangle (political opponent) overlapped by a yellow triangle (Jew) to form a Star of David.

SUGGESTED READING: Guido Kisch, "The Yellow Badge in History," *Historia Judaica* 19 (October 1957).

JEW-BAIL. "Insufficient bail."

JEWBIE. (British, U.S. slur) Someone who behaves in a stereotypical Jewish manner; a Jewish wannabe.
SUGGESTED READING: "List of Ethnic Slurs," *Wikipedia*, http://en.wikipedia.org/wiki/List_of_ethnic_slurs.

JEW BILL. The British naturalization bill of 1753. The measure to make **citizenship** for Jews easier passed the House of Lords, but was withdrawn in the Commons because of the public outcry against it. During the debate, many raised medieval **defamations** against Jews: that the Jews were **deicides**, adherents of the Devil and the **Antichrist**, and Christianity's permanent enemies.
SUGGESTED READING: Cecil Roth, *History of the Jews in England* (Oxford: Clarendon, Press, 1988).

JEWBIRD. Bird with an "ugly, conspicuous beak."

JEW BOY. (British, U.S. slur) Adult Jewish male.
SUGGESTED READING: "List of Ethnic Slurs," *Wikipedia*, http://en.wikipedia.org/wiki/List_of_ethnic_slurs.

JEWBUSH. A bush "characterized by powerful emetic and drastic properties," that is, it makes one vomit and die.

JEW CENSUS. In 1914, at the start of World War I, a hundred thousand German Jews volunteered to fight for Germany. This was far above the proportion of non-Jews who entered the military. During the war, 12,000 Jews died in combat, 78 percent fought at the front, 30,000 were decorated, and 2,000 were awarded battlefield commissions as officers. Nevertheless, because of the stereotype of Jews as exploiters of a nation, not as defenders, in 1916 the German minister of war carried out a "Jew census" to prove that Jews were "shirkers." When the contrary was shown to be the case, the German government refused to release the figures. *See also* TWAIN, MARK.

SUGGESTED READING: Bill Niven, "Questions of Responsibility in Past and Present: New Research into the Holocaust," *German Politics* 13, no. 1 (March 2004).

"JEW DEAL." Derogatory term for President **Franklin Roosevelt**'s New Deal of the 1930s to deal with the Great Depression. Conservatives alleged that FDR was surrounded by Jewish advisors and that he himself was descended from Sephardic Jews, a charge later made by the **Nazis** as well. Although "President Rosenstein's" (another derogatory term at the time for FDR) staff contained several Jewish advisors, Roosevelt disregarded calls for humane and generous action to help the Jews of Europe, even when such action could have been accomplished at negligible cost both politically and in terms of the war effort.

SUGGESTED READING: Robert E. Herzstein, *Roosevelt and Hitler: Prelude to War* (New York: Paragon Books, 1989).

JEWFISH. Fish, member of the grouper family, with an ugly, prominent nose.

JEWFORD. (U.S. slur) A Jewish Southerner; a contraction of Jew and Buford.

SUGGESTED READING: "List of Ethnic Slurs," *Wikipedia*, http://en.wikipedia.org/wiki/List_of_ethnic_slurs.

JEWGABOO. (U.S. slur) A child of Jewish-black parentage.

SUGGESTED READING: "List of Ethnic Slurs," *Wikipedia*, http://en.wikipedia.org/wiki/List_of_ethnic_slurs.

JEWGENE. (U.S. slur) A Jew who behaves in a stereotypical Italian manner.

SUGGESTED READING: "List of Ethnic Slurs," *Wikipedia*, http://en.wikipedia.org/wiki/List_of_ethnic_slurs.

JEW HAT (*JUDENHUT*). *See* STIGMATIC EMBLEMS.

JEW HATE. Traditional term for **antisemitism**. *See also* JUDENHAß.

JEWIES. "I'm told those *Jewies* does have a sort of a queer odour coming off them for dogs" (James Joyce, *Ulysses*, chap. 12). *See also* FOETOR JUDAICUS.

JEW IN THE THORNBUSH. In the fairytale "The Jew in the Thornbush" from the Brothers **Grimm**, a Jewish tradesman is shown as an untrustworthy, un-German alien, despite the fact that in small German towns much of the Christian–Jewish interaction was harmonious.

SUGGESTED READING: Robertson Ritchie, ed., *The German-Jewish Dialogue: An Anthology of Literary Texts, 1749–1993* (Oxford: Oxford University Press, 1999).

JEWISH-AMERICAN PRINCESS (JAP). Antisemitic and sexist stereotype of Jewish girls and young women in America. They are seen as pampered, spoiled, shallow, and materialistic and are accused of having an obsession with clothes and shopping. In addition, they are characterized as demanding yet dependent on a man, be it their father or husband, and guilty of dominating and infantilizing him. Sexually, they are seen as frigid and unresponsive.

SUGGESTED READING: Janice Becker, *The Jewish-American Princess and Other Myths: The Many Forms of Self-Hatred* (New York: Shapolsky, 1991).

JEWISH ANTI-FASCIST COMMITTEE (JAFC). Group formed in 1942 when the Communist government under **Joseph Stalin** sought support from American Jews during World War II. The JAFC came to the United States in 1943 to get money and gain goodwill. Prominent Russian Jewish artists such as Solomon Mikoels and Itsik Fefer told audiences in Yiddish about the **Holocaust**, despite the Allies', including the USSR's, unwillingness to publicize it. When Golda Meir, premier of Israel, visited the USSR in 1948 and was very warmly greeted, Stalin disbanded the JAFC in his first move toward his planned **genocide** of Soviet Jews. Most members were subsequently arrested and murdered.

SUGGESTED READING: Arnold Lustiger, *Stalin and the Jews*, trans. Roman Brackman (New York: Enigma Books, 2000).

JEWISH CONDITION IN POLAND. While Jews were an unprotected minority in England, France, Portugal, Spain, France, and Italy, in Poland from at least the 13th century they were a protected "estate." A document known as "The General Charter of Jewish Liberties" was issued in 1264 in the town of Kalisz by Boleslaw Pobozny (Boleslau the Pius, 1221–1279). The charter, also called the Statute of Kalisz, created the climate that enabled the Jews to set up their own autonomous nation, which existed until Poland's dissolution in 1795. Jews were regarded as different but not as inferiors, and their rights were spelled out in great detail: "Our Jews are treasures" read section 36 of the charter. In the 19th and 20th centuries, the Jewish condition in Poland suffered from the growing importance of the Roman Catholic Church as the rallying point for Polish nationalism. During World War II, the Germans murdered almost all the Polish Jews. Although the Yad Vashem Holocaust Memorial in Jerusalem contains more individual Polish names on its Avenue of the Just than of any other nation (the whole country of Denmark is also listed), the high level of **antisemitism** in Poland contributed to German success in pursuing their **Final Solution**.

SUGGESTED READING: Bernard Weinryb, *The Jews of Poland* (Philadelphia: Jewish Publication Society, 1972); Simon Dubnow, *A History of the Jews in Russia and Poland from the Earliest Times to the Present Day* (New York: Ktav, 1975); David Biale, *Power and Powerlessness in Jewish History* (New York: Schocken, 1987).

JEWISH COUNCIL OF BUDAPEST (1944). Germany occupied Hungary in March 1944. With the invasion came **Adolf Eichmann**, whose role was to implement the **Final Solution**. Jewish organizations were dissolved and a Jewish Council of Budapest set up. The council agreed to relay German and Hungarian orders to the Jewish community of Budapest and to the other Jewish councils throughout Hungary. Jews were **ghettoized**, coerced to wear the **yellow** star, and used as **forced labor**. About 400,000 Hungarian Jews were deported to and murdered in **Auschwitz-Birkenau**, and 30,000 Budapest Jews were killed. Intervention by foreign embassies and the advance of the Red Army saved 120,000 Budapest Jews. Randolph L. Braham in his *Politics of Genocide* claims that the council agreed to keep the Final Solution quiet and to reassure the Jewish masses of their safety. In return, some of the leadership were saved. He considered that a betrayal. **Hannah Arendt** in her *Eichmann in Jerusalem* thought the council should have warned the Jews and encouraged them to do everything possible to escape rather than cooperate. Yehuda Bauer in his *Jews for Sale?* says that the council Jews did the best they could under the circumstances and saved as many as they could. In his *Destruction of European Jews*, Raul Hilberg states that the Palestine Zionist leadership also was indifferent to the fate of European Jews. *See also* ARROW CROSS; BLOOD FOR TRUCKS; HORTHY, MIKLÓS.

SUGGESTED READING: Yehuda Bauer, *Jews for Sale? Nazi–Jewish Negotiations, 1939–1945* (New Haven, CT: Yale University Press, 1994); Randolph Braham, *The Politics of Genocide: The Holocaust in Hungary* (New York: Rosenthal Institute for Holocaust Studies of the City University of New York, 1994); Raul Hilberg, *The Destruction of European Jews* (New York: Holmes & Meier, 1985).

JEWISH LIGHTNING. (British, U.S. slur) Arson commissioned or committed by Jews on their own property so that they can collect on the insurance.

SUGGESTED READING: "List of Ethnic Slurs," *Wikipedia*, http://en .wikipedia.org/wiki/List_of_ethnic_slurs.

JEWISH ORDER SERVICE (JÜDISCHER ORDNUNGSDIENST). Jewish **Ghetto** Police, 1940–44. This unarmed police force within Nazi ghettos was affiliated with the Judenrat (**Nazi**-appointed governing councils). They assisted the Nazis in rounding up Jews for **selection**s and **deportations** to concentration camps. Their collaboration caused great hatred and resentment against them and the Judenrat among the other ghetto Jews.

SUGGESTED READING: Calel Perechodnik, ed., *Am I a Murderer? Testament of a Jewish Ghetto Policeman*, trans. Frank Fox (Boulder, CO: Westview Press, 1996).

JEWISH QUESTION AS A RACIAL, MORAL, CULTURAL PROBLEM, THE (DIE JUDENFRAGE ALS RASSEN-, SITTEN-, UND KULTURFRAGE). An 1881 book by **Eugen Karl Dühring**, arguing for a **final solution** of the "Jewish question." It proposed that Jews were causing Germany's decline and that they constituted an evil, eternal "counter-race" immune to conversion and assimilation.

SUGGESTED READING: Ritchie Robertson, *The Jewish Question in German Literature, 1789–1939* (Oxford: Oxford University Press, 1999).

JEWISH SPIRIT. Nazi dictator **Adolf Hitler** concluded near the end of his life that biological racism was a sham. It was the Jewish mind and values, the "Jewish spirit," that he hated. The only way to rid the world of this "virus," Hitler concluded, was to destroy the Jewish bodies that housed it.

SUGGESTED READING: Adolf Hitler, Martin Bormann, and François Genoud, *The Testament of Adolf Hitler: The Hitler-Bormann Documents, February–April 1945* (London: Cassell, 1960).

JEWISH SUPERSTITIONS, ON. Agobard gave currency to the common **defamations** against the Jews and at great length cited passages from the **Church Fathers** to show how they hated the Jews. His statement that the Jews are accused of cursing Christ introduced the theme of the curse that underlies the legend of the eternal or **wandering Jew**.

SUGGESTED READING: James Carroll, *Constantine's Sword: The Church and the Jews—A History* (Boston: Mariner Books, 2002).

JEW KILLERS (*JUDENSCHLÄCHTER*). *See* ARMLEDER MASSACRE.

JEW LIZARD. Lizard with a prominent nose.

JEWMAN. Stereotypical Jew.

JEWOP. (U.S. slur) Jew who behaves like a stereotypical Italian; combination of Jew and "wop."

SUGGESTED READING: "List of Ethnic Slurs," *Wikipedia*, http://en .wikipedia.org/wiki/List_of_ethnic_slurs.

JEW ORDERS. *See* GRANT, ULYSSES S.

JEWS, KINGS OF THE EPOCH, THE. *See* TOUSSENEL, ALPHONSE.

JEWS AND THEIR LIES, ON THE. *See* LUTHER, MARTIN.

JEWS' BEECH-TREE, THE (*DIE JUDENBUCHE*). An 1842 murder mystery by **Annette von Droste-Hülshoff**, among the best analyses of human guilt in 19th-century German realist narratives. It reflects the double standard German society used in the 18th and 19th centuries for Christians compared to Jews. The Jews in the story are compared with **pigs** and dogs, portrayed as demanding and avenging, ruthless aliens, damned infidels, and murderous crucifiers, whereas the Christians for the most part are pious and sensitive. *See also* JUDENSAU.

SUGGESTED READING: Karin Doerr, "The Specter of Antisemitism in and around Annette von Droste-Hülshoff's *Judenbuche*," *German Studies Review* 17, no. 3 (October 1994); Kuno Francke and W. G. Howard, *The German Classics of the Nineteenth and Twentieth Centuries*, 20 vols. (New York: German Publication Society, 1913–15).

JEWS' HOUSES. "Distorted and crumbling remains of ancient tin-smelting furnaces."

JEWS' LETTER. Stigmatic emblem indicating the mark of Cain.

JEWS' MYRTLE. A plant that, "in popular belief, served as Christ's crown of thorns."

JEW SOMEONE OUT OF SOMETHING, TO. (British, U.S. slur) To cheat or deprive a person of something.
SUGGESTED READING: "List of Ethnic Slurs," *Wikipedia*, http://en .wikipedia.org/wiki/List_of_ethnic_slurs.

JEWS' SLIME. Asphalt or bitumen.

JEW SÜSS. See JUD SÜSS.

JEWY. Stereotypically Jewish.

JEW YORK CITY. (U.S. slur) New York City.
SUGGESTED READING: "List of Ethnic Slurs," *Wikipedia*, http://en .wikipedia.org/wiki/List_of_ethnic_slurs.

JEW YORKER. (U.S. slur) A Jew, especially from New York City, which has a large Jewish population.
SUGGESTED READING: "List of Ethnic Slurs," *Wikipedia*, http://en .wikipedia.org/wiki/List_of_ethnic_slurs.

JIDAN; JIDOV. (Romanian slur) Offensive word for Jew, the more neutral word being "evreu" (Hebrew); derived from the Slavic *Zhid*.
SUGGESTED READING: "List of Ethnic Slurs," *Wikipedia*, http://en .wikipedia.org/wiki/List_of_ethnic_slurs.

JIGGER. (U.S. slur) A Jew behaving in a combined stereotypical Jewish and black behavior, that is, someone accused of being cheap and lazy; combination of Jew and nigger.
SUGGESTED READING: "List of Ethnic Slurs," *Wikipedia*, http://en .wikipedia.org/wiki/List_of_ethnic_slurs.

JIHAD. Arabic for "holy war." The term has a number of meanings, but in the context of conflict in the Middle East, it signifies a Muslim war against the West and, especially, Israel. Daniel Pipes has further expanded this definition to encompass "the legal, compulsory, and communal effort to expand territories ruled by Muslims at the expense of territories ruled by non-Muslims." The former president of **Iran**, Ali Akbar Hashemi Rafsanjani, advocated that "one atomic bomb would wipe out Israel without a trace," whereas any Israeli retaliation would only "damage" the Islamic world. Iran's current president, Mahmoud Ahmadinejad, supported by Iran's supreme leader Ayatollah Ali Khamenei and Rafsanjani, has called on Muslim nations to "wipe Israel off the map" and to destroy the West in a jihad.

SUGGESTED READING: Daniel Pipes, "What is Jihad?" *New York Post*, December 31, 2000; Cyril Glasse, *The New Encyclopedia of Islam* (Walnut Creek, CA: Rowman & Littlefield, 2002); Robert S. Wistrich, *Muslim Antisemitism: A Clear and Present Danger* (New York: American Jewish Committee, 2002); Marvin Perry and Frederick M. Schweitzer, *Antisemitism: Myth and Hate from Antiquity to the Present* (New York: Palgrave Macmillan, 2002); "Iran's Conference on Holocaust Denial Begins on Tuesday," *Iran Focus*, March 21, 2006, http://www.iranfocus.com/modules/news/article.php?storyid = 6082.

JOG. White supremacist and antigovernment extremist acronym for Jew(ish) Occupied Government. It reflects the belief that Jews occupy and control the U.S. government and media. The letters often appear in a circle with a slash. *See also* ZOG.

SUGGESTED READING: Anti-Defamation League, *Hate on Display: Extremist Symbols, Logos, and Tattoos* (New York: Anti-Defamation League, 2006); ADL Law Enforcement Agency Resource Network, *A Visual Database of Extremist Symbols, Logos, and Tattoos*, http://www.adl.org/hate_symbols/default.asp.

JOHN I (1167–1216). King of England, 1199–1216. As King John put it, the English Jews were under the monarchy's protection as royal property and should live in peace. "We say this not only for our Jews, . . . for if we gave our peace to a dog it should be inviolably observed."

SUGGESTED READING: Cecil Roth, *History of the Jews of England* (Oxford, England: Clarendon Press, 1988).

JOHN I (1358–1390). King of Castile and León, 1379–90. John was convinced by **Dominican** friar **Vincent Ferrer** to expel the Jews unless they **converted**. He aimed to reduce Jews to pariah status and to isolate them by forcing them into unhealthy **ghettos**. This, he hoped, would coerce them into conversion.

SUGGESTED READING: Yitzhak Baer, *A History of Jews in Christian Spain*, 2 vols. (Philadelphia: Jewish Publication Society, 1992).

JOHN I (1357–1433). King of Portugal, 1385–1433. At the end of the 14th century, in response to King John's petition, Pope Boniface IX implicitly sanctioned the idea of Jewish **desecration of the Host** by approving the extension of a Christian church, hermitage, and hospital in Coimbra, commemorating the supposed desecration.

SUGGESTED READING: Shlomo Simonsohn, *The Apostolic See and the Jews: Documents, 492–1404* (Toronto: Pontifical Institute of Mediaeval Studies, 1988); Shlomo Simonsohn, *The Apostolic See and the Jews: Documents, 1394–1464* (Toronto: Pontifical Institute of Mediaeval Studies, 1989).

JOHN II (1319–1364). King of France, 1350–64. A charter of the 14th-century French king stated that Jews

> have no place of their own in all Christendom, where they can live and move and take up their dwelling; they can only live at the entire discretion and purely by the permission of the prince or princes under whose government they wish to settle as subjects, and who are willing to receive them as such.

SUGGESTED READING: James Carroll, *Constantine's Sword: The Church and the Jews—A History* (New York: Mariner Books, 2002).

JOHN XXII (1249–1334). Pope, 1316–34. John XXII expelled the Jews from the **Papal States** in the south of France and granted absolution to Christians who had persecuted or participated in the murder of Jews. During the **Shepherds' Crusade**, following **St. Augustine**'s dictum that the Jews were the Witness People, the pope reminded the Christian secular authorities in France that Jews should be "defended since they bear witness to [the validity of] the Catholic faith." Even here, however, John did not specify any penalty for noncompliance with his directives. He noted "the blindness of Judaism" and his "detestation of the old Jewish treachery." In September 1320, when the Shepherds were suppressed, Pope John authorized another assault on the **Talmud** for blasphemy and error. Noting "the damned initiatives of the **perfidious** Jews," he ordered that "the plague and deadly diseased weed [of Judaism] must be pulled out by its roots." John also took advantage of the Jews' vulnerability at this time and sent special preachers to them in the papal cities of southern France, hoping for mass **conversions**. When the Jews still refused **baptism**, their **synagogues** were destroyed in three papal towns and they were sent into exile. "The filth of the Jewish superstition" was to be replaced by Christian chapels.

SUGGESTED READING: Eamon Duffy, *Saints and Sinners: History of the Popes* (New Haven, CT: Yale University Press, 2002).

JOHN XXIII (1881–1963). Pope, 1958–63. Before he became Pope John XXIII, Angelo Roncalli's efforts during World War II illustrate what might have been done by others to rescue Jews. He issued baptismal certicates and sent letters to leaders of nations warning them of the dire results of Jewish **deportations**. When he was elected pope in 1958, he tried to repair relations between Jews and Catholics. John XXIII summoned the Vatican Council II, which revised negative prayers against Jews and promoted the Declaration on the Relationship of the Church to Non-Christian Religions, which tried to eliminate **antisemitism** in the church, admit past mistakes, brand antisemitism a violation of church doctrine, and promote positive feelings between Jews and Catholics. Nevertheless, while he was the apostolic delegate at Istanbul during the **Holocaust**, Roncalli had written to Pope **Pius XII**'s secretary of state, Cardinal Luigi Maglione, that he did not want Catholic charity to lead to Jewish control of the Holy Land. He was disturbed by the possibility of increased Jewish immigration to the Holy Land:

> I admit that the idea of seeing the Holy See concern itself with helping Italian Jews escape to Palestine where they could build a Jewish state arouses in my mind a kind of anxiety. . . . It does not seem good to me that a simple act of charity by the Holy See may encourage the possibility of or give the appearance of a collaboration, even indirect, in the establishment of a messianic dream. This may be perhaps only a personal qualm. . . . The reconstruction of a Jewish state can never amount to anything more than a utopian dream.

SUGGESTED READING: Peter Hebblethwaite and Margaret Hebblethwaite, *John XXIII: Pope of the Century* (New York: Continuum, 2000); Joseph D'Hippolite, "Pope John XXIII," *FrontPagemagazine.com*, August 20, 2004, http://www.frontpagemagazine.com/article/readarticle.asp?ID = 14732.

JOHN 8:44. Christian Scriptural passage: "Ye [Jews] are of your father, the devil, and the lust of your father ye will do." This became one of the classic bits of evidence supporting Christian **antisemitism**.

SUGGESTED READING: William Nicholls, *Christian Antisemitism: A History of Hate* (Northvale, NJ: Jason Aronson, 1995).

JOHN 15:16. Christian Scriptural passage: "If a man abide not in me, he is cast forth as a branch and is withered; and men gather them and cast them into the fire, and they are burned." This verse was the basis of the **auto-da-fé**.

SUGGESTED READING: William Nicholls, *Christian Antisemitism: A History of Hate* (Northvale, NJ: Jason Aronson, 1995).

JOHN OF DAMASCUS, ST. (675–749). **Church Father** and Doctor of the Roman Catholic Church; theologian. John held that God gave the Jews their **Sabbath** because of their "grossness and sensuality . . . and absolute propensity for material things."

SUGGESTED READING: Rosemary Radford Ruether, *Faith and Fratricide* (New York, Seabury Press, 1974).

JOHN PAUL II (1920–2005). Pope, 1978–2005. Born Karol Józef Wojtyla. John Paul recognized Judaism as a valid religion and established diplomatic relations between the **Vatican** and Israel. The pope apologized for Catholic persecution of Jews in the past and Catholics' lack of action during the **Holocaust**. He encouraged Jewish–Christian dialogue, visited Rome's **synagogue**, and called **antisemitism** a sin. John Paul held individual Catholics responsible for crimes against Jews but failed to hold the church as an institution responsible for persecutions in Jewish history. He also made saints of Catholic figures who persecuted Jews, such as Queen Isabella of Spain, and attempted to canonize Pope **Pius XII**. John Paul approved a Carmelite convent at **Auschwitz**, and he embraced **Yassir Arafat**, met with Austria's Kurt Waldheim, and refused to completely open Vatican archives.

SUGGESTED READING: George Weigel, *Witness to Hope: The Biography of John Paul* (New York: HarperPerennial, 2001).

JOHNSON-REED ACT. Also known as the Immigration Restriction Act of 1924 and the National Origins Act. In the 1920s, the Congressional Committee on Immigration and Naturalization was determined to reduce or end Jewish immigration and its "dangers"—**pogroms** in Russia and Poland in 1919 and 1920 had caused a significant rise in Jewish immigration to the United States. Lawmakers complained about Chinese, Italian, and other immigrants as well. The committee was chaired by Albert Johnson of Washington, Congress's leading nativist. After presidents William Taft and **Woodrow Wilson** vetoed anti-immigration bills, President Warren Harding called Congress into special session in 1921, when it approved an act that temporarily curbed immigration, passing the House on a voice vote and the Senate 78–1. The 1921 Quota Act set the first immigration quotas in the nation's history, equal to 3 percent of the foreign born of admissible nationality in the 1910 census. There was no limit on immigration from the Western Hemisphere. The 1924 Johnson-Reed Act set an annual ceiling of 154,227 for the Eastern Hemisphere, each country having a quota representative of its population in the United States as of the 1920 census. Despite protests from minority representatives, in 1924 Congress overwhelmingly voted to establish a permanent immigration law containing a yearly quota system. The number of immigrants allowed into the United States from any foreign country was restricted to no more than 2 percent of that country's national-origin group residing in the United States in 1890, and Chinese immigration was shut off completely. The final vote count on the bill was 323–71 in the House and 62–6 in the Senate. President Harding signed it without hesitation. With the gates of the United States—along with those of most of the free world—virtually closed to Jews, the **Holocaust** was even more effective. *See also* BERMUDA CONFERENCE; BRIGHAM, CARL; EUGENICS; EVIAN CONFERENCE; GRANT, MADISON; IMMIGRATION RESTRICTION LEAGUE; LAUGHLIN, HARRY; ROOSEVELT, FRANKLIN D.

SUGGESTED READING: Daniel Tichenor, *Dividing Lines: The Politics of Immigration Control in America* (Princeton, NJ: Princeton University Press, 2002).

JOKES, ANTI-JEWISH. Anti-Jewish jokes reinforce **antisemitic** stereotypes of Jews, their "race," religion, and/or ethnic origin. These jokes portray Jews as cheap, cowardly, or disloyal to their country; as tricksters taking unfair advantage of, and outwitting, innocent Gentiles; or as rich, money-hungry, unethical, dishonest, prideful, conceited, and clannish.

SUGGESTED READING: Christie Davies, "Jewish Jokes, Antisemitic Jokes and Hebedonian Jokes," in *Jewish Humor*, ed. Avner Ziv (Tel Aviv: Papyrus Publishing House at Tel Aviv University, 1986).

JONES, LEROI (AMIRI BARAKA) (1934–). African-American poet, writer, and activist. When civil rights activist James Chaney and Jewish civil rights workers Michael Schwerner and Andrew Goodman were killed by the **Ku Klux Klan** in June 1964 in Mississippi, Jones remarked that "those white boys were only seeking to assuage their own leaking consciences." The 1965 death of **Malcolm X** played a pivotal role in shaping Jones's worldview, leading him to become a hard-core black nationalist, anti-white racist, and the clarion voice of black **antisemitism**. In his poem "For Tom Postell, Dead Black Poet," Jones referred to his ex-wife as a "fat jew girl." In another poem, he wrote of the Jews as "double crossers" who convinced blacks "to worship a dead Jew" instead of themselves. In a 1967 poem, "The Black Man Is Making New Gods," he called Jews "little arty bastards" using arithmetic that they "sucked from the Arab's head." In 1966, the same year as he published "Black Art" ("We want . . . dagger poems in the slimy bells of the owner-Jews," "Look at the Liberal Spokesman for the jews clutch his throat and puke himself into eternity," "Another bad poem cracking steel knuckles in a jewlady's mouth"), Jones became a Muslim and changed his name to Amiri Baraka. His antisemitism has transmuted into **anti-Zionism**. *See also* COX, WILLIAM HAROLD.

SUGGESTED READING: Imanu Ami Baraka et al., *The LeRoi Jones/Amiri Baraka Reader* (New York: Thunder's Mouth Press, 1999).

JOSEPH II (1741–1790). Holy Roman emperor, 1765–90. Joseph's Edict of Toleration (*Toleranzpatent*) of 1782 permitted Jews to enter the Austrian economy, remove **stigmatic emblems,** have Christian servants, appear in public on Sunday, and wear swords. But the decree did not allow Jews to own land or shops outside the **ghetto** or to have public **synagogues** in Vienna. They were still required to pay a special Jew **tax**, to speak German in their business transactions, and to take German names. Pope Paul VI and the Austrian bishops opposed any and all rights being granted to the Jews.

SUGGESTED READING: Owen Chadwick, *The Popes and European Revolution* (Oxford: Oxford University Press, 1981); Gotthard Deutsch, "Joseph II," *JewishEncyclopedia.com*, http://www.jewishencyclopedia.com/view.jsp?artid = 443&letter = J.

JOYCE, WILLIAM (1906–1946). American-born British **fascist**, known as "Lord Haw Haw." Joyce, a savage **antisemite**, joined the **British Union of Fascists** in 1932. He left that group in 1937 and formed the British National Socialist Party. In 1939, just before war broke out between Germany and Britain, he fled to Berlin. From there, he broadcast pro-German, anti-British government radio messages. Joyce blamed the war on the Jews and favored a quick peace settlement. He was tried for treason and executed by the British after World War II.

SUGGESTED READING: Francis Solgyn, *Hitler's Henchmen: The Crime of Lord Haw Haw* (Harmondsworth, England: Penguin, 1992).

J STAMP. With the failure of the international **Evian Conference** in July and Germany's *Anschluss* of Austria in October 1938, increasing numbers of Jews sought asylum in Switzerland. Heinrich Rothmund, head of the Swiss federal police, requested that the German government recall all Jewish passports and mark them with a large red letter *J* to prevent Jews from smuggling themselves into Switzerland. Swiss anxieties about *Überfremdung* ("being overrun by foreigners") prevailing over moral or humanitarian concerns, Switzerland adopted a policy of *refoulement*, sealing its borders to all "illegal" immigrants. Moreover, in February 1940, the British discovered that the German government was issuing passports to some

Jews without the red *J* stamped therein. As a result, the Italian and Yugoslav authorities could issue transit visas to Palestine and safety to Jews despite British pressure not to. The British ambassador made "urgent requests" to the Yugoslavs "to take particular care that the [Jewish] passports are labelled with the necessary letter 'J' [and the appropriate visas]." The effect was to close this European border entirely to Jews. This policy and the red *J* were a death sentence for Jewish refugees who were sent back to the **Gestapo**.

SUGGESTED READING: Alfred Haesler, *The Lifeboat Is Full: Switzerland and the Refugees, 1933–1945* (New York: Funk & Wagnalls, 1969); David Kranzler, *Heroine of Rescue: The Incredible Story of Rita Sternbuch* (Brooklyn, NY: Mesorah, 1984); Ronald Zweig, *Britain and Palestine during the Second World War* (London: Oxford University Press, 1986); Bernard Wasserstein, *Britain and the Jews of Europe, 1939–1945* (London: Institute of Jewish Affairs, 1979).

JUDAISM IN MUSIC. An 1869 book by composer **Richard Wagner—Adolf Hitler**'s favorite composer. In this work, Wagner claimed that Jews, because they lacked the German **Aryan** spirit, could not be truly creative. Wagner called Jewish melodies bland and poorly constructed with repeated notes. Jews, he said, could only imitate great music.

SUGGESTED READING: Paul Rose, *Antisemitism in Germany, from Kant to Wagner* (Princeton, NJ: Princeton University Press, 1997).

JUDAIZERS. Christians who observed even the smallest Jewish rituals disapproved by the Church were considered judaizers, that is, **heretics**.

SUGGESTED READING: Yitzhak Baer, *A History of Jews in Christian Spain*, 2 vols. (Philadelphia: Jewish Publication Society, 1992).

JUDASBAUM **(JUDAS TREE).** The tree upon which **Judas Iscariot** supposedly hung himself in response to allegedly betraying Jesus of Nazareth.

SUGGESTED READING: Jacob Grimm and Wilhelm Grimm, *Deutsches Wörterbuch* (Leipzig: Verlag von S. Hirzel, 1877).

JUDASBRUDER **(JUDAS'S BROTHER).** A false or faithless brother or friend.

SUGGESTED READING: Jacob Grimm and Wilhelm Grimm, *Deutsches Wörterbuch* (Leipzig: Verlag von S. Hirzel, 1877).

JUDASGRUSZ. Treacherous greeting.

SUGGESTED READING: Jacob Grimm and Wilhelm Grimm, *Deutsches Wörterbuch* (Leipzig: Verlag von S. Hirzel, 1877).

JUDAS ISCARIOT. Disciple of Jesus of Nazareth who may have betrayed him. In traditional Christian **antisemitism**, all Jews are seen as Judases. The first clear enunciator of this comparison was **St. Jerome**. In 2006, a gnostic Gospel of Judas was restored, authenticated, and translated from Coptic into English after being lost for 1,700 years. This ancient manuscript tells the story of Judas as Jesus of Nazareth's favorite disciple. Bart D. Ehrman, chairman of the Department of Religious Studies at the University of North Carolina–Chapel Hill, described the document as "a gnostic gospel [showing] Jesus and Judas in a very different perspective. Judas is Jesus's closest intimate. Rather than betraying Jesus, he actually did what Jesus wanted him to do."

SUGGESTED READING: Charles A. Radin, "A New Judas Emerges from Rediscovered Gospel," *Boston Globe*, April 7, 2006; Herbert Krosney, *The Lost Gospel: The Quest for the Gospel of Judas Iscariot* (Washington, DC: National Geographic, 2006).

JUDASKUSS. Treacherous kiss.

SUGGESTED READING: Jacob Grimm and Wilhelm Grimm, *Deutsches Wörterbuch* (Leipzig: Verlag von S. Hirzel, 1877).

JUDE. (German, Swedish slur) A Jew. The Brothers **Grimm** quote the German saying, "It takes a Jew to cheat a Jew."

SUGGESTED READING: Jacob Grimm and Wilhelm Grimm, *Deutsches Wörterbuch* (Leipzig: Verlag von S. Hirzel, 1877); "List of Ethnic Slurs," *Wikipedia*, http://en.wikipedia.org/wiki/List_of_ethnic_slurs.

JUDELEI. The way Jews speak and do business.

SUGGESTED READING: Jacob Grimm and Wilhelm Grimm, *Deutsches Wörterbuch* (Leipzig: Verlag von S. Hirzel, 1877).

JÜDELN. To speak like a Jew.

SUGGESTED READING: Jacob Grimm and Wilhelm Grimm, *Deutsches Wörterbuch* (Leipzig: Verlag von S. Hirzel, 1877).

JUDEN. To **jew**; to do business like a Jew.

SUGGESTED READING: Jacob Grimm and Wilhelm Grimm, *Deutsches Wörterbuch* (Leipzig: Verlag von S. Hirzel, 1877).

JUDENAPFEL **(JEW APPLE).** The apple of the Tree of Knowledge that Satan convinced Eve to pursuade Adam to eat; the act that caused calamity forever after.

SUGGESTED READING: Jacob Grimm and Wilhelm Grimm, *Deutsches Wörterbuch* (Leipzig: Verlag von S. Hirzel, 1877).

JUDENBAUM (**JEW TREE**). *See* JEW'S MYRTLE; JUDENDORN.
SUGGESTED READING: Jacob Grimm and Wilhelm Grimm, *Deutsches Wörterbuch* (Leipzig: Verlag von S. Hirzel, 1877).

JUDENBENGEL. Jew rascal; Jewish young man.
SUGGESTED READING: Jacob Grimm and Wilhelm Grimm, *Deutsches Wörterbuch* (Leipzig: Verlag von S. Hirzel, 1877).

JUDENBUCHE, DIE. See JEWS' BEECH-TREE, THE.

JUDENDEUTSCH. Jewish German; the German language as spoken by Jews with a Hebrew accent.
SUGGESTED READING: Jacob Grimm and Wilhelm Grimm, *Deutsches Wörterbuch* (Leipzig: Verlag von S. Hirzel, 1877).

JUDENDORN (**JEW THORN**). The bush of thorns from which "the Jews twisted Jesus's crown."
SUGGESTED READING: Jacob Grimm and Wilhelm Grimm, *Deutsches Wörterbuch* (Leipzig: Verlag von S. Hirzel, 1877).

JUDENFRAGE (**JEWISH QUESTION; JEWISH PROBLEM**). The mere presence of Jews in many countries of Europe was believed by **anti-semites** to be a "problem." Jews, they theorized, were a contamination, an alien element that harmed society. Antisemites came up with solutions, often implemented, such as denying full political rights and refusing Jews social and economic intercourse. In addition, **ghettoization**, **expulsion**, and extermination as a **Final Solution** were all utilized in an attempt to "solve" the issue.
SUGGESTED READING: Jacob Towry, "The Jewish Question: A Semantic Approach," *Leo Baeck Institute Yearbook* 2 (1966).

JUDENGASSE. See GHETTOS.

JUDENHARZ (**JEW RESIN**). Asphalt.
SUGGESTED READING: Jacob Grimm and Wilhelm Grimm, *Deutsches Wörterbuch* (Leipzig: Verlag von S. Hirzel, 1877).

JUDENHAß; *JUDENHASS*. German for "**Jew hate**"; the traditional German term for anti-Judaism, *Judenfeinschaft*, softened and made more polite by **Wilhelm Marr**.

SUGGESTED READING: Robert S. Wistrich, *Anti-Semitism: The Longest Hatred* (New York: Schocken, 1994).

JUDENHUT. See STIGMATIC EMBLEMS.

JUDENMAUSCHEL. Jewish jabbering.

SUGGESTED READING: Jacob Grimm and Wilhelm Grimm, *Deutsches Wörterbuch* (Leipzig: Verlag von S. Hirzel, 1877).

JUDENREIN; *JUDENFREI.* Cleansed of Jews; rid of Jews. This was **Nazi** terminology for the **Final Solution**. The Nazi goal was a "Europe rid of Jews." Towns and areas where all Jews were **deported** were considered Judenrein, in official **Nazideutsch** language.

SUGGESTED READING: Robert Michael and Karin Doerr, *Nazi-Deutsch/ Nazi German* (Westport, CT: Greenwood, 2001).

JUDENSAU. The scatological medieval Judensau motif pictured the Jews as sucking a sow's teats and eating its feces, identified with the **Talmud**. **Martin Luther** was the first to write of this **defamation**.

SUGGESTED READING: Isaiah Shachar, *The Judensau: A Medieval Anti-Jewish Motif and Its History* (London: Warburg Institute, 1974).

JUDENSCHLÄCHTER **(JEW-SLAUGHTERERS).** *See* JEW KILLERS.

JUDENSEELE **(JEW SOUL).** "Lost like the soul of a Jew."

SUGGESTED READING: Jacob Grimm and Wilhelm Grimm, *Deutsches Wörterbuch* (Leipzig: Verlag von S. Hirzel, 1877).

JUDENSPIESZ; *JUDENSPIEß* **(JEW SPEAR).** The spear with which Jesus Christ's side was stabbed.

SUGGESTED READING: Jacob Grimm and Wilhelm Grimm, *Deutsches Wörterbuch* (Leipzig: Verlag von S. Hirzel, 1877).

JUDEO-BOLSHEVISM. A central theme of **fascism** sets up a mythical, devilish alliance between Jews and **Bolsheviks** (Communists) as the heart of the Russian Revolution and future Marxist revolutions. Judeo-Bolshevism claims that demonic Jews are the authentic instigators of social crises intended to destroy the status quo. This fantasy enabled the **Nazis** to present Jewish communism as the bogeyman of the German middle class, thereby gaining the support of German conservatives and capitalists.

SUGGESTED READING: Léon Poliakov, *La causalité diabolique* (Paris: Calmann-Lévy, 1980); David Hogan, ed., *The Holocaust Chronicle* (Lincolnwood, IL: Publications International, 2000).

JUDEOPHOBIA. Fear of Jews. Before the term *antisemitism* came into use in the late 19th century, *Judeophobia* was often used. It was employed by Christians and had less of a racial overtone and more of a religious one. Christians, particularly authorities, saw Judaism as a challenge and threat to the faith. They also feared that **New Christians** would revert to Judaism upon contact with true Jews. *See also* MARR, WILHELM.

SUGGESTED READING: Robert Chazan and Marc Lee Raphael, *Modern Jewish History: A Source Reader* (New York: Schocken, 1974).

JUDEU. (Portuguese slur) A Jew.

SUGGESTED READING: "List of Ethnic Slurs," *Wikipedia*, http://en.wikipedia.org/wiki/List_of_ethnic_slurs.

JUDGMENT OF THE JEWS. *See* EXCOMMUNICATION OF JEWS.

JUDICIUM JUDAEORUM. See EXCOMMUNICATION OF JEWS.

JUDÍO. (Spanish slur) A Jew.

SUGGESTED READING: "List of Ethnic Slurs," *Wikipedia*, http://en.wikipedia.org/wiki/List_of_ethnic_slurs.

JUD SÜSS. Mock-historical **Nazi** propaganda film of 1940. One of three films (along with *Ewige Jude* and *Die* **Rothschilds**) commissioned by the Nazi Propaganda Ministry. *Jud Süss* proved to be one of the most popular films throughout occupied Europe. Beyond its entertainment value and the purported historical import of its subject, there was a 1924 best-selling novel by the Jewish novelist Lion Feuchtwanger and an English film of 1934 from which the historically distorted Nazi film derived much impact. By Nazi direction, the main character, a **Court Jew**, uses his position to seduce Gentile women and cheat Gentiles.

SUGGESTED READING: Rolf Giesen, *Nazi Propaganda Films: A History and Filmography* (Jefferson, NC: McFarland, 2003); Linda Schulte-Sasse, *Entertaining the Third Reich: Illusions of Wholeness in Nazi Cinema* (Durham, NC: Duke University Press, 1996).

JUIF ERRANT. See WANDERING JEW.

JULIAN (331–363). Full name Flavius Claudias Julianus. An "apostate" Roman emperor, Julian was devoted to pagan gods, whereas other emperors of the period were Christian. In *Against the Galilaeans*, he wrote that the Jewish law was

> harsh and stern and contains much that is savage and barbarous. . . . The rages and the bitterness of the Jews, who destroy temples and overturn altars. . . . This hard-hearted and stubborn-necked people. . . . Their generals are . . . inferior. . . . Their statecraft and learning and arts are miserable and barbarous. . . . What kind of healing art has ever appeared among the Hebrews . . . ? . . . Is their "wisest" man Solomon at all comparable with Phocylides?

SUGGESTED READING: Simon Dubnov, *History of the Jews*, vol. 2, *From the Roman Empire to the Early Medieval Period*, trans. Moshe Spiegel (South Brunswick, NJ: Thomas Yoseloff, 1968).

JUNG, CARL (1875–1961). Swiss psychoanalyst. Once a colleague of **Sigmund Freud**'s, Jung broke with Freud in 1913. Jung viewed **Aryanism** as part of German collective unconsciousness, which Jews did not have, and remained in the **Third Reich** during the World War II. He wrote that **Adolf Hitler** may have started with good intentions but then an evil spirit took possession of him. Hitler was the tool of the German unconscious. "German policy is not made; it is revealed through Hitler. He is the mouthpiece of the gods as of old." In Jung's words, "I am absolutely not an opponent of the Jews, even though I am an opponent of Freud's. I criticize him because of his materialistic and intellectualistic . . . irreligious attitude and not because he is Jewish." The **Nazis** fascinated Jung because he believed that his theory of archetypes was best able to explain them. He believed that the Germans were reintegrating archaic elements. By 1936, Jung had recognized Hitler's and the Nazis' demonic nature. Still, he hoped that their evil would turn to goodness. His mythological descriptions of history may have obscured his view of events. Those close to him claim that he never supported the Nazis nor **antisemitism** but spoke out against them, and that many of his students were Jews. Besides, he had many Jewish students.

SUGGESTED READING: Deirdre Bair, *Jung: A Biography* (Boston: Little, Brown, 2003); Mark Medweth, "Jung and the Nazis," *Psybernetika*, Winter 1996.

JUNIOR ORDER OF UNITED AMERICAN MECHANICS. One of the most vigorous and largest of the nativist organizations opposing the **Wagner-Rogers Bill** in 1939.

SUGGESTED READING: Arthur Morse, *While Six Million Died: A Chronicle of American Apathy* (New York: Overlook Press, 1998).

***JURAMENTUM JUDAEORUM. See* OATHS, JEWISH.**

JUSTIN, ST. *See* JUSTIN MARTYR.

JUSTINIAN I (483–565). Byzantine Roman emperor, 527–65. Justinian promulgated several laws that undermined Judaism economically, politically, and religiously, classifying Judaism as a kind of **heresy**. Justinian invited ecclesiastical authorities to oversee laws affecting the Jews' status and rights. The Church's canons concerning the Jews then had the force of law. *See also* JUSTINIAN CODE.

SUGGESTED READING: Simon Dubnov, *History of the Jews*, vol. 2, *From the Roman Empire to the Early Medieval Period*, trans. Moshe Spiegel (South Brunswick, NJ: Thomas Yoseloff, 1968).

JUSTINIAN CODE. Emperor **Justinian**'s collection of laws concerning the Jews were promulgated in 529–34. They became the standard basis of medieval European law from the 12th century forward, reducing Jewish status to "permanent inferiority." Some of Justinian's laws removed Jewish rights and classified Jews, along with other non-Christians, as **heretics**, punished Jewish marriages as "abominable," forbade **circumcision** of converts, and limited the way Jews could worship. Justinian's Novella 146 stated that the Jewish **Talmud** intentionally distorted the authentic "christological" meanings of the Jewish Scriptures, and therefore it should be forbidden to the Jews.

SUGGESTED READING: James Parkes, *The Conflict of the Church and the Synagogue* (New York: Atheneum, 1979).

JUSTIN MARTYR (100–165). Christian apologist. Because Jews were permanently evil, or so the **Church Father** Justin Martyr believed, the sacrament of Christian baptism would not work to wash away the stink of Jewish unbelief. Associating the Jews with **heresy**, he argued that God had given Moses' Law to the Jews because God wanted to keep the inherently sinful Jews' evil in check. "**Circumcision** was given to you as a sign that you may be separated . . . from us, and that you alone may suffer that which you now justly suffer, and that your land may be desolate, and your cities burnt with fire. These things have happened to you in fairness and justice."

SUGGESTED READING: "Justin Martyr," in *Encyclopedia Judaica*, ed. Geoffrey Wigoder (Philadelphia: Jewish Publication Society, 2004).

JUTKU; LUTIKKA. (Finnish slur) A Jew.

SUGGESTED READING: "List of Ethnic Slurs," *Wikipedia*, http://en
.wikipedia.org/wiki/List_of_ethnic_slurs.

JUVENAL (60–140). Roman satirist. Juvenal wrote about Jews that they
"revere the **Sabbath**, worship nothing but the clouds."

SUGGESTED READING: Menahem Stern, *Greek and Latin Authors on
Jews and Judaism* (Jerusalem: Israel Academy of Sciences and Humanities, 1984).

– K –

KALTENBRUNNER, ERNST (1903–1946). Austrian **Nazi** police official.
Kaltenbrunner was the successor to **Reinhard Heydrich,** becoming head
of the Reich Security Service (RSHA). In that capacity he was complicit
in the **genocide** of the Jews because RSHA controlled the concentration
camps. He was hanged at Nuremberg in 1946. *See also* NUREMBERG
WAR CRIMES TRIALS.

SUGGESTED READING: Peter Black, *Ernst Kaltenbrunner: Ideological
Soldier of the Third Reich* (Princeton, NJ: Princeton University Press,
1985).

KAMMERKNECHTSCHAFT. *See* SERFS.

KANT, IMMANUEL (1724–1804). German philosopher. Although he was
friendly with a few individual Jews, such as **Moses Mendelssohn**, for
Kant, Judaism lacked a clear formulation of morality and view of the afterlife. He disliked the ideas of revelation and chosen people. Kant's lectures
"Anthropology from a Pragmatic Point of View" indicated:

> All [Jewish] talents revolve around stratagems and cunning. . . . They are a nation
> of swindlers that for the most part does not attain to civic honor. . . . As long as
> the Jews are Jews and allow themselves to be **circumcized**, they never will be-
> come more useful than harmful to civil society. They are now vampires of so-
> ciety.

These ideas and Kant's advocacy of a *"Euthanasie des Judentums"* fore-
shadowed the **Holocaust**. **Johann Gottlieb Fichte** was one of his students.

SUGGESTED READING: Paul Rose, *Antisemitism in Germany: From Kant
to Wagner* (Princeton, NJ: Princeton University Press, 1997); Micha Brum-
lik, *Deutscher Geist und Judenhass: Das Verhältnis des philosophischen
Idealismus zum Judentum* (Munich: Luchterhand-Verlag, 2000).

KASH ROOT. (U.S. slur) A Jew obsessed with money; a play on "cash" and *Kashrut* (Jewish kosher laws).

SUGGESTED READING: "List of Ethnic Slurs," *Wikipedia*, http://en .wikipedia.org/wiki/List_of_ethnic_slurs.

KENT, JAMES (1763–1847). American jurist. As Chief Justice of the New York State Supreme Court, Kent ruled:

> We are a Christian people, and the morality of the country is deeply engrafted upon Christianity, and not upon the doctrines or worship of those impostors [other religions]. . . . [We are] people whose manners . . . and whose morals have been elevated and inspired . . . by means of the Christian religion.

SUGGESTED READING: Jacob Marcus, *United States Jewry, 1776–1985* (Detroit: Wayne State University Press, 1989).

KEROUAC, JACK (1922–1969). American poet and novelist. Author Ann Douglas noted that in his final years, as a drug addict, Kerouac became "ever more paranoid," believing that "the New York Jewish critics [such as Jewish authors Joseph Heller and Norman Mailer] were plotting against him. He joked about titling *Big Sur* (1962) 'Another big idea for the Jews to steal.'" Kerouac became a virulent **antisemite** despite the fact that his best friend, Alan Ginsberg, was a Jew. He told a friend that Sen. Joseph McCarthy had "all the dope on the Jews and the fairies."

SUGGESTED READING: Ann Douglas, "Dharma Bum," *Village Voice*, October 1999.

KHAKI SHIRTS. U.S. **fascist** organization of the 1930s and 1940s. In the fall of 1933, Americans learned of a sensational plot by Gen. Art Smith—a soldier of fortune—and his Khaki Shirts. Smith's idol was **Benito Mussolini**, and he boasted that a million men would follow him and, as committed **antisemites**, that they would "kill every damn Jew in the United States." In 1933, the Khaki Shirts killed a heckler in New York City. *See also* SECRET ORGANIZATIONS, 20TH CENTURY.

SUGGESTED READING: Glen Jeansonne, *Gerald L. K. Smith, Minister of Hate* (Baton Rouge: Louisiana State University, 1997).

KHOMEINI, RUHOLLAH (1902–1989). Ayatollah; supreme leader of **Iran**, 1979–89. Popularly acclaimed as leader in 1979, Khomeini established a clerical state in Iran with himself at the top and run by Shiite Muslim clergy. Later in the year, Khomeini's forces seized the U.S. embassy and 52 hostages. As ruthless as the shah he replaced, Khomeini had thousands of secular leftists murdered and indoctrinated the bureaucracy, schools, media, military, and security services with his brand of Islam. He also exported his ideas to other Muslim nations. An eight-year war with Iraq began in 1980 and cost a million lives. He issued a notorious *fatwa* (clerical opinion) condemning writer Salman Rushdie to death for **heresy**. Khomeini died a few months later. Khomeini's legacy is his defiance of the so-called American Great Satan (Israel being the "Little Satan"). *See also* ANTI-ZIONIST ANTISEMITISM.

SUGGESTED READING: Baqer Moin, *Khomeini: Life of the Ayatollah* (New York: St. Martin's Press, 1999).

KICHKO, TROFIM. Author; member Ukrainian Academy of Sciences. Kichko wrote a book entitled *Judaism without Embellishment* (1963), which was replete with **antisemitic** slurs. The cartoons were similar in offensive style to those found in the **Nazi** *Der Stürmer*. Kichko asserted that Jewish **bankers** were allied with Western imperialists in an international conspiracy against the USSR. In his book, he wrote: "It is in the teachings of Judaism, in the Old Testament, and in the **Talmud**, that the Israeli militarists find inspiration for their inhuman deeds, racist theories, and expansionist designs." Western Communist parties protested the work, so Soviet premier Nikita Khrushchev had copies burned and Kichko dismissed. However, after the **Six Day War** in 1967, Kichko was given a medal, restored to grace, and wrote another book, *Judaism and Zionism* (1968), reiterating the hoax of a world Jewish conspiracy.

SUGGESTED READING: William Korey, *The Soviet Cage: Antisemitism in Russia* (New York: Viking, 1973).

KIDDUSH HA CHAIM. Hebrew for "sanctification of life." It indicates active Jewish cultural, spiritual, and especially religious responses— specifically, those of Jews during the **Holocaust** attempting to persist in their Jewish values as a means of resisting the **Nazis**. The term was coined by Rabbi Yitzhak Nissenbaum in the Warsaw **Ghetto**, who said that "this is the hour of Kiddush ha Chaim, and not **Kiddush ha Shem** by death. The enemy demands the physical Jew, and it is incumbent upon every Jew to defend, to guard his own life."

SUGGESTED READING: Joseph Gottfarstein, "Kiddush Ha-Hayim," *Judaism*, Summer 1970.

KIDDUSH HA SHEM. Hebrew for "sanctification of God's name." It denotes the highest standard of Jewish ethics: One should do everything possible to glorify the name of God and conversely not bring discredit on Judaism and Jews, thereby injuring the Lord's name, *Hilul ha Shem*. Historically, martyrdom/suicide in the cause of Jews and Judaism has been deemed *Kiddush ha Shem. See also* CRUSADES.

SUGGESTED READING: Philip Birnbaum, *Encyclopedia of Jewish Concepts* (New York: Hebrew Publishing Company, 1979).

KIELCE. A town in Poland that witnessed a post-**Holocaust pogrom** on July 4, 1946. About 200 survivors of the **Nazis** sought to reestablish the Jewish community there after the war. **Antisemites** who opposed this started a pogrom based on the false charge that a Jewish home was the site of kidnapped and **ritually murdered** Christian-Polish children. Forty-two Jews were killed. This encouraged survivors to go to Western-controlled displaced persons camps rather than return to their homes in Poland. Also, the Biricha movement, fleeing to the Jewish settlement in Palestine, was invigorated.

SUGGESTED READING: Peter Meyer et al., *The Jews in the Soviet Satellites* (Westport, CT: Greenwood Press, 1971).

KIGY. Klansman, I Greet You. Shorthand indication of membership/affiliation with the **Ku Klux Klan**. It is used primarily as a salutation, but also in e-mail addresses and Web page addresses. KIGY originated with the revival of the Ku Klux Klan after 1915, along with two other acronyms: AKIA for "A Klansman I Am" and AYAK for "Are You a Klansman?"

SUGGESTED READING: Anti-Defamation League, *Hate on Display: Extremist Symbols, Logos, and Tattoos* (New York: Anti-Defamation League, 2006).

KIKE. (U.S. slur) Common denigration of Jews. Perhaps deriving from *Kikel*, a German and Yiddish term for "circle," a mark often used by illiterate Eastern European Jewish immigrants processed through Ellis Island to sign documents. Jews saw the traditional Christian "X" as bad luck, perhaps representing the Christian cross. Others believe *kike* derives from the Latin *caeca* ("blind"), a common traditional Christian **defamation** of Jews, referring to Jewish blindness to the so-called true faith.

SUGGESTED READING: "List of Ethnic Slurs," *Wikipedia*, http://en.wikipedia.org/wiki/List_of_ethnic_slurs; "Kike," *Answers.com*, http://www.answers.com/topic/kike.

KIPLING, RUDYARD (1865–1936). Indian-born British novelist, poet, and short-story writer. In his novel *Puck of Pook's Hill* (1906), in the chapter "The Treasure and the Law," Kipling has an old Jewish physician named Kadmiel state:

My Prince saw peace or war decided not once, but many times, by the fall of a coin spun between a Jew from Bury and a Jewess from Alexandria, in his father's house, when the Great Candle was lit. Such power had we Jews among the Gentiles. . . . A Jew is as free as a sparrow—or a dog.

Angry that Jewish attorney-general Rufus Isaacs (Lord Reading), who had been implicated in a financial scandal, could become Lord Chief Justice, Kipling wrote the bitter **antisemitic** poem "Gehazi," attacking his elevation in 1913:

> The boils that shine and burrow,
> The sores that slough and bleed—
> The leprosy of Naaman
> On thee and all thy seed?
> Stand up, stand up, Gehazi,
> Draw close thy robe and go,
> Gehazi, Judge in Israel,
> A leper white as snow!

Kipling regarded *The Protocols of the Elders of Zion* as "exactly what the international Jew has accomplished, and is accomplishing, at the present moment."

SUGGESTED READING: Keith Wilson, "The *Protocols* and the *Morning Post*, 1919–1920," *Patterns of Prejudice* 19, no. 3 (1985).

KISHINEV. City in Bessarabia (now Moldavia). In the first decade of the 20th century, this city of 60,000 Jews, 46 percent of the population, was the site of two **pogroms**. The first occurred around Easter, April 6–7, 1903. The death of a Christian child led to a **ritual murder** charge. Both Romanians and Russians, with large contingents of students, attacked the Jewish quarter with encouragement by the local and central tsarist government. The result was 49 dead, 500 injured, 600 businesses gutted, and 2,500 homeless. On October 19–20, 1905, rioters struck again; this time with 19 deaths. The earlier riot led to worldwide protests that had little effect on the tsar. However, the attacks spurred Jewish self-defense groups in Russia.

SUGGESTED READING: Howard H. Judge, *Easter in Kishinev: An Anatomy of a Pogrom* (New York: New York University Press, 1995).

KLAGES, LUDWIG. German ecological pacifist. Klages attacked reason and the critical intellectual spirit, thereby serving the reactionary wing of the *Völkisch* Movement and paving the way for **Nazism**. He defended the German *Volk* against the destructive forces of modernity, which he associated with the Jews. Jews were seen as visible signs of capitalism and communism and as hostile to the nature-loving, völkisch cause. As George Mosse observed:

> According to many Völkisch theorists, the nature of the soul of a volk is determined by native landscape. Thus the Jews, being a desert people, are viewed as shallow, arid, "dry people. . . . a spiritually barren people [unlike the Germans,] who, living in the dark, mist-shrouded forests, are deep, mysterious, and profound."

SUGGESTED READING: George Mosse, *The Crisis of German Ideology: Intellectual Origins of the Third Reich* (New York: Grosset & Dunlap, 1964).

KLARSFELD, SERGE AND BEATE (1935–, 1935–). Professional **Nazi** hunters. Serge Klarsfeld was a Jewish-French lawyer and Beate Kunzel Klarsfeld a German-Lutheran. In 1968 Beate publicly slapped West German chancellor Kurt Kiesinger, who was known to be a **Third Reich** propagandist. This launched her nearly 40-year career as a professional Nazi hunter. The Klarsfelds kept the issue of justice for Nazi **war criminals** alive by dramatizing the issue and ferreting out a number of Nazi and collaborationist officials. Most noted were the discovery and apprehension of **Gestapo** captain **Klaus Barbie** and the prosecution of **René Bousquet** (1989), Paul Touvier (1994), and Maurice Papon (2002), all of whom were involved in **deporting** Jews.

SUGGESTED READING: Erna Paris, *Unhealed Wounds: France and the Klaus Barbie Affair* (New York: Grove Press, 1985).

KNIFE-NOSE. (U.S. slur) A reference to the stereotyped Jewish nose.

SUGGESTED READING: "List of Ethnic Slurs," *Wikipedia*, http://en .wikipedia.org/wiki/List_of_ethnic_slurs.

KNOW NOTHINGS. Also known as the American Party. Secret nativist movement originating in the 1850s, which was anti-Catholic and anti-Jewish. The slavery issue overshadowed its religious issues, and the party petered out before 1960. General **Ulysses S. Grant** was a member, as was President Millard Fillmore.

SUGGESTED READING: *The Party of Fear: Nativist Movements to the New Right in American History* (New York: Vintage, 1995).

KONITZ AFFAIR. Ritual murder **defamation** of March 1900. In the last decade of the 19th century, more than 100 **ritual murders** were charged against the Jews of Europe. In Konitz, Germany, the accusation was that the victim's blood was drained so that Jews could use it for making matzoh for Passover. Journalists from **antisemitic** newspapers stirred the unstable to fabricate horror stories about Jews until riots had to be suppressed by the Prussian police. Because the authorities did not want to indict a Christian, the real murderer was never apprehended. Though no Jews were killed, local Christians threw stones, tried to set the **synagogue** on fire, and shouted "Beat the Jews to death." Many of Konitz's Jews emigrated to Berlin or the United States.

SUGGESTED READING: Helmut Smith, *The Butcher's Tale: Murder and Antisemitism in a German Town* (New York: W. W. Norton, 2002).

KORAN; QURAN. Holy Book of Islam. According to Arab tradition, these scriptures were transmitted to **Muhammad** by the angel Gabriel in the early seventh century. The Koran reiterates many of the Bible narratives, changing some. For this reason, Jews and Christians are considered "People of the Book" and are to be given tolerance and protection while living under Islamic rule, but only as second-class citizens, **dhimmis**. Muslim attitudes toward Jews are reflected in the Koran. Sura (chapter) 2:61 states: "[The Children of Israel] were consigned to humiliation and wretchedness. They brought the wrath of God upon themselves, and this is because they used to deny God's signs and kill His Prophets unjustly and because they disobeyed and were transgressors." Other suras say that Jews introduce corruption (5:64), have been always disobedient (5:78), and are enemies of Allah, the Prophet, and the angels (2:97–98). *See also* HADITH.

SUGGESTED READING: Robert S. Wistrich, *Muslim Antisemitism: A Clear and Present Danger* (New York: American Jewish Committee, 2002); Mitchell Bard, "The Treatment of Jews in Arab/Islamic Countries," *Jewish Virtual Library*, http://www.jewishvirtuallibrary.org/jsource/anti-semitism/Jews_in_Arab_lands_(gen).html..

KOSHER GHOST. (U.S. slur) A Hassidic or Orthodox Jew; a reference to the belief that these Jews have sexual intercourse through a hole in a sheet.

SUGGESTED READING: "List of Ethnic Slurs," *Wikipedia*, http://en.wikipedia.org/wiki/List_of_ethnic_slurs.

KRAMER, JOSEF (1906–1945). **Nazi** camp commandant. Kramer served in a number of camps: he was in charge of the Birkenau mass murder facilities at **Auschwitz,** where he was active **selecting** inmates for the **gas chambers**. Promoted to commandant of **Bergen-Belsen** from December 1944 to April 1945, he was noted for cruelty. He beat and machine-gunned inmates, earning him the title "Beast of Belsen." His administration was so apathetic that even former Auschwitz inmates were shocked at the horrible, unsanitary, chaotic conditions at Bergen-Belsen. Kramer was executed by the British, who had liberated the camp. *See also* GRESE, IRMA.

SUGGESTED READING: United States Holocaust Memorial Museum, *1945, Year of Liberation* (Washington, DC: U.S. Holocaust Memorial Museum, 1995).

KRAUS, KARL (1874–1936). Austrian writer, editor, and satirist. The son of a Jewish paper merchant, Kraus moved with his family in 1877 to Vienna, where he studied philosophy. He became the editor and publisher of the satirical magazine *Die Fackel* (*The Torch*, 1899–1936), in which he attacked Jews. He wrote that **Freudian** psychoanalysis was the illness it pretended to be able to cure. Kraus attacked the Jews' "**ghetto**-mentality" and urged Jews to reject their Jewish ethnicity and their Judaism in order to assimilate into Christian society. In *Eine Krone für Zion* (1898), Kraus ridiculed the views of Theodor Herzl, the founder of Zionism. He has been described as "an exquisitely Jewish **antisemite**."

SUGGESTED READING: John Theobald, *The Paper Ghetto: Karl Kraus and Antisemitism* (Frankfurt am Main: P. Lang, 1996).

KREUZZEITUNG. 19th-century conservative German journal. *Kreuzzeitung* and its circle argued that the Jews and their allies controlled the German press, economy, and state. The group argued that Jews were to be granted hospitality and protection, but not the right to positions of authority in the bureaucracy, judiciary, and education, for these institutions symbolized the Christian-German national spirit and should never fall into the hands of Jews.

SUGGESTED READING: Simon Dubnov, *History of the Jews*, vol. 5, *From the Congress of Vienna to the Emergence of Hitler*, trans. Moshe Spiegel (South Brunswick, NJ: Thomas Yoseloff, 1973).

KRISTALLNACHT. The Night of Broken Glass, November 9/10, 1938. At the suggestion of **Josef Goebbels** and with the cooperation of **Reinhard Heydrich,** the **SA** and **SS** staged a **pogrom** against the Jewish communities of Germany, Austria, Danzig, and the Sudetenland. The excuse given was that it was a "spontaneous retaliation" for the murder of Ernst vom Rath, a minor German diplomat in Paris by a Polish-Jewish teenager. Upward of 30,000 Jews were arrested and sent to concentration camps; those who survived were released in a few months. The **Nazis** estimated that 267 **synagogues** were burned—nearly every one in Germany and Austria. In actuality, estimates of the number of synagogues destroyed range from 500 to 1,200. In addition, 815 shops, 29 department stores, and 171 dwellings belonging to Jews were destroyed. There were at least 91 deaths, not including those who committed suicide or died in the camps. In addition, hundreds of other Jews were brutally beaten and some raped. In Austria alone, there were at least 680 suicides. There were only about 9,000 Jewish shops remaining in Germany in 1938, of which Heydrich estimated that 7,500 were destroyed or damaged. Many Western nations condemned the pogrom, causing the **Third Reich** to keep such attacks secret thereafter, and with the war breaking out removing the violence beyond German borders.

SUGGESTED READING: Martin Gilbert, *Kristallnacht: Prelude to Destruction* (New York: HarperCollins, 2006); Gerald Schwab, *The Day the Holocaust Began* (New York: Praeger, 1990); Anthony Read, *Kristallnacht* (New York: Crown, 1990); Holocaust History Project, "What Was Kristallnacht?" 2003, http://www.holocaust-history.org/short-essays/kristallnacht .shtml.

KRUPP. *See* HUGENBERG, ALFRED.

KRUSHEVAN, PAVOLAKI (PAVEL ALEKSANDROVICH KRU-SHEVAN) (1860–1909). Russian journalist, editor, publisher, and official. Krushevan was active in the **Black Hundreds** and was known for his far-right, ultranationalist, and openly **antisemitic** views. He was the first publisher of the fraudulent *Protocols of the Elders of Zion*.

SUGGESTED READING: David Vital, *A People Apart: A Political History of the Jews of Europe, 1789–1939* (New York: Oxford University Press, 2001).

KUGEL. (South African slur) A rich Jewish woman; from the sweet or savory pudding of that name.

SUGGESTED READING: "List of Ethnic Slurs," *Wikipedia*, http://en .wikipedia.org/wiki/List_of_ethnic_slurs.

KUHN, FRITZ (1896–1951). "Fuehrer" (leader) of the pro-Nazi **German-American Bund**. Kuhn worked at the Ford Motor Car Company in Detroit off and on from 1928 until 1936. Harry Bennett, **Henry Ford**'s plant strongman, once confessed to the FBI that Kuhn had been caught during work hours "practicing speeches in a dark room."

SUGGESTED READING: Robert Herzstein, *Roosevelt and Hitler: Prelude to War* (New York: Paragon House, 1988).

KU KLUX KLAN (KKK). Secret and violent U.S. Protestant white-supremacist organization, originally founded by ex-servicemen of the Confederate Army in 1865 and refounded in 1915 as a response to the **Leo Frank** case. By 1924 the KKK had four million members, including 40,000 Protestant ministers. Although the Klan's anti-Jewish sentiments appealed particularly to fundamentalist Christians, Klan ideas were widely held. Its intent was to reestablish Protestant Christian values in America by any means possible. In the **xenophobic** atmosphere following World War I, the Klan attacked "niggers, Catholics, Jews." At its peak in 1924, 40,000 uniformed Klansmen paraded through the streets of Washington, DC, during the Democratic National Convention.

Mixing nationalism, nativism, and religion, the KKK was the first organized American anti-Jewish movement. As an Imperial Giant (senior leader) of the Klan affirmed: "The Ku Klux Klan stands primarily for the principles of Jesus Christ and that explains why . . . Christian white men are . . . to give the Jews some of their own medicine." Klansmen believe "in the tenets of the Christian religion"—that "the Bible [stood] as the basis of our Constitution. . . . We honor Christ as the Klansman's Only Criterion of Character." The so-called Kloran (guidebook) of the 1920s contained a catechism that asked, "Are you a native-born white, Gentile American citizen? . . . Do you believe in the tenets of the Christian religion?" Like generations of other **triumphalistic** Christians, the Klan perceived Jews as **Judases** and **Shylocks**, **Christ-killing** monsters who specialized in the immoral use of money. In a Klan magazine called the *Kourier*, a minister wrote in 1925: "As a Protestant minister of the **Gospel**, I joined the Knights of the Ku Klux Klan because: I believed in Jesus Christ and His church; I believed in a militant Christianity; I believed in the Cross." A Klan pamphlet of 1924, "Christ and Other Klansmen," indicated that Jesus was the first and ideal Klansman and blamed the Jews for his murder. In the 1920s, the Klan's anti-Jewish attitudes corresponded to the **antisemitism** in American culture. Senators, congressmen, governors, judges at all levels, and even future president **Harry Truman** joined. The Klan may have initiated President Warren G. Harding as a member in a private ceremony in the White House itself.

Although suffering a drastic loss of membership during the final years of World War II, the Ku Klux Klan made great gains after the war by championing Christian supremacy and antisemitism, thereby assuring themselves of support among many fundamentalists. Although black Americans have been the special targets of their nativist violence, many Klansmen have proclaimed that they feared Jews most of all. In April 1991, Ku Klux Klan representatives continued to maintain that the Bible indicated that the true Israel was white Christian America. The KKK is sometimes symbolized by a cross in a circle with a drop of blood in the center, other times by a fiery cross. *See also* FORD, HENRY; SHELTON, ROBERT.

SUGGESTED READING: James Ridgeway, *Blood in the Face: The Ku Klux Klan, Aryan Nations, Nazi Skinheads and the Rise of the New White Culture* (New York: Thunder's Mouth Press, 1990).

KULTURKAMPF. German for "culture battle." In the early years of the German Empire, established in 1870–71—contemporaneously with **Vatican Council I**'s claim to papal infallibility—*Reichskanzler* **Otto von Bismarck** attempted to reduce the influence of the Catholic Church in a Germany that was dominated by Protestant Prussia but faced with a growing Catholic population in the Rhineland, the Slavic peoples of eastern Germany, and Bavaria. Catholics formed about a third of Germany's population. In 1871, a German law threatened criminal prosecution of clergy discussing politics and established a secular court for court cases. In 1872, the **Jesuits** were banned; in 1875 civil weddings were made mandatory. After 1878, Bismarck joined forces with the **Catholic Center Party** to oppose socialism. Catholic leaders accused "liberal" Jews (that is, all Jews) of supporting Kulturkampf legislation. Even when Bismarck and Pope **Leo XIII** reached an accord in 1887 ending the struggle, Catholic **antisemitism** persisted.

SUGGESTED READING: Ellen Evans, *The German Center Party, 1870–1983: A Study in Political Catholicism* (Carbondale: Southern Illinois Press, 1981); Margaret Anderson, *Windhorst: A Political Biography* (Oxford, England: Clarendon Press, 1981).

KUN, BÉLA (1886–1939?). Hungarian Communist leader. Kun was a founder of the Hungarian Communist Party in 1918. In 1919 he became the dictator of Hungary. The next year, with the help of Romania, Admiral **Miklós Horthy** overthrew Kun's regime, whose army refused to fight for him. In the **white terror** that followed, all Jews were considered Communists, and many were murdered. Kun escaped and served in the Comintern (Communist International for subversion) in the USSR. Falling out of favor with Soviet dictator **Joseph Stalin**, he later "disappeared." The **Nazis** used his picture as an example of Jewish attempts to communize Christian nations.

SUGGESTED READING: Miklos Molnar and Arnold Pomerans, *From Béla Kun to Janos Kadar* (Oxfordshire, England: Berg, 1991).

– L –

LACHRYMOSE THEORY OF JEWISH HISTORY. The lachrymose theory considers Jewish history as always tragic. The theory states that the medieval Jews

> lived in a condition of extreme wretchedness . . . , subject to incessant persecution and violence. . . . Prisoner in the **Ghetto**, denied access to the resources and activities of Western society, distorted intellectually, morally, spiritually by centuries of isolation and torture, the Jew was set free by the Emancipation.

The eminent Jewish historian Salo Baron (1895–1998) criticized this theory as overstating the historical case, but other historians claim he has significantly underestimated the harm Church policy and Christian theology inflicted on the Jews of Europe.

SUGGESTED READING: Israel Shanker, *Coat of Many Colors* (London: Doubleday, 1985); Salo Baron, "Ghetto and Emancipation: Shall We Revise the Traditional View?" *Menorah Journal* (June 1928).

LAGARDE, PAUL ANTON DE (1827–1891). Born Paul Bötticher. German cultural writer. Lagarde's major work was *German Literature* (1881), in which he propounded "cleansing German life" by ending Jewish economic and spiritual power. For Lagarde, Jews were responsible for materialism and commercialism and were "purveyors of decadence." Lagarde coined the terms "**Blood and Soil**" and "Master **Volk**," which reverberated later with the **Nazis**. His most notorious proclamation was: "Hate the Jews and despise those who—out of humanity!—defend these Jews or who are too cowardly to trample this usurious vermin to death." In 1899, in a manifesto published in Hamburg, Lagarde warned that in the 20th century, the Jewish problem "will become a world problem solved . . . in the end by the extermination of the Jewish people."

SUGGESTED READING: Robert W. Lougee, *Paul de Lagarde, 1827–1891: A Study of Radical Conservatism in Germany* (Cambridge, MA: Harvard University Press, 1962); Walter Bacharach, *Anti-Jewish Prejudices in German-Catholic Sermons* (Lewiston, NY: Mellen Press, 1993).

LA GUARDIA BLOOD LIBEL. Spanish **ritual murder** trial of 1490. **Dominican** Grand Inquisitor **Tomás de Torquemada** (1420–1498) staged a show trial against eight Jews in the town of La Guardia. He was out to prove that Jews were dangerous to Spain. The defendants were charged with ritual murder of a Christian boy, though there was no body found. The accused were all burned at the stake.

SUGGESTED READING: Thomas Hope, *Torquemada, Scourge of the Jews* (Worthing, England: Unwin, 1939).

LAMB, CHARLES (1775–1834). English poet, story writer, and essayist. In his essay "Imperfect Sympathies," Lamb writes of his **antisemitism** when he confesses that he has

> not the nerves to enter their **synagogues**. Old prejudices cling about me. I cannot shake off the story of Hugh of Lincoln. Centuries of injury, contempt, and hate, on the one side—of cloaked revenge, dissimulation, and hate, on the other, between our and their fathers, must, and ought, to affect the blood of the children . . . so deadly a disunion. A Hebrew is nowhere congenial to me.

SUGGESTED READING: Frank Felsenstein, *Antisemitic Stereotypes: A Paradigm of Otherness in English Popular Culture, 1660–1830* (Baltimore: Johns Hopkins University Press, 1995).

LAMENNAIS, FÉLICITÉ ROBERT DE (1782–1852). French priest and philosopher. Liberal Catholics like Lamennais still affirmed Catholic **triumphalism** with regard to the Jews. Though disillusioned with the Church, Lamennais repeated its traditional teachings about the Jews as blind to the truth and replaced by Christians as the true Israel. The **Diaspora** and persecutions of Jews historically proved this fall from grace. Lamennais called the Jews "coarsely carnal," a "perverse race," and called the Jewish leadership the "enemies who plotted [Jesus'] destruction." He believed that no amount of "suffering and disgrace" has been able to rid the Jews of "their pride and their curse." Living Jews were as sinful as those who killed Christ, inherently evil, and capable of any crime. The Jews' "suffering and disgrace has become second nature. [The Jewish people] exists . . . always as strangers, its course painful and vagabond . . . marked with a most terrible sign of Cain on its forehead, . . . **DEICIDE!**"

SUGGESTED READING: Arnold Ages, "Lamennais and the Jews," *Jewish Quarterly Review* 63 (1972).

LAMMERS, HANS HEINRICH (1879–1962). **Nazi** jurist. Lammers was a close aide to **Adolf Hitler** and served as state secretary in the Reich Chancellery from 1933 to 1944. Every anti-Jewish measure passed through his desk. His legal advice made him a paper criminal in the **Final Solution**. This Nazi lawyer was tried at the **Nuremberg War Crimes Trials** in 1949 for giving anti-Jewish measures legal sanction. Lammers's 20-year sentence was cut short by a pardon in 1954 due to Cold War politics.

SUGGESTED READING: Louis L. Snyder, *Encyclopedia of the Third Reich* (New York: Paragon House, 1989).

LANC (LIGA APARARII NATIONALE CRESTINE). *See* NATIONAL CHRISTIAN DEFENSE LEAGUE.

LANGBEHN, JULIUS (1851–1907). German writer. Langbehn's most famous work was *Rembrandt as Teacher* (1890). He believed Germans were a superior group, and those Germans who were least mixed with other groups were most superior. All the virtues of the *Volk* (German spirit) were carried by the blood. Intermarriage polluted this strain and weakened the German people. Jews, according to Langbehn, not being part of the Volk, could never be true Germans. In 1899, Langbehn proclaimed that Jews sucked the blood of Christian flesh and of Christian nations. *See also* NUREMBERG LAWS OF 1935; *RASSENSCHANDE*.

SUGGESTED READING: Fritz Stern, *The Politics of Cultural Despair: A Study of Germanic Ideology* (Berkeley: University of California Press, 1974); Walter Bacharach, *Anti-Jewish Prejudices in German-Catholic Sermons* (Lewiston, NY: Mellen Press, 1993).

LANSING, ROBERT (1864–1928). President **Woodrow Wilson**'s secretary of state. Lansing opposed the Balfour Declaration, which recognized Jewish rights in Palestine: "Many Christian sects and individuals would undoubtedly resent turning the Holy Land over to the absolute control of the race credited with the death of Christ."

SUGGESTED READING: Norman Cohn, *Warrant for Genocide* (London: Serif, 1996).

LAODICEA, COUNCIL OF. In 360, this Church council in present-day Turkey forbade Christians from resting on the **Sabbath** rather than on the Lord's Day and required that if Christians worship on the Sabbath, they must read the **Gospels** along with the other Scriptures. The church body forbade Christians from participating in Jewish feasts and ceremonies. Similar prohibitions appear in canons from the Council of Antioch (341), forbidding Christians to eat Passover Seder with Jews, and the Council of Elvira (c. 300) prohibited the blessing of fields by Jews and the sharing of feasts with Jews.

SUGGESTED READING: Jacob Marcus, *The Jew in the Medieval World: A Source Book, 315–1791* (New York: New York University Press, 1979).

LAPOUGE, GEORGES VACHER DE (1854–1936). French anthropologist and racial **antisemite**. Lapouge's major work was *The Aryan and His Social Role* (1899). A **eugenicist** and **Social Darwinist**, he believed "Race is everything." As an advocate of Aryan supremacy, he classified the "races" (ethnic groups) by various measurements, particularly the head shape, and urged scientists to engage in selective breeding to improve the human race. For him a good society would be antidemocratic, anticapitalist, and antisemitic. His extreme eugenic views provided **völkisch nationalists** grist for the elimination of the "lower races" in Nazi Germany. *See also* HAECKEL, ERNST.

SUGGESTED READING: Jennifer Michael Hecht, *The End of the Soul: Scientific Modernity, Atheism, and Anthropology in France, 1876–1936* (New York: Columbia University Press, 2003); Jennifer Michael Hecht, "Vacher de Lapouge and the Rise of Nazi Science," *Journal of Ideas* 61, no. 2 (April 2000): 285–304.

LAROUCHE, LYNDON (1933–). American political activist. In 1989, though jailed for tax and securities fraud, LaRouche remained the head of an **anti-Zionist** and **antisemitic** movement. LaRouche has run for president under different party names many times. He has claimed knowledge of a conspiracy of Jewish **bankers**, espoused **Holocaust denial**, and accused Jews and the British queen of running the international drug trade. *See also PROTOCOLS OF THE ELDERS OF ZION, THE.*

SUGGESTED READING: Dennis King, *Lyndon LaRouche and the New American Fascism* (New York: Doubleday, 1989).

LASSEN, CHRISTIAN (1800–1876). German orientalist. The Norwegian-German Lassen and French writer **Ernest Renan** were the first scholars to popularize "**Aryans**" and "Semites" as racial concepts, borrowing the terms from the names of language groups and claiming that Semites were racially egotistical and exclusive.

SUGGESTED READINGS: George Moss, *Toward the Final Solution* (Madison: University of Wisconsin, 1985).

LATERAN COUNCIL, THIRD. *See* GRATIAN.

LATERAN COUNCIL, FOURTH. Roman Catholic Church conclave called by and presided over by Pope **Innocent III** in 1215. Its first canon (church law) clarified "*Salus non est extra ecclesiam*" (There is no salvation outside the Church). Stating "There is one universal Church of the faithful, outside of which absolutely no one is saved, and in which Jesus Christ is himself at once both priest and sacrifice," the council reaffirmed that only through the Church could a soul be saved from Hell, thus condemning all Jews to eternal suffering in the afterlife. It passed a number of anti-Jewish decrees: Baptized Jews were forbidden to practice Jewish customs; Jews were not to appear in public at Easter time; they were barred from public office; their interest rates were to be modest (if a Jew practiced "immoderate **usury**" against a Christian, then "all relations with Christians shall be denied him"); and secular Catholic authorities were required to order their Jews to wear distinctive dress and **stigmatic emblems (Jew badges)**. The council also canceled Christians' debts to Jews if the former went on **Crusade**. It furthermore called for secular powers to exterminate all **heretics**. See also ALBIGENSIAN CRUSADE; EXCOMMUNICATION OF JEWS.

SUGGESTED READING: Jacob Rader Marcus, *The Jew in the Modern World* (Cincinnati, OH: Hebrew Union College, 1999); William Nichols, *Christian Antisemitism: A History of Hate* (Northvale, NJ: Jason Aronson, 1993).

LAUGHLIN, HARRY (1880–1943). American **eugenicist**. Laughlin, editor of *Eugenical News* and executive of the Eugenics Record Office, was appointed as the U.S. House of Representatives' Committee on Naturalization and Immigration's "expert eugenics agent" (1921–31). He warned the committee of the "inborn social inadequacy" among Jews and Italians and of the threat that real Americans could be conquered "by other racial stocks" that were "not assimilable." In 1934, Laughlin opposed any "special . . . provisions for . . . Jews persecuted in Germany," and in 1939, he "recommended a substantial reduction of immigration quotas, together with procedures to denaturalize and deport some immigrants who had already obtained citizenship." Laughlin doubted that Jews would be loyal to "American institutions and people . . . the Nordics' task was to prevent more of them from coming." *See also* DAVENPORT, CHARLES BENEDICT.

SUGGESTED READING: Edwin Black, *The War against the Weak: Eugenics and America's Campaign to Create a Master Race* (New York: Four Walls, Eight Windows, 2003).

LAVATER, JOHANN KASPAR (1741–1801). Swiss theologian and pseudoscientist. In 1768, with Christian **triumphalism** in mind, Lavater publicly challenged the brilliant and widely respected Jewish intellectual **Moses Mendelssohn** to either prove the Christian notion of the soul false or else **convert** to Christianity. Ultimately, Mendelssohn wrote *Jerusalem: Religious Power and Judaism* (1783), which argues that the assumed universality of Christianity results in coercive religious beliefs. In *Physiognomy of Nations* (first published in German in 1775), Lavater developed the idea that a person's inner life was revealed in his or her body's features.

Lavater's illustrations of Jewish figures have the following characteristics: The body is exceptionally fat or thin; the posture is crooked; the feet are flat; the hair is dark; the body hair is thick and coarse; the eyes are dark and bulging; the nose is bent; the eyelids and lower lip are drooping; and the men's beards are heavy. Lavater's scheme of negative physical traits attributed to Jews as an indication of their evil nature was used by **Nazi** racial ideologists.

SUGGESTED READING: Richard Gray, *About Face: German Physiognomic Thought from Lavater to Auschwitz* (Detroit: Wayne State University Press, 2004); Mary Mills, "Propaganda and Children during the Hitler Years," *Jewish Virtual Library*, http://www.jewishvirtuallibrary.org/jsource/Holocaust/propchil.html; Jonathon Kahn, "Which Enlightenment? Moses Mendelssohn and the Haskalah," *Books & Culture: A Christian Review* (May 2004).

LEAGUE OF RUSSIAN PEOPLE. *See* BLACK HUNDREDS.

LEBENSRAUM. German for "living space"; used as a geopolitical term. Although the concept predated him, **Adolf Hitler** wanted Germany to expand east into Poland and Russia to provide raw materials, slave labor, and land for Germans. He wanted to "liberate" Russia from what he considered Jewish domination. The overtones of this idea were ethnic cleansing of native peoples, including Jews, and **deportation**. *See also* JUDENREIN, JUDENFREI; *MEIN KAMPF.*

SUGGESTED READING: Martyn Housden, *Hans Frank: Lebensraum and the Final Solution* (New York: Palgrave Macmillan, 2004); Jeremy Noakes, "Hitler and 'Lebensraum' in the East," BBC, 2004, http://www.bbc.co.uk/history/war/wwtwo/hitler_lebensraum_01.shtml; "Lebensraum," *Wikipedia*, http://en.wikipedia.org/wiki/lebensraum.

LEBENSUNWERTES LEBEN. German for "Life unworthy of life." *Die Freigabe der Vernichtung lebensunwerten Lebens* (*The Permission to Destroy Life Unworthy of Life*) by Karl Binding and Alfred Hoche was published in 1920. This work advocated the murder of the mentally and physically handicapped. Bills were introduced in the 1920s and 1930s into the **Weimar Republic** parliament for the prevention of the birth of those with mental and physical handicaps, *unwertes Leben und lebensunwerte Menschen.* In 1940, **Adolf Hitler** ordered the systematic murder of those with fatal and hereditary diseases, the mentally ill, and the disabled. **Euthanasia** centers were established in order to rid the country of these so-called undesirable people. All Jews fell into this category and were to be euthanized.

SUGGESTED READING: Michael Burleigh and Wolfgang Wipperman, *The Racial State: Germany, 1933–1945* (Cambridge: Cambridge University Press, 1991).

LEECH. (International, esp. Muslim, slur) A reference to the medieval Christian **defamation** that Jews drank the blood of Christian children. The modern myth holds that Israelis murder Palestinian children and drink their blood. *See also* RITUAL MURDER.

SUGGESTED READING: "List of Ethnic Slurs," *Wikipedia*, http://en .wikipedia.org/wiki/List_of_ethnic_slurs.

LEGION OF ARCHANGEL MICHAEL. Right-wing Romanian political party formed by **Corneliu Codreanu** in 1927. The Legion opposed capitalism, Communism, and modernity, accusing them all of Jewish inspiration. Its military wing was the **Iron Guard**, which committed atrocities against Jews. In 1940, Horia Sima (1906–?) took over the leadership, but he was ousted by Ion Antonescu (1882–1946).

SUGGESTED READING: Radu Ioanid, *The Sword of the Archangel: Fascist Ideology in Romania* (New York: Columbia University Press, 1990).

LENARD, PHILIPP (1862–1947). German **Nazi** physicist who won a Nobel Prize in 1905 for his work on cathode rays. An ardent supporter of **Adolf Hitler** and Nazism since 1924, Lenard denounced Albert Einstein, "Jewish physics," and Jewish scientists in favor of "**Aryan** physics." He believed scholarship was conditioned by race and "blood."

SUGGESTED READING: John Cornwell, *Hitler's Scientist* (New York: Viking, 2003).

LEO I, ST. (THE GREAT) (c. 400–461). Pope, 440–61. The man who dissuaded Attila the Hun from attacking Rome in 452, Leo I also claimed universal authority for the Church and supreme authority for the pope within the Church. This pope had stated that "**usurious** profit from money means the death of the soul." Leo regarded Jews as malicious murderers of Christ and also believed that Jews were blind and carnal.

SUGGESTED READING: Jacques Le Goff, *Your Money or Your Life* (New York: Zone/MIT, 1990).

LEO III (THE ISAURIAN) (680–741). Byzantine emperor, 717–41. Emperor Leo III unsuccessfully attempted to **convert** Jews forcibly, as did

Byzantine emperors Maurice (d. 602), Phocas (d. 610), Heraklios (d. 641), Basil I (d. 886), Romanos I Lekapenos (d. 944), and John Vatatzes (d. 1254). Although the Orthodox Church officially opposed forced conversions, its theology, propaganda, and liturgy supported imperial hostility toward Jews.

SUGGESTED READING: David I. Kertzer, *The Popes against the Jews* (New York: Knopf, 2001).

LEO VII (d. 939). Pope, 936–39. In 937 Leo VII wrote that Jews should not be **converted** by force—but in the same letter ordered that if preaching did not convert these Jewish "enemies of God," they should be expelled, for Christians must not allow "God's enemies" to live among them.

SUGGESTED READING: Shlomo Simonsohn, *The Apostolic See and the Jews: Documents, 492–1404* (Toronto: Pontifical Institute of Mediaeval Studies, 1988).

LEO XII (1760–1829). Pope, 1823–29. Annibale della Genga, the cardinal vicar of Rome who would later become Pope Leo XII, inspired Rome's *Ecclesiastical Journal* to attack Jews for more than a century for **deicide**, lust for money, conspiracy to destroy Christianity, **ritual murder**, **desecration of the Host**, Church burning, blood libel, and violation of Christian virgins. As pope, Leo XII rebuilt the Roman Jewish **ghetto**, which **Napoleon**'s troops had torn down, and reestablished **sermons** of **conversion** to Jews. He revoked all civil rights for Jews under his control. It took the destruction of the **Papal States** and the secular unification of Italy by Victor Emmanuel II in 1870 to destroy the ghetto completely.

SUGGESTED READING: David I. Kertzer, *The Popes against the Jews* (New York: Knopf, 2001).

LEO XIII (1810–1903). Pope, 1878–1903. Leo XIII permitted the more closely controlled international Catholic press—the **Vatican**'s own *Osservatore Romano* and the **Jesuits'** *Civiltà Cattolica*—to print **antisemitic** articles hostile to Alfred **Dreyfus** and Jews until 1899. In 1894 and 1895, Leo blessed and treasured the Austrian Christian-Social Party—also called the Antisemitic Party—and its newspaper, the *Reichspost*. *See also* LUEGER, KARL.

SUGGESTED READING: David I. Kertzer, *The Popes against the Jews* (New York: Knopf, 2001).

LETTER OF BARNABAS. Also known as the Epistle of Barnabas. Written around 100 CE, this letter declared that the Jews had forfeited their Covenant with God just after Moses had received it, and Christians had replaced them as God's Chosen.

SUGGESTED READING: Michael Grant, *The Jews in the Roman World* (New York: Macmillan, 1973).

LEUCHTER, FRED (1943–). American self-proclaimed expert on poison gas and **Holocaust denier**. Leuchter was sent by **Ernst Zundel** to investigate the ruins of the **gas chambers** at **Auschwitz-Birkenau**, and **Majdanek**, Nazi **extermination camps**. Leuchter claimed at **Zundel**'s 1988 trial in Toronto that he had found no traces of **Zyklon** gas. His four reports, known as the Leuchter Reports, denied the use of gas chambers in the **genocide** of Jews. However, Leuchter did not have training as an engineer nor an engineer's license to qualify him to make such judgments.

SUGGESTED READING: Deborah Lipstadt, *Denying the Holocaust* (New York: Free Press, 1993).

LEWIS, WYNDHAM (1882–1957). English painter and writer. Lewis's *The Apes of God* (1930), a satire on wealthy bohemians, contained undercurrents of **antisemitism**. After World War I, Lewis believed society and the individual were under attack from democracy, liberalism, and communism—all Jewish plots. His fiction holds several antisemitic portraits: Jan Pochinsky in *Tarr* (1928), Julius Ratner in *The Apes of God*, Peter Wallace and Isaac Wohl in *The Revenge for Love* (1937). In the latter, Lewis described Wohl as someone who prefers "to be somebody else than to 'be himself,'" and this parallels a widespread antisemitic attitude toward Jews from **Richard Wagner**'s "plastic demons" to **Martin Heidegger**'s "infinitely mimetic beings . . . producing no art and achieving no appropriation." Lewis was an early supporter of **Adolf Hitler** in 1931. He wrote the first biography of Hitler and agreed with the **Nazis** on nationalism and racism in opposition to a mythologized Jewish enemy.

SUGGESTED READING: John Constable, "Review of David Ayers, Wyndham Lewis and Western Man," *Essays in Criticism* 43, no. 3 (July 1993): 265–71, http://mysite.wanadoo-members.co.uk/jbcpub/ayersrev.html.

LEY, ROBERT (1890–1945). Head of the **Nazi** Labor Front. Ley abolished democratic labor unions in Nazi Germany. He was responsible for **forced labor camps**. Jews worked as slave laborers, receiving starvation rations, in unsanitary conditions, for seven days a week, 12 hours a day, and were subject to brutality. *Arbeitsjuden* were "work Jews" capable of laboring for the German war industry, ultimately to be worked to death. *Arbeitsunfähig* meant "unable to work"—such prisoners to be killed on the spot or transferred to death camps to be killed. This included the disabled and the old. Condemned to death by the **Nuremberg War Crimes Trials**, Ley committed suicide in his cell. *See also* LODZ.

SUGGESTED READING: Joachim C. Fest, *The Face of the Third Reich: Portraits of Nazi Leadership*, trans. Michael Bullock (New York: Pantheon, 1970).

LIBERATION. **Antisemitic** 1930s U.S. periodical financed and published by **William Pelley**, becoming virtually an overnight success by attracting not only numerous financial supporters but also expressive writers such as Pelley and hundreds of unemployed men anxious to sell the publication from street corners.

SUGGESTED READING: Leo Ribuffo, *Protestants on the Right: William Dudley Pelley, Gerald B. Winrod and Gerald L. K. Smith* (New Haven, CT: Yale University Press, 1976).

LIBERTY LOBBY. 20th-century U.S. extremist group. Arguably the most powerful purveyor of **Holocaust denial** over the past quarter-century has been **Willis Carto**. Carto is the founder and main leader behind the Washington, DC–based Liberty Lobby and its offshoots, the **Noontide Press** and the most well known denial organization, the **Institute for Historical Review** (IHR).

SUGGESTED READING: Frank P. Mintz, *The Liberty Lobby and the American Right: Race, Conspiracy, and Culture* (Westport, CT: Greenwood Press, 1985).

LIBRE PAROLE, LA (THE FREE WORD). Viciously **antisemitic** newspaper founded by **Edouard Drumont** in France in 1892. It preached that the "Jewish question" was the key to French history. The lower classes, he proclaimed, should revolt against the Jewish oppressors, who should be expelled and their property confiscated and redistributed. The newspaper's "exposés" excited mobs against Captain Alfred **Dreyfus**.

SUGGESTED READING: Stephen Wilson, *Ideology and Experience: Antisemitism in France at the Time of the Dreyfus Affair* (Rutherford, NJ: Farleigh Dickinson University Press, 1982).

LIEBENFELS, LANZ VON (1884–1954). Viennese writer and publisher. From 1905 to 1914, Liebenfels published a newspaper, *Ostara*, named after a sun goddess, filled with *völkisch* racist views. He wanted blond supermen to be bred; dark people were to be exterminated and the sick sterilized. Liebenfels greatly influenced the young **Adolf Hitler**, who snatched up back copies during his pre–World War I sojourn in Vienna.

SUGGESTED READING: George L. Mosse, *Toward the Final Solution* (Madison: University of Wisconsin Press, 1985).

LIEBERMANN VON SONNENBERG, MAX. *See* SONNENBERG, MAX LIEBERMANN VON.

LIENHARD, FRIEDRICH (1865–1929). Prominent *völkisch* writer, publisher, and leader of "idealistic **antisemitism**."

SUGGESTED READING: Uwe Puschner, Walter Schmitz, and Justus H. Ulbricht, eds., *Handbuch zur Völkischen Bewegung, 1871–1918* (Munich: Saur, 1996).

LIFE RUNE. Elhaz rune, Algis rune. **Neo-Nazi**, racist **skinhead**, white supremacy symbol consisting of a *Y* with a vertical line through it. This rune in pagan Europe related to hunting stags, as well as honor, nobility, and protection. Often called the "life rune" (*Lebensrune*), during World War II it was the symbol of the **SS**'s Lebensborn project, which encouraged SS men to have children out of wedlock with "**Aryan**" mothers and kidnapped children of "Aryan" appearance from German-occupied Europe to raise as Germans. The neo-Nazi **National Alliance** adopted this symbol as part of its logo.

SUGGESTED READING: Anti-Defamation League, *Hate on Display: Extremist Symbols, Logos, and Tattoos* (New York: Anti-Defamation League, 2006).

LILIENTHAL, MAX (1815–1882). German rabbi and educator who traveled to tsarist Russia. Fresh from running a very successful school in Riga, Latvia, and an advocate of *Haskalah*, the rabbi was asked by Tsar **Nicholas I** and his minister of education, Sergey Urarov (1766–1865), to establish state schools to teach both secular and Jewish religious subjects. Lilienthal had many consultations with Jews to convince them that attendance at the schools was a good idea, but Jews in the **Pale of Settlement** warned that the schools would serve only to proselytize the youngsters into Christianity. After failing to convince most Jewish leaders, and soon afterward convinced that they were right, Lilienthal slipped off to the United States. He became a leader and professor for the Jewish Reform Movement in Cincinnati.

SUGGESTED READING: Max Lilienthal, *My Life as an American Rabbi* (New York: Bloch, 1915).

LIMPIEZA DE SANGRE. Spanish for "**purity of blood**." Racist **Judeophobia** of 15th- to 17th-century Spain. The **New Christians**, or **conversos**, who remained in Spain after the **expulsion** in 1492 were so dynamic and enterprising that they edged out ancestral Christians, who sought a way to neutralize these former Jews by passing legislation requiring that important functions in society should be exercised only by pure-blooded Christians. The conversos thereafter were excluded from public office, **guilds**, religious offices, colleges, military orders, and some towns. *See also* MARRANOS; NUREMBERG LAWS OF 1935.

SUGGESTED READING: Albert Sicroff, *Les controverses des statuts de "pureté de sang" en Espagne du XVe au XVIIe siècle* (Paris, 1960); Maria Martinez, "Limpieza de Sangre," in *Encyclopedia of Mexico*, ed. Michael Werner (Chicago: Fitzroy Dearborn, 1997).

LINDBERGH, CHARLES (1902–1974). Internationally renowned pilot and conservative isolationist. In 1936, Lindbergh stated that **Adolf Hitler** had "done much for the German people." In the same year, he attended the Berlin **Olympics** as **Hermann Goering**'s personal guest. At an official state dinner in October 1938, Goering, "by order of the Führer," presented Lindbergh with the Service Cross of the German Eagle. Even after **Kristallnacht**, Hitler's *Anschluss* of Austria, and his invasion of Czechoslovakia, Lindbergh continued to justify **Nazi** behavior. "Germany has pursued the only consistent policy in Europe in recent years," he wrote (April 1939 diary entry). During the 1939–41 period, Lindbergh emerged as the most prominent public spokesman for the **America First Committee**. In a radio address on October 13, 1939, shortly after Germany's invasion of Poland and the start of World War II, Lindbergh blamed the British and French for the war. Even after Germany's 1940 occupation of Norway, Denmark, the Netherlands, Belgium, and France, Lindbergh refused to reconsider his position. "Nothing is to be gained by shouting names and pointing the finger of blame across the ocean." At an America First Committee rally in Des Moines in September 1941, Lindbergh blamed Jewish people for "agitating for war . . . for reasons that are not American." He also claimed that the Jews' "greatest danger to this country lies in their large ownership and influence in our motion pictures, our press, our radio, and our Government." He warned American Jews that "instead of agitating for war, [they] should be opposing it in every possible way for they will be among the first to feel its consequences." Secretary of the Interior Harold Ickes called him "the number one fellow-traveler of the Nazis in the United States." Even after visiting postwar Germany and its **extermination camps**, in his

Wartime Journals (1970), Lindbergh insisted that he still held the same prewar beliefs, with no criticism of the Nazis.

SUGGESTED READING: Rafael Medoff, "Lindbergh's Public Statements Were More Troubling Than His Private Affairs," David S. Wyman Institute for Holocaust Studies, November 2003, http://www.wymaninstitute.org/articles/2003-11-lindbergh.php; Victor Ferkiss, "Populist Influences on American Fascism," *Western Political Quarterly* (June 1957).

LINZ PROGRAM (*LINZER PROGRAMM*). Concept of **Georg von Schönerer**, Austria's most prominent Pan-German, nationalist, and *völkisch* political leader. In 1882 in Parliament, Schönerer proclaimed: "We do not gravitate toward Vienna. Rather, we gravitate to wherever there are Germans." In the same year, the Austrian government banned a meeting to found a German People's Party in Linz. Therefore, Schönerer published his "Linz program," comprising völkisch goals, social reform, and all-German power. His motto was "Through Purity to Unity." The program demanded the removal of Jewish influence from all spheres of public life. It influenced all subsequent conservative political parties (e.g., the Christian Social Party, German People's Party, and German Agrarian Party).

SUGGESTED READING: Jeremy King, *Budweisers into Czechs and Germans: A Local History of Bohemian Politics, 1848–1948* (Princeton, NJ: Princeton University Press, 2005).

LIST, GUIDO VON (1848–1919). Austrian runes expert. An investigator of the ancient Teutonic symbols and writers, List publicized what would become the **SS** lightning symbol. In 1911, he formed an occultist **Aryan** organization, the Armonen Order. It called for a pan-German empire, subjecting non-Aryans to Aryans. He and his Order preached racial purity, visualizing a struggle between the forces of light (Aryans) and of darkness (Jews).

SUGGESTED READING: Peter Levenda, *Unholy Alliances: The History of Nazi Involvement in the Occult* (New York: Avon, 1995).

LISZT, FRANZ (1811–1886). Hungarian musician. Perhaps influenced by his **antisemitic** son-in-law **Richard Wagner**, Liszt deprecated the Jews' "clawed, pale hands" and avaricious stares. His book *The Gypsy in Music* captured the imagination of Europe's middle classes and was translated into English in 1860. In it, he argued that persecution and statelessness did not "excuse" the Jews for their material success and ambition. Jews could not produce glorious music but could only manage money and crafted goods. In a letter written late in life, he observed that "the Jews loathe me, my music and myself, for no reason at all."

SUGGESTED READING: Dan Damon, "Chasms of Perdition," *Central Europe Review*, http://www.tol.cz/look/cer/article.tpl?idlanguage = 1&id publication = 14&nrissue = 23&nrsection = 2&nrarticle = 12502.

LITURGY, CHRISTIAN. *See* GENUFLECTION; GOOD FRIDAY.

LIUTOSTANSKII, IPPOLIT. *See* RUSSIAN POGROMS, 1881–1884.

LJOTI, DIMITRIJE (1891–1945). Yugoslavian minister of justice, 1931; major general commanding Serbian volunteer corps, 1941–44. Ljoti was the head of the national movement Zbor, whose slogans were "The Jews are our tragedy" and "Ruthless and uncompromising fight against the Jews."

SUGGESTED READING: Ivo Goldstein, *Antisemitism, Holocaust, Antifascism* (Zagreb: Židovska općina, 1996.

LODZ. Large industrial city in western Poland. Lodz became the first major **ghetto** established by the **Nazis** (December 1939), and the last to be liquidated (August 1944). It had 220,000 Jewish residents, of whom only 870 survived. Chaim Rumkowski, the head of the Judenrat, sought to save lives by having the ghetto perform useful work for the Germans and to save the community by sending the aged and the sick to fill Nazi **deportation** quotas. When this did not work, he committed suicide. The slave labor only temporarily staved off deportation.

SUGGESTED READING: Lucjan Dobroszycki, *The Chronicle of the Lodz Ghetto, 1941–1944* (New Haven, CT: Yale University Press, 1984).

LONDON, JACK (1876–1916). American novelist and short-story writer. In his novel *Martin Eden* (1909), London wrote:

> The speaker, a clever Jew . . . stood forth representative of the whole miserable mass of weaklings and inefficients who perished according to biological law on the ragged confines of life. They were the unfit. In spite of their cunning philosophy and of their antlike proclivities for cooperation, Nature rejected them for the exceptional man. . . . Of course, they could squirm as they perished.

In *Michael, Brother of Jerry* (1917), he wrote:

> Vainly striving to paint, [the Jew, Simon Nishikanta] would . . . get out his large-calibred automatic rifle, . . . and try to shoot any stray porpoise, albacore, or dolphin. It seemed to give him great relief to send a bullet home into the body of some surging, gorgeous-hued fish, arrest its glorious flashing motion for ever, and turn it on its side slowly to sink down into the death and depth of the sea. . . . Nishikanta would be beside himself in the ecstasy of inflicting pain.

Another character observed, "In the good old days up in Colusa [County, California], we used to hang men like him just to keep the air we breathed clean and wholesome."

SUGGESTED READING: Louis Harap, *The Image of the Jew in American Literature* (Syracuse, NY: Syracuse University Press, 2003).

LONG, BRECKINRIDGE (1881–1958). U.S. undersecretary of state, 1940–44. In charge of immigration affairs and the issuing of visas at the **State Department**, Long orchestrated restrictive policies designed to prevent European Jews from escaping **Nazi** persecution. In testimony before Congress on November 26, 1943, Long misled and exaggerated regarding the number of refugee Jews admitted to the United States. *See also* BERMUDA CONFERENCE; ROOSEVELT, FRANKLIN D.

SUGGESTED READING: Henry Feingold, *The Politics of Rescue: The Roosevelt Administration and the Holocaust*, rev. ed. (New York: Holocaust Library, 1980).

LONGFELLOW, HENRY WADSWORTH (1807–1882). American poet. In the prelude to *Tales of a Wayside Inn* (1863), Longfellow wrote, "How the Jews, the tribe accursed, / Mocked him, scourged him, crucified him." In "The Jewish Cemetery at Newport" (1852), he compared the Jewish gravestones to "the tablets of the Law, thrown down / And broken by Moses." To Longfellow, the Jewish names in the cemetery seemed un-American, "strange," and "foreign." He conceded that the Jews arrived on these shores because of a "burst of Christian hate," yet like **St. Paul**, he pictured these Jews as the "Ishmaels and Hagars of mankind," referring to "the deep mark of Cain" and observing that "the dead nations never rise again."

SUGGESTED READING: Louis Harap, *The Image of the Jew in American Literature* (Syracuse, NY: Syracuse University Press, 2003).

LOPE DE VEGA CARPIO, FÉLIX (1562–1635). Spanish dramatist; one of the world's great playwrights, who wholeheartedly supported the **expulsion** of the Jews in 1492. Lope de Vega called Jews "this inhuman enemy of our land" and repeated the defamatory story of Jewish collusion with the Moors against Spanish Christians. He also employed alleged Jewish **ritual murder** as a plot in one of his plays.

SUGGESTED READING: Paul Johnson, *A History of the Jews* (New York: HarperPerennial, 1987); Richard Gottheil et al., "Blood Accusation," *JewishEncyclopedia.com*, http://www.jewishencyclopedia.com/view.jsp ?artid = 1173&letter = B.

LOPEZ, RODERIGO. *See* COKE, EDWARD.

LOUIS I (778–840). Also known as Louis the Pious or Louis the Fair. Frankish king, 814–40; son of Charlemagne and Holy Roman emperor. When he tried to treat Jews fairly, in 833 an assembly of bishops deposed him and compelled him to appear in a penitent's garb.

SUGGESTED READING: Robert Chazan, *Medieval Jewry in Northern France: A Social and Political History* (Baltimore: Johns Hopkins University Press, 1973).

LOUIS IV (1282–1347). Also known as Louis the Bavarian. Holy Roman emperor, 1314–47. Louis IV proclaimed: "You, the Jews, your bodies—as well as your property—belong to us and to the empire, and we can do to you, treat you, and handle you the way we want and consider proper."

SUGGESTED READING: Joseph Schatzmiller, *Shylock Reconsidered: Jews, Moneylending, and Medieval Society* (Berkeley: University of California Press, 1990).

LOUIS VII (1120–1180). French king, 1137–80. Louis VII allowed **Crusaders** to refuse Jewish moneylenders both interest and principal, in effect, expropriating the Jewish community in France. He also punished former Jews who reverted to Judaism by banishment, though he responded to a petition of the Jews of Paris by clearing them of responsibility for the death of a Christian child, "St." Richard, by issuing a decree of protection, and by condemning the **ritual murder** accusation at **Blois**.

SUGGESTED READING: Robert Chazan, *Medieval Jewry in Northern France: A Social and Political History* (Baltimore: Johns Hopkins University Press, 1973).

LOUIS IX, ST. (1214–1270). French king, 1226–70. Louis IX collaborated with the **Inquisition**, the popes (seven held office during his reign), and the friars in anti-Jewish policies. He mercilessly punished blasphemers and **heretics** of all sorts, especially Jews. His campaign against the sanctums of Judaism and the lives and the livelihoods of Jews not only resulted in the destruction of Jewish culture in France during the period but also set a model for the anti-Jewish decrees of the Cortes of Gerona in Spain in 1241. Jewish money-lending was attacked and the **Talmud** was tried and condemned as blasphemous and burned; French **Crusaders** massacred Jews in 1236 and 1251 in Anjou and Poitou with impunity. Louis also **confiscated Jewish property**, including homes and fields, schools, **synagogues**, and even cemeteries. When he returned from the Crusades in

1254, he canceled all debts owed to Jews, taking 20 percent for himself, and expelled the Jews from France. He had copies of the Talmud seized in March 1240 and ordered a **disputation** that took place in June in Paris, probably conducted with the cooperation of the Inquisition.

SUGGESTED READING: Robert Chazan, *Medieval Jewry in Northern France: A Social and Political History* (Baltimore: Johns Hopkins University Press, 1973).

LOWELL, ABBOTT LAWRENCE (1856–1943). Harvard University president, 1909–33. Lowell's plan to restrict Jewish admissions to Harvard was formally rejected by a faculty committee that insisted on character and scholarship as the only acceptable criteria for admissions. Lowell claimed that limiting the number of Jews at colleges would help reduce **antisemitism**. His plan was gradually effected in an informal way. He believed that only the Protestant aristocracy should be educated in the elite schools. Jews and Christians "just don't mix," he said. This kind of anti-Jewish discrimination in Ivy League graduate school admissions continued into the 1950s. *See also* QUOTAS, COLLEGE.

SUGGESTED READING: Henry Feingold, *Zion in America* (Mineola, NY: Dover, 2002); Beth Wenger, *New York Jews and the Great Depression* (New Haven, CT: Yale University Press, 1996); Henry Feingold, *Time for Searching* (Baltimore: Johns Hopkins University Press, 1992).

LOWELL, JAMES RUSSELL (1819–1891). American poet, critic, satirist, writer, diplomat, and abolitionist. In his poem "Bibliolatres" (1849), Lowell regarded the Jewish Bible as useless and rigid, broken and dead, unconnected with the living God. He addressed the Jews as "blind and unconverted." Judaism he saw as merely a "dry and sapless rod." As U.S. ambassador to Great Britain, he noted that the passion in Spanish politics was due to the Jewish blood that had mingled into the Spanish upper and middle classes, the Jewish blood being "the most intense, restless, aspiring and unscrupulous blood of all." In an address to an English audience in 1884, he remarked, "We drove them into a corner, but they had their [Jews'] revenge. . . . They made their corner the counter and **banking-house** of the world, and thence they rule it with the ignobler scepter of finance."

SUGGESTED READING: Henry Feingold, *Zion in America* (Mineola, NY: Dover, 2002); Howard Elisha Scudder, *James Russell Lowell: A Biography* (Boston: Houghton Mifflin, 1901).

LUDENDORFF, ERICH (1865–1931). German general and politician; commander-in-chief of German forces at the end of World War I. After the war, Ludendorff joined the **Nazi Party** under **Adolf Hitler**. The former chief of staff participated in the Beer Hall Putsch in 1923, Hitler's failed attempt at a rebellion in Bavaria. Ludendorff denounced the "Jewish-**Bolshevik**-Masonic conspiracy" for Germany's ills. He also promoted *The Protocols of the Elders of Zion* in the **Weimar Republic**. *See also* LUDENDORFF, MATHILDE; TANNENBERGERBUND.

SUGGESTED READING: Charles B. Flood, *Hitler: The Path to Power* (Boston: Houghton Mifflin 1989).

LUDENDORFF, MATHILDE (1877–1966). German schoolteacher, neurologist, and occultist. A pioneer of the environmentalist movement in Germany, Mathilde Ludendorff (wife of General **Erich Ludendorff**) blamed the Jews for the destruction of nature. In works like *Triumph of the Will to Immortality* (1921), she reflected the tendency of rightist reactionary environmentalists to disseminate **antisemitic** and world conspiracy theories. She believed that she was a prophet who carried divine inspiration for the spiritual enlightenment of Germany only because she understood her racial heritage. Strict adherence to racial unity and a unique conception of the divine would inevitably lead to German liberation. She believed that the *Volk* had inherited its spirituality, so for Germany to regain confidence, spiritual strength, and material greatness, it had to expel the alien influences of Christianity, the French **Enlightenment**, and Judaism. She and her husband associated Jews with **Freemasonry**, liberalism, and democracy, which, they argued, were scornful of moral principles, lacking national traditions and a sense of cultural history, instead dreaming of an impersonal internationalism that nourished alienation. *See also* TANNENBERGERBUND.

SUGGESTED READING: Heinz P. Wassermann, ed., *Antisemitismus in Österreich nach 1945: Ergebnisse, Positionen und Perspektiven der Forschung. Schriften des Centrums für Jüdische Studien* 3 (Innsbruck: Studien Verlag, 2002); Alison Rose, "Review of Heinz P. Wassermann, ed., *Antisemitismus in Österreich nach 1945,*" *Hapsburg* (September 2003).

LUEGER, KARL (1844–1910). Mayor of Vienna, 1897–1910. Lueger pioneered political **antisemitism** as a means of electing a political party and was the first politician in Europe to be elected on a strictly antisemitic platform. He founded the Christian Social Party specifically to stop "Jewish domination." Once in office, he established *numerus clausus* in higher education. Although his antisemitic speeches were virulent, Lueger claimed that "I myself decide who is a Jew"—a comment later echoed by **Hermann Goering**—as a way of keeping the peace with prominent Vien-

LUTHER, MARTIN • 287

nese Jews. In 1897, Lueger supported a bill in the Austrian parliament designed to end Jewish immigration into the Austro-Hungarian Empire. The bill described Jews as foreigners and "enemies of Christian culture and of nations of **Aryan** descent." **Adolf Hitler** spent formative years in Vienna and learned from Lueger's popular antisemitism.

SUGGESTED READING: Richard S. Geehr, *Karl Lueger, Mayor of Fin-de-Siècle Vienna* (Detroit: Wayne State University Press, 1990).

LUMBROZO, JACOB (d. 1666?). Jewish physician and merchant of Maryland, Lumbrozo in 1658 was indicted for "blasphemy against our blessed Savior, Jesus Christ"—an accusation to which all Jews were vulnerable—because he had denied "the doctrine of the Trinity." As a Jew, he had no choice but to deny Jesus' divinity or else he could not consider himself a Jew. He **converted** to Christianity and only then was allowed all the rights of a Christian.

SUGGESTED READING: "A Case of Blasphemy," *American Jewish Historical Society*, 2005, http://www.ajhs.org/publications/chapters/chapter .cfm?documentID = 250.

LUTHER, MARTIN (1483–1546). German founder of Lutheranism, and Protestantism generally. Luther's last major writings on the Jews are an excellent compendium of nearly all the anti-Jewish ideas written, spoken, painted, or sung in the Catholic tradition: Jews were "the devil's people." He advocated a plan to deal with Jews that served as a model for **Adolf Hitler** and the **Nazis**. The **synagogue** is "a defiled bride, yes, an incorrigible whore and an evil slut." He advocated: Burn their synagogues and their houses; confiscate their prayer books and **Talmud**.

> We must not consider the mouth of the Jews as worthy of uttering the name of God within our hearing. He who hears this name from a Jew must inform the authorities, or else throw sow dung at him when he sees him and chase him away. And may no one be merciful and kind in this regard.

> Forbid their rabbis to teach, abolish safe-conduct on the highways, prohibit money-lending, force Jews into manual labor, "for it is not fitting that they sit behind the stove, feasting and farting."

He seemed to want to murder them if all else failed—and he often believed that all else *would* fail. Luther successfully campaigned against the Jews in Saxony, Brandenburg, and Silesia. *See also DAS IST DER JUDE!*

SUGGESTED READING: Diane Prevary Kramer, *Who Shall Inherit the Kingdom of God? A Study of the Writing of Martin Luther on the Jews* (Fredericksburg, VA: Mary Washington College, 1979).

LUTHER, MARTIN (1896–1945). **Nazi** foreign office official. Luther attended the **Wannsee Conference** to help coordinate the **Final Solution**. He wrote the 1942 Luther Memorandum, which urged the Hungarian government to more vigorously persecute Jews. *See also* HORTHY, MIKLÓS.

SUGGESTED READING: John Weitz, *Hitler's Diplomat* (New York: Ticknor & Fields, 1992).

LUXEMBURG, ROSA (1871–1919). Revolutionary Communist. Born in tsarist Poland, Luxemberg acquired German citizenship by marriage. She was the brains behind the Spartacists League in Berlin. She teamed up with Karl Liebknecht, the Spartacist leader opposing Germany's participation in World War I. Although her parents were Orthodox Jews, Luxemberg had no Jewish sympathies, saying: "I cannot find a corner in my heart for the **ghetto**." She saw **antisemitism** as a function of capitalism. Nevertheless, German socialists and trade unionists attacked Luxemberg as a Jew. She and Liebknecht formed the German Communist Party. Liebknecht pushed her and the party to a premature *Putsch* (failed revolution) in 1918. **Freikorps** officers beat her up, shouting antisemitic insults, then shot her, on January 16, 1919, and threw her body into a Berlin canal.

SUGGESTED READING: Peter Nettl, *Rosa Luxemburg* (New York: Oxford University Press, 1969).

LYSIMACHUS (4th cent. BCE). Greco-Egyptian writer in Thrace. Lysimachus was the most **antisemitic** pagan writer besides **Apion**. Jews to him were among the "impure and impious." Moses instructed them "to show goodwill to no man, to offer . . . the worst advice, and to destroy any temples and overturn altars of the gods. . . . They maltreated . . . and plundered and set fire to the temples" and had "sacrilegious tendencies."

SUGGESTED READING: Menahem Stern, ed., *Greek and Latin Authors on Jews and Judaism* (Jerusalem: Israel Academy of Sciences and Humanities, 1984).

– M –

MacDONALD, KEVIN. *See* EVOLUTIONARY PSYCHOLOGY.

MADAGASCAR PLAN. Adolf Hitler and **Heinrich Himmler** planned to ship millions of European Jews to Madagascar. But with the powerful British Royal Navy intact and dominating the seas and a diversion of efforts with the invasion of USSR, the plan was abandoned.

SUGGESTED READING: Richard Breitman, *The Architect of Genocide* (New York: Knopf, 1991).

MAJDANEK. Nazi **forced labor** and **extermination camp** near Lublin, Poland. This camp emphasized destruction through work (***Vernichtung durch Arbeit***). Established July 21, 1941, and liberated by the Red Army on July 23, 1944, this hellhole claimed the lives of more than 230,000. Among the victims, 88 percent were Jews.
SUGGESTED READING: Daniel Jonah Goldhagen, *Hitler's Willing Executioners* (New York: Knopf, 1996).

MALANETS. (Russian slur) Jew.
SUGGESTED READING: "List of Ethnic Slurs," *Wikipedia*, http://en.wiki pedia.org/wiki/List_of_ethnic_slurs.

MALCOLM X (1925–1965). Born Malcolm Little; later known as El-Hajj Malik El-Shabazz. African-American leader. In a *Playboy* interview in May 1963, Malcolm stated:

> Anybody that gives even a just criticism of the Jew is instantly labeled **antisemite**. The Jew cries louder than anybody else if anybody criticizes him. You can tell the truth about any minority in America, but make a true observation about the Jew, and if it doesn't pat him on the back, then he uses his grip on the news media to label you antisemite. . . . Who owns Hollywood? Who runs the garment industry . . . ? [The Jew] never shows [the Negro] how to set up factories and hotels. Never advises him how to own what he wants. No, when there's something worth owning, the Jew's got it. Walk up and down in any Negro ghetto in America. Ninety percent of the worthwhile businesses you see are Jew-owned. Every night they take the money out. This helps the black man's community stay a ghetto.

SUGGESTED READING: Alex Haley, "Interview of Malcolm X," *Playboy*, May 1963; Clayborne Carson and David Gallen, *Malcolm X: The FBI File* (New York: Carroll & Graf, 1991).

MANDEL, MARIA (1912–1947). Chief female **SS** camp supervisor. After serving in Lichtenburg and Ravensbrück, Mandel obtained her post at **Auschwitz-Birkenau**. The Austrian matron was noted for her cruelty and active part in **selections** of Jews for the **gas chambers**. *See also* GRESE, IRMA.
SUGGESTED READING: Danuta Czech, *Auschwitz Chronicle, 1939–1945* (New York: Henry Holt, 1990).

MANETHO (3d cent. BCE). Greco-Egyptian priest and historian. In his *History of Egypt* (271 BCE), he claimed that the Jews were Hyksos, a Semitic tribe who ruled Egypt cruelly for 500 years. One division of them became identified with the Israelites. Led by Moses, a renegade priest of Heliopolis, this subgroup were lepers, finally driven out by Egyptians. Jews were "polluted" and suffering from "leprosy." The Jewish historian Josephus accused Manetho of abetting the slander of Jews by providing fodder for the anti-Jewish polemicist **Apion**.

SUGGESTED READING: Victor Tcherikover, *Hellenistic Civilization and the Jews* (Philadelphia: Jewish Publication Society, 1959).

MANIFESTO OF RACIAL SCIENTISTS. Neither racism nor **antisemitism** were initially an essential aspect of Italian **Fascism**. Indeed, for its first 15 years, Italian Fascism was **philosemitic**. Until the late 1930s, **Benito Mussolini** ridiculed **Nazi** racism, and many German Jews found refuge in Fascist Italy. The Manifesto of Racial Scientists was a pseudoscientific document supposedly written by Guido Lando, a Fascist scholar heading up the Italian Ministry of Popular Culture in 1938, and published in the Italian press. It marked a decisive turn in Mussolini's policy toward Jews. The Manifesto's purpose was to define the Italian Fascist position concerning race. It represented the Italians as a Nordic, **Aryan** race and included antisemitism and **eugenics**. As in Nazi racism, the Manifesto regarded Jews as an **alien race** and forbade Italians from marrying Jews, who were seen as **Bolsheviks** and **Freemasons**. In September 1938, Jewish schoolchildren found elementary and secondary schools closed to them. Foreign-born Jews could not have legal residence in Italy, and Jews who became naturalized citizens after January 1, 1919, were denaturalized.

SUGGESTED READING: Susan Zuccotti, *Under His Very Windows: The Vatican and the Holocaust in Italy* (New Haven, CT: Yale University Press, 2000); Aaron Gillette, *Racial Theories in Fascist Italy* (New York: Routledge 2002).

MANN, THOMAS (1875–1955). Noted German writer. With regard to Jews, Mann was a paradox. He was married to Katia Pringsheim, a wealthy assimilated Jew, yet much of his writing may be interpreted as **antisemitic**. Mann identified himself with Jews as outsiders; like himself, many Jews were writers not fully accepted into society, people who had to construct their own identity through the creative process. Mann's short story "Wälsungenblut" (1905) may be interpreted as antisemitic or as a story about Jews protesting the pressure to assimilate. Another short story, "Tristan," may also be interpreted as antisemitic or as reflecting Mann's artistic need to create his own identity and accept his Otherness. In 1895 and 1896, Mann and his brother Heinrich worked on an antisemitic nationalist journal, *Das Zwanzigste Jahrhundert* (*The Twentieth Century*). Thomas never explicitly disassociated himself from his brother Heinrich's admitted racism, and he continued to create negative Jewish stereotypes in his fiction even after Heinrich had undergone a political conversion to the left and disavowed his antisemitism.

SUGGESTED READING: Manfred Dierks and Ruprecht Wimmer, eds., *Thomas Mann und das Judentum* (Frankfurt am Main: Vittorio Klosterman, 2004); George Bridges, review of Dierks and Wimmer, *Thomas Mann und das Judentum*, in *Shofar Book Reviews*, Midwest Jewish Studies Association, Case Western Reserve University (Fall 2004).

MANOEL (1469–1521). King of Portugal, 1495–1521. In 1497 Manoel baptized all Jewish children, ages 4 to 14, in order to force their parents to **convert** to Christianity. The plan was not effective. The more successful conversions were accomplished by the kidnapping of Jewish children, who were then scattered and raised as Christians apart from their parents. *See also* BAPTISM, FORCED.

SUGGESTED READING: Heinrich Graetz, *History of the Jews*, vol. 4 (Philadelphia: Jewish Publication Society, 1898).

MARIA THERESA (1719–1780). Queen of Hungary and Moravia; archduchess of Austria. Maria Theresa believed the Jews were the embodiment of the **Antichrist**. In 1744 she expelled Jews from Bohemia and Moravia. After protests from the European Great Powers (Russia, France, Great Britain, and Prussia), she quickly admitted them back, though not into Prague. Jews had to pay a **tax** every 10 years for staying in the Austrian Empire. In 1752 she decreed that Jewish families were limited to one son. Conditions for Jews improved under her son, Joseph.

SUGGESTED READING: William McCagg, *A History of Hapsburg Jews, 1670–1918* (Bloomington: Indiana University Press, 1989).

MARITAIN, JACQUES (1882–1973). Eminent French-Catholic philosopher; before 1937, the theological sage of the **Action Française**. Maritain noted that behind the Jewish people's suffering was its "failure to understand the cross, its refusal of the cross." Only with baptism would Jewish suffering cease, he said. Maritain emigrated to the United States and taught philosophy at Columbia University in 1940–44.

SUGGESTED READING: Robert Royal, *Jacques Maritain and the Jews* (South Bend, IN: University of Notre Dame Press, 1994).

MARKOV, NIKOLAI E. Leader of the Union of Russian People. In 1911 Markov, before the Duma and at the Congress of the United Nobility, of which he was also a member, called the Jews criminals and enemies of humanity. The latter congress charged the Jews with **ritual murder** and resolved that "All the Jews must be driven within the **Pale [of Settlement]**, this is the first act. The second act is to drive them out of Russia entirely."

SUGGESTED READING: Louis Greenberg, *The Jews in Russia* (New Haven, CT: Yale University Press, 1965).

MARLOWE, CHRISTOPHER (1564–1593). English playwright. Marlowe, a major Elizabethan figure who introduced blank verse, wrote *The Jew of Malta* (1589). The central figure in this work possessed all the **antisemitic** stereotypes. As in Shakespeare's *Merchant of Venice*, this merchant's daughter **converts** to Christianity. *See also* SHYLOCK.

MARR, WILHELM (1818–1904). German writer, political theorist, and agitator. In 1879, Marr founded the **Antisemites' League**, the first organization devoted exclusively to promoting political **antisemitism**. Marr's organization reflected his secular racism, which existed inconsistently alongside his religious antisemitism. His self-proclaimed goal was "to free Christianity from the yoke of Judaism." Marr coined the term *Antisemitismus*, "antisemitism," which for him denoted a secular-racial hatred of Jews. He used the word *antisemitism* to make **Jew-hatred** seem rational, sanctioned by science—polite. *See also* VICTORY OF THE JEWS OVER THE GERMANS, THE.

SUGGESTED READING: Moshe Zimmerman, *Wilhelm Marr: The Patriarch of Antisemitism* (New York: Oxford University Press, 1986).

MARRANOS. (Spanish slur) Spanish for "swine." Crypto-Jews; Jewish **converts** to Christianity; Jews married to Catholics. An insulting term applied to Jews who either were forced or willingly converted to Catholicism in the Iberian Peninsula starting in the 15th century. They secretly practiced some of the Jewish rituals, customs, and commandments while outwardly pretending they were Catholics. The **Inquisition**, devoted to rooting out **heretics**, focused on suspected crypto-Jews. The Marranos themselves preferred the term *Anusim*, meaning "forced ones." Christians used other negative terms such as **"New Christians"** and "Alboraycos" (like **Muhammad**'s magical "lightning bolt" that transported him to heaven—a white animal with the body of a mule, the head of a woman, and the tail of a peacock—the baptized Jews seemed neither Jewish nor Christian). **Con-**

versos ("converted ones") was a neutral term. *See also* AUTO-DA-FÉ; TORQUEMADA, TOMÁS DE.

SUGGESTED READING: Cecil Roth, *A History of the Marranos* (North Stratford, NH: Ayer, 1975); "List of Ethnic Slurs," *Wikipedia*, http://en .wikipedia.org/wiki/List_of_ethnic_slurs.

MARRIAGE RESTRICTIONS. As early as 388 the Christian-Roman law prohibited marriage between Christians and Jews. Such liaisons were to be treated like adultery—punished by exile, expropriation, or death. In 506 the Arian king Alaric II, in his **Breviary**, ordered that intermarriage among Christians and Jews was forbidden. In 18th-century Germany, Jewish marriages were limited so that the Jewish population would not increase. The **Nazis** incorporated intermarriage restrictions in the **Nuremberg Laws of 1935**.

SUGGESTED READING: Paul Rose, *Revolutionary Antisemitism in Germany from Kant to Wagner* (Princeton, NJ: Princeton University Press, 1990).

MARSDEN, VICTOR. Marsden translated *The Protocols of the Elders of Zion* from Russian into English. He was a member of the Britons Society, an English organization founded in 1918 by **Henry Hamilton Beamish**.

SUGGESTED READING: Richard Thurlow, *Fascism in Britain: A History, 1918–1985* (Oxford: Blackwell, 1987).

MARTIN V (1368–1431). Pope, 1417–31. Martin V appointed the anti-Jewish Franciscan **St. Giovanni di Capistrano** as head of the **Inquisition** for Germany, the Slavic countries, and Italy. In nearly 100 bulls, this pope alternated protection of the Jews with papal assaults on them, changing his mind as he was lobbied first by Jews and then, and more frequently, by anti-Jewish friars. The Jews used money to gain his help; Christians employed arguments of faith.

SUGGESTED READING: Cecil Roth, *History of the Jews in Italy* (Philadelphia: Jewish Publication Society, 1946).

MARTIN, TONY. History professor in the Africana Studies Department of Wellesley College in Massachusetts. In 1993, for his African-American history course, Martin assigned *The Secret Relationship between Blacks and Jews*. He wrote pamphlets accusing Jews of controlling the African slave trade, the civil rights movement, and scholarship on African-American culture and history. Moreover, he argued that today's Jews are conservative racists who squelch black progress. In *The Jewish Onslaught* (1993),

Martin portrays a "conspiracy" against him at Wellesley by Jewish students and the **Anti-Defamation League**. Martin attacked his black critics as "handkerchief heads," "Uncle Tom house Negroes," and "unthinking Negro stooges." In 1994, Wellesley denied Martin a merit raise on the basis of poor scholarship. The History Department dropped his classes. Like **Leonard Jeffries**, Martin spoke at the "Black Holocaust" conference.

SUGGESTED READING: Anti-Defamation League, "Schooled in Hate: Antisemitism on Campus," 1997, http://www.jewishvirtuallibrary.org/jsource/anti-semitism/Black_student_groups.html.

MARTINEZ, FERRANT. Also spelled Ferrand. Archdean of Ecija; vicar-general of the archbishop of Seville. Martinez led a massive anti-Jewish campaign at the end of the 14th century (1373–91). He demanded the destruction of Jews and Judaism. His beliefs and sermons instigated an anti-Jewish movement that spread to Andalusia, Castile, and most of Spain. Christians, both municipal officials and common people, looted and massacred perhaps 50,000 Jews, forcing thousands of others to be **baptized**.

SUGGESTED READING: Cecil Roth, *A History of the Marranos* (New York: Schocken, 1974).

MARTINI, RAYMOND (RAYMUND MARTIN) (d. 1285). Spanish-Christian theologian. In his diatribe *Dagger of Faith against the Moors and the Jews*, Martini argued that the **Talmud** was not a holy book of the Jews, for it contained all the fundamental doctrines of Christianity, and he later forged Talmudic passages to prove his point. He paired the Jews with the Devil who, following the Talmud, deliberately attacked Christians by killing them and their children. He defined Jews as even worse enemies of Christianity than the Muslims.

SUGGESTED READING: Edward Kessler and Neil Wenborn, *A Dictionary of Jewish–Christian Relations* (Cambridge: Cambridge University Press, 2005).

MARWITZ, FRIEDRICH VON DER. Prussian-German aristocrat and writer. In 1811, with the Jews gaining some civil rights in Prussia, Baron Marwitz wrote: "The Jews' long-awaited **Messiah** is Mammon, and they will rule the world with money."

SUGGESTED READING: H. W. Koch, *A History of Prussia* (London: Longman, 1987); Léon Poliakov, *The History of Antisemitism*, 4 vols. (New York: Vanguard, 1965–86).

MARX, KARL (1818–1883). German economist and philosopher. Born into a family of rabbis, Marx's father, a lawyer, converted himself and his family to Lutheranism to further his career. Karl Marx, the founder of modern communism, wrote in his essay "On the Jewish Question" (1844) that Jewishness means moneymaking, merchant hucksterism, self-interest, crass commercialism, and exploitative capitalism. The negative stereotypes stuck among Marxists of every stripe.

SUGGESTED READING: Dennis K. Fishman, *Political Discourse in Exile: Karl Marx and the Jewish Question* (Amherst: University of Massachusetts Press, 1991).

MARYLAND. *See* LUMBROZO, JACOB.

MASSACRES DISBELIEVED, HOLOCAUST. News of massacres was received among the Allies during World War II in two different ways, depending on the identity of the victim group. Massacres that took place against non-Jews (e.g., at Lidice, Czechoslovakia, in June 1942 and Oradour sur Glane, France, in June 1944) were believed and understood as horrific events. In contrast, atrocities taking place against Jews were downplayed or even dismissed. This predisposition was found in the American press, including the editors of *Time* and the *New York Times*, and among U.S. government officials such as President **Franklin D. Roosevelt**, Secretary of War **Henry Stimson**, and Assistant Secretary of State **Breckinridge Long**, as well as by many ordinary Americans. For several members of the U.S. **State Department**, it was not their inability to understand what was happening to the Jews, but rather their **antisemitic** bigotry that primarily motivated their indifference.

SUGGESTED READING: David Wyman, *The Abandonment of the Jews* (New York: Pantheon Books, 1984).

MATCHSTICK. (European slur) Reference to starved or cremated Jews in **Nazi** concentration camps.

SUGGESTED READING: "List of Ethnic Slurs," *Wikipedia*, http://en.wiki pedia.org/wiki/List_of_ethnic_slurs.

MATTHEW. Gospel; the first book of the Christian Scriptures. Matthew 27:25 depicts a scene in the courtyard of Roman governor Pontius Pilate where a Jewish crowd is gathered. It relates that Pilate, who did not want responsibility for Jesus' death, asks the crowd whether to execute him. The assembled Jews cry, "Crucify him!" and added, "His [Jesus'] blood be on us and on all our children." This was one of several Christian rationales "justifying" the persecution of Jews throughout two millennia while exonerating the Romans.

SUGGESTED READING: Peter Richardson and David Granshaw, *Anti-Judaism in Early Christianity* (Waterloo, ON: Wilfred Laurier University Press, 1986).

MATZAH OF ZION, THE. See TLASS, MUSTAFA.

MATZO BALLER. (U.S. slur) Reference to the Jewish food product.

SUGGESTED READING: "List of Ethnic Slurs," *Wikipedia*, http://en.wikipedia.org/wiki/List_of_ethnic_slurs.

MAURRAS, CHARLES (1868–1952). French politician and journalist. Maurras was the founder, along with **Léon Daudet**, of the **Action Française**. The two believed the concept of human rights and popular sovereignty were godless Jewish plots to destroy French society. The exoneration of Capt. Alfred **Dreyfus** they believed was an illustration of Jewish dominance. When the **Nazi** armies occupied France, Maurras welcomed them and supported the collaborationist **Vichy** regime.

SUGGESTED READING: Edward Tannenbaum, *The Action Française: Diehard Reactionaries of the Twentienth Century* (New York: John Wiley & Sons, 1962).

MAURY, JEAN-SIFFREIN (1746–1817). French cardinal and politician. Maury led the Court and Church party and the anti-Jewish forces in the French National Assembly during the **French Revolution**, along with **Bishop Henry de la Fare** of Nancy. Maury argued that the Jews were religiously alien to France and inherently evil.

SUGGESTED READING: Jay P. Berkevitz, "The French Revolution and the Jew: Assessing the Cultural Impact," *Association for Jewish Studies Review* 20, no. 1 (1995).

MAUTHAUSEN. Nazi forced labor concentration camp operating from 1938 to 1945 near Linz, northwest Austria. Mauthausen was established to exploit nearby stone quarries and was classified by the **SS** as a camp of utmost severity. It had the highest death-to-inmate ratio among the camps not specifically designated as **extermination camps**. More than 120,000 prisoners, including 38,000 Jews, were worked so hard and treated so brutally that they perished quickly. It was also a test camp for food experiments that led to increased prisoner sickness and fatalities.

SUGGESTED READING: Konnilyn G. Feig, *Hitler's Death Camps: The Sanity of Madness* (New York: Holmes & Meier, 1981).

MAXIMILIAN I (1459–1519). Holy Roman emperor, 1493–1519. Maximilian banned Jews from several of his territories. In 1509 he authorized a **converted** Jew, **Johannes Pfefferkorn**, to confiscate and destroy all Jewish books, especially the **Talmud**.
SUGGESTED READING: Heinrich Graetz, *History of the Jews*, vol. 4 (Philadelphia: Jewish Publication Society, 1898).

MAXIMILIAN I (1573–1651). Duke of Bavaria, 1597–1651. Maximilian renewed his grandfather Duke **Albrecht V**'s decree banning Jews from his territory:

> Whereas our respected predecessors and sovereign princes, with the gracious consent of His Majesty the Roman Emperor, and on the advice of our Council, have removed the Jews, their wives, and children . . . from our Principalities, so We herewith desire and ordain most solemnly that no Jew or Jewess may enter our Principality to have their residence nor to pursue any trade or profession, nor may they be tolerated by anyone whatsoever, or be given shelter.

SUGGESTED READING: Michael Kunze, *Highroad to the Stake: A Tale of Witchcraft* (Chicago: University of Chicago Press, 1987).

MAY LAWS (1882–1914). Anti-Jewish Russian laws. Tsar **Alexander III** was advised by his minister **Konstantin Petrovich Pobedonostsev** that **pogroms** were a reaction of common people because of their supposed exploitation by Jews who controlled commerce and industry. Restrictions had to be placed on Jews since they had been "pampered" by Tsar Alexander II. The May Laws, passed in 1882, restricted the **Pale of Settlement** even more tightly. Jews were forbidden to settle outside of towns, Jewish real estate deeds outside towns were voided, and Jews could not conduct commerce on Sundays or Christian holidays. The effect was to initiate a mass emigration of Jews to the United States. *See also* IGNATIEV, NIKOLAI PAVLOVITCH.
SUGGESTED READING: Simon Dubnow and Israel Friedlaender, *History of the Jews of Russia and Poland* (Bergenfeld, NJ: Avotaynu, 2000).

McFADDEN, LOUIS (1876–1936). Republican congressman, 1914–31; chair of the House Committee on **Banking** and Currency. McFadden inveighed against international Jewish money powers, denounced Jews, and praised the **Nazis** from the floor of the U.S. House of Representatives. In 1933, McFadden warned that America would have to choose between God and the "money changers." He claimed that Jewish bankers intended "to paralyze industry, to destroy patriotism, and, finally, to secure the overthrow of government itself in the United States." He also sympathized with the anti-Jewish policies of the **Third Reich**. Defeated in his bid for reelection in 1934, McFadden ran for the presidency in 1936 on a platform one of whose planks was "Christianity instead of Judaism." The notorious Jew-baiter **Charles Coughlin** drew material from this openly **antisemitic** congressman.

SUGGESTED READING: David Wyman, *The Abandonment of the Jews* (New York: Pantheon Books, 1984).

MEAUX, COUNCIL OF. At the Church councils held in Meaux in 845 and in Paris in 846, **Amulo** lobbied for the passage of a number of anti-Jewish canons, some of which admonished Christians not to protect Jews and required that Jewish children be separated from their parents. Fortunately for the Jews, King Charles the Bald of France rejected these canons.

SUGGESTED READING: Esther Genbasa, *The Jews of France: A History from Antiquity to the Present*, trans. M. B. Debevoise (Princeton, NJ: Princeton University Press, 1999).

MÉDICIS, MARIE DE (1573–1642). French queen-regent who expelled Jews from France in 1615 on the grounds they were "the sworn enemies of Christianity."

MEIN KAMPF (*MY STRUGGLE*). **Adolf Hitler**'s autobiography. Hitler wrote his blueprint for the future while jailed in 1924. The major concepts of National Socialism were set forth, including vituperative **antisemitism** and canards such as that Jews had caused Germany's ills and had corrupted German "**Aryan**" purity and made Germany lose World War I. This work also made the charge that Jews enabled **Bolshevism** to triumph in Russia. Furthermore, Jews were culture destroyers, parasites, and manipulators of the world's finances and governments. Hitler mentioned gassing Jews and attacking eastward to destroy the Jewish-controlled Soviets. *See also* CHAMBERLAIN, HOUSTON STEWART; EUGENICS; *LEBENSRAUM*; SOCIAL DARWINISM; *VICTORY OF JEWS OVER THE GERMANS, THE*.

MEINVILLE, JULIO (d. 1970?). **Argentinian** antisemitic priest active in the 1930s. A prolific writer and the spiritual leader of Tacuara, a violent, **anti-Semitic**, anti-American **fascistic** group of upper-class youth, active in the 1960s. Argentina's history is marked both by social antisemitism and official antisemitism.

SUGGESTED READING: Haim Avni, *Antisemitism in Argentina: The Dimensions of Danger* (New York: American Jewish Committee and the International Center for University Teaching of Jewish Civilization, 1994); Stephen Roth Institute for the Study of Contemporary Antisemitism and Racism, "Why Argentina? Police Involvement in Argentinean Antisemitism," 1997, http://www.tau.ac.il/Anti-Semitism/asw97-8/la-int.html.

MELANCHTHON, PHILIPP. 16th-century reformer and colleague of **Martin Luther**. In his *Loci Communes* (1543), Melanchthon argued for the kingdom of Christ being spiritual and against the Anabaptists' "Jewish error" of the church as a "civil and worldly state ruled by the godly."

SUGGESTED READING: Philipp Melanchthon, *Loci Communes, 1543* (St. Louis: Concordia, 1992).

MELLAH. Moroccan **ghetto**. Moroccan Jews have been ghettoized for two millennia, before and after the establishment of Islam. Moroccan ghettos for Jews were established in Fez, Rabat, and Marrakesh. *See also* ANTI-SEMITISM, MUSLIM.

SUGGESTED READING: Michael Laskier, *North African Jewry in the Twentieth Century: The Jews of Morocco, Tunisia, and Algeria* (New York: New York University Press, 1997); Mitchell Bard, "The Treatment of Jews in Arab/Islamic Countries," *Jewish Virtual Library*, http://www.jewishvirtuallibrary.org/jsource/anti-semitism/Jews_in_Arab_lands_(gen).html.

MELVILLE, HERMAN (1819–1891). American novelist. *Redburn* (1849), Melville's only novel with Jewish characters, describes a Jewish pawnbroker as "a curly-headed little man with a dark oily face, and a hooked nose, like the pictures of **Judas Iscariot**." Later in the book, praising German-Americans as "the most orderly and valuable of her foreign population," Melville observed that America is special because its ethnic diversity makes Americans noble and prejudice-free. Ironically, he completed his image with an **antisemitic** allusion:

> There is something in . . . the mode in which America has been settled, that in a noble breast, should forever extinguish the prejudices of national dislikes. Settled by people of all nations, all nations may claim her for their own. You can not spill a drop of American blood without spilling the blood of the whole world. Be he Englishman, Frenchman, German, Dane, or Scot. . . . We are not a narrow tribe of men, with a bigoted Hebrew nationality—whose blood has been debased in the attempt to ennoble it.

In *The Confidence Man* (1857), Melville concluded a list of criminals—a horse-thief, an assassin, a treaty-breaker, and a judicial murderer—with "a Jew with hospitable speeches cozening some fainting stranger into ambuscade, there to burk him, and account it a deed grateful to Manitou [Mammon], his God." An entry in his journal refers to the Jews in Palestine: "In the emptiness of the lifeless antiquity of Jerusalem the emigrant Jews are like flies who have taken up their abode in a skull."

SUGGESTED READING: Bernard Rosenthal, "Herman Melville's Wandering Jews," in *Puritan Influences in American Literature*, ed. Emery Elliot (Urbana: University of Illinois Press, 1978).

MEMOIRS ILLUSTRATING THE HISTORY OF JACOBINISM. A 1797–99 book by **Jesuit** Abbé **Augustin Barruel** describing an "Illuminist plot" in France. In it, Barruel affirms that "the grand object of this conspiracy was to overturn every altar where Christ was adored." Theirs was an "unrelenting hatred for Christ and kings." **Illuminati** "adepts of revolutionary Equality and Liberty had buried themselves in the Lodges of Masonry," where they caused the **French Revolution** and then ordered "all the adepts in their public prints to cry up the revolution and its principles." Soon, every nation had its "apostle of Equality, Liberty, and Sovereignty of the People." This book has been regarded as the conceptual inspiration for *The Protocols of the Elders of Zion*.

Although he did not mention Jews in his earlier work, in 1806 Barruel circulated a forged letter alleging that the Jews had been involved in the conspiracy he had earlier attributed to the "Lodges of Masonry." This **defamation** of an international Jewish conspiracy reappeared later in the century all across Europe.

SUGGESTED READING: "Antisemitism" and "Elders of Zion, Protocols of the Learned," in *Encyclopaedia Judaica* (Jerusalem: Keter, 1971).

MENCKEN, H. L. (1880–1956). German-American social and literary critic, essayist, journalist, and curmudgeon. References to Jews pepper his diaries: "a brisk, clever Jew," "a French Jewess," "a young Harvard Jew," "New York Jews," "an elderly and palpably Jewish gentleman," "they had not suspected he was a Jew," "there is a shrewd Jew in him at bottom," "a great many of the richer Jewish firms in Baltimore," "he is a highly dubious Jew," "he, too, is a Jew, and moreover, a jackass," "the only Jew on the guest list," "the Jew who owns it never spends a cent on decorations," "it appeared to me, in the rather dim light, that many of them were Jews," "the Jews of Hollywood have certainly not given him [**Theodore Dreiser**] much money," "a smart Jew," "most of them are Jewish Communists," "did not enjoy being bracketed with two Jews," "the donors were Jews." Mencken's letters also demonstrate his anti-Jewish attitudes. In a letter of May 29, 1919, he prophetically wrote, "There is a good ground for hoping that, as a Jew, [**Sigmund Freud**] will fall a victim to some obscure race war in Vienna." On November 15, 1934, Mencken wrote his friend, poet **Ezra Pound**, "All the ideas you have labored for so many years are now taken over by a gang of Communists (chiefly **kikes**) and reduced to complete absurdity."

SUGGESTED READING: Terry Teachout, *The Skeptic: A Life of H. L. Mencken* (New York: HarperCollins, 2002).

MENDELSSOHN, MOSES (1729–1796). Jewish philosopher and scholar and one of the greatest minds of the 18th century. Mendelssohn realized that, despite his personal prestige, his people were held in great contempt. In Frankfurt in the late 18th century, Jews had to step aside before Christians who ordered them to "Obey, Jew," Jewish **marriages** were limited so that the Jewish population would not increase, Jews were barred from the law and public office, and Jewish passports were stamped with the word *Jew*. A public promenade was posted, "No Jews and no **pigs**," and the Jews were confined to a **ghetto** whose gates were shut from sunset to sunrise. In July 1770 Mendelssohn wrote to a friend that in Germany he had to

> live so constricted, hemmed in on all sides by true intolerance. . . . I talk of it with my wife and children. "Father," [his] innocent child asks, "what does that fellow have against us? Why do people throw stones after us? What have we done to them?" "Yes, father dear," [his other child] says, "they chase after us in the streets and abuse us: Jews! Jews! Is it then such a reproach in people's eyes, to be a Jew?"

SUGGESTED READING: E. Jospe and Moses Mendelssohn, *Moses Mendelssohn: Selections from His Writings* (New York: Viking Press, 1975).

MENGELE, JOSEF (1911–1979?). Also known as the "Angel of Death." **SS** physician at **Auschwitz-Birkenau** death camp. After serving at the Russian Front, Mengele practiced at Auschwitz. Besides sending thousands to the **gas chambers** by **selection**, often at random, he performed sadistic, inhuman experiments on prisoners. A great believer in **Adolf Hitler**'s German superiority based on *völkisch* race theory, he sought ways to create Nordic twins by experimenting on Jewish twins at Birkenau. After using them, Mengele gave most youngsters fatal injections. He eluded capture using the **Ratline** (a **Vatican** escape route). It is believed he drowned in Brazil in 1979.

SUGGESTED READING: Gerald Posner and John Ware, *Mengele: The Complete Story* (New York: Dell, 1987).

MERCHANT OF VENICE, THE. Play by William Shakespeare (1596). The work focuses on **Shylock**, the Jewish moneylender, and Antonio, the Christian merchant who borrows from him, agreeing to a contract that indicates if he defaults on his loan, Shylock may extract a pound of flesh. Antonio defaults, and Shylock demands his pound of flesh. But if a drop of Christian blood is spilled, Shylock forfeits his life; besides, all his possessions are forfeit for his attempt to enact revenge. In the end, Shylock is coerced into becoming a Christian. Shylock's evil traits, his use of and relentless search for revenge through the "legal" murder of an innocent Christian, reminds the audience of Judas' betrayal. Shakespeare's story signifies the victory of Christianity and God's withholding of grace from the Jews.

SUGGESTED READING: Howard Bloom, *Shylock* (New York: Chelsea House, 1991).

MERRY DEL VAL, RAFAEL (1865–1930). Anglo-Spanish cardinal; secretary of state to Pope **Pius X**. Theodor Herzl—one of the principal founders of Zionism, who was making a plea in 1904 for **Vatican** support for a Jewish homeland—mentions in his diaries that Merry del Val stated to him:

> As long as the Jews deny the divinity of Jesus, we certainly cannot make a declaration in their favor. . . . To us they are the indispensable witnesses to the phenomenon of God's term on earth. . . . In order for us to come out for the Jewish People in the way you desire, they would first have to be converted.

SUGGESTED READING: Theodor Herzl, *The Complete Diaries of Theodor Herzl* (New York: Herzl Press, 1960).

MESSIAH. The Jews maintain that they are still awaiting the true messiah, God's agent whose arrival will be disclosed by the establishment of justice, peace, and harmony for all living beings. Until he comes, Jews themselves work to change the world for the better. However, Christians reply that the predicted messiah has already come; he was the redeeming God, Jesus Christ. That the Jews were still awaiting their messiah, an essential aspect of their self-identity, became further reason for Christians to oppress them. Because they continued to deny Christ while awaiting their "false messiah," the Jews were considered allies of the **Antichrist**, as well as **deicides**.

SUGGESTED READING: Jacob Neusner and Alan Avery-Peck, *The Blackwell Companion to Judaism* (Oxford, England: Blackwell, 2000).

METTERNICH, KLEMENS VON (1773–1859). Austrian diplomat. Although Metternich was not an **antisemite**, and although the Congress of Vienna in 1815, which Metternich led, placed some Jewish civil rights on paper, the principle of restoration—a return to pre-**Napoleonic** times—disenfranchised Jews and re-**ghettoized** them in many areas of Europe.

SUGGESTED READING: "Jews in the Age of Metternich," in *Leo Baeck Yearbook* (London: East & West Library, 2001).

METZGER, TOM (1938–). California **Ku Klux Klan** leader, a former member of the John Birch Society, a Grand Dragon of the Knights of the Ku Klux Klan, and a **Christian Identity** minister. Metzger in 1983 founded the White Aryan Resistance (WAR), which is symbolized by a skull, with a patch over one eye, and crossbones headed by the banner "WAR." He is also connected to the **Aryan Nations**, the **Silent Brotherhood**, and the **World Church of the Creator**. Metzger promotes **Holocaust denial** and preaches a fierce brand of antisemitic, racist, and anti-immigrant invective, combined with a leftist-leaning revolutionary ideology known as the "Third Position." He has been the principal mentor of the **neo-Nazi skinhead** movement since its appearance in America during the mid-1980s.

SUGGESTED READING: Leonard Zeskind, *Peddling Racist Violence for a New Generation: A Profile of Tom Metzger and the White Aryan Resistance* (New York: Center for Democratic Renewal, 1987); Anti-Defamation League, "Tom Metzger, White Aryan Resistance," 2002, http://www.adl .org/learn/ext_us/metzger.asp.

MEXICO. Although there were no acts of violence against Jews or their property, there were more than 130 **antisemitic** incidents reported in Mexico in 2002, considerably more than in previous years. Also, Mexico's universities, aided by the mass media, were the center of an anti-Zionist campaign, comparing Israel with **Nazi** Germany. In March 2002, the largest circulation newspaper, *La Prensa*, published an article by Lisandro Otero stating that "ultra-orthodox Israelis, followers of one of the most fundamentalist trends of Judaism supporting [Israeli prime minister Ariel] Sharon, are the panthers of extermination and hate." In April, Jose Antonio O'Farril Avila, editor of *Novedades*, one of the oldest newspapers in Mexico, and the English-language *News*, claimed that Jews knew in advance about the 2001 attack on the World Trade Center. *The Protocols of the Elders of Zion* and *The International Jew* continued to be available in bookstores. Anti-Jewish graffiti, in particular **swastikas**, have appeared in Jewish neighborhoods of Mexico City. On the other hand, in April 2003, the Mexican Congress unanimously approved a law to prevent and eliminate all forms of discrimination, including antisemitism.

SUGGESTED READING: Steven Roth Institute for the Study of Antisemitism and Racism, "Mexico," n.d., http://www.tau.ac.il/Anti-Semitism/asw2002-3/mexico.htm.

MEXIJEW. (U.S. slur) Reference to mixed Jewish and Hispanic parentage, or a Hispanic person practicing Judaism.

SUGGESTED READING: "List of Ethnic Slurs," *Wikipedia*, http://en.wiki pedia.org/wiki/List_of_ethnic_slurs.

MÉZIÈRES, PHILIPPE DE. Medieval French aristocrat, bureaucrat, and writer. In the late 14th century, Mézières held that Spain's comparative tolerance for Jews was a disaster for the state and the Church. He wrote of the "destructive ferment of the Old Testament and the maliciousness of the Jews that has been responsible for the horrible tyrannies of Pedro I the Cruel [1357–67] and for most of the ruination of the Holy Catholic Faith in [Spain]."

SUGGESTED READING: Philippe de Mézières, *Le Songe du Vieil Pelerin* (1389), ed. G. W. Coopland (Cambridge: Cambridge University Press, 1969).

MICHAELIS, JOHANN DAVID (1717–1791). A Lutheran theologian and Göttingen Hebraist, Michaelis was, as Frank Manuel calls him, "a pivotal figure in the contemporary German perception of Judaism." Michaelis observed that it was not likely that a people like the Jews could produce a man with "a noble disposition. . . . Even average virtue and honesty is found among this people so seldom that even the few exemplars of them cannot reduce the hatred of the Jews as much as one would wish." Michaelis argued that because of the Jews' own religious principles and their bad treatment at the hands of Christians, which made cheating and dishonesty a way of life, Christians hated Jews. Like other French and German thinkers of the time, Michaelis concluded that Judaism and Jews were morally deficient. But unlike liberal writers, he held that Jews could never become authentic **citizens**. "As long as Jews keep the laws of Moses, [they will not be able to make friends nor] fuse with us like Catholics and Lutherans . . . living in the same State."

SUGGESTED READING: Frank Manuel, *Broken Shaft* (Cambridge, MA: Harvard University Press, 1992); Alex Bein, *The Jewish Question* (New York: Simon & Schuster, 1990).

MILITIA MOVEMENT. U.S. paramilitary organizations, most of them located west of the Mississippi River, who regard government as the enemy of American freedom. They range from harmless protesters, through strong anti–gun law advocates and survivalists, to confrontational revolutionaries seeking military skirmishes with government agencies. Membership is estimated between 10,000 and 40,000. Many members believe that Jews control the U.S. government, calling Washington, DC, "**ZOG**"—Zionist-Occupied Government. They claim that Jews support United Nations control of the United States. Some militias are allied with the **Christian Identity Movement**, claiming that Jews are the "spawn of Satan," whereas Gentile whites are the truly chosen people.

SUGGESTED READING: Kenneth S. Stern, *Force upon the Plain: The American Militia Movement and the Politics of Hate* (New York: Simon & Schuster, 1995).

MINIM. Hebrew for "**heretics.**" In the first two centuries after the destruction of the Temple in Jerusalem in 70 CE, the Jewish Patriarch Rabbi Gamaliel II—to distinguish Jews from Christians of Jewish background and to exclude the latter from the **synagogue** itself—ordered that an alternative form of the **Amidah,** or *Shemoneh Esreh* (The Eighteen Blessings), be included in the Jewish liturgy. The 12th benediction, the *Birkat ha-Minim* or "Blessing" of the Heretics (c. 1st century), was originally intended simply to prevent these heretics and Jewish-Christians from participating in the synagogue service, not to curse them or to expel them from Judaism.

SUGGESTED READING: Simon Dubnov, *History of the Jews*, vol. 2, *From the Roman Empire to the Early Medieval Period*, trans. Moshe Spiegel (South Brunswick, NJ: Thomas Yoseloff, 1968).

MINORITY TREATIES. The League of Nations declared Jews to be a national minority. A series of treaties filed with the League in the 1920s prompted by Jewish groups, pertaining to East European states such as Poland and Romania, prohibited **antisemitic** legislation and guaranteed equal treatment of Jews. However, these minority treaties were not very successful, leaving the Jews and other minorities with great promises but very little actual protection because the League of Nations was extremely weak. Many states only partially implemented the treaties and then began to regress on even those measures. By the time of the Munich Crisis in 1938 (when **Adolf Hitler** demanded control of the Sudetenland in western Czechoslovakia, which was once Austrian, and Britain and France, along with Hitler's ally Italy, awarded him this territory in the Munich Pact), the minority treaties and their protections were almost totally in abeyance. *See also* VERSAILLES PEACE CONFERENCE.

SUGGESTED READING: Celia S. Heller, *On the Edge of Destruction* (Detroit: Wayne State University Press, 1994).

MIRANDOLA, GIOVANNI PICO DELLA (1463–1494). Italian count, scholar, philosopher, and humanist. Despite his friendship with the Jew Elias del Medigo and his study of Kabbalah, Mirandola believed that the **expulsion** of the Spanish Jews represented a victory for Christianity, an exaltation of the Catholic religion through the "Most Christian King [**Ferdinand**] who is beyond all praise."

SUGGESTED READING: Shlomo Simonsohn, *The Apostolic See and the Jews: History* (Toronto: Pontifical Institute of Mediaeval Studies, 1991); Joseph Dan, *The Christian Kabbalah: Jewish Mystical Books and Their Christian Interpreters* (Cambridge, MA: Harvard University Houghton Library, 1998).

MIRROR TO THE JEWS. In this 1862 book, its author, **Wilhelm Marr**, refers to the Jews as "this alien people."

MISANTHROPY. Hatred of humankind; a Hellenistic **defamation** of Jews. Greeks regarded Jews as misanthropes because it seemed Jews denied the Hellenistic principle of the unity of humankind. They bristled at the failure of Jews to share the joys of the table with them, intermarry with them, give gifts to the pagan temples, and partake in pagan sacrifices. During the **Enlightenment**, thinkers such as **Voltaire** denounced Jewish particularism, faulting them for not adopting a religion of reason that would unite humankind.

SUGGESTED READING: Paul Johnson, *A History of the Jews* (New York: Perennial/Harper & Row, 1987).

MR. CHRISTIAN'S CRUSADERS. *See* SECRET ORGANIZATIONS, 20TH CENTURY.

MIT BRENNENDER SORGE (*WITH BURNING ANXIETY*). Papal encyclical. Pope **Pius XI** wrote this letter on March 14, 1937, four years after the **Vatican**'s Concordat with the **Third Reich**. It condemned the regime for not living up to the Concordat and for persecuting the Catholic Church. A long section was devoted to damning the **Nazi** theory of **Blood and Soil** and Nazi race theories, considering the latter the "Cult of Idols." However, not only did the persecution of Jews go unmentioned, but the Jews were cited as **deicides**.

SUGGESTED READING: Anthony Rhoads, *The Vatican in the Age of the Dictators, 1922–1945* (New York: Rinehart & Winston, 1973).

MNASEAS OF PATROS. 2nd-century BCE Greek author. Mnaseas reported that the Jews worship a donkey's head in the Holy of Holies [most sacred section of Jerusalem Temple]. This legend was repeated by several other pagan authors.

SUGGESTED READING: Kaufmann Kohler, "Ass-Worship," *Jewish Encyclopedia.com*, http://www.jewishencyclopedia.com/view.jsp?artid = 2027&letter = A.

MOCZAR, MIECZYSLAW (1913–1986). Polish Communist general officer and nationalist. The **anti-Zionist** campaign of 1967–68 contained themes of traditional Polish **antisemitism**. It was also a power struggle between Moczar and Communist leader Wladyslaw Gomulka, as well as a conflict between those advocating Polish interests and those advocating Moscow's. Moczar was in charge of the secret police; Gomulka had Jews in his entourage. Moczar lamented that Soviet-influenced Jews claimed to have the right to leadership and "a monopoly over deciding what was right for the Polish nation." In a radio broadcast, Moczar proclaimed that there was no difference between Israeli behavior toward the Arabs and the way the **Nazis** had treated Poles and Polish Jews. His program, a mixture of intense nationalism and primitive antisemitism, resulted in 1967 in a systematic purge of Jewish officials. This antisemitic campaign in Poland resulted in the mass **expulsion** of approximately 15,000 Polish citizens of Jewish nationality or Jewish ancestry between 1968 and 1972, the largest anti-Jewish action in Europe in the postwar period.

SUGGESTED READING: Paul Lendvai, "Poland: The Party and the Jews," *Commentary* 46, no. 3 (September 1968).

MOLL, OTTO (1915–1946). **SS** concentration camp captain. Moll managed the **gas chambers** and **crematoria** at **Auschwitz-Birkenau** and supervised the murder of Hungarian Jews. He designed pits to drain off fat from burning corpses and threw live babies into pits. In 1945 he managed Gleiwitz camp until its liberation by the Americans, who executed him.

SUGGESTED READING: Kazimierz Smolen et al., eds., *KL Auschwitz Seen by the SS* (Warsaw: Interpress Publishers, 1991).

MOMMSEN, CHRISTIAN MATTHIAS THEODOR (1817–1903). German historian and writer. Mommsen was the major Christian intellectual challenging Prussian state historiographer **Heinrich von Treitschke**'s **antisemitism**. Mommsen attacked the 1878–90 antisemitic campaign and called Treitschke's "suicidal agitation of national sentiment" one of "the most silly perversions" and "a national calamity." But the liberal Mommsen rejected the Jews' desire to maintain their cultural and religious identity. He suggested that Jews renounce their Judaism and **convert** to Christianity as the price of breaking down the barriers between Jews and their fellow Christian citizens—that is, of entry into the great German nation. Mommsen also asserted that the Jews were "an element of decomposition" in the Roman Empire. Mommsen later explained that he had not intended the word "decomposition" to demean the Jews but to compliment them. Nevertheless, his phrase was widely misunderstood at the time as an insult to the Jews and was later quoted by the **Nazis**.

SUGGESTED READING: Paul Mendes Flohr and Jehuda Reinharz, *The Jew in the Modern World*, 2nd ed. (New York: Oxford University Press, 1995).

MONEYLENDER. (European, North American slur) Reference to **usury** allegedly involving all Jews.

SUGGESTED READING: "List of Ethnic Slurs," *Wikipedia*, http://en.wikipedia.org/wiki/List_of_ethnic_slurs.

MONEY-LENDING. *See* USURY.

MONTBOISIER, PIERRE DE. *See* PETER THE VENERABLE (PETER OF CLUNY).

MONTESQUIEU, CHARLES-LOUIS DE SECONDAT, BARON DE LA BRÈDE ET DE (1689–1755). French philosopher and satirist. In letter 60 of his *Persian Letters* (1721)—an epistolary novel consisting of letters about Europe sent to and from two fictional Persians—Montesquieu wrote:

> You ask me if there are Jews in France. Know that wherever there is money, there are Jews. You ask me what they do. Exactly what they do in Persia: nothing is more like an Asiatic Jew than a European one. They exhibit among the Christians, as among ourselves, an invincible attachment to their religion, amounting to folly. The Jewish religion is like the trunk of an old tree which has produced two branches that cover the whole earth—I mean Mohammedanism and Christianity: or rather, she is the mother of two daughters that have loaded her with a thousand bruises; for, in religious matters, the nearest relations are the bitterest foes.

SUGGESTED READING: Charles Lehrmann, *The Jewish Element in French Literature* (Cranbury, NJ: Thomas Yoseloff, 1961).

MONUMENT HENRY. Memorial to Commandant **Hubert Henry**, the **antidreyfusard** officer who forged evidence during the **Dreyfus Case**. During the Christmas season of 1898, **Edouard Drumont**'s *Libre Parole* initiated a contribution campaign to raise money for Berthe Henry, the major's widow, in order to sue Joseph Reinach for describing Henry's forgery role in the Dreyfus Affair, which she claimed defamed her husband's character. Twenty-five thousand French people contributed to what became known as the Henry Memorial. The contributors' comments, printed in *La Libre Parole*, demonstrated the continuing influence of traditional **antisemitism** on the French people. French men, women, children—and their pets—wrote that they planned to flay and butcher and boil the Jewish **vampires** alive, or bake them in the ovens of Baccarat. A certain Abbé Cros donated three francs for a bedside rug made of "'Yids' skins' to trample on morning and evenings." Contributors to the fund expressed a variety of discontents: fears of economic and social change and of poverty, resentment of liberal intellectuals and professors, and anger at capitalist exploitation. The contributors strongly supported the Church and the army as the basic institutions of the French nation. They regarded the Jews as paradigmatically evil creatures who were polluting France, corrupting the national spirit and honor through capitalistic enterprise, and destroying the most cherished Christian-French values.

SUGGESTED READING: Stephen Wilson, "Le Monument Henry: La structure de l'antisemitisme en France, 1898–1899," *Annales* 32 (1977): 279; Pierre Quillard, *Le Monument Henry* (Paris: Stock, 1899).

MOODY, DWIGHT (1837–1899). Preeminent American revivalist crusader of the 1870s. Moody not only condemned the Jews for **deicide** but also asserted that in Paris in 1873 a meeting of a thousand Jews bragged about killing the Christian God. Although he claimed that he respected the Jews as a people who would transform the non-Christian world to Christianity, in reality he wanted to **convert** the Jews themselves to Christianity. Years later, in 1893, he invited the **antisemitic** German Lutheran court-preacher **Adolf Stöcker**—another example of the interlocking relationship between European and American antisemites—to share a pulpit with him. Moody was not a rabble-rouser, but a man whose ideas and values, although expressed emotionally, coincided perfectly with those of middle-class Protestant America.

SUGGESTED READING: Naomi Cohen, *Encounter with Emancipation: The German Jews in the United States, 1830–1914* (Philadelphia: Jewish Publication Society, 1984).

MORTARA ABDUCTION CASE. Notorious kidnapping case. In 1858, a very sick seven-year-old Jewish child, Edgardo Mortara, was baptized by his teenage Catholic nursemaid in Bologna, Italy, then part of the **Papal States**. A year later, papal gendarmes took the child away from his parents to be raised a Catholic, as Pope **Pius IX** had directed. Edgardo was brought up in the **Vatican** and given special attention by the pope despite worldwide protests. He became a priest. The Alliance Israelite Universelle was founded in 1860 to defend Jewish rights as an outgrowth of this case.

SUGGESTED READING: David I. Kertzer, *The Kidnapping of Edgardo Mortara* (New York: Vintage, 1998).

MOSLEY, OSWALD. *See* BRITISH UNION OF FASCISTS.

MOTHER GOOSE. Pseudonymous author of a traditional nursery rhyme collection. In "Jack and the Beanstalk," "Jack sold his egg to a rogue of a Jew, who cheated him out of half his due." This **antisemitic** stereotype is no longer included in modern editions. *See also* GRIMM, JACOB AND WILHELM.

SUGGESTED READING: M. Leuthe, *Once upon a Time: On the Nature of the Fairy Tale* (Bloomington: Indiana University Press, 1976).

MUDARIS, IBRAHIM. Sheikh and Muslim cleric. On May 13, 2005, from a Gaza mosque, Mudaris proclaimed:

> The Jews are the cancer spreading all over the world . . . the Jews are a virus like AIDS hitting humankind . . . Jews are responsible for all wars and conflicts. . . . Do not ask what Germany did to the Jews but what the Jews did to Germany. True, the Germans killed and burned Jews but the Jews exaggerate the numbers to gain propaganda advantages and sympathy.

SUGGESTED READING: "News Alert: Simon Wiesenthal Center Calls on PA President to Dismiss TV Chief after Live Broadcast of Antisemitic Sermon," Simon Wiesenthal Center, http://www.wiesenthal.com/site/apps/nl/content2.asp?c = fwLYKnN8LzH&b = 312451&ct = 941645.

MUHAMMAD (570–632). Prophet; founder of Islam. Those who accept Muhammad as the Prophet are called Muslims, and his teachings, Islam. The book compiled from what Muslims believe the angel Gabriel dictated to Mohammed is called the **Koran**. Muhammad tried to get the Jewish clans of Arabia to recognize him as a prophet but the Jews refused. He then forcibly subdued the Jewish clans, particularly in Medina. One clan, Quraiza, was subject to beheading; other clans paid a **tax** of half of their produce but survived as "People of the Book" (a term that denotes both Christians and Jews because they revere the Bible). *See also* JIHAD.

SUGGESTED READING: Robert Spencer, *Onward Muslim Soldiers* (Washington, DC: Regnery, 2003).

MUHAMMAD, KHALID ABDUL (1948–2001). Formerly national spokesman of **Louis Farrakhan**'s Nation of Islam and, later, leader of the New **Black Panther Party**; **Holocaust denier**. On November 29, 1993, at Kean College in New Jersey, Muhammad demonstrated the extreme of black **antisemitism** in a diatribe he gave:

> You see everybody always talk about **Hitler** exterminating six million Jews. That's right. But don't nobody ever ask what did they do to Hitler? What did they do to them folks? They went in there, in Germany, the way they do everywhere they go, and they supplanted, they usurped, and a German, in his own country, would almost have to go to a Jew to get money. They had undermined the very fabric of the society. Now he was an arrogant no-good devil bastard, Hitler, no question about it. He was wickedly great. Yes, he was. He used his greatness for evil and wickedness. But they are wickedly great too, brother. Everywhere they go, and they always do it and hide their head.

"Brother, I don't care who sits in the seat at the White House," he said. "You can believe that the Jews control that seat and they sit in from behind the scenes. They control the finance, and not only that, they influence the policy-making." He continued:

> I called them [Jews] bloodsuckers. I'm not going to change that. Our lessons talk about the bloodsuckers of the poor in the supreme wisdom of the Nation of Islam. It's that old no-good Jew, that old imposter Jew, that old hooked-nose, bagel-eating, lox-eating, Johnny-come-lately perpetrating a fraud, just crawled out of the caves and hills of Europe, so-called damn Jew . . . and I feel everything I'm saying up here is kosher.

It took months for national black leaders to speak out against Muhammad's address. Moreover, the Kean College students attending his speech apparently agreed with it, as demonstrated by their uproarious approval, as heard on tapes of the event. This affair demonstrates the difficulties that black leaders have dealing with avowed black antisemites.

SUGGESTED READING: A. M. Rosenthal, "On Black Antisemitism," *New York Times*, January 11, 1994; Anti-Defamation League Special Report, "Khalid Abdul Muhammad: In His Own Words," http://www.adl.org/special_reports/khalid_own_words/khalid_own_words.asp.

MUHLENBERG, HENRY MELCHIOR (1711–1787). The founder of Lutheranism in America. At the Pennsylvania Constitutional Convention in

October 1776, the German-born and -trained Muhlenberg advocated a strict Christian oath be required of public officials, arguing that "it now seems as if a Christian people were ruled by Jews, Turks, Spinozists, Deists, perverted naturalists. They were learned pillars and would have much to answer for if they were now silent." The influential Pennsylvanian held that the only way for Jews to escape damnation was to **convert** to Christianity.

SUGGESTED READING: Henry Muhlenberg, *The Journals of Henry Melchior Muhlenberg*, 3 vols. (Philadelphia: Evangelical Lutheran Ministerium and Muhlenberg Press, 1942–43).

MÜLLER, HEINRICH (1900–?). **SS** major general. As head of Department IV, which investigated and indicted **Nazi** enemies, and **Gestapo** chief, Müller ordered **protective custody** for thousands. This meant transferring a suspect to a concentration camp without due process of law. He was a figure at the **Wannsee Conference**, where the mass extermination of Jews was planned. Müller supervised **Adolf Eichmann**. He disappeared from **Adolf Hitler**'s bunker in 1945 and was last seen in Damascus, Syria.

SUGGESTED READING: Edward Crankshaw, *Gestapo: Instrument of Tyranny* (New York: Viking, 1956).

MÜLLER-GUTTENBRUNN, ADAM (1851–1923). Austrian poet and theatrical director. *See also* ARYAN THEATER.

MULTICULTURALISM. A multicultural environment promotes cultural diversity within social cohesion, a community of citizens and a society of subcommunities, with each subcommunity maintaining its own distinctiveness and making its own unique contribution to society as a whole. Yet many European Jews fear an inauthentic multiculturalism that has come to mean that those who are ideologically and theologically opposed to Western liberalism and democracy and advocate the destruction of Western civilization are offered the freedom to propagate their views. The fact is that few European nations embrace authentic multiculturalism.

SUGGESTED READING: Antony Lerman, "Europe, Antisemitism, and Multiculturalism," *Sh'ma* (2000).

MUSIC, NAZI PURGE OF JEWISH INFLUENCE IN. After **Adolf Hitler**'s appointment as German chancellor in January 1933, one of the **Third Reich**'s major goals was to purge Germany of all "degenerate" modern art, music, and literature. In an important sense, German **fascism** was a revolution against modernism. Since the expressions of modernism were most obvious in the arts, they became the special targets of **Nazi** propaganda. Wanting to create an environment for "healthy," native, German arts, the Nazi regime declared all modernist art **"degenerate art"** (*Entartete Kunst*), and official policy was to rid the nation of this art and artists. Modernism, seen as essentially Jewish, was defined as a disease threatening the health of an **Aryan** Germanic nation. "Racial alien" arts were considered carriers of disease infecting the German mind and soul. Jews and their kind were to be removed from the body of the Third Reich along with their culture. Before the mass murders of World War II and along with preliminary **eugenic** "cleansing" of the *Volk*, the Nazis forced the emigration of hundreds of Jewish, half-Jewish, and other musicians and composers, as well as artists, writers, film directors, actors, professors, scientists, and intellectuals.

SUGGESTED READING: Harald Hagemann and Claus-Dieter Krohn, *Biographische Handbuch der deutschsprachigen Emigration nach 1933* (Munich: Saur, 1999); Stephanie Barron, *Degenerate Art* (New York: Harry Abrams, 1991); Alan E. Steinweis, *Art, Ideology, and Economics in Nazi Germany: The Reich Chambers of Music, Theater, and the Visual Arts* (Chapel Hill: University of North Carolina Press, 1996).

MUSLIM ORAL TRADITION. *See* HADITH.

MUSLIM BROTHERHOOD. Islamic Arab fundamentalist, social-reform organization. Imam **Hassan al-Banna** founded the Brotherhood in 1929 in Egypt. The Muslim Brotherhood is a social-reform movement, a leading advocate of political Islam, and has inspired the deadliest terror movements of the past two decades, including **Hamas** and **al-Qaeda**. Its branches are found in 70 countries. Egypt banned the Muslim Brotherhood in 1954. Political allies of the Muslim Brotherhood now dominate organized Islamic life in much of Western Europe. The Brotherhood's goal is to isolate Europe's Muslims from Western culture. This aim has resulted in stimulating violent ideas—and actions. Islamic terrorists are using Europe to launch their attacks on the West, including the September 11, 2001, assault on the United States and the 2004 train bombing in Madrid. After 9/11, the Brotherhood hailed **Osama bin Laden** as "a hero in the full sense of the word" and prayed that al-Qaeda would eventually "eradicate America." The terror strike against New York was considered "divine retribution," because America "preferred [Jewish] apes to human beings [and supported] homosexuals and **usury**." *See also* RADICAL ISLAM.

SUGGESTED READING: Robert S. Wistrich, *Muslim Antisemitism: A Clear and Present Danger* (New York: American Jewish Committee,

2002); Ian Johnson, "A Mosque for Ex-Nazis Became Center of Radical Islam," *Pittsburgh Post Gazette*, July 21, 2005.

MUSSOLINI, BENITO (1883–1945). Dictator of Italy, 1922–43. The architect of Italian **Fascism** introduced anti-Jewish legislation in 1938, but did not actively enforce **antisemitic** provisions. The Italian Army protected Jews in areas of its control. In September 1943, Mussolini was overthrown but rescued by German commandos. A puppet government was set up for him near Lake Como under **SS** control. Jews were rounded up with the aid of Fascist militia. Mussolini was assassinated by Italian partisans in April 1945. *See also* MANIFESTO OF RACIAL SCIENTISTS.

SUGGESTED READING: Meir Michaels, *Mussolini and the Jews* (Oxford, UK: Clarendon Press for the Institute of Jewish Affairs, 1978).

MYSTERY PLAYS. Medieval mystery plays denigrated the Jews, who refused to depart from their Torah and accept the divinity, or **messiahship**, of Jesus. Jews were portrayed as demons who, blind to the truth of Christianity, stubbornly insisted on their own religion. The Jews were shown seizing, torturing, and murdering Christ, doing most of what the **Gospels** assigned to the Romans.

SUGGESTED READING: Joel Carmichael, *The Satanizing of the Jews* (New York: Fromm International, 1993).

MYTH OF THE TWENTIETH CENTURY. Book by **Alfred Rosenberg** (1925). Rosenberg borrowed from **Friedrich Nietzsche**, **Arthur de Gobineau**, and **Houston Stewart Chamberlain** in his racial thought. He believed that Germans were the superior race corrupted by Jews, who were cultural destroyers, ignoble, and parasitic. Jews were behind Christianity, which he wanted purged of all Jewish aspects. He claimed that Jesus was not a Jew, but an **Aryan**. Believing Christianity was too infiltrated by Judaism, he preferred to return Germany to paganism. Like **Adolf Hitler**'s *Mein Kampf*, Rosenberg's *Myth* wanted Jews rooted out of German life. *See also* MARR, WILHELM.

SUGGESTED READING: Joachim C. Fest, *The Face of the Third Reich: Portraits of the Nazi Leadership*, trans. Michael Bullock (New York: Pantheon Books, 1970).

– N –

NAPOLEON (1769–1821). French emperor, 1804–15. Napoleon Bonaparte was the first European leader to emancipate Jews. His *Code Napoléon*, which granted equal rights, spread to all the countries he conquered or dominated. As early as 1794, as a general entering the Italian **Papal States**, Napoleon freed the Jews, had the **ghetto** walls pulled down, and lifted restrictions such as dress codes. In 1806 he convened the **Assembly of Notables** and in 1807 the Grand **Sanhedrin** of leading rabbis. They assured him Judaism had no conflict with the French state. He required the Jews to form *consistories*, communal offices for overseeing individual and communal Jewish affairs. Napoleon sought to integrate Jews into national French life and ordered consistory rabbis to promote military service as a sacred duty. One deviation from total emancipation was the **Infamous Decree** (1808), a series of special laws for Jews. The decree held that the state could exercise control over Jewish loans, require permits to engage in trade, prohibit moves to northeast France, and forbid replacements for military service. *See also* BARRUEL, AUGUSTIN; METTERNICH, KLEMENS VON; PIUS IX.

SUGGESTED READING: Franz Kobler, *Napoleon and the Jews* (New York: Schocken, 1988).

NARODOWE SILY ZBROJNE (NSZ). Polish Armed National Force formed in 1942, with 70,000 members. The NSZ was strongly anticommunist and **antisemitic**. It fought the German occupation forces in Poland but also murdered hundreds of Jewish partisans and Jews seeking refuge from the **Nazis**. It did not recognize the official Polish Home Army. After the war, the NSZ opposed Soviet forces and continued to murder **Holocaust** survivors.

SUGGESTED READING: Yisrael Gutman and Shmuel Krakowski, *Unequal Victims: Poles and Jews during World War II* (New York: Holocaust Library, 1986).

NASSER, GAMAL ABDEL (1918–1970). Egyptian head of state, 1954–70. After Nasser overthrew the Egyptian monarchy and became head of state, he adopted a belligerent attitude toward Israel. He instituted an economic boycott, promoted armed infiltration, initiated an arms race, and in 1956, closed the Suez Canal to Israeli shipping. In 1967, he provoked the **Six Day War** and, after its conclusion, moved the Arab world to a policy of "no relations, no negotiations" with Israel. Nasser claimed to distinguish between Jews, Judaism, and Zionism, asserting that his hostility was confined to Zionists. This kind of stance—claiming that **anti-Zionism** is not a form of **antisemitism**, when in fact it is simply another form of anti-Jewish hatred—is held by many Muslims living in the West.

SUGGESTED READING: Said Karurish, *Nasser the Last Arab* (New York: Dunne Books, 2004).

NATIONAL ALLIANCE. Neo-Nazi group in the United States. Led by veteran **antisemite** and racist **William Pierce**, the National Alliance has grown to become a large and active neo-Nazi organization. National Alliance members have engaged in plotting violent crimes, and its propaganda appears to have inspired others to carry out murder, bombings, and robberies. With 16 active cells from coast to coast and a growing membership, the National Alliance has been visible in at least 26 states, most notably in Ohio, Florida, Michigan, New York, Maryland, North Carolina, Virginia, and New Mexico. It is the largest and most active racist group in the United States and is sometimes symbolized by a **life rune**, which was also used on Nazi **SS** gravestones.

SUGGESTED READING: Robert Griffin, *The Fame of a Dead Man's Deeds: An Up-Close Portrait of White Nationalist William Pierce* (Bloomington, IN: Authorhouse, 2001); Anti-Defamation League, "William Pierce," 2004, http://www.adl.org/learn/ext_us/pierce.asp.

NATIONAL ASSOCIATION FOR THE ADVANCEMENT OF WHITE PEOPLE (NAAWP). Symbolized by a tiger surrounded by the group's name. A self-proclaimed civil rights organization for white people founded by former Klan leader **David Duke** and currently led by Ray Thomas in Tampa, Florida.

SUGGESTED READING: Anti-Defamation League, *Hate on Display: Extremist Symbols, Logos, and Tattoos* (New York: Anti-Defamation League, 2006).

NATIONAL CATHOLIC WELFARE CONFERENCE (NCWC). U.S. Catholic organization. Although the Catholic press had information about the Jewish predicament in Europe during World War II, editors opposed raising immigration **quotas**. The NCWC and the Catholic Committee for Refugees worked to rescue non-Jews, but these organizations looked on Jewish immigration as wrong in principle. Jews were "too prosperous, too successfully grasping." Officials of the NCWC's Bureau of Immigration in 1939 questioned whether Jewish refugees "might sell [their quota numbers for admission to America]." In 1945, the same group questioned the actions of the **War Refugee Board**, the only governmental organization dealing with Jewish refugees, albeit on a limited basis. "We have never seen any worthwhile results . . . plenty of money was wasted in the operation."

SUGGESTED READING: David S. Wyman, ed., *America and the Holocaust*, a 13-volume set documenting the acclaimed book *The Abandonment of the Jews*, 13 vols. (New York: Garland, 1989–91).

NATIONAL CHRISTIAN DEFENSE LEAGUE (LIGA APARARII NATIONALE CRESTINE, LANC). In 1923, Romania's National Christian Defense League was founded by one of the nation's leading scholars, A. C. Cuza, professor of law in the University of Iasi. The league, headed by scholars, had great influence among university students and educated men in general, and it became a force of very considerable political importance, particularly after it merged in 1935 with the political party headed by poet and politician **Octavian Goga**. LANC enlisted the support of both Christians and seculars, based on its hostility to Jews and **Bolsheviks**.

SUGGESTED READING: Josef Ebner, "From the World of Yesterday in the Jewish Renaissance Movement," in *History of the Jews in the Bukowina*, 1962, http://www.jewishgen.org/yizkor/bukowinabook/buk2_125.html.

NATIONAL DEMOCRATIC PARTY (GERMANY). German far-right, **xenophobic, antisemitic**, antiparliamentary party formed in 1964 in a merger of far-right parties. The National Democratic Party is home to a number of **skinheads** and is a refuge for **neo-Nazis**. While not receiving the necessary 5 percent of the federal votes to gain representation, it still has influence and greater strength in local elections in Saxony and Brandenburg. Thousands of its members marched in Dresden in February 2005, to the embarrassment of Chancellor Helmut Schroeder.

SUGGESTED READING: David Grossland, "Germans Want to Outlaw Nationalist Political Party," *Washington Times*, January 25, 2005.

NATIONAL DEMOCRATIC PARTY (POLAND). Also known as Endejca. Intensely nationalistic and **antisemitic** 20th-century Polish political movement. The party became powerful during World War I and held a plurality in the Polish Parliament after the war. It passed laws against Jews such as *numerus clausus* and encouraged college students to attack Jews. Its slogans included such lines as "Poland is composed of a nation, not of nationalities" and "Poland for Poles only." As part of the Polish underground Home Army, it fought against **Nazis** and persecuted Jews at the same time. *See also* DMOWSKI, ROMAN; PILSUDSKI, JÓZEF.

SUGGESTED READING: Celia S. Heller, *On the Edge of Destruction* (Detroit: Wayne State University Press, 1994).

NATIONALIST MOVEMENT, THE. Symbolized by crossed arrows. Also known as Hungarian **Arrow Cross**; Victory Flag; Battle Flag. This symbol originated in Hungary in the 1930s as the symbol of the leading Hungarian **fascist** political party, the Arrow Cross party. The symbol came to be used by other racist and **antisemitic** groups. The crossed arrows in red, white, and blue is the official symbol of this white supremacist, anti-immigrant, antigay Nationalist Movement operating in Mississippi.

SUGGESTED READING: Anti-Defamation League, *Hate on Display: Extremist Symbols, Logos, and Tattoos* (New York: Anti-Defamation League, 2006).

NATIONAL SOCIALIST AMERICAN WORKERS FREEDOM MOVEMENT. *See* NATIONAL SOCIALIST MOVEMENT.

NATIONAL SOCIALIST GERMAN WORKERS PARTY. *See* NAZI PARTY.

NATIONAL SOCIALIST MOVEMENT (NSM). Originally, the National Socialist American Workers Freedom Movement. NSM is the largest **neo-Nazi** group in the United States. This Minneapolis, Minnesota–based hate group—founded by two former George Lincoln Rockwell stormtroopers, Robert Brannen and Cliff Herrington, in 1974—is a throwback to the 1960s-era American Nazi Party: members wear **Nazi** uniforms and openly display **swastikas**. It has grown considerably in membership and influence, with dozens of chapters across the country. Part of the reason for the group's growth has been its appeal to racist **skinheads** and other young white supremacists, who join in NSM activities ranging from literature distribution to armed paramilitary training. NSM calls for a "greater America" that would deny citizenship to Jews, nonwhites, and homosexuals. With contact points throughout the United States, the NSM, led by Jeff Schoep in Minneapolis, is a virulently racist and **antisemitic** neo-Nazi group. The movement's symbol consists of the letters *NSM* superimposed on a swastika overlaying a shield—black and red from the flag of Nazi Germany, stars and stripes from the U.S. flag.

SUGGESTED READING: Howard L. Bushart et al., *Soldiers of God: White Supremists and Their Holy War for America* (New York: Kensington, 2000).

NATIONAL SOCIALIST WHITE PEOPLE'S PARTY. *See* AMERICAN NAZI PARTY.

NATIONALSOZIALISTISCHE FRAUENSCHAFT. *See* PASSOW, HILDEGARD.

NATIONAL STATES RIGHTS PARTY (NSRP). Avowed "white racist political party" founded by Edward Fields in 1958 in Indiana. Fields was a significant force in the racist world, known both for his collaboration with notorious racist bomber J. B. Stoner and as publisher of the NSRP's *Thunderbolt* newspaper, which attacked Jews as fiercely as it did integration. An Alabama version of the Hitler Youth, NSRP members wore white shirts, black ties, black pants, and armbands with the **Nazi thunderbolt** symbol; they aimed to "save Alabama and the nation from Jew Communists and their nigger allies."

SUGGESTED READING: Federal Bureau of Investigation, "National States Rights Party," http://foia.fbi.gov/foiaindex/national_states_rights_party .htm.

NATION OF ISLAM. See FARRAKHAN, LOUIS; *SECRET RELATIONSHIP BETWEEN BLACKS AND JEWS.*

NATURALIZATION BILL. See JEW BILL.

NAZI-CHRISTIANS. See GERMAN-CHRISTIANS.

NAZIDEUTSCH (NATIONAL SOCIALIST GERMAN). The German language as created, used, and distorted by the **Nazis**. Nazideutsch disguised Nazi programs, policies, attitudes, and behaviors from the outside world, from their Jewish and other victims, and perhaps from themselves. The Nazis created terms to disguise the true purpose of their activities, although the insiders knew they referred to the **Third Reich**'s policies and actions against the Jews. Examples include:

- *abdirigieren*: literally, "to direct away," but actually a bureaucratic euphemism for murdering someone because of an inability to work
- *Marschketten*: literally, "expeditionary force," but actually a Ukrainian militia collaborating with the Germans to round up, rob, and murder Jews
- *Zyklon*: literally, "cyclone," but actually an insecticide used to kill the Jews and others in **gas chambers** at several concentration camps, especially the six **extermination camps** in Poland

SUGGESTED READING: Robert Michael and Karin Doerr, *Nazi-Deutsch/ Nazi-German: An English Lexicon of the Language of the Third Reich* (New York: Greenwood Press, 2001).

NAZI LEGAL MEASURES AGAINST JEWS. Two months after **Adolf Hitler** assumed the office of chancellor, the rubber-stamp Reichstag on

April 7, 1933, passed the Law for the Reestablishment of the Professional Civil Service, which prohibited Jews from holding public offices. Hitler issued an edict that day restricting the number of Jewish lawyers admitted to the bar. Two days later an **Aryan** Paragraph was added, defining a Jew as a person with one parent or one grandparent who followed Judaism. On April 24, Jewish doctors were banned from government-sponsored health insurance programs. The next day the Law against the Overcrowding of German Schools and Universities was passed, establishing *numerus clausus*. On July 14, 1933, the government revoked the citizenship of *Ostjuden* who entered Germany after World War I. The **Nuremberg Laws** were passed on September 15, 1935. On November 12, 1938, **Hermann Goering** proclaimed the Elimination of Jews from German Economic Life, which barred Jews from all businesses as of January 1, 1939. *See also* ARYANIZATION.

SUGGESTED READING: Raul Hilberg, *The Destruction of European Jews* (Chicago: Quadrangle, 1967); Saul Friedlander, *Nazi Germany and the Jews* (New York: HarperCollins, 1997).

NAZI LOW RIDERS (NLR). A U.S.-based **neo-Nazi** group. First organized as a criminal gang in the early to mid-1970s among inmates housed by the California Youth Authority, the NLR's ideology is based on white supremacy. Located primarily in Southern California, members are also scattered among other states, including Arizona, Colorado, Florida, and Illinois. It is allied with the **Aryan Brotherhood**, which helped build NLR's brutal and ambitious reputation and created new criminal opportunities, including narcotics trafficking, murder, assault, extortion, and armed robbery. NLR champions its whiteness, especially when recruiting members from **skinhead** gangs and among new inmates, but it is primarily driven by criminal profit. So-called race traitors—those in interracial relationships or who demonstrate an affinity for what members consider to be black culture—have also been targeted, as have Jews, Asians, and other minorities. The letters *NLR* are also a prison tattoo, combined with **Nazi** symbols and icons, including eagles, **swastikas**, and skulls.

SUGGESTED READING: Southern Poverty Law Center, "Age of Rage," *Intelligence Report* no. 114 (Summer 2004).

NAZI PARTY. The National Socialist German Workers Party or Nazi Party was created in 1920 by **Adolf Hitler**, who had earlier joined the **German Workers Party**. By 1932, the Nazi Party was the largest political party in Germany, polling 37 percent of the vote. Its popularity pushed Hitler into the chancellery. A number of factors attributed to its success, including the

German defeat in World War I, the huge inflation of the mid-1930s, the Great Depression, political instability, the ultraliberal **Weimar** Constitution, nationalism, and **antisemitism**. *See also* DREXLER, ANTON; FINAL SOLUTION OF THE JEWISH PROBLEM; GERMAN WORKERS PARTY; GESTAPO; GOEBBELS, JOSEF PAUL; GOERING, HERMANN; HIMMLER, HEINRICH; SWASTIKA; THULE SOCIETY.

SUGGESTED READING: Charles B. Flood, *Hitler: The Path to Power* (Boston: Houghton Mifflin, 1989).

NAZI PARTY PLATFORM. Nazi propaganda proudly declared, "The Party Program of the NSDAP was proclaimed on the 24 February 1920 by Adolf Hitler at the first large Party gathering in Munich and since that day has remained unaltered. Within the national socialist philosophy is summarized in 25 points." Several points apply indirectly or directly to Jews, in particular:

> 4. Only a member of the race can be a citizen. A member of the race can only be one who is of German blood, without consideration of creed. Consequently no Jew can be a member of the race. 5. Whoever has no **citizenship** is to be able to live in Germany only as a guest, and must be under the authority of legislation for foreigners. 6. The right to determine matters concerning administration and law belongs only to the citizen. Therefore we demand that every public office, of any sort whatsoever, whether in the Reich, the county or municipality, be filled only by citizens. We combat the corrupting parliamentary economy, office-holding only according to party inclinations without consideration of character or abilities. . . . 24. We demand freedom of religion for all religious denominations within the state so long as they do not endanger its existence or oppose the moral senses of the Germanic race. The Party as such advocates the standpoint of a positive Christianity without binding itself confessionally to any one denomination. It combats the Jewish-materialistic spirit within and around us, and is convinced that a lasting recovery of our nation can only succeed from within on the framework: common utility precedes individual utility.

See also IF I WERE KAISER; PAN-GERMAN LEAGUE.

SUGGESTED READING: Office of the United States Counsel for the Prosecution of Axis Criminals, *Nazi Conspiracy and Aggression*, vol. 4 (Washington, DC: GPO, 1946); David Hogan, ed., *The Holocaust Chronicle* (Lincolnwood, IL: Publications International, 2000).

NEO-NAZI ROCK. *See* GERMAN FAR-RIGHT ROCK MUSIC; WHITE POWER MUSIC.

NEO-NAZIS. Post–World War II **Nazi** sympathizers. Neo-Nazis today are found in a number of countries, including the United States, France, Great

Britain, the Scandinavian states, Russia, Germany, and Austria. They look back with admiration to **Adolf Hitler** and Nazi Germany. The **swastika** or a facsimile remains their symbol. Their **antisemitic** beliefs include **Holocaust denial**, hatred of Israel, and the myth of Jewish domination of economics and politics. Some **skinheads** provide bullying. Many flock to extremely ultranationalistic, **xenophobic** political parties such as the **National Democratic Party** in Germany. Neo-Nazi hate groups pollute the Internet. Muslim fanatics often ally themselves with the Neo-Nazis. *See also* ARYAN NATIONS; CHRISTIAN IDENTITY MOVEMENT; GERMAN FAR-RIGHT ROCK MUSIC; KU KLUX KLAN; NATIONAL ALLIANCE; WHITE POWER MUSIC.

SUGGESTED READING: Howard Bushart, *Soldiers of God: White Supremists and Their Holy War for America* (New York: Kensington, 2000).

NEUES WIENER TAGBLATT. Vienna newspaper (1867–1945) published initially by Jews. In 1888, followers of Austrian politician and founder of the Pan-German Party **Georg Schönerer** ransacked the offices of this newspaper and beat up its employees.

SUGGESTED READING: Nicholas Goodrick-Clarke, *The Occult Roots of Nazism* (New York: New York University Press, 1992).

NEUMANN AFFAIR. In March 1881 the antisemitic German newspaper *Norddeutsche Presse* reported a brutal attack on a Jewish household on February 12 in the village of Bandsburg, West Prussia, which resulted in the murder of a Jewish merchant named Neumann and serious injuries to his wife. The reporter concluded his account with the comment that "this deed proved how deeply outraged the people were by *Semitentum* if they had to resort to such an act of mad revenge." At the same time, the *Deutsche Landeszeitung* reported: "As a result of the peripatetic agitation of Dr. [**Ernst**] **Henrici**, we are pleased to announce that the farmers no longer tolerate the presence of any Jew, whatever his standing, on their farms, and that they now refuse to do business with him." These are the probable facts of the attack on the Neumanns:

> At 5 o'clock in the morning of the 12 February, a man broke into the household of the Jewish merchant, Neumann, severely beat up his wife, killed the merchant, smashed the skull of the maid, and escaped. The murderer was believed to be a miller, who had previously been in the employment of the merchant and from whom he had stolen a document. The miller had later been apprehended, tried and sentenced to four months' imprisonment as a result of Neumann's testimony.

As a result of the attack and the inflammatory **antisemitic** articles and statements in the press, Jewish representatives sent a delegation to the kaiser asking for protection.

SUGGESTED READING: Stephen C. J. Nicholls, "The Burning of the Synagogue in Neustettin: Ideological Arson in the 1880s," in "Jews and Christians in Pomerania, 1800–1918," Ph.D. diss., University of Sussex Centre for German-Jewish Studies.

NEUSTETTIN POGROM. On February 18, 1881, the Neustettin **synagogue** was burned to the ground, the result of the **antisemitic** mood in Germany in the last quarter of the 19th century. It was through **Ernst Henrici**'s visits to the area that the slogans of the leading antisemites in Berlin were transplanted to Neustettin. The fire itself disrupted social and business relations between the Jewish and Christian communities. There was a **boycott of Jewish shops**, Jews were expelled from singing clubs, and Jewish children attending the local grammar school were abused and molested. On February 13 a *Norddeutsche Presse* article entitled "Dr. **Martin Luther** and the Jewish Question" repeated Luther's program of violence. The German government did not act effectively to stop the looting and rioting that followed. After a protracted investigation, five *Jewish* citizens were arrested for burning their own synagogue down. The public prosecutor followed the reasoning of anti-Jewish propagandists, who alleged that the synagogue fire was a case of **Jewish lightning**. Four of the five were sent to prison. When the case went to appeal in March 1884, the jury acquitted all the defendants of any involvement. Jewish-owned shops in Neustettin were plundered, and five Jews were physically assaulted. Despite Jewish attempts to defend themselves, a series of anti-Jewish disturbances continued throughout the summer. Even Kaiser Wilhelm II believed that the authorities had not displayed enough energy in dealing with the riots. The Neustettin affair provides a model for the way in which agitators, supported by tendentious and irresponsible reporting in the press, can exploit an isolated event to create an atmosphere of national crisis. Complaints in the press about the Jews' "sucking even the smallest villages dry" and "choking the life out of the peasant with exorbitant interest rates" anticipated Nazi **Blood and Soil**.

SUGGESTED READING: Stephen C. J. Nicholls, "The Burning of the Synagogue in Neustettin: Ideological Arson in the 1880s," in "Jews and Christians in Pomerania, 1800–1918," Ph.D. diss., University of Sussex Centre for German-Jewish Studies.

NEW AGE MOVEMENT. Within the literature of the New Age Movement is a subtle attack on Jewish identity. New Agers see a "Jewish problem," with Jews needing to solve their "problems" for the good of all mankind. Jews are represented as people adhering to an outdated religion harmful to them and disruptive to the world. New Agers hold that the "Jewish problem" results from the Jews' belief in their ancient identity, so they urge complete Jewish assimilation. *See also* BAILEY, ALICE A.

SUGGESTED READING: Clifford Denton, "The Subtle Antisemitism of the New Age Movement," *Community* 2, no. 4 (Summer 1994), reprinted in *Tishrei* (July 2003); Hannah Newman, "Rainbow Swastika: A Report to the Jewish People about New Age Antisemitism," *Philologos.org*, http://www.lermanet.com/rainbow-swaztika.

NEW ANTISEMITISM. The old **antisemitism** in the Western world was largely rightist politically. In the 21st century, the mainstream right is increasingly sympathetic to Jews and Israel, while the Western political left is becoming hostile. Antisemitism was historically a Christian phenomenon; now many Muslims have become antisemitic and have appropriated the Christian canards. Muslim antisemitism, unlike the Christian which had its enmity based on religion, grew out of a hostility based on the concept that Jews must be subject to Islam in the Arab world (as **dhimmis**). In the late 19th and 20th century, racial or secular antisemitism—in existence for millennia—grew in prominence. Today, both Europeans and the Islamic world see Israel as a great threat. With Palestinian Liberation Organization leader **Yassir Arafat'**s death in February 2005, there are signs that the Palestinians and Israelis may forge an agreement that, in turn, may improve Israel's international standing and thus, reduce the growth of the New Antisemitism.

SUGGESTED READING: Phyllis Chesler, *The New Antisemitism* (San Francisco: Jossey-Bass, 2003); Ron Rosenbaum, ed., *Those Who Forget the Past: The Question of Anti-Semitism* (New York: Random House, 2004).

NEW LEFT. Established in the 1960s in the United States, the New Left consists of students, peaceniks, anticapitalists, those hostile to U.S. foreign policy, anti-imperialists, and Third World idealists. The New Left is rather undoctrinaire and utopian regarding major issues, but it favors the Arabs and Palestinians, viewing them as oppressed, and is unsympathetic toward Israel. New Leftists oppose Zionism, yet claim they are not **antisemitic**. Still, they use traditional antisemitic symbols, cartoons, and accusations, comparing Israeli policies to those of the **Nazis**. They attack Israel with a focus on the Occupied Territories in Palestine, but often ignore obvious violations of human rights in Arab lands and other parts of the world. *See also* ANTI-ZIONIST ANTISEMITISM.

SUGGESTED READING: George Jochnowiz, *The New Left and Its New Antisemitism: An Article from Midstream* (New York: Theodore Herzl Foundation, 2004).

NEW YORK LIBERAL. (U.S. slur) Reference to the large number of Jews living in New York City and their historic support for liberalism and the Democratic Party.

SUGGESTED READING: "List of Ethnic Slurs," *Wikipedia*, http://en.wik ipedia.org/wiki/List_of_ethnic_slurs.

NEW YORK SUPREME COURT. *See* KENT, JAMES.

NICAEA, COUNCIL OF. Ecumenical conclave of Catholic bishops called by Emperor **Constantine** in 325 to resolve the Arian controversy (Arians denied divinity of Christ) and establish religious peace and Christian uniformity in his newly united empire. The council defined the nature of Jesus, developed a uniform Christian creed, declared Arianism a **heresy**, and clearly distinguished the celebration of the Christian Easter from the Jewish Passover. The council's decisions were sanctioned and published to the empire on June 19, 325, in a letter by Constantine. Its anti-Jewish rhetoric echoed that of **Church Fathers** such as **Tertullian** and **Cyprian** and signaled that the break with Judaism would be official and emotional.

> [The Jews are] a people who, having imbued their hands in a most heinous outrage [Jesus' crucifixion], have thus polluted their souls and are deservedly blind. . . . Therefore we have nothing in common with that most hostile of people the Jews. We have received from the Savior another way . . . our holy religion. . . . On what subject will that detestable association be competent to form a correct judgment, who after that murder of their Lord . . . are led . . . by . . . their innate fury . . .?

SUGGESTED READING: C.-J. Hefele and H. Leclercq, *Histoire des conciles d'après les documents originaux* (Paris: Librairie Letouzey et Ané, 1938).

NICHOLAS I (1786–1855). Russian tsar, 1825–55. Nicholas I regarded Jews as harmful aliens and sought to assimilate them by divorcing them from their traditions. He set up compulsory military service for children down to 12 years old—and strict quotas on Jewish communities led to the drafting of nearly 50,000 children as young as five years old, who were often forcibly **converted** to Christianity (called Cantonists). He also reduced the **Pale of Settlement**, established proselytizing government schools, instituted official progovernment rabbis, and prohibited traditional

Jewish garb. In 1844 Nicholas received a report that a secret book existed that ordered Jews to **ritually murder** Christian children and consume their blood. In the same year, the tsar's public education law contained this secret supplement: "The purpose of educating the Jews is to bring about their gradual merging with the Christian nationalities, and to uproot those superstitions and harmful prejudices which are instilled by the teachings of the **Talmud**." *See also* LILIENTHAL, MAX.

SUGGESTED READING: N. V. Riasanovsky, *Nicholas I and Official Nationality in Russia, 1825–1855* (Berkeley: University of California Press, 1967).

NICHOLAS II (d. 1061). Pope, 1058–61. Nicholas II wrote that Jewish authority over Christians violated theological precepts that have concerned the Church since the beginnings of Christianity. Furthermore, Jewish authority in matters such as military service contravened the **Theodosian Code**.

NICHOLAS II (1868–1918). Russian tsar, 1894–1917. Nicholas II was a patron and honorary member of the **Black Hundreds** and wore its symbol at every opportunity. He told his minister of war, Gen. A. N. Kuropatkin, that the Jews deserved their fate because of their revolutionary activities. In his **antisemitism**, Nicholas was joined by the tsarina, Alexandra. They evidently believed that the Jews were behind the 1905 Revolution and posed a permanent danger to Russia. When a police chief, General Drachevsky, told him that many Jews had died in **pogroms**, Nicholas replied, "No. Not enough. I expected that more would die."

SUGGESTED READING: Hans Rogger, *Jewish Policies and Right-Wing Politics in Imperial Russia* (Berkeley: University of California Press, 1986).

NICHOLAS III (1216–1280). Pope, 1277–80. Nicholas III ordered the **Dominicans** and Franciscans to renew their conversionary preaching. He ruled that Jews who were **baptized** while fearing for their lives but who later returned to their Judaism were to be considered relapsed **heretics** and burned at the stake.

SUGGESTED READING: Paul E. Grosser and Edwin G. Halperin, *Anti-Semitism: The Causes and Effects of a Prejudice* (Secaucus, NJ: Citadel Press, 1979).

NICHOLAS IV (d. 1292). Pope, 1288–92. In 1288, Nicholas IV ordered Hugo de Biondes and Peter Arlin, **Dominican** Inquisitors in France, to proceed against relapsed Jewish **converts** as **heretics**, since forced **baptism** was valid even when in fear for their lives. In 1290, Nicholas, a Franciscan, complained that Jews and **judaized** Christians infected the faithful with **heresy**. He instructed the Franciscan **Inquisition** and other ecclesiastical and civil authorities to "pull out the deadly plant by its roots, . . . purge the infected provinces, . . . and punish these idolators and **heretics**, denying them any right of appeal."

SUGGESTED READING: Solomon Grayzel, *The Church and the Jews in the XIII Century*, ed. Kenneth R. Stow (Detroit: Wayne State University Press, 1989).

NICHOLAS V (1397–1455). Pope, 1447–55. The **Inquisition** in Spain, requested by Spanish monarchs and first established in 1451 by Pope Nicholas V, employed secular force extensively and targeted the **converted** Jews (**conversos**). With the full support of the papacy, the Inquisition could fine, imprison, humiliate, expropriate, torture, and murder "**heretical**" conversos, as well as those who sympathized with, protected, or sheltered them. The Spanish Inquisition was established to root out apostasy, real or imagined.

SUGGESTED READING: Simon Dubnov, *History of the Jews*, vol. 5, *From the Congress of Vienna to the Emergence of Hitler*, trans. Moshe Spiegel (South Brunswick, NJ: Thomas Yoseloff, 1973).

NICKEL NOSE. (U.S. slur) Reference to the stereotypical Jewish nose.

SUGGESTED READING: "List of Ethnic Slurs," *Wikipedia*, http://en.wik ipedia.org/wiki/List_of_ethnic_slurs.

NIEMÖLLER, MARTIN (1892–1984). Lutheran pastor and leader of the German Lutheran opposition to **Adolf Hitler**. A sermon given by Niemöller in August 1935 is replete with anti-Jewish Christian myths and comparisons between Hitler and the Jews. Jewish history was "dark and sinister." At the same time the Nazis were vilifying the Jews within German society as the most evil and cursed of people, eternally held in contempt, the most prestigious, charismatic leader of the German Protestant dissenters was doing the very same thing within his Church. The **antisemitic** logic of Niemöller's position is unassailable: since the Jews are the model of evil in Christendom, the Nazis can and should be compared with them. Although he did warn his listeners not to hate the Jews, his reason was that the Jews were already hated and cursed by God. After the war, Niemöller wrote that each German was as guilty as an **SS** man.

SUGGESTED READING: Richard Gutteridge, *Open Thy Month for the Dumb: The German Evangelical Church and the Jews, 1879–1950* (Southhampton, England: Camelot, 1976).

NIETZSCHE, FRIEDRICH (1844–1900). German philosopher. Nietzsche was not an **antisemite** nor an admirer of German people. However, **Nazis** twisted his ideas of the "will to power" and the "Superman" who was beyond good and evil to suit their expansionist, racist, and immoral *Weltanschauung* (worldview).

SUGGESTED READING: Walter Kaufman, ed., *The Portable Nietzsche* (New York: Penguin, 1977).

NIGHT AND FOG DECREE. *Nacht und Nebel* in German, *Nuit et Brouillard* in French. A secret order given December 7, 1941, by **Adolf Hitler** to arrest "persons endangering German security." As the German Army aided in these roundups rather than solely acting as soldiers at the war front, they became complicit in **crimes against humanity**. These actions grew out of increased anti-Nazi resistance, particularly in France. The suspect would disappear without legal recourse into the "night and fog"—to a concentration camp, summary execution, or gassing.

SUGGESTED READING: Ingo Mueller, *Hitler's Justice: The Courts of the Third Reich*, trans. Deborah Lucas Schneider (Cambridge, MA: Harvard University Press, 1991).

NILUS, SERGEI (1862–1929). Russian writer and publicist. In 1905, Nilus published a book entitled *The Great in the Small: The Coming of the Anti-Christ and the Rule of Satan on Earth*. A section of the book consisted of *The Protocols of the Elders of Zion*, which purported to be the minutes of a world Jewish plot to dominate Gentile society. When it was presented to Tsar **Nicholas II**, he dismissed the book as a fraud, burned copies, and banished Nilus. A fervent Orthodox Christian, Nilus was arrested by the Soviets and detained briefly in 1924 and 1927.

SUGGESTED READING: Norman Cohn, *Warrant for Genocide* (Chico, CA: Scholars Press, 1981).

NIXON, RICHARD M. (1913–1994). U.S. president, 1969–74. Nixon often referred to Jews as **"kikes"** and "left-wing." He fantasized that "the Jews in the U.S. control the entire information and propaganda machine, the large newspapers, the motion pictures, radio and television, and the big companies. And there is a force that we have to take into consideration." The tapes of White House conversations kept by Nixon reveal that in February 1972, after a prayer breakfast with the Reverend Billy Graham, Nixon's chief of staff, H. R. Haldeman, made an **antisemitic** wisecrack about the Jews at *Time* magazine—"You meet with all their editors, you better take your Jewish beanie"—which was followed by Nixon's ranting about the Jews controlling Hollywood and the media. The conversation continued:

> BILLY GRAHAM: This stranglehold has got to be broken or the country's going down the drain. . . .
> PRESIDENT NIXON: You believe that?
> GRAHAM: Yes, sir.
> NIXON: Oh boy. So do I. I can't ever say that [in public], but I believe it.
> GRAHAM: No, but if you get elected a second time, then we might be able to do something.
> NIXON: Well, it's also the Jews are irreligious, atheistic, immoral bunch of bastards.

SUGGESTED READING: James Warren, "Nixon, Billy Graham, Antisemitism on Tape," *Chicago Tribune*, March 1, 2001.

NOLDE, EMIL (1867–1956). German expressionist artist. Nolde's paintings, often in watercolor, exhibited supernatural and mystical themes. He joined the **Nazi Party** in 1920 and expressed extreme German nationalism and **antisemitic** views. He was shocked when the **Nazi** government labeled his work **degenerate art** and banned a thousand of his paintings in 1936.

SUGGESTED READING: Eric Michaud and Janet Lloyd, *The Cult of Art in Nazi Germany* (Stanford, CA: Stanford University Press, 2004).

NON-JEWS, HELP FOR, BY U.S. GOVERNMENT DURING THE HOLOCAUST. The U.S. government made many decisions and carried out actions that both complicated and delayed winning the war. Some of these extraordinarily demanding efforts were performed for non-Jews, such as the Anglo-American-Nazi agreement to feed millions of non-Jewish Greeks during a midwar famine; the ineffectual and self-defeating attempts to aid the non-Jewish Polish Warsaw uprising in 1944; the bypassing of the U.S. Neutrality Act, the use of Presidential slush funds, and the manipulation of the Immigration Law quotas to allow thousands of non-Jewish children to immigrate to the United States in 1941; and the transportation of thousands of non-Jewish Europeans all over the world, including the United States, during the war.

SUGGESTED READING: Arthur Morse, *While Six Million Died: A Chronicle of American Apathy* (New York: Overlook Press, 1998).

NOONTIDE PRESS. The most well-established U.S. publishing house catering to American bigots and extremists. Noontide Press has published material promoting **Holocaust denial**, bigotry, and bomb making; the antisemitic *Protocols of the Elders of Zion*, *The International Jew*, and *Mein Kampf*; the **Holocaust denial** tract *Hoax of the Twentieth Century*; and *The Road Back*, a terrorist manual with an ideological bent, popular with the antigovernment **militia movement** in the United States.

SUGGESTED READING: Anti-Defamation League, "Extremist Literature as a Recipe for Murder," press release, February 29, 1996, http://www.adl.org/presrele/militi_71/2682_71.asp.

NORDIC SUPERIORITY. The view that Nordics—misnamed **Aryans**—from the northern tier of Europe (Scandinavia, Germany, Great Britain, Holland, and Denmark) were superior: more intelligent, more orderly, cleaner, more civic-minded, and more energetic than anyone else. The U.S. immigration laws until 1965 were based on this view. *See also* DAVENPORT, CHARLES BENEDICT; GRANT, MADISON; LAUGHLIN, HARRY; QUOTAS, IMMIGRATION; STODDARD, LOTHROP.

SUGGESTED READING: Stefan Kuhl, *The Nazi Connection* (New York: Oxford University Press, 1994).

NORRIS, FRANK (1870–1902). American novelist. Norris's 1899 novel *McTeague*, generally acclaimed as a classic, portrays a Polish Jew, Zerkow, as the incarnation of greed. The eloquent passage describing his incredible lust for gold—to the point of sleeping in a pile of it—is memorable. McTeague abounds with racial stereotypes. Zerkow fulfills **antisemitic** stereotypes: money-hungry, leering, with "claw-like, prehensile fingers—the fingers of a man who accumulates, but never disburses," greedy, unclean, a "red-headed Polish Jew who took Maria [an allusion to the Virgin Mary] home to his wretched hovel . . . [where] Maria gave birth to a child, a wretched, sickly child, with not even strength enough nor wits enough to cry."

SUGGESTED READING: Louis Harap, *Creative Awakening: The Jewish Presence in Twentieth-Century American Literature, 1900–1940s* (Westport, CT: Greenwood Press, 1987).

NORWICH BLOOD LIBEL. First recorded accusation of **ritual murder** in the Middle Ages. In Norwich, England, in 1144, the false charge stated that Jews of the town bought a Christian boy, tortured him, and crucified him near Easter. In response, the town executed Jewish community leaders. *See also* APION; BEILIS CASE; BLOIS; FULDA.

SUGGESTED READING: Gerd Mentgen, "The Origins of the Blood Libel," *Zion* 5, no. 2 (1994).

NOSTRA AETATE. See DECLARATION ON THE RELATIONSHIP OF THE CHURCH TO NON-CHRISTIAN RELIGIONS.

NOVELLA 146. Part of the **Justinian Code** that attempted to determine the tenets of Jewish belief. The novella decreed that the Jewish **Talmud** intentionally distorted the authentic "christological" meanings of the Jewish Testament and therefore should be forbidden to the Jews. The novella also stated that Jews should interpret their holy books only as "announcing the Great God and the Savior of the human race, Jesus Christ," not for their "literal" meaning. Jewish exegesis was "malignant," "extraneous and unwritten . . . ungodly nonsense."

SUGGESTED READING: Eberhard Klingenber, "Justinian Novellae Concerning the Jews," *Jewish Law Association Studies* 8 (1996).

NUMERUS CLAUSUS. Latin for "restricted number." The amount fixed against Jews regarding admission to certain professions, educational institutions, and public office starting in the 19th century, particularly in Russia, Hungary, and Romania. In the United States, **quota systems** in higher education remained in effect until the 1950s. During the 1930s, the **Nazis** initially instituted *numerus clausus* for professions and civil service positions, as well as within educational institutions of all levels in Germany. Subsequently, the concept of restriction was abandoned in favor of wholesale **expulsion** of Jews from public and civic life. Throughout Russia and the former Soviet Union, such quotas continue unofficially. *See also* LOWELL, JAMES RUSSELL; MINORITY TREATIES; REVERSE DISCRIMINATION.

SUGGESTED READING: David Vital, *A People Apart: A Political History of the Jews in Europe, 1789–1939* (New York: Oxford University Press, 1999).

NUREMBERG LAWS OF 1935. The Law for the Protection of German Blood and Honor prohibited both **marriages** and extramarital relations between Jews and Gentile Germans. The Reich Citizenship Law took **citizenship** away from Jews. It established the legal concept of *Mischling*, or part-Jew, which gave the **Nazis** enormous difficulties in definition. In 1938 supplementary decrees to the Reich Citizenship Law excluded physicians and lawyers from practicing. These anti-Jewish laws used the religious affiliation of Jews in order to identify them for discrimination. There was no authentic scientific way to detect the racial nature of a Jew, so the Nazis had to resort to using birth and baptismal records. A German could provide proof of not being a Jew through the records of four grandparents, two parents, and the person himself or herself. The churches often collaborated with the **Third Reich** in determining who was a Jew by supplying baptismal records.

SUGGESTED READING: Daniel Jonah Goldhagen, *Hitler's Willing Executioners* (New York: Knopf, 1996); Saul Friedlander, *Nazi Germany and the Jews* (New York: HarperCollins, 1997).

NUREMBERG WAR CRIMES TRIALS. Twenty-four top Nazis stood before an International Military Tribunal at the Nuremberg Palace of Justice on November 20, 1945. They were charged with waging aggressive war; the arrest, **deportation**, and enslavement of millions; and **crimes against humanity**. The latter charge included the **genocide** of six million Jews. The prosecutors and judges were from the victorious Allies in World War II: Great Britain, France, the Soviet Union, and the United States. The trial lasted 21 days and the proceedings filled 17,000 pages. Various treaties Germany had signed, including the Hague and Geneva Conventions—all of which the **Nazis** had broken—were produced as evidence. **Heinrich Himmler**, **Robert Ley** (who committed suicide before the trials), and **Hermann Goering** cheated the hangman's noose. Ten others were executed on October 16, 1946, while the rest received prison sentences.

Under U.S. jurisdiction and judges, 12 Subsequent Nuremberg War Crimes Trials followed at the Palace of Justice at Nuremberg between 1946 and 1949, involving **SS** officers, collaborators, physicians, and industrialists who were tried for crimes ranging from waging aggressive war and violating international law concerning soldiers and civilians to crimes against humanity (maltreatment of minorities). Most notable among these additional trials were the Medical Trial, the **I. G. Farben** Trial, the Justice Trial, and the **Einsatzgruppen** Trial. While most of the defendants were convicted, because of Cold War politics John McCloy, the U.S. high commissioner for Germany, pardoned or commuted the sentences of many of those. The trials were unprecedented in that individuals were held responsible as **war criminals** or for crimes against innocent civilians. *See also* FRANK, HANS; LAMMERS, HANS HEINRICH; SAUCKEL, FRITZ; SPEER, ALBERT; STREICHER, JULIUS.

SUGGESTED READING: Whitney R. Harris, *Tyranny on Trial* (New York: Barnes & Noble, 1995); The Avalon Project at Yale Law School, *Trial of the Major War Criminals Before the International Military Tribunal*, http://www.yale.edu/lawweb/avalon/imt/imt.htm.

NYE, GERALD (1892–1971). U.S. senator (R-ND), 1925–45. Nye was the Senate's leading isolationist, associated with the **America First Committee**. In August 1941, Nye, along with Champ Clark (D-MO), Burton Wheeler (D-MT), and other senators, launched an investigation of Hollywood's film industry. They legitimized their **antisemitism** by claiming that Hollywood was "dedicated to warmongering, that it constituted a Jewish-controlled monopoly, and that it was engaged in covert dealings with the [**Franklin**] **Roosevelt** administration." Ironically, after the United States entered World War II, Nye and other isolationists promptly enlisted Hollywood to develop films about the **Nazis**.

SUGGESTED READING: Michael E. Birdwell, *Celluloid Soldiers: Warner Bros.'s Campaign against Nazism* (New York: New York University Press, 1999).

– O –

OATHS, JEWISH. Statements required of Jews and converts from Judaism; originally established by Emperor **Justinian** in 540. The idea was based on the concept that no **heretic** could be believed in court against a Christian. The Jewish **convert** was required to renounce the "errors of our fathers" and to undertake not to

> associate with the accursed Jews who remain unbaptized . . . the evil tradition.
> . . . I will never return to the vomit of Jewish superstition, the vomit of my former error, or [associate] with the wicked Jews. . . . If I wander from the straight path
> . . . I shall be handed over to the eternal fire, in the company of the Devil . . .
> sharing . . . with **Judas [Iscariot]** the punishment of burning.

Various methods were used to ensure that the Jew was telling the truth. These included swearing on an opened Torah scroll while standing on a bloody **pigskin** or while wearing a belt of thorns, or even standing on a stool wearing a **Jew hat**. In 1555 the oath became standardized throughout Europe; in Romania, it was not totally abolished until 1914.

SUGGESTED READING: Jacob Marcus, *The Jew in the Medieval World: A Source Book, 315–1791* (New York: New York University Press, 1979).

OBERAMMERGAU. Traditional **passion play**. This pageant depicts the last days of the life of Jesus. It was first performed in 1634—and repeated every decade—following a vow taken by the residents of Oberammergau, Bavaria, thanking God for being spared the Black Death, at the time striking nearby Munich. The play originally portrayed Jews as sinister **Christ-killers**. Four times, actors cried out, "May His blood be on us and our children!" Caiaphas, the high priest, had horns. **Judas Iscariot** was bedecked in yellow (considered an outcast color), and the Jews were shown as hostile and menacing to Jesus. **Adolf Hitler** praised the play "as a convincing portrayal of the menace of Jewry" and admired it as **Aryan** peasant art and culture. Hitler approved the special tricentennial jubilee performances in 1934. Because of World War II, the play was not again performed until 1950. Jews and others denounced the portrayals of the high priest and members of the Jewish **Sanhedrin** as **antisemitic** stereotypes. Beginning in 1960, reforms were made in the performances of the eight-hour passion play. In 1970, the playing time was reduced to five hours. In 2010 the Oberammergau Passion Play will have new sets and costumes.

SUGGESTED READING: James Shapiro, *Oberammergau: The Troubling Story of the World's Most Famous Passion Play* (New York: Vintage, 2001).

OCTOBER ROUNDUP, ROME. Italy was occupied by German troops after September 8, 1943. **Benito Mussolini** had been overthrown, but then rescued by the Germans and set up near Lake Como. The **SS**-backed **Fascist** government thereafter sought to **deport** Jews from Italy. The Germans had anticipated that Pope **Pius XII**, as bishop of Rome, would lead the way and publicly protest against German deportation of the Jews of Rome. However, at a time when he knew that arrest was a prelude to the mass murder of Jews, the pope refused to enter any public protest when in October 1943 the Germans rounded up the Jews of Rome. Ironically, had Pius taken an assertive stance in trying to prevent the roundup of Roman Jews, he apparently would have gotten support from the local German authorities, none of whom wanted a **pogrom** against the Jewish community that would result in their deportation and death. On October 16, Pius ordered **Vatican** secretary of state Giuseppe Maglione to discuss the Roman raid with German ambassador Ernst von Weizsäcker. Maglione noted that the pope was being "cautious so as not to give the German people the impression that [he] has done or has wished to do even the smallest thing against Germany during this terrible war." **Heinrich Himmler** issued no stop order; on the contrary, the arrests of Italian Jews continued on the very

next day. The SS deported 1,259 Jews. *See also* MANIFESTO OF RA-
CIAL SCIENTISTS.

SUGGESTED READING: Susan Zuccotti, *Under His Very Windows: The
Vatican and the Holocaust in Italy* (New Haven, CT: Yale University Press,
2000); Meir Michaelis, *Mussolini and the Jews: German Italian Relations
and the Jewish Question in Italy, 1922–1945* (New York: Oxford University Press, 1978).

ODESSA POGROMS. Odessa, a Black Sea port in the Ukraine, was the site
of many **pogroms** during the reign of the tsars. By 1905, the year of the
largest pogrom, Jews constituted one-third of the city's diverse population
of 403,000. There were clashes between the anti-tsarist revolutionary
groups, in which Jews were overrepresented, and the patriotic conservative
right wing, complicated by the enmity between Jewish and Greek businessmen. The Russian Army garrison was not activated quickly or efficiently
to quell the violence. More than 400 Jews were killed between October 18
and 22, 1905, while 1,500 Jewish properties were gutted. The pogroms
encouraged the growth of Jewish self-defense, the Zionist movement, and
Jewish migration to the United States. *See also* BLACK HUNDREDS; KI-
SHINEV.

SUGGESTED READING: Patricia Herlsky, *Odessa: A History, 1794–1914*
(Cambridge, MA: Harvard University Press, 1986); Michael Lynch, *Reaction and Revolutionaries in Russia, 1881–1924* (London: Hodder, 2005);
Robert Weinberg, "The Pogrom of 1905 in Odessa: A Case Study," in *Pogroms: Anti-Jewish Violence in Modern Russian History*, ed. John D. Klier
and Shlomo Lambroza (Cambridge: Cambridge University Press, 1992).

ODO (c. 1208–1273). Bishop of Chateauroux and papal legate to the king
of France. Odo headed a papal commission evaluating the **Talmud**. He
concluded that the Talmud "contained so many unspeakable insults that it
arouses shame in those who read it, and horror in those who hear it"; containing "errors, abuses, blasphemies, and wickness" and injurious to the
Christian faith, these talmudic books are essentially **heretical** and deserve
to be burned, which he ordered in 1248.

SUGGESTED READING: Jacob Rader Marcus, *The Jew in the Medieval
World: A Source Book, 315–1791* (Cincinnati, OH: Hebrew Union College
Press, 1999).

OESTERREICHISCHER BEOBACHTER. Viennese newspaper, **Austria**'s
most prestigious. On March 4, 1934, with Austria still independent from
Germany, it urged that Jews be removed from leading positions in Austria.

SUGGESTED READING: Bruce Pauley, *From Prejudice to Persecution: A History of Austrian Antisemitism* (Chapel Hill: University of North Carolina Press, 1998).

OFFENSIVE WORDS FOR JEWS. Some of the most popular slurs for Jews around the world include the Dutch *smous*, English *kike*, French *you-pin*, German *Jude*, Greek *Ellenike*, Italian *giudeo*, Palestinian Arabic *al Halsuada* (evil dogs), Polish *Zhid*, Portuguese *judeu*, Russian *Yevryee*, Spanish *judío*, and Swedish *jude*.
SUGGESTED READING: "List of Ethnic Slurs," *Wikipedia*, http://en.wikipedia.org/wiki/List_of_ethnic_slurs.

OFFICE OF WAR INFORMATION (OWI). During World War II, this U.S. organization led the way in reporting stories, even concerning mass murder; the secular press usually followed. But OWI, working in collaboration with the **Franklin D. Roosevelt** administration, tried to suppress news concerning anti-Jewish atrocities. When John Pehle's **War Refugee Board** released some stories about **Auschwitz** in November 1944, Elmer Davis, the head of OWI, complained bitterly. Several broadcasts to Europe were also canceled when it was discovered that they included references to the **Final Solution**. The OWI's censorship of Jewish news may have been why no reporter asked the president at his twice-weekly news conferences about the **Nazi** Final Solution; nor did Roosevelt address the issue until March 1944, when most of the **Holocaust**'s Jewish victims were already dead. The OWI claimed that if the Jewish predicament were exposed and treated with sympathy, then it could hurt American war interests in occupied countries, where a high level of native anti-Jewish feeling existed. *See also* EVIDENCE OF THE HOLOCAUST, SUPPRESSION OF.
SUGGESTED READING: Deborah Lipstadt, *Beyond Belief* (New York: Free Press, 1999).

OHLENDORFF, OTTO (1907–1951). German lawyer and **SS** general. As commander of the mobile killing squad **Einsatzgruppe** D, Ohlendorf was responsible for the murder of more than 90,000 Jews. He was the chief defendant at the Einsatzgruppen Trial of the Subsequent **Nuremberg War Crimes Trials** and was sentenced to death in 1951.
SUGGESTED READING: Yitzhad Arad et al., eds., *The Einsatzgruppen Reports* (New York: Holocaust Library, 1989).

OKHRANA. Tsarist secret political police unit charged to spy and apprehend citizens whom it considered dangerous to the state. It was started by

Tsar **Alexander III** in 1881 and directed against revolutionaries. Having extralegal powers, the Okhrana could execute suspects or deport them to prison camps. It employed informers and double agents, who often provoked violence and revolutionary activity. The Okhrana penetrated the **Bund**. Its agents in Paris during the **Dreyfus** Trial composed a forgery from French sources, *The Protocols of the Elders of Zion*, the notorious **antisemitic** work, and publicized it.

SUGGESTED READING: Norman Cohn, *Warrant for Genocide* (London: Serif, 1996).

OLYMPIC GAMES, BERLIN. On August 1, 1936, **Adolf Hitler** opened the summer Olympic Games in Berlin. During the Olympics, the **Third Reich** muted its anti-Jewish propaganda. **Antisemitic** signs were taken down, and the Nazi-controlled press refrained from public attacks on Jews, although German Jews had been excluded from official German sports and from competition. A movement to boycott the event failed. In the United States, Avery Brundage, president of the U.S. Olympic Committee, stated that Jewish athletes in Germany were treated fairly and insisted on U.S. participation. Brundage dismissively described the plight of Jews in Germany as "the present Jew-Nazi altercation." He claimed that opposition to U.S. participation in the Berlin Olympics was "a Jewish-Communist conspiracy" to "make the American athlete a martyr to a cause not his own." Even after Hitler blatantly exploited the games for propaganda purposes, and even after the Nazis' demand for the U.S. team to bar two U.S. Jewish track stars from competing (which Brundage accepted), Brundage continued to insist that the games had contributed to "international peace and harmony." Soon after the Olympics ended, persecution of the Jews recommenced.

SUGGESTED READING: Susan D. Bachrach, *Nazi Olympics: Berlin 1936* (Boston: Little, Brown, 2000).

OLYMPIC GAMES, MUNICH. Scene of terrorist attack. On September 6, 1972, 11 Israeli athletes were murdered at the Munich Olympic Village. The perpetrators were a Palestinian group called **Black September**. When the members of the Israeli wrestling team were taken hostage, a German SWAT team tried but failed to stop the kidnappers. A one-day Olympic memorial stoppage ensued, but Avery Brundage, head of the International Olympic Committee, insisted the games continue. Later, the Israeli Mossad launched a secret strike force that ferreted out and eliminated all but one of the eight killers. *See also* ARAFAT, YASSIR.

SUGGESTED READING: Simon Rieve, *One Day in September: The Full Story of the 1972 Munich Olympic Massacre and the Israeli Revenge Operation, "Wrath of God"* (New York: Arcade Publishing, 2001).

OMAR, PACT OF. Restrictive rules for non-Muslims issued by Caliph Omar I in Arabia in 638. Christians and Jews were to live under Muslim rule with religious freedom, unmolested. Since these minorities were "People of the Book," they were to be protected **dhimmis**. However, they were subjected to certain Islamic prohibitions. Omar II in 1717–20 crystallized the Pact: For Jews, no new **synagogues**, no Muslim slaves or employees, no horses, no military arms, and no authority over a Muslim. Jews had to wear distinctive dress, often **yellow** garb. A special poll **tax** (*jizya*) had to be paid. These rules were inconsistently enforced.

SUGGESTED READING: Mark R. Cohen, *Under Crescent and Cross: The Jews in the Middle Ages* (Princeton, NJ: Princeton University Press, 1994).

ON THE JEWS AND THEIR LIES (DIE JUDEN UND IHREN LÜGEN). Book written in 1543 by **Martin Luther** as he grew increasingly impatient that Jews would not **convert** to his brand of Christianity. This work is particularly vituperative. It was quoted by **antisemitic** editor **Julius Streicher** at the **Nuremberg War Crimes Trials** in justifying his actions. In it, Luther urges burning Jewish **synagogues**, razing and destroying Jewish houses, taking away Jewish prayer books and the **Talmud**, forbidding rabbis to teach, banning Jews from travel, and forcing them to do hard physical labor. In another section of the book, he advocated **expulsion**, and, if that did not work, he condoned mass murder.

SUGGESTED READING: Heiko Oberman, *The Roots of Antisemitism in the Age of Renaissance and Reformation* (Philadelphia: Fortress Press, 1981).

OPERATION REINHARD. Nazi **genocidal** program of revenge. This plan was named after Security Chief **Reinhard Heydrich** soon after he was assassinated in Prague in 1942. Jews were **deported** from Lublin, Poland, and their property plundered. As a result, the death camps **Sobibor**, **Belzec**, and Treblinka—Operation Reinhard camps—were established to facilitate this part of the **Holocaust**.

SUGGESTED READING: Yitzhak Arad, *Belzec, Sobibor, Treblinka: The Operation Reinhard Camps* (Bloomington: Indiana University Press, 1987).

ORDER, THE. *See* SILENT BROTHERHOOD.

ORDER OF SEVENTY-SIX. *See* SECRET ORGANIZATIONS, 20TH CENTURY.

OREGLIA, GIUSEPPE. Italian **Jesuit** priest. In the late 19th century, in the Jesuit journal *Civiltà Cattolica*, Oreglia argued that Pope **Innocent IV**'s 13th-century skepticism in regard to Jewish **ritual murder** was in error since the pope was ignorant of the fact that the Jews consumed Christian children's blood while leaving the hearts intact. He **defamed** Jews as capable of any crime, any sin. Oreglia fantasized that Jews ritualistically mixed blood with wine and flour to make the Passover ceremony valid, that Jews needed Christian blood for other religious ceremonies, and that during **Purim** each Jew was allowed to get drunk and kill one Christian.

SUGGESTED READING: Andrew M. Canepa, "Cattolici ed Ebrei nell'Italia Liberale," *Comunità* 32 (April 1978); David I. Kertzer, *The Popes against the Jews* (New York: Knopf, 2001).

O'REILLY, BILL (1949–). Fox network radio and television personality. On the December 3, 2004, broadcast of the nationally syndicated *The Radio Factor with Bill O'Reilly*, O'Reilly engaged in a dialogue with a Jewish caller, during which O'Reilly said:

> All right. Well, what I'm tellin' you, [caller], is I think you're takin' it too seriously. You have a predominantly Christian nation. You have a federal holiday based on the philosopher Jesus. And you don't wanna hear about it? Come on, [caller]—if you are really offended, you gotta go to Israel then. I mean because we live in a country founded on Judeo—and that's your guys'—Christian, that's my guys', philosophy. But overwhelmingly, America is Christian. And the holiday is a federal holiday honoring the philosopher Jesus. So, you don't wanna hear about it? Impossible. And that is an affront to the majority. You know, the majority can be insulted, too. And that's what this anti-Christmas thing is all about.

A few days later, on the December 9 program, O'Reilly called Media Matters in America (a watchdog group that monitors **antisemitism** in the media) "the most vile, despicable human beings in the country"; the **Anti-Defamation League**, "an extremist group that finds offense in pretty much everything"; and ADL president Abraham Foxman "a nut." On December 15, O'Reilly called Media Matters in America "character assassins," adding, "You guys really are despicable weasels."

On February 26, 2004, on *The O'Reilly Factor*, a television program on the Fox News Network, during an interview with Mel Gibson in regard to the movie *The Passion of the Christ*, O'Reilly defended Gibson, saying: "OK, it's a very, very difficult question. And I'm asking this question respectfully. Is it because . . . the major media in Hollywood and a lot of the secular press is controlled by Jewish people?"

SUGGESTED READING: Peter Hart, *The Oh Really? Factor: Unspinning Fox News Channel's Bill O'Reilly* (New York: Seven Stories Press, 2003);

National Jewish Democratic Council, "Conservative Pundit Bill O'Reilly Discusses Jewish Control of Media," 2004, http://njdc.org/emet/detail .php?id=361; "O'Reilly to Jewish Caller: 'If You Are Really Offended, You Gotta Go to Israel,'" Media Matters for America, 2004, http://media matters.org/items/200412070004; "O'Reilly Attacked *Media Matters*: 'The Most Vile, Despicable Human Beings in the Country'; Called ADL President 'a Nut,'" Media Matters for America, 2004, http://media matters.org/items/200412100002; Eric Boehlert, "The Grinch Who Saved Christmas," *Salon.com*, 2004, http://www.salon.com/news/feature/2004/ 12/16/grinch/index_np.html; Steve Rendall, "The Mainstreaming of Anti-Semitism," *Extra!* (May–June 2005), http://www.fair.org/index.php?page =2535; National Jewish Democratic Council, "Bill O'Reilly to Jewish Caller: 'If You Are Really Offended, You Gotta Go to Israel,' More," *News Digest*, December 8, 2004, http://209.59.159.153/newsdigest/detail .php?id=423; "Battle Lines Drawn between O'Reilly and Rich," *News-Max.com*, March 11, 2004, http://www.newsmax.com/archives/ic/2004/3/ 11/171859.shtml.

OREMUS. Latin for "Let us pray." The prayer that starts the **Good Friday** liturgy, instructing the faithful to pray for the welfare of other Christians and for God's help in ending evil in the world. Prayers for **heretics**, schismatics, pagans, and Jews follow. The tone is conciliatory and mild except toward the Jews. The faithful are instructed to **genuflect** and say "Amen" at the conclusion of each of these prayers, but not after the prayer for the Jews. The Oremus singles out the "**perfidious**" Jews for special treatment. Pope **John XXIII** had this bias in the prayer removed. *See also* AMULO.

SUGGESTED READING: Shlomo Simonsohn, *The Apostolic See and the Jews: History* (Toronto: Pontifical Institute of Mediaeval Studies, 1991).

ORGANIZATION FOR SECURITY AND COOPERATION IN EUROPE (OSCE). *See* ANTISEMITISM, WORKING DEFINITION OF; BERLIN DECLARATION.

ORIGEN (184–253). Alexandrian **Church Father**. Origen perceived Jews as hating their neighbors and the law. He believed that God punished the Jews with perpetual slavery for the murder of the Christian **messiah**. The Jews will never regain their former situation, since "they committed a despicable crime by conspiring against the savior of humankind."

SUGGESTED READING: *Contra Celsum* 4, 22, in *Patrologiae, Cursus Completus: Series Graeca*, ed. Jacques-Paul Migne (Paris: Garnier, 1857–66), 11:1060.

ORION. Neo-Nazi, white supremacist, **Ku Klux Klan, Christian Identity**, and racist **skinhead** acronym for "Our Race Is Our Nation." This racist slogan emphasizes the paramount importance of racial ties compared to national or other identifications.

SUGGESTED READING: Anti-Defamation League, *Hate on Display: Extremist Symbols, Logos, and Tattoos* (New York: Anti-Defamation League, 2006).

ORLÉANS, THIRD SYNOD OF. Church conclave in France in 538. It ruled that Jews were not allowed to employ Christian servants or to possess Christian slaves. During the early Middle Ages, the good relations that sometimes existed between Jews and Christians troubled Churchmen, and several Church councils ordered the isolation of Jews from Christians in order to prevent such positive interaction. *See also* LAODICEA, COUNCIL OF; NICAEA, COUNCIL OF; OXFORD, COUNCIL OF.

SUGGESTED READING: William Nichols, *Christian Antisemitism: A History of Hate* (Northvale, NJ: Jason Aronson, 1995).

OSSERVATORE ROMANO, L'. Official newspaper of the **Vatican**. It joined **Civiltà Cattolica** in expressing anti-Jewish themes beginning with the last decade of the 19th century. In 1892, *L'Osservatore Romano* warned the Jews that "they had better beware, for . . . God would inevitably grow intolerant of their behavior and then people's patience would be at an end. Then disturbances and horrible crimes could result, but who will be responsible [if not the Jews themselves]?" During this same period, the apostolic nuncio (**Vatican** diplomat) to France made an equally disturbing threat when he wrote that "the Jewish danger is everywhere, it threatens all of Christianity . . . and all means should be used to crush it. . . . The Catholic Church has reserved special indulgences for those who, when the good cause demands it, spill the blood of Jews and pagans."

SUGGESTED READING: David I. Kertzer, *The Popes against the Jews* (New York: Knopf, 2001).

OSTJUDEN. The German term for Eastern Europe Jews. Assimilated German Jews (*Westjuden*), like their assimilated liberal French, English, and **Austrian** brethren, regarded their unassimilated Ostjuden coreligionists warily, concerned that their traditional lifestyle, Yiddish language, and Hassidic Judaism—that is, their refusal to assimilate or modernize—would endanger the vain Jewish hope for acceptance by German society. **Antisemites** regarded Ostenjuden with even more horror than they regarded assimilated Jews.

SUGGESTED READING: Amos Elon, *The Pity of It All: A Portrait of the German-Jewish Epoch* (New York: Picarda, 2002).

OSWEGO. From August 1944 to February 1946, Fort Ontario at Oswego, NY, was the site of the only U.S. refugee center established during World War II. The 874 Jews and 108 other nationalities were kept under guard and behind barbed wire. It was initially intended that they should be returned to their nations of origin. The U.S. government was bombarded by letters of complaint from local residents about the Jews interned at the camp. The temporary acceptance of these refugees was a small part of the efforts of the **War Refugee Board** and was supported by Harold Ickes, secretary of the interior. After the war ended, President **Harry Truman** allowed the refugees to remain in the U.S. as citizens.

SUGGESTED READING: David Wyman, *The Abandonment of the Jews* (New York: Free Press, 1995); Ruth Gruber, *Haven* (New York: Random House, 2000).

OTHALA RUNE. Norse/Viking rune. **Neo-Nazi** symbol. **Nazi** Germany glorified an idealized "**Aryan**/Norse" heritage; consequently extremists have appropriated many symbols from pagan Europe for their own uses. They give such symbols a racist significance, even though the symbols did not originally have such meaning and are often used by nonracists today, especially practitioners of modern pagan religions.

SUGGESTED READING: Anti-Defamation League, *Hate on Display: Extremist Symbols, Logos, and Tattoos* (New York: Anti-Defamation League, 2006).

OUR DEMANDS ON MODERN JEWRY. See STÖCKER, ADOLF.

OVEN DODGER. (Australian slur) Reference to Jews who survived the Nazi **Holocaust**.

SUGGESTED READING: "List of Ethnic Slurs," *Wikipedia*, http://en.wikipedia.org/wiki/List_of_ethnic_slurs.

OXFORD, COUNCIL OF. Church council in 1222 that prohibited the construction of new **synagogues**.

SUGGESTED READING: William Nichols, *Christian Anti-Semitism: A History of Hate* (Northvale, NJ: Jason Aronson, 1995).

OXFORD ENGLISH DICTIONARY. The foremost dictionary of the English language lists dozens of historical examples of the use of the words

Jew and *Jewish*. Fully half the definitions are offensive; for example, a *Jew* is a "grasping or extortionate money-lender or **usurer**" and *to Jew* is to cheat. Historically oriented dictionaries in French (Émile Littré's *Dictionnaire de la langue française*), German (the **Grimm** Brothers' *Deutsches Wörterbuch*), Portuguese (Célia Szniter Mentlik, "História, linguagem e preconceito: Ressonâncias do período inquisitorial sobre o mundo contemporâneo," *Revista História Hoje* 2, no. 5 [November 2004]), and other languages reflect the same definitions, and worse.

– P –

PAINE, THOMAS (1737–1809). Anglo-American political theorist and writer. Weaving together an assault on ecclesiastical Christianity and an even stronger attack on Judaism and Jews, Paine held that "Christian priests [were only] sometimes as corrupt and often as cruel" as their Jewish counterparts. Paine stereotyped the nature of all Jews from the alleged behavior of some, 3,000 years earlier. He wrote that the Jewish Bible was chock full of "lies, wickedness, and blasphemy" and that Jews were thoroughly evil. In 1775 Paine retold "The Monk and the Jew," a story of a Jew forced into **conversion** to Catholicism and then drowned so that he would not return to Judaism. Although apparently a satire on Catholicism, Paine ridiculed the Jewish victim, using Yiddish-accented English.

SUGGESTED READING: Louis Harap, *The Image of the Jew in American Literature* (Syracuse, NY: Syracuse University Press, 2003).

PALE OF SETTLEMENT. Area restricted for Russian Jews. In 1794 Tsarina Catherine II inherited a huge tract of land that was once part of the Polish kingdom, where great numbers of Jews lived. It extended from the Baltic Sea to the Black Sea, encompassing Russia's 25 western provinces and about 396,000 square miles. Jews could not travel or live outside it without permission. Jewish occupations were restricted to commerce and crafts. Jews developed a degree of self-government and used Yiddish as their main language. Under various tsars, the Pale was either expanded or contracted. In 1915, faced with invading German armies, Tsar **Nicholas II** ordered huge areas of Jews evacuated because he distrusted their loyalty, thus causing a de facto end to much of the Pale. It was officially dissolved with the revolutionary Provisional Government in 1917. *See also* ALEXANDER II; ALEXANDER III (TSAR); ELIZABETH II; MAY LAWS; NICHOLAS I.

SUGGESTED READING: Simon Dubnow and Israel Friedlaender, *History of the Jews in Russia and Poland* (Bergenfield, NJ: Avotaynu, 2000).

PALESTINE LIBERATION ORGANIZATION. *See* ARAFAT, YASSIR.

PALESTINE MUSLIM BROTHERHOOD. *See* HAMAS; MUSLIM BROTHERHOOD.

PALT, JOHANNES VON. Erfurt (Germany) Augustinian Magister (one who makes spells). In the early 16th century, Palt accused the Jews of knowingly and willingly torturing Christ.

PAMYAT. (Russian) People's National Patriotic Orthodox Christian Union. Drawing on **antisemitic, xenophobic**, and monarchist elements, Pamyat ("Memory") was organized in 1985 by Demitri Vassilyev. Its slogan was "God, Tsar, and Nation." *Zionists*—the code word for Jews—were blamed for the **Bolshevik** Revolution, **Joseph Stalin**'s excesses, and Russia's social ills. The Soviet state was termed a "Zionist-Occupied Government." Pamyat reinvigorated *The Protocols of the Elders of Zion*. With the death of its two dynamic leaders, the organization faded away in 1999 in numbers and relevance. *See also* BLACK HUNDREDS.

SUGGESTED READING: William Korey, *Russian Antisemitism, Pamyat and the Demonology of Zionism* (Chur, Switzerland: Harwood Academic Publishers, 1995).

PANAMA CANAL SCANDAL. The French failed venture to build a Panama canal in 1888–89. Tropical disease, insufficient funds, defaulted loans, and bankruptcy of the venture company led to the ruin of investors. Some well-known Jews were involved, providing grist for conspiratorial **antisemitism** in France.

SUGGESTED READING: David Vital, *A People Apart: A Political History of the Jews in Europe, 1789–1939* (New York: Oxford University Press, 1999).

PANCAKES. (U.S. slur) Reference to the Jewish skullcap (yarmulke), or the Jewish food item, *latkes*.

SUGGESTED READING: "List of Ethnic Slurs," *Wikipedia*, http://en.wiki pedia.org/wiki/List_of_ethnic_slurs.

PAN-GERMAN LEAGUE. Expansionist, racist, **antisemitic** organization founded in 1896. Henrich Class (Daniel Frymann, 1868–1953), president of the league in Germany became enamored with the **Aryan** superiority ideas of Frenchman **Arthur de Gobineau**, except he applied them to German racial superiority. Made up largely of schoolteachers, the league, which lasted until 1914, blamed Jews for Germany's problems because of supposed Jewish opposition to militarism and expansion. One symbol used by the Pan-German League showed a Jew hanging from gallows. The league favored uniting all German-speaking peoples, colonial expansion, and putting an end to Jewish immigration, as well as making Jews resident aliens. It also opposed Jewish-Christian **marriages**.

SUGGESTED READING: Mildred S. Wertheimer, *The Pan German League, 1890–1914* (New York: Columbia University Press, 1924).

PAN-SLAVISM. 19th-century Russian intellectual movement to unite all Slavic peoples. Nationalists wanted to unite Slavs in the Austro-Hungarian Empire and Ottoman Empire with Russia. Their efforts led to Balkan wars and triggered World War I. It led to extreme nationalism and intolerance of non-Slavic minorities, such as the Jews, who lacked a "Slavic soul." The victorious **Bolsheviks** renounced it in 1917.

SUGGESTED READING: Hans Kohn, *Pan Slavism: Its History and Ideology* (Notre Dame, IN: University of Notre Dame Press, 1953).

PAPAL ANTI-JEWISH RHETORIC, MEDIEVAL. The 13th and 14th centuries alone indicate the extent to which the popes denigrated the Jews in their letters to a variety of Christian princes and Catholic hierarchs, calling them "the sons of the crucifiers, against whom to this day the blood cries to the Father's ears," "slaves rejected by God, in whose death they wickedly conspired," a "deadly weed," and a "dangerous sickness"; decrying the "damned faithlessness of the Jews" and their "malicious deceit"; and disparaging their "accursed rite" and "death-dealing study [and] poisonous diet."

SUGGESTED READING: Shlomo Simonsohn, *The Apostolic See and the Jews: Documents, 492–1404* (Toronto: Pontifical Institute of Mediaeval Studies, 1988).

PAPAL JEWISH POLICY. As represented by the popes' decrees, pronouncements, encyclicals, bulls, letters, and **canon law** (*corpus juris canonici*), the policy of the popes toward the Jews influenced medieval secular law. The three bases of early papal Jewish policy were **St. Augustine**'s theological construct, the "Witness People"; the fading influence of Roman law; and the arbitrary exercise of "Christian mercy and pity."

However, protection was set aside when Jews did not suffer to the degree they "should."

Since the Middle Ages, the papacy has associated Jews with everything it hated about modern liberal society: freedom of speech and religion, legal equality, and respect for the rights of others. Using the Catholic press to revive traditional defamations such as the **ritual murder** charge, and cozying up to **fascist** regimes as dams against liberalism, the Holy See fought what it considered "Jewish capitalism" as well as "Jewish **bolshevism**." The papacy's traditional **antisemitism**, the most deep-seated of any Western institution's, made the Church the natural ally of fascist regimes and prepared the faithful to be their supporters. In 1894 Father Henri Delassus wrote in a well-known French Catholic weekly that "antisemitism and Catholicism are one and the same thing"; in 1911, Pope **Pius X** appointed him apostolic prothonotary (first officer of the papal court) and monsignor, and later personally congratulated him on his golden anniversary as a priest. Despite proclamations to the contrary, the 20th-century popes before **John XXIII** still believed that the Jews were **Christ-killers** with no fundamental right to reside among Christians. Like their medieval counterparts, popes **Pius XI** and **Pius XII** adhered to a Jewish policy that mixed *Realpolitik* with half-hearted protection and degradation of Jews, a program rooted in the basic canons of the Church's anti-Jewish theology. *See also* DECLARATION ON THE RELATIONSHIP OF THE CHURCH TO NON-CHRISTIAN RELIGIONS.

SUGGESTED READING: Shlomo Simonsohn, *The Apostolic See and the Jews: Documents, 492–1404* (Toronto: Pontifical Institute of Mediaeval Studies, 1988); David I. Kertzer, *The Popes against the Jews* (New York: Knopf, 2001).

PAPAL STATES. European territories under the rule of the popes between 754 and 1870. The territories varied in size, but were most located in Italy, with some in France. Jews of the Papal States were generally confined to **ghettos**, were forced to listen to Christianizing **sermons** and to wear **stigmatic emblems**, and were subject to ownership restrictions, **Talmud** burning, and **expulsion**. Jews in the 19th-century Papal States lived as though they were still in the Middle Ages: restricted to ghettos; forced to wear **Jew badges**, prohibited from social relations with Christians; and forbidden to own property, to enter the professions or university, or to travel without permission. *See also* MORTARA ABDUCTION CASE; PAUL IV; PIUS IX; TAXATION OF JEWS.

SUGGESTED READING: David I. Kertzer, *The Popes against the Jews* (New York: Knopf, 2001).

PARASITISM CHARGE. One of dozens of antisemitic **defamations**. It states that Jews do not contribute real productive work for the betterment of society; rather, they scheme to defraud Gentiles.

SUGGESTED READING: Bernard Lewis, *Semites and Anti-Semites: An Inquiry into Conflict and Prejudice* (New York: Norton, 1986).

PARIS, MATTHEW (1200–1259). English Benedictine monk and chronicler. Paris claimed that Jews tortured and crucified "Little St. Hugh," an alleged victim of Jewish **ritual murder**. He noted that the Jews had collaborated in their crime with Jews in "almost all the cities of England" and that they tortured and had "crucified [Hugh] in contempt and reproach of Jesus Christ."

SUGGESTED READING: Gavin Langmuir, *Toward a Definition of Antisemitism* (Berkeley: University of California Press, 1996).

PARIS MERCHANTS GUILD. Association of Christian merchants. Six **guilds** in 1777 petitioned King Louis XV to deny Jews entry into France. They claimed Jews cooperated with each other, "running together like quicksilver," thus creating unfair competition.

PARTI POPULAIRE FRANÇAISE. Working-class pro-**Nazi**, **antisemitic** party in France, 1936–45. Its founder, Jacques Doriot (1898–1945), was once an active Communist. This organization sought to wean Frenchmen away from the Communists. It helped round up Jews for **deportation** and became an arm of **Klaus Barbie**'s **Gestapo** during the Nazi occupation of France.

SUGGESTED READING: David Littleton, *Foreign Legions of the Third Reich* (San Jose, CA: James Bender, 1998).

PASSAU DESECRATION. In 1478 in Passau, Bavaria, Jews were accused of conspiring with Jews in Prague and Regensburg in the **desecration of the Hosts**. Jews were called "avaricious dogs" and "blasphemers of God [who] crucif[ied God] with savage eagerness." The Jews of Passau were executed, **baptized**, or expelled. The "miracle" of Passau was that the Host was not—could not be—destroyed by Jews. The reports of Jewish profanation of the Host were, however, fundamentally based on Christian theological anti-Jewishness. *See also* DEFAMATIONS, ANTI-JEWISH.

SUGGESTED READING: Jacob Marcus, *The Jew in the Medieval World: A Source Book, 315–1791* (New York: New York University Press, 1979).

PASSING OF A GREAT RACE. *See* GRANT, MADISON.

PASSION PLAYS. In these religious Christian plays in Europe. Jews were portrayed as morally blind, deceitful, **perfidious**, damned murderers, **Judases** who were traitors for money, cohorts of the Devil. *See also* MYSTERY PLAYS; OBERAMMERGAU.

SUGGESTED READING: Leonard J. Greenspoon, ed., *Representations of Jews through the Ages* (Omaha, NE: Creighton University Press, 1996).

PASSOW, HILDEGARD. Leader of the **Nazi** Women's Organization *Nationalsozialistische Frauenschaft*, 1933–45. Passow noted that "at no time does the Lord God require of us charitable conciliation with the Jews, the moral enemy of the **Aryan** character. Christ himself called the Jews 'the sons of the Devil, a brood of snakes,' and drove the dealers and money-changers from the house of God with a whip."

SUGGESTED READING: Cate Haste, *Nazi Women: Hitler's Seduction of a Nation* (London: Channel 4 Books, 2001); Jill Stephenson, *Women in Nazi Germany* (New York: Longman, 2001); Michael Kater, "Everyday Anti-semitism in Prewar Nazi Germany: The Popular Bases," *Yad Vashem Studies* 16 (1984).

PASTOUREAUX. *See* SHEPHERDS' CRUSADE.

PASTRAMI EATER. (U.S. slur) Reference to the cured beef widely served by Jewish delicatessens.

SUGGESTED READING: "List of Ethnic Slurs," *Wikipedia*, http://en.wiki pedia.org/wiki/List_of_ethnic_slurs.

PATTON, GEORGE S. (1885–1945). U.S. Army general in World War II. When Patton received a report about Jewish survivors, Patton wrote in his diary:

> We frequently have to use force in order to prevent the inmates—Germans, Jews and other people—from defecating on the floor when ample facilities are provided outside. . . . Evidently the virus started by [Treasury Secretary] Henry Morgenthau and [**Franklin Roosevelt** advisor] **Bernard Baruch** of a Semitic revenge against all Germans is still working. [Jew lovers?] believe that the Displaced Person is a human being which he is not, and this applies particularly to the Jews who are lower than animals. . . . The Jews were only forced to desist from their nastiness and clean up the mess by the threat of the butt ends of rifles. Of course, I know the expression "lost tribes of Israel" applied to the tribes which disappeared—not to the tribe of Judah from which the current sons of bitches are descended. However, it is my personal opinion that this too is a lost tribe—lost to all decency.

SUGGESTED READING: Carlo D'Este, *Patton: Genius for War* (New York: HarperCollins, 1995); Abram L. Sachar, *The Redemption of the Unwanted* (New York: St. Martin's, 1983).

PAUKER, ANA (1893–1960). Born Hannah Robinsohn of Orthodox Jewish parents, she reacted to the extreme **antisemitism** in Romania by joining, then heading, the Communist movement in that country. During World War II she fled to the USSR and then returned to her native land with the Red Army in 1944. In 1947, she was appointed foreign minister, the first Jew and first woman to hold such a post. Some portray her as a rigid Stalinist, but others claim she opposed collectivization, opposed **Joseph Stalin**'s anti-Jewish purges, promoted emigration of 100,000 Jews to Israel, and was a universalist and internationalist socialist. For these reasons, antisemites accused her of espionage in the service of the United States and the "Zionist International." When Stalin died in 1953, she was released from jail. *See also* ANTI-ZIONIST ANTISEMITISM; COSMOPOLITANISM; PRAGUE TRIALS.

SUGGESTED READING: Robert Levy, *Ana Pauker: The Rise and Fall of a Jewish Communist* (Berkeley: University of California Press, 1991).

PAUL, ST. (d. c. 65). Also known as Paul of Tarsus. Paul rarely attributed lasting value to Judaism. In the Biblical book of Romans, Paul acknowledges the glory, the covenants, the Torah, the promises, the patriarchs, and the **messiah** as Jewish, but he rejects Jews as the true descendants of Abraham. Jews must serve Christians. In Galatians, he compares Jews with "Hagar, from Mount Sinai, bearing children for slavery." Christians, on the other hand, Paul related to Sarah, the free woman. Christians, not Jews, were "children of the promise." To live according to Torah means to be cut off from Christ, and only through faith in Christ can Jews attain grace. Living according to Torah meant living to "gratify the desires of the flesh," whereas to "live by the spirit" meant not to be not subject to Torah.

SUGGESTED READING: Peter Richardson, ed., *Anti-Judaism in Early Christianity: Studies in Christianity and Judaism* (Waterloo, ON: Wilfrid Laurier University Press, 1986).

PAUL II (1417–1471). Pope, 1464–71. In 1466 Paul II forced young Jews to race every day of the Roman *Carnivale* in the nude. They were ridiculed, harassed, and humiliated. "Races were run . . . by horses, asses, buffaloes, old men, lads, children, and Jews. Before they were to run, the Jews were richly fed to make the race more difficult for them. . . . The Holy Father stood upon a richly ornamented balcony and laughed heartily."

SUGGESTED READING: Edward Synan, *The Popes and the Jews in the Middle Ages* (New York: Macmillan, 1965); Cecil Roth, *A History of the Jews of Italy* (Philadelphia: Jewish Publication Society, 1946); Sam Waagenaar, *The Pope's Jews* (La Salle, IL: Open Court Publishers, 1974).

PAUL IV (1476–1559). Pope, 1555–59. Born Giovanni Pietro Caraffa. As late as 1553, Cardinal Caraffa, head of the **Inquisition**, ordered copies of the **Talmud** burned in the **Papal States** and all across Italy. In 1555, as Paul IV, he required that Jews living under papal authority earn a living by selling old clothes and used goods. He attempted to coerce Jews into **conversion** and required Jews residing in the small, unsanitary **ghettos** of the Papal States to listen to weekly **sermons**; those Jews who did not pay attention were flogged. His anti-Jewish bull *Cum nimis absurdum* stated that it was

> utterly absurd and impermissible that the Jews, whom God has condemned to eternal slavery for their guilt [in the crucifixion], should enjoy our Christian love and toleration . . . [and] that Jews venture to show themselves in the midst of Christians and even in the immediate vicinity of churches without displaying any badge.

In 1556, Paul ordered 20 Portuguese **conversos** burned on the grounds of **heresy**, for any contact between conversos and Jews was deemed **heretical**.

SUGGESTED READING: Cecil Roth, *A History of the Jews of Italy* (Philadelphia: Jewish Publication Society, 1946); Sam Waagenaar, *The Pope's Jews* (La Salle, IL: Open Court Publishers, 1974); Max Margolis and Alexander Marx, *History of the Jewish People* (Philadelphia: Jewish Publication Society, 1927).

PAUL V (1550–1621). Pope, 1605–21. Following his predecessors' policies, Paul V **ghettoized** those Jews living in Rome and other papal cities, required them to wear **Jew badges** as a sign of the stigma of their Jewishness, and forced other restrictions on them, such as conversionary **sermons**.

SUGGESTED READING: Cecil Roth, *A History of the Jews of Italy* (Philadelphia: Jewish Publication Society, 1946); Sam Waagenaar, *The Pope's Jews* (La Salle, IL: Open Court Publishers, 1974).

PAUL DE BURGOS (1350–1435). Also known as Pablo de Santa Maria; born Solomon Halevi. Spanish apostate and archbishop. In his youth, he was a Jewish scholar in Burgos, Spain. As an advisor to King **Henry II** of Castile, he drew up a law (1412) with 10 clauses designed to humiliate and impoverish Spanish Jews: Jews had to live in a prescribed **ghetto** area, the Juderia; could not practice medicine or surgery, deal in bread, wine, flour, or meat, or engage in trades or handicraft; were forbidden to engage in normal social intercourse with Christians or hire Christian servants; and had to wear only coarse clothing. *See also* FERRER, VINCENT.

SUGGESTED READING: Yitzhak Baer, *A History of Jews in Christian Spain*, 2 vols. (Philadelphia: Jewish Publication Society, 1992).

PAVELIC, ANTE (1889–1959). Croatian chief of state, 1941–45; **Ustasha** leader. Pavelic gained power when **Nazi** Germany set up a satellite state, Croatia, out of the former Yugoslavia. Racist and brutal, he undertook ethnic cleansing on non-Croatians. Jews were **deported** to a concentration camp, Jasenovac, where more than 32,000 Jews were murdered.

SUGGESTED READING: J. Romans, *The Jews of Yugoslavia, 1941–1945* (Belgrade, Yugoslavia: Savez Jevreskiik, Opstisa Jugoslavje, 1982).

PECKERWOOD; WOOD. White youths with loose ties to white power gangs in and out of prison and racist **skinhead** gangs concentrated in California, where they participate in the drug trade and have ties to the **Nazi Low Riders**. Many gang members carry Peckerwood tattoos—the letters *PW* (Peckerwood) or *APW* (American Peckerwood) along with a wood-pecker head and beak.

SUGGESTED READING: Anti-Defamation League, *Hate on Display: Extremist Symbols, Logos, and Tattoos* (New York: Anti-Defamation League, 2006).

PEDRO III (1239–1285). King of **Aragón**, 1276–85, and of Sicily (as Pedro I, 1282–85). A warrior king who exploited Jews as sources of heavy **taxes** for his military campaigns and as translators for his negotiations with the Muslims. In April 1279, Pedro complied with the wishes of Pope **Nicholas III** that the **Dominican** order renew its conversionary preaching. Pedro continued this anti-Jewish trend, although he reversed himself when the economic value of his Jews seemed threatened by his decrees.

SUGGESTED READING: Judah Gribetz, Edward L. Greenstein, and Regina S. Stein, *The Timetables of Jewish History* (New York: Simon & Schuster, 1993).

PELLEPOIX, LOUIS DARQUIER (1897–1980). **Vichy** chief of Jewish affairs, 1942–44. Replacing **Xavier de Vallat**, Pellepoix founded Rassemblement, an organization whose magazine called for the **expulsion** of Jews and reprinted *The Protocols of the Elders of Zion*. As commissioner of

Jewish affairs, he facilitated **deportation** of the Jews from France. While in exile in Madrid in 1978, he characterized the **Holocaust** as a "Jewish invention."

SUGGESTED READING: Michael R. Marrus and Robert O. Paxton, *Vichy France and the Jews* (New York: Schocken Books, 1983).

PELLEY, WILLIAM (1890–1965). American political activist. Pelley claimed to be fighting for the Christian nature of public life against the Jewish assault. He believed that the Jews were out to destroy Christian society and deserved their divinely ordained punishment. He called for the establishment of a Christian commonwealth. Focusing his attack on the Jews, Pelley founded a group of disciples, the Silver Shirts (Christian American Patriots), based on the **fascist** model. In his words, the internationalist Jews "have turned the Christian United States into a vast civic **synagogue**."

SUGGESTED READING: David H. Bennett, *The Party of Fear*, 2nd rev. ed. (New York: Vintage, 1995); "William Pelley Dies, Founded Silver Shirts," *New York Times*, July 2, 1965.

PEÑAFORTE, RAYMOND DE (1180–1275). A major spiritual influence in Western Christendom at the time, an anti-Jewish Spanish **Dominican**, and confessor of Spanish king **James I**—whose anti-Jewish decrees may have resulted from Peñaforte's influence. Peñaforte was also an eminent jurist who opined that the Church "can inflict temporal penalties . . . and even spiritual penalties indirectly, by removing Christians from communion with [Jews]."

SUGGESTED READING: Robert Chazan, *Church, State, and Jew in the Middle Ages* (New York: Behrman House, 1980).

PENN, WILLIAM (1644–1718). English Quaker leader; founder of Pennsylvania. In Pennsylvania's constitution, "The Frame of Government," Penn required that all electors and elected officials profess faith in Jesus Christ. Penn's "Holy Experiment" restricted Jews more than the other pariah group, the Catholics. Penn dreamed of Jews' **conversion**. Their misfortune, he believed, derived from their rejection of Christ as savior.

SUGGESTED READING: Egal Feldman, *Dual Destinies: The Jewish Encounter with Protestant America* (Chicago: University of Illinois Press, 1990).

PENNY CHEWS. (British slur) British rhyming slang—rhymes with "Jews."

Suggested Reading: "List of Ethnic Slurs," *Wikipedia*, http://en.wiki
pedia.org/wiki/List_of_ethnic_slurs.

PEPYS, SAMUEL (1633–1703). English diarist and public official. In his
diary entry of October 14, 1663, Pepys wrote:

> After dinner my wife and I, by Mr. Rawlinson's conduct, to the Jewish **Syna-
> gogue**: . . . Lord! to see the disorder, laughing, sporting, and no attention, but
> confusion in all their service, more like brutes than people knowing the true God,
> would make a man forswear ever seeing them more and indeed I never did see so
> much, or could have imagined there had been any religion in the whole world so
> absurdly performed as this. Away thence with my mind strongly disturbed with
> them.

Suggested Reading: Frank Felsenstein, *Antisemitic Stereotypes: A
Paradigm of Otherness in English Popular Culture, 1660–1830* (Baltimore: Johns Hopkins University Press, 1995).

PERFIDIA. Slur against Jews. Initially, the term may have simply meant
"unfaithful." But because of its association with the Jews as faithless in
regard to Christianity, *perfidia* collected the pejorative connotations of
stubbornness, blindness, hostility, intentional disbelief, malicious infidelity, malevolence, and treachery. As late as 1962, the Good Friday Prayer
instructed Catholics to pray for the "perfidious Jews" that they might convert to the truth. In response to Pope **John XXIII** and **Vatican Council II**,
the current prayer prays for "the Jewish people, first to hear the word of
God, that they may continue to grow in the love of his name and in faithful-
ness to his covenant."

Suggested Reading: Judah Gribetz, Edward L. Greenstein, and Regina
S. Stein, *The Timetables of Jewish History* (New York: Simon & Schuster,
1993); Judith Herschcopf, *Vatican Council Statement and the Jews* (New
York: Institute on Human Relations, 1971).

PETER I (THE GREAT) (1672–1725). Tsar, 1682–1725. Westernized Russian reformer. Despite Peter's desire for Russia to become an advanced
European state, as in the West, he was not ready to invite Jews into the
country, claiming that Jews were all too shrewd as businessmen.

Suggested Reading: Simon Dubnow, *History of the Jews in Russia
and Poland* (Bergenfield, NJ: Avotaynu, 2000).

PETER III. *See* PEDRO III.

PETER OF BLOIS (1135–1205). French statesman and theologian. Peter
believed that the Jews should be permitted to live for two reasons only:

because they act as the "enslaved book-bearers" of Christianity and because their very faces remind Christians of "the passion of Christ." Yet Peter warned that the **messiah** for whom the Jews awaited was in reality the **Antichrist** and "after the manner of his father the devil [the Jew] often changes into monstrous shapes."

SUGGESTED READING: Peter of Blois, *Against the Perfidy of the Jews*, http://www.fordham.edu/halsall/source/1198peterblois-jews.html.

PETER THE HERMIT (1050–1115). An important French preacher for the First **Crusade**. The former soldier joined the knights and often led them, instituting **pogroms** in the Rhineland and plundering and massacring Jews in Speyer, Mainz, and Cologne.

SUGGESTED READING: Robert Chazan, *European Jewry and the First Crusade* (Berkeley: University of California Press, 1996).

PETER THE VENERABLE (PETER OF CLUNY) (1092–1156). Church polemicist. A Benedictine abbot of Cluny, France, the greatest monastery in the West, Peter addressed the Jews directly as progenitors of the **Antichrist**: "I am talking to you, you Jews, who to this very day deny the Son of God. How long, you miserable people, will you deny the truth? How long will you fight against God? [You will] produce the Antichrist, the king of all the ungodly." Peter advised King **Louis VII** of France to take harsh measures against Jews. He considered the **Talmud** foolish insanity and attacked it viciously. Peter would **confiscate Jewish property** acquired by **usury** and did not believe Jews were part of humanity. *See also* BASILISK.

SUGGESTED READING: Dominique Logna-Prat, *Order and Exclusion: Cluny and Christendom Face Heresy, Judaism and Islam, 1000–1150*, trans. Graham R. Edwards (Ithaca, NY: Cornell University Press, 2002).

PETLYURA, SIMON (1879–1926). Ukranian independence leader, 1918–26. After the Russian Revolution in 1917–18, Petlyura helped establish an independent Ukrainian state and became its president in 1919. In the course of the war with the **Bolshevik** Red Army in 1918–21, his forces committed 897 **pogroms**, killing 28,000 Jews. His defenders said this was not a result of planning by Petlyura, but because of undisciplined soldiers in a chaotic situation. Defeated by the Reds, he escaped to Poland, then to Paris, where he was assassinated by a Jewish student, Shalom Schartzbard, in 1926.

SUGGESTED READING: Saul Friedman, *Pogromchik: The Assassination of Simon Petlyura* (Oxford, England: Hart, 1976); "The Pogroms in the Ukraine, 1918–1921," *YIVO: Annuals of Jewish Social Science* 6 (1951).

PETRONIUS ARBITER (fl. 1st cent. CE). Roman writer; perhaps advisor to Emperor Nero. Apparently misinterpreting the Jewish refusal to eat pork, Petronius claimed that Jews worship a "**pig**-god."

SUGGESTED READING: Menahem Stern, ed., *Greek and Latin Authors on Jews and Judaism* (Jerusalem: Israel Academy of Sciences and Humanities, 1984).

PFEFFERKORN, JOHANNES (1469–1521). German apostate and **Dominican** friar who attacked the **Talmud**. A former butcher, Pfefferkorn convinced Holy Roman Emperor **Maximilian I** in 1509 to destroy everything hostile to Christianity. In 1505–09, the friar wrote vitriolic pieces against Jews, urging an end to **usury**, advocating forced **sermons** upon Jews, and seeking the **expulsion** of Jews from **Frankfurt, Worms**, and Regensburg. **Johannes Reuchlin**, the humanist scholar, successfully rebutted Pfefferkorn's attacks on the Talmud.

SUGGESTED READING: Paul E. Grosser and Edwin G. Halperin, *Anti-Semitism: The Causes and Effects of a Prejudice* (Secaucus, NJ: Citadel Press, 1979).

PHARISEES. Jewish religious party in ancient Palestine; believers in Oral Law and developers of the **Talmud.** The Pharisees evolved around the first century BCE. They believed that the Oral Law (oral interpretations of written scripture) was holy and that the original Jewish Scriptures needed further amplification. The Pharisees became the party of poor and common folk, developing into mainstream Judaism. The **Gospels** in **Matthew** 23 and Luke 18 called them hypocrites and the "offspring of vipers." Jewish tradition sees them as flexible and humane rather than stubborn and hard. There is evidence that Jesus may have belonged to one of the schools of the Pharisees. *See also* SADDUCEES.

SUGGESTED READING: Alan T. Davies, ed., *Antisemitism and the Foundations of Christianity* (New York: Paulist Press, 1979).

PHILIP AUGUSTUS (1179–1223). French king, 1180–1223. Philip Augustus's policies included repeated extortions of money from the Jews and **confiscation of Jewish property**, including **synagogues**, which he donated to the Church as Christian places of worship. Philip also ordered the murder of Jews.

SUGGESTED READING: Jim Bradbury, *Philip Augustus: King of France, 1180–1223* (New York: Longman, 1998).

PHILIP THE FAIR (1268–1314). French king, 1285–1314. Philip the Fair arrested Jews so he could seize their goods to accommodate his lavish lifestyle.

SUGGESTED READING: Jeffrey Howard Denton, *Philip the Fair and the Ecclesiatical Assemblies of 1294–95* (Philadelphia: American Philosophical Society, 1991).

PHILOSEMITISM. Any pro-Jewish or pro-Judaic utterance or act, such as non-Jewish defense of Jews, Judaism, and Jewishness or befriending Jews. Although the term *philosemitism* was established at the same time as *antisemitism*, philosemitism has existed since the birth of Judaism. Even during the worst periods of Christian antisemitism during the Middle Ages, there were always Christians who befriended Jews—from Boccaccio to the anonymous Christians the church and papacy attempted to penalize in its conciliar decrees.

SUGGESTED READING: Alan T. Levenson, *Between Philosemitism and Antisemitism: Defenses of Jews and Judaism in Germany, 1871–1932* (Lincoln: University of Nebraska Press, 2004).

PHILOSTRATUS. 3rd-century Greek pagan. Philostratus reproached the Jews for keeping themselves apart:

> For the Jews have long been in revolt not only against the Romans, but against humanity; and a race that has made its own life apart and irreconcilable, that cannot share with the rest of mankind in the pleasures of the table, nor join in their libations or prayers or sacrifices, are separated from ourselves by a greater gulf than divides us from Sura or Bactra of the more distant Indies.

SUGGESTED READING: Menahem Stern, ed., *Greek and Latin Authors on Jews and Judaism* (Jerusalem: Israel Academy of Sciences and Humanities, 1984).

PHINEAS PRIEST. Symbolized by the letter *P* with a horizontal line drawn through it. Extremists have claimed to be Phineas Priests after committing violent acts against people they consider to be breaking "Biblical Law," including interracial couples, abortion providers, and homosexuals. Most people who have declared themselves Phineas Priests are adherents to **Christian Identity**. The concept of the Phineas Priesthood comes from a 1990 book by white supremacist and Christian Identity follower Richard Kelly Hoskins, *Vigilantes of Christendom: The Story of the Phineas Priesthood.* In the book, Hoskins describes a continuous priesthood of "avengers" who, throughout the centuries, have committed violent acts in order to defend racial purity and "God's Law." According to Hoskins, these avengers have been inspired by, and thus take their name from Phinehas who, in order to protect the purity of the Israelites and keep them from harm, killed a fellow Israelite who had taken up with a Midianite woman (Num. 25:6–15).

SUGGESTED READING: Anti-Defamation League, *Hate on Display: Extremist Symbols, Logos, and Tattoos* (New York: Anti-Defamation League, 2006).

PHOCAS (d. 610). Eastern Roman emperor, 602–10. Phocas was one of several Byzantine emperors who unsuccessfully attempted to **convert** Jews forcibly.

SUGGESTED READING: Menahem Stern, ed., *Greek and Latin Authors on Jews and Judaism* (Jerusalem: Israel Academy of Sciences and Humanities, 1984).

PHYSICS, GERMAN VERSUS JEWISH. With the rise of **Nazism** in Germany, science, according to Nazi ideology, became either German-**Aryan** or Jewish. Jewish scientists were dismissed from posts in labs and universities. In 1936, **Philipp Lenard** wrote *German Physics*, in which he distinguished between German and Jewish physics, claiming that all real advances in science were a product of German blood and Aryan race. Lenard and Johannes Stark (1874–1957) asserted that Jewish physics was too abstract, too vague, and too mathematical and was riddled with moral relativism. They opposed Albert Einstein and his Theory of Relativity and quantum mechanics. Because of Nazi ideology, Jewish atomic physicists emigrated to England and the United States and, in the end, the Allies developed the atomic bomb before the Germans did. *See also DEGENERATION.*

SUGGESTED READING: Alan D. Beyechen, *Scientists under Hitler: Politics and the Physics Community in the Third Reich* (New Haven, CT: Yale University Press, 1977); Lewis Elton Einstein, "General Relativity and the German Press, 1919–1920," *Isis* 77 (March 1986).

PICARD, EDMUND (1836–1929). Belgian journalist and writer. A racist and **Aryan** supremacist, Picard claimed he was a socialist. His articles in the socialist daily *Le Peuple* railed against intermingling of Jews and Aryans. He also disliked Arabs because they were Semites, and he called Jews "Asiatics." Picard believed Jews committed bourgeois crimes against Gentiles. He was influential in turning Belgian socialists against Jews.

SUGGESTED READING: Robert F. Byrnes, *Antisemitism in Modern France* (New York: H. Fertig, 1969).

PICQUART, GEORGES (1854–1914). French intelligence officer. When Picquart became head of the French counterintelligence in 1896, he examined the letters and details of the **Dreyfus Case**. Although he was an **antisemite**, it was he, along with Matthieu Dreyfus, Alfred's brother, who broke open the case and established the innocence of Dreyfus. Before he was shipped to Tunisia on a dangerous assignment, he left the evidence with his lawyer, who leaked it to the press.

SUGGESTED READING: Jean-Denis Bredin, *The Affair: The Case of Alfred Dreyfus* (New York: George Brazilla, 1986).

PICTURE OF DORIAN GRAY, THE. An 1891 novel by Anglo-Irish playwright Oscar Wilde (1854–1900). In *The Picture of Dorian Gray*, Wilde has Gray describe Isaacs as

> a hideous Jew, in the most amazing waistcoat I ever beheld in my life, was standing at the entrance, smoking a vile cigar. He had greasy ringlets and an enormous diamond blazed in the centre of a soiled shirt. "Have a box, my Lord?" he said when he saw me, and he took off his hat with an air of gorgeous servility. There was something about him, Harry, that amused me. He was such a monster . . . the horrid old Jew came around to the box after the performance was over and offered to take me behind the scenes and introduce me to her.

Wilde's narrator later observes about Isaacs:

> For some reason or other, the house was crowded that night, and the fat Jew manager who met them at the door was beaming from ear to ear with an oily, tremulous smile. He escorted them to their box with a sort of pompous humility, waving his fat jewelled hands, and talking at the top of his voice. Dorian Gray loathed him more than ever. He felt as if he had come to look for Miranda and had been met by Caliban.

Wilde also has Dorian say in describing a theater orchestra: "There was a dreadful orchestra, presided over by a young Hebrew who sat at a cracked piano, that nearly drove me away." As Christopher Nassaar writes, "This . . . extends the **antisemitic** overtones beyond the figure of Isaacs." Nassaar notes that Wilde is attacking "**George Eliot**'s highly sympathetic and unrealistically idealized portrait of Daniel Deronda and the English Jewish community." He observes that Wilde expressed antisemitism nowhere else and that he had excellent relationships with Jews. Nassaar concludes that Wilde was at worst "insensitive" and that "it is difficult to imagine a Jew reading Wilde's novel without being offended by the passages on Isaacs."

SUGGESTED READING: Christopher Nassaar, "The Problem of the Jewish Manager in *The Picture of Dorian Gray,*" *The Wildean: A Journal of Oscar Wilde Studies* (January 2003).

PIERCE, WILLIAM (1934–2002). U.S. leader of the **neo-Nazi National Alliance**. Pierce wrote the novel *The Turner Diaries* (1978), which depicts the **Aryan** takeover of the world. He may have inspired Timothy McVeigh to carry out the Oklahoma City bombing in 1995, the most deadly act of domestic terrorism ever in the United States. Pierce used the Internet to spread his anti-Jewish, anti-black, and antigovernment propaganda, to recruit potential members, and to maintain contact with like-minded haters. He was actively linked to racists and neo-**fascist** and right-wing parties in Germany, Great Britain, France, and Holland.

SUGGESTED READING: Robert Griffin, *The Fame of a Dead Man's Deeds: An Up-Close Portrait of White Nationalist William Pierce* (Bloomington, IN: Authorhouse, 2001); Anti-Defamation League, "William Pierce," 2004, http://www.adl.org/learn/ext_us/pierce.asp.

PIG. The Torah, **Talmud,** and Jewish Apocrypha agreed that the pig was the symbol of filth and of all that was abominable. Since they associated the sacrifice of pigs with idolatrous worship, Jewish authorities condemned even swine farmers. For a Jew, the refusal to eat swine, even when threatened with death, became a test of one's Jewishness. Yet from earliest Christian times through the late Middle Ages Christian theologians charged that Jews not only associated with the pig, but worshipped it. *See also* JUDENSAU.

PILEUS CORNUTUS. *See* STIGMATIC EMBLEMS.

PILSUDSKI, JÓZEF (1867–1935). Polish statesman. Pilsudski represented Poland at the **Versailles Peace Conference** in 1919. When his Polish armies defeated the Red Army in 1920, he became the virtual dictator of Poland (1926–35). Not an **antisemite**, Pilsudski tried to better Polish–Jewish relations. But after his death in 1935, those relations deteriorated.

SUGGESTED READING: Celia S. Heller, *On the Edge of Destruction* (Detroit: Wayne State University Press, 1994).

PIUS II (1405–1464). Pope, 1458–64. The first papal sanction of racial discrimination against Jews occurred in 1461, when Pius II decreed that the administrators of a loan fund must be "Old Christians" with four generations of purely Christian blood on both the mother's and father's sides. Even the National Socialist **Nuremberg Decrees of 1935** were less exclusive, defining a Jew as having one parent or two grandparents who were Jewish by religious identity. *See also* PURITY OF BLOOD.

SUGGESTED READING: "The Popes," in *Jewish Encyclopedia*, ed. Isadore Singer (New York: Funk & Wagnalls, 1909).

PIUS V (1504–1572). Pope, 1566–72. Pius V expelled Jews from most of the **Papal States** in 1569 as criminal "dead sheep," hopelessly unconvertible.

SUGGESTED READING: Owen Chadwick, *The Popes and European Revolution* (New York: Oxford University Press, 1981).

PIUS VI (1717–1799). Pope, 1775–99. Near the end of the 18th century, as the Jewish "Middle Ages" came to a close, Pius VI ordered Jews who lived in any **Papal State** to listen to conversionary **sermons** delivered in the **synagogues** after the **Sabbath** services; forbade them to associate in any way with Christians, ride in carriages, leave the **ghetto**, sell food to Christians, sing religious songs, or erect tombstones over their dead; and prohibited the study of the **Talmud**.

SUGGESTED READING: "Pius VI," in *Jewish Encyclopedia*, ed. Isadore Singer (New York: Funk & Wagnalls, 1909).

PIUS VII (1740–1823). Pope, 1800–23. When Pius VII was restored to Rome in 1815 after his **Napoleonic** exile, he stripped Jews of whatever freedoms they had achieved under the French occupation and reinstituted the embarrassing and painful Jewish participation in the Roman *Carnivale*, conversionary **sermons**, and the **Inquisition**.

SUGGESTED READING: David I. Kertzer, *The Popes against the Jews* (New York: Knopf, 2001).

PIUS IX (1792–1878). Pope, 1846–78. Born Giovanni Mastai-Ferretti. Pius IX was beatified by Pope **John Paul II** despite protests by Jews. He **ghettoized** the Jews in 1850 and had them wear distinctive clothes. At his orders, a Jewish child, Edgardo Mortara, was kidnapped and raised Catholic because he had been baptized as an infant by a Catholic nursemaid. This pope experienced the liquidation of the **Papal States** when Italy was unified in 1861, and the Rome ghetto was opened up in 1870. *See also* MORTARA ABDUCTION CASE.

SUGGESTED READING: David I. Kertzer, *The Popes against the Jews* (New York: Knopf, 2001).

PIUS X, ST. (1835–1914). Pope, 1903–14. Pius X informed Theodor Herzl, the founder of modern Zionism:

The soil of Jerusalem . . . has been sanctified by the life of Jesus Christ. . . . The Jews have not recognized our Lord, therefore we cannot recognize the Jewish people. . . . If you come to Palestine, . . . we shall have churches and priests ready to baptize all of you. . . . I know, it is not pleasant to see the Turks in possession of our Holy Places. We simply have to put up with it. But to support the Jews in the acquisition of the Holy Places, that we cannot do.

SUGGESTED READING: Sergio I. Minerbi, *The Vatican and Zionism* (New York: Oxford University Press, 1990).

PIUS XI (1857–1939). Pope, 1922–39. Born Achille Ratti. Pius XI negotiated a Concordat with **Benito Mussolini**, the Italian dictator, then later with **Adolf Hitler**. He opposed race laws, but not **antisemitism**. Recognizing that Hitler was not honoring the treaty, he wrote the encyclical *Mit brennender Sorge*. Pius ignored German Jewish-born nun **Edith Stein**'s plea about laws against Jews in 1933. It was the substitution of **blood and soil** for God and Christianity that troubled him. While a cardinal and later as pope, he considered Jews dangerous, as attackers of the Church and Communists. It was brutal antisemitic excesses he opposed. A planned but never executed encyclical not released by the **Vatican** stated in part: "In the case of the Jews, its flagrant denial of human rights sends many thousands of helpless persons out over the face of the earth without any resources; wandering from frontier to frontier, they are a burden to humanity and to themselves." But the encyclical still regarded the Jews as **Christ-killers**.

SUGGESTED READING: David I. Kertzer, *The Popes against the Jews* (New York: Knopf, 2001).

PIUS XII (1876–1958). Pope, 1939–58. As secretary of state for Pope **Pius XI,** Eugenio Pacelli negotiated the Concordat**,** a treaty between **Nazi** Germany and the Catholic Church. As pope, his reign was a subject of controversy regarding his actions or lack of actions during the **Holocaust**. He was a source of diplomatic information for the United States confirming the destruction of European Jewry. His defenders claim that the Italian resistance to the **Final Solution** was prompted by Pius XII's covert interventions. He did permit clergy and Catholic institutions to shelter Jews, though just how many were saved is a matter of dispute. Yet, he ordered that Jewish children under Catholic control or who had been baptized need not be returned to the Jewish community.

In September 1943 SS Lt. Col. Herbert Kappler, chief of security in Rome, tried to extort 50 kilograms of gold from the already condemned Jewish community; Pius assented to a loan if the Jewish attempt to secure the gold fell short. Many individual Catholics, including a few priests, contributed their own gold. During the Nazi **deportation** of Jews from Rome in the **October roundup** of 1943, the pope was silent. Although Pius did not speak out in December when Mussolini ordered all Jews living in Italy to be interned and expropriated, he did relax canonical restrictions to allow about 5,000 Jews to be hidden on Church property. The pope may have feared making matters worse for the Jews, Italians, German Catholics, or himself by a strong intervention.

Pius asked **Josef Tiso**, the dictator of Slovakia, to spare **converted** Jews. He also pleaded with **Miklós Horthy** to stop deporting Hungarian Jews in 1944. While strongly condemning **euthanasia** in an encyclical, he did not use the full force of his authority in condemning the **genocide** of Jews. After the war, Pius requested mercy for all Nazi **war criminals**, and the **Vatican** helped a number of Nazi war criminals escape justice through the so-called **Ratline**.

SUGGESTED READING: Margherita Marchione, *Pope Pius XII, Architect for Peace* (New York: Paulist Press, 2000); Daniel Jonah Goldhagen, *A Moral Reckoning: The Role of the Catholic Church in the Holocaust and the Unfulfilled Duty of Repair* (New York: Knopf, 2002).

PIZZA BAGEL. (North American slur) A person of Italian and Jewish parentage.

SUGGESTED READING: "List of Ethnic Slurs," *Wikipedia*, http://en.wiki pedia.org/wiki/List_of_ethnic_slurs.

PLEHVE, VYACHESLAV VON (1846–1906). Tsarist minister of the interior and member of the anti-Jewish Russian Assembly; reactionary Jew-hater. Plehve instigated the **pogroms** in **Kishinev** in 1903 and in Gomel. His goal was to eliminate Jews from Russia. Plehve told Theodor Herzl that Russian Jews had to be suppressed since they were an alien minority.

SUGGESTED READING: Simon Dubnow, *History of the Jews in Russia and Poland* (Bergenfield, NJ: Avotaynu, 2000).

PLUTARCH (46?–c. 120). Greek priest of Delphi who lived in Athens and Rome. He listed Greeks as "discovering evil barbarian [Jewish] ways," that is, "superstitions such as . . . wallowing in filth, keeping the **Sabbath**," and so forth. The Jews rested on the Sabbath even while the enemy captured their defenses, remaining "fast bound in the toils of superstition as in one great net."

SUGGESTED READING: Menahem Stern, ed., *Greek and Latin Authors on Jews and Judaism* (Jerusalem: Israel Academy of Sciences and Humanities, 1984).

POBEDONOSTSEV, KONSTANTIN PETROVICH (1827–1907). Chief procurator of the Holy Synod and advisor to tsars **Alexander III** and **Nicholas II**. Pobedonostsev's advice for Jews, whom he considered **Christkillers** and radical revolutionaries, was that one-third emigrate, one-third **convert**, and one-third be killed. To aid in **pogroms**, he sponsored a secret society, the Sacred Legion of 300 army officers. He wrote to **Fyodor Dostoyevsky**:

> The **Yids** . . . have taken everything over, they have undermined everything. . . . They are at the root of the revolutionary-social movement and regicide, they control the periodical press, they have the money market in their hands, they are enslaving the popular masses financially, they are even guiding the principles of present-day science that is seeking to place itself *outside of* Christianity.

SUGGESTED READING: Edward Flannery, *The Anguish of the Jews* (New York: Paulist Press, 1985).

POGROM. Russian for "attack." Jews have been subject to pogroms throughout their history, including destruction of property, murder, looting, rape, torture, and burning. Often pogroms were triggered by false accusations against Jews such as the **ritual murder** and **desecration of the Host**. Government officials and religious authorities were at best indifferent to, and were often complicit in, pogroms. *See also* BLACK HUNDREDS; CHMIELNICKI MASSACRES; CRUSADES; DENIKIN, ANTON; FERRER, VINCENT; HAIDAMACKS; KISHINEV; ODESSA POGROMS; PETLYURA, SIMON.

POHL, OSWALD (1892–1951). Overseer of **SS** economic enterprises, 1942–45. Pohl looted goods from concentration camp inmates and sent the spoils back to Germany. He made available thousands of concentration camp slave laborers for 40 large companies and 150 factories. His department, the Economic and Administrative Office, had responsibility to construct and oversee concentration camps. He was tried and executed in 1951 by a U.S. military tribunal. *See also* FORCED LABOR CAMPS; I. G. FARBEN.

SUGGESTED READING: Benjamin Ferencz, *Less Than Slaves* (Cambridge, MA: Harvard University Press, 1979).

POIRÉ, EMMANUEL (1858–1909). Russian-born French artist, caricaturist, and illustrator. One of the brilliant **antisemitic** cartoonists in the "stable" of **Edouard Drumont**, using the name Caran d'Ache. *See also* DREYFUS CASE.

SUGGESTED READING: Robert Byrnes, *Antisemitism in Modern France* (New Brunswick, NJ: Rutgers University Press, 1950); Norman Kleeblatt, "The Dreyfus Affair: A Visual Record," in *The Dreyfus Affair: Art, Truth, and Justice* (Berkeley: University of California Press, 1987).

POISONING OF WELLS ACCUSATION. Medieval false charge of Jewish conspiracy. When the **Black Death**, bubonic plague, was decimating Europe in 1347–50, Jews were accused of poisoning the wells and rivers near towns, causing the plague. The poisonous concoction supposedly had ingredients that included Christian flesh, hearts, and the sacred Host; another fantastic recipe combined a consecrated Host and menstrual blood. As a result, 60 major cities and 150 minor ones witnessed Jews tortured and burned and their homes destroyed with the occupants inside. *See also* DEFAMATIONS, ANTI-JEWISH.

SUGGESTED READING: Norman Cantor, *In the Wake of the Plague: The Black Death and the World That It Made* (New York: Free Press, 2001).

POLAND. *See* JEWISH CONDITION IN POLAND; MOCZAR, MIECZYSLAW.

POLL TAX. *See* TAXATION OF JEWS.

POLNA RITUAL MURDER. An accusation of **ritual murder** in Polna, Bohemia, resulting from the murder of Agnes Hruza in March 1899. Hruza was a 19-year-old seamstress whose body was found in a forest, her throat cut and her clothes torn. Suspician fell on a 23-year-old Jewish vagrant with limited mental and physical abilities, Leopold Hilsner. Both the state's attorney and the attorney for the Hruza family made clear suggestions of ritual murder. Despite the lack of convincing evidence, he was sentenced to death. *Vaterland*, the leading Catholic periodical, restated the blood libel and claimed that the Church had confirmed it. Attacks on Jews took place. When a second body was discovered in October, Hilsner was charged with this murder as well, witnesses claiming they saw him with a ritual slaughtering knife. Hilsner was sentenced to death amid **antisemitic** agitation, his sentence commuted to life in prison.

SUGGESTED READING: Arthur Nussbaum, "The Ritual-Murder Trial of Polna," *Historica Judaica* 9 (1947); Gotthard Deutsch, "Polna Affair," *JewishEncyclopedia.com*, http://www.jewishencyclopedia.com/view.jsp?artid=420&letter=P.

POLYCARP, ST. (69–155?). Apostolic Father of Smyrna. Polycarp wrote to the church at Phillipi (Asia Minor): "To deny that Jesus Christ has come in the flesh is to be **Antichrist**. To contradict the evidence of the Cross is to be of the devil."

SUGGESTED READING: Maxwell Staniforth, ed. and trans., *Early Christian Writings: The Apostolic Fathers* (Harmondsworth, England: Penguin, 1968).

POPE, ALEXANDER (1688–1744). English poet and satirist. Pope wrote about "barbarous and cruel Jews, who . . . thirst vehemently after the blood of the white ones." In a letter to Robert Digby in 1720, he listed Jews along with "Jobbers, Bubblers, Subscribers, Projectors," and others. He also wrote *A Strange but True Relation How Edmund Curl, of Fleet street, Stationer, Out of an extraordinary Desire of Lucre, went into Change-Alley, and was converted from the Christian Religion by certain Eminent Jews: And how he was circumcis'd and initiated into their Mysteries.*

SUGGESTED READING: Frank Felsenstein, *Antisemitic Stereotypes: A Paradigm of Otherness in English Popular Culture, 1660–1830* (Baltimore: Johns Hopkins University Press, 1995).

POPULAR FRONT. Socialist government of 1930s France, led by the Jewish politician Léon Blum. **Action Française** deplored the Popular Front as a "**kike**'s" revolution and called Blum's Popular Front government a "cabinet of the **Talmud**."

SUGGESTED READING: Julian Jackson, *The Popular Front in France: Defending Democracy, 1934–1938* (Cambridge: Cambridge University Press, 1990).

POPULAR FRONT FOR THE LIBERATION OF PALESTINE. Arab rejectionist liberation organization founded by George Habash in 1967 in the aftermath of the **Six Day War**. Marxist-Leninist in doctrine, its ultimate goal is the elimination of the State of Israel, substituting a Palestinian socialist state. It became part of the Palestine Liberation Organization. *See also* FATAH.

SUGGESTED READING: Yaakov Shimoni, Evyatar Levine, et al., eds., *Political Dictionary of the Middle East in the 20th Century* (New York: Quadrangle/New York Times, 1974).

POPULISTS, U.S. Powerful third-party movement in the rural western and southern United States at the turn of the 19th century. Although some populists were sympathetic, most expressed the sometimes latent and often manifest **antisemitism** of their time. The 1896 the Democratic and Populist Party platforms declared: "The influence of European moneychangers has been more potent in shaping legislation than the voice of the American people," and they attacked a conspiracy of "the money-lending class at home and abroad." "Moneychangers" and "money-lending class," like "international **bankers**," were code words for **Shylocks**, and "Shylocks" a code word for Jews. **Tom Watson**, the Georgia Populist who ran for president in 1904 and 1908, attacked Catholics and their allies, "the opulent Jews." William Jennings Bryan's (1860–1925) striking metaphor reminded his audience of Jesus' crucifixion when he warned, "You shall not crucify mankind upon a cross of gold!" Evidently aware of the charges of antisemitism leveled at the populist movement, Bryan affirmed, during his 1896 campaign for president, "We are not attacking a race; we are attacking greed, and avarice which knows no race or religion."

SUGGESTED READING: Richard Hofstadler, "The Folklore of Populism," in *Antisemitism in the United States*, ed. Leonard Dinnerstein (New York: Holt, Rinehart and Winston, 1971); Arnon Gutfeld and Robert Rockaway, "Demonic Images of the Jew in the Nineteenth Century," *American Jewish History* 89, no. 4 (2000); Leonard Dinnerstein, *Anti-Semitism in America* (Oxford: Oxford University Press, 2001); Naomi Cohen, *Encounter with Emancipation: The German Jews in the United States, 1830–1914* (Philadelphia: Jewish Publication Society, 1984); Thomas Curran, *Xenophobia and Immigration, 1820–1930* (Boston: Twayne, 1975).

PORK. *See* JUDENSAU; PIG.

PORPHYRY (232–c. 304). Greek scholar, historian, and philosopher; native of Tyre, Lebanon. In 280, in *Against Christianity*, Porphyry criticized those he considered Christianity's forebears: "The foreign mythologies of the Jews are of evil reputation among all men."

SUGGESTED READING: Menahem Stern, ed., *Greek and Latin Authors on Jews and Judaism* (Jerusalem: Israel Academy of Sciences and Humanities, 1984).

PORTER, KATHERINE ANNE (1890–1980). American novelist, journalist, essayist, and short-story writer. Porter's 1962 novel *Ship of Fools* contains one timid, forlorn Jewish character, Julius Loewenthal, without any counterbalancing positive Jewish figure. When interviewed a few years after the novel's publication, Porter admitted:

> I am an old American. . . . We are in the direct legitimate line; we are people based in English as our mother tongue. . . . These others have fallen into a curious kind of argot, more or less originating in New York, a deadly mixture of academic, guttersnipe, gangster, fake-Yiddish, and dull old wornout dirty words—an

appalling bankruptcy in language, as if they hate English and are trying to destroy it along with all other living things they touch.

Her mention of New York and Yiddish indicates that she was most likely talking about Jews.

SUGGESTED READING: Guy Stern, "The Rhetoric of Antisemitism in Postwar American Literature," in *Anti-semitism in Times of Crisis*, ed. Sander Gilman and Steven Katz (New York: New York University Press, 1991).

POSIDONIUS (155–131 BCE). Syrian Stoic. According to Roman geographer Strabo, Posidonius claimed that the Jews were "sorcerers" who used incantations, urine, and "other malodorous liquids."

SUGGESTED READING: Menahem Stern, *Greek and Latin Authors on Jews and Judaism* (Jerusalem: Israel Academy of Sciences and Humanities, 1984).

POSSE COMITATUS. Latin for "power of the county." The forerunner of the 1990s Freemen Movement, Posse Comitatus is an **antisemitic**, antitax extremist organization founded in 1969. It has attracted **Christian Identity Movement** members, **Ku Klux Klansmen**, and other rabid antisemites. Opposing the federal government, claiming the government is controlled by Jews, in 1983 Posse member Gordon Kahl killed two U.S. marshals in Medina, ND. Its symbol is a sheriff's star with a noose, sword, and book in the center and the words "Sheriff's Posse Comitatus" written across the top.

SUGGESTED READING: Brian Levin, "The Patriot Movement: Past, Present, and Future," http://hatemonitor.csusb.edu/research_articles/patriot .html.

POUND, EZRA (1885–1972). U.S. poet and critic. No 20th-century American author wrote so vituperatively about Jews. Pound regarded the Jews as aliens, enemies, children of darkness, haters of life, and parasitic destroyers of individuals and nations. He condemned Jews in almost all of the more than 120 wartime broadcasts he made on Rome Radio. In 1942 and 1943, he blamed the Jews for exploiting Gentiles, starting World War II, and corrupting the world. England, France, Russia, and the U.S.A., he said, were all "under **yidd** control. Lousy with **kikes**." He noted in **Nazi** metaphors: "You let in the Jew and the Jew rotted your empire, . . . And the big Jew has rotted *every* nation he has wormed into. . . . It were better you were infected with typhus." He repeated on May 9, 1942, "You would do better to inoculate your children with typhus and syphilis than to let in the Sas-

soons, **Rothschilds**, and Warburgs [prominent Jewish **banking** families]."
Americans "are now ruled by Jews, and by the dirtiest dirt from the bottom
of the Jew's ash can." Reflecting ideas common among Jew-haters for a
millennium, Pound claimed that the anti-Christian **Talmud** caused the evil
Jewish character. He told his audience that "the sixty Kikes who started
this war . . . got their inspiration from the Talmud, [which has] corrupted
the Jews." In his prose and broadcasts, he called the Jews "rats," "bed-
bugs," "vermin," "worms," "bacilli," and "parasites" who constitute an
overwhelming "power of putrefaction." Pound's solution to the Jewish
problem mirrored that of **Adolf Hitler**. He insisted that a few hundred
American Jews and **Franklin D. Roosevelt** should be hung for their crimes
and insisted that "all the kike congressmen" should be "bumped off"
without delay. Pound joked about the mass murder of Jews as "fresh meat
on the Russian steppes."

SUGGESTED READING: Robert Casillo, *The Genealogy of Demons: Antisemitism, Fascism, and the Myths of Ezra Pound* (Evanston, IL: Northwestern University Press, 1988); Leon Surette, *Pound in Purgatory: From
Economic Radicalism to Antisemitism* (Champaign: University of Illinois
Press, 2000).

PRAGUE MASSACRE. On March 18, 1389, a priest was hit with a few
grains of sand by small Jewish boys playing in the street. He became insulted and insisted that the Jewish community purposely plotted against
him. A Prague mob then slaughtered 3,000 Jews, many of whom had
sought refuge in the Staranova **Synagogue**; the mob destroyed the synagogue and Jewish cemetery, burned Jewish books, and pillaged Jewish
homes. King Wenceslaus ruled that the responsibility lay with the Jews for
showing themselves outside the **ghetto** during Holy Week.

SUGGESTED READING: Heinrich Graetz, *History of the Jews*, vol. 4 (Philadelphia: Jewish Publication Society, 1898).

PRAGUE TRIALS. Czech show trials manipulated by **Joseph Stalin** in
1952. After the Communist takeover in 1948, Stalin began his **antisemitic**
campaign. In 1952 nine top Czech Communist leaders were tried for treason, **Trotskyism**, and Titoism. While the trials took place in Prague, they
were orchestrated by Stalin against Jews to show they were "imperialist
agents." It was the first time in the history of Communism that an authori-
tative body openly proclaimed a worldwide Jewish conspiracy. The main
victim was Rudolf Slansky (1901–1952), secretary of the Czech Communist Party. He and 11 other Jews defendants were hanged on the trumped

up charge of "conspiracy against the state." What followed was persecution of Jews both in Czechoslovakia and the USSR.

SUGGESTED READING: Meir Cotic, *The Prague Trial: The First Anti-Zionist Show Trial of the Communist Bloc* (New York: Herzl Press, 1987); Avigdor Dagan, *The Slansky Trial* (Jerusalem: Keter, 1971).

PRANAITIS, JUSTIN. Turn-of-the-20th-century Polish priest and professor in St. Petersburg and so-called Catholic expert on Judaism who described a Jewish "dogma of blood." In 1893 Pranaitis authored a pamphlet, charging Jews with **ritual murder**. In 1911 he served the **antisemitic** Russian government as an "expert witness" against the Jew Mendel **Beilis** at his ritual-murder trial in Kiev when no important Russian Orthodox priest could be found to support the government's case. According to Pranaitis, the **Talmud** urged Jews to murder Christians, as each death of a Christian, serving as a substitute for the Temple sacrifices, would hasten the arrival of the Jewish **messiah**. The Talmudic and Torah prohibitions about consuming blood were circumvented, according to Pranaitis, by boiling the blood. Rabbis at the trial revealed his lack of knowledge about the Talmud.

SUGGESTED READING: Louis Greenberg, *The Jews in Russia* (New Haven, CT: Yale University Press, 1965); David S. Maddison, "Who Was Pranaitis and What Did He Do?" http://www.geocities.com/athens/cyprus/8815/pranaitis.html.

PREZIOSI, GIOVANNI. In 1921, Giovanni Preziosi published *The Protocols of the Elders of Zion* in Italy.

PRINCETON UNIVERSITY EATING CLUBS. At least through 1998, not one of Princeton's 13 "eating clubs," the centers of social life at the university, offered kosher meals. In *Frank v. Ivy Club*, 120 N.J. 73 (1990), cert. denied, 498 U.S. 1073, 111 S.Ct. 799, 112 L.Ed. 2d 860 (1991), the issue was whether Princeton University's private eating clubs were "distinctly private" and thus exempt from New Jersey's law against discrimination. Membership in five eating clubs (the Cap and Gown Club, Cottage Club, Ivy Club, Tiger Inn, and Tower Club) was by invitation only after the applicant submitted to interviews and a demanding selection process. However, the court concluded that the eating clubs were subject to New Jersey's law notwithstanding these selective membership criteria because of the integral and "symbiotic relationship" between the eating club and the university, a place of public accommodation. As pointed out in 2004 by Russell Nieli of the Princeton University Politics Department, Princeton's eating clubs are but one manifestation of discrimination.

SUGGESTED READING: William Selden, *Club Life at Princeton: An Historical Account of the Eating Clubs at Princeton University* (Princeton, NJ: Princeton Prospect Foundation, 1994); *Dale v. Boy Scouts of America*, Superior Court of New Jersey, Appellate Division, A-2427-95T3, http://lw.bna.com/lw/19980317/a242795.htm; Ben Gose, "Princeton Tries to Explain Drop in Jewish Enrollment," *Yggdrasil*, http://home.ddc.net/ygg/rj/rj-32.htm.

PRIVILEGIA. Pro-Jewish charters; concessions granted to the Jews by local political authorities in Europe in medieval times. These charters were the best protection the Jews had in the Middle Ages and were probably purchased at great expense. It cost the English Jews 4,000 marks to have their charters confirmed in 1201. These *privilegia* were awarded the Jews because the sovereign authority who "owned" them meant to make a profit by **taxing** Jewish wealth. *See also PRIVILEGIA ODIOSA.*

SUGGESTED READING: Joseph Jacobs, *The Jews of Angevin England: Documents and Records* (London: David Nutt, 1893); Jacob Marcus, *The Jew in the Medieval World: A Source Book, 315–1791* (New York: New York University, 1979).

PRIVILEGIA ODIOSA. Official discrimination (against Jews) in medieval Europe. *See also PRIVILEGIA.*

PROGRESSIVE LABOR PARTY. Ultraleft-wing U.S. political party, a splinter of the Communist Party. Its propaganda speaks of a workers' revolution. It criticizes Israel for aiding the U.S. "imperialistic endeavors." *See also* NEW LEFT.

PROTECTIVE CUSTODY. Arrest without due process of law by the **Gestapo** of those considered enemies of the **Third Reich**. Jews were classified within this category; their "crime" was being born Jewish. Usually, the destination was the **concentration camp.** During **Kristallnacht**, 20,000 Jews were arrested and sent to concentration camps to persuade them to leave the Reich. The expression used by **Hermann Goering** was *Schutzhaft*. The term of confinement was indefinite, and the prisoner had no recourse to judicial proceedings.

SUGGESTED READING: Whitney Harris, *Tyranny on Trial* (New York: Barnes & Noble, 1995).

PROTOCOLS OF THE ELDERS OF ZION, THE. A book written by Elie de Cyon (Ilya Tsion), a Russian journalist living in Paris in the late 19th century, in an attempt to discredit the modernizing economic policies of Sergei Witte, the Russian minister of finance. The tract was expanded in 1895 by the tsarist opponents of Witte and, in a slightly abridged form, was published in the St. Petersburg newspaper *Znamya* (*The Banner*) in August and September 1903. In 1897, Witte—who called the Jews "poor," "filthy," and "repulsive" and said they engaged in "pimping and **usury**," were cursed with "racial peculiarities," and were "one of the malignant factors of our accursed revolution"—instructed Russian general Pyotr Rachkovsky, head of the Russian Secret Police in Paris, to break into Cyon's home. There, the agents discovered *The Protocols*. The general used the work against the Jews and Cyon, who was himself Jewish. In 1909 **Sergei Nilus** revealed to a Russian count that *The Protocols* was fraudulent and that General Rachkovsky had sent the manuscript to him. Later, Nilus included this material as an appendix to his book, *The Great in the Small*.

The text, purporting to be the minutes of a secret meeting of Jewish leaders, advanced the idea of a worldwide Jewish conspiracy to dominate Gentile society. Modeled on earlier French works, it blamed revolutions and civil disorder on Jewish plots. During the Russian Civil War, White Russians declared the **Bolshevik** Revolution a Jewish invention based on *The Protocols*. Detroit industrialist **Henry Ford** thought World War I was caused by Jews, and serialized *The Protocols* in his *Dearborn Independent* newspaper in 1920. **Adolf Hitler** also widely used the ideas of Jewish domination and plotting in his diatribes. Arab states and writers still popularize *The Protocols* today.

In the 1930s, the Jewish community of Switzerland sued the Swiss National Socialist League for publishing offensive literature that might encourage crime. In 1935, the trial judge declared *The Protocols* a forgery "liable to excite hatred." In 1937, another court stated that *The Protocols* was "scurrilous and immoral" but did not fall under Bern's offensive-literature law. Many **antisemites** considered this ruling "proof" of the truth of *The Protocols*. More recently, *The Protocols* has become a staple of Islamic antisemitism, "dramatized" in a 30-part series by Arab Radio and Television. According to an Egyptian weekly, the series exposed Arab viewers to the central strategy "that to this very day dominates Israel's policy, political aspirations, and racism." *See also BIARRITZ 1868*; FREEMASONS; GOEDSCHE, HERMANN.

SUGGESTED READING: Hadassah Ben-Itto, *The Lie That Would Not Die: The Protocols of the Elders of Zion* (London: Vallentine Mitchell, 2005); Norman Cohn, *Warrant for Genocide* (New York: Harper & Row, 1967); Robert S. Wistrich, *Muslim Antisemitism: A Clear and Present Danger* (New York: American Jewish Committee, 2002).

PROUDHON, PIERRE-JOSEPH (1809–1865). French founder of anarchism. Proudhon believed Jews were unsociable and obstinate poisoners of commerce. He wrote that Jews were "often unfaithful to Jehovah, but always faithful to Mammon." He thought that they should not be admitted to any kind of employment and should be expelled to Asia or exterminated.

SUGGESTED READING: Léon Poliakov, *The History of Antisemitism*, 4 vols. (New York: Vanguard, 1965–86).

PRYNNE, WILLIAM (1600–1669). Radical Puritan minister and English pamphleteer. Prynne campaigned to block Oliver Cromwell's plan to reopen England to the Jews. Cromwell finally settled the issue by simply letting the Jews return surreptitiously. According to Prynne, Jewish methods included "Usuries and Deceits, clipping and falsifying monies, ingrossing all sorts of commodities into their hands, [and] usurping the Nations' trades." "They are all turned Devils already, and now we must all turn Jews." Jews were "not fit for our land nor yet for our dung-hills."

SUGGESTED READING: Cecil Roth, *History of the Jews in England* (Oxford: Oxford University Press, 1965).

PSEUDO-AMBROSE. Christian writer confused with **St. Ambrose**; possibly St. Nicetas of Remesiana (335–414). Pseudo-Ambrose saw all Jews as "apostates, for denial of Christ is essentially a violation of the Law."

SUGGESTED READING: Marcel Simon, *Verus Israel* (Oxford: Oxford University Press, 1986).

PSEUDO-CYPRIAN. Fourth-century Christian writer confused with **St. Cyprian**. In his *Adversus Judaeos*, III, Pseudo-Cyprian stated: "Moses they [the Jews] cursed because he proclaimed Christ, . . . David they hated because he sang of Christ, . . . Isaiah they sawed asunder shouting His glories, . . . John they slew revealing Christ, . . . **Judas** they loved betraying Him."

SUGGESTED READING: Marcel Simon, *Verus Israel* (Oxford: Oxford University Press, 1986).

PSEUDO-METHODIUS, APOCALYPSE OF (690). Scholarly medieval tract authored by an anonymous writer confused with St. Methodius. He regarded the Jews as soldiers of the **Antichrist** who lived off human flesh.

SUGGESTED READING: Norman Cohen, *The Pursuit of the Millennium* (Oxford: Oxford University Press, 1980).

PSYCHOANALYSIS. Antisemities regard psychoanalysis as a "Jewish pseudo-science." *See* FREUD, SIGMUND; JUNG, CARL.

PTOLEMY (100–170). Greco-Egyptian astronomer and mathematician. Ptolemy wrote that Jews are "more gifted in trade and exchange; they are unscrupulous, despicable cowards, treacherous, servile, and in general fickle . . . bold, godless, and scheming."

SUGGESTED READING: Menahem Stern, ed., *Greek and Latin Authors on Jews and Judaism* (Jerusalem: Israel Academy of Sciences and Humanities, 1984).

PUBLIC OPINION REGARDING JEWS, 1930s AND 1940s, U.S. Several public-opinion polls taken in the 1930s and 1940s testify that most Americans perceived **Nazi** persecution of Jews as in part the fault of the victims, a finding which may express the respondents' own negative feelings toward Jews. During the Depression, polls demonstrated a widespread fantasy that Jews ran the **banking** system and caused the stock market crash. In actuality, Jews held very few major positions in American banking and had very little influence on the banking industry. In addition, the few international Jewish investing houses had smaller overseas loans than any of the powerful Gentile establishments. Indeed, the U.S. government effectively kept Jews out of banking by not issuing bank charters to Jewish bankers. At the time of the Wall Street crash in 1929, only one small Jewish-owned bank existed. It was forced into bankruptcy because no other bank was willing to grant it a loan. In 1935, *Fortune*, one of America's most influential journals, reported that more than half of those surveyed in the Farm Belt and the West were indifferent to Nazism in Germany or thought that the exclusion of Jews helped Germany as a country. A Gallup poll of 1939 reported that 83 percent of Americans opposed the admission of a larger number of Jewish refugees. In the same year, *Fortune* concluded that **Adolf Hitler** would rejoice because the results of its public-opinion polls indicated that "Americans don't like the Jews much better than do the Nazis." The Office of Public Opinion Research found that in 1942, only about 1 percent of Americans polled believed that Nazi hatred of the Jews was bad. Polls indicated that between 1940 and 1945 about 70 percent of those polled would have supported a campaign against Jews *in* the United States or would have refused to take a stand. A June 1944 poll indicated that 57 percent of Americans anticipated "a widespread campaign in this country" against Jews. In June 1945, Jews were considered a far greater threat to America than German- or Japanese-Americans. As late as the 1960s, polls showed that half of the American people were still **antisemitic** and that religious bigotry was the most important factor behind this anti-Jewishness.

SUGGESTED READING: Charles Stember et al., *Jews in the Mind of America* (New York: Basic Books, 1966).

PUNCH. British humor magazine. By the turn of the 19th century, *Punch* had become a national institution, its weekly political cartoon reflecting national attitudes. *Punch*'s cartoons reflected British **antisemitic** stereotyping. British Prime Minister **Benjamin Disraeli** was depicted as "Ben JuJu"; he became a standard point of identification for cartoonists in *Punch* and elsewhere to exaggerate and caricature. His ethnicity was frequently depicted as un-English and non-Christian. A June 1875 article in *Punch* reflected the fashionable antisemitism of the time, depicting Jews at a furniture sale as greedy, money-hungry, filthy individuals—all with hooked noses: "I am aware that . . . beaks will swoop down upon me, as a hawk on a lamb. . . . They are one and all of the Hebrew persuasion." A Jewish broker responded to that article, saying:

> Most indignantly do I deny every assertion contained in your article . . . as to the broken English you so glibly put into the mouths of the Jews who addressed you. . . . I am only a Broker, and have been unable to study since the age of sixteen, yet I am quite willing to read or speak in English, French, German, or Italian, side by side with yourself. . . . It is a presumption to call us Jews unclean.

SUGGESTED READING: Anthony S. Wohl, "'Ben JuJu': Representations of Disraeli's Jewishness in the Victorian Political Cartoon," *Jewish History* 10, no. 2 (Fall 1996).

PURGE OF 1968 (POLAND). *See* MOCZAR, MIECZYSLAW.

PURIM. Jewish holiday in early spring based on the Biblical Book of Esther. The protagonist of the story is **Haman**, who states the classical **antisemitic** canard that Jews are unpatriotic and do not follow the customs and laws of the host society. He casts lots (*Pur*) to determine when the Jews of Persia should be murdered but is foiled by Queen Esther.

SUGGESTED READING: Kaufmann Kohler and Henry Malter, "Purim," *JewishEncyclopedia.com*, 2002, http://www.jewishencyclopedia.com/view.jsp?artid=613&letter=P.

PURISHKEVICH, VLADIMIR MITROFANOVICH. Russian politican and right-wing extremist. In 1905, Purishkevich helped found the Union of the Russian People and the Union of Archangel Michael. *See also* BLACK HUNDREDS.

SUGGESTED READING: Walter Laqueur, *Black Hundreds: The Rise of the Extreme Right in Russia* (New York: HarperCollins, 1993).

PURITY OF BLOOD. Starting in 1449, Spanish Christians believed that the **conversos** threatened the Christian community's spiritual health. They doubted the **New Christians'** sincerity. An economic motive also troubled them, since the conversos were very successful competitors. They therefore passed purity-of-blood laws barring **converts** and their descendants from positions of power and prestige and intermarrying "natural Christians." Purity of blood required tracing one's ancestors back five generations, proving no Jewish intermarriage. The **Jesuits** also demanded purity of blood for their members back to 1750, as did the **Nazi SS**. *See also* LIMPIEZA DE SANGRE; MARR, WILHELM; NUREMBERG LAWS OF 1935.

SUGGESTED READING: Yitzhak Baer, *A History of Jews in Christian Spain*, 2 vols. (Philadelphia: Jewish Publication Society, 1992).

PUSHKIN, ALEKSANDR (1799–1837). Russian writer. In *Black Shawl* (1831), a lyric poem often set to music, he wrote: "One day I'd invited of guests a gay crew, / Then to me there came creeping an infamous Jew."

– Q –

QUINTILLIAN (35–96). Spanish-Roman orator and rhetorician. "[Moses is] detested for concentrating a race that is a curse to others, the founder of the Jewish superstition." *See also* JUVENAL.

SUGGESTED READING: Menahem Stern, ed., *Greek and Latin Authors on Jews and Judaism* (Jerusalem: Israel Academy of Sciences and Humanities, 1984).

QUISLING, VIDKUN (1887–1945). Norwegian prime minister and collaborator with the **Nazis**. When the Nazis invaded Norway in 1940, Quisling, who had already formed his own **fascist** organization, aided in the persecution, roundup, and **deportation** of Jews. Quisling was executed in Norway in 1945. His name became synonymous with collaboration.

SUGGESTED READING: Samuel Abrahamsen, *Norway's Response to the Holocaust* (New York: Holocaust Library, 1991).

QUOTA SYSTEM. Until rather recent times, the Jews in most lands faced quota systems. There were restrictions on employment, professional advancement, college entry, camps, private schools, and other institutions. Often these quotas were unofficial, quiet, or underground. Sometimes they were expressed as a *numerus clausus.* The British who ruled Palestine from 1920 to 1948 imposed quotas for Jewish immigration to placate the Arabs. In the United States the 1960s saw the demise of quotas. Since 1921 in the former Soviet Union, and now Russia, government officials have tried to reduce the number of Jews in important positions and higher education. *See also* QUOTAS, COLLEGE; QUOTAS, IMMIGRATION; REVERSE DISCRIMINATION; STALIN, JOSEPH; WHITE PAPER OF 1939.

QUOTAS, COLLEGE. With the huge immigration to the United States from Eastern Europe between 1890 and 1924, the number of Jews in the United States increased to more than 3 percent. The new Americans sought to enter prestigious colleges and universities. However, because college administrators wanted to preserve the "Christian gentleman" nature of higher education, most Ivy League schools instituted informal quota systems. *See also* LOWELL, ABBOTT LAWRENCE.

SUGGESTED READING: Edward Flannery, *The Anguish of the Jews* (New York: Paulist Press, 1985).

QUOTAS, IMMIGRATION. The U.S. immigration laws of 1921 and 1924 were, in effect, discriminatory anti-Jewish acts, motivated in great part by **antisemitism**. The 1921 Quota Law was based on the quota at 2 percent of those nationalities already in the United States as of 1910. The Act of 1924 based its restrictionist quotas on the population of ethnic stocks already in the United States as of 1890. This meant that Jewish immigrants from countries such as Russia, Poland, and Romania, where Jews—mostly orthodox Jews—were attempting to flee persecution, would have very limited quotas; the grand total of immigrants annually allowed into the United States from all three of these nations was 8,899 (the German quota was more than 27,000). Both laws were based on antisemitism and belief in **Nordic superiority**. *See also* EUGENICS; IMMIGRATION RESTRICTION LEAGUE; JOHNSON-REED ACT; LAUGHLIN, HARRY.

SUGGESTED READING: John Higham, *Strangers in the Land: Patterns of American Nativism, 1860–1925* (New Brunswick, NJ: Rutgers University Press, 1955); Naomi Cohen, *Encounter with Emancipation: The German Jews in the United States, 1830–1914* (Philadelphia: Jewish Publication Society, 1984); Arthur Morse, *While Six Million Died: A Chronicle of American Apathy* (New York: Overlook Press, 1983).

QUTB, SAYYID (1906–1966). Egyptian author and **Muslim Brotherhood** activist. A leading Islamic ideologue of the 1950s, Qutb was the author of a seminal essay on the Jews, "Our Struggle with the Jews," which argues that Muslim **antisemitism** is consistent with the **Koran**, that the eternal Jew conspires constantly against Islam, and that the existence of Israel and the success of the Jews reflect the failures of Islamic civilization, which is under further attack by secularity, modernity, sexuality, and American culture. According to Qutb, Jews created the modern ideologies of communism and psychoanalysis to destroy the Muslim "family and shatter the sacred relationships in society." His ideas form a backdrop for Muslim terrorism. Egypt's secular Muslim president **Gamal Abdel Nasser** had Qutb hanged for his attack on Nasser's authority.

SUGGESTED READING: Robert S. Wistrich, *Muslim Antisemitism: A Clear and Present Danger* (New York: American Jewish Committee, 2002); Ronald L. Nettler, *Past Trials and Present Tribulation: A Muslim Fundamentalist View of the Jews* (Oxford, England: Pergamon, 1987).

– R –

RAC. *See* ROCK AGAINST COMMUNISM.

RACE, ADOLF HITLER'S FINAL VIEWS ON. A few months before his death in April 1945, **Adolf Hitler** told his private secretary **Martin Bormann**:

> We use the term *Jewish race* as a matter of convenience, for in reality and from the genetic point of view there is no such thing as the Jewish race. There does, however, exist a community. . . . It is [a] spiritually homogeneous group [to] which all Jews throughout the world deliberately adhere . . . and it is this group of human beings to which we give the title *Jewish race*.

Denying that the Jews were only "a religious entity," since Jewish atheists existed, Hitler described the Jews as "an abstract race of the mind [that] has its origins, admittedly, in the Hebrew religion. . . . A race of the mind is something more solid, more durable that just a [biological] race, pure and simple."

SUGGESTED READING: *The Testament of Adolf Hitler: The Hitler-Bormann Documents, February–April 1945* (London: World Service, 1978).

RACISM. *See* ANTISEMITISM, RACIAL.

RADEMACHER, FRANZ (1906–1973). **SS** general and administrator. Rademacher headed the department in the German Foreign Ministry that dealt with Jews. Working along with **Adolf Eichmann**, he aided in the **deportations** of Jews from Belgium, France, Slovakia, and Yugoslavia, ordering mass executions of Serbian Jews. After making a postwar escape, he was arrested and convicted by a German court and died in prison.

SUGGESTED READING: Christopher Browning, *The Final Solution and the German Foreign Office* (New York: Holmes & Meier, 1978).

RADICAL ISLAM. Currently, radical Islam is a major force in the Islamic world. It interprets traditional Islam as a 20th-century ideology at war with the West and the Jews. Its leaders want Muslims to live in strict accordance with the sacred religious law of the Shari'a. In this way, the Islamic world would regain the wealth, strength, and glory it had during the Middle Ages. Radical Islam believes that Jews spare no effort to dominate the world, especially the Muslim nations. Therefore, a ruthless war against Jews wherever they are located is an urgent necessity for radical Muslims everywhere. *See also* HAMAS; HEZBOLLAH; MUSLIM BROTHERHOOD; *PROTOCOLS OF THE ELDERS OF ZION, THE.*

SUGGESTED READING: Daniel Pipes, *Militant Islam Reaches America* (New York: W. W. Norton, 2003).

RADULF. *See* RODOLPHE.

RAHOWA. White supremacist and **World Church of the Creator** contraction of "racial holy war." RAHOWA signifies the battle that will pit the white race against minorities and Jews and lead to **Aryan** rule over the world.

SUGGESTED READING: Anti-Defamation League, *Hate on Display: Extremist Symbols, Logos, and Tattoos* (New York: Anti-Defamation League, 2006); ADL Law Enforcement Agency Resource Network, *A Visual Database of Extremist Symbols, Logos, and Tattoos*, http://www.adl.org/hate_symbols/default.asp.

RAMI, AHMED. *See* HOLOCAUST DENIAL.

RAMPOLLA DEL TINDARO, MARIANO (1843–1913). Pope **Leo XIII**'s secretary of state, Cardinal Rampolla rejoiced at the overwhelming victory by the Austrian Christian-Social Party (Antisemitic Party) in Vienna's municipal elections in the mid-1890s: "You see, we have triumphed."

SUGGESTED READING: Henry Cohn, "Theodore Herzl's Conversion to Zionism," *Jewish Social Studies* 32 (April 1970).

RANKIN, JOHN (1882–1960). U.S. Representative from Mississippi, 1921–53. Although no one in Congress publicly advocated anti-Jewish violence in the 1930s and 1940s, several members openly expressed **antisemitism**. Rankin called the Jewish commentator Walter Winchell "a little slime-mongering **kike**." From the floor of the House of Representatives in 1939, he complained that the Jewish money-changers want "us to go into war, but not to protect Christianity. It is about 2,000 years too late for them to wrap the cloak of Christianity about themselves." The Jews caused "strikes in the Midwest, inflation and then depression in Germany, the starvation of millions of Christian farmers in the Ukraine, and race-mixing in South America." Rankin complained in 1941 that the Jews were again "crucifying civilization on a cross of gold." In 1949, he blamed the deaths of "30 million Christians" during the war on "the same gang that composed the fifth column of the crucifixion." Jews hounded, persecuted, derided "the Savior." In addition, for two millennia Jews had attempted to "destroy Christianity and everything that is based on Christian principles. They have overrun and virtually destroyed Europe. They are now trying to undermine and destroy America." In 1952, he railed in Congress against insidious alien enemies who are now "plotting . . . the wiping of Christianity from the face of the earth."

SUGGESTED READING: Steven Alan Carr, *Hollywood and Antisemitism: A Cultural History to World War II* (Cambridge: Cambridge University Press, 2001).

RASSENSCHANDE. German for "race defilement." Sexual contact between Jewish Germans and non-Jewish Germans—between Jews and those related to German citizens by blood—was forbidden and punishable under the **Nuremberg Laws of 1935**. On February 10, 1944, Security Chief **Ernst Kaltenbrunner** ruled that violations warranted the death penalty. The term was extended to sexual relations between Germans and Slavic workers as well. *See also* MARRIAGE RESTRICTIONS; RHINELAND OCCUPATION; WAGNER, GERHART.

SUGGESTED READING: Irene Eckler, *A Family Torn Apart by "Rassenschande": Political Persecution in the Third Reich* (Schwetzingen, Germany: Horneburg Verlag, 1998); Robert Michael and Karin Doerr, *Nazi-Deutsch/Nazi-German: An English Lexicon of the Language of the Third Reich* (Westport, CT: Greenwood Press, 2001).

RASSINIER, PAUL (1906–1967). **Holocaust denier** and professor of literature at Lyons, France. Rassinier stated that a Jewish conspiracy accounts for the "myth" of the **Holocaust**. He denied that the **gas chambers** were used to murder Jews; rather, they were for lice extermination. The loss of Jewish life at concentration camps, Rassiner claimed, was due to typhus. *See also* BUTZ, ARTHUR; INSTITUTE FOR HISTORICAL REVIEW; LEUCHTER, FRED.

SUGGESTED READING: Florent Brayard, *Comment l'idée vint à M. Rassinier: Naissance du Révisionnisme* (Paris: Fayard, 1996); Ben S. Austin, "A Brief History of Holocaust Denial," http://www.jewishvirtuallibrary.org/jsource/Holocaust/denialbrief.html.

RATH, ERNST VOM (1911–1938). Minor German diplomat. Herschel Grynszpan, a Jewish teenager tormented by the news of his parents' **deportation** to Poland in 1938, shot and killed vom Rath, third secretary at the German embassy in Paris. This act was the pretext for the preplanned German **pogrom** known as **Kristallnacht**.

SUGGESTED READING: Anthony Read and David Fisher, *Kristallnacht: The Nazi Night of Terror* (New York: Random House, 1989).

RATHENAU, WALTHER (1867–1922). German Jewish industrialist and statesman. Rathenau helped to negotiate the **Versailles** Treaty and was the German minister of reconstruction and foreign minister in the **Weimar Republic** in 1922. Right-wing racists and **Nazis** accused him of criminal treasonous activity for what they considered the "stab in the back," the betrayal of the German Army by Jews, socialists, and liberals that forced a premature signing of the armistice to end World War I.

SUGGESTED READING: Charles B. Flood, *Hitler: The Path to Power* (Boston: Houghton Mifflin, 1989).

RATLINE. Post–World War II organization for the escape of **Nazi war criminals** from Europe. It was an informal secret association of Catholic clergy and **Vatican** officials with the U.S. Office of Strategic Services, an intelligence gathering unit that later formed the core of the CIA. The ratline provided safe houses, fake passports, and new identities and used Catholic institutions to enable Nazis to reach South America, the United States, **Australia**, and **Canada**. *See also* BARBIE, KLAUS; BRUNNER, ALOIS; EICHMANN, ADOLF; HUDAL, ALOIS; PAVELIC, ANTE; STANGL, FRANZ.

SUGGESTED READING: Christopher Simpson, *Blowback: America's Recruitment of Nazis and Its Effects on the Cold War* (London: Weidenfeld & Nicolson, 1988).

RAYMOND OF PEÑAFORT, ST. *See* PÑNAFORTE, RAYMOND DE.

REBATET, LUCIEN (1903–1972). French **fascist** intellectual, journalist, and author; music and film critic for *Action Française* and contributor to the right-wing *Je Suis Partout*, for which he wrote until the liberation of France in 1944. In 1938 Rebatet became head of information for Action Française and worked closely with **Charles Maurras**. Expressing sympathy for National Socialism, Rebatet accused Jews of wanting a war to destroy the **Third Reich**. In 1942, Rebatet published *Les Decombres* (*The Ruins*), arguing that France's politicians and military as well as French Jews—especially, the Jew—caused France's defeat.
SUGGESTED READING: Frédéric Vitoux, *Céline: A Biography* (New York: Marlowe, 1994).

RECCARED. Spanish **Visigothic king**, 586–601; first Catholic Visigothic king. Reccared passed an anti-Jewish law code that forbade Jews from owning slaves, prevented intermarriage, and denied Jews important offices. The code so impressed Pope **Gregory I** that the pope wrote Reccared a letter in August 599 congratulating him for his "regulations against the *perfidia* of the Jews" and supporting Reccared's refusal to accept the Jews' pleas and their offer of a bribe to rescind his anti-Jewish legislation.
SUGGESTED READING: Shlomo Simonsohn, *The Apostolic See and the Jews: Documents, 492–1404* (Toronto: Pontifical Institute of Mediaeval Studies, 1988); Solomon Grayzel, "The Papal Bull *Sicut Judeis*," in *Essential Papers on Judaism and Christianity in Conflict*, ed. Jeremy Cohen (New York: New York University Press, 1991).

RECCESWINTH. Spanish Catholic **Visigothic king**, 649–72. Recceswinth prohibited Jewish **circumcision** and observance of Jewish holy days.
SUGGESTED READING: "The Jews of Spain and the Visigothic Code, 654–681 CE," *Internet Jewish History Sourcebook*, http://www.fordham.edu/halsall/jewish/jews-visigothic1.html.

RECONQUISTA. Also known as the Spanish Crusade. Reconquest of Spain by Christians from Moors (Muslim Arabs). In the 11th century Christian monarchs began their campaign, and in 1492, Granada, the last Muslim holding, was captured by **Ferdinand** and Isabella. In that same year, more than 200,000 Jews were expelled from Spain. The Moors had tolerated— even welcomed—the Jewish presence, with a Golden Age occurring between the 10th and 12th centuries. But with the reconquest, Jews became subject to forced **conversions** and mass slaughter (such as at Seville in 1391).

SUGGESTED READING: Bernard F. Reilly, *The Medieval Spains* (New York: Cambridge University Press, 1993).

RED SEA PEDESTRIAN. (British slur) A phrase, referring to the biblical book Exodus, used in Monty Python's *The Life of Brian*.

SUGGESTED READING: "List of Ethnic Slurs," *Wikipedia*, http://en.wiki pedia.org/wiki/List_of_ethnic_slurs.

REFORMATION. *See* CALVIN, JOHN; LUTHER, MARTIN (1483–1546).

REFUGEE PROBLEM. During the 1930s and 1940s, while **Adolf Hitler** persecuted Jews first in Germany and then in the rest of Europe, potential safe havens disappeared. The United States would not revise its restrictive immigration policies. Great Britain drastically limited the number of refugees who could enter Palestine. Even underpopulated **Australia** held that "We don't have a racial problem and we don't want one." **Canada**'s leaders believed that "none is too many." The word *refugee* became a code word for Jew. Conferences such as **Evian** and **Bermuda** found no resolution to the situation. **Antisemitism** precluded any Free World solution to the refugee "problem." *See also* LONG, BRECKINRIDGE; ROOSEVELT, FRANKLIN D.; *ST. LOUIS*; WAR REFUGEE BOARD; WHITE PAPER OF 1939.

SUGGESTED READING: Arthur Morse, *While Six Million Died* (New York: Random House, 1968).

REGNARD, ALBERT (1836–1903). French socialist writer. At the end of the 19th century, Regnard praised the work of the antisemitic **Edouard Drumont** for raising the alarm concerning Judaism and Jewish capitalism, which were blamed for ruining Catholicism. He celebrated the **Aryan** race.

SUGGESTED READING: Robert Byrnes, *Antisemitism in Modern France* (New Brunswick, NJ: Rutgers University Press, 1950).

REICHENAU, WALTER VON (1884–1942). **Nazi** German field marshal. As commander of the German Sixth Army in Russia, Reichenau supported the **SS Einsatzgruppen** mobile murder units against Jews. One of **Adolf Hitler**'s favorites, Reichenau told his troops, "We have to exact a harsh but just retribution on the Jewish **subhumans**." He died in a plane crash after suffering a heart attack.

SUGGESTED READING: Robert S. Wistrich, *Who's Who in Nazi Germany* (London: Rutledge, 1995).

REICHSKRISTALLNACHT. *See* KRISTALLNACHT.

REICHSTHEOLOGIE. A movement mainly within Protestantism during the **Nazi** period to de-**judaize** the Protestant churches. It consisted of using only the New Testament Scriptures of the Bible, eliminating Hebrew words such as *amen*, and admitting to the church only Germans of pure Christian descent. The churches accepted the primacy of the state over the church. *See also* BONHOEFFER, DIETRICH; CONFESSING CHURCH; PURITY OF BLOOD.

SUGGESTED READING: Eberhard Bethge, *Dietrich Bonhoeffer: Man of Vision, Man of Courage* (New York: Harper & Row, 1970).

REINACH, JOSEPH. *See* MONUMENT HENRY.

RENAN, ERNEST (1823–1892). French philosopher and orientalist. In Renan's work on general history and Semitic languages in 1848, he distinguished between the naturally gifted **Aryan** race and the Semitic (Jewish) race and claimed that the Jews' monotheism stifled creativity and science. In 1862, he observed that although Semites had some admirable qualities, they almost always lacked "that keenness of moral feeling that seems to be above all natural to the Germanic and Celtic races." In the next year, he argued that Jesus obviously belonged to a superior race and, therefore, could not have been a true Semite. Whereas Christianity was purely spiritual, "Judaism contained the principle of a narrow formalism, of exclusive fanaticism disdainful of strangers; this was the Pharisaic spirit, which later became the talmudic spirit." And although he denied the responsibility of individual Jews for Jesus' crucifixion, he argued that Jews themselves were responsible for Christian intolerance of them. Whole nations can have a moral responsibility, he claimed, and "If ever there was a crime of a nation, it was the death of Jesus." *See also* LASSEN, CHRISTIAN.

SUGGESTED READING: Shmuel Almog, *Antisemitism through the Ages* (Elmsford, NY: Pergamon, 1988).

RENNES, GUILLAUME DE (d. 1264). French **Dominican** who declared that because Jews were the slaves of the princes (kings and rulers in Europe), their children could be removed "without any injury" to the parents.

SUGGESTED READING: Walter Pakter, "*De his qui foris sunt*: The Teachings of the Medieval Canon and Civil Lawyers Concerning the Jews,"

Ph.D. diss., Johns Hopkins University, 1974; David Nirenberg, *Communities of Violence: Persecution of Minorities in the Middle Ages* (Princeton, NJ: Princeton University Press, 1996).

"REPORT TO THE SECRETARY" ON THE ACQUIESCENCE OF THIS GOVERNMENT IN THE MURDER OF THE JEWS." A 1944 report mainly written by Josiah DuBois, a lawyer in the U.S. Treasury Department, that maintained that several **State Department** officials were fearful the U.S. government might act to save the Jews of Europe if the gruesome facts relating to **Adolf Hitler**'s plans to exterminate them were to become known. For this reason, these State Department officials not only attempted to suppress the **evidence of the Holocaust** but also secretly countermanded the instructions of the acting secretary of state (Sumner Welles) ordering such facts to be reported. The Treasury report stated:

> We leave it for your judgment whether this action made such officials the accomplices of Hitler in this program and whether or not these officials are not **war criminals** in every sense of the term. . . . We don't shoot them [Jews]. We let other people shoot them, and let them starve. . . . When you get through with it, the [State Department's] attitude to date is no different from Hitler's attitude. [The State Department officials involved in America's refugee policy are an] underground movement . . . to let the Jews be killed.

As to the British, the report concluded that they, "by doing nothing, are condemning these people [Jews] to death. [How can they] blame the Germans for killing them when we are doing this? The law calls them para-delicto, of equal guilt."

SUGGESTED READING: Foreign Funds Control Staff, memorandum, "For Secretary Morgenthau's Information Only," December 23, 1943, in *America and the Holocaust*, vol. 6, ed. David Wyman (New York: Garland, 1989–91); David Wyman, *The Abandonment of the Jews* (New York: New Press, 1998); Yitshaq Ben-Ami, *Years of Wrath, Days of Glory* (New York: Robert Speller & Sons, 1982).

REPROACHES. *See* IMPROPERIA.

RESTRICTIVE COVENANTS. Contracts prohibiting occupancy or use of real estate by Jews in the United States that began appearing in the 19th century. The Supreme Court in *Shelley v. Kramer* (1948) ruled such covenants regarding race and ethnicity unconstitutional. But newspapers nevertheless continued to advertise properties for "Christians only." The practice continued informally as "gentlemen's agreements."

SUGGESTED READING: Ruth B. Weintraub, *How Secure These Rights? Antisemitism in the United States in 1948* (Berkeley: University of California Press, 1949).

REUCHLIN, JOHANNES (1455–1522). German humanist. Reuchlin, Germany's foremost student of Jewish literature and mysticism, was of the opinion that "the Jew belongs to God just as much as I do." In his youth a follower of **St. Jerome**, Reuchlin at first accused the Jews of hating and persecuting Christians, of unbelief and depravity, and of blasphemy against Jesus Christ and Mary. But he later argued that the Jews were **citizens** of the Holy Roman Empire, that they deserved its full privileges and protection, and that the medieval accusations of **heresy** against Jews were false. Reuchlin was keenly interested in Hebrew and Hebrew religious texts. He believed that Kabbalistic writings, the Jewish mystical tradition, verified Christianity. His major work, *Rudiments of Hebrew*, was used by theologian **Martin Luther**. In the latter part of his life, Reuchlin vigorously and successfully defended the **Talmud** against the attacks by **Johannes Pfefferkorn,** who wished to have it banned in Germany.

SUGGESTED READING: Erika Rummel, *The Case against Johannes Reuchlin* (Toronto: University of Toronto Press, 2002).

REVENTLOW, ERNST ZU (1869–1943). In 1937, in *Judas Kampf und Niederlage in Deutschland*, Count Reventlow wrote: "Experience shows that Jewish blood is frequently stronger than **Aryan** blood, not only in grandchildren, but also in great-grandchildren and even further on down the line." Believing that Jews were the "lightning rods for all grievances," Reventlow believed that the Russian Revolution was caused by Jews. This confirmed **Adolf Hitler**'s idea that Jews were revolutionaries. The antisemitic *völkisch* right admitted exploiting political chaos and "using the situation for fanfares against Jewry, and the Jews as lightning conductors for all grievances."

SUGGESTED READING: Michael Burleigh, *The Third Reich: A New History* (New York: Hill & Wang, 2001).

REVERSE DISCRIMINATION. Governments as varied as the USSR's and the United States's have pursued a policy of preferential treatment, or affirmative action, in order to redress past discrimination through the improvement of the economic and education conditions for groups that were previously discriminated against. When the **Bolsheviks** consolidated their power in Russia in the 1920s, they gave preference to peasants and workers, indirectly discriminating against Jews, many of whom were professionals and small businessmen. Some believe that U.S. policies based on race discriminate against Jews and others.

SUGGESTED READING: Arkady Vaksberg, *Stalin against the Jews* (New York: Knopf, 1994).

REVISIONISM. *See* HOLOCAUST DENIAL.

REVOLUTIONS OF 1848. A series of European revolutions resulting from the growing power of the middle classes and demands for guaranteed civil liberties to all individual citizens, including Jews. Jews fought beside their fellow Christian citizens and helped write the new constitutions that resulted. Many liberals advocated Jewish emancipation and opposed the notion that European nations were only Christian nations. However, many Christians feared that Jewish emancipation would lead to Jewish domination; for example, conservatives like Prussian minister of the interior Hermann von Thile argued that granting Jews civil rights was inconsistent with Christian principles. In the first half of the 19th century, France, The Netherlands, and Great Britain had emancipated Jews, while most other nations, except for Russia, had been gradually eliminating legal discriminations against Jews. In much of the Austrian Empire, as elsewhere in Europe, 1848 provided a convenient pretext for popular attacks on Jews associated with the bourgeoisie, who intended to bring capitalism to society; many farmers and artisans also blamed the Jews for their economic troubles. In May, the Empire's Jews were given full rights, but when the Austrian monarchy recaptured the city, the new emperor, Franz Joseph, dissolved the Reichstag and nullified the "Basic Laws." By 1853, bans against Jews buying property and moving to certain areas of the empire were reconstituted. Soon "Jewish **oaths**" were restored and Jews were forbidden to hire Christian servants. Similarly, Hungarian Jews suffered from special **taxes**. In many nations, Jews kept some of their newly won freedoms, but in others, emancipation was repealed. In Germany the "Basic Rights of the German People" granted in 1848-49 was abolished a few years later, and Jews were once again subject to discrimination. Prussian law included a paragraph stating: "The Christian religion shall be the basis in all government institutions that are associated with religion." Jews would have to wait until 1871 for legal emancipation in Germany.

SUGGESTED READING: Glenn R. Sharfman, "Jewish Emancipation," 2004, http://www.ohiou.edu/~Chastain/ip/jewemanc.htm; Werner Mosse, Arnold Paucker, and Reinhard Rürup, eds., *Revolution and Evolution: 1848 in German-Jewish History* (Tübingen, Germany: J. C. B. Mohr, 1981).

REWBELL, JEAN-FRANÇOIS (1747–1807). Jacobin Alsatian deputy during **French Revolution**. Rewbell helped persuade the Jacobin deputies to defeat the extension of civil liberties to Jews. He stated, "The Jews are the alien despoilers of the peasants, and they will turn against the Revolution if they are abandoned to these oppressors." He also disputed the Jewish demand for private communal [*kahal*] officials, saying: "What do you think of individuals who want to become French but who want nonetheless to keep Jewish administrators, Jewish judges, Jewish notaries, and all this within their own confines?"

SUGGESTED READING: Béatrice Philippe, *Être Juif dans la société française* (Paris: Montalba, 1979).

RHINELAND OCCUPATION, ALLIED. As a result of the Allied victory in World War I, Allied troops, particularly French, occupied the Rhineland between 1918 and 1929. Many of these troops were Black African, part of French colonial forces. **Adolf Hitler**, among others, blamed the occupation and the use of such troops on the Jews who sought "racial shame" (*Rassenschande*) on the Germans.

SUGGESTED READING: Robert N. Proctor, *Racial Hygiene: Medicine under the Nazis* (Cambridge, MA: Harvard University Press, 1988).

RICHARD I (1157–1199). King of England, 1189–99. Also known as Richard the Lionheart; Coeur de Lion and Oc et No (Yes and No) by the French; and Melek-Ric (King Rick) by the Saracens. In 1190 Richard noted that the Jews should be treated as "our [the king's] property." At Richard's coronation, wrote William of Newburgh (d. 1198), a Christian struck a Jew with his hand. A melee ensue and several Jews died. Although Richard had ordered that all the Jews be left alone, William wrote of subsequent attacks that "an agreeable rumor pervaded the whole of London that the king had ordered all Jews exterminated. An innumerable mob . . . soon assembled in arms, eager for plunder and for the blood of a people hateful to all men, by the judgment of God."

SUGGESTED READING: Albert M. Hyamson, *A History of the Jews of England* (Portland, OR: University Press of the Pacific, 2001).

RICHARD OF DEVIZES. Late 12th-century English monk in Winchester. In his book *Chronicon*, Devizes associated the Jews with the Devil, bloodsucking vermin, vomit, and feces.

SUGGESTED READING: Anthony Bale, "Richard of Devizes and the Fictions of Judaism," *Jewish Cultural History* 3, no. 2 (2001): 46–65.

RICKOVER, HYMAN GEORGE (1900–1986). Admiral and father of the nuclear submarine. Rickover took the U.S. Navy into the atomic age with his persistence that the U.S. Navy build the first nuclear-powered submarine. In 1918, Rickover received an appointment to the U.S. Naval Academy, where he was often confronted with **antisemitism**. After he had been twice passed over for promotion to admiral (the naval codes require retirement if promotion is twice denied), congressional leaders suspected that he was a victim of "foul play." Following an investigation that uncovered antisemitism, he was named a rear admiral in 1953.

SUGGESTED READING: Francis Duncan, *Rickover: The Struggle for Excellence* (Annapolis: Naval Institute Press, 2001).

RIGORD (1150–1209). French chronicler, physician, and monk who wrote the *Gesta Philippi Augusti*, dealing with the life of the French king **Philip Augustus**. Rigord praised this "most Christian king's" **expulsions** of the Jews and argued that the king had an obligation to safeguard the religious purity of France from the perverse, religiously unclean Jews, whose malicious behavior (including **ritual murder**, **usury**, and **desecration of the Host**) stemmed from their Jewishness. Although King Philip's anti-Jewish policies had obvious economic and political benefits to the crown, Rigord explained that Philip chose his anti-Jewish policies based on the stories the king had heard as a youth of Jewish ritual murder of a Christian child. Rigord complained that chalices pledged to Jewish usurers as security for loans were "used so vilely, in their impiety and scorn of the Christian religion, that from the cups in which the body and blood of our Lord Jesus Christ was consecrated they gave their children cakes soaked in wine."

SUGGESTED READING: Jacob Marcus, *The Jew in the Medieval World: A Source Book, 315–1791* (New York: New York University, 1979).

RINDFLEISCH. Late 13th-century German knight. The worst massacre of Jews who were charged with **desecration of the Host** occurred in 1298 at Röttingen, where Jews were accused of pounding a consecrated wafer until blood flowed. Under the age-old and persistent influence of Christian anti-Jewishness, the killing spread through much of central Germany and Austria between 1298 and 1303, when the vengeful followers of the German nobleman Rindfleisch traveled beyond the local area in a "divinely ordained" attempt to murder all the Jews. Some local burghers and bishops vainly tried to protect their Jewish neighbors, as did Holy Roman Emperor Albert of Austria (d. 1308). All Jews were held responsible for the imaginary actions of a few local Jews. Perhaps 100,000 Jews, including **con-**

verts to Christianity, in 146 German communities were massacred during this period. *See also* DEFAMATIONS, ANTI-JEWISH.

SUGGESTED READING: Miri Rubin, *Gentile Tales: The Narrative Assault on Late Medieval Jews* (Philadelphia: University of Pennsylvania Press, 2004).

RITUAL MURDER. From the 12th to the 20th centuries, accusations of ritual murder were often made against Jews in Europe. Imagined to be in league with sorcerers, devils, and **heretics**, the Jews were accused of annually murdering a Christian child, usually at Passover-Easter time or sometimes at **Purim**, using the techniques of *shechita*, Jewish ritual slaughter, and draining the child's blood for consumption. This accusation most likely stemmed from the myth of the Jews' unending role in Jesus' crucifixion. The triumph of Christianity and the vindication of Jesus' sacrifice were confirmed by the exposure of the Jews' "crimes" and by their punishment. In May 1934, the **Nazi** *Der Stürmer* ran an article listing 131 cases of alleged Jewish ritual murder. The ritual-murder and blood-libel **defamations**—originally circulated in the 19th century by resident Christians—also occurred in Muslim areas: Beirut (1824), Antioch (1826), Hama (1829), Damascus (1840), and the Ottoman Empire, leading to **pogroms** in Smyrna (1872) and Constantinople (1874). *See also* ANDERL OF RINN; APION; BLACK HUNDREDS; BLOIS; BEILIS CASE; CHAUCER, GEOFFREY; FULDA; LA GUARDIA BLOOD LIBEL; NORWICH BLOOD LIBEL; SIMON OF TRENT; TÍSZA-ESZLÁR.

SUGGESTED READING: Marvin Perry and Frederick M. Schweitzer, *Antisemitism: Myth and Hate from Antiquity to the Present* (New York: Palgrave Macmillan, 2002); Alan Dundes, *The Blood Libel Legend: A Casebook in Antisemitic Folklore* (Madison: University of Wisconsin Press, 1991); Robert S. Wistrich, *Muslim Antisemitism: A Clear and Present Danger* (New York: American Jewish Committee, 2002).

RITUAL SLAUGHTER (*SHECHITA*). Jewish law demands swift death of kosher animals when they are killed for food. The animals should experience virtually no pain. However, there have been movements to ban shechita based on distortions of the **Talmud**—often as an indirect form of **antisemitism**. Other times, animal rights groups have opposed it. The anti-shechita movement started in Germany in the mid-19th century. Switzerland was the first with an outright ban in 1893. Other countries followed in the 1930s. In the West, many countries, including the United States, have special laws permitting shechita. *See also* DIETARY LAWS, JEWISH.

SUGGESTED READING: Samuel Dresner and Seymour Siegel, *Jewish Dietary Laws* (New York: United Synagogue Book Service, 1980).

RIVALTO, GIORDANO DA (1260–1311). Tuscan **Dominican** preacher. Rivalto wrote that the Jews continued to murder Christ by stealing the Host and, in a repetition of the crucifixion, attacking it as if it were Christ's body. Giordano himself claimed that he was present when the boy Jesus miraculously appeared at a **desecration of the Host** by the Jews, and he proudly claimed that this miracle stirred Christians to murder 24,000 Jews as punishment for their evil deed. *See also* DEFAMATIONS, ANTI-JEWISH.

SUGGESTED READING: Jeremy Cohen, *The Friars and the Jews* (Ithaca, NY: Cornell University Press, 1982).

ROBERTSON, PAT (1930–). Leading American revivalist preacher. Although he has made antisemitic remarks—for example, "The **Antichrist** is probably a Jew alive in Israel today"—Robertson is also a supporter of the Jewish state of Israel.

SUGGESTED READING: Bill McKibben, "The Christian Paradox," *Harper's Magazine*, August 2005.

ROBESPIERRE, MAXIMILIEN. *See* FRENCH REVOLUTION.

ROCK AGAINST COMMUNISM. Symbolized by *RAC* with a skull superimposed on a hammer-and-sickle. Associated with racist **skinheads, neo-Nazis**, and White Power hate music focusing on racism and **antisemitism**. In the 1980s, rock promoters in Great Britain put on a series of "Rock against Racism" concerts. In response, various white supremacist bands, led by Ian Stuart and Skrewdriver, held "Rock against Communism" concerts. The term eventually became used to describe the style of music, and later still came to be used as a general term for **white power music**.

SUGGESTED READING: Anti-Defamation League, *Hate on Display: Extremist Symbols, Logos, and Tattoos* (New York: Anti-Defamation League, 2006).

ROCKWELL, GEORGE LINCOLN. *See* AMERICAN NAZI PARTY.

RODOLPHE. French Cistercian monk. In 1146, at the start of the Second **Crusade**, Rodolphe, who was believed to perform miracles and who attracted enormous crowds, preached that the Jewish enemies of God must be punished. Anti-Jewish riots broke out in Strasbourg, Cologne, Mainz,

Worms, Speyer, Würzburg, and other French and German cities. **St. Bernard of Clairvaux**, the most influential Christian of his time, denounced Rodolphe and came in person to Germany to force the monk to return to his monastery.

SUGGESTED READING: Edward Flannery, *The Anguish of the Jews* (New York: Macmillan, 1965).

ROHLING, AUGUST (1839–1931). German Roman Catholic priest, professor of theology in Prague. Rohling believed that the **ritual murder defamation** was true and thought he could prove it. He sought to be a witness at the Hungarian **Tísza-Eszlár** Trial in 1882, but scholars discredited him. In 1887 he published *The Talmud Jew*. When Samuel Bloch (1850–1933), a Jewish scholar, refuted his work, Rohling sued Bloch, but the priest, recognizing the weakness of his arguments, withdrew. Nevertheless, *The Talmud Jew* continued to be reprinted and was used by **Nazis** as a sourcebook.

SUGGESTED READING: Max Raisin, *A History of the Jews in Modern Times*, rev. ed. (New York: Hebrew Publishing, 1949).

ROMAN LAW. *See* JUSTINIAN CODE; THEODOSIAN CODE.

ROOSEVELT, FRANKLIN D. (1882–1945). President of the United States, 1933–45. Although his administrations contained more Jews than any other, Roosevelt delivered two inaugural speeches in which he employed language that many Americans would have related to the **antisemitic** rhetoric of Father **Charles Coughlin**: he condemned the "unscrupulous money changers . . . in the temple" as causing the Depression and noted that "We of the Republic pledged ourselves to drive from the temple of our ancient faith those who had profaned it." "Money changers" and "driven from the temple" are key anti-Jewish phrases, code words used by many antisemites.

In 1939 the **Wagner-Rogers Bill** to permit Jewish refugee children into the United States died in committee, in part because Roosevelt gave it no support. That was also the year when the refugee ship *St. Louis* sought to land its cargo of Jewish escapees from **Nazi** Germany—most of whom had U.S. **quota** numbers that should have permitted them entry; Roosevelt ordered the Coast Guard to prevent any of them from landing. Roosevelt appointed the antisemitic **Breckinridge Long** to head that part of the **State Department** that pragmatically determined U.S. refugee policy.

At the 1943 Casablanca Conference, Roosevelt, who knew a great deal about the **Third Reich**'s atrocities, nevertheless seemed to sympathize with the **Nazis**. He proposed that the French government in North Africa discriminate against the Jews: "the number of Jews engaged in the practice of the professions . . . should be definitely limited to the percentage that the Jewish population in North Africa bears to the whole North African population." He endorsed the same plan for Nazi Germany. Limiting the number of Jews in the professions, he stated, "would further eliminate the specific and understandable complaints which the Germans bore toward the Jews in Germany, namely, that while they represented a single part of the population, over 50 percent of the lawyers, doctors, school teachers, college professors, etc., in Germany were Jews." The errors in Roosevelt's statements were telling, because they mirrored modern antisemitic stereotypes. In the interwar period, the facts are that Jews in Germany comprised about 16 percent of the lawyers, 11 percent of physicians, 4 percent of the university teachers, and 1 percent of teachers in lower grades. *See also* "JEW DEAL."

SUGGESTED READING: Henry L. Feingold, *The Politics of Rescue: The Roosevelt Administration and the Holocaust, 1938–1945* (New Brunswick, NJ: Rutgers University Press, 1970); Robert Michael, *A Concise History of American Antisemitism* (Lanham, MD: Rowman & Littlefield, 2005).

ROOTLESS COSMOPOLITAN. (Former Soviet Union slur) Reference to the alleged rootless nature of Jews.

SUGGESTED READING: B. Z. Goldberg, *The Jewish Problem in the Soviet Union* (New York: Crown, 1961); "List of Ethnic Slurs," *Wikipedia*, http://en.wikipedia.org/wiki/List_of_ethnic_slurs.

ROSENBERG, ALFRED (1893–1946). Major **Nazi** ideologist. An émigré from Estonia, Rosenberg influenced **Adolf Hitler** through his 1930 book *Myth of the Twentieth Century*. He joined the **Nazi Party** at its beginnings and was a member of its inner circle. Rosenberg headed the Institute for the Study on Jewish Questions. He initiated the idea of concentrating Jews in Lublin, Poland. In 1941 he became Reich Minister for the Occupied Eastern Territories, where Jews were mass murdered. Convicted of **war crimes** at the **Nuremberg War Crimes Trials**, he was hanged in 1946.

SUGGESTED READING: Fritz Nova, *Alfred Rosenberg: Nazi Theorist of the Holocaust* (New York: Buccaneer Books, 1986).

ROSENBERG TRIAL. In the early 1950s, America was in the middle of Cold War hysteria. The USSR has detonated an atomic bomb, and South Korea had been invaded by Communist North Korea. In this background, Julius and Ethel Rosenberg went on trial in New York on the charge of criminal conspiracy to commit espionage. All the principals in the trial were Jewish: the defendants, Julius and Ethel Rosenberg; the federal judge, Irving R. Kaufman; the district attorney, Irving Saypol; his special assistant, Roy Cohn; the major prosecution witnesses, Max Eitcher, Harry Gold, and David Greenglass; and the defense lawyer, Emanuel Bloch. The court case was fraught with irregularities and misinterpretation of law, but on March 29, the couple was found guilty. On June 16, 1953, Supreme Court Justice William O. Douglas stayed the execution, but a rare immediate session of the whole Court overruled the stay, and the Rosenbergs were electrocuted. In contrast to the death penalties assigned to the Rosenbergs, the British atomic scientist Klaus Fuchs—whose information supplied to the Soviets was much more important concerning the atomic bomb—spent only nine years in a British prison.

The most that could convincingly be proved is that Julius Rosenberg supplied nonatomic industrial secrets to the KGB and that Ethel, having no contact with the Russians herself, did nothing to stop him. Even J. Edgar Hoover, head of the FBI, felt that Ethel's sentence was excessive. A January 22, 1953, CIA memorandum provides some clues to **antisemitic** prejudice among government officials:

> PROPOSAL: A concerted effort to convince Julius and Ethel Rosenberg, convicted atom spies now under sentence of death, that the Soviet regime they serve is persecuting and ultimately bent on exterminating the Jews under its sovereignty. The action desired of the Rosenbergs is that they appeal to Jews in all countries to get out of the communist movement and seek to destroy it. In return, death sentence would be commuted.

SUGGESTED READING: Richard J. Aldrich, *The Hidden Hand: Britain, America and the Cold War Secret Intelligence* (New York: Overlook Press, 2000); Lucy S. Dawidowitz, "Antisemitism and the Rosenberg Case," *Commentary* 4, no. 1 (July 1952); Sam Roberts, *The Brother: The Untold Story of Atomic Spy David Greenglass* (New York: Random House, 2001).

ROTHSCHILD FAMILY. Prominent European Jewish family of **bankers**. Mayer Amschel (1744–1812) was the patriarch in Frankfurt-am-Main. Starting as a moneylender, he founded a banking empire. His 10 children managed a number of banking houses throughout Europe—in Paris, Berlin, London, Naples, and Vienna. The family was the chief financial power in 19th-century Europe. **Antisemites**, on both the left and right politically, used them as an example of the evils of capitalism and "proof" of a Jewish worldwide conspiracy. *See also* BISMARCK, OTTO VON; HEP HEP RIOTS; ILLUMINATI; *ROTHSCHILDS, DIE*; SCHÖNERER, GEORG RITTER VON.

SUGGESTED READING: Niall Ferguson, *The House of Rothschild* (London: Penguin, 2000).

ROTHSCHILDS, DIE (THE ROTHSCHILDS). One of three films (*Der Ewige Jude, Jud Süss*, and *Die Rothschilds*) commissioned by the **Nazi** Propaganda Ministry. A pseudodocumentary with a distorted history of the Rothschild family, the 1940 film purported to show how Jews sought to start a world war.

SUGGESTED READING: Rolf Giesen, *Nazi Propaganda Films: A History and Filmography* (Jefferson, NC, and London: McFarland, 2003).

RÖTTINGEN. *See* RINDFLEISCH.

ROUSSEAU, JEAN-JACQUES (1712–1778). French writer and philosopher. Rousseau marveled at Jewish survival: "What a marvelous and truly unique spectacle it is to see . . . a people, spread, dispersed over the earth, enslaved, persecuted, despised by all the nations, that nevertheless preserves its customs, its laws, its manners, its love of country, and its first social bond." He attributed Jewish survival to the power of Moses' legal code, "capable of effecting such wonders, capable of braving the conquests, the dispersions, the revolutions, the centuries, capable of surviving the customs, laws, and dominion of all nations, [capable] of lasting as long as the world." Although Christians believe that God punishes the Jewish nation, everyone "must recognize here a singular marvel . . . more than anything admirable that Greece and Rome have to offer us in political institutions and human establishments." Yet Rousseau's *Creed of a Savoyard Vicar* attacked the Jewish God as angry and hating men. Several of his letters refer to the Jews as "the vilest of peoples" and "incapable of any virtue." In the novel *Emile*, he criticized the Jews' "most furious fanaticism" and called them "the basest of all peoples." He found Jews contemptuous and arrogant and regarded their sad history as the result of God's rejection of their evil ways.

SUGGESTED READING: Léon Poliakov, *The History of Antisemitism*, 4 vols. (New York: Vanguard, 1965–86).

ROWLANDSON, THOMAS (1756–1827). English caricaturist; major successor of **William Hogarth**. Rowlandson developed the character John Bull, representing the British Empire. He published *Family Quarrels; or, The Jew and the Gentile*, which later became the operatic play *Family Quarrels* (1802). "The Jew and the Gentile" may refer to the depiction of the two figures in a Rowlandson print. On the right is a caricature of a Jew, recognizable as John Braham (considered the greatest tenor of his age); on the left is a Gentile. The Jew's labored singing is characterized by a musical notation "Allegro Squekando," while two bearded figures to the bottom right show their appreciation, one of them remarking "Mine Cod, How he shing." By contrast, the Gentile is easily singing "Moderato con expressione." The print is a graphic representation of tensions between Jew and Christian in a period when political emancipation was entering the political agenda.

SUGGESTED READING: Todd M. Endelman, *The Jews of Georgian England* (Philadelphia; Jewish Publication Society of America, 1979); Jewish Theological Seminary, "The Jew as Other: A Century of English Caricatures: 1730–1830," http://www.jtsa.edu/library/exhib/jewoth.

ROZANOV, VASILII (1856–1919). According to Rozanov, one of Russia's most articulate fin-de-siècle **antisemites**, all Jewish qualities stemmed from "their femininity—their devotion, cleaving, their almost erotic attachment, to the particular person each one of them is dealing with, as well as to the tribe, atmosphere, landscape, and everyday life that they are surrounded by (as witness both the prophets' reproaches and the obvious facts)."

SUGGESTED READING: Yuri Slezkine, *The Jewish Century* (Princeton, NJ: Princeton University Press, 2004).

RÜDIGER (fl. late 11th cent.). Bishop of Speyer. The first walled **ghetto** for Jews may have been located in Speyer, Germany, where in 1084 Rüdiger gave the Jews a charter in which they were to live in an area encircled by a wall and rationalized as a place where "they not be easily disrupted by the insolence of the mob." By the end of the 12th century, the crowded and unhealthy walled ghetto marked most of Christian Europe's towns.

SUGGESTED READING: Robert Chazan, *Church, State, and Jew in the Middle Ages* (New York: Behrman House, 1980).

RUSSIA, POST-SOVIET. In the period of *perestroika* to the present, intellectuals in the group dominating the Russian Federation's Writers' Union have expressed a high degree of **antisemitism**. They argue that non-Jewish Russians are hospitable people with a unique cultural mission expressed through their Orthodox religion, the traditional village, and Russia's geopolitical position. They associate Jews with industrial and democratic values and treat Jews as power-hungry aliens. These antisemites adhere to the myth of an organized cabalistic Jewish conspiracy and Jewish **ritual murder**. A second type of Russian antisemitism depicts Jews as opponents of socialism and supporters of the foreign values of individualism and profit. A third type of antisemitism is disguised as **anti-Zionism**. Zionism is seen as an international conspiracy for universal Jewish domination, and every Russian Jew is seen as an agent of Jewish domination. The final group of Russian antisemites sees all Jews as sinister, malevolent, satanic, evil **Christ-killers**. This brand of Russian antisemitism stems from Christian **triumphalism**. Significantly, the revival of public religious activity in Russia has *not* been accompanied by the Church propagation of antisemitism.

SUGGESTED READING: Theodore Friedgut, "Antisemitism and Its Opponents in the Russian Press: From Perestroika until the Present," *Acta* no. 3 (1994).

RUSSIAN ORTHODOX CHURCH. The condition of the Jews in Russia replicated that of Western Europe except that the Russian Orthodox Church played a lesser role in the conduct of state Jewish policy than the Roman Catholic Church did in the West. **Antisemitic** policies were not conducted in the name of the Russian Orthodox Church, even though attacks on Jews can be found in Orthodox polemics and in the sermons and speeches of the most illustrious clerics and hierarchs of the Russian Orthodox Church— they reflected not church policy but the widely held negative attitudes of the general population toward the Jews. Indeed, an equal number of Russian Orthodox clerics, including senior hierarchs, openly defended persecuted Jews from the second half of the 19th century. In Russia, hierarchs of the church and professors in the theological academies refuted the accusations that Jews conducted **pogroms** and **ritual murder** and were organizing a "worldwide conspiracy," as they fought for the social rights of Jews. But nothing seemed able to ameliorate the general hatred of Jews characteristic of the Russian population, the state, and religious laws.

SUGGESTED READING: Hans Rogger, *Jewish Policies and Right-Wing Politics in Imperial Russia* (Berkeley: University of California Press, 1986); Yuri Tabak, "Relations between the Russian Orthodox Church and Judaism: Past and Present," *JCRelations.net*, http://www.jcrelations.net/en/?id = 787.

RUSSIAN POGROMS, 1881–1884. The widespread **pogroms** of 1881–84 may have resulted from the failure of reforms climaxed by Tsar Alexander II's assassination, after which the Russian press opposed equal rights for Jews, alleging that Jews conspired to control the world through their secret societies and international organizations. Rumors that Jews had killed the tsar spread throughout Russia. In St. Petersburg, Ippolit Liutostanskii, a propagator of the blood libel, claimed that Jews had offered him up to 100,000 rubles to prevent him from publishing his works. The situation was widely reported in the press. Rumors of impending attacks by "warring Israel" and revolutionary propaganda aggravated the situation. Once the pogroms broke out, mostly in the Ukraine, reports that authorities refused to intervene to suppress the plundering and the riots contributed to the belief that Christians were given three days to "beat the Jews." Many of the *pogromchiks* were merchants and artisans—that is, those most threatened by modern capitalism and Jewish competition—as well as railroad and migrant workers who looked down on the Jews. In the Ukraine, peasants may have reacted to the old tradition that linked Polish landlords, Catholic priests, and Jews, which had caused atrocities against all three groups during the **Chmielnicki massacres**. The only group among the three remaining to attack were the Jews. By the end of 1881 more than 200 Jewish communities within the **Pale of Settlement** had suffered looting, burning, and devastation, leaving 100,000 Jews without means of livelihood and 20,000 without homes.

SUGGESTED READING: Martin Gilbert, *Exile and Return: The Emergence of Jewish Statehood* (London: Weidenfeld & Nicolson, 1978).

RUTHARD. Archbishop of Mainz, 1089–1109. When **Emicho** and his **Crusaders** arrived in Mainz, Germany, in 1096, Ruthard invited all Jews to seek protection in his palace. The Jews thereupon gave him their possessions for safekeeping and 1,300 of them camped in the courtyard and the attic, trying to calm their fears with prayer. When a mob appeared in front of the gates of the palace and demanded the Jews, the Jews found out that they had been lured into a trap. The archbishop, a close relative of Emicho, left the Jews to be massacred, their property divided between Emicho and Ruthard.

SUGGESTED READING: Jacob Marcus, *The Jew in the Medieval World: A Sourcebook, 315–1791* (New York: Jewish Publication Society, 1999).

RUTILIUS NAMATIANUS (fl. early 5th cent. CE). Roman poet; the last non-Christian Latin writer to express **antisemitism**. In his epic poem *De Reditu Suo* (*On His Return*), Rutilius wrote:

> The filthy race that infamously practices **circumcision**; a root of silliness: chill **Sabbaths** are after their own heart, yet their heart is chillier than their creed. Each seventh day is condemned to ignoble sloth. . . . I think not even a child in his sleep could believe the wild ravings from their lying bazaar. . . . The infection of this plague . . . still creeps abroad.

He cursed the Jews for having engendered Christianity. *See also* VOLTAIRE.

SUGGESTED READING: Menahem Stern, ed., *Greek and Latin Authors on Jews and Judaism* (Jerusalem: Israel Academy of Sciences and Humanities, 1984).

– S –

SA (STURMABTEILUNG). Also known as Brown Shirts and Stormtroopers. A paramilitary organization started in 1922 that protected **Nazi Party** rallies and acted as a street force until 1934. They battled Communists and social democrats and attacked and persecuted Jews. Their importance diminished greatly after **Adolf Hitler** had their leaders murdered in 1934, substituting the **SS** as the main instrument of terror and security.

Also, a modern **neo-Nazi**, white supremacist organization, whose symbol consists of the letters *S* and *A* combined within a circle; the *S* is a lightning bolt with an arrow on the bottom.

SUGGESTED READING: David Littlejohn and Ronald Volstad, *The SA, 1921–1945: Hitler's Stormtroopers* (London: Osprey, 1990); "Sturmabteilung," *Axis History Factbook*, http://www.axishistory.com/index.php?id = 2870.

SABATINI, RAFAEL (1875–1950). Anglo-Italian writer. In Sabatini's 1913 history *Torquemada and the Spanish Inquisition*, Sabatini accused the Jews of Spain of **usury**, ostentation, and **ritual murder**.

SABBATH. Jewish day of rest that begins at sundown on Friday and runs to sundown on Saturday. Observance of the Sabbath had many meanings for Jews as a way to sanctify time, to reestablish community, and to contemplate one's life and one's relationship with God. Some pagans interpreted Jewish Sabbath behavior as indicative of laziness, but in the eyes of early Christian writers, the Sabbath became a time when the Jews plotted their evil deeds. Early Christians secularized the Jewish Sabbath and replaced it by a new Sabbath, the Lord's Day, Sunday.

SUGGESTED READING: Judith M. Lieu, *The Jews among Pagans and Christians in the Roman Empire* (New York: Routledge, 1992).

SACHS, HANS (1494–1576). German poet and *Meistersinger*. Many of Sachs's more than 6,200 dramas dealt with deceptive and evil Jews. He was idealized by composer **Richard Wagner** in the opera *Die Meister-singer von Nürnberg*.

SADAT, ANWAR AL- (1918–1981). President of Egypt, 1970–81. Upon President **Gamal Abdel Nasser**'s death in 1970, Sadat became president. In 1972, Sadat referred to the Jews as "a nation of liars and traitors, contrivers of plots, a people born for deeds of treachery," who would soon be "condemned to humiliation and misery," as prophesied in the **Koran**. In 1973, Egypt and Syria initiated a surprise attack on Israel on Yom Kippur, the holiest day in the Jewish calendar. Iraq, Saudi Arabia, Tunisia, Sudan, Jordan, Lebanon, Morocco, and the Palestinians supplied men and/or equipment to the Egyptian-Syrian war effort. Israel mobilized its reserves and eventually repulsed the invaders and carried the war deep into Syria and Egypt. Egypt was saved from a disastrous defeat by the UN Security Council, which had failed to act while the tide of war favored the Arabs. Sadat decided to make peace and visited Jerusalem, unprecedented at the time. With the aid of U.S. President Jimmy Carter, Sadat signed the Camp David Accords in 1979 with Israeli Prime Minister Menachem Begin (1913–1992). The Islamic fundamentalist group **Tanzim al-Jihad** assassinated Sadat in 1981 for daring to negotiate with the Israelis, the "enemies of God" and "enemies of humanity."

SUGGESTED READING: Robert S. Wistrich, *Muslim Antisemitism: A Clear and Present Danger* (New York: American Jewish Committee, 2002).

SADDUCEES. One of several politico-religious parties in Judea in the period 200 BCE–70 CE. Made up of priests and wealthy aristocrats, the Sadducees dominated the Temple worship and the judicial body, the **Sanhedrin**. As literalists, they held to the written Torah and rejected the Oral Law (**Talmud**) and the concepts of immortality and resurrection. During Jesus' lifetime, they held power because of their alliance with the occupying Romans. Zealots, another party of Jews, many of whom traveled with Jesus as disciples, were intent on destroying both Sadducee and Roman power in Palestine. **Matthew**'s **Gospel** labeled Sadducees and **Pharisees** "a generation of vipers."

ST. LOUIS. **Nazi** German cruise ship that held 933 Jews fleeing Germany in 1939. When the president of Cuba would not permit the German-Jewish passengers of the *St. Louis* to disembark there in May 1939, the vessel sailed near the Florida coast. Despite frantic negotiations in May–June 1939, President **Franklin D. Roosevelt** ignored all appeals, upholding the restrictive immigration laws, and ordered the Coast Guard to prevent any passengers from the ship from debarking in the United States, despite the knowledge that a return to Hamburg meant certain **deportation** to concentration camps. Nor would any Latin American country accept the passengers. In June 1939, England, France, Belgium, and the Netherlands agreed among themselves to give temporary haven to 933 Jewish refugees. When the ship docked at Antwerp on June 17, 181 passengers went to the Netherlands, 224 to France, and 240 stayed in Belgium. Only those 288 that Britain accepted, however, survived. The voyage of the *St. Louis* underscored Roosevelt's callousness toward the plight of the refugees.

SUGGESTED READING: Gordon Thomas and Max Morgan-Witts, *Voyage of the Damned* (New York: Stein & Day, 1974).

SAINT-SIMON, CLAUDE-HENRI DE ROUVROY, COMTE DE (1760–1825). French social theorist. Saint-Simon described Jews as "a morose people, egotistical, and devoured by pride."

SUGGESTED READING: Zosa Szajkowski, "The Jewish Saint-Simonians and Socialist Antisemites in France," *Jewish Social Studies* 9 (1947).

SALUS NON EST EXTRA ECCLESIAM. *See* LATERAN COUNCIL, FOURTH.

SAMISDAT PUBLISHERS. One of the largest distributors of **Nazi** and **neo-Nazi** propaganda and memorabilia in the world, run since the late 1970s by **Ernst Zundel**.

SANDOMIERZ. Town in Poland with a Jewish settlement that dates back to the 13th century. The level of crown **taxes** paid in 1507 suggests that Sandomierz was one of the largest and wealthiest Jewish communities in Poland at that time. Because of competition from Jewish merchants and artisans, in 1521 Sandomierz became part of a coalition of towns demanding that the king limit Jews' freedom to trade. Trials involving accusations of **desecration of the Host** (1639) and **ritual murder** (1698 and 1710) sparked riots and looting of Jewish homes.

After the town was occupied by the Germans at the start of World War II, the Germans staged a violent **pogrom**. In June 1942, they created a **ghetto** where Jews from the surrounding area were resettled; its total population was approximately 5,200. Almost all perished in the death camp in **Belzec** in October 1942. Some 7,000 Jews were murdered in January 1943: about 1,000 able-bodied people were sent to the **forced labor camp** in Skarzysk-Kamienna; the rest were killed in Treblinka.

SUGGESTED READING: Alina Cala, Hanna Wegrzynek, and Gabriela Zalewska, "Historia i kultura Zydow polskich. Slownik," *Diapositive Dictionary*, http://www.diapozytyw.pl/en/site/slownik_terminow/sandomierz.

SANHEDRIN. Supreme Jewish political, religious, and judicial body in Judea during Roman rule (6–425). The Christian **Gospels** describe three different trials of Jesus. Even though the most critical one, often the subject of later **passion plays**, was before the Roman procurator Pontius Pilate, **antisemities** often focus on the hearing that supposedly took place before the Sanhedrin on the night of Passover. Jewish scholars and the **Talmud** assert that the Sanhedrin, usually made up of 71 members, never met on holidays or at night. *See also* NAPOLEON; OBERAMMERGAU; SADDUCEES.

SUGGESTED READING: Solomon Zeitlin, *The Rise and Fall of the Judean State* (Philadelphia: Jewish Publication Society, 1967).

SARGENT, JOHN SINGER (1856–1925). Anglo-American painter. Sargent was called **antisemitic** when his 1919 fresco for the Boston Public Library showed "Judaism" [**Synagoga**] as a woman on her knees with bandaged eyes. He replied that he was only following medieval artistic traditions and refused to change the depiction.

SAUCKEL, FRITZ (1894–1946). Head of **Nazi** labor mobilization. Sauckel was the ruthless coordinator of **forced labor** for German war production. He bragged that "of five million foreign workers, less than 200,000 came voluntarily." He was held accountable as a **war criminal** for thousands of deaths of workers, mostly Jews, in Poland. His sentence at the **Nuremberg War Crimes Trials** was death.

SUGGESTED READING: Eugene Davidson, *The Trial of the Germans* (New York: Macmillan, 1966).

SAUL OF TARSUS. *See* PAUL, ST.

SAYYID QUTB. *See* QUTB, SAYYID.

SCHELLING, FRIEDRICH WILHELM JOSEPH VON (1775–1854). Philosopher of Romanticism. Visiting Berlin in 1787, Schelling criticized the local intellectuals, especially the Jews, among whom he found a "vermin" of unbearable young scholars.

SUGGESTED READING: Alfred Low, *Jews in the Eyes of the Germans* (Philadelphia: Institute for Study of Human Issues, 1979).

SCHEMANN, LUDWIG (1852–1935). German racial scholar. Schemann was active in German nationalist, **antisemitic**, and racist organizations, a member of **Richard Wagner**'s Bayreuth circle, and most noted for his dissemination of the racial theories of **Arthur de Gobineau** in the Gobineau Vereinigung (Gobineau Society) in 1894 in Freiburg, Germany. Schemann's German patriotism, militarism, and attack on "everything that was un-German in and around us" were praised in **Erich Ludendorff**'s *Kriegführung und Politik* (1922).

SUGGESTED READING: Léon Poliakov, *The Aryan Myth*, trans. Edmund Howard (New York: Barnes & Noble, 1974).

SCHEUNENVIERTEL POGROM. A 1923 **pogrom** against Jewish immigrants from Eastern Europe residing in the Scheunenviertel, a poor district in central Berlin with a large Eastern European Jewish population. **Völkisch nationalists** (proclaiming that they were for the German Empire, German culture, and the unity of the nation) *and* Communist workers plundered and destroyed Jewish shops. This pogrom resulted from the unification of right and left, of the völkisch elements as well as the masses organized by the Communist Party against "Jewish capital."

SUGGESTED READING: Christhard Hoffmann, Werner Bergmann, and Helmut W. Smith, *Exclusionary Violence: Antisemitic Riots in Modern Germany* (Ann Arbor: University of Michigan Press, 2002).

SCHINDLER, OSKAR (1908–1974). Sudeten-German industrialist and **Nazi Party** member. In 1939 Schindler followed the German Army into Krakow, Poland. He befriended and ingratiated himself with the officers of the **SS**, but after witnessing a German attack on Jews, he was heard to say: "I am now resolved to do everything in my power to defeat the system." He operated an enamelware and shell-casing plant near the Krakow **ghetto** and Plaszow concentration camp. By 1942 he had 500 Jews working for him there. Bribing German officials, Schindler insisted that his factory site be protected and, when they liquidated the Krakow ghetto in 1943, he paid them for 900 more Jews. Even those actually unfit or unqualified to work were housed safely in his compound. Although the "SchindlerJuden" worked very long shifts, they suffered no beatings or executions and were provided with food and medicine. His wife assisted him. Honored as a Righteous Gentile (one who saved Jews during the **Holocaust**) by Yad Vashem, his wartime efforts demonstrate what more might have been done to save Jews.

SUGGESTED READING: Elinor Brecher, *Schindler's Legacy* (New York: Plume, 1994).

SCHLEGEL, KARL WILHELM FRIEDRICH VON (1772–1829). German poet and critic, statesman and novelist. Schlegel rejected full civil rights for contemporary Jews.

SCHLEIERMACHER, FRIEDRICH (1768–1834). Influential German Protestant theologian and philosopher. Schleiermacher denounced **antisemitism** but asserted that Judaism was nothing but "a system of universal immediate retribution." Jews, he thought, should cease to be Jews culturally, politically, and religiously.

SUGGESTED READING: Alfred Low, *Jews in the Eyes of the Germans* (Philadelphia: Institute for Study of Human Issues, 1979).

SCHÖNERER, GEORG RITTER VON (1842–1921). **Austrian** politician. Von Schönerer founded the Pan-German Party, which advocated the union of Austria with Germany. Its **antisemitic** platform attacked the **Rothschild family** of Jewish **bankers** and sought to nationalize the Rothschilds' railroads. The Pan-Germans believed that through money, Jews controlled whole nations. **Adolf Hitler** had pictures of Schönerer in his room in Vienna.

SUGGESTED READING: Nicholas Goodrick-Clarke, *The Occult Roots of Nazism* (New York: New York University Press, 1992).

SCHOPENHAUER, ARTHUR (1788–1860). German philosopher. Schopenhauer believed that in order to receive full rights in a Christian state, the Jews would have to **convert** to Christianity. Like **Martin Luther**, he blamed the Jews for having gained control of whole nations through robbery and murder.

SCHWABENSPIEGEL. The South German law code and the Viennese Stadtrechtsbuch were two secular law codes based on Church teachings. The clerical author of the Schwabenspiegel in 1275 was a Franciscan friar who believed that nothing in secular law should conflict with **canon law** and the Christian faith. He helped transpose ecclesiastical legislation into Jewish secular life. The codes sought to prevent Christians and Jews from sharing meals; prohibited Jews from holding public office and Jewish doctors from treating Christians; and forbade Jews to leave the **ghetto**, or to open their doors or windows, on **Good Friday**. It assumed that Jews were essentially **perfidious**, that is, treacherous and prone to perjury, and required Jews to take a humiliating **oath** while standing on a bloody **pigskin**.

SUGGESTED READING: Shlomo Simonsohn, *The Apostolic See and the Jews: History* (Toronto: Pontifical Institute of Mediaeval Studies, 1991).

SCHWARZE KORPS, DAS. *See* SS.

SCOTT, JOHN (1751–1838). Earl of Eldon; English Lord Chancellor. Scott ruled against Jews claiming a right to the benefits of the Belford Charity. He noted: "I apprehend that it is the duty of every judge presiding in an English Court of Justice, when he is told that there is no difference between worshipping the Supreme Being in chapel, church, or **synagogue**, to recollect that Christianity is part of the law of England."

SUGGESTED READING: Todd Endelman, *The Jews of Georgian England, 1714–1830* (Philadelphia: Jewish Publication Society, 1979).

SCOTT, WALTER (1771–1832). Scots writer and historical novelist. The Jews in Scott's novel *Ivanhoe* (1820) are cast as the text's eternal Others, set outside English society. "The leopard will not change his spots," Friar Tuck says at one point, "and a Jew he will continue to be." Yet the Jews in *Ivanhoe* are also sympathetic. Although cowardly and avaricious, Isaac is as eloquent as **Shylock** in exposing the hypocrisy of both Saxon and Norman societies. Rebecca is admirable for her strength of character under duress and her eloquent descriptions of the pain of exile. But Scott wrote critically in his journal on November 25, 1825, about Jewish merchants and middlemen:

> After all, it is hard that the vagabond stock-jobbing Jews should, for their own purposes, make such a shake of credit as now exists in London. . . . It is just like a set of pickpockets, who raise a mob, in which honest folks are knocked down and plundered, that they may pillage safely in the midst of the confusion they have excited. Side note: I was obliged to give this up in consequence of my own misfortunes.

In a letter to Joanna Bailie in 1817, Scott wrote:

> Jews will always be to me Jews. One does not naturally or easily combine with their habits and pursuits any great liberality of principle. . . . They are moneymakers and moneybrokers by profession and it is a trade which narrows the mind. I own I breathed more freely when I found that Miss Montenero [the heroine of a novel he had just read] was not an actual Jewess.

SUGGESTED READING: Frank Felsenstein, *Antisemitic Stereotypes: A Paradigm of Otherness in English Popular Culture, 1660–1830* (Baltimore: Johns Hopkins University Press, 1995).

SD (SICHERDIENST). Security service within the **SS**. This intelligence-gathering arm of the SS included the dreaded **Gestapo**. **Reinhard Heydrich** headed it beginning in 1936. **Adolf Eichmann** began his career in the SD.

SUGGESTED READING: Abraham and Hershel Edelheit, *History of the Holocaust* (Boulder, CO: Westview Press, 1994).

SECRET DOCTRINE. See BLAVATSKY, HELENE.

SECRET ORGANIZATIONS, 20TH CENTURY. Stimulated by the Great Depression, the *American Fascistic Association*, also known as the *Order of Black Shirts*, was organized in 1930. It followed the traditions of the Ku Klux Klan and was headquartered near Atlanta. Its slogans were "Drive the Negroes out of jobs and put whites in their place" and "Fight [Jew] Communism in Georgia." The *Silver Shirts* had their headquarters in San Francisco. Their battle cry was "The Jews must go, the Pope must go, democracy must go." Their scheme was to secure the reign of Christ on Earth. The Silver Shirts adopted the **swastika** and professed sympathy with **Adolf Hitler** and the **National Socialist Movement**. The *Crusaders for Economic Liberty* attracted the leading congressional antisemite **Louis T. McFadden.** *Mr. Christian's Crusaders* sought to establish economic liberty under capitalism by destroying the Jewish money monopoly and by inaugurating the Golden Rule. The *Order of Seventy-Six*, the *Khaki Shirts*, and the *Black Legion* launched attacks against communists, blacks, Jews, Catholics, and the foreign-born, mixing criticisms of capitalism with Christian beliefs.

SUGGESTED READING: David H. Bennett, *The Party of Fear*, 2nd rev. ed. (New York: Vintage, 1995).

SECRET RELATIONSHIP BETWEEN BLACKS AND JEWS. **Antisemitic** propaganda published by the Historical Research Department of the Nation of Islam in 1991 that presents a multilayered attack against the Jewish people. It assaults the integrity of the Jewish religion, the meaning of Jewish history, and the foundations of Jewish scholarship. The anonymous authors argue that the history of slavery in the New World was initiated by Jewish shipowners and merchants, who as a group remained the main beneficiaries of the slave economy and who "carved for themselves a monumental culpability in slavery." The authors advance this bizarre thesis by unscrupulously distorting the findings of legitimate authors writing on the history of Jews in the New World. In the process, they rationalize and demean the centuries of suffering that brought Jews to the Americas. Rather than attribute Jewish **expulsions** to enduring antisemitism, the authors provide a list of "reasons" for these expulsions: the Jews were monopolizers and **usurers**, they engaged in "sharp practices" and sold "cheap" goods, they filed for frequent bankruptcies. Each of these charges stems from antisemitic stereotypes. The African-American authors have ironically drawn on the rhetoric of white supremacists.

SUGGESTED READING: Harold Brackman, *Ministry of Lies: The Truth behind the Nation of Islam's "The Secret Relationship between Blacks and Jews"* (New York: Four Walls, Eight Windows, 1994).

SELECTION. A **Nazideutsch** word really meaning the choosing of Jews for **deportation** or death by Nazis. Jews selected either in **ghettos** or concentration camps by Nazi **SS** doctors and others for death were initially identified as too young, too sick, too old, or too weak for **forced labor**. But often these criteria did not hold, and the Nazis selected able-bodied Jews for death. *See also* GAS CHAMBERS; MENGELE, JOSEF.

SUGGESTED READING: George Annas and Michael A. Grodin, eds., *The Nazi Doctors and the Nuremberg Code* (New York: Oxford University Press, 1992).

SELIGMAN, JOSEPH (1819–1880). German-Jewish-American who rose from peddler to international **banker**. Seligman's firm helped finance the Northern effort in the U.S. **Civil War** by obtaining European capital. His service to the Union was described as "equal perhaps to the service of the general[s] who stopped Lee at Gettysburg." He declined the post of secretary of the treasury offered to him by President **Ulysses S. Grant**. Seligman was later involved in a cause célèbre when in 1877 he was refused admittance into the Grand Union Hotel in Saratoga Springs, NY, because he was a Jew.

SUGGESTED READING: Steven Birmingham, *Our Crowd: The Great Jewish Families of New York* (Syracuse, NY: Syracuse University Press, 1962).

SENECA (5 BCE–65 CE). Spanish-Roman Stoic philosopher; advisor and tutor to Emperor Nero. Seneca claimed the **Sabbath** encouraged idleness in Jews. He wrote in a work on superstitions: "The customs of this accursed race have gained such influence that they are now received throughout all the world. The vanquished have given laws to their victors."

SUGGESTED READING: Menahem Stern, ed., *Greek and Latin Authors on Jews and Judaism* (Jerusalem: Israel Academy of Sciences and Humanities, 1984).

SEPARATION OF CHURCH AND STATE IN THE UNITED STATES. The words *separation*, *church*, and *state* do not appear in the First Amendment. The First Amendment reads, "Congress shall make no law respecting an establishment of religion, or prohibiting the free exercise thereof. . . ." The phrase "separation between church and state" was **Thomas Jefferson**'s: "I contemplate with solemn reverence that act of the whole American people which declared that their legislature should 'make no law respecting an establishment of religion, or prohibiting the free exercise thereof,' thus building a wall of separation between Church and State." The principle of separation has been expanded by and defined by the U.S. Supreme Court over the years. It has afforded Jews in America greater religious freedom than they have known under any other government. *See also* HOLY TRINITY CHURCH CASE.

SUGGESTED READING: George Harmon Knoles, "The Religious Ideas of Thomas Jefferson," *Mississippi Valley Historical Review* (June 1943); Robert Healey, "Jefferson on Judaism and the Jews," *American Jewish History* (June 1984).

SERFS. Also termed *servi camerae* (servants of the treasury), *servi regis* (servants of the king), *servi nostrae* (our servants), *servi camerae regis* (servants of the king's treasury), and *servi camerae imperialis* (servants of the imperial treasury). The Church allowed the Jews no inherent right to exist as a free people among Christians. Although as a medieval corporation the Jews sometimes enjoyed a degree of self-government, the Jews' right to exist at all was often challenged. The idea of the Jews as slaves began with the Apostle **St. Paul**, who compared the Jews with slaves and Christians with free men. **St. Augustine** put it bluntly: "The Jew is the slave of the Christian." **St. Origen, St. Jerome, St. John Chrysostom**, and other **Church Fathers** argued that God was punishing the Jews with perpetual slavery for their murder of Jesus. Although the Jews (*Judei*) had a status distinct from slaves, serfs, or any other Christian, Christian princes found them economically and practically useful, and reduced the Jews to servile status. Jewish servitude was evident since the early 12th century. The 12th-century town charters in **Aragón** and Castile confirmed that "Jews are the slaves of the crown and belong exclusively to the royal treasury." In 1190, English King **Richard I** gave a charter to a leading English Jew, Isaac, son of Joce, but it repeated twice that the Jews should be treated "as our property." In 1236, the German emperor **Frederick II** coined the term "household serf" ("serfs of our court," "servants," "our serfs, the Jews") to indicate the Jews' personal, involuntary, and hereditary dependence on the emperor alone. The Church sanctioned Christian princes' treatment of Jews as property that could be sold, traded, or lent; the only traditional restrictions—often violated—were those against murder and forced **conversion**. As late as 1581, Pope **Gregory XIII** concluded that the Jews were to be "eternal slaves" since their guilt for murdering Jesus grew deeper with each generation.

SUGGESTED READING: Robert Chazan, ed., *Medieval Jewish Life* (New York: Ktav, 1976).

SERMONS, MANDATORY. Sermons to Jews for **conversion** purposes from the 9th century through the 19th, often containing traditional Christian **antisemitism**. In the ninth century, Archbishop **Agobard** instructed Catholic clergy in Lyons to preach every Saturday in the **synagogues**. When the **Dominican** order was founded in 1216, the friars started preaching in **Aragón**. In the 13th century, **Pablo Christiani** preached in both Spain and France and the kings of Aragón and France ordered conversionary sermons. In the 15th century, **Vincent Ferrer** preached throughout Europe. Pope **Gregory XIII** in 1577 ordered Jews in the **Papal States** to attend sermons, a practice that did not end until 1846 under **Pius IX**.

SUGGESTED READING: Solomon Grayzel, *Church and Jews in the XIII Century* (Detroit: Wayne State University, 1989).

SERVI CAMERAE; SERVI NOSTRAE; SERVI REGIS. *See* SERFS.

SETTLEMENT HEIMLAND. In 1896, **Theodor Fritsch** published his *völkisch* book *Die Stadt der Zukunft* (*City of the Future*), reflecting an extreme racist perspective (he argued for the "establishment of a new blond Germanic race") that later contributed to National Socialist ideology and resulted in Fritsch being revered as a prophet of **Nazism**.

SUGGESTED READING: Dirk Schubert, ed., *Die Gartenstadtidee zwischen reaktionärer Ideologie und pragmatischer Umsetzung* (The Garden City Idea between Reactionary Ideology and Pragmatic Realization) (Dortmund: Institute of Spatial Planning, University of Dortmund, 2004).

SEYSS-INQUART, ARTHUR (1892–1946.) Austrian **Nazi** politician. For a short time, Seyss-Inquart was Austrian chancellor, then governor of the annexed **Austria** in 1938. He became a deputy to **Hans Frank** in conquered Poland. As *Reichskommissar* (military governor) for the Netherlands, he oversaw the destruction of 105,000 Dutch Jews.

SUGGESTED READING: Florence R. Miale and Michael Selzer, *The Nuremberg Mind: The Psychology of Nazi Leaders* (New York: Quadrangle Books, 1977).

SHAKESPEARE, WILLIAM. *See MERCHANT OF VENICE, THE*; SHYLOCK.

SHAW, GEORGE BERNARD (1856–1950). British playwright and Fabian Socialist. Shaw wrote in his 1902 play *Man and Superman* that "Jews who still want to be the chosen race should go to Palestine and stew in their own juice." A portion of Shaw's preface to *On the Rocks* (1933), entitled "Present Exterminations," reads: "The extermination of whole races and classes has been not only advocated but actually attempted. The extirpation of the Jew as such figured for a few mad moments in the program of the **Nazi Party** in Germany." Two months into war, he urged that Great Britain and France make peace with Germany and that **Winston Churchill** be overthrown before **Adolf Hitler**; he added that the Führer had overturned "our wicked work" at **Versailles**. Shaw welcomed the German occupation of **Austria** in 1938 and that year wrote to Beatrice Webb: "I think we ought to tackle the Jewish question by admitting the right of the State to make **eugenic** experiments by weeding out any strains they think undesirable." Though he warned the Irish Republican Army that Hitler was anti-Catholic, he declared that Hitler was "nine-tenths right"—the only "hitch in his statesmanship" being his "bee in the bonnet" about the Jews. As late as 1942 Shaw noted that Hitler was "a remarkable fellow" who took "the courage of his convictions to a sublime height." He regarded Germany as an unmalicious "terror of Europe." Shaw defended Nazi policies on the grounds that nations possessed the inherent right to define **citizenship**, and Germany had the right to decide whether the Jews were fit or "unfit to enjoy the privilege" of living in Germany. Shaw denied the existence of the **Holocaust**. In the preface to his play *Geneva* (1945), Shaw portrayed the death camp murders as having been caused by overcrowding and lack of food. Atrocities resulted from the "natural percentage of callous toughs" among the guards and take place "in every war when troops get out of hand." Although he admitted Hitler was a "mad messiah," Shaw also regarded him as "a poor devil, . . . a national hero, as [he] will become in Germany presently."

SUGGESTED READING: Benedict Nightingale, "Shaw—and a Lesson in Evil," *Times* (London), August 29, 2000.

SHECHITA. See DIETARY LAWS, JEWISH; RITUAL SLAUGHTER (*SHECHITA*).

SHEENIE; SHEENY; SHENY; SHENEY; SHEENEY. (British, North American, former Soviet Union slur) Reference to the gabardine Jews often wore, which became shiny after prolonged use. *See also* GABARDINE-STROKING MONKEY.

SUGGESTED READING: "List of Ethnic Slurs," *Wikipedia*, http://en.wiki pedia.org/wiki/List_of_ethnic_slurs.

SHELLEY, PERCY BYSSHE (1792–1822). British poet. Shelley's *Oedipus Tyrannus; or, Swellfoot the Tyrant* was a political satire with three absurd Jewish characters: Moses, a "sow-gelder"; Solomon, a "porkman"; and Zephaniah, a butcher. They are summoned by King Swellfoot and ordered to slay all their **pigs**. Some Shelley experts believe that Zephaniah may have been a spoof on financier Nathan **Rothschild**.

SUGGESTED READING: Frank Felsenstein, *Antisemitic Stereotypes: A Paradigm of Otherness in English Popular Culture, 1660–1830* (Baltimore: Johns Hopkins University Press, 1995).

SHELTON, ROBERT (1930–2003). A leader of the United Klans of America of the **Ku Klux Klan** in the 1960s. A devout Methodist, Shelton believed in a strong Christian foundation for the Klan. He distinguished between the two groups he feared the most, blacks and Jews, as follows: "I don't hate niggers, but I hate the Jews. The nigger's a child, but the Jews are dangerous people. . . . All they want is control and domination of the Gentiles through a conspiracy with the niggers."

SUGGESTED READING: Warren Prichard, "Interview with a Former Grand Dragon," *New South* 24 (Summer 1969).

SHEMONEH ESREH. The Eighteen Benedictions in the Jewish daily prayer book. Christian critics from late antiquity through the Middle Ages viewed denunciations aimed at pagans in the prayers as veiled criticisms of Christianity.

SUGGESTED READING: Cyrus Adler, ed., "Articles of Faith," *The Jewish Encyclopedia* (New York: Funk and Wagnalls, 1906–1910).

SHEPHERDS' CRUSADE. Also known as Pastoureaux or Pastorelli. In 1315, perhaps the worst famine in European history occurred. The long-lasting suffering and dislocations resulted in a series of riots in France that focused in 1320 into a movement called the Shepherds' Crusade. The "crusading" shepherds attacked communities of Jews, who were regarded as Europe's primary evildoers. The shepherds found many sympathizers among the Christian townspeople when they did violence to Jews and their property. Although there may have been economic motives for such collaboration, the primary cause was religious. In 1321, during the continuing Shepherds' Crusade, false rumors were put forth that lepers were **poisoning wells** in order to kill all Christians. The Jews of France and Spain were believed part of the conspiracy, and perhaps an additional 5,000 were burned in the south of France.

SUGGESTED READING: Margaret Wade Laburge, *Saint Louis: The Life of Louis IX of France* (Boston: Little, Brown, 1968).

SHERIDAN, RICHARD BRINSLEY (1751–1816). Irish-born dramatist. In Sheridan's comic ballet *The Duenna* (1775), the Jew Isaac Mendoza is ridiculed. "The most remarkable part of his character is his passion for deceit and tricks of cunning," says one character of him; but Mendoza's compulsive attempts to swindle are foiled. The play *School for Scandal* (1777) has similar Jewish types.

SHERMAN, WILLIAM TECUMSEH (1820–1891). U.S. soldier; **Civil War** general. In a letter that predated the Civil War, Sherman wrote that Jews were "without pity, soul, heart or bowels of compassion." More letters written in 1862 concerning Jewish merchants in Tennessee reflect not only his opposition to all commerce in the area, but his contempt specifically for Jewish merchants; phrases include "Jews and speculators," "swarms of Jews," "Jews . . . will again overrun us," and "the country will swarm with dishonest Jews."

SUGGESTED READING: Bertram Korn, *American Jewry and the Civil War* (Philadelphia: Jewish Publication Society, 1951).

SHONK; SHONKER. (British slur) Derived from the Yiddish *shoniker*, meaning "shopkeeper."

SUGGESTED READING: "List of Ethnic Slurs," *Wikipedia*, http://en.wikipedia.org/wiki/List_of_ethnic_slurs.

SHYLOCK. The Jewish moneylender in Shakespeare's play *The Merchant of Venice* can be played in different ways: as a villain, as a pitiable character, or as a tragic figure. Attempts have been made to emphasize Shylock's humanity, but most often the Shylock character is treated as malignant, bloodthirsty, unscrupulous, and greedy. The Arabs, in particular the Syrian literary magazine *al-Usbu al Adabt*, today use the the stereotype of Shylock as an evil, sinister Jew. "Shylock" has also become a U.S., British, and British Commonwealth slur for "Jew," referencing the Shakespearean character. *See also* USURY.

SUGGESTED READING: John Gross, *Shylock: A Legend and Its Legacy* (New York: Touchstone, 1994); Marvin Perry and Frederick M. Schweitzer, *Antisemitism: Myth and Hate from Antiquity to the Present* (New

York: Palgrave Macmillan, 2002); "List of Ethnic Slurs," *Wikipedia*, http://en.wikipedia.org/wiki/List_of_ethnic_slurs.

SHYSTER; SCHEISTER. (U.S., British, British Commonwealth slur) Reference to lawyers, especially Jewish lawyers, or to unscrupulous businessmen, especially Jewish businessmen. Possibly derived from **Shylock** or from the German or Yiddish word *scheißer* or *scheißter*, "shitter."
   SUGGESTED READING: "List of Ethnic Slurs," *Wikipedia*, http://en .wikipedia.org/wiki/List_of_ethnic_slurs.

SICHERDIENST. *See* SD.

SID. (U.S. slur) A Hassidic Jew; also, a reference to the common Jewish name Sidney.
   SUGGESTED READING: "List of Ethnic Slurs," *Wikipedia*, http://en .wikipedia.org/wiki/List_of_ethnic_slurs.

SIETE PARTIDAS. Spanish law code of 1263. The establishment of this law code marked the beginning of the end of the Spanish Jews' glorious history. Henceforth, mistreatment of the Jews would be justified, as the law put it, because "they crucified Our Lord Jesus Christ." Further laws within the code stated that Jews were permitted to reside in the kingdom so "that they might live forever in captivity and serve as a reminder to mankind that they are descended from those who crucified Our Lord Jesus Christ." Although the **synagogues** were protected by the laws as a "place where the name of God is praised," the **ritual-murder** myth was mentioned, and Jews who **converted** Christians to Judaism were to suffer the death penalty along with the convert. In the eyes of the law, the convert was to be treated "just as though he had become a **heretic**." Jews could not appear in public on **Good Friday** nor hold public office, since the Jews had lost their chosen status as "people of God" when they murdered Jesus. *See also* ALFONSO X.
   SUGGESTED READING: Mark Cohen, *Under Crescent and Cross: The Jews of the Middle Ages* (Princeton, NJ: Princeton University Press, 1994).

SILENT BROTHERHOOD. Also known as *Bruder Schweigen* or the Order. Perhaps the most violent post–World War II **antisemitic** organization in the United States. While largely defunct today, in the 1980s it committed violent acts in the West. Led by founder Robert Jay Mathews, a **neo-Nazi** and white supremacist, the Silent Brotherhood preached violent revolution against the U.S. government and **genocide** against Jews and African Americans. Based in the Northwest, the group robbed banks, bombed **synagogues**, and murdered Denver radio talk-show host Alan Berg in the 1980s. Symbolized by the words "Hail the Order" positioned above an ax and a Bruder Schweigen crest and banner with the proclamation "Thou Art My Battle Axe and Weapons of War."

SUGGESTED READING: Kevin Flynn and Gary Gerhardt, *The Silent Brotherhood* (New York: Signet, 1990); Anti-Defamation League, "The New Order Hate Group," 1998, http://www.nizkor.org/hweb/orgs/American/adl/paranoia_as_patriotism/theorder_.html.

SILVER SHIRTS. *See* SECRET ORGANIZATIONS, 20TH CENTURY.

SIMBALAR. (Tatar slur) A reference to Saturdays, the day of the Jewish **Sabbath**.

SUGGESTED READING: "List of Ethnic Slurs," *Wikipedia*, http://en.wikipedia.org/wiki/List_of_ethnic_slurs.

SIMON OF TRENT (1472–1475). A three-year-old Christian boy who drowned in Trento, Italy. Since his body washed aground at the grating of a Jewish home on the shore, the Jews of Trento were accused of **ritual murder** and blood libel. **Bernardinus of Feltre**, a Franciscan friar and rabid Jew-hater, stirred up the town with trumped-up charges. The local bishop, eager to gain Jewish property, collaborated. Despite a papal envoy and commission from Pope **Sixtus IV** attesting to Jewish innocence, Jews of the town were burned or beheaded. One hundred years later, both Simon and Bernardinus were canonized by Gregory XIII; however, in 1965, the canonization was repealed.

SUGGESTED READING: Paul E. Grosser and Edwin G. Halperin, *Anti-Semitism: The Causes and Effects of a Prejudice* (Secaucus, NJ: Citadel Press, 1979).

SIN AGAINST THE BLOOD. *See* DINTER, ARTUR.

SIX DAY WAR. War between Israel and its Arab neighbors Egypt, Syria, Lebanon, and Jordan June 5–10, 1967. A massive buildup of Egyptian armor in the Sinai Desert close to the Israeli border on June 5 prompted an Israeli preemptive attack. The Israeli Air Force knocked out Arab air forces on the ground in Egypt, Syria, and Iraq. Israel warned Jordan not to join the battle, but it struck Israel anyway. By its victory, Israel gained control of all of Jerusalem and the West Bank, and all of prewar Palestine. Israel also took possession of the Sinai Peninsula and the Golan Heights. Even though Israel's actions were defensive, world opinion turned against Israel as persecutor of the Palestinian Arabs in particular.

SUGGESTED READING: Michael Oren, *Six Days of War: June 1967 and the Making of the Modern Middle East* (Novato, CA: Presidio Press, 2003).

SIXTUS IV (1414–1484). Pope, 1471–84. In 1478, Spanish rulers **Ferdinand** and Isabella petitioned Sixtus IV to clamp down on Spanish Jews who were only superficially **converted**, many through coercion. He empowered the Spanish monarchs to eliminate **heresy** by means of the **Inquisition** and approved of **Tomás de Torquemada** as Grand Inquisitor. **Conversos**, in the pope's words, "observe Jewish superstition and the dogmas and precepts of **perfidy** . . . the depravity of heresy. . . . They not only persist in their blindness, but they also infect with their perfidy others [their children and spouses]." The conversos were "a pernicious sect" to be extirpated by the roots. Sixtus later abrogated all privileges the conversos had been granted.

SUGGESTED READING: Shlomo Simonsohn, *The Apostolic See and the Jews, Documents: 1465–1521* (Toronto: Pontifical Institute of Mediaeval Studies, 1990).

SIXTUS V (1520–1590). Pope, 1585–90. Born Francesco della Revere. In response to Jewish bribes, Sixtus V removed most restrictions on Jews in the **Papal States**. However, in 1588, he approved a Portuguese law forbidding **converted** Jews from being ordained as priests.

SUGGESTED READING: Edward A. Synan, *Popes and Jews in the Middle Ages* (Hampshire, England: Macmillan, 1967).

SKID, FRONT-WHEEL. (British slur) Rhyming slang for **Yid**.

SUGGESTED READING: "List of Ethnic Slurs," *Wikipedia*, http://en .wikipedia.org/wiki/List_of_ethnic_slurs.

SKIN. Racist and **skinhead** symbol of a fist with the letters "S-K-I-N" tattooed on the fingers.

SUGGESTED READING: Anti-Defamation League, *Hate on Display: Extremist Symbols, Logos, and Tattoos* (New York: Anti-Defamation League, 2006).

SKINHEADS. The skinheads originated in England in gangs of shaven-headed, tattooed, threatening youths in combat boots in the 1970s—tough, patriotic, and working-class. Some skinheads are law-abiding, indulging only in this skinhead style. But many are racists, bigots, and **antisemites**.

Racist skinheads are found today in almost every industrialized country whose majority population is of European stock. Viking imagery offers the skinhead a perception of himself as a race warrior. Many skinheads glorify **Adolf Hitler** and aspire to create his vision of a worldwide, pan-**Aryan** Reich. These skinheads desecrate Jewish **synagogues**, cemeteries, and memorials to the **Holocaust**.

SUGGESTED READING: Mark S. Hamm, *American Skinheads: The Criminology and Control of Hate Crime* (Westport, CT: Praeger, 1993).

SKOKIE, NAZI MARCH IN. In 1977 and 1978 the American Civil Liberties Union (ACLU) fought successfully for the rights of **American Nazis** to march in Skokie, IL, a community with a significant population of Jewish survivors of **Nazi** concentration camps. The Nazis never marched in the city, but had a park rally instead. The ACLU subsequently lost 30,000 members and many of its largest financial contributors.

SUGGESTED READING: Judah Gribetz, Edward L. Greenstein, and Regina S. Stein, *The Timetables of Jewish History* (New York: Simon & Schuster, 1993).

SKREWDRIVER. Skinhead, **neo-Nazi**, white supremacist band whose name is displayed with a large scripted *S* combined with other symbols frequently used by white supremacists, such as an eagle or the **Aryan** fist. Many fans wear Skrewdriver tattoos and pins, patches, and clothing.

SUGGESTED READING: Anti-Defamation League, *Hate on Display: Extremist Symbols, Logos, and Tattoos* (New York: Anti-Defamation League, 2006).

SKULL AND CROSSBONES. Also called the "Death's Head" or *Totenkopf*; symbol of the **Nazi SS** now used by **neo-Nazis**, racist **skinheads**, and **white supremacists**. The "Death's Head" was the symbol of the SS-Totenkopfverbände (one of the original three branches of the SS, along with the Algemeine SS and the Waffen SS), whose purpose was to guard the concentration camps. Later, SS-Totenkopfverbände became the core of a Waffen-SS division, the Death's Head Division. The symbol often comprises a tattoo, which sometimes indicates that its wearer has murdered a Jew or other minority.

SUGGESTED READING: Anti-Defamation League, *Hate on Display: Extremist Symbols, Logos, and Tattoos* (New York: Anti-Defamation League, 2006).

SLANSKY TRIAL. *See* PRAGUE TRIALS.

SLAPPED WITH A YARMULKE. (U.S. slur) Reference to someone with stereotypical Jewish facial features.

SUGGESTED READING: "List of Ethnic Slurs," *Wikipedia*, http://en .wikipedia.org/wiki/List_of_ethnic_slurs.

SLAVOPHILE. Lover of Slavs; a movement claiming superiority of Slavic peoples in the mid-19th century. This intellectual upper-class movement, Slavophilism, believed Russia's future development should be based on traditional Russian values, namely, Orthodox Christianity, autocracy, aid to a free peasant class, and decentralization. A more conservative version, Doehvennichestve ("Back to the Soil"), articulated by tsarist minister **Konstantin Petrovich Pobedonostsev,** was rabidly **antisemitic**. Jews, he believed, did not have a "Slavic soul."

SUGGESTED READING: John Klier, *The Origins of the Jewish Question in Russia* (Dekalb: Illinois University Press, 1986).

SLOVAKIA, HOLOCAUST IN. *See* TISO, JOSEF.

SMITH, BAILEY (1939–). President of the Southern Baptist Convention, the largest Protestant denomination in the United States. In 1980, Smith preached:

> It's interesting at great political rallies how you have a Protestant to pray, a Catholic to pray, and then you have a Jew to pray. With all due respect to those dear people, my friends, God Almighty does not hear the prayer of a Jew. For how in the world can God hear the prayer of a man who says that Jesus Christ is not the true **Messiah**? That is blasphemy.

SUGGESTED READING: Norma Sherry, "Never Again, According to the Gospels," *OpEdNews*, http://www.opednews.com/sherry022804_never_ again.htm.

SMITH, BRADLEY. Chief propagandist for the **Holocaust denial** movement in America since 1983. Smith achieved his greatest notoriety as the director of the now-defunct Committee for Open Debate on the **Holocaust,** whose mission was to disseminate Holocaust denial to students on college campuses.

SUGGESTED READING: Michael Shermer and Alex Grobman, *Denying History* (Berkeley: University of California Press, 2000).

SMITH, GERALD L. K. (1898–1976). An influential **antisemitic** U.S. Protestant minister. Smith came from three generations of Protestant preachers, was raised on the teachings of the Bible, and admired **Adolf**

Hitler's and **Henry Ford**'s antisemitism. His mother was antisemitic, and he was most likely taught religious anti-Jewishness during his childhood. In 1933 and 1942 he received "calls" from God "to save Christian America from the invasion of the enemies of Christ." He fervently believed that "the crucifiers of Christ were not God's Chosen People. They were a throng of devil-possessed agents of the **Antichrist**." After the war, he insisted that the **Holocaust** was invented by Jews to gain sympathy.

SUGGESTED READING: Glen Jeansonne, *Gerald L. K. Smith, Minister of Hate* (Baton Rouge: Louisiana State University, 1997); Jim Saleam, *American Nazism in the Context of the American Extreme Right, 1960–1978*, http://www.alphalink.com.au/~radnat/usanazis.

SMITH, GOLDWIN (1823–1910). British historian and journalist. Smith was a professor of modern history at Oxford University and a leading late 19th-century intellectual, outspoken Jew-hater in Toronto. He wrote: "The Jew alone regards his race as superior to humanity, and looks forward not to its ultimate union with other races, but to its triumph over them all and to its final ascendancy under the leadership of a tribal **Messiah**." Smith called British Prime Minister **Benjamin Disraeli** a "contemptible trickster and adventurer. He couldn't help it because he was a Jew." Smith condoned Russian **pogroms** and wanted Jews sterilized.

SUGGESTED READING: Goldwin Smith, "Can Jews Be Patriots? Response to Hermann Adler," *Nineteenth Century* 3 (March 1878); Goldwin Smith, "The Jewish Question," *Nineteenth Century* 10 (October 1881).

SMOLETT, TOBIAS (1721–1771). British novelist and translator. Smolett wrote in *The Adventure of Sir Launcelot Greaves* (1760) about an Isaac Vanderpelft, "a stock-jobber of foreign extract, not without a mixture of Hebrew blood, immensely rich." His rival, Mr. Quickset, says, "We are no upstarts, nor foreigners, nor have we any Jewish blood in our veins." *The Adventures of Roderick Random* (1748) portrays scenes between a whore and "the old cent-per-cent fornicator," Isaac Rapine, a grasping [Jewish] moneylender.

SMOUS. (Dutch slur) Jew.

SUGGESTED READING: "List of Ethnic Slurs," *Wikipedia*, http://en.wikipedia.org/wiki/List_of_ethnic_slurs.

SNIP-TIP. (U.S. slur) Reference to Jewish **circumcision**.

SUGGESTED READING: "List of Ethnic Slurs," *Wikipedia*, http://en.wikipedia.org/wiki/List_of_ethnic_slurs.

SNOZZO. (U.S. slur) Reference to the stereotypical Jewish oversized nose.
SUGGESTED READING: "List of Ethnic Slurs," *Wikipedia*, http://en.wiki
pedia.org/wiki/List_of_ethnic_slurs.

SOBIBOR. Nazi **extermination camp** located in eastern Poland. More than
250,000 Jews were gassed there from May 1942 to October 1943. Sobibor
was staffed with veterans of the Nazi **euthanasia** program, Ukrainian
guards, and a skeleton crew of Jewish inmates. The 600 inmates staged a
successful revolt and breakout on October 14, 1943, after which the camp
was closed. *See also* ZYKLON.
SUGGESTED READING: Miriam Novitch, ed., *Sobibor, Martyrdom and
Revolt* (New York: Holocaust Library, 1980).

SOCIAL DARWINISM. Application of Charles Darwin's works to human
society, developed about 1870. The **Nazis** took Darwin's ideas on biological evolution, survival of the fittest, and natural selection to justify their
murder of Jews and other non-**Aryan** peoples. For the Nazis, Aryans were
supermen, destroyed by intermingling with non-Aryans, especially the
Jews. *See also* CHAMBERLAIN, HOUSTON STEWART; DAVENPORT,
CHARLES BENEDICT; EUGENICS; GOBINEAU, ARTHUR DE;
HAECKEL, ERNST; *MEIN KAMPF.*
SUGGESTED READING: Daniel J. Kevles, *In the Name of Eugenics* (Cambridge, MA: Harvard University Press, 1995).

SOCIAL JUSTICE. A weekly newspaper founded by radio priest **Charles
Coughlin**. In 1934 Coughlin formed the National Union for Social Justice
and its newspaper *Social Justice*. The group claimed that Jewish manipulation of the economy had caused the Great Depression and that Jews were
behind the **Bolsheviks** and Communism. *Social Justice* was banned by the
U.S. Post Office in 1942 for alleged subversion.
SUGGESTED READING: Donald Warren, *Radio Priest: Charles Coughlin,
the Father of Hate Radio* (New York: Free Press, 1996).

SOLZHENITSYN, ALEKSANDR (1918–). Russian novelist, dramatist,
and historian. In Solzhenitsyn's works, Jews are portrayed unfavorably—
overrepresented in the **Bolshevik** Revolution, in the leadership after the
revolution, and in the Communist Party bureaucracy, including the political police, NKVD. He attributed many of the faults of Communist rule in
the USSR to Jewish involvement.
SUGGESTED READING: Richard Pipes, "Alone Together: Solzhenitsyn
and the Jews Revisited," *New Republic*, November 25, 2002.

SOMBART, WERNER (1803–1941). German political economist. Sombart traced the development of capitalism from the late Middle Ages to the 20th century. His most controversial book was *The Jews and Modern Capitalism* (1911), in which he argued that deriving from Jewish **messianism**, Jews were restless revolutionaries who seek to dominate the world through money, and he called for a freeing of modern life in general and German culture in particular from the corruptions of "the Jewish spirit." The **Nazis** admired his work, pointing to crass Jewish commercialism versus the honest **Nordic** farmer. Sombart became a Nazi, and his last work, *The New Social Philosophy* (1934), was a Nazi textbook.

SUGGESTED READING: Werner Sombart, *The Jews and Modern Capitalism* (1911; reprint, New York: Free Press, 1951).

SONDERKOMMANDO. Special **Nazi** squad, usually consisting of Jewish prisoners the Nazis assigned to the most degrading tasks: cleaning up emptied **ghettos**, emptying gas vans and **gas chambers** of bodies, removing gold teeth and other valuables from the corpses, and shoveling bodies into ovens. Periodically, the Nazis killed off an entire Sonderkommando. The term also applied to a division of **Einsatzgruppen** generally smaller than Einsatzkommando, but also a more general term for special military units assigned particular murder functions. *See also* SONDERWAGON.

SUGGESTED READING: Yisrael Gutman and Michael Berenbaum, eds., *Anatomy of Auschwitz Death Camp* (Bloomington: Indiana University Press, 1994).

SONDERWAGON. Special **Nazi** killing van that killed its Jewish victims by means of circulating its exhaust gas into a sealed compartment. They were used at Chelmno and **Mauthausen** death camps. Because the Nazis found this method inefficient, they developed **gas chambers** using **Zyklon** gas. *See also* SONDERKOMMANDO.

SUGGESTED READING: Konnilyn G. Feig, *Hitler's Death Camps: The Sanity of Madness* (New York: Holmes & Meier, 1981).

SONNENBERG, MAX LIEBERMANN VON (1848–1911). German Army officer, politician, and **antisemitic** publicist. A member of the *Völkisch* Movement, he helped found the **Antisemitic League** in 1870 along with **Wilhelm Marr** and organized the **Antisemites' Petition** along with Bernhard Förster, husband of **Elisabeth Förster-Nietzsche**, and **Ernst Henrici**. Elected to the Reichstag in 1881, Sonnenberg developed a nationwide following. In the 1880s he and Förster founded the antisemitic Deutscher Volksverein, along with newspapers *Deutsche Volkszeitung* and

Deutschsozialen Blätter, wherein Sonnenberg blamed the "Jewish race" for Germany's social upheavals during industrialization. In 1889 Sonnenberg united the Vereinigung der Christlichsozialen Partei with other antisemitic organizations to create the Antisemitischen Deutschsozialen Partei (or Deutsch-Soziale Antisemitische Partei), which he represented in the Reichstag from 1890 to 1911. In 1900, he and **Otto Böckel** founded the Deutschsozialen Reformpartei, whose platform was based on the racist theories of **Houston Stewart Chamberlain**; it was dedicated to the weakening of Jewish life in Germany, the **"final solution of the Jewish problem"** (*"Endlösung der Judenfrage"*), and the "destruction of the Jewish people" (*"Vernichtung des Judenvolks"*). In the same year, he suggested that the **Konitz Affair** be publicized.

SUGGESTED READING: Alan T. Levenson, *Between Philosemitism and Antisemitism: Defense of Jews and Judaism in Germany, 1871–1912* (Lincoln: University of Nebraska Press, 2004); *German-Social Pages*, 10th Annual, no. 374 (Leipzig, 1895).

SONS OF ABRAHAM. (International slur) Term used sarcastically to refer to Jews.

SUGGESTED READING: "List of Ethnic Slurs," *Wikipedia*, http://en.wiki pedia.org/wiki/List_of_ethnic_slurs.

SORCERY. *See* ANCRE, PIERRE DE L'; DEFAMATIONS, ANTI-JEWISH; JEW BADGE.

SOREL, GEORGES (1847–1922). French socialist revolutionary. Sorel believed the working class was sleeping, inert, and needed a violent revolution. In 1909, he joined the antisemitic **Action Française**. Sorel believed Jewish finance had orchestrated World War I, and he attacked Jewish writers, saying they corrupted society and fought against the spiritual heritage of the nation they lived in.

SUGGESTED READING: Zeev Sternhell, *Neither Right nor Left: Fascist Ideology in France*, trans. David Maisel (Berkeley: University of California Press, 1998).

SPANISH INQUISITION. *See* INQUISITION, SPANISH.

SPANKNOEBEL, HEINZ. The **American Nazi Party**'s first president. Spanknoebel was an employee at the Ford Motor Company. *See also* FORD, HENRY.

SPEER, ALBERT (1905–1981). **Nazi** minister of armaments. Speer ruthlessly exploited slave labor from the concentration camps, later admitting his awareness of the murderous aspects of **forced labor**. Convicted of the mistreatment of the slave laborers, he was sentenced at the **Nuremberg War Crimes Trials** to 20 years' imprisonment. *See also* SAUCKEL, FRITZ.

SUGGESTED READING: Gitta Sereny, *Albert Speer: His Battle with Truth* (New York: Vintage, 1996).

SS (SCHUTZSTAFFEL). Nazi Security Squad. These detachments were originally formed in 1925 as **Adolf Hitler**'s personal guard. From 1929, under **Heinrich Himmler,** the SS developed into the elite of the Nazi Party. SS members had to prove their racial purity back to 1700, and membership was also based on **Aryan** appearance. In mid-1934, they took over the political police and the concentration camps. Their goal was, in Nazi terms, to achieve a **Final Solution of the Jewish Problem**. In reality they were used to round up and murder Jews and undesirable non-Jews. For its emblem, the SS used two Teutonic runes, a parallel jagged double *S*. The SS grew into a state within the state. Its divisions included the armed SS, or Waffen-SS, which fought as elite German military units; the general SS, or Allgemeine-SS; and the SS-Totenkopfverbände, SS "Death's Head" units that acted as concentration camp staff and guards. The SS contained Germanic units composed of Flemish, Danish, or Dutch from 1942 on. Later, as manpower demands grew greater, even units of Poles, Ukrainians, and Turkish Muslims who possessed the requisite racial qualities were formed. At the **Nuremberg War Crimes Trials**, the SS was labeled a criminal organization and cited for its "persecution and extermination of Jews." *See also* BRUNNER, ALOIS; EICHMANN, ADOLF; EXTERMINATION CAMPS; HEYDRICH, REINHARD; MENGELE, JOSEF; ZYKLON.

SUGGESTED READING: Charles W. Sydnor, *Soldiers of Destruction* (Princeton, NJ: Princeton University Press, 1977).

STADTRECHTSBUCH. *See* SCHWABENSPIEGEL.

STALIN, JOSEPH (1879–1953). Dictator of the Soviet Union, 1928–53. Stalin's pact with Germany in 1939 trapped three million Jews in Poland. The Soviet press suppressed all information about the **Nazi** persecution of Jews. With the German invasion of the Soviet Union in June 1941, thousands of Jews in the Baltics and USSR were relocated to *gulags*, Soviet concentration camps. After World War II, Joseph Stalin and the Soviet

Union put increased pressure on the Jews to surrender their Jewishness. Attempting to hide their **antisemitism**, the Soviets called the Jews "**cosmopolitans**" and "bourgeoisie nationalists." In 1948 Stalin ordered the deaths of the **Jewish Anti-Fascist Committee** and began his purge of Jewish artists and intellectuals. The dictator also sought to destroy Israel by providing massive aid to its Arab enemies. In 1952, 110 eminent Jewish academics were put on trial, accused of attempting to begin an underground Zionist-Nationalist party. This trial resulted in 13 Jews being put to death and initiated the end of Jews openly practicing their religion within Poland and the Soviet Union. Jews stopped speaking Yiddish and attempted to hide their Jewish origins. Stalin continued his move toward a **genocide** of Soviet Jews with the trumped-up **Doctors' Plot** and the execution of Jewish Communists such as Rudolf Slansky. On Stalin's death, he was preparing for mass Jewish deportations. *See also* BIROBIDZHAN; BOLSHEVIKS; BUND; COSMOPOLITANISM; ZINOVIEV, GREGORY.

SUGGESTED READING: Arkady Vaksberg, *Stalin against the Jews*, trans. Antonina W. Bouis (New York: Alfred Knopf, 1994).

STALINIZATION OF EASTERN EUROPE. *See* PRAGUE TRIALS; SLANSKY TRIAL; STALIN, JOSEPH.

STANGL, FRANZ (1908–1971). Austrian commandant. Stangl served the Nazi **euthanasia** program at a killing center for the crippled in 1939–40. In 1942, he oversaw construction of the **Sobibor** death camp. During 1942–43 he was in charge of the murder of 870,000 Jews at Treblinka. Stangl escaped after the war to Brazil with the aid of the **Ratline**'s Bishop **Alois Hudal**. Eventually he was extradited and died in a German prison in 1971.

SUGGESTED READING: Gita Sereny, *Into that Darkness* (New York: Vintage, 1983).

STARK, RODNEY. *See* CHRISTIAN BELIEFS AND ANTISEMITISM.

STATE DEPARTMENT, U.S., DURING WORLD WAR II. U.S. government officials, until much too late, despite knowing of the realities of the **Holocaust**, refused to fill U.S. immigration **quotas**. Moreover, they actively resisted allowing the United States to be used as a potential safe haven. A State Department document of November 1938, just after the massive German **pogrom** of **Kristallnacht**, indicates that pressure on the Department to "do something" immediately increased. It was obvious that this pressure was going to be both exceedingly strong and prolonged. The Secretary, Mr. [Sumner] Welles, Mr. [George] Messersmith and Mr. [J. P.] Moffat decided that it will be inadvisable for the Department to attempt merely to resist the pressure, and that it will be far preferable to get out in front and attempt to guide the pressure, primarily with a view toward forestalling attempts to have the immigration laws liberalized.

The highest-ranking U.S. officials involved in foreign policy used a double standard in regard to Europe's non-Jews on the one hand and the Jews on the other. This policy was exemplified in one instance by the refusal of the U.S. government to fill cargo ships returning to the United States with Jews who had escaped to North Africa, even though these same ships were empty and in need of ballast. More dismally, the U.S. government, along with the British, refused to deal with the **Nazis** to save Jewish lives, in contrast to their dealings with the Germans to save non-Jewish lives. *See also* EVIDENCE OF THE HOLOCAUST, SUPPRESSION OF; LONG, BRECKINRIDGE; NON-JEWS, HELP FOR, BY U.S. GOVERNMENT DURING THE HOLOCAUST; "REPORT TO THE SECRETARY ON THE ACQUIESCENCE OF THIS GOVERNMENT IN THE MURDER OF THE JEWS"; ROOSEVELT, FRANKLIN D.

SUGGESTED READING: David Wyman, *Paper Walls* (New York: Pantheon Books, 1968); David Wyman, *The Abandonment of the Jews* (New York: Pantheon Books, 1986).

STATUT DES JUIFS. **Vichy** France's first comprehensive anti-Jewish statute, passed on October 3, 1940, that defined a Jew more harshly and more inclusively than that stipulated by the Germans in the occupied zone of France and elsewhere. The law, formulated purely on French initiative, provided the basis for drastically reducing the role of Jews in French society. It excluded Jews from top positions in the French civil service, army, and professions that helped shape public opinion—teaching, the press, radio, cinema, and theater. Jews could hold menial public-service positions, provided they had served in the armed forces between 1914 and 1918 or had distinguished themselves in the campaign of 1939–40. The statute also stated that a **quota system** would be devised to limit the presence of Jews in the liberal professions (law, medicine, etc.).

Vichy's efforts to apply this statute effectively and toughen some of its provisions led to a second Statut des Juifs on June 2, 1941. This law opened the way for a massive removal of Jews from the liberal professions, commerce, and industry. Its provisions applied to Jews living in Algeria, Morocco, and Tunisia as well as France. Jews had to wear a **Jew badge** and lost businesses to **Aryanization**. Naturalized Jews were denaturalized.

Thousands of foreign Jews, mostly German and Austrian refugees, were later interned in French concentration camps and shipped to death camps in Poland. *See also* PELLEPOIX, LOUIS DARQUIER; VALLAT, XAVIER DE.

SUGGESTED READING: Michael R. Marrus and Robert O. Paxton, *Vichy France and the Jews* (New York: Schocken Books, 1983).

STAUFF, PHILIP (1876–1923). *Völkisch* journalist. In May 1910, Stauff mentioned the idea of an **antisemitic** lodge, with the names of members kept secret to offset the supposed conspiracy that enabled Jews to influence German life. In 1912 Stauff moved to Berlin where he soon published a directory of Pan-German and antisemitic groups, *Das deutsche Wehrbuch* (*German Defense Book*). In 1913 Stauff was involved in a series of spiritualist séances that claimed to communicate with the long-dead priest-kings of the old Germanic religion. In the same year, he published *Semi-Kürschner oder literarisches Lexikon der Schriftsteller, Dichter, Bankiers, Geldleute, Ärzte, Schauspieler, Künstler, Musiker, Offiziere, Rechtsanwälte, Revolutionäre, Frauenrechtlerinnen, Sozialdemokraten usw., jüdischer Rasse und Versippung, die von 1813–1913 in Deutschland tätig oder bekannt ware* (*A Literary Lexicon of the Writers, Poets, Bankers, Money People, Physicians, Actors, Artists, Musicians, Officers, Attorneys, Revolutionaries, Suffragettes, Social Democrats, and so forth, of Jewish Race and Heritage, who from 1813–1913 were active or known in Germany*). In 1916 Stauff became a principal officer of the Berlin chapter of the **Germanenorden**.

SUGGESTED READING: Christian Weikop, "Culture Wars: 'The Enemy Within,'" *Art History* 24, no. 5 (November 2001).

STAUPITZ, JOHANNES VON (1460–1524). German abbot. The vicar of the Augustinian Order and **Martin Luther**'s early superior, Staupitz charged the Jews with inflicting the "harshest" torments on Christ, "savagely" striking him: "O you evil Jew! Pilate teaches you that your character is harsher than a **pig**'s; the pig at least knows mercy."

SUGGESTED READING: Johannes von Staupitz, *Salzburger Passionspredigten*, 1512, Sermon X, in *Sämtliche Schriften*, ed. Graf zu Dohna von Lothar and R. Wetzel (Berlin, 1983).

STAVISKY AFFAIR. In the context of economic worries and unstable governments, riots in Paris in 1934 staged by French rightists and monarchists in opposition to Camille Chautemps's Radical-Socialist government (neither radical nor socialist—nor a party—but a centrist coalition), which they accused of having corrupt dealings with a Russian Jew, Serge Alexandre

Stavisky, involved in financial fraud. Following his capture and death in January 1934, the Right accused the police of killing Stavisky to cover up the involvement of government officials in the scandal. Though the affair toppled the Chautemps government (replaced by Édouard Daladier, then by Gaston Doumergue), a long trial in 1935–36 acquitted all those accused of being involved in the scandal. The affair discredited the Radical-Socialist Party in particular as well as parliamentary democracy in general.

SUGGESTED READING: Alexandre Werth, *France in Ferment* (Gloucester, MA: Smith, 1968).

STEIN, EDITH (ST. TERESA BENEDICTA OF THE CROSS) (1891–1942). German philosopher. Born to an Orthodox Jewish family, Stein converted to Catholicism in 1922 and became a nun. Her writings played an important part in the phenomenological movement (study of people's inner life). In 1933, she tried to persuade Pope **Pius XI** to openly denounce Nazi **antisemitism**, but to no avail. She saw herself as the biblical Queen Esther pleading for her people. Stein fled Germany in 1938 to Holland. In 1942, because Dutch Catholic bishops criticized **Nazi** treatment of Dutch Jews, in retaliation, she, although a nun, was deported to **Auschwitz** and gassed with her sister (also a nun). Canonized in 1998 by Pope **John Paul II**, Jewish organizations and writers objected on the grounds that Edith died because of her Jewish background, not because she belonged to the Roman Catholic Church, and that her canonization was a cooption of the **Holocaust**.

SUGGESTED READING: Waltraud Herbstreth, *Never Forget: Christian and Jewish Perspectives on Edith Stein* (Glasgow, Scotland: ICS Books, 1998).

STEINER, RUDOLF (1861–1925). German anthroposophist. Steiner's anthroposophy and its techniques of biodynamic cultivation had a profound effect on **Walther Darré**, providing a basis for the **Third Reich**'s agricultural policy and an ecological rationalization for the German colonization of Eastern Europe.

SUGGESTED READING: Anna Bramwell, *Ecology in the 20th Century: A History* (New Haven, CT: Yale University Press, 1989).

STEPHEN (1097–1154). King of England, 1135–54. Until the time of Stephen, the Jews had prospered. He sought to protect them, but he also **taxed** up to one-quarter of their liquid assets.

STEPHEN III (720–772). Pope, 768–72. Stephen III complained to the archbishop of Narbonne and the kings of Spain and Septimania that the "**deicidal**" Jews of the Frankish Kingdom should not prosper: "The Jewish people, ever rebellious against God and derogatory of our rites . . . own hereditary estates . . . as if they were Christian residents; for they are the Lord's enemies . . . liars . . . miserable dogs. [They must have no such benefit] in vengeance for the crucified Savior."

SUGGESTED READING: Shlomo Simonsohn, *The Apostolic See and the Jews: Documents, 492–1404* (Toronto: Pontifical Institute of Mediaeval Studies, 1988).

STEPHENSON, D. C. (1891–1966). Grand Dragon of the Indiana **Ku Klux Klan**. Stephenson became Grand Dragon in 1922. The position led to the acquisition of great wealth, which he used to support political candidates. Publicly a Prohibitionist and a defender of "Protestant womanhood," his spectacular trial and conviction for abduction and rape led to the end of Indiana Klan activity.

SUGGESTED READING: Wyn Craig Wade, *The Fiery Cross: The Ku Klux Klan in America* (New York: Oxford University Press, 1998).

STEVENSON, ROBERT LOUIS (1850–1894). Scots writer. In his memory adventure *Across the Plains* (1892), a story of traveling between New York and San Francisco, Stevenson wrote:

> Jew storekeepers have already learned the advantage to be gained from this [unlimited credit]; they lead on the farmer into irretrievable indebtedness, and keep him ever after as their bond-slave hopelessly grinding in the mill. So the whirligig of time brings its revenges, and except that the Jew knows better than to foreclose, you may see Americans bound in the same chains with which they themselves had formerly bound the Mexicans.

STIGMATIC EMBLEMS. Distinctive discriminatory badges or types of apparel that Jews have been forced to wear. Caliph Omar II (717–720) ordered Jews in Muslim lands to wear colored clothing. In Sicily, the Turkish governor in 887 ordered Jews to don **yellow** hats. The Fourth **Lateran Council** in 1215 ordered Christian princes to require a distinctive badge or clothing for Jews. In 1267, the Council of Vienna, an ecclesiastical body, ruled that Jews must wear horned hats. The Jew hat and yellow or silver circular **Jew badges** were most often employed to stigmatize Jews. *See also* BRESLAU, COUNCIL OF.

SUGGESTED READING: Alfred Rubens, *A History of Jewish Costume* (New Hyde Park, NY: Learning Links, 1981); Jewish Theological Seminary, "The Jew as Other: A Century of English Caricatures: 1730–1830," http://www.jtsa.edu/library/exhib/jewoth.

STILES, EZRA (1778–1795). Late 18th-century Puritan divine and advocate of religious liberty; president of Yale University and founder of Brown University. In many ways, Stiles seemed a **philosemite**. He admired Hebrew (the language of the "psalms sung in heaven"), knew all of the Newport (RI) Jews, seemed sympathetic to the tribulations of this "distinct people," and cherished the "sweetness of behavior" of his Jewish friend Aaron Lopez. Yet he observed in 1762, just two years after calling religious liberty a "precious jewel," that America was a Christian commonwealth that had little if any place for the Jews. And 20 years later when his friend Lopez drowned, he "wished that sincere pious and candid mind could have perceived the evidences of Christianity, perceived the truth as it is in Jesus Christ, known that Jesus was the **Messiah** predicted by Moses and the prophets!" He observed in his diary that the Jews were "professed enemies to a crucified Christ!"

SUGGESTED READING: Franklin Dexter, *Extracts from the Itineraries and Other Miscellanies of Ezra Stiles, D.D., LL.D., 1755–1794* (New Haven, CT: Yale University Press, 1916); Franklin Dexter, *The Literary Diary of Ezra Stiles* (New York: C. Scribner's Sons, 1901).

STIMSON, HENRY (1867–1950). U.S. secretary of state under President Herbert Hoover, 1924–33, and secretary of war under President **Franklin D. Roosevelt**, 1940–45. For Stimson and many ordinary Americans, there existed during the **Holocaust** a predisposition to disbelieve that atrocities were taking place against Jews. Stimson's diaries rarely mention the **Nazi** war against the Jews, and he opposed postwar Jewish immigration. In his diary entry of September 14, 1944, Stimson had complained that Henry Morgenthau was "biased by his Semitic grievances." Stimson blocked a proposal for temporary havens for Jews in the United States. In March 1944 he argued that a "Jewish problem" disquieted this country, since the European Jews did not assimilate well, and so **quotas** on postwar immigration had to take precedence over other considerations (even after the extent of Nazi anti-Jewish atrocities were revealed). He justified himself by observing that elements of the U.S. population feared that Jews would remain in this country after the war. At a time when more than 90 percent of immigration quotas from Nazi Europe were unfilled, Stimson argued that **Adolf Hitler** would expel Jews, forcing them to flee to the United States. *See also* WAR REFUGEE BOARD.

SUGGESTED READING: Henry Lewis Stimson Diaries, McKeldin Library, Yale University.

STIRNER, MAX (1806–1856). Pseudonym of Johann Kaspar Schmidt. German author, philosopher, and teacher. In *The Ego and His Own* (1844), Stirner wrote:

> The ancient acuteness and profundity lies as far from the spirit and the spirituality of the Christian world as earth from heaven. . . . The man who is set free is nothing but a freed man, a libertinus, a dog dragging a piece of chain with him: he is an unfree man in the garment of freedom, like the ass in the lion's skin. . . . Emancipated or not emancipated, Jew remains Jew.

SUGGESTED READING: Nicholas Goodrick-Clarke, *The Occult Roots of Nazism* (New York: New York University Press, 1992).

STÖCKER, ADOLF (1835–1909). German chaplain and politician. In 1878, Stöcker founded the Christian Social Party. Grounding his political policy on **antisemitism**, his platform included as key goals the restriction of civil rights for Jews, limiting Jewish immigration, *numerus clausus*, and exclusion of Jews from public office. He also inspired an antisemitic student movement, the German Students Union, and held an International Anti-Jewish Congress in 1882. His solution to the "Jewish problem" was to eliminate the Jews from all influential sections of German life. Only this "would restore Germany to blessedness, or the cancer from which we suffer will continue to eat away at us. Our future will then be imperiled, our German spirit will be Jewified." By the 1890s, his influence dramatically declined, only to be reborn with the **Nazis**.

SUGGESTED READING: George L. Mosse, *The Crisis of German Ideology: Intellectual Origins of the Third Reich* (New York: H. Fertig, 1998).

STODDARD, LOTHROP (1883–1950). **Eugenicist** and racist; **Madison Grant**'s protégé. In *The Rising Tide of Color against White World-Supremacy* (1922), Stoddard wrote of the need to maintain "white political domination" in the face of the colored threat—not so much from blacks, who were dismissed as inferior savages, but from "Asiatics" (of which Jews were a subset) who, according to Stoddard, constituted the main danger in an impending struggle for control of Africa and "mongrel-ruled" South America. He saw in the Jews "a dwarfish stature, flat faces, high cheekbones, and other Mongoloid traits," and a "Negroid strain" as well, noting the Jews' frizzy or woolly hair and thick lips.

SUGGESTED READING: Edwin Black, *The War against the Weak* (New York: Four Walls, Eight Windows, 2003).

STOKER, BRAM. *See* DRACULA.

STONER. *See* NATIONAL STATES RIGHTS PARTY.

STORMFRONT. Symbolized by a **Celtic Cross** or Odin's Cross surrounded by the phrase "White Pride World Wide." White power website created by Don Black, out of West Palm Beach, Florida. One of the first hate sites on the Internet, it is still widely accessed and has links to hate groups all over the world.

SUGGESTED READING: Anti-Defamation League, *Hate on Display: Extremist Symbols, Logos, and Tattoos* (New York: Anti-Defamation League, 2006).

STORY, JOSEPH (1779–1845). Supreme Court justice; poet. Story's inaugural discourse after accepting the Dane Professorship at Harvard in 1829 stated:

> Christianity is a part of the Common Law, . . . the boast is as true as it is beautiful. There never has been a period, in which the Common Law did not recognize Christianity as lying at its foundations. [For Christianity] now repudiates every act done in violation of its duties of perfect obligation. It pronounces illegal every contract offensive to its morals. . . . It still attaches to persons believing in its divine authority the highest degrees of competency as witnesses.

See also VIDAL v. GIRARD'S EXECUTORS.
SUGGESTED READING: William Story, *Life and Letters of Joseph Story* (Boston: Little, Brown, 1851).

STREICHER, JULIUS (1885–1946). Editor and publisher. A personal friend of **Adolf Hitler**'s, Streicher was a fanatic **antisemite**. He was the chairman of the committee on the **boycott of Jewish shops** in March 1933. In Franconia he embezzled Jewish property. But Streicher is best known for his vicious attacks on Jews in the paper he founded and published from 1925 to 1945, *Der Stürmer* (*The Attacker*). Its motto was "The Jews Are Our Misfortune," straight from **Martin Luther** and **Heinrich von Treitschke**. He printed the **ritual murder** myth and urged violence against **synagogues**. Streicher advocated annihilation of Jews as early as 1939 in his paper and also published children's books full of antisemitic stories. Unrepentant, he was hanged after the **Nuremberg War Crimes Trials,** saying that Luther should have been there with him.

SUGGESTED READING: Louis L. Snyder, *Hitler's Elite* (New York: Berkeley Books, 1992).

STROOP, JÜRGEN (1885–1946). **SS** general. Stroop directed the liquidation of the **Warsaw Ghetto**, its destruction "a gift to **Adolf Hitler**." In his "Stroop Report," the general bragged that thousands of Jews were killed in **ghetto** fighting. He was then sent to Athens to **deport** 5,000–7,000 Jews but caught only 800. Violating the Geneva Convention, he also had American POWs killed. The Poles hanged him on March 6, 1952.

SUGGESTED READING: *Revolt amid the Darkness, 1942–1943: Days of Remembrance* (Washington, DC: United States Holocaust Memorial Museum, 1995).

STRUMA. Jewish Palestine Party–sponsored refugee ship. The *Struma* was an unseaworthy vessel carrying 769 mostly Romanian Jewish refugees seeking to escape **deportation** in December 1941. They were refused permission to land in Istanbul largely through the influence of the British Foreign Office, who feared the refugees would reach Palestine. The Turkish officials forced the ship out to sea, where a mysterious explosion drowned all but one refugee, who had been hospitalized and left behind. *See also* WHITE PAPER OF 1939.

SUGGESTED READING: Ira Hirschmann, *Lifeline to a Promised Land* (New York: Vanguard, 1946).

STUCKART, WILHELM (1902–1953). Nazi jurist. Stuckart played a key role in drafting and implementing the **Nuremberg Laws of 1935**. A member of the **Wannsee Conference**, he was complicit in planning the **Final Solution**. After the war, he was arrested but served only four years in prison.

SUGGESTED READING: Louis Snyder, *Encyclopedia of the Third Reich* (New York: Paragon House, 1989); Joseph Tenenbaum, *Race and Reich: The Story of an Epoch* (New York: Twayne, 1956).

STURMABTEILUNG. *See* SA.

STÜRMER, DER. *See* STREICHER, JULIUS.

STUYVESANT, PETER (1592–1672). Dutch governor of New Amsterdam (later New York). In 1654, 23 Jewish refugees fleeing from Recife, Brazil, landed in New Amsterdam. The local merchants complained to Stuyvesant that the Jews intended to remain as residents. The governor wrote to the offices of the Dutch West India Company, which sponsored the colony, that Jews were "repugnant, deceitful, enemies and blasphemous of Christ." He wanted them expelled. The Dutch West India Company, having some Jewish investors, wrote back that the Jews must stay, but must not be allowed to practice their Judaism outside of their homes and must be kept from corrupting the "tender lambs of Christ."

SUGGESTED READING: David A. Gerber, *Antisemitism in American History* (Chicago: University of Illinois Press, 1986).

STYLITES, ST. SIMEON (390–459). Ascetic monk in Syria. In 420 and 423, Emperor Theodosius II had to issue further laws protecting Jewish lives and property. Incensed at the **Theodosian code** protecting **synagogues**, as limited as it was, militant Christians prevailed on Simeon Stylites to oppose it and to prevent its application in the Eastern Empire. Simeon ordered the synagogue at Amida in Mesopotamia, not far from Callinicum, burned down and in its place a small chapel built dedicated to the Blessed Virgin. The Jews of Amida were prevented from replacing their destroyed synagogue on land that they already owned. When the emperor ordered another Christian-occupied synagogue at Antioch be returned to the Jewish community, Simeon, like **St. Ambrose**, chastized the emperor for seeming to protect Jews rather than make concessions to Christians. As a result, Theodosius apologized to the Christians, changed his mind about restoring the synagogue, and gave up his attempt to protect both the Jews and their synagogues.

SUGGESTED READING: Jean Juster, *Les Juifs dans l'empire romain* (Paris: P. Geuthner, 1914).

SUBHUMAN. In the **Nazi** worldview, Gypsies (i.e., Romani and Sinti), Slavs, blacks, and the physically and mentally handicapped were *Untermenschen*, subhuman. This dehumanization justified to the Nazis their cruel, and often murderous, practices. Sometimes the Nazis regarded the Jews as subhuman, too, but often they put the Jews into another category, that of the inhuman, associating them with vermin, parasites, and disease, as well as with the powers of evil—and treating them as a danger and threat to the very existence of the **Third Reich. Heinrich Himmler** himself clearly made this distinction: He spoke to **SS** officers at Posen, Poland, in 1943 and defined Germany's goal of murdering all Jews as

a really grave matter. Among ourselves, this once, it shall be uttered quite frankly; but in public we will never speak of it. . . . I am referring to the evacuation of the Jews, the annihilation of the Jewish people. . . . In our history, this is an unwritten and never-to-be-written page of glory. . . . The wealth they had we have taken from them. . . . We had the moral right, we had the duty toward our people, to kill this people which wanted to kill us.

See also ANTISEMITISM, MYSTICAL.

SUGGESTED READING: Richard Breitman, *The Architect of Genocide*: *Himmler and the Final Solution* (Boston: University Press of New England, 1992).

SUBSEQUENT NUREMBERG WAR CRIMES TRIALS. *See* NUREMBERG WAR CRIMES TRIALS.

SUE, EUGÈNE (1804–1857). Sue's novel *Le Juif Errant* (*The Wandering Jew*, 1844), even though it has as its protagonist villain a **Jesuit** priest, propagated the myth and **defamation** of the **Wandering Jew**, Ahasuerus, associated with the story of Herodias, who caused John the Baptist's death and who accompanies Ahasuerus through history. It is from this 1844 book, which associates Jews with money and maliciousness (*Schadenfreude*), that most people derive their knowledge of the Wandering Jew.

SUGGESTED READING: Dietrich Schwanitz, *Shylock: Von Shakespeare bis zum Nuernberger Prozess, mit einem Abdruck von "Shylock's Revenge" by David Henry Wilson* (Hamburg: Verlag Dr. R. Kraemer, 1989).

SUPERCESSIONISM. *See* TRIUMPHALISM.

SVENGALI. The main character in English novelist **George du Maurier**'s 1894 novel *Trilby*. Svengali is described as an unpleasant Jew who exerts hypnotic powers over a young Irish woman named Trilby. The pianist and music teacher can make her sing beautifully when he hypnotizes her, but otherwise she has a poor singing voice. The novel expresses the negative stereotype of an avaricious Jew corrupting a pure white woman.

SUGGESTED READING: Edgar Rosenberg, *From Shylock to Svengali: Jewish Stereotypes in English Literature* (Stanford, CA: Stanford University Press, 1960).

SWASTIKA. *Hakenkreuz.* Hooked cross. Swastika was the most important **Nazi** symbol. In ancient India, it was a symbol of purity. Nazis employed it to symbolize **Aryan** blood and destiny. It was first used as a political symbol by the Heimwehr and Freikorps in 1918. Today, the Swastika is a **neo-Nazi**, racist **skinhead**, and white supremacist symbol. **Hitler** made the Nazi swastika unique to his party by reversing the normal direction of the symbol so that it appeared to spin clockwise. *See also* SWASTIKA WITH IRON CROSS, NAZI.

SUGGESTED READING: Robert Michael and Karin Doerr, *Nazi-Deutsch/ Nazi-German: An English Lexicon of the Language of the Third Reich*

(New York: Greenwood Press, 2001); Anti-Defamation League, *Hate on Display: Extremist Symbols, Logos, and Tattoos* (New York: Anti-Defamation League, 2006).

SWASTIKA WITH IRON CROSS, NAZI. The Iron Cross (without the **swastika**) was a Prussian-German medal for bravery that originated during the **Napoleonic** Wars. In 1939, **Adolf Hitler** renewed use of the Iron Cross, superimposed the **Nazi** swastika in its center. Following the fall of the **Third Reich**, Germany banned the use of this symbol. Today, the Iron Cross, with or without the **swastika**, is displayed by **neo-Nazi** groups as a hate symbol on clothing and jewelry.

SUGGESTED READING: Anti-Defamation League, *Hate on Display: Extremist Symbols, Logos, and Tattoos* (New York: Anti-Defamation League, 2006).

SWIFT, JONATHAN (1667–1745). Anglo-Irish satirist and clergyman. In his "Miscellanies" (1711), Swift wrote of a run on a bank:

> On Thursday morning there was little or nothing transacted in Change-alley; there were a multitude of sellers, but so few buyers, that one cannot affirm the stocks bore any certain price except among the Jews; who this day reaped great profit by their infidelity. There were many who called themselves Christians, who offered to buy for time; but as these were people of great distinction, I choose not to mention them, because in effect it would seem to accuse them both of avarice and infidelity.

SUGGESTED READING: Jonathan Swift et al., *Miscellanies in Prose and Verse* (London: Pickering & Chatto, 2003).

SWIFT, WESLEY (d. 1971). A Methodist minister from Alabama and former **Ku Klux Klan** Kleagle; editor of **Gerald L. K. Smith**'s *The Cross and the Flag*. Swift founded the Church of Jesus Christ–Christian and was national director of the **Christian Defense League**. He was also associated with such racist paramilitary groups as the California Rangers and the Minutemen. "All Jews must be destroyed," he said. "I prophesy that before November 1953, there will not be a Jew in the United States, and by that I mean a Jew that will be able to walk or talk." *See also* ARYAN NATIONS.

SUGGESTED READING: ADL Law Enforcement Agency Resource Network, "Richard Butler," http://www.adl.org/learn/ext_us/butler.asp?&x picked = 2&item = butler.

SWITZERLAND. Neutral country bordering Germany, Austria, France, and Italy. This traditional refuge for persecuted people admitted 23,000 Jews out of 200,000 refugees it accepted during World War II. Switzerland prompted Germany to introduce the *J* **stamp** in its Jewish passports in 1938 so that it could stem the flow of German refugees. Switzerland permitted German trains transporting concentration-camp inmates free passage through the country to Italy. The Swiss administrative and banking industry laundered money for the **Nazis**. German assets—including assets stolen from Jews, possibly gold from Jewish corpses—were deposited in Swiss banks up to 1943. Jews who had deposited money for safekeeping in Swiss banks before the war have had great difficulty gaining access to these funds in the postwar period.

SUGGESTED READING: Adam LeBor, *Hitler's Secret Bankers: The Myth of Swiss Neutrality During the Holocaust* (Secaucus, NJ: Carol Publishing Group, 1997).

SWP. Racist abbreviation for "Supreme White Power."

SUGGESTED READING: Anti-Defamation League, *Hate on Display: Extremist Symbols, Logos, and Tattoos* (New York: Anti-Defamation League, 2006); ADL Law Enforcement Agency Resource Network, *A Visual Database of Extremist Symbols, Logos, and Tattoos*, http://www.adl.org/hate_symbols/default.asp.

SYLVESTER, JAMES JOSEPH (1814–1897). Prominent British mathematician. Sylvester was also a lawyer and the first Jewish professor at the University of Virginia. In 1842 the university administration allowed him to be hounded from his position after being assaulted by two **antisemitic** students. The Presbyterian Church commented that most Virginians were Christians and the university should require of its professors a "pure morality based upon Christian principles." Sylvester went on to positions at Johns Hopkins and Oxford universities.

SUGGESTED READING: Naomi Cohen, ed., *Essential Papers on Jewish–Christian Relations in the United States: Imagery and Reality* (New York: New York University Press, 1990).

SYNAGOGA. Medieval artistic symbol of the Jews. The defeated Synagoga was positioned in medieval Christian art on the left of cathedral entrances or statues or paintings of Jesus, thereby associating the Jews with hell, strife, and danger. The triumphant figure of Ecclesia was positioned on the right, thereby associating Christians with heaven, election, and safety. By the end of the Middle Ages, the artistic trappings of Ecclesia would be transferred to Mary, *mater et sponsa Christi* (mother and bride of Christ), as the universal symbol of Christian belief. Synagoga was depicted as a defeated adversary. As hatred of Jews increased, so did "the gracelessness of Synagoga's image." Christian artists associated her more and more with the Jewish **"Christ killers"** and sometimes provided her with all the instruments of Christ's murder: the spear, sponge, vinegar, and crown of thorns. She was usually blinded or blindfolded, often by the Devil. Frequently, her head was bowed, her spear (perhaps an allusion to the spear that stabbed Christ on the cross or symbolic of the Jewish Scriptures breaking upon contact with Christianity) was broken into three parts, the tablets of the law were falling from her hand, and her crown lay at her feet.

SUGGESTED READING: Wolfgang S. Seiferth, *Synagogue and Church in the Middle Ages: Two Symbols in Art and Literature*, trans. L. Chadeayne and P. Gottwald (New York: Frederick Ungar, 1970); Abba Eban, *My People* (New York: Behrman House, 1996).

SYNAGOGUE. Jewish place of worship, study, and fellowship. Christian theologians have systematically reinterpreted the meaning of the synagogue. Perhaps because it symbolized Judaism in general as well as representing the various Jewish communities in particular, the **Church Fathers'** disparaging and insulting rhetoric threatened the synagogue. Ephrem the Syrian (306–373) described the synagogue as a whore, as did Church Father **St. John Chrysostom. St. Jerome**'s opinion was that "if you call it a brothel, a den of vice, the devil's refuge, Satan's fortress, a place to deprave the soul, an abyss of every conceivable disaster or whatever else you will, you are still saying less than it deserves." **St. Ambrose** called the synagogue "a refuge of insanity." Christianized Roman law reflected these attitudes as well. To Christian theologians, the synagogue represented Judaism, the hated rival of Christianity. Destroying or damaging the synagogue building, transforming it into a church, and preventing the construction of a new synagogue were means for the politically empowered and theologically motivated Church to persecute the Jews, lower their prestige, and destroy their attraction for the Christian faithful.

SUGGESTED READING: Vincent Martin, *A House Divided: The Parting of the Ways between Church and Synagogue* (New York: Paulist Press, 1995); Friedrich Heer, *God's First Love* (New York: Weybright and Talley, 1967).

SZALASI, FERENC (1897–1946). Founder of **Arrow Cross**; head of the Hungarian government from October 15, 1944, to January 1945. On the day Szalasi came to power, a **pogrom** by Arrow Cross members took the lives of thousands of Jews. He and the pro-**Nazi** Arrow Cross instituted a

death march of 80,000 Jews to the **Austrian** border. Survivors were to be used as slave labor.

SUGGESTED READING: David Cesarani, ed., *Genocide and Rescue: The Holocaust in Hungary 1944* (Oxford, England: Berg, 1997).

– T –

TACITUS, CORNELIUS (56–120). Roman historian. Tacitus wrote this in his book *The Histories* (110):

> Most authors agree . . . this race . . . was hateful to the gods. . . . The Jews regard as profane all that we hold sacred. . . . They permit all that we abhor. . . . Customs of the Jews are base and abominable, and owe their persistence to their depravity. . . . The are extremely loyal toward one another . . . but toward every other people they feel only hate and enmity. . . . As a race, they are prone to lust. . . . Among themselves nothing is unlawful. . . . Those who are converted . . . despise the gods . . . disown their country . . . and regard their parents, children, and brothers as of little account. . . . The ways of the Jews are absurd and filthy.

SUGGESTED READING: John G. Gager, *The Origins of Anti-Semitism: Attitudes toward Judaism in Pagan and Christian Antiquity* (Oxford: Oxford University Press, 1985).

TACUARA GROUP. Rightist **Argentinian** political movement. During Juan Perón's dictatorship (1946–55), **antisemitism** declined in Argentina, as it did under the democratic rule of President Arturo Frondizi (1958–62), but during the unstable post-Perón period, fear of communism led to Argentina's dependency on rightist movements. Argentina's antidemocratic opposition consisted of Catholic conservatives, the military, and the Tacuara Group, which used the violation of Argentinian sovereignty involved in the Israeli capture of **Adolf Eichmann** to accuse Argentina's Jews of "dual loyalty" and to launch a wave of antisemitic actions. Many Argentinian Jews emigrated to Israel.

SUGGESTED READING: Raanan Rein, *Argentina, Israel, and the Jews: Peron, the Eichmann Capture and After* (Bethesda: University Press of Maryland, 2003).

TAGBLATT. See NEUES WIENER TAGBLATT.

TALMUD. Multivolume series of rabbinic interpretations of the Jewish Scriptures, Jewish civil and canonical law not collected in the Pentateuch, and the collection of ancient rabbinic writings on Jewish law and tradition (the Mishna and the Gemara) that constitute the basis of religious authority in Orthodox Judaism. An attack on the Jews through the assault on the Talmud spread throughout medieval Christendom. Several condemnations and **book burnings** of the Talmud took place, along with the writing of anti-talmudic treatises, confiscations of the Talmud by popes and kings, and **Inquisitional** censorings of the Talmud and other Jewish holy books. *See also* DISPUTATIONS.

SUGGESTED READING: Hyam Maccoby, *Judaism on Trial: Jewish–Christian Disputations in the Middle Ages* (London: Litman Library, 1982); Marc-Alain Ouaknin, *The Burnt Book: Reading the Talmud* (Princeton: Princeton University Press, 1995); Aaron Parry, *The Complete Idiots' Guide to the Talmud* (New York: Alpha, 2004).

TALMUD JEW, THE. An **antisemitic** publication by **August Rohling** in Germany in 1871. *The Talmud Jew* is largely based on **Johann Eisenmenger's** *Entdecktes Judentum* (*Judaism Unmasked*). Rohling twisted, misinterpreted, fabricated, and misquoted parts of the **Talmud** to show that the work slandered Christianity and Jesus. Nevertheless, Parisian publisher **Edouard Drumont** introduced the work to France. Later, antisemites and **Nazis** quoted it. *See also* CHRISTIANI, PABLO; DONIN, NICHOLAS; FRANKISTS; PETER THE VENERABLE (PETER OF CLUNY); PFEFFERKORN, JOHANNES.

SUGGESTED READING: Ismar Elbogen, *A Century of Jewish Life*, trans. Moses Hados (Philadelphia: Jewish Publication Society, 1945).

TANNENBERGERBUND. Antisemitic German organization formed in 1925 by General **Erich Ludendorff** and his wife, **Mathilde Ludendorff**. The Tannenbergerbund demanded the elimination of Jewish influence in German affairs and the expansion of German power. Members believed that the German people could achieve freedom only by expelling foreign influences from Germany. The Bible was seen as a Jewish fraud that destroyed every *völkisch* impulse toward racial purity. The search for God was to lead to the German "**blood and soil**." The Bund attacks Jews, Communists, Catholics, and **Freemasons** and was involved in a **pogrom** in Lüneburg, Germany.

SUGGESTED READING: Dirk Stegmann, *Kleinstadtgesellschaft und Nationalsozialismus* (Hamburg: VSA-Verlag, 1984); Heinz P. Wassermann, ed., *Antisemitismus in Österreich nach 1945: Ergebnisse, Positionen und Perspektiven der Forschung; Schriften des Centrums für Jüdische Studien*, vol. 3 (Innsbruck: Studien Verlag, 2002).

TANZIM AL-JIHAD. Arabic for "the Holy War Organization." Tanzim started as an Egyptian fundamentalist terrorist group. Four of its members assassinated Egyptian president **Anwar al-Sadat**. It played a major role in the al-Aqsa **Intifada** and has ambushed and bombed civilians in Israel. Tanzim has support on the West Bank. *See also* JIHAD; MUSLIM BROTHERHOOD; RADICAL ISLAM.

SUGGESTED READING: Cyril Glasse, *The New Encyclopedia of Islam* (Walnut Creek, CA: Altamira Press, 2002).

TAXATION OF JEWS (*FISCUS JUDAICUS*). After the Jewish Temple in Jerusalem fell in 70 CE, Emperor **Vespasian** decreed an annual tax on all Jews living in the Roman Empire to finance a temple to Jupiter. The tax lasted until the fourth century and was collected by severe measures. It was revived during the Middle Ages as a personal tax (poll tax) on Jews by the Holy Roman emperor, who considered the Jews his property; all taxes on them went directly to him. From the 13th century, individual rulers within the empire often taxed the Jews as well. In the medieval German states, officials could find 38 excuses for taxes from birth to death. The Muslims levied a *khara*, a tax for exemption from military service, and also a *jrzya*, a tax to permit the practice of the Jewish religion. In 1219 the English monarchy established the Exchequer of the Jews to levy and collect taxes. In 1342, Louis the Bavarian (1314–1347) introduced the *Goldener Opferpfennig*, a one-florin tax on Jewish adults. The Jewish inhabitants of the Roman **ghetto** (1555–1808, 1815–1870) paid taxes, one of which paid for the House of Catechumens. Almost all these taxes were paid communally.

SUGGESTED READING: Edwin Mendelssohn, "Fiscus judaicus," *Shekel* 19, no. 3 (May–June 1986), 3–5; Gotthard Deutsch, "Opferpfennig, Goldener," *JewishEncyclopedia.com*, http://www.jewishencyclopedia.com/view.jsp?artid=80&letter=O; Bernard Lewis, *The Jews of Islam* (Princeton, NJ: Princeton University Press, 1987).

TEACHING OF CONTEMPT. Roman Catholic approach to Jews and Judaism historically. Judaism was considered old, out of date, and superceded by Christianity. Jews worshipped a God of vengeance rather than of love. The Jews were considered a **deicide** people whose guilt for the rejection and murder of Jesus passed down through the generations. The Jewish people were considered abandoned by the Lord, rejected, heretical, blind, and stubborn. They were to suffer as punishment for their evil deeds. *See also* ANTISEMITISM IN THE CHRISTIAN SCRIPTURES; TRIUMPHALISM; VATICAN COUNCIL II.

SUGGESTED READING: Jules Isaac, *The Teaching of Contempt: Christian Roots of Antisemitism*, trans. Helen Weaver (New York: Holt, Rinehart & Winston, 1968).

TEN PERCENT OFF. (U.S., British slur) Reference both to **circumcision** and discount prices.

SUGGESTED READING: "List of Ethnic Slurs," *Wikipedia*, http://en.wiki pedia.org/wiki/List_of_ethnic_slurs.

TERBOVEN, JOSEF (1898–1945). **Nazi** German head of conquered Norway, 1940–45. As governor appointed by **Adolf Hitler**, Terboven was the true ruler, rather than the Norwegian **Vidkun Quisling**. Terboven began rounding up Jews in June 1941, planning to confine them to five internment camps. However, the Norwegian underground smuggled 900 of 1,700 Jews to safety in Sweden.

SUGGESTED READING: Samuel Abrahamsen, *Norway's Response to the Holocaust* (New York: Holocaust Library, 1991).

TEREZÍN (THERESIENSTADT). **Ghetto** and concentration camp in Czechoslovakia, 1941–45. This complex also contained a **Gestapo** prison known as the "small fortress." It was falsely promoted by the Germans as a model camp. At first, elderly Jewish World War I veterans and prominent Jews were **deported** there. Others came from 30 nations. More than 90,000 Jews were shipped from Terezín (Theresienstadt to the Germans) to death camps, mainly **Auschwitz-Birkenau**. Only 100 of 15,000 children survived. The Red Cross uncritically accepted the camp at face value when it visited the camp in June 1944.

SUGGESTED READING: Norbert Troller, *Theresienstadt: Hitler's Gift to the Jews*, ed. Joel Shatzsky, trans. Susan E. Cernyak-Spatz (Chapel Hill: University of North Carolina Press, 1991).

TERTULLIAN (160–240). Ecclesiastical writer and **Church Father** from Carthage, North Africa. Tertullian wrote *Adversus Judaeos*, a tract that questioned Moses as prophet, Jewish religious understandings, and the need to observe the **Sabbath**. Tertullian argued that Jews were murderers of God and "the very anti-type of true virtue."

SUGGESTED READING: Robert Wilde, *The Treatment of the Jews in the Greek Christian Writers of the First Three Centuries* (Washington, DC: Catholic University Press, 1949).

THACKERAY, WILLIAM MAKEPEACE (1811–1863). British novelist. In *Vanity Fair* (1847–48), Thackeray's characters speak of "Jewboy,"

"Jew banker," and "Jew's eye," and he quotes "The Rape of the Lock" about Belinda's diamonds, "which Jews might kiss and infidels adore." In *Notes of a Journey from Cornhill to Grand Cairo* (1846), the chapter on Rhodes says:

> Think of the centuries during which these wonderful people [Jews] have remained unchanged; and how, from the days of Jacob downwards, they have believed and swindled! The Rhodian Jews, with their genius for filth, have made their quarter of the noble desolate old town the most ruinous and wretched of all.

In 1847, Thackeray published *Codlingsby*, an "**antisemitic** burlesque."

SUGGESTED READING: Daniel Denecke, "The Motivation of Tennyson's Reader: Privacy and the Politics of Literary Ambiguity in *The Princess*," *Victorian Studies* 43, no. 2 (Winter 2001).

THEATER, NAZI PURGE OF. In Germany during the **Weimar Republic**, as under the kaisers—and as in Austria, Great Britain, France, and Russia—Jews were in the forefront of the performing arts, both as artists and performers, as well as in the audiences. German-Jewish playwrights tended to be pro-republic, leftist, and sexually experimental—all of which traits infuriated the **Nazis**. In September 1933 **Adolf Hitler** apppointed **Josef Goebbels** to head the Reich Chambers of Culture, creating mandatory **guilds** for employees in the fields of film, theater, music, the fine arts, and journalism. Jews were forbidden from joining these guilds, and therefore were purged from working in these professions. In November 1938, Jews were prohibited from attending theaters, movies, concerts, and exhibits. *See also* DEGENERATE ART; FILM INDUSTRY, NAZI PURGE OF.

SUGGESTED READING: Alan E. Steinweis, *Art, Ideology, and Economics in Nazi Germany: The Reich Chambers of Music, Theater, and the Visual Arts* (Chapel Hill: University of North Carolina Press, 1996); John London, ed., *Theatre and the Nazis* (Manchester, England: Manchester University Press, 2000).

THEODOSIAN CODE (CODEX THEODOSIANUS). Compiled in 438, this was the first official collection of imperial [Roman] constitutions. It was ordered by Emperor Theodosius II (401–450) as part of his concern with legal education. The code was adopted in both the eastern and western portions of the Roman Empire and provides much incidental information about social and economic conditions in the late empire. The *Codex Theodosianus* followed the Church's principle that Jews should never be put in a position of authority over any of the faithful, thus excluding Jews from military rank and its accompanying privileges. For a Jew to serve in the military, the law required that he be baptized as a Christian. Although neither the Church nor the empire ever outlawed Judaism itself, one of the first laws of the Christianized empire made it a criminal offense to become a Jew. Moreover, exile or death was the fate of Jews who prevented their coreligionists from apostatizing to Christianity or who encouraged Romans to convert to Judaism. Note the hateful language of the following laws:

- "The Jews must be informed that if they . . . dare attack anyone escaping from their deadly sect and choosing to join the cult of God [Christianity] . . . they shall be delivered immediately to the flames and burnt with all their associates."
- "The blind and senseless Jews [are] **heretics** [and] abominable. . . . Whoever coerces or persuades any Roman, slave or free, to leave the cult of the Christian religion and join instead that abominable sect and rite [Judaism] shall be sentenced to death and expropriation."
- "[It is prohibited to] cease being a Christian and adopt the abominable and disgusting name of the Jews [that is,] to adopt the Jewish perversity, which is alien to the Roman Empire which has now become Christianized. . . . For it is an issue of life and death when someone rejects the Christian faith and replaces it with the disgusting Jewish form of perverse belief."

SUGGESTED READING: James Everett Seaver, *The Persecution of Jews in the Roman Empire* (Lawrence: University Press of Kansas, 1952), 300–428.

THEOLOGIA GLORIAE. See TRIUMPHALISM.

THEOSOPHY. *See* BAILEY, ALICE A.

THIRD REICH. Adolf Hitler's Nazi regime, 1933–45. The First Reich (empire) was the Holy Roman Empire; the second was the **Otto von Bismarck**–Kaiser period (1871–1918). The Third Reich, Hitler envisioned, would last for a thousand years. This New Order would be *Judenfrei* (free of Jews) and would include all Europe. It was a totalitarian dictatorship, consisting of one leader (*der Führer*), one political party (the Nazi Party), monopolies on armed force and terror and on communications, and a partial monopoly on the economy, with strict control of labor unions but much less control of management and ownership. The eliminationist Nazi ideology held the Jews to be the regime's most dangerous enemies.

SUGGESTED READING: William L. Shirer, *The Rise and Fall of the Third Reich* (New York: Simon & Schuster, 1960).

THREE HUNDRED, THE. An **antisemitic** fantasy and **defamation**. In December 1921, German-Jewish politician, industrialist, and economist **Walther Rathenau** wrote in the *Wiener Freie Presse* (*Vienna Free Press*): "Three hundred men, all of whom are known to one another, guide the economic destinies of the Continent and seek their successors among their followers." Six months later, Rathenau was assassinated. Nowhere in Rathenau's article were Jews mentioned in any context. However, like many other German antisemites, including General **Erich Ludendorff**, one of his murderers claimed at his trial that Rathenau himself was "one of the three hundred Elders of Zion," and that Rathenau's policy of fulfilling the terms of the **Versailles** Treaty was dictated by an international Jewish plot against Germany. *See also PROTOCOLS OF THE ELDERS OF ZION, THE.*

SUGGESTED READING: Vamberto Morais, *A Short History of Anti-Semitism* (New York: Norton, 1976).

THULE SOCIETY. Nationalist and **Aryan** supremacist literary circle formed in 1912 in Munich. The word *Thule* was taken from Ultima Thule, the Land at the End of the World, the mythical birthplace of the Germanic race. The circle promoted the ancient Teutonic religion, including the Norse runes and beliefs and festivals. After 1918 the Thule Society accepted workers as members and assumed anti-**Bolshevik** and **antisemitic** postures. It financed the **Freikorps** and hosted the **German Workers Party**. Thule's symbol was the **swastika**. **Adolf Hitler**'s mentor, **Dietrich Eckart**, was a prominent member. *See also* LIST, GUIDO VON; SS.

SUGGESTED READING: Wulf Schwartzwaller, *The Unknown Hitler* (Berkeley: University of California Press, 1990); Nicholas Goodrick-Clarke, *The Occult Roots of Nazism* (New York: New York University Press, 1992).

THUNDERBOLT, THE. Extreme racist newspaper of the U.S. **National States Rights Party** (NSRP), 1958–88. The brainchild of Edward Field (1932–), the *Thunderbolt*'s ideology was white supremacist and was extremely **anti-Semitic**, with **genocidal** overtones. When Field was eased out of the NSRP, the paper dissolved.

SUGGESTED READING: Forster A. Epstein, *The Radical Right* (New York: Vintage, 1967).

THUNDERBOLTS/LIGHTNING BOLTS. **Nazi** symbol signifying **Heinrich Himmler**'s Schutzstaffel (**SS**). The symbol is frequently seen in **neo-Nazi** and racist **skinhead** tattoos and graffiti indicating violence, **antisemi-**

tism, white supremacy, and **fascism**. Originally, the Sigrune or Sowilo or Victory rune.

SUGGESTED READING: Anti-Defamation League, *Hate on Display: Extremist Symbols, Logos, and Tattoos* (New York: Anti-Defamation League, 2006).

TILLMAN, "PITCHFORK" BEN (1847–1918). **Populist** U.S. senator from South Carolina. Tillman was an up-and-coming Democrat in 1896, elected to the Senate in 1894. In discussing the gold standard, he said:

> **Rothschild** and his American agents graciously condescended to come to the help of the United States treasury in maintaining the gold standard. . . . Great God, that this proud government, the richest, most powerful on the globe, should have been brought to so low a pass that a London Jew should have been appointed its receiver to have charge of the treasury.

SUGGESTED READING: Francis Butler Simkins and Orville Vernon Burton, *Pitchfork Ben Tillman, South Carolinian* (Columbia: University of South Carolina Press, 2002).

TISO, JOSEF (1887–1947). Catholic priest; pro-**Nazi** president of Slovakia, 1939–45. During Tiso's reign of the **fascist** state, he introduced anti-Jewish legislation: Jewish property was expropriated; Jews were placed in slave labor camps and 20,000 were deported. It is reported that Rabbi Michael Ber Weissmandl managed to escape from one of these trains and made it to the residency of the papal nuncio, the **Vatican**'s ambassador to the Slovak republic. He pleaded with the nuncio to pressure Tiso to stop the trains and thereby save the lives of thousands of innocent Jewish children. The nuncio replied, "There is no such thing as an innocent Jewish child! You will all pay with your blood for the killing of our Savior!" *See also* TUKA, VOJTECH.

SUGGESTED READING: Gerald Reitlinger, *The Final Solution* (New York: Perpetua/Barnes & Noble, 1961).

TÍSZA-ESZLÁR. Hungarian village that was the scene of a **ritual murder** accusation. In 1882, a 14-year-old Christian girl disappeared. A local Catholic priest accused the Jews, and an unstable Jewish youth "confessed" that he had witnessed the murder in a **synagogue**. A grand jury investigated the charge and acquitted all Jews. The Budapest government's inquiry confirmed the acquittal, but anti-Jewish riots followed anyway. Gyozo Istoczy then formed an antisemitic party. *See also* ROHLING, AUGUST.

SUGGESTED READING: Andrew Handler, *Blood Libel at Tiszaeszlar* (New York: Columbia University Press, 1980).

TITUS, FLAVIUS VESPASIANUS (39–81). **Vespasian**'s son; Roman general and emperor, 79–81. In 70 CE, Titus destroyed the Second Temple, and along with it Jewish Judea. He demolished the city of Jerusalem, pillaged the Temple's holy objects, and desecrated the Holy of Holies, the inner sanctum of the Temple of Solomon where the Ark of the Covenant between God and the Jews was said to reside. He tortured and disemboweled Jews who tried to escape and forced Jews to engage in murderous gladiatorial contests.

SUGGESTED READING: Chaim Raphael, *Walls of Jerusalem* (New York: Knopf, 1968).

TIVOLI PROGRAM. At the Tivoli Congress of the German Conservative Party in 1892, the party officially adopted **antisemitism** as a plank in its platform, saying: "We combat the widely oppressive and decomposing Jewish influence on our national life; we demand for our Christian people a Christian magistracy and Christian teachers for Christian pupils."

SUGGESTED READING: James Retallack, "Antisemitism, Conservative Propaganda and Racial Politics in Late 19th-Century Germany," *German Studies Review* 11, no. 3 (October 1985).

TLASS, MUSTAFA (b. 1932). Syrian defense minister for decades at the end of the 20th century. Combining the **Damascus Affair**, based on the medieval **ritual murder** defamation, and *The Protocols of the Elders of Zion*, Tlass has argued that Jews are **vampires** who murder Christians and Muslims and drink their blood. In his book *The Matzoh of Zion* (1983), Tlass wrote:

> The Jew can kill you and take your blood in order to make his Zionist bread. Here opens before us a page more ugly than the crime itself: the religious beliefs of the Jews and the perversions they contain, which draw their orientation from a dark hate towards all humankind and all religions.

Based on Tlass's book, in 2002 an Egyptian film company produced the **antisemitic** series *Horseman without a Horse*.

SUGGESTED READING: Robert S. Wistrich, *Muslim Antisemitism: A Clear and Present Danger* (New York: American Jewish Committee, 2002).

TOLEDO, FOURTH COUNCIL OF. Church lawmaking body convened in 636. The council required Jewish parents who had **converted** to Christianity but then reverted to Judaism to either return to Christianity or give up their children to the Church, which would place them in monasteries or among Christian families. That is, the council sanctioned forced **baptism** of children, reasoning that Jewish children were slaves who must be set free into Christian homes. Jews and converted Jews were banned from public office that put them in any position of authority over Christians. The Church's discrimination against even baptized Jews was a precursor to the later Spanish race laws. *See also* ISIDORE OF SEVILLE, ST.

TOLEDO, 12TH COUNCIL OF. Church lawmaking body convened in 681. The faithful were admonished to "Tear the Jewish pest out by the root!" *See also* ERWIG.

TOLERANZPATENT. See JOSEPH II.

TORQUEMADA, TOMÁS DE (1420–1494). **Dominican** friar and Grand Inquisitor in Spain. As confessor to Queen Isabella, Torquemada was her choice for Grand Inquisitor in 1478. He set up **Inquisition** courts all over Spain. Under him **conversos** suspected of returning in any way of practicing to Judaism were sentenced as **heretics**. Torture, dispossession of worldly goods, and **auto-da-fé** characterized Torquemada's Inquisition. Torquemada was most influential in the issuance of the 1492 Edict of **Expulsion** by Isabella and Ferdinand. His name became synonymous with fanatical religious persecution. *See also* CRUSADES; INQUISITION, SPANISH.

SUGGESTED READING: Simon Whitechapel, *Flesh Inferno: Torquemada and the Spanish Inquisition* (New York: Creation Books, 2003).

TORTOSA DISPUTATION. Greatest medieval **disputation**, presided over in 1413–14 by Antipope **Benedict XIII**, that condemned the **Talmud** as prelude to mass **conversion** of the Spanish Jews. Although the Jewish apostate Gerónimo de Santa Fé conducted the Christian case, Benedict himself was heavily involved. Losing patience after dozens of sessions over nearly two years, the antipope demanded that the Jews adhere to the Church's restrictions on Jewish life. When they did not accept Gerónimo's arguments, the Jewish representatives at Tortosa were detained for months by Benedict and the civil authorities, and their Jewish communities were exposed to intimidation and physical attack by priests such as **Vincent Ferrer** and Christian mobs. Once several Jewish leaders escaped from Tortosa in mid-1413, Benedict ordered them to return to answer charges of **heresy** and defend the Talmud against charges of blasphemy. Although the disputation failed to achieve an intellectual success, the events surrounding the debate intimidated perhaps 3,000 Jews into converting to Christianity.

SUGGESTED READING: Yitzhak Baer, *A History of Jews in Christian Spain*, vol. 1 (Philadelphia: Jewish Publication Society, 1992).

TOUCAN SAM. (U.S. slur) Reference to the bird's large beak, said to resemble the stereotypical Jewish nose.

SUGGESTED READING: "List of Ethnic Slurs," *Wikipedia*, http://en.wiki pedia.org/wiki/List_of_ethnic_slurs.

TOUSSENEL, ALPHONSE (1803–1885). French publicist and ornithologist. Toussenel wrote the book *The Jews, Kings of the Epoch* (1845), in which he claimed that Jews had complete control over the monetary affairs of Europe. He also defended past persecutions of Jews as justified. A **Fourierist**, Toussenel blamed a Jewish oligarchy for social unrest and bemoaned the **Rothschild family**'s railroads for destroying pristine forests. He wrote that "the Jew reigns and governs France." To him, the Jews were "merchants and birds of prey," and parasites, and he called for a "war on the Jews."

SUGGESTED READING: Robert Byrnes, *Antisemitism in Modern France* (New Brunswick, NJ: Rutgers University Press, 1950).

TRANSMOGRIFICATION OF JEWISH VALUES. Through anti-Jewish theological myths and **defamations**, the **Church Fathers** pictured the Jews no longer as the chosen people, no longer heroes of holiness and moral living; they were instead the earthly representatives of the powers of evil. The Church countered the Jewish belief in the possibility of Gentile salvation with assertions that only Christian nations should exist and that salvation was inconceivable outside the Church. To provide the Church with a clear identity for itself, the Church Fathers turned Jewish values and practices on their heads by misrepresenting them as their opposites. Christian theologians attacked the Jews' Covenant with the One God, their Chosenness, **circumcision**, ethical laws, God-wrestling, the **messiah**, **dietary laws**, the **Sabbath**, holy days, patriarchs, and the Holy Scriptures. *See also* TRIUMPHALISM.

SUGGESTED READING: Robert Markus, *The End of Ancient Christianity* (Cambridge: Cambridge University Press, 1990); Ben Zion Bokser, *Judaism and the Christian Predicament* (New York: Knopf, 1967); Gavin Langmuir, *History, Religion, and Antisemitism* (Berkeley: University of California Press, 1990).

TREITSCHKE, HEINRICH VON (1839–1896). German historian. A Berlin University professor, Treitschke repopularized **Martin Luther**'s slogan "The Jews Are Our Misfortune," in his 1880 essay, "A Word About Our Jews." Treitschke accused Jews of conducting dishonest business practices, displaying crass materialism, belittling German customs and Christianity, dominating the press, and adhering to Jewish nationalism while demanding complete emancipation and acceptance in German society. He chastised Jews for creating a mongrel "German-Jewish culture." Treitschke justified **antisemitic** campaigns, claiming they were a "proper feeling against a foreign element." He helped make antisemitism respectable among German intellectuals. *See also* PAN-GERMAN LEAGUE; STREICHER, JULIUS.

SUGGESTED READING: Paul Mendes Flohr and Jehudah Reinhart, *The Jew in the Modern World* (New York: Oxford University Press, 1995).

TRIDON, GUSTAVE. 19th-century French social reformer. In *Du Molochisme Juif* (1884), Tridon stated that the Jew is "the stain in the picture of civilization, the bad genius of the earth. His gifts are pests. To fight Semitic ideas is the duty of the **Aryan** race."

TRILBY. See DU MAURIER, GEORGE; SVENGALI.

TRISKELE; TRISKELION; THREE-BLADED SWASTIKA. Three "sevens" spiraling from a common center are a White supremacy, **neo-Nazi**, and **skinhead** symbol. The triskele is an ancient symbol used widely in pagan Europe. Some versions—seen, for example, in Celtic jewelry and artwork—are not racist. The symbol was used by the **Nazi** regime. One South African group, the AWB (Afrikaner Resistance Movement), used it as its flag, claiming that the three sevens symbolized supremacy over the devil (frequently represented by "**666**"). The symbol is also used as part of the logo of the international racist skinhead group, Blood & Honour.

SUGGESTED READING: Anti-Defamation League, *Hate on Display: Extremist Symbols, Logos, and Tattoos* (New York: Anti-Defamation League, 2006).

TRIUMPHALISM. Also called *theologia gloriae*, theology of glory. A theological position adopted by all early Churchmen and many modern ones that the Jewish people are archetypal evildoers and that any injustice done to them, short of murder, is justified. A reaction to the majority of Jews' rejection of Jesus of Nazareth as their **messiah**, this anti-Jewish attitude became a permanent element in the fundamental identity of Western

Christian civilization. Triumphalistic writers transformed Jewish virtues into vices and **transmogrified Jewish values** into sins. This theology assumed that the Christian Church, the "new Israel"—ordained and sanctioned by God—succeeded the cursed and rejected old Israel morally, historically, and metaphysically.

SUGGESTED READING: Rosemary Ruether, *Faith and Fratricide: The Theological Roots of Antisemitism* (New York: Seabury Press, 1974).

TROGUS, GNAEUS POMPEIUS (end of 1st cent. BCE–start of 1st cent. CE). Roman historian. Trogus claimed that ancestors of the Jews were cast out of Egypt because they were lepers. *See also* APION.

TROLLOPE, ANTHONY (1815–1822). British novelist. Trollope's **anti-semitism** is ambiguous. His villains in *The Way We Live Now* (1875) and Lopez in *The Prime Minister* (1876) are rumored to be Jewish. Augustus Melmotte is a fantastically wicked Jewish swindler and financier of mysterious origins and demoniacal powers. Trollope uses "Jew" as a pejorative adjective, and his descriptions of Jewish characters are unflattering and stereotypical. Mr. Hart, a London tailor who runs for a seat in Parliament in *Rachel Ray* (1863), is described as a

> Jewish hero [who] did not pronounce his words with any of those soft slushy Judaic utterances by which they had been taught to believe he would disgrace himself. His nose was not hookey, with any especial hook, nor was it thicker at the bridge than was becoming. He was a dapper little man, with bright eyes, quick motion, ready tongue, and a very new hat. It seemed that he knew well how to canvass. He had a smile and a good word for all—enemies as well as friends.

In the same work, Trollope went on to comment: "They in England who are now keenest against the Jews, who would again take from them rights that they have lately won, are certainly those who think most of the faith of a Christian." In *Nina Balatka* (1867), Trollope wrote:

> To those who know the outward types of his race there could be no doubt that Anton Trendellsohn was a very Jew among Jews. He was certainly a handsome man. . . . No white man could be more dark and swarthy . . . but his eyes were somewhat too close together in his face, and the bridge of his aquiline nose was not sharply cut, as is mostly the case with such a nose on a Christian face. The olive oval face was without doubt the face of a Jew, and the mouth was greedy, and the teeth were perfect and bright, and the movement of the man's body was the movement of a Jew.

But in *Nina Balatka* Trollope also contrasts the behaviors of other Jewish and Christian characters. Trendellsohn's father allowed Nina and her father to remain in their house without paying rent. Nina's Christian aunt says,

"Oh, I hate them! I do hate them! Anything is fair against a Jew." And during a meeting with Anton, she exclaims, "How dares he come here to talk of his love? It is filthy—it is worse than filthy—it is profane." Most of Trollope's Jewish characters are kind.

SUGGESTED READING: Bryan Cheyette, ed., *Between Race and Culture: Representations of "The Jew" in English and American Culture* (Stanford, CA: Stanford University Press, 1996).

TROTSKY, LEON (LEV BRONSTEIN) (1879–1940). **Bolshevik** military leader. Trotsky was second to Vladimir Lenin in directing the Communist revolution in tsarist Russia and headed the Red Army from 1917 to 1921. Trotsky regarded himself as an internationalist rather than a Jew. He argued for total assimilation of Jews, rejecting the Jewish **Bund** and Zionists. However, his (stereotypical) Jewish "looks" and birth name triggered **antisemitism** among Russian peasants. **Judeophobes** worldwide used Trotsky to "prove" the Bolshevik Revolution was a sinister Jewish plot. *See also PROTOCOLS OF THE ELDERS OF ZION, THE.*

SUGGESTED READING: Isaac Deutscher, *The Prophet Armed: Trotsky, 1879–1921*; *The Prophet Unarmed: Trotsky, 1921–1929*; and *The Prophet Outcast: Trotsky, 1929–1940* (London: Verso, 2003).

TRUMAN, HARRY (1884–1972). U.S. president, 1945–52. In 1922, Truman—like many other senators, congressmen, governors, and judges at all levels at that time—joined the **Ku Klux Klan,** though he quit it shortly afterward. Yet in 1946, Truman expressed in a diary that was recently released by the National Archives these anti-Jewish stereotypes:

> The Jews, I find, are very, very selfish. They care not how many Estonians, Latvians, Finns, Poles, Yugoslavs or Greeks get murdered or mistreated as DP [displaced persons] as long as the Jews get special treatment. Yet when they have power, physical, financial or political neither **Hitler** nor **Stalin** has anything on them for cruelty or mistreatment to the underdog.

Henry Wallace, Truman's secretary of commerce, noted in his own diary: "Truman . . . said that 'Jesus Christ couldn't please them when he was on earth, so how could anyone expect that I would have any luck?' Pres. Truman said he had no use for them and didn't care what happened to them." While Truman quickly gave diplomatic recognition to the new state of Israel, he issued an arms embargo against the new state at a crucial time in its history.

SUGGESTED READING: Michael Beschloss, *The Conquerers: Roosevelt, Truman and the Destruction of Hitler's Germany, 1941–1945* (New York: Simon & Schuster, 2002); Mark Franklin, "Gentile Leaders Have Not

Liked Jews," *History News Network*, July 11, 2003, http://www.hnn.us/comments/15664.html.

TSIFOUTIS. (Former Yugoslav, Bulgarian, Greek slur) A Jew.
    SUGGESTED READING: "List of Ethnic Slurs," *Wikipedia*, http://en.wiki pedia.org/wiki/List_of_ethnic_slurs.

TUKA, VOJTECH (1890–1946). Prime minister of Slovakia, 1939–44. Tuka was the prime mover in Jewish persecution in Slovakia. The **Hlinka Guardist** requested **Nazi** help in June 1942 to facilitate **deportations** to concentration camps. The **war criminal** was hanged after World War II in Bratislava. *See also* TISO, JOSEF.
    SUGGESTED READING: Emanuel Frieder, *To Deliver Their Souls* (New York: Holocaust Library, 1987).

TURGENEV, IVAN (1818–1883). Russian author, librettist, poet, journalist, and playwright. Turgenev's literary *Memoirs* spoke of *Zhidovtsvo* (**kikery**) and Jews as "having seized power over the pockets of the entire world" and likely "in a short time to get hold of everything else." *See also* ZHID.

TURNER DIARIES, THE. Violent, apocalyptic, misogynistic, racist, and **antisemitic** book published in 1978 by **William Pierce**, leader of the **neo-Nazi National Alliance**. The alleged diaries of Earl Turner, a member of an underground white supremacist army, provide an inside account of an **Aryan** revolution that overturns the U.S. government in 2099. One of the most widely read and cited books on the Far Right; it has influenced the **Silent Brotherhood**, the Aryan Republican Army, the New Order, and Oklahoma City bomber Timothy McVeigh.
    SUGGESTED READING: James Ridgeway, *Blood in the Face: The Ku Klux Klan, Aryan Nations, Nazi Skinheads, and the Rise of a New White Culture* (New York: Thunder's Mouth Press, 1995); Anti-Defamation League, "Q & A on *The Turner Diaries*," press release, May 16, 1996, www.adl .org/presRele/militi_71/2737_71.asp.

TWAIN, MARK (SAMUEL CLEMENS) (1835–1910). One of America's greatest writers. Although Twain praised the Jews for their charity, close family life, hard work, and "genius," in his essay "Concerning the Jews," published in *Harper's New Monthly Magazine* in September 1899, he wrote: "I was raised to a prejudice against Jews—Christians always are, you know—but such as I had was in my head, there wasn't any in my heart." But there was in his writing.

In 1879 Twain observed that "the Jews are the only race who work wholly with their brains and never with their hands. . . . They are peculiarly and conspicuously the world's intellectual aristocracy." He repeated the slander that the Jews had an "unpatriotic disinclination to stand by the flag as a soldier" (despite the fact that thousands of Jews fought in the Civil War—a much higher proportion than their percentage of the general population). His solution was for regiments of Jews and Jews only to enlist in the army so as to prove false the charge that "you feed on a country but don't like to fight for it." In reaction to angry letters from American Jews who read the essay, Twain later retracted this statement.

Twain also wrote: "There was no way to successfully compete with [the Jew] in any vocation, the law had to step in and save the Christian from the poorhouse. . . . Even the seats of learning . . . had to be closed against this tremendous antagonist. [The Jew] has made it the end and aim of his life to get [money]." He opposed Theodor Herzl's plan for a homeland for the Jews in Palestine, arguing that "if that concentration of the cunningest brains in the world was going to be made in a free country . . . , I think it would be politic to stop it. It will not be well to let that race find out its strength." At the close of his essay, he observed that the Jews would always be unwanted and disliked aliens wherever they lived outside of their own land:

> By his make and ways [the Jew] is substantially a foreigner wherever he may be, and even the angels dislike a foreigner. I am using this word foreigner in the German sense—stranger. . . . You [Jews] will always be by ways and habits and predilections substantially strangers—foreigners—wherever you are, and that will probably keep the race prejudice against you alive.

SUGGESTED READING: Bryan Cheyette, *Between Race and Culture: Representations of "The Jew" in English and American Literature* (Stanford, CA: Stanford University Press, 1996).

TWENTY-FIVE POINTS. *See* NAZI PARTY PLATFORM.

TWO KINGDOMS, LUTHER'S IDEA OF. For **Martin Luther**, there are two kingdoms: the state as the judging left hand of God, and the church as the merciful right hand of God. Christian faith had to accept these two sides of divine rule without question. For Luther, an uprising of the believers against the state was a grave sin against God. Luther condemned, for example, the German peasants who revolted violently against their princes. He proclaimed that a Christian could be a hangman and express God's judicial wrath over criminals and, at the same time, a loving and forgiving person in his private life. Many Nazi-era Lutherans interpreted Luther to mean that they had no right to criticize the **Third Reich**, for it had exclusive authority in the secular, political arena of German life. This "justified" loving one's wife and children and at the same time overseeing the murder of millions of Jews and other human beings.

SUGGESTED READING: Richard Gutteridge, *Open Thy Mouth for the Dumb* (Oxford, England: Blackwell, 1976).

TYR RUNE. Teiwaz, tiewaz. **Neo-Nazi** symbol of upward pointing arrow. The Tyr rune was named after the Norse god of warfare. Because **Nazi** Germany glorified an idealized "**Aryan**/Norse" heritage and used the Tyr rune as a symbol for the leadership schools *(Reichsführerschulen)* of the **SA**, neo-Nazis, white supremacists, and racist **skinheads** use this pagan symbol, even though it did not originally have such meaning and is often used by nonracists and modern pagans.

SUGGESTED READING: Anti-Defamation League, *Hate on Display: Extremist Symbols, Logos, and Tattoos* (New York: Anti-Defamation League, 2006).

– U –

UAO. Racist abbreviation for "United as One." A greeting used by white supremacists to signify the need to unite for the common cause of preserving the white race.

SUGGESTED READING: Anti-Defamation League, *Hate on Display: Extremist Symbols, Logos, and Tattoos* (New York: Anti-Defamation League, 2006).

UKRAINE, POST-SOVIET. Both **antisemitism** and opposition to it became tools for the political parties and movements of the post-Soviet Ukraine in their ideological and political struggles after the breakup of the USSR. In contrast to Russia, which remains a center of antisemitic activity, the independent Ukraine has experienced much less antisemitism. Indeed, the forces establishing democracy in the Ukraine have been fighting antisemitism. Nevertheless, the state of crisis in Ukraine facilitated the establishment of extreme nationalist organizations. Before 1992 these groups resorted to antisemitism only sporadically, but since that time it has been increasingly exploited as an ideological tool for expressing opposition to (Western and "Jewish") democracy. The Ukrainian extreme nationalists— only 2–3 percent of the population—have created their own version of the **Aryan** myth in which the Ukrainian nation is seen as the "progenitor of the Indo-European race." Its destiny is to become a superpower that will lead the Aryan world in fighting the forces of evil and destruction, behind which hide the Jews bent on world domination. The antisemitic press is also only 2–3 percent of the total.

SUGGESTED READING: Liudmila Dymerskaya-Tsigelman and Leonid Finberg, "Antisemitism of the Ukrainian Radical Nationalists: Ideology and Policy," ACTA no. 14 (Jerusalem: Vidal Sassoon International Center for the Study of Antisemitism, 1999), http://sicsa.huji.ac.il/14liud.html.

UKRAINIAN REPUBLIC. Short-lived republic, 1917–20. After the turmoil of the March and October 1917 revolutions in tsarist Russia, Ukraine declared itself an independent republic in January 1918. However, many **pogroms** broke out while fighting raged between Ukrainian and Red Army forces. Tens of thousands of Jews were murdered, the worst massacres in 300 years, as the new Ukrainian Republic was unable to save the Jews from Ukrainian **antisemites** and the Ukrainian army. *See also* PETLYURA, SIMON; WHITE TERROR (RUSSIA).

SUGGESTED READING: Henry Abramson, *A Prayer for the Government: Ukrainians and Jews in Revolutionary Times, 1917–1920* (Cambridge, MA: Harvard University Press, 1999).

ULTRAMONTANISM. Supremacy of the pope within the Catholic Church. A conservative revival led by Joseph de Maistre, **Louis de Bonald**, and **Louis Veuillot** defended ultramontanism as a papal theocracy to preserve Christian morality and the Catholic religion from the "dangers" of the **Enlightenment**, the **French Revolution**, and the international Judeo-Masonic conspiracy that controlled the press and sponsored modern, progressive, and "anti-Catholic" ideologies such as liberalism, radicalism, and secularism.

SUGGESTED READING: Joseph de Maistre, *The Works of Joseph de Maistre*, trans. and ed. Jack Lively (New York: Schocken Books, 1971).

UMSCHLAGPLATZ. Assembly and transfer point for Jewish **deportation** by **Nazis**. This area often separated the Jewish **ghetto** from Christian dwellings. In the **Warsaw Ghetto**, it was the site of a railway siding where 300,000 Jews boarded trains for concentration camps, mainly Treblinka. Often the Umschlagplatz was the scene of both Nazi-German and native **antisemitic** brutality against helpless Jewish civilians.

SUGGESTED READING: Vladka Meed, *On Both Sides of the Wall: Memoirs of the Warsaw Ghetto*, trans. Steven Meed (New York: Holocaust Library, 1979); Robert Michael and Karin Doerr, *Nazi-Deutsch/Nazi-*

German: An English Lexicon of the Language of the Third Reich (New York: Greenwood Press, 2001).

UNION OF RUSSIAN PEOPLE. *See* BLACK HUNDREDS.

UNITED NATIONS RESOLUTIONS. Since the 1960s, 30 percent of the resolutions by the UN Commission on Human Rights to condemn specific state abuses have been against Israel. Of 10 emergency sessions called by the UN General Assembly, six have been directed against the Jewish state. In 2003, 18 resolutions regarding violations of human rights concerned Israel while all other states received a total of four. Fifty-six Islamic nations sit in the United Nations and vote as a bloc against Israel. The double standard reveals a profound bias against Jews and the Jewish state.

SUGGESTED READING: Anne Bayefsky, "One Small Step," *Wall Street Journal*, June 21, 2004; Anne Bayefsky, "The United Nations and Israel," *National Review*, February 26, 2004.

"UNSERE EHRE HEISST TREUE." Nazi **SS** slogan. Used as well by **neo-Nazis** in the original German or its English translation, "Our Honor Is Loyalty," to demonstrate allegiance to the white supremacist movement. Neo-Nazi **skinheads** also have the slogan tattooed on their bodies. The expression was also used by Ernest Windholz, a member of the far-right Austrian Freedom Party, during a ceremony honoring activists from that party in the year 2000.

SUGGESTED READING: Anti-Defamation League, *Hate on Display: Extremist Symbols, Logos, and Tattoos* (New York: Anti-Defamation League, 2006).

URBAN II (1035–1097). Pope, 1088–97. The first of the **Crusades** took place under Urban II's inspiration; Jewish communities in the Rhineland and Jerusalem were destroyed. *See also* WORMS.

SUGGESTED READING: Colin Morris, *The Papal Monarchy: The Western Church from 1050 to 1250* (Cambridge: Cambridge University Press, 1990).

USTASHA. Croatian **fascist** movement; a political party and paramilitary force created in 1930. Once **Nazi** Germany invaded and defeated Yugoslavia in April 1941, it set aside Croatia as a separate satellite state. Its head, **Ante Pavelic**, leader of the pro-Nazi Ustasha, was responsible for the murder of 60,000 Jews along with many hundreds of thousands of other victims, mainly Serbs.

SUGGESTED READING: Michael Berenbaum, *A Mosaic of Victims: Non-Jews Persecuted and Murdered by Nazis* (New York: New York University Press, 1990).

USURY. Lending money at excessive interest. The Jewish Scriptures state that no interest should be collected on loans to a fellow Jew, whereas a Gentile could be charged interest. The Roman Catholic Church prohibited usury—which it defined as taking *any* interest—by Christians. In many areas of medieval Europe, Jews were blocked from owning land, from farming, from hiring Christian employees, from the military, and from the Christian **guilds**. Given these extensive restrictions on economic and professional life, many Jews came to money-lending by default, as this was one of the few avenues open to support both themselves and their families. In this way, money-lending became the chief occupation of Jews from the 12th to the 14th centuries. In the Dark Ages, Jews were known as *merchants*, but in the Middle Ages, they were termed *usurers*. Money was borrowed by Christians for a number of reasons, especially to finance the medieval **Crusades** and for building projects, but sometimes simply surviving daily life required a loan. The Church regarded money as dirty and lending for interest as immoral, and given their attitudes toward Jews, who better to lend money at interest than the immoral "**Christ-killing** Jews"? Jews often charged high rates of interest because retrieving the money lent was very difficult, because courts and judges were Christians and because various clerics and nobles, popes and kings canceled debts owed to Jews on the flimsiest of pretexts. Often, Crusaders did not have to pay back loans to Jews, or at least not the interest. Once the Church realized that money-lending was a way to make money, it relaxed its prohibition against usury for Christians. This pushed most Jews into the interstices of the European economy, such as pawn shops and dealing in used clothes. *See also* EDWARD I; SHYLOCK; SOMBART, WERNER.

SUGGESTED READING: Joseph Shatzmiller, *Shylock Reconsidered: Jews, Moneylending and Medieval Society* (Berkeley: University of California Press, 1989).

UVAROV, SERGEI (1786–1855). Count; minister of education in tsarist Russia, 1833–49. In 1848, Uvarov established public schools for Russian Jews, hoping to integrate them and assimilate them into Russian society. He approved of the *Haskalah* movement. Demanding that the Jews abandon the **Talmud**, Uvarov believed the schools would wean Jewish children away from Judaism to Christianity. He enlisted **Max Lilienthal**, a Jewish educator, to aid him in the project. Jewish leaders were suspicious of the program. Uvarov coined the slogan "Orthodoxy, Autocracy, Nationhood," which was picked up by the **Slavophiles**. *See also* NICHOLAS I.

SUGGESTED READING: Simon Dubnow, *History of the Jews of Russia and Poland*, trans. I. Friedlander (Bergenfield, NJ: Avotaynu, 2000).

– V –

VALKNOT. Valknut, valknutr, Hrungnir's Heart. **Neo-Nazi**, racist **skinhead**, white supremacy symbol consisting of three interlocking triangles. A symbol of the Norse god Odin, the Valknot, or "knot of the slain," often represented the afterlife in old Norse carvings and designs. Used as a sign of willingness to give one's life to Odin, generally in battle. Nonracist pagans also use this symbol.

SUGGESTED READING: Anti-Defamation League, *Hate on Display: Extremist Symbols, Logos, and Tattoos* (New York: Anti-Defamation League, 2006).

VALLAT, XAVIER DE (1891–1972). **Vichy**'s first commissioner-general for Jewish affairs, who coordinated Vichy France's anti-Jewish program, the *Statuts des Juifs*. Vallat's pro-French and anti-German attitude caused his dismissal. He was replaced by **Louis Darquier Pellepoix** in late 1942.

SUGGESTED READING: Michael R. Marrus, "Coming to Terms with Vichy," *Holocaust and Genocide Studies* 1, no. 1 (Spring 1995).

VAMPIRES. (International slur). A reference to the medieval myth that Jews drank the blood of Christian children as part of **ritual murder** and to the modern myth that Israelis murder Palestinian children and drink their blood.

SUGGESTED READING: "List of Ethnic Slurs," *Wikipedia*, http://en .wikipedia.org/wiki/List_of_ethnic_slurs.

VANNES, COUNCIL OF. Church lawmaking body convened in 465. The council prohibited the Christian clergy from participating in Jewish feasts.

SUGGESTED READING: Shlomo Simonsohn, *The Apostolic See and the Jews: History* (Toronto: Pontifical Institute of Mediaeval Studies, 1991); Heinrich Graetz, *History of the Jews*, vol. 3 (Philadelphia; Jewish Publication Society, 1898).

VATICAN. Papal headquarters in Rome, also called the Holy See or Vatican City. This tiny enclave is the administrative and spiritual capital of Roman

Catholicism, and the world's smallest independent, sovereign state. The Vatican is probably per square foot the richest country in the world, making up for its total lack of natural resources with an astonishing collection of priceless art treasures. Through its nuncios and apostolic visitors (ambassadors), it was well informed about the **Holocaust**. Although Pope **Pius XII** tried several times indirectly to slow the **deportations** of Jews, and several Catholic prelates and priests (Righteous Gentiles) took independent initiatives to help Jews, the Vatican's main goal was to protect Catholic interests in **Nazi** Europe rather than to protect or rescue Jews. No direct censure was made regarding the **genocide** of the Jews even when opportunities presented themselves. After the defeat of Germany, Vatican offices were used to help Nazi **war criminals** escape. *See also* HUDAL, ALOIS; JOHN XXIII; PIUS XI; RATLINE; VATICAN COUNCIL I; VATICAN COUNCIL II.

SUGGESTED READING: Anthony Roads, *The Vatican in the Age of the Dictators, 1922–1945* (New York: Holt, Rinehart & Winston, 1973); Guenter Lewy, *The Catholic Church and Nazi Germany* (New York: McGraw-Hill, 1964); Susan Zuccotti, *Under His Very Windows* (New Haven, CT: Yale University Press, 2000).

VATICAN COUNCIL I. This Roman Catholic Council of 1869–70, noted for its affirmation of papal infallibility, also proclaimed a **triumphalistic** "Prayer for Jewish '**Conversion**,'" as a postulatum approved by Pope **Pius IX**:

> The undersigned Fathers of the Council humbly yet urgently beseechingly pray that the Holy Ecumenical Council of the Vatican deign to come to the aid of the unfortunate nation of Israel with an entirely paternal invitation; that is, that it express the wish that, finally exhausted by a wait no less futile than long, the Israelites hasten to recognize the **Messiah**, our Savior Jesus Christ, truly promised to Abraham and announced by Moses; thus completing and crowning, not changing, the Mosaic religion.
>
> On one hand, the undersigned Fathers have the very firm confidence that the holy Council will have compassion on the Israelites, because they are always very dear to God on account of their fathers, and because it is from them that the Christ was born according to the flesh.
>
> On the other hand, the same Fathers share the sweet and intimate hope that this ardent desire of tenderness and honor will be, with the aid of the Holy Spirit, well received by many of the sons of Abraham, because the obstacles which have held them back until now appear to be disappearing more and more, the ancient wall of separation now having fallen.
>
> Would that they then speedily acclaim the Christ, saying "Hosanna to the Son of David! Blessed be He who comes in the name of the Lord!"
>
> Would that they hurl themselves into the arms of the Immaculate Virgin Mary,

even now their sister according to the flesh, who wishes likewise to be their mother according to grace as she is ours!

SUGGESTED READING: *Dogmatic Canons and Decrees of the Council of Trent, Vatican Council I, Plus the Decree on the Immaculate Conception and the Syllabus of Errors* (Rockford, IL: Tan Books, 1977); Roy Schoeman, "Salvation Is from the Jews," http://www.salvationisfromthejews.com/postulatum.html.

VATICAN COUNCIL II. Roman Catholic ecumenical council, 1962–65. Called by Pope **John XXIII**, the council attempted to change Catholic thinking about Jews and Judaism. The results of the proceedings were published as the Declaration on the Relationship of the Church to Non-Christian Religions (*Nostra Aetate [In Our Time]*). Jews were no longer to be considered a **deicide** people, nor cursed, nor rejected by God. The term *perfidious* as applied to Jews was eliminated from a **Good Friday** prayer. Jew-hatred and **antisemitism** were forbidden. The hand of the Church was extended to Jews in friendship and dialogue. The results have been mixed. *See also* TEACHING OF CONTEMPT.

SUGGESTED READING: Judith Herschcopf, *Statement on Jews* (New York: American Jewish Committee, 1971).

VEESENMAYER, EDMUND (1904–1977). **SS** brigadier general and diplomat. Veesenmayer was the **Nazi** envoy to Zagreb, **Croatia**, and was complicit in the **deportations** and murder of Jews in Croatia and Serbia in 1942. As Reich plenipotentiary of Hungary, he pressured Hungarian officials to participate in the **Final Solution** in 1944. *See also* HORTHY, MIKLÓS.

SUGGESTED READING: Christopher Browning, *The Final Solution and the German Foreign Office* (New York: HarperCollins, 1993).

VERJUDUNG. German for "Jewification" or "**Judaization**"; traditional belief in the "noxious" Jewish influence on all aspects of German life. An often-used **Nazi** propaganda term. In his section on prostitution in *Mein Kampf*, **Adolf Hitler** wrote, "*Diese Verjudung unseres Seelenlebens und Mammonisierung unseres Paarungstriebes werden früher oder später unseren gesamten Nachwuchs verderben*" (Sooner or later, this Jewification of our soul-life and Mammonizing of our mating impulse will ruin our entire new generation). Even German anti-Nazi exiles approved discriminatory measures against the Jews because they shared with the Nazis the belief that the Jews Jewified German society and therefore that the Jews themselves were responsible for **antisemitism** in the sense that Jews allegedly created animosity by seeking power and being too conspicuous.

SUGGESTED READING: George Mosse, *Toward the Final Solution* (Madison: University of Wisconsin Press, 1988); George Mosse, *Germans and Jews* (Detroit: Wayne State University Press, 1987).

VERNICHTUNG DURCH ARBEIT. German for "destruction through work"; the general **Nazi** policy of working Jews and other prisoners to death. An agreement was reached in September 1942 between **SS** Chief **Heinrich Himmler** and Reich Minister of Justice Otto Thierack whereby Jews and others serving in prisons were to be transferred to the SS so that they could be worked to death. *See also* FORCED LABOR CAMPS.

SUGGESTED READING: Benjamin Ferenz, *Less than Slaves* (Cambridge, MA: Harvard University Press, 1979); Robert Michael and Karin Doerr, *Nazi-Deutsch/Nazi-German: An English Lexicon of the Language of the Third Reich* (New York: Greenwood Press, 2001).

VERSAILLES PEACE CONFERENCE. The Allied Powers meeting in 1919 to conclude peace treaties among the belligerents engaged in World War I. More than 100 Jewish representatives were present. They were concerned that the new states created by the conference would exhibit **antisemitism**. Article 12 of the League of Nations Charter, **Minority Treaties**, set up after Versailles, was to guarantee racial, language, and religious safeguards in the new Baltic and East European states. It was widely ignored.

SUGGESTED READING: Avraham Greenbaum, ed., *Minority Problem in Eastern Europe between the World Wars, with Emphasis on Jewish Minority* (Jerusalem: Hebrew University Press, 1988).

VESPASIAN, TITUS FLAVIUS (9–79). General; Roman emperor, 69–79. As commander in Judea, Vespasian crushed the Jewish revolt in 66–70. He executed the Jewish general Simon Giora in Rome and had the Jerusalem Temple dedicated to Jupiter. His son **Titus** finished the conquest of Judea.

SUGGESTED READING: Flavius Josephus, *Josephus: The Essential Works*, ed. Paul Maier (Grand Rapids, MI: Krezel, 1987).

VEUILLOT, LOUIS (1813–1883). One of the most influential French-Catholics of his time. In regard to the **Mortara Abduction Case,** Veuillot wrote that Jewish children could be **baptized** without parental consent in order to "snatch a soul from Satan." He attacked Jews as "the **deicide**

people" who **ritually murdered** Christians. Jews were a foreign element in Catholic France that plotted to control all of French society.

SUGGESTED READING: Zosa Szajkowski, "The Jewish Saint-Simonians and Socialist Antisemites in France," *Jewish Social Studies* 9 (1947).

VICHY. The Vichy regime (which called itself *État Français*, French State) was the French puppet government under **Nazi** influence in 1940–44, opposed by the Free French Forces. It was established after France surrendered to Germany in 1940 and took its name from the government's capital in Vichy. Its civil service and police were active in identifying, rounding up, and **deporting** thousands of Jews to the East, most of them to their deaths. The Nazis took control of all France in November 1942; however, Vichy's officials continued to collaborate. *See also* BARBIE, KLAUS; DARNAND, JOSEPH; PELLEPOIX, LOUIS DARQUIER; *STATUT DE JUIFS*; VALLAT, XAVIER DE.

SUGGESTED READING: Michael R. Marrus and Robert O. Paxton, *Vichy France and the Jews* (New York: Schocken Books, 1983).

VICTORY OF THE JEWS OVER THE GERMANS, THE (DER SIEG DES JUDENTHUMS ÜBER DAS GERMANENTHUM). 1879 book by German politician **Wilhelm Marr**. Marr used the term *antisemitism* in this book as a substitute for *Judenhass*, Jew hatred. Since Jewish traits were inborn, he argued, **conversion** and assimilation were futile—they only enabled Jews to conquer Gentile society from within. He complained that Jews voted liberal and favored equal rights, religious toleration, and capitalism in order to gain power. Marr bemoaned alleged Jewish ownership of the press, which, he claimed, encouraged fraud, sensationalism, and crass commercialism. Marr's anti-Jewish political coalition ran an electoral campaign in 1889 whose slogan was "Christianity, Kaiserism, Fatherland."

SUGGESTED READING: Moshe Zimmerman, *Wilhelm Marr: The Patriarch of Antisemitism* (New York: Oxford University Press, 1986).

VIDAL, GORE (1925–). American novelist and essayist. Hostile to Israel, Vidal attacked Jews as being more interested in Israel than the interests of the United States, a traditional **antisemitic** stance, as was Vidal's claim that Jews use their influence to manipulate U.S. foreign policy. He warned that Jews should be careful because they are guests in the United States. In *Live from Golgotha* (1992), Vidal attacked the Israelis, the "Jewish Lobby," Jews who are "Jews first," "self-loving" Jews, and "narrow-minded Temple Hebrews." He claims that Jesus is "Lucifer incarnate" and wears "a beanie on the back of his head in the best—that is, pious—Jewish fashion."

SUGGESTED READING: Richard Peabody et al., *Conversations with Gore Vidal* (Jackson: University Press of Mississippi, 2005); David Klinghoffer, "Review of *Live from Golgotha,*" *National Review,* November 30, 1992.

VIDAL v. GIRARD'S EXECUTORS. **Daniel Webster,** the eminent lawyer and statesman, represented one of the parties in this 1844 case before the U.S. Supreme Court. Girard's will had funded a college in Pennsylvania but prohibited any clergyman from appearing on campus. This had incensed many Protestants, and one of them, Vidal, hired Webster to try to overturn this provision. Though Vidal and his attorney lost on this narrow issue, the broader principle argued by Webster—conceded by opposing counsel and ultimately agreed to by a unanimous court—was that the United States was a Christian country and all other religions held an inferior status. Justice **Joseph Story,** writing for a unanimous court, affirmed that America was a thoroughly Christian nation. Story made four fundamental points:

1. blasphemy against Christ or Christianity should be punished
2. "the truth of Christianity [was] a divine revelation. . . ."
3. even though the Pennsylvania constitution protected all religions, "[only] the Christian religion is a part of the common law"
4. only the Christian Scriptures teach the purest, clearest, and most perfect principles of morality, and it would be impossible "in a Christian country" like the United States for a school to be established "for the propagation of Judaism, or Deism, or any other form of infidelity. . . . [This right] is not to be presumed to exist in a Christian country."

SUGGESTED READING: William Story, *Life and Letters of Joseph Story* (Boston: Little, Brown, 1851).

VIGNY, ALFRED DE (1797–1863). French poet, playwright, and novelist. Vigny pictured his character Samuel Montalto in the play *La Mareschale d'Ancre* (1831) as "rich and avaricious, meek and deceitful, a **Court Jew.** Not too dirty on the outside, very dirty on the inside. . . . This Jew would obviously have a soul as dark as his body."

SUGGESTED READING: Béatrice Philippe, *Etre Juif dans la société française* (Paris: Montalba, 1979).

VISIGOTHIC KINGS. Early Spanish kings of the fourth through eighth centuries. Although these kings were Arian Christians (Arians held that

Jesus Christ was not coequal with God, the Father), the Visigothic kings treated the Jews as Roman citizens, for the Jews predated the kings, coming during the expansion of the Roman Empire. Since the Jews were not a military or political threat to these kings, they seemed less concerned about religious differences. Arian Visigothic laws were relatively mild toward Jews: Christians were not permitted to participate in Jewish rituals, and intermarriage between Christians and Jews was forbidden, but **synagogues** were to be protected and Jewish holidays respected. But when Iberian rulers became Roman Christians late in the sixth century, the level of social **antisemitism** increased, causing segregation, discrimination, and forced **baptisms**. Many Jews secretly practiced their faith in Spain until the Arab conquest in 711. The Arabs were more tolerant of Jews and Judaism, considering them as **dhimmis**, a People of the Book, and not **deicides**. *See also* ANUSIM; MARRANOS.

SUGGESTED READING: Yitzhak Baer, *A History of Jews in Christian Spain*, vol. 1 (Philadelphia: Jewish Publication Society, 1992).

VOGELSANG, KARL VON (1818–1890). Prussian noble, convert to Catholicism, founder and ideologist of the Christian-Social Movement, and owner of the newspaper *Das Vaterland*. Vogelsang was a traditional religious **antisemite**. He wrote: "The Jew should no longer be our master. Christ must once again become our master. That is the only moral and Catholic antisemitism." *See also* LUEGER, KARL.

SUGGESTED READING: Peter Pulzer, *The Rise of Political Antisemitism in Germany and Austria* (Cambridge, MA: Harvard University Press, 1988).

VOLK. German for "people," "folk," "nation," or "race." *Volk* indicates the German nation as a community defined and unified by blood, place, history, and language, an organic collectivity of Germanic people, a common creative energy, and a cultural essence with a special "soul" or "spirit." Developers of the concept were **Johann Gottfried von Herder**, in his 1773 book *Voices of the German People and Their Songs*, and **Johann Gottlieb Fichte** in his 1803 book *Addresses to the German Nation*. Volkist ideologues claimed Jews could never possess such a soul or spirit or be part of its collectivity. *See also* BÖCKEL, OTTO; CHAMBERLAIN, HOUSTON STEWART; DÜHRING, EUGEN KARL; HITLER, ADOLF; LANGBEHN, JULIUS; LIST, GUIDO VON; NUREMBERG LAWS OF 1935; PAN-GERMAN LEAGUE; ROHLING, AUGUST; ROSENBERG, ALFRED; SCHÖNERER, GEORG RITTER VON; VÖLKISCH NATIONALISM.

SUGGESTED READING: George L. Mosse, *Toward the Final Solution* (New York: Harper & Row, 1978); Peter Viereck, *Metapolitics: The Roots of the Nazi Mind* (New York: Capricorn, 1961); John Weiss, *Ideology of Death* (Chicago: Ivan Dee, 1996).

VÖLKISCH NATIONALISM. In the face of dislocations created by industrial capitalism and political upheaval, *völkisch* thinkers preached a return to nature. Völkisch leaders advocated "aggressive nationalism, mystically charged racism, and environmentalist predilections" and opposed the rationalism, cosmopolitanism, and urban civilization represented by the Jews. The purpose of the state was to embrace and enhance the **Volk**, which overlapped and ignored political boundaries. Those not members of the Volk were considered aliens. They might be subject to a German government but were not citizens because they did not participate in the Volk soul. *See also MEIN KAMPF*; NUREMBERG LAWS.

SUGGESTED READING: Peter Viereck, *Metapolitics: The Roots of the Nazi Mind* (New York: Capricorn, 1961); Peter Staudenmaier, "Fascist Ecology: The 'Green Wing' of the Nazi Party and Its Historical Antecedents," in Janet Biehl and Peter Staudenmaier, *Ecofascism: Lessons from the German Experience* (Edinburgh: AK Press, 1995), available at http://www.spunk.org/library/places/germany/sp001630/peter.html.

VOLKSFRONT. Life rune in a circle with a *VF* superimposed. **Neo-Nazi,** racist **skinhead**, white supremacist symbol. Volksfront is a neo-Nazi group headquartered in Oregon and based primarily in the Pacific Northwest.

SUGGESTED READING: Anti-Defamation League, *Hate on Display: Extremist Symbols, Logos, and Tattoos* (New York: Anti-Defamation League, 2006).

VOLTAIRE (FRANÇOIS MARIE AROUET) (1694–1778). French **Enlightenment** philosopher. Raised in a devoted Catholic family and educated at the **Jesuit** Collège Louis le Grand, Voltaire turned against the Church but adopted Catholic **antisemitism**. In his various writings, Voltaire described Jews as ignorant, barbarous, avaricious, **misanthropic**, and fanatical. He attacked the Hebrew Bible, describing the ancient Jews as "monsters of cruelty." His attack on Jews and Judaism was an indirect way of assaulting the Catholic Church, which he despised as superstitious quackery. In effect, Voltaire was arguing: "If it were not for the damned Jews, we would not have damned Christians."

SUGGESTED READING: Arthur Hertzberg, *The French Enlightenment and the Jews* (New York: Columbia University Press, 1990).

– W –

WAGENER, HERMANN (1815–1889). Director of the German counterrevolutionary Protestant journal *Kreuzzeitung*. Wagener collaborated with **Bruno Bauer** from 1859 to 1867 on the conservative *Neues Conversations-Lexikon: Staats- und Gesellschafts-Lexikon*, editing most of its 23 volumes and himself writing many of the articles—several of which had **antisemitic** themes, scapegoating Jews for all the ills of the modern era.

SUGGESTED READING: Theodor Nipperdey, *Deutsche Geschichte, 1866–1918* (Munich, 1990).

WAGNER, COSIMA (1837–1930). Born Cosima Liszt-Bülow; illegitimate daughter of **Franz Liszt**. She was **Richard Wagner**'s mistress from 1864 and wife from 1870. A devoted **antisemite** in her own right, Cosima managed the **Bayreuth Festivals** and organized a circle of friends dedicated to promoting her husband's memory, listening to his music, and discussing racism, nationalism, and antisemitism. Her son-in-law **Houston Stewart Chamberlain** was also a member of the Bayreuth Circle, to which in 1923 **Dietrich Eckart** and **Alfred Rosenberg** introduced **Adolf Hitler**.

SUGGESTED READING: Peter Viereck, *Metapolitics: The Roots of the Nazi Mind* (New York: Capricorn Books, 1965).

WAGNER, GERHART (1892–1938). Chief physician of the **Third Reich**. Wagner distrusted academic medicine and pure science, favoring instead a racist "people's medicine." He was active in expelling Jewish physicians from their medical practices from 1929 on. In September 1935, Wagner urged "a law for the protection of German blood." It was passed as part of the **Nuremberg Laws**. This prohibited **marriages** and sexual intercourse between German Gentiles and German Jews. Such relations were considered a crime of *Rassenschande*—racial defilement. Wagner was the inspiration behind the **euthanasia** program, the killing of disabled people and those with incurable diseases. He also urged sterilization for Jews.

SUGGESTED READING: Michael H. Kater, *Doctors under Hitler* (Chapel Hill: University of North Carolina Press, 1989).

WAGNER, RICHARD (1813–1883). German composer. Wagner was an extreme **antisemite** whom **Adolf Hitler** considered his teacher. For Wagner, the Jews represented the multifaceted power of evil: Jews were the "plastic demon" responsible for the decadence of all human society. Wagner thought that the Jewish spirit distorted the life-giving principles of compassion and love contained in authentic Christianity (not ecclesiastical

Christianity, which he rejected), but it had also distorted the church, troubled his nation, corrupted Western civilization, and intended to dominate the world. He called moneylenders "damned Jewish slime." Only Christians could be "purely human"; the Jews were hardly human beings at all in his mind. Hitler claimed inspiration from Wagner, but there is no real proof of it. Whether Wagner would have objected to Hitler's radical answers to the Jewish problem is unknowable. Wagner himself was not clear about what to do with the Jews. Hitler copied from Wagner operatic pageantry at **Nazi** rallies, and Wagner's music was sometimes played at the entrance to the **Auschwitz gas chambers**. *See also* GOBINEAU, ARTHUR DE; VÖLKISCH NATIONALISM; WAGNER, COSIMA.

SUGGESTED READING: Jacob Katz, *The Darker Side of Genius: Richard Wagner's Antisemtism* (Hanover, NH: University Press of New England for Brandeis University Press, 1986); Léon Poliakov, *The History of Antisemitism*, vol. 3, *From Voltaire to Wagner* (New York: Vanguard, 1976); Marc A. Weiner, *Wagner and the Antisemitic Imagination* (Lincoln: University of Nebraska Press, 1995).

WAGNER-ROGERS BILL. U.S. congressional bill proposed in 1939 to allow 20,000 German-Jewish children into the United States. Prominent Christian Americans, the major labor unions, the American Friends and Unitarians, representatives of the YMCA and YWCA, family-service experts, and Jewish groups advocated the passage of the bill. Dozens of favorable editorials from both the secular and Christian press were sent to the joint congressional committee from all over the country. However, the bill was opposed by representatives of "patriotic" organizations, who represented most public opinion. The committee never voted the bill out to the floor of Congress. A typical response to the bill was the view expressed by Laura Delano Houghteling, wife of the commissioner of immigration and a cousin of President **Franklin D. Roosevelt**, who confided at a Washington cocktail party that the major problem with the bill was "that 20,000 [Jewish] children would all too soon grow up into 20,000 ugly adults." The United States gave refuge to fewer Jewish children—about 1,000 between 1934 and 1945—than did Holland, Belgium, France, Switzerland, Sweden, or Great Britain, both relative to their population and in absolute numbers.

SUGGESTED READINGS: Arthur Morse, *While Six Million Died: A Chronicle of American Apathy* (New York: Overlook Press, 1998); Henry Feingold, *The Politics of Rescue* (New York: Holocaust Library, 1980).

WALLACE, LEW (1827–1905). **Civil War** Union general and novelist. Wallace wrote the enormously popular *Ben-Hur, a Tale of Christ* (1880), which contained anti-Jewish material. The Christian ideas and values expressed by Wallace in *Ben-Hur* captured the nation and President James Garfield. As a play, it filled theaters all across the English-speaking world for more than 20 years. In *Ben-Hur*, Wallace associated the Jews with **deicide**, for which they had to suffer, and he made Judaism appear only as the groundwork for Christianity with no justification in itself for existence—a pure elaboration of Christian **triumphalism**. In the novel, after Jesus' crucifixion, the Jewish people "stared at each other aghast. His blood was upon them! . . . They beat their breasts and shrieked with fear. His blood was upon them!" Wallace also maintained that only the Jews "could have cried, Better a law without love than a love without law. . . . Revenge is a Jew's of right; it is the law." In the end, Ben-Hur and his family "saw the light," and, after having wrongly adhered to Judaism, were saved—as Christians. In *The Prince of India* (1893), Wallace portrayed the **Wandering Jew** as all Jews, like "the type Rabbinical that sat with Caiaphas in judgment on the gentle Nazarene."

SUGGESTED READING: Louis Harap, *The Image of the Jew in American Literature* (Syracuse, NY: Syracuse University Press, 2003).

WALPOLE, HORACE (1717–1797). English historian, member of Parliament, novelist, playwright, political writer, and publisher. Writing to a friend in 1857, Walpole commented on the recently retired Lord Chancellor: "the late Chancellor **Shylock**, that Jew who loves human blood better than anything but money . . . even for murder I believe he would grudge a penny."

SUGGESTED READING: Frank Felsenstein, *Antisemitic Stereotypes: A Paradigm of Otherness in English Popular Culture, 1660–1830* (Baltimore: Johns Hopkins University Press, 1995).

WANDERING JEW. Legend and **defamation**. The Wandering Jew was a Jew who allegedly refused Jesus Christ a place to rest on his way to Calvary. Jesus supposedly cursed him—and in Christian legend, all Jews—to wander the Earth in punishment until Christ's Second Coming. The story portrays Jews as obstinate rejectors of Christ for selfish and mean-spirited reasons. The Jew has been given various names—*Der ewige Jude* (Eternal Jew), *le Juif errant* (Wandering Jew), and Ahasuerus, among others. This legend has been expanded as the explanation for the Jewish dispersion or **Diaspora**. A demonic and **vampiric** Wandering Jew image appears in several Gothic novels such as Charles Maturin's *Melmoth the Wanderer* (1820), Bram Stoker's *Dracula* (1897), **George du Maurier**'s *Trilby* (1894), **H. Rider Haggard**'s *She*, and Oscar Wilde's *Picture of Dorian*

Gray and in theories about the identity and motives of Jack the Ripper. Thus, approaching the 20th century, the Wandering Jew became identified with the Devil, a **Christ-killer**, the **Antichrist**, **ritual murderer**, anti-Christian **usurer**, bloodsucking capitalist *and* Marxist, alien, terrorist, and anarchist.

SUGGESTED READING: Yvonne Glikson, "Wandering Jew," in *Antisemitism* (Jerusalem: Keter, 1974); Carol Davison, *Antisemitism and British Gothic Literature* (New York: Palgrave Macmillan, 2004).

WANNSEE CONFERENCE. Meeting held on January 20, 1942, outside Berlin, ordered by **Hermann Goering** and including 14 leaders of the German political, military, police, **SS**, and **Nazi Party** bureaucracy to coordinate plans to effect a **final solution to the Jewish problem**. The 90-minute conference was chaired by **Reinhard Heydrich**, with **Adolf Eichmann** taking minutes. The plans involved internment and murder of all 11 million Jews in Europe. *See also* STUCKART, WILHELM.

SUGGESTED READING: Richard Breitman, *The Architect of Genocide: Himmler and the Final Solution* (New York: Knopf, 1991); Joseph Tenenbaum, *Race and Reich* (New York: Twayne, 1956); Minutes of the Wannsee Conference, *Progressive Review*, http://www.prorev.com/wannsee.htm.

WAR (WHITE ARYAN RESISTANCE). *See* METZGER, TOM.

WAR CRIMES TRIALS. *See* NUREMBERG WAR CRIMES TRIALS.

WAR CRIMINAL. According to the Allied Powers at the **Nuremberg War Crimes Trials** in 1945–46, a war criminal was anyone who was a principal, accessory to, or connected in the commission of war crimes (violation of the rules of war established by international law), or anyone who was a member of an organization or group connected with the commission of such crimes.

SUGGESTED READING: Eugene Davidson, *The Trial of the Germans* (New York: Macmillan, 1966); Richard A. Falk, Gabriel Kolko, and Robert Jay Lifton, *Crimes of War* (New York: Vintage, 1971); John Weiss, *Ideology of Death* (Chicago: Ivan Dee, 1996).

WAR REFUGEE BOARD. Pressured by the Treasury Department's "**Report to the Secretary on the Acquiescence of This Government in the Murder of the Jews**" and embarrassed by the public exposure of **Breckinridge Long**'s misrepresentations to Congress on the refugee issue, President **Franklin D. Roosevelt** established the WRB in January 1944. He ordered it "to take all measures in its authority to rescue the victims of oppression in immediate threat of death and to provide those victims with all aid consistent with the successful prosecution of the war." The WRB acted as an intermediary between private Jewish agencies and rescue operations. It was supported almost exclusively from private Jewish funds. Jewish Americans were the only Americans who had to pay privately for the rescue of their coreligionists. In contrast, the U.S. government appropriated $1.34 billion for the United Nations Relief and Rehabilitation Administration, whose function was to help those already liberated, that is, mostly non-Jews. The WRB estimated it saved 20,000 Jews. Its plan to establish temporary havens for endangered Jews resulted in one success, a haven for about 1,000 refugees in Fort Ontario at **Oswego**, NY. Its attempts to have the U.S. Army Air Forces bomb **Auschwitz** met with failure. *See also* STATE DEPARTMENT, U.S.

SUGGESTED READING: David Wyman, *The Abandonment of the Jews* (New York: New Press, 1998); Henry Feingold, *The Politics of Rescue* (New York: Holocaust Library, 1980).

WARSAW GHETTO UPRISING, THE *NEW YORK TIMES* TREATMENT OF. The *New York Times* in the 1930s had downgraded Jewish stories so as to prove the newspaper did not favor Jews. In 1943, when fewer war stories were competing for the headlines, the Jewish **ghetto** revolt made the front page only once, at the less-read bottom. The ghetto uprising was mentioned a few more times but buried in the back pages, on one occasion next to an article on a pet show in Greenwich Village. The *Times* neglected the Warsaw ghetto uprising, although it was the first urban revolt against the **Nazis**, and the poorly armed Jews of the ghetto held out against the Nazis longer than the nations of Poland, Luxembourg, Belgium, Holland, Denmark, Norway, and France had resisted the German invasions in 1939–40. But the story was a nonevent for the *Times* and the American press in general. In contrast, although other competing war stories of great significance to the war effort were breaking in 1944, the non-Jewish Warsaw uprising made the front pages almost every day.

SUGGESTED READING: Laurel Leff, *Buried by the Times: The Holocaust and America's Most Important Newspaper* (New York: Cambridge University Press, 2005).

WATSON, TOM (1856–1922). Georgia **Populist** who ran for president in 1904 and 1908. In 1915 in his two periodicals, *Watson's Magazine* and the *Weekly Jeffersonian*, Watson attacked Catholics and their allies "the opulent Jews." He demanded that **Leo Frank**, in a Georgia prison in 1915, be hanged, charging that he was a "typical young libertine Jew" who had attacked his pencil factory employee, Mary Phagan, because of his "lustful eagerness enhanced by the racial novelty of the girl of the uncircumcized." "Frank belongs to the Jewish aristocracy. . . . Our Little Girl—ours by the Eternal God—has been pursued to a hideous death and a bloody grave by this filthy perverted Jew of New York." Watson argued that the Jews of the world would see to it that Frank would not be convicted, since "no aristocrat of their race should die for the death of a working-class Gentile." Watson saw a worldwide Jewish conspiracy, an "Invisible Power," at work in Governor John Slaton's commutation of Frank's death sentence. Combining racial and religious **antisemitism** with nationalism, Watson went beyond the Frank case to oppose Jewish immigration in his periodicals: "From all over the world, the Children of Israel are flocking to this country, and plans are on foot to move them from Europe en masse . . . to empty upon our shores the very scum and dregs of the Parasite Race." In 1920, Georgia sent Watson to the U.S. Senate.

SUGGESTED READING: C. Vann Woodward, *Tom Watson, Agrarian Rebel* (New York: Oxford University Press, 1963).

WATSON'S MAGAZINE. *See* WATSON, TOM.

WATTS, ISAAC (1674–1748). English poet and hymnologist. Watts wrote "Praise for the **Gospel**," a child's hymn whose lyrics begin:

> Lord, I ascribe it to thy Grace,
> And not to Chance as others do,
> That I was born of *Christian* race,
> And not a *heathen* or a *Jew*.

SUGGESTED READING: Frank Felsenstein, *Antisemitic Stereotypes: A Paradigm of Otherness in English Popular Culture, 1660–1830* (Baltimore: Johns Hopkins University Press, 1995).

WEBB, BEATRICE (1858–1943). Early 20th-century social reformer and writer. Webb believed in racial determinants and in the alleged purity of the Jewish "race," and she warned about the "greed of the Jews" and their conspiracy to dominate the societies in which they lived. In a diary entry of October 30, 1930, Webb asked, "Why is it that everyone who has dealings with Jewry ends by being prejudiced against the Jew?"

SUGGESTED READING: Shalom Lappin, "The Rise of a New Antisemitism in the UK," *Engage* 1 (January 2006).

WEBSTER, DANIEL (1782–1852). Eminent lawyer and U.S. secretary of state, 1841–43 and 1850–52. Webster considered himself an enemy of religious bigotry and a supporter of the **separation of church and state**, yet he believed that America was a Christian nation. In the Massachusetts Constitutional Convention of 1820, he had argued for a "recognition of the Christian religion." In the case of *Vidal v. Girard's Executors*, he contrasted the "Christian" morality of Jesus with the immorality of Jesus' Jewish contemporaries and disciples:

> When little children were brought into the presence of the Son of God, his disciples proposed to send them away; but he said, "Suffer little children to come unto me." Unto me; he did not send them first for lessons in morals to the schools of the **Pharisees** or to the unbelieving **Sadducees**, nor to read the precepts and lessons phylacteried on the garments of the Jewish priesthood.

Webster went on to assert that Christianity is the law of the land in all America, "a country of Christianity and religion." America was based on "Christian origin, a Christian code of laws [and] a firm and sincere belief in the divine authority and great importance of the truths of the Christian religion. . . . Christianity is part of the law of the land."

SUGGESTED READING: Daniel Webster, *The Great Speeches and Orations of Daniel Webster* (Boston: Houghton Mifflin, 1889).

WEBSTER, NESTA (1876–1960). Prominent English **antisemite** and author. Webster's books, such as her *Secret Societies and Subversive Movement* (1921), trace all revolutions back to the Jews of Jesus' day. Her *Surrender of an Empire* (1931) identifies the Sinn Fein, Zionism, and **Bolshevism** as the same. Denying any antisemitism, she stated that there existed a coordinated and continuous Jewish conspiracy to destroy Christianity and dominate the world. Webster took every opportunity to imply or suggest that many of the persons mentioned in her books were Jews. Despite denying the historical validity of *The Protocols of the Elders of Zion*, she makes several references to *The Protocols* as if it were true. In *Secret Societies and Subversive Movements*, Webster argues that the five major conspiracies in the world—**Freemasonry**, theosophy, Pan-Germanism, international finance, and social revolution—"all contain a Jewish element."

SUGGESTED READING: Richard Gilman, *Behind World Revolution: The Strange Career of Nesta H. Webster* (Ann Arbor, MI: Insight Books, 1982); Ephraim Radner, "New World Order, Old World Antisemitism— Pat Robertson of the Christian Coalition," *Christian Century*, September 13, 1995.

WEIMAR REPUBLIC. The republic that governed Germany between 1919 and 1933. This time frame is also known as the Weimar Period. The republic was named after the city of Weimar, Germany, where a national assembly convened to produce a new constitution following the nation's defeat in World War I, although the Republic still called itself *Deutsches Reich* (German Empire). This attempt to establish a liberal democracy in Germany was born during a disastrous period of history, 1918–23, a period of anarchy and civil conflict followed by history's greatest currency inflation and a French invasion. **Antisemitism** was characterized by disorganized street violence and hostage-taking by older street gangs. During the "Locarno period" of more stability at home and abroad, 1924–29, antisemitic activity became less violent, consisting of desecrations of **synagogues** and Jewish cemeteries (200 such attacks between 1923 and 1932) committed mostly by German youth. After 1929, the Great Depression helped cause more instability. Anti-Jewish violence became better organized than before, coming under the direction of the **SA** and the **Nazi Party**. Also during this period, there was renewed interest among antisemites in the spurious *Protocols of the Elders of Zion* and in the **defamation** of the **Talmud**. De facto, the Weimar Republic died with the ascent of **Adolf Hitler** and the Nazi Party, though the Weimar constitution was not invalidated until after World War II. The legal measures taken by the Nazi **Third Reich** in the months and years after Hitler came to power (*Gleichschaltung*) destroyed the Republic's democratic system. Once Hitler had the power of chancellor, he concentrated complete power in his hands, establishing a totalitarian system. Some 40 parties were represented in the Reichstag, fragmenting political power.

Suggested Reading: Dirk Walter, *Antisemitische Kriminalitaet und Gewalt: Judenfeindschaft in der Weimarer Republik* (Antisemitic Criminality and Violence: Jew-Hatred in the Weimar Republic) (Bonn: J. H. W. Dietz Verlag, 1999); Donald I. Niewyk, *The Jews in Weimar Germany* (New Brunswick, NJ: Transaction Publishers, 2001).

WEININGER, OTTO (1880–1903). Jewish Austrian philosopher. Weininger wrote only one book, *Sex and Character* (1903), after which the 23-year-old committed suicide. He argued that all people have male and female elements, with Jewish males having more female characteristics than Gentile males. Hostile toward women, he attributed to them negative traits: lack of spirituality, lack of ethics, illogical thinking, and materialism. Jews, he claimed, were like women having the above traits; also they believed in nothing, which led them to atheism and Communism. Weininger's Jewish self-hating analysis was used by the **Nazis**.

SUGGESTED READING: Otto Weininger, *Sex and Character: An Investigation of Fundamental Principles* (Bloomington: Indiana University Press, 2005).

WEIRD BEARD. (U.S. slur) Hassidic Jewish male.
SUGGESTED READING: "List of Ethnic Slurs," *Wikipedia*, http://en.wiki pedia.org/wiki/List_of_ethnic_slurs.

WEIZMANN, CHAIM (1874–1952). Scientist, president of the World Zionist Organization (1920–31, 1935–46), and first president of the State of Israel (1949–52). When one of Weizmann's teachers at Freiberg University in Germany assured him that Germans would give up their **antisemitism** once they realized how much Jews had contributed to their prosperity and their rich culture, Weizmann perceptively analyzed the whole Jewish **Diaspora** experience: "Herr Doktor, if a man has a piece of something in his eye, he doesn't want to know whether it's a piece of mud or a piece of gold. He just wants to get it out."
SUGGESTED READING: Fritz Stern, "The Burden of Success: Reflections on German Jewry," in *Dreams and Delusions* (New York: Knopf, 1987); Norman Rose, *Chaim Weizmann: A Biography* (New York: Viking, 1986).

WELLS, H. G. (1866–1946). English novelist; the father of science fiction. In 1933 Wells refused to join a committee against **antisemitism** because of "a natural reaction to the intense nationalism of the Jews and to the very distinctive role they play in the world of art and business." He was in the habit of referring to **Karl Marx** as "a shallow, third-rate Jew" and "a lousy Jew" in private correspondence. In his *Outline of History* (1920), he maintained: "The main part of Jewry never was in Judea and had never come out of Judea."
SUGGESTED READING: Michael Coren, *The Invisible Man: The Life and Liberties of H. G. Wells* (New York: Atheneum, 1993); Michael Foot, *The History of Mr. Wells* (New York: Counterpoint, 1993).

WESLEY, JOHN (1703–1791). English founder of Methodism. Wesley wrote this poem of the Jews:

> Outcasts from thee, and scattered wide
> Blaspheming whom they crucified,
> Unsaved, unpitied, unforgiven,
> Branded like Cain, they bear their load,
> Abhorred of men, and cursed of God.

In his sermon "The Righteousness of Faith" (1746), Wesley declaimed on the Jewish adherence to the Torah: "What stupidity, what senselessness must it be for such an unclean, guilty, helpless worm as this [the Jew], to dream of seeking acceptance by his own righteousness, of living by 'the righteousness which is of the law!'"

SUGGESTED READING: Egal Feldman, *Dual Destinies: The Jewish Encounter with Protestant America* (Chicago: University of Illinois Press, 1990).

WHARTON, EDITH (1862–1937). American writer. Wharton's novel *The House of Mirth* (1905) portrayed a Jew, Simon Rosendale, a new millionaire, as trying desperately to break into high society. Others of her novels have similar Jewish types. When **F. Scott Fitzgerald** published *The Great Gatsby* in 1925, Wharton wrote him, saying that he had discovered the cause of America's problems. The character, the crook Meyer Wolfsheim, she said, was "the perfect Jew."

SUGGESTED READING: Irene Goldman-Price, "The Perfect Jew and *The House of Mirth*: A Study in Point of View," *Edith Wharton Review* 16, no. 1 (Spring 2000).

WHEELER, BURTON (1882–1975). U.S. senator from Montana, 1923–47. The zealous isolationist hated the prowar "Hollywood Hitlers" (code for "Jews"). When a special assistant to the U.S. attorney general, William Maloney, accused Wheeler and other members of Congress of receiving money from **Nazi** Germany, Wheeler successfully exerted pressure to have Maloney removed. *See also* NYE, GERALD.

SUGGESTED READING: David H. Bennett, *The Party of Fear*, 2nd rev. ed. (New York: Vintage, 1995); "The 1930s: Nazis Parading on Main Street," part 5, "Congressmen and Seditionist," http://www.spiritone.com/~gdy 52150/1930sp5.html.

WHITE PAPER OF 1939. British foreign policy memorandum regarding Palestine, issued May 17, 1939. The White Paper declared that 75,000 Jewish immigrants would be allowed to enter Palestine over a five-year period and that any subsequent increase would require the acquiescence of the Arabs. The British thus repudiated the Balfour Declaration and their commitments under the League of Nations (to keep Palestine open for Jewish immigration with a view toward Jewish statehood) at the time of greatest need for a sanctuary for Jewish refugees. The British, though at war with the Axis powers, committed its navy to implement this policy. The White Paper trapped the Jews of Europe, exposing them to the coming **Holo-**

caust. *See also* BERMUDA CONFERENCE; EVIAN CONFERENCE; *STRUMA*.

SUGGESTED READING: Bernard Wasserstein, *Britain and the Jews of Europe, 1939–1945* (Oxford, England: Clarendon Press for the Institute of Jewish Affairs, 1979).

WHITE POWER MUSIC. This music provides a focus for many racist **skinheads** from the United States and overseas. "White power" bands attack and dehumanize Jews, blacks, and other minorities. These bands create their own logos and proudly display them on CDs that glorify violence against minorities, in particular Jews. "White power, Oi!" (Oi! is a skinhead way of saying hello or goodbye) music was born out of a skinhead and punk music subculture that made its way into the United States from Great Britain in the mid-1970s. The lyrics attack Jews, blacks, Mexicans, liberals, feminists, gays, and others, whom they blame for society's ills and the failings in their own lives. White power band members are typically covered with tattoos ranging from various **neo-Nazi** symbols to other more general racist symbols and slogans. Resistance Records, Panzerfaust Records, Tri-State Terror, and Micetrap Records sell the music of white-power bands such as **Skrewdriver**, Blue Eyed Devils, **RAHOWA**, Extreme Hatred, Angry **Aryans**, **Nordic** Thunder, **Blood & Honour**, Brutal Attack, Racist Redneck Rebels, Race War, Attack We Must, Ethnic Cleansing, Stromschlag, Der Angriff, and Kill or Be Killed. The cover of Kill or Be Killed's latest album, for example, *The ABC's of Hate*, shows a **Holocaust** photograph of a German soldier with a raised rifle about to shoot a woman carrying a child. The cover of the Racist Redneck Rebels' album *Keep the Hate Alive* shows a rebel battle flag and a hooded **Ku Klux Klan** hanging a black man. Other groups have songs like "Bagels and Blood" and "Piles of Dead Jews."

SUGGESTED READING: Anti-Defamation League, *Hate on Display: Extremist Symbols, Logos, and Tattoos* (New York: Anti-Defamation League, 2006).

WHITE REVOLUTION. The Arkansas-based White Revolution, founded in 2002 by Billy Roper, is a relatively new **neo-Nazi** organization that seeks to promote unity and cooperation among white supremacist groups. It attracts a wide array of racist participants, ranging from young **skinheads** to the **Christian Identity Movement** to **neo-Nazis** and **Ku Klux Klansmen**. The group has put leaders of other organizations, for example, the West Virginia Skinheads and the White Wolves (a racist skinhead group based in Connecticut), in leadership positions. After the September

11, 2001, attacks, Roper organized rallies in November and December 2001 in front of the Israeli embassy in Washington, DC, to blame Israel and Jews for the tragedy. The group's symbol is a Greek letter lambda (λ) on an orange background, based on an image from an ancient Spartan shield (each man carried the letter lambda for Lakedaimon, another name for Sparta, on his shield for identification in battle), because of the Spartan defense at Thermopylae against the Persians, which signifies to White Revolution the defense of Europe against "nonwhite hordes."

SUGGESTED READING: ADL Law Enforcement Agency Resource Network, "White Revolution/Billy Roper," 2005, http://www.adl.org/learn/ext_us/w_revolution.asp?xpicked = 3&item = whiterevolution.

WHITE TERROR (HUNGARY). In November 1919, Admiral **Miklós Horthy** led right-wing counterrevolutionaries (Whites) into Budapest after a Romanian army had ousted the Communist regime of **Béla Kun**. Between March 1920 and the end of 1921, a White Terror led to the imprisonment of 75,000 and the torture and murder of 5,000 of Kun's supporters, including Communists, socialists, Jews, leftist intellectuals, and others who threatened the traditional Hungarian political order. Jews in particular were targeted. Appointed regent and head of state in a restored monarchy, Horthy also established a *numerus clausus* against Jews in education, dismissed all Jews in government and the army, forbade Jewish trade in tobacco, and closed scientific institutions to them. Ultimately, the White Terror forced nearly 100,000 people to leave the country, most of them socialists, intellectuals, and Jews.

SUGGESTED READING: Andrew Janos, *The Politics of Backwardness in Hungary* (Princeton, NJ: Princeton University Press, 1982); Thomas Sakkuyster, *Hungary's Admiral on Horseback, Miklós Horthy* (New York: Columbia University Press, 1994).

WHITE TERROR (RUSSIA). The Whites were reactionary military forces fighting the Red Army to undo the **Bolshevik** revolution in Russia in 1917–21. Some were tsarists, others non-Russian nationalists. In the course of the Russian **Civil War**, there were 2,000 **pogroms** in Poland and the Ukraine causing the deaths of 30,000 Jews, and 120,000 more deaths from wounds and disease. The Jews were perceived by the Whites and their supporters as favoring the Bolsheviks, although the vast majority of Jews were moderate Mensheviks. *See also* DENIKIN, ANTON; TROTSKY, LEON.

SUGGESTED READING: Zvi Y. Gitelman, *A Century of Ambivalence: The Jews in Russia and the Soviet Union, 1881 to the Present* (Bloomington: Indiana University Press, 2001).

WHITMAN, WALT (1819–1892). American poet. An admirer of ancient Judaism and the Hebrew Bible, Whitman nevertheless mentioned contemporary Jews negatively. In *New York Dissected*, looking at the scene on Broadway, New York, in August 1856, for example, he wrote about "dirty looking German Jews . . . with a sharp nasal twang and flat squalling enunciation to which the worst Yankee brogue is sweet music."

SUGGESTED READING: Louis Harap, *The Image of the Jew in American Literature* (Syracuse, NY: Syracuse University Press, 2003).

WIESENTHAL-KREISKY CONTROVERSY. Austrian "Nazi-hunter" Simon Wiesenthal (1908–2005) discovered that Austrian Chancellor Bruno Kreisky (1911–1990) had selected four ministers with Nazi pasts for his 1970 cabinet. Kreisky claimed that Wiesenthal lived to tell "the world that Austria is **antisemitic**. What else can he do?" Wiesenthal responded that "Kreisky has a disturbed relationship to Nazism and Judaism." Although a Jew himself, Kreisky complained, about Wiesenthal, "The Eastern Jews [*Ostjuden*] are alienated from normal ways of thinking." He also called Wiesenthal a Mafioso, expressed doubt about his engineering credentials, and suggested he had been cozy with the **Gestapo**. When Kreisky considered appointing Frederick Peter, the head of the Austrian Freedom Party (a group rife with ex-Nazis), as Austrian vice chancellor, Wiesenthal revealed that Peter had served as an officer in an **SS** battalion that was part of an **Einsatzgruppe**. The controversy revealed the continuing hostility between assimilated Jews of the West and Eastern Jews, as well as the Austrian struggle with their role during the Nazi era. Despite Kreisky's ambiguous attitude toward Jewish issues, Austria remained a transit point for Jews leaving the Soviet Union for Israel and the West.

SUGGESTED READING: Alan Levy, *The Wiesenthal File* (Grand Rapids, MI: Eerdmans, 1994).

WILDE, OSCAR. *See PICTURE OF DORIAN GRAY, THE.*

WILLETTE, ADOLPHE (1857–1926). French painter, illustrator, caricaturist, lithographer, and antisemitic cartoonist. In an 1886 campaign poster for the National Assembly, Willette stated: "The Jews are great only because we are on our knees. 50,000 alone benefit from the constant and hopeless work of 30,000,000 French slaves."

SUGGESTED READING: Robert Byrnes, *Antisemitism in Modern France* (New Brunswick, NJ: Rutgers University Press, 1950); Norman Kleeblatt,

"The Dreyfus Affair: A Visual Record," in *The Dreyfus Affair: Art, Truth, and Justice* (Berkeley: University of California Press, 1987).

WILLIAMS, ROGER (1603–1683). Governor of Rhode Island, 1654–57. Williams invited Jews to settle in Newport—the first Jewish community in New England. The new colony's charter declared "that no person within the said colony shall hereafter be any wise molested or called in question for any difference in opinion in matters of religion." Williams insisted that State and Church should be separate; none were to be forced into the majority religion. But many of Williams's beliefs were anti-Jewish. Biblical Jews—in his mind, the only authentic Jews—no longer existed. This position justified an attempt to **convert** his Jewish neighbors. Williams insisted on "a spiritual war against Judaism." His list of those to be converted consisted of "Jewes, Turks, and Infidels."

SUGGESTED READING: Arthur Hertzberg, "The New England Puritans and the Jews," in *Hebrew and the Bible in America: The First Two Centuries*, ed. Shalom Goldman (Hanover, NH: University Press of New England, 1993); Frederick Tyvie Bruce and David Payne, *Israel and the Nations* (Downers Grove, IL: InterVarsity Press, 1995).

WILSON, WOODROW (1856–1924). U.S. president, 1912–20. When Wilson once discussed a position for **Bernard Baruch** in his administration with Secretary of the Navy Josephus Daniels, Daniels reminded him that Baruch was "somewhat vain," to which Wilson responded, "Did you ever see a Jew who was not?"

SUGGESTED READING: Jordan A. Schwartz, "The Leading Jew in America," *Commentary* 70 (December 1980).

WINROD, GERALD (1900–1957). U.S. clergyman and politician. Winrod fell in love with **Nazi** Germany when he visited it in 1934 and returned to the United States inspired by Nazi ideology. In 1938 he unsuccessfully ran for the Senate in Kansas, preaching against the Jews and in favor of Christian values and American isolation. His slogan was "Keep Christian America Christian."

SUGGESTED READING: David H. Bennett, *The Party of Fear*, 2nd rev. ed. (New York: Vintage, 1995).

WIRTH, CHRISTIAN (1885–1944). **Nazi** concentration camp commander. Wirth was the innovator implementing the use of poison gas in the **euthanasia** killing of the German mentally and physically handicapped. He applied these murder techniques at Chelmno. Wirth was the first

Kommandant at **Bergen-Belsen,** then head of **Belzec**, a position that earned him the nickname "Christian the Terrible" because of his brutality. Wirth was killed by Italian partisans in Trieste in 1944.

SUGGESTED READING: Henry Friedlander, *The Origins of the Nazi Genocide: From Euthanasia to the Final Solution* (Chapel Hill: University of North Carolina Press, 1995).

WISLICENY, DIETER (1911–1948). **SS** officer; **Adolf Eichmann**'s deputy. Wisliceny was an active participant in the mass murder of Slovakian, Greek, and Hungarian Jews. He implicated **Heinrich Himmler** and **Adolf Hitler** in the Jewish **genocide** at the **Nuremberg War Crimes Trials** in 1946. Wisliceny was executed in Czechoslovakia in 1948.

SUGGESTED READING: Joseph Tenenbaum, *Race and Reich* (New York: Twayne, 1956); Joseph E. Persico, *Nuremberg: Infamy on Trial* (New York: Viking, 1994).

WITH BURNING ANXIETY. *See MIT BRENNENDER SORGE.*

WITNESS PEOPLE. *See* AUGUSTINE, ST.

WOLFE, THOMAS (1900–1938). American novelist. Wolfe seemed fascinated by Jews his whole life long, and for years had a Jewish mistress. In his autobiographical novel *Look Homeward Angel* (1929), he wrote that "Eugene, Max and Harry ruled their little neighborhood: they made war upon the negroes and the Jews." They had "spat joyously on the Jews," and their desire was to "drown a Jew and hit a nigger." A child is called "you little **Kike**." In the same novel, after a young Jew has killed himself, Wolfe's characters are cruelly "shaken by sudden glee as they saw his father, a bearded orthodox old Jew . . . approach . . . holding his hands in the air and wailing rhythmically." Yet Wolfe's travels in **Nazi** Germany sobered him to the "genuinely evil" in mankind. By the late 1930s, in *You Can't Go Home Again* (1940), he wrote with sympathy about the Jewish victims of Nazism.

SUGGESTED READING: Louis Harap, *The Image of the Jew in American Literature* (Syracuse, NY: Syracuse University Press, 2003).

WOLFF, KARL (1900–1984). **SS** general; part of **Heinrich Himmler**'s personal staff. In April 1945, Wolff surrendered all German forces in Italy to the Allies and subsequently gave testimony at the **Nuremberg War Crimes Trials**. He was charged and convicted with complicity in the murder of 300,000 Jews at Treblinka, but he served only six years in prison.

SUGGESTED READING: Jochen von Lang, *Top Nazi, Karl Wolff: The Man between Hitler and Himmler* (New York: Enigma Books, 2004).

WOLFSANGEL. Wolf's Hook, Dopplehaken. **Neo-Nazi** symbol consisting of a straight line (horizontal or vertical) with sharp hooks on each end and a short line intersecting it in the middle. The Wolfsangel is an ancient runic symbol that was believed to ward off wolves. The symbol appeared in Germany as guidestones on the sides of roads and in the coats of arms of various towns; there is even a German city called Wolfsangel. Along with many other runic symbols, the Wolfsangel was adopted by the Waffen-**SS** during the **Nazi** era, including the divisional insignia of the notorious 2nd SS "Das Reich" Panzer Division. As a result, it became a symbol of choice for neo-Nazis in Europe and the United States. The **Aryan Nations'** logo is derived from the Wolfsangel.

SUGGESTED READING: Anti-Defamation League, *Hate on Display: Extremist Symbols, Logos, and Tattoos* (New York: Anti-Defamation League, 2006).

WORD ABOUT OUR JEWS, A. *See* TREITSCHKE, HEINRICH VON.

WORLD CHURCH OF THE CREATOR. Racist and **antisemitic** group led by Matt Hale. (Not to be confused with World Church of the Creator, a trademark of TE-TA-MA Truth Foundation.) Their main objective is "the Survival, Expansion, and Advancement of the White Race" and their motto is **RAHOWA**. The World Church of the Creator maintains an important hate website. Hale claims that the **JOG** (Jewish-occupied government) is run by criminals violating the Constitution who should be treated "like the criminal dogs they are" and that the World Church should "take the law into our own hands." Ben Klassen (who killed himself in 1993) originally founded the anti-Christian Church in 1973. World Church of the Creator members have been linked to murders, armed robberies, assaults, and Benjamin "August" Smith's July 4, 1999, murder of two, wounding of nine, and suicide. His victims were blacks, Jews, and Asian Americans. The group is symbolized by a *W* representing the white race, along with a crown and halo above it signifying the group's belief in the elite and sacred nature of the white race.

SUGGESTED READING: ADL Law Enforcement Agency Resource Network, "World Church of the Creator 'Moves' to Wyoming," December 12, 2002, http://www.adl.org/learn/news/wcotc_wyoming.asp.

WORMS. City in the German Rhineland; site of mass murder of Jews during the First **Crusade** in 1096. Crusader Count **Emicho** murdered 800 Jews and seized Jewish children for **baptism**; the **synagogue** was destroyed, then was rebuilt only to be destroyed again in the Second Crusade in 1146. Jews suffered once more when the synagogue was damaged by riots during the time of the **Black Death** (1348–50). In 1938, during **Kristallnacht**, **Nazis** burned the synagogue down and even its ruins were despoiled. In 1961, because of the religious and historical importance of the synagogue, the town of Worms, the county, and the German government rebuilt the synagogue yet again and donated it to the Jewish community of Mainz since the Jewish community of Worms was no longer in existence.

SUGGESTED READING: Robert Chazan, *European Jewry and the First Crusade* (Berkeley: University of California Press, 1996).

WPWW. Racist abbreviation for "White Pride World Wide." "WPWW" is used around the world as a greeting by white supremacists to show pride in the white race.

SUGGESTED READING: Anti-Defamation League, *Hate on Display: Extremist Symbols, Logos, and Tattoos* (New York: Anti-Defamation League, 2006); ADL Law Enforcement Agency Resource Network, *A Visual Database of Extremist Symbols, Logos, and Tattoos*, http://www.adl.org/hate_symbols/default.asp.

WRIGHT, RICHARD (1908–1960). African-American novelist. Wright observed in his famous autobiographical novel *Black Boy* (1945) that the black folks he knew at the start of the 20th century expressed an antagonism to Jews paralleling that of whites. Raised in Mississippi and Arkansas, Wright's anti-Jewish attitude was created and nurtured at home, and by the time he was six or seven became almost second nature to him. Although themselves victimized by racial prejudice, poverty, hunger, and ignorance, Wright's main character and his playmates were enabled, through Christian **antisemitism**, to feel superior to the **"Christ-killing"** Jews. Coming from a religious Christian background, Wright's character's perceptions concerning Jews had been set in his mind before he ever met an actual Jew:

> All of us black people who lived in the neighborhood hated Jews, not because they exploited us, but because we had been taught at home and in Sunday school that Jews were "Christ killers." With the Jews thus singled out for us, we made them fair game for ridicule.

His black Christian friends, with the approval of their elders, would proudly shout at the Jews their

> folk ditties, some mean, others filthy, all of them cruel. No one ever thought of questioning our right to do this; our mothers and parents generally approved, ei-

ther actively or passively. To hold an attitude of antagonism or distrust toward Jews was bred in us from childhood; it was not merely racial prejudice, it was a part of our cultural heritage.

See also ANTISEMITISM, BLACK.

– X –

XANTEN RITUAL MURDER. Xanten, located in the German Rhineland and the scene of medieval attacks on Jews, was the location of a **ritual-murder** charge in June 1891. A five-year-old boy, John Hegmann, was found dead, his throat cut. A neighbor accused a Jewish butcher, Adolf Buschoff, of the murder. The local priest, Father Bresser, published articles on ritual murder in the *Bote für Stadt und Land*, of which he was the editor, which led to agitation in the **antisemitic** press, as well as to antisemitic meetings, where it was claimed that the Jews had bribed the authorities to prevent the discovery of the ritual murder. This forced the government to arrest Buschoff and his family in October 1891. Buschoff's first trial was dismissed for lack of evidence. **Adolf Stöcker**, leader of the Christian Social Party, insisted on a jury trial, which was granted. The jury, too, found Buschoff not guilty. Rioters then vandalized Jewish property in Xanten. Buschoff left town and made his way to the United States.

SUGGESTED READING: Paul Massing, *Rehearsal for Destruction* (Ann Arbor, MI: University Microfilms, 1979).

XENOPHOBIA. Hatred or fear of the alien, the foreigner. This psychosocial factor stands behind much **antisemitism**. It manifests itself in racism, segregation, scapegoating, civic and religious intolerance, nationalism, **expulsion**, and **genocide**. Theodore Herzl, founder of modern Zionism, believed this was the major cause of antisemitism, hence as long as Jews live in the **Diaspora**, Herzl believed it would continue to exist.

SUGGESTED READING: Paul M. Johnson, *A History of the Jews* (New York: HarperPerennial, 1987); Shlomo Avineri, "Herzl's Road to Zionism," http://www.wzo.org.il/en/resources/view.asp?id=1273.

– Y –

YAHOODI; YAHUDI; YAHOODEE. (U.S. slur) From the Arabic *Yahood* and/or Hebrew *Yehudi* (Jew).

SUGGESTED READING: "List of Ethnic Slurs," *Wikipedia*, http://.wiki pedia.org/wiki/List_of_ethnic_slurs.

YAHOODI AND THE BLOWFISH. (U.S slur) A Jew who adopts black culture; from Hootie and the Blowfish, a 1990s music group.
SUGGESTED READING: "List of Ethnic Slurs," *Wikipedia*, http://en.wiki pedia.org/wiki/List_of_ethnic_slurs.

YASSIN, AHMED (1932–2004). Palestinian Arab cofounder and leader of **Hamas**, the terrorist party in the Gaza Strip. The wheelchair-bound Yassin was committed to the complete destruction of Israel and its replacement with an Arab Islamic state. He encouraged suicide bombings and opposed peace accords with Israel. He stated that he would favor a Palestinian state on the West Bank only as a base to destroy Israel. Yassin died after an Israeli helicopter bomb targeted him.
SUGGESTED READING: Simon Robinson,"How Will Hamas Rule?" *Time*, February 27, 2006; Dan Cohn-Sherbok and Dawoud el-Alami, *The Palestine-Israeli Conflict* (New York: One World [Oxford], 2002); "Hamas Covenant, 1988," Avalon Project at Yale Law School, http://www.yale .edu/lawweb/avalon/mideast/hamas.htm; "Yassin Was the Ideological Force behind Hamas," MSNBC News, March 22, 2004.

YELLOW. Johann Wolfgang von Goethe's observations in *Theory of Colors* (1810) associated Jews with a negative description of the color yellow.

> Through a slight and imperceptible movement the fine impression of fire and gold is transformed into a perception of something dirty and the color of honor and joy is converted into a color of shame, disgust, and displeasure. This is how the yellow hats of bankrupt persons and the yellow rings on the cloaks of the Jews may have originated.

Yellow is the color traditionally associated with gold and was sometimes used around medieval **Jew badges**. A yellow star for Jews was required by the **Nazis**; in the concentration camps, Jews had to sew on a yellow Star of David for identification. *See also* STIGMATIC EMBLEMS.
SUGGESTED READING: Shlomo Simonsohn, *The Apostolic See and the Jews: History* (Toronto: Pontifical Institute of Mediaeval Studies, 1991); Alfred D. Low, *Jews in the Eyes of Germans: From the Enlightenment to Imperial Germany* (Philadelphia: Institute for the Study of Human Issues, 1979); Myriam Yardeni, *Anti-Jewish Mentalities in Early Modern Europe* (Lanham, MD: University Press of America, 1990).

YEMEN. Country at tip of Arabian Peninsula. In 1165, fanatical Shi'ite Arabs forced Jews to **convert** to Islam. In 1172, forced conversions and a false **messiah** prompted a letter from Maimonides to the Jews of Yemen, urging them to convert only outwardly and to reject messiahs. In 1586, Yemeni Jews were accused of aiding the Ottoman Turks; special headgear and garments were imposed. **Synagogues** were destroyed in 1676 and 1724. In 1947 bloody **pogroms** took place there. Airlifts by Israel in 1949 brought Jewish Yemenis to Israel.

SUGGESTED READING: Joseph Tobi, *The Jews of Yemen: Their History and Culture* (Boston: Brill, 1999).

YENTA. (North American slur) An annoying Jewish woman gossip.

SUGGESTED READING: "List of Ethnic Slurs," *Wikipedia*, http://en.wiki pedia.org/wiki/List_of_ethnic_slurs.

YEVRYEE. (Russian slur) A Jew.

SUGGESTED READING: "List of Ethnic Slurs," *Wikipedia*, http://en.wiki pedia.org/wiki/List_of_ethnic_slurs.

YEVSEKTSIA. Jewish section of Soviet Communist Party, made up of Jews who were strictly secular and very hostile to Judaism. Beginning in 1919, the Soviets sought to use Yevsektsia to make Communists of the Jews in the Soviet Union. With the complete backing of a totalitarian government, they outlawed Hebrew, encouraged Yiddish, destroyed the Jewish **Bund**, and closed down Zionist and traditional Jewish religious institutions. Officially, this division of the Communist Party disbanded in 1929. *See also* BIROBIDZHAN; BOLSHEVIKS.

SUGGESTED READING: Martin Gilbert, *The Jews in the Twentieth Century* (New York: Schocken Books, 2001).

YID. (U.S., British slur) A Jew; from "Yiddish."

SUGGESTED READING: "List of Ethnic Slurs," *Wikipedia*, http://en.wiki pedia.org/wiki/List_of_ethnic_slurs.

YIDDIOT. (U.S. slur) A stupid Jew, combination of *yid* and *idiot*.

SUGGESTED READING: "List of Ethnic Slurs," *Wikipedia*, http://en.wiki pedia.org/wiki/List_of_ethnic_slurs.

YID-LID. (U.S. slur) *Yid* and *lid* refers to the Jewish yarmulke.

SUGGESTED READING: "List of Ethnic Slurs," *Wikipedia*, http://en.wiki pedia.org/wiki/List_of_ethnic_slurs.

YOM KIPPUR WAR. *See* SADAT, ANWAR AL-.

YORK MASSACRE. At York, England, in March 1190, a Christian crowd—stirred up by **Crusaders'** propaganda, unrestrained by the government, and motivated by religion and greed—attacked the Jewish community on the **Sabbath** evening before Passover. Most of York's Jews retired to the royal constable's castle, where mutual suspicions led to his ordering the Jews out. Most Jews committed suicide, *Kiddush ha Shem*, rather than be killed by Christians. As during the First Crusade massacres, in a religious frenzy the mob murdered those Jews who appealed for mercy in return for **baptism**. Clergymen, especially impoverished priests, "who had personally held the Jews in hatred," led the mob against the Jews.

SUGGESTED READING: R. B. Dobson, *The Jews of Medieval York and Massacre of 1190* (York, England: University of York, Borthwick Institute Publications, 2002).

YOUNG EGYPT. Secularist, nationalist, antiforeign movement in Egypt that began in 1933 in Cairo. It was anti-British, admired **Adolf Hitler** and **Benito Mussolini**, and had the support of the Royal Palace. Its military arm was the Greenshirts. In 1946 Young Egypt became a political party and reinvented itself as the Islamic Nationalist Party, boycotting Jewish merchants and espousing the Palestinian cause. In 1948 its **anti-Zionism** slipped into **antisemitism**.

SUGGESTED READING: Meyer Weinberg, *Because They Were Jews: A History of Antisemitism* (Westport, CT: Greenwood Press, 1986).

YOUNG GERMANY. The German Youth Movement. It consisted of the Bündische Jugend, German Scouting, Jungenschaft, and the Wandervogel. Wandervogel means "migratory bird," and the intention of Young Germany was to break out of society's restrictions and return to nature and freedom. After World War I, the Wandervogel emphasized hiking, adventure, tours to far-off places, romanticism, and more youthful leaders, adopting uniforms, flags, and camps. The **Nazis** adopted the methods and symbols of the German Youth Movement for the Hitler Youth. Some of the Wandervogel groups had Jewish members; other groups within the movement were *völkisch*, **antisemitic**, and close to the Nazis, adopting the "Sieg Heil" greeting. Aside from church-affiliated groups, from 1933 the Nazis outlawed all youth groups independent of the Hitler Youth.

SUGGESTED READING: Walter Laqueur, *Young Germany: A History of the German Youth Movement* (New Brunswick, NJ: Transaction Books, 1984).

YOUNG HEGELIANS. Thinkers in Germany in 1840–45 who applied **Georg Hegel**'s dialectics to society. Young Hegelians were made up of students and young teachers, Jews and Gentiles, who after Hegel's death in 1840 attacked the Prussian establishment and religion in general, which they saw as a mask for privilege and delusion of the masses. **Bruno Bauer, Friederich Engels**, and **Karl Marx** were among its members in Berlin. Bauer and Marx decided that Jews must give their Judaism up and eventually become atheists. Highly critical of capitalist society, they believed **antisemitic** attacks were in reality an indirect attack on capitalist exploitation.

Suggested Reading: Lawrence Stepelvich, "The Young Hegelians," *Philosophical Forum* 8, nos. 2–4 (1978).

YOUPIN. (French slur) A Jew.

Suggested Reading: "List of Ethnic Slurs," *Wikipedia*, http://en.wiki pedia.org/wiki/List_of_ethnic_slurs.

YOUTH MOVEMENT IN GERMANY. *See* YOUNG GERMANY.

YOUTRE; YOUTE. (French slur) A Jew.

Suggested Reading: "List of Ethnic Slurs," *Wikipedia*, http://en.wiki pedia.org/wiki/List_of_ethnic_slurs.

– Z –

ZAMORA, COUNCIL OF. Ecclesiastical Church council convened in 1313. Meeting in Zamora, Spain, the conclave decreed the imposition of the **Jew badge**, the segregation of the Jewish from the Christian population, and a ban against the employment of Jewish physicians by Christians or of Christian servants by Jews. The council also imposed the prohibition of Jews holding public office. Jews could no longer bear Christian names nor associate in any way with Christians, and Jewesses could wear no ornaments whatever, whether pearls, gold, or silver. The claims of Jewish creditors were reduced, but no Christian debtor could appeal to a papal bull for the cancellation of his indebtedness to a Jewish creditor.

Suggested Reading: Henry Charles Lea, "The Jews and the Moors," in *A History of the Inquisition of Spain* (New York: Macmillan, 1906), http://libro.uca.edu/lea1/1lea2.htm.

ZENO (c. 450–491). Byzantine emperor, 474–91. Zeno asked at the burning of Jewish corpses in the Antioch **synagogue** in 489: "Why did they not burn the living Jews along with the dead? And then the affair would be over."

SUGGESTED READING: Robert Grant, *Augustine to Constantine: The Rise and Triumph of Christianity in the Roman World* (New York: Harper & Row, 1970).

ZHANDOV, ANDRE. *See* DOCTORS' PLOT.

ZHID; ZYD. (Polish, Russian, Ukrainian slur) Mean and rough people; Jews. By the 12th century, with Christianity as Russia's state religion, the Jews were called Zhids, enemies of Christ and of the Russian people.

SUGGESTED READING: "List of Ethnic Slurs," *Wikipedia*, http://en.wiki pedia.org/wiki/List_of_ethnic_slurs.

ZINOVIEV, GREGORY (RADOMYSLSKI) (1883–1936). Jewish **Bolshevik** revolutionary; senior Soviet politician. Zinoviev was a collaborator of Vladimir Lenin, a major figure in the Bolshevik Revolution, a Politburo leader, and the architect of the Communist International. He was the target of White counterrevolutionaries. **Antisemites** both within and outside Russia pointed to him along with other Jewish revolutionaries as proof that the Bolsheviks and government in Russia were part of a Jewish plot. In the 1920s Zinoviev joined **Leon Trotsky** against **Joseph Stalin**, which turned the Stalinists against Jews. Zinoviev was executed on false charges of murder in 1936 during Stalin's Great Purge of old Bolsheviks. *See also* WHITE TERROR (RUSSIA).

SUGGESTED READING: Arkody Vaksberg, *Stalin against the Jews* (New York: Knopf, 1994).

ZIONAZI. (International slur) Combination of *Zionist* and *Nazi*, a reference to Israelis and their alleged mistreatment of Palestinians.

SUGGESTED READING: "List of Ethnic Slurs," *Wikipedia*, http://en.wiki pedia.org/wiki/List_of_ethnic_slurs.

ZIONISM. *See* ANTISEMITISM, MUSLIM; ANTI-ZIONIST ANTISEMITISM; BLACK HUNDREDS; CHRISTIAN MOBILIZERS; JONES, LEROI; KICHKO, TROFIM; MERRY DEL VAL, RAFAEL; NASSER, GAMAL ABDEL; NEW LEFT; PAMYAT; PIUS X, ST.; RAMPOLLA DEL TINDARO, MARIANO; UNITED NATIONS RESOLUTIONS; XENOPHOBIA; YOUNG EGYPT.

ZIONISM AS RACISM. *See* UNITED NATIONS RESOLUTIONS.

ZOG (ZIONIST-OCCUPIED GOVERNMENT). (U.S. slur) Racist, white supremist, and neo-Nazi belief that the U.S. government is dominated by Jews (Zionists). It a variation of *The Protocols of the Elders of Zion* myth. *See also* PAMYAT.
SUGGESTED READING: "List of Ethnic Slurs," *Wikipedia*, http://en.wiki pedia.org/wiki/List_of_ethnic_slurs; Anti-Defamation League, *Hate on Display: Extremist Symbols, Logos, and Tattoos* (New York: Anti-Defamation League, 2006); ADL Law Enforcement Agency Resource Network, *A Visual Database of Extremist Symbols, Logos, and Tattoos*, http://www .adl.org/hate_symbols/default.asp.

ZOLA, EMILE (1840–1904). French novelist and reformer. Zola is remembered as the great defender of Capt. Alfred Dreyfus in the **Dreyfus Case** in 1898. In his earlier novels, he included several Jewish characters in the French financial world as unscrupulous and unsavory. An example is the Jewish **banker** Gunderman in the novel *D'Argent* (1891).

ZOSSIMA. 15th-century Muscovite metropolitan. The status of the Jews in Russia began to decline in the 15th century because of the reaction of Orthodox Christianity and the monarchy to the conversion of many Christians to Judaism, including some aristocrats and even Zossima. Aristocrats and Zossima "seduced the simple, plying them with Jewish poison."
SUGGESTED READING: Léon Poliakov, *The History of Antisemitism*, 4 vols. (New York: Vanguard, 1965–86).

ZUNDEL, ERNST (1939–). German-born founder of **Samisdat Publishers** in Toronto, Canada, active both in the United States and **Canada**. A leading **Holocaust denier**, Zundel wrote *The Hitler We Loved and Why* in 1977. He is the inspiration for and key content provider of an online repository of Holocaust-denial propaganda. His activities have led to numerous trials in Canada, whose government deported him to Germany, where he maintains an **antisemitic** website under his name. Adept at attracting media attention, Zundel has usually relished his legal battles with what he calls the "**Holocaust** industry."
SUGGESTED READING: Michael Posner, "Silence Is Golden: After Four Decades of Spreading Lies, Holocaust Denier Ernst Zundel Was Finally Sent Packing," *Toronto Life*, May 1, 2005; ADL Law Enforcement Agency Resource Network, "Ernst Zundel," 2005, http://www.adl.org/learn/ext_ US/zundel.asp?xpicked = 2&item = zundel; "Zundel Deported to Ger-

many, March 1, 2005," CBC News (Toronto), http://www.nsm88.com/
articles/ernst%20zundel%20deported.html.

ZYGELBOYM, SHMUEL (1895–1943). Jewish member of the Polish
government-in-exile during the **Holocaust**. Zygelboym's May 1943 suicide note written in London read:

> From the latest information from Poland, it is evident that the Germans, with the
> most ruthless cruelty, are now murdering the few remaining Jews in Poland. . . .
> The responsibility for the crime of murdering the entire Jewish population of Po-
> land falls in the first instance on the perpetrators, but indirectly it is also a burden
> of the whole of humanity, the people and governments of the Allied States which
> thus far have made no effort toward concrete action for the purpose of curtailing
> this crime. . . . By the passive observation of the murder of defenseless millions,
> and of the maltreatment of children, women, and old men, these countries have
> become the criminals' accomplices. . . . By my death I wish to express my strong-
> est protest against the inactivity with which the world is looking on and permit-
> ting the extermination of my people.

Zygelboym's death was widely reported, but his motives as expressed in
his suicide note were ignored.

SUGGESTED READING: Eliezer L. Ehrman, ed., *Readings in Modern Jewish History* (New York: Ktav, 1977).

ZYKLON. Pesticide; prussic acid developed in 1920 as a fumigant and used
at **Auschwitz-Birkenau** and other death camps on Jews in **gas chambers**.
The patent on the pellets was held by **I. G. Farben**, a company that knew
full well its deadly use. After exposure to the air, the crystals changed into
a deadly gas that killed victims in minutes. (This technique was called
Zyklon B; Zyklon A combined Zyklon pellets with water.) Nazi Commandant **Rudolf Höβ** pioneered its application on Soviet POWs in September
1941. **Heinrich Himmler** believed its use was more "humane than shooting." The **SS** calculated that it cost five cents per victim at 2,000 inmates
per application. *See also* DEGESCH.

SUGGESTED READING: Josiah DuBois with Edward Johnson, *The Devil's
Chemists: The International Farben Cartel Who Manufacture Wars* (Boston: Beacon Press, 1952).

About the Authors

Robert Michael is professor emeritus of history at the University of Massachusetts–Dartmouth, founder of the scholarly e-mail list H-ANTISEMI-TISM, and a recipient of the American Historical Association's James Harvey Robinson Prize for the "most outstanding contribution to the teaching and learning of history." Dr. Michael was a Phi Beta Kappa graduate of Boston University in philosophy, a Woodrow Wilson Fellow at Columbia University, and an NDEA Fellow at the University of Connecticut. He has taught classes at Central European University in Budapest and Inter-American University in Puerto Rico and has delivered lectures at the University of Vienna, the Ateneo Veneto, and the University of Venice (Italy). Dr. Michael has published poetry and more than 50 articles and a dozen books on the Holocaust and history of antisemitism. He served in the U.S. Army from 1958 to 1961 and worked as a book editor in New York City publishing for six years. Professor Michael currently teaches on the graduate faculty of Florida Gulf Coast University and the University of South Florida and Ringling School of Art & Design.

Philip Rosen received his doctorate degree from Carnegie-Mellon University researching American ethnicity. He was the director of the Holocaust Museum at Gratz College in Philadelphia and has authored two books on the Holocaust. He is currently teaching at Temple University and Arcadia University in the Greater Philadelphia area, where he lives with his wife, Lillian.